LITERARY THEORIES
A READER AND GUIDE

Edited by
Julian Wolfreys

NEW YORK UNIVERSITY PRESS

Washington Square, New York

© Introductions, selection and editorial
materials, the contributors, 1999

First published in the U.S.A. in 1999 by
NEW YORK UNIVERSITY PRESS
Washington Square
New York, NY 10003

Typeset in Sabon and Gill Sans
by Bibliocraft Ltd, Dundee, and
printed and bound in Great Britain
by The Cromwell Press, Trowbridge, UK

Library of Congress Cataloging-in-Publication Data
Literary theories : a reader and guide / edited by Julian Wolfreys.
p.   cm.
Originally published : Edinburgh : Edinburgh University Press.
1999.
Includes bibliographical references (p.) and index.
ISBN 0-8147-9360-6 (alk. paper). – ISBN 0-8147-9361-4 (pbk. :
alk. paper)
1. Criticism.   2. Literature–History and criticism–Theory, etc.
I. Wolfreys, Julian, 1958-
PN81.L58   1999
801'.95–dc21   99-20887
                    CIP

CONTENTS

ACKNOWLEDGEMENTS

I would like to thank Jill Barker, John Brannigan, Mark Currie, Jane Goldman, Moyra Haslett, Gail Ching-Liang Low, Martin McQuillan, Ken Newton, Ruth Robbins, Leah Wain and Ken Womack for their ready, willing and enthusiastic participation in this project. In particular, I would like to thank Ken Womack for some eleventh-hour editorial aid. I would also like to thank Jackie Jones at Edinburgh University Press, for her help, enthusiasm and faith, and Peter Williams for his invaluable and, as ever, scrupulous editorial work.

A NOTE ON REFERENCES

All notes are those of the individual authors unless otherwise annotated. Abbreviations at ends of notes other than those marked JW (which indicate the current editor's inclusions) indicate the editor or translator of the volume from which the essay in question is reproduced. For the purposes of consistency throughout, all bibliographical notes have been changed to parenthetical references, citing author's surname, date of publication and, where relevant, page or pages. Full bibliographical details for all parenthetical citations are given in the Works Cited section at the end of this volume.

FOREWORD

What is literary theory? How has it developed? What does it do? Why is it necessary, and/or what is it good for? What are the arguments for it and why the resistance to it? All of these questions sound as if they belong in an exam, none of them are easy to answer, certainly not in so short a space as a foreword. But I want to begin by outlining very broadly a few responses.

Literary theory is the name given to a range of disparate critical practices and approaches which are used by members of the humanities in the exploration of literary texts, films and aspects of contemporary and past cultures. Literary theory is also the name given to the teaching of such practices and approaches in the university, particularly in English departments. Literary theory is an umbrella term which gathers together conveniently and for the purpose of identification or definition various texts concerned with the study of literature and culture by, amongst others, feminists, Marxists, and those who teach literature but are interested in certain branches of linguistics, psychoanalysis or philosophy.

Literary theory, as a convenience term or label, defines work influenced by the practices, discourses (language and its power relations within specific disciplines) and texts of feminism, Marxism, psychoanalysis, linguistics, semiotics (the study of signs) and continental philosophy of the last 40 years, including all the various disciplines, fields and, again, discourses, ideas and approaches gathered together under the label 'structuralism' or 'poststructuralism'. Literary Theory is, then, the name given to a number of different, differing, occasionallly overlapping or related ways of reading and interpreting, and is defined thus for economical purposes, first within the university, and subsequently beyond the university, in publishers' catalogues, in reviews, journals and news media.

Before moving on to the next question, 'How has it developed?', I would like to point to what is, for me, a problem with the term 'literary theory'. As everything in the previous paragraph should suggest, the nature of literary theory is complex and multiple. There is more than one aspect or identity for/to literary theory. Hence the plural used in the title of this reader: Literary Theories. 'Literary Theory' is problematic for me because it names a singular object or point of focus. However implicitly, 'literary theory' names a single focal point, rather than something composed, constructed or comprised of many aspects or multiple, often quite different identities. If we name several identities or objects as one, not only do we not respect the separateness or singularity of each of those subjects or identities, we also move in some measure towards erasing our comprehension of the difference between those objects and identities, making them in the process invisible.

Indeed some would say that the act of providing a single name or single identity is done precisely to make things simple for ourselves, or for whoever does the naming. If we can reduce, say, feminist literary criticism, Marxist literary criticism, psychoanalytic approaches to literature, to 'literary theory', we have a catch-all term which puts everything together effortlessly. The act of naming implies a great power for whoever controls the act, whoever has the ability. At the same time, the act of naming does a degree of violence to the different objects. In making the different identities all the same, we make them manageable, we contain them, we don't respect their differences, we make life a little bit easier for ourselves.

This may seem to be making too much of this question of a single identity, but the harm implicit in such an act cannot be underestimated. The importance of the point can be seen if we think for a moment, not of literary study but of attitudes towards cultures, or, even more simply, if we name everyone who comes from some place other than where we are from, foreigners. In doing so, we immediately engage in a way of thinking about the world which is reliant on an ability to define, and separate, an 'us' from a 'them'. And as an example of 'literary theory' demonstrates, the act of separation is also an act of containment. All those feminists, all those Marxists, all those ... well it's all just literary theory, isn't it?

This leads me to the second question, though with a qualification, given that I wish to resist thinking about 'literary theory' in the singular. How has it developed? Let's begin straight away by saying that 'literary theory' is not an 'it', and precisely for the kinds of reasons I've already suggested or at least implied. If we accept the argument that literary theory is composed of many strands, the question of how 'it' developed can be re-cast as 'how have theories developed?'. Various theoretical approaches to literature have evolved and developed in part because in the twentieth century the study of literature had itself developed from a limited range of perspectives, beliefs, and ideological or philosophical assumptions which had not been questioned from other places and the proponents of which largely did not examine their own assumptions or grounds of articulation. This meant, in brief, that certain questions could not be asked about literature or even that only certain works were deemed worthy of study in the first place.

Theoretical approaches developed, employing the language of other disciplines from outside the field of literary studies as a means of redressing the balance, of finding ways of asking previously unarticulated questions, and as a means of bringing back into focus texts which have been neglected. At the same time, theoretically informed approaches to the study of literature and culture provided various vantage points from which different 'voices' could be heard, different identities other than those implicitly understood (Christian, humanist, western, male European) in the conventional institutional approaches to literary study. Not all these voices agreed with each other, although out of the disagreement and debate came yet other inflections, further positions and identities, yet more ways of addressing what it is we call 'literature', as Ruth Robbins suggests in her introduction to feminism, where she makes the point that there are various feminist discourses and philosophies, and that feminisms themselves cannot, today as we come towards the end of the twentieth century, be reduced to a single feminism.

All questions of what has been termed 'literary theory' come down therefore, as Martin McQuillan suggests, to questions of reading. Not just reading in the narrow sense of picking up a novel and gleaning the story from it; rather 'reading' suggests a manner of interpreting our world and the texts which comprise that world. No one single manner of reading will do, so heterogenous is the world, so diverse are its peoples and cultures, so different are the texts, whether literary, cultural or symbolic by which we tell ourselves and others about ourselves, and by which others speak to us about their differences from us, whether from the present, from some other culture, or from the past, from whatever we may think of as our own culture.

Theoretical approaches to literary study have developed and established themselves in part in the academic world, though not without often bitter struggles which still persist, as a means of comprehending, acknowledging and respecting heterogeneity and difference, rather than seeking to reduce the difference to one identity which is either a version of ourselves, a version of the same, or otherwise as an other which cannot be incorporated into a single identity. This is what theoretical approaches to literary and cultural studies can do, what they are 'good for' to put it both baldly and pragmatically; it is also why they are necessary: as the beginning steps in a process of revising how one sees, how one reads. Such approaches are also necessary because they provide the means, as already remarked, for alternative voices, even dissenting voices, instead of being spoken for by some single authoritative voice, to challenge the power of those who had previously assumed the right to speak for all, whether in the form of a single, dominant political party or politician, or through the voice of a critic such as F. R. Leavis, who presumed to tell us that there was a 'great tradition' in English literature and what exactly did or did not belong to that tradition. Literary theories contest not only the composition of the tradition but also the right of any one voice or group of aligned voices to argue for a single tradition.

This point is argued in part by K. M. Newton (1997) whom I quote in the introduction on this issue. Newton, as you'll read, has pointed out that any form of reading, 'even the most naive' (1997, xv) is in some way theoretically formed. One of the reasons why the various literary theories have proved challenging, provoking and have caused on some occasions hostile resistance, is because they insist on this theoretical aspect in reading. Newton points out that critics and scholars who are threatened by theoretical approaches are resistant to what they call 'literary theory' precisely because in the face of theory it is impossible to maintain a calm, undisturbed vision of a 'single community'.

Michael Payne (1991), who is also cited, points to how theoretically informed approaches to literature have led to both the broadening of the literary canon, the texts we study, and to the raising of questions, concerning, for example, race, gender, national identity, which previously had not been asked – which could not be asked because of the implicit ideological and philosophical assumptions behind the study of so-called great literature. Forty years ago it would hardly have been appropriate to raise the issue of either Shakespeare's or Dickens's depiction of Jews or women. Today, Caliban can no longer be considered merely as a somewhat fantastic figure, the offspring of a witch; instead, his role and *The Tempest* in general are explored in relation to questions of race, of miscegenation, and the cultural history of England's colonial expansion.

If you look at Gail Low's exemplary reading of Kipling as another example of the exploration of the ways in which colonial ideology is mediated in literary forms in this collection of essays, you will understand how necessary it is to ask different questions, to move beyond aesthetic considerations which had always been the purview of conventional literary criticism, in order to see how the literary is not separate from the world in which we live.

Finally, the other aspect of theoretical discourse which encounters objection raised by Payne is its difficulty. The obviously political question aside, there is, as Payne points out (1991, vii) the sense, especially expressed by those who are 'anti-theory' that it is, well, hard to read, drawing as it does on the specialised languages of other disciplines. As I discuss below, such a reaction has more to do with the challenge felt to the identity of literary studies as, in Newton's words a 'single community' on the part of members of that community, than it has to do with theoretical discourse itself. Theoretical discourse often is difficult, not simply because of the way in which theories of literature are expressed but also because of the questions differing approaches to the literary text demand we ask, often of ourselves and our understanding of what we think of as literature, as 'good' or 'great' literature, and how we come to think of the literary in such a manner in the first place. The language of some of the essays contained herein will, no doubt, seem difficult. It will require that you approach the essays openly, responsively, reading attentively and patiently for what they have to say, rather than rushing through in order to get the gist of the argument, so to speak.

What follows in the introduction is not then an introduction to literary theory, strictly speaking. There are in this volume numerous introductions to different theoretical approaches, all of which, explicitly or implicitly stress the plurality of their own approaches. What I seek to do here is place you in the midst of particular debates while, at the same time, introducing the study of literary theories in the broader context of literary study in the university, The most significant introduction to the subject still remains Terry Eagleton's

Literary Theory: An Introduction. Indeed it is Eagleton to whom I first turn. In order to introduce the study of literary theories in the broader context of literary study in the university, I turn to particular debates, using the work of Terry Eagleton as an example. Beginning with the epigraph which opens the introduction, I draw on Eagleton's agricultural or rural metaphor as a means of introducing the debates around so-called 'literary theory'. Looking at how Eagleton has returned over the years from his position as a Marxist to question the need for theoretical approaches, I move from this and from Eagleton's own arguments to a consideration of the significance of theory and its sometimes fraught relation to the more conservative elements in the institution of literary study.

Following Eagleton's metaphors as a means of addressing the movement of theory, I develop the idea of theory as something which crosses over the border of literary studies from other places. In doing so, I suggest that the various identities of theories, in being perceived as 'foreign' to some 'native' identity of literary studies, have had to undergo some form of naturalization process, some reinvention of their identities in order to allow them into the field of literary studies. Yet, this being the case, it is now necessary to recognise what has happened and to find ways of reading, looking again at literary theories so as to return to the theoretical a sense of the radical difference of theories in order to question the very process of institutionalization which Terry Eagleton had been concerned with, back in 1976.

INTRODUCTION: BORDER CROSSINGS, OR CLOSE ENCOUNTERS OF THE TEXTUAL KIND

Julian Wolfreys

> ... yet one more stimulating academic 'approach', one more well-tilled field for students to tramp ...
>
> Terry Eagleton

FROM THE COUNTRY TO THE CITY

The epigraph – that sneaking rhetorical device which insinuates itself onto the page between the title and the body of the text, and yet which has the hubris to assume the role of summarising, encapsulating, the argument of the entire essay or book in a nutshell – is taken, as you'll see, from Terry Eagleton, in 1976. Eagleton is bemoaning the possible, perhaps even inevitable, institution-alisation and canonisation of Marxist politics in the form of a literary approach to texts. Politics diluted to a method. In Eagleton's view, the translation from the realm of politics to that of literary studies signalled some form of entry into academia, which was also a form of domestication for Marxism. To enter the 'United States of Criticism', if not of 'theory', meant that the discourse or practice in question had been suitably vetted, vetoed if and where necessary, and granted the requisite visa for entry into the land of literary studies.

Eagleton's metaphor of the field and students tramping across the Marxist farmland is instructive. It ties the practice of Marxism, once located within the study of literature and English departments, to an agrarian way of life, perhaps even one that is feudal. Marxism, once the wild and glorious countryside of ideological practice, has been transformed into manageable soil. Interesting also is the pessimistic manner in which the critic invokes hoards of ramblers pursuing their path unthinkingly across arable and fertile land. It does not seem to occur to Eagleton in his vision of the study of literary criticism and theory that there might be a form of crop rotation at work here, where a Jethro Tull-like figure (the agricultural theorist, not the band) sets out the theory of circulating the seeds of Marxism, feminism and so on, in order to produce a varied crop and to maintain the fertility of the soil at the same time, through the process of rotation. Be that as it may, the field has been entered. The topographical image serves a useful starting point here. It speaks of the land, suggesting an act of trespass. The boundary line broken, the well-ordered soil is churned up, the field will need to be reworked.

This was in fact to be the case with Eagleton himself. For, only seven years after his concerned and somewhat cynical caveat, there occurred the publication of a book which served, to a great extent, to change the outlook on literary study for a generation of students in Great Britain, *Literary Theory: An Introduction*. As is well known, Eagleton was the author of this book. Instead of standing by like some alarmed woodsman watching in disbelief as packs of day-trippers disported themselves in so cavalier a fashion across his land, here is the same author helping in the reconstruction of the landscape. The landscape has changed, however, and we will find ourselves no longer, like Tess, rooting for the dirt covered crops of critical thinking, but being brought face to face with an imposing architectural structure.

Beginning with the assertion that, if there is something called literary theory then there must equally be something called literature, about which theory can circulate, about which it can make its theoretical statements (1983, 1), Eagleton traces the question of what is to be considered 'literature'. He concludes his introduction by stating, correctly, that what we term 'literature' relies for its identity on a complex and interrelated series of value-judgements relating to 'deeper structures of belief', the 'roots' of which are 'as apparently as unshakeable as the Empire State Building' (1983, 16). I'm not sure whether buildings have roots (I know they have foundations). However, if literature, or rather its ideological, cultural and institutional maintenance, is now akin to the structure which supports an undeniably urban architecture, the implication is that theory is there in order to comprehend the structure, the structures of the text and the 'deeper structures' out of which the structure of literature grows or is constructed. What is the purpose of a theoretical approach to the structure beyond merely seeing how the structure functions? Eagleton concludes his book, in a discussion of political criticism, by asking a similar question: 'What is the *point* of literary theory?' (1983, 194). The brief answer is that literature is not value free, nor is it merely a question of aesthetic evaluation, as though aesthetics were themselves somehow outside the realm of the political or economic. As Eagleton puts it, 'the history of modern literary theory is part of the political and ideological history of our epoch ... literary theory [is] ... indissociably bound up with political beliefs and ideological values. Indeed literary theory is less an object of intellectual enquiry in its own right than a particular perspective in which to view the history of our times' (1983, 194–5).

Continuing, Eagleton points out that 'Departments of literature in higher education, then, are part of the ideological apparatus of the modern capitalist state' (1983, 200). The purpose of the various methods of criticism and theory is to work to expose the ideological apparatus, to show its workings and structures, and to question an immovable notion of 'literature', to understand 'literature' not as being distinct from other cultural forms or having some immutable and universal value, but as itself being the product of broader discursive and ideological practices. The feminist theorist, Eagleton argues by example, 'is not studying representations of gender simply because she believes that this will further her political ends. She also believes that gender and sexuality are central themes in literature and other sorts of discourse, and that any critical account which suppresses them is seriously defective' (1983, 209). Thus the purpose of the theoretical analysis of literature is not solely for the purpose of looking at literature in another way, taking one more 'approach'. 'Literature' and its conventional study are wholly conventional constructs of the societies in which we live and the systems of belief which maintain the operation of those societies. The theorised – and for Eagleton, politicised – study of the literary is not an end in itself, but, rather, a means of making oneself capable of seeing beyond literature, to see how literature functions and is made to function in silent and invisible ways.

The Significance of Theory

I don't want to spend too much more time with Terry Eagleton (not because the debate is done; this is, however, an introduction, and we need to move on), but because of his central significance to 'literary theory', it is necessary and instructive to take the measure of literary theory through brief consideration of Eagleton's move from worried sceptic in 1976 to advocate of the theoretical in 1983, which is a wholly understandable move for the politicised critic. In a sense, this also helps to explain, in retrospect, Eagleton's adoption of various critical-political positions throughout his writing career; from Marxist to Althusserian Marxist, to postcolonial Marxist.[1] Eagleton's breathless and trenchant political commentaries on the literary and its institutionalised positions have demonstrated the political necessity not only of adopting theoretical positions but also of shaping one's political response in different ways strategically as a means of resisting becoming solidified into a single position, which itself is then accommodated by the 'ideological state apparatus'. Eagleton's shift is part of an attempt to prevent the fall of theory into the hands of those who he sees serving the institutional and ideological needs of dominant discourses and structures. Theory in the 'wrong hands', say that of the 'dominant political order' (Eagleton, 1990, 37), becomes merely one more tool, one more weapon, involved in acts, to paraphrase Eagleton of intensive colonisation (1990, 36, 37). Who gets colonised? We do, says Eagleton, as subjects disciplined and contained within various social modes of production, in which modes of production literature serves as an apparatus for colonisation of the subject (1990, 37). What this means is that, in being told that literature has a restricted range of timeless humanist values, which it is your purpose to comprehend through a literary education, you are being asked to accept these values as a form of truth. Thus, as a reader, you are 'colonised' through being asked to accept such values as your own. Theory, if divorced from its often political contexts, can be transformed – if it has not been altogether rejected – into a merely formal method of proving the same or similar values as those produced by conventional criticism. Retaining the radicality of theory is, for Eagleton, a means of comprehending the cultural, historical and material aspects of literary texts, while also providing forms of resistance to 'colonisation', ideologically speaking. The image of colonisation is an important one, for it suggests the use of force to take over what is assumed to be a sovereign state. It speaks to the image in my title of border crossings. Theory, for Eagleton, and, indeed for me, provides a means not only of understanding how borders get crossed, how locations become colonised and made to speak almost unconsciously in a voice we never realised we had (see Martin McQuillan in this volume on the novels of Jane Austen or Claire Kahane's reading of *The Bostonians*); the significance of theory, for Eagleton in 1990, is that it helps to keep alive 'radical ideas' in the face of the attempted erasure of those very same radical ideas in both Britain and the USA (1990, 38).

Crossing the Border

Theory has always been understood, in its various guises and manifestations, to have arrived from elsewhere. Most immediately, theory, in the forms of 'poststructuralism', 'psychoanalytic literary criticism', 'deconstruction', is usually identified, in introductions, encyclopedias, guides and so on, as the result of the import of French theoretical discourses prevalent in the 1960s, which subsequently became translated into English and into departments of English. There were also some German incursions, in the form of one version of Reader-Response theory, the influence of members of the Frankfurt School and other hermeneuticists, but the simple narrative of theory is that its origins were markedly Francophone, if not specifically Parisian. Like so many tourists on a trip to Britain and the USA, theoretical discourses arrived, dressed themselves up in Anglo-American guise and had the nerve to stay, long after the visa expired. What occurred is, as they say, history, but English and criticism have never been the same since, and the change in the national identities of literary study has lasted now for more than thirty years.

Two commentators on the import of theory and the subsequent changes in literary studies are Michael Payne and K. M. Newton. First, Michael Payne:

> Fundamental and far-reaching changes in literary studies, often compared to paradigmatic shifts in the sciences, have been taking place in the last

thirty years. These changes have included enlarging the literary canon not only to include novels, poems and plays by writers whose race, gender or nationality had marginalized their work but also to include texts by philosophers, psychoanalysts, historians, anthropologists, social and religious thinkers, who previously were studied by critics merely as 'background' ... Many practising writers and teachers of literature, however, see recent developments in literary theory as dangerous and anti-humanistic. (Payne, 1991, vi–vii)

Now, K. M. Newton:

> ... theory or critical principles that have some theoretical base underlie *any* form of reading, even the most naïve, of a literary text ... The reason that there is so much controversy and debate in literary studies ... is that critics and readers feel they belong to a single community, even though they may have made quite different choices as to how they read literary texts ... [However,] literary criticism ... is like a parliament ... in which two parties dominated ... What has happened to the 'parliament' recently is that this two-party dominance has been threatened because numerous small parties have entered the parliament, depriving any single party of an overall majority ... Literary criticism is thus revealed as a struggle for power among parties ... The debate also has significance for society in general in that it raises questions that have implications beyond the purely literary sphere. (Newton, 1997, xv, xviii, xix)

Between Terry Eagleton, Michael Payne and K. M. Newton, you might get the sense that literary theory is something to be feared; indeed many do fear it, often without knowing exactly what it is, other than it does derive from numerous disciplines outside literary studies, such as feminism, Marxism, psychoanalysis and philosophy, and, worst of all, *continental* philosophy, not the good old, home-grown varieties of the analytical tradition in Britain or pragmatism in the USA.

Another fear, already mentioned, both within and outside universities, is that theory is difficult, as Michael Payne suggests in pointing to the worries of the detractors (see Payne, 1991, vii). What could represent more of an affront than language about literature, about material which is supposedly part of a cultural heritage – that which puts the *English* in *English Literature* and also in *English Departments* – yet which is hard to understand? Canonical Literature should be taught either historically, from Beowulf to, well, Virginia Woolf and cultural studies should be abandoned; or literature should be taught because of its timeless, formal and aesthetic qualities which transcend cultural and political issues; what we need is a sense of *value*. You can find letters of objection similar in content or tone in, for example, *The New York Review of Books*, the *Times Literary Supplement*, the *Times Higher Education Supplement*, *The Chronicle of Higher Education*, even in non-specialist newspapers, such as *The Guardian* or the *Los Angeles Times*. What is the reason for this? Largely it's a question of media misrepresentation, because, to assume an Eagletonian tone for a moment, the newspapers and other forms of media are all part of the dominant order, they all serve in the colonisation of the subject, of which Eagleton speaks.

Literary theory is, then, something to be afraid of, like so many illegal immigrants, like the 'contamination' of the English language with *modish* foreign words or, as far as some Britons are concerned, with the importation of 'Americanisms'. The fear of theory on the part of many, whether inside or outside the university, is precisely a fear of the foreign, the alien, the intruder, that which gets across the national boundaries, that which crosses the borders and comes to live in the homeland of English Literature, eventually taking it over, and changing its terrain forever. To borrow K. M. Newton's analogy, even the consensus politics of English Literature is no longer a safe discourse between ruling parties, assaulted as it is by those who no longer speak the same language. Literary Theory speaks in tongues, a Babelian hoard not even waiting at the checkpoints to have its passports stamped. Perhaps the most far-reaching challenge which theory represents in its many forms is to the inadequacy of the representation of the literary on the part of traditional and institutional beliefs as the 'best' that can be known and taught, to paraphrase Matthew Arnold. And the extent to which theory has already crossed the border, infiltrated the mother country of English Literature, is marked by, on the one hand, the native distrust of whatever theory may be (mis)taken to be, and, on the other, the way in which the institution of higher education, as a representative of Eagleton's dominant social order, has sought to quiet it down, to domesticate it, to reify it in English departments.

One way in which theory has been given its rabies shots, put into quarantine, and then, having been taught to sit up and pay attention, let into its new homeland, is through the establishment of courses on literary theory. This is an effective form of containment, because it marks theory off from, say, Shakespeare or the Victorian novel as merely one more subject to study. In this form it has become that which Eagleton in 1976 feared it would: a series of approaches (if this is week six it must be feminism). Even with the best will in the world on the part of those of us who teach on Literary Theory courses, the danger of such an approach is double: on the one hand, we isolate theory from its engagement with literature, because if the course is about theory, then to a certain extent, we have to trust in the student's – that's to say your – willingness to go away and address literary texts from theoretical perspectives. With so much to study, this doesn't always happen. Theory merely ends up an adjunct of literary studies, an optional course for those who wish to take it. What could be better for those who fear theory than this version of events. Theory is not going to represent a threat to anyone or anything if it's put in its place. (This is assuming of course that theory is a threat; it may or may not be radical or political, but it is only a threat if you fear being asked to think differently from the usual tired complacent habits of thought and belief which can come to constitute an identity for you, without your awareness.)

On the other hand, the other form of theory's institutionalisation is its absorption into the mainstream. Take the following statement: 'These days most academics are, to some extent, theorised.' These are the words of an ex-colleague, or as close to what he said as I can remember (though I believe it's fairly accurate). I'm not going to suggest that there is any overt agenda behind the utterance of this statement, in fact I believe it was uttered, as far as was possible for him, in absolute good faith. Yet, it can be read in a number of ways which suggests something of the institutional fortunes of theory. While theory may be contained through being given its own place in the curriculum as yet one more course, it can also be consumed, rendered relatively ineffectual and reduced to a series of formalist tools. To simplify greatly: the study of the function of metaphors and rhetorical figures has been replaced, as a result of, for example, the influence of Foucault and the Anglicisation of his radical foreign identity, with the study of images of the body, or of incarceration, acts of policing, and so forth. Feminism, to take another example, is merely the examination of the depiction of women, of female characters and women writers. One can read the formalist domestication of theory everywhere in literary studies, where 'domestication' means simply the replacement of old figures of analysis with newer ones, while maintaining the same principles behind the act of reading. If we are all, to greater or lesser extents, theorised, then the debates and battles, spoken of by Newton, Payne and Eagleton, are won. Aren't they? Theory, in this formula, has done well and no longer needs to keep going on about political issues or to insist on being political. One can't keep waging a war with the foreign, so one has to find ways of accommodating it, always supposing of course that this accommodation occurs according to one's own identity and values. If we are all more or less theorised, then theory no longer has to be an issue, its erasure begun as surely as that of radical thought gestured towards by Eagleton.

BORDER CROSSINGS

As if to anticipate the institutionalisation and domestication of 'Literary Theory', critical theories have, repeatedly, energetically and ceaselessly, formed and reformed themselves, forging allegiances with, and involving themselves in, critical debate with other theoretical discourses, models, paradigms. There is no single literary theory, if there ever was, even though the anti-theorists make the mistake of assuming a single identity for theory. The application of the title 'Literary Theory' is merely one form of domestication. The title operates to silence and erase differences, to hide contention, to ignore the complications, the heterogeneity, the protean energies, not only of disparate theories, but also within any supposedly single theory, such as, for example 'feminism'. As Ruth Robbins' title, 'Will the Real Feminist Theory Please Stand Up?' suggests, it is impossible to tell which is the 'real' theory, if only because, as she goes on to argue, there is no single true feminist theory. And this perhaps is feminism's, or any theory's, 'threat', that being hybrid, heterogeneous and protean, 'it' is not an 'it'; the theoretical discourse, by virtue of its own nature, resists all efforts at identification. This can be seen in a number of the introductory essays in this collection. Martin McQuillan states that there is no such thing as reader-response theory, precisely because what is called reader-response theory draws upon so many other theoretical discourses, and all theoretical discourses are, in a sense, responses of the reader. Postmodernism cannot be represented because the discourses called 'postmodernism' are, themselves, so diverse and differentiated, while at the same time, the discourse on postmodernism is a postmodernist discourse inasmuch as it seeks to stress the unrepresentable. K. M. Newton's article on Roland Barthes and structuralism similarly stresses that Barthes was a critic who never stood still, and could not therefore be pinned down as a structuralist critic (even supposing some simple identity called 'structuralism' existed, which, as Newton shows in differentiating Barthes from other structuralist critics, it did not).

Thus there are border crossings from one theory to another, and within theoretical positions. To return to the image of countries and states, theories exist in a state of productive tension, rather than in some utopian location of pluralist consensus, as is imagined by those, such as my previously mentioned acquaintance, for whom theory represents a club, determined to exclude those who don't know the language. It is not the case that there is the land of non-theory, and that of theory, where, like the Lilliputians and Brobdingnagians, wars are waged over which end one's egg should be opened (a case might be made for the comparison to be made in terms of Yahoos and Houyhnhnms, although this is not the place to do so), even though anti-theorists might wish it were that simple (as their anti-theoretical narratives seem to suggest they do). Rather, theories cross each others' borders constantly; there are borders, limits, the demarcation of lines, to be certain. But these get redrawn constantly, as you will see from the essays in this collection, both those which are collected and reprinted here, and those which serve as introductions and which are commissioned for this collection. As an example of this, take the annotated bibliographies. In the sections on Deconstruction, Poststructuralism and Reader-Response Theory, you will find three entries for the same title by Paul de Man. Similarly, in the feminist section of this book, the reprinted essay by Terry Castle (from her book *The Apparitional Lesbian*) is as much an essay belonging to the discourse of 'queer theory' as it is a feminist essay, and enters into a debate with the work of Eve Kosofsky Sedgwick, who is represented by the essay 'Queer and Now' in the section on Gay Studies/Queer Theory. Similarly, if you examine the reprinted essays which make up the reader, you will find the work of Jacques Derrida as an implicit or explicit influence in a number of places, including Feminism, Queer Theory, Postcolonial Discourse, Poststructuralism and so on. By the same token, the effects and legacies of various structuralisms mark theoretical readings of textual forms in a number of places. Theories not only cross the borders of an assumed identity in order to demonstrate the unspoken assumptions which serve to articulate that identity in the first place, they also, to reiterate the point, cross and recross each other's borders, remapping their own boundaries as they go. It is perhaps this very sense of vitality, of energy and survival, and of the constant outgrowing of a self which so troubles those who need the definition 'Literary Theory', if only so as to keep 'it' in 'its' place, in their minds at least. 'Literary Theory' is itself a form of border erected so as to keep 'theory' contained. It names an act also of border patrol, of policing, keeping the foreign, the other, the potentially dangerous under surveillance. The border patrol operates in a number of ways, for it seeks to erect a boundary within its own territory, rather than ultimately expelling the theoretical. To take the example of 'deconstruction', a very singular example unquestionably, and yet an example which serves to exemplify the treatment accorded all such singular examples, whether we name these feminism, Marxism, postcolonial or gay theories, the institutionalised response is summed up by Peggy Kamuf: 'Concerning the institution that is the university put in question by the PC debate, the term "deconstruction" is most often presumed to refer to a theory, a method, a school, perhaps even a doctrine, in any case, some identifiable or localizable "thing" that can be positioned – posed and opposed – within that institution, but also that can be excluded from this defined enclosure' (1997, 141).

CLOSE ENCOUNTERS OF THE TEXTUAL KIND

As Peggy Kamuf continues, what is more interesting than the reasons for establishing boundaries – the reasons present themselves more or less obviously or immediately, as the reasons *for* identification and location – is the revelation of a certain 'unfigurable space . . . the space for different kinds of effects' (1997, 141). It is precisely the opening of a space, unfigurable by any border, which gives rise to such animosity in the face of the perceived threat of theory or theories. Indeed, the use of the plural *theories* is intended to signal that the opening of the space is already underway. If the work of Jacques Derrida in a certain way, in a translated form, is remarked in Queer Theory or Postcolonial Studies for example, this is less a comment on the signal importance of Derrida's work to a number of areas and disciplines, discourses and practices in the twentieth century, than it is an exemplary sign of the opening of channels of virtual communication which pass easily across all imagined borders and boundaries. The virtualisation of theoretical movements reinscribes the space of the theoretical with a certain haunted quality, an uncanny effect as one of the possible effects described by Kamuf, in the unfigurable space of theories. Another effect, if it can be described this way, is to counter the formalisation of critical thinking in the institution of literary criticism. For what has emerged have been new forms of political thinking, which, in adapting radical discourse and crossing the borders of literary study, have reinvented textual encounters, as the examples of Postcolonial Theory, Queer Theory and gay and lesbian studies, and Cultural Studies show. Critical practices such as these address not only questions of what we read, but also how we reread what we've already been told how to read, such as the works of Jane Austen, William Shakespeare, Oscar Wilde or Rudyard Kipling. This is not to say that other theoretical discourses have not been political, have not stressed the necessity for rereading in ways which seek to emancipate the differences of the text. Rather, it is to suggest that literary theories have responded to the immediate danger of institutional enclosure through redrawing the political lines of analysis, of textual encounter. The textual encounter has become one, once more, of proximity, the close encounter of this introduction's title. If theoretical discourse is markedly political, it also, by virtue of its production of different effects, has come close to the text, to read with energy and urgency textual structures.

That theoretical engagements with textual forms are capable of crossing borders with rapidity is suggested most immediately by the range of textual encounters to be found, first of all, in the essays collected in this anthology, and, beyond this, in the various books, journals and collections to which the various essays and extracts belong. Here you will find close encounters with, among others, Balzac, the Bible, Henry James, Sylvia Townsend Warner, Colette, Oscar Wilde, Marcel Duchamp, Charles Baudelaire, Virginia Woolf, Samuel Taylor Coleridge, Jean-Paul Sartre, Thomas Hardy, Samuel Beckett, David Lynch, Shakespeare, Rudyard Kipling, Jean Genet, Joe Orton, Zhang YiMou. At the same time, you will also encounter discussions of theoretical positions alongside readings of film, art and literature.

The essays reprinted in this collection represent a constant commitment on the part of each of the critics represented to addressing the need to reread the text, to re-evaluate the critical act and what we understand by terms such as 'literature' and 'culture'. Each essay indicates, directly or obliquely, an ideological, philosophical or political engagement in its approach and with its subject; each changes our knowledge of the textual and the terrain on which criticism stands. The range of essays covers approximately the thirty years of theoretical involvement in critical studies, that period which critics such as Eagleton and Newton identify as the time of literary theory. In relation to these essays, the introductions commissioned for *Literary Theories: A Reader and Guide*, address the principal arguments of the reprinted pieces while also exceeding the function of faithful paraphrase by seeking to present in an exploratory and introductory fashion the artificially and institutionally defined fields within 'literary theory'. In doing so, each piece also attempts to use the institutional definition as a springboard, from which to leap, in order to move the reader beyond the notion of a 'feminism', a 'Marxism' a 'psychoanalytic practice', and so on. Also, each introduction suggests possible overlaps with other theoretical paradigms. *Literary Theories: A Reader and Guide* offers readers the chance to encounter various border crossings, and, in coming to terms with these critical acts, to begin the process of crossing various epistemological, political and critical borders themselves.

NOTE

1. This sentence sketches Eagleton's engagement with different theoretical discourses, none of which he has simply accepted. Rather he has sought to mediate the insights of various theories from a Marxist orientation. Louis Althusser was a French Marxist whose own work engaged with structuralism and aspects of psychoanalysis.

PART I
STRUCTURALISM

INTRODUCTION:
NEVER STANDING STILL, OR IS
ROLAND BARTHES STRUCTURALISM?

K. M. Newton

A common description of structuralism is that it is a method of analysing cultural phenomena founded on Saussurian linguistics. This description is borne out if one reads such structuralist critics as Roman Jakobson, in his later critical writings, Tzvetan Todorov, A. J. Greimas, Gérard Genette. These critics were concerned to apply structuralist methodology – in Jakobson's case to the analysis of poetic language and in the case of Todorov, Greimas and Genette to the study of narrative – without explicitly engaging in philosophical or ideological conflict with non-structuralist forms of analysis. Roland Barthes, the most famous of structuralists, was also capable of such neutral forms of structuralist analysis, notably in one long essay entitled 'The Structural Analysis of Narratives'. However, Barthes was essentially a critical contro-versialist. For him, structuralism was primarily important as a weapon that could be used to attack two of the dominant forces in western ideology – science and its counterpart in the social sciences, positivism – both of which had their basis in empiricism.

One might see Barthes as fighting an old battle here. The French tradition of thought had been predominantly based on rationalism, a form of thinking that posited that knowledge of reality is possible without reference to sensory experience, Descartes being the major French philosopher in this tradition. Opposed to this rationalist tradition was empiricism, the theory that all knowledge is derived from sense experience and that no knowledge is innate or a priori. The latter tradition had been dominated by Anglo-Saxon thinkers such as Locke and Hume, and this tradition was much more in tune with science than the rationalist tradition. Since the rise of science in the seventeenth and eighteenth centuries, therefore, empiricism can be seen as the major influence on Western thinking. In the conflict between rationalism in the philosophical sense and empiricism, the latter could be said to have prevailed.

Yet it could be argued that the rationalist tradition encouraged critique much more forcibly than the empiricist tradition. In the empiricist tradition the world was seen as an independent structure which it was the task of the human mind to try to understand. The mind's relation to the world could then be seen as essentially passive, thus encouraging conservative attitudes. Marx, one recalls, blamed philosophers for only interpreting the world instead of endeavouring to change it. The attraction of structuralism for a radical like Barthes was that it had the potential to reassert rationalist critique and undermine empiricist passivity, for central to structuralist thinking is that the mind's relation to the world is active and not passive.

Before Saussure, linguistics had tended to be studied on a positivistic basis grounded in empirical investigation. Language was treated in historical terms, with the emphasis being on how language had developed and changed over time. Saussure shifted the emphasis from this diachronic aspect of language to the synchronic aspect. His predominant concern was with how language as a system of signs functioned at a particular point in time rather than with language as a historical product. For Saussure, language has two fundamental aspects: *langue* or the underlying system that governs language use, and *parole*, how language is employed for communicative purposes through the use of words and sentences. Saussure's overriding interest was in *langue*. One can see that this is a return to a more rationalistic approach in the philosophical sense, since *langue* is not empirically present as the object of investigation but is a mental construct. *Langue* governs *parole* but it can only be reconstructed from *parole*, that is from empirically existing linguistic data, but such data are essentially secondary. Noam Chomsky's linguistic theory departs from Saussure's in important respects but for Chomsky also it is the linguistic system that allows individual users to generate sentences which may never have been uttered before yet which can be understood by others, and significantly the title of one of Chomsky's books is *Cartesian Linguistics*, indicating his identification with a rationalist tradition of thought.

An implication of Saussurian linguistics is that language structures the world since language as a system of signs mediates between the human mind and external reality. For Saussure words are arbitrary signs and, more important, meaning is relational: it is produced by the differences between linguistic signs and not by words having discrete independent meanings. In the relation between mind and world, therefore, one cannot forget about language: it refracts the mind's relation to the world. In 'From Science to Literature', Barthes attacks science for viewing language as 'an instrument' and as 'transparent' and 'neutral' so that it is 'subjugated to scientific matters (operations, hypotheses, results) which are said to exist outside it and to precede it'. Literature, in contrast, is made up only of language – 'language is the *being* of literature, its very world' – and this allows it to question reality and not merely accept it passively: 'Ethically, it is solely by its passage through language that literature pursues the disturbance of the essential concepts of our culture, "reality" chief among them'. The rise of science had seemingly consigned the study of rhetoric to the dustbin of history but Barthes claims that the discrediting of rhetoric – 'grandiose effort of an entire culture to analyze and classify the forms of speech, to render the world of language intelligible' – was ideological and that it is structuralism's 'glamorous ancestor'.

However, Barthes goes on to argue that structuralism has itself been infected by the scientific aspiration towards objectivity, and in contrast argues that its 'logical extension can only be to join literature, no longer as "object" of analysis but as activity of writing'. This involves recognising the role of the subject in any analysis of the object. This will allow structuralism more effectively to contest the view of positivistic science that 'a neutral state of language exists, from which would branch off, like so many gaps and ornaments, a certain number of specialized languages, such as the literary language or the poetic language'. Science has no claim to be 'a superior code; writing seeks to be a total code, including its own forces of destruction'. Barthes makes clear the social and ideological implications of this when he writes: 'It follows that only writing alone can break the theological image imposed by science'.

This literary writing is called by Barthes *écriture*. Writing which seeks to be transparent and is thus complicit with the prevailing dominant ideology with its basis in positivistic science is, in contrast, *écrivance*. For Barthes the objection to the realist novel is that it has its basis in *écrivance* rather than *écriture*, and throughout his writing Barthes is hostile to realist fiction because it is seen as reinforcing a conservative ideology that essentially accepts the world as given. However, there would seem to be an obvious distinction between formulaic realist novels that have no claim to literary merit or interest and novels by writers such as Balzac or Stendhal who are categorised as realists by literary historians. It is perhaps the need to distinguish between different types of realism that leads Barthes to produce *S/Z*, his study of Balzac's novella, *Sarrasine*.

In the introductory sections of *S/Z*, Barthes introduces a distinction that qualifies his earlier distinction between *écriture* and *écrivance*, namely that between *scriptible* and *lisible*, usually translated as 'writerly' and 'readerly' respectively. *S/Z* can be seen as a transitional work in which Barthes is moving beyond structuralism into poststructuralism, with the emphasis being on textual rather than structural analysis. It is generally agreed that poststructuralist thinking emerged most powerfully in 1966 with Jacques Derrida's paper 'Structure, Sign and Play in the Discourse of the Human Sciences', first delivered at a conference at Johns Hopkins University, a conference Barthes had attended. Derrida followed this up with the publication of three major texts in 1967, notably *Of Grammatology*. In the opening section of *S/Z* Barthes distances himself from the earlier structuralist project:

> Precisely what the first analysts of narrative were attempting: to see all the world's stories ... within a single structure [is] a task as exhausting (ninety-nine percent perspiration, as the saying goes) as it is ultimately undesirable, for the text thereby loses its difference.

Barthes then goes on to discuss this 'difference' and the word has a distinctly Derridean ring. He shifts the focus from narrative in the general sense, which was the main preoccupation of structuralist narratology, to the individual text: 'the single text is valid for all texts of literature, not in the sense that it represents them ... but in that literature itself is never anything but a single text: the one text is not an (inductive) access to a Model, but entrance into a network with a thousand entrances'.

However, Barthes maintains his hostility to realism. The 'writerly' is from the beginning elevated above the 'readerly' text: 'Why is the writerly our value? Because the goal of literary work (of literature as work) is to make the reader no longer a consumer, but a producer of the text'. The 'writerly' text 'is a perpetual present, upon which no *consequent* language ... can be super-imposed'; it is '*ourselves writing*, before the infinite play of the world ... is traversed, intersected, stopped, plasticized by some singular system ... which reduces the plurality of entrances, the opening of networks, the infinity of languages'. This is very like Derrida's second form of interpretation in his 'Structure, Sign and Play' essay which 'affirms freeplay and tries to pass beyond man and humanism' (Macksey, 1972, 265), yet it could be argued that both owe something to Barthes's concept of 'writing degree zero' in his first important book of that name, published in 1953. In contrast 'readerly' texts 'are products (and not productions), they make up the enormous mass of our literature'. Whereas the 'writerly' text is 'a galaxy of signifiers' and 'the codes it mobilizes extend as far *as the eye can reach*', the readerly text is open to interpretation and governed by a restricted number of codes. However, Barthes accepts that certain 'readerly' texts have a limited plurality, texts by such writers as Balzac and other literary realists. The basis of that limited plurality is 'connotation'. The aim of his study of Balzac's *Sarrasine* is to reveal the 'difference' at work within the text, that difference being created by the space between 'denotation' and 'connotation' in a text. Connotation, for Barthes, is 'a correlation immanent in the text ... one may say that it is an association made by the text-as-subject within its own system ... connotations are mean-ings which are neither in the dictionary nor in the grammar of the language in which the text is written'.

Conventionally connotation is contrasted with denotation in language, that is meaning in a literal sense, the meaning that can be found in a dictionary. But Barthes claims that denotation has no intrinsic priority over connotation: 'denotation is not the first meaning, but pretends to be so; under this illusion, it is ultimately no more than the *last* of the connotations (the one which seems both to establish and close the reading). This suggests that denotation or literal meaning is more of an ideological than a linguistic product. Certain meanings have a greater power than others for ideological reasons and these meanings are termed denotative or literal.

In demonstrating that a text is a plurality of connotations, with denotation being displaced from the centre of meaning and having no separate existence from connotation, one can see Barthes's structuralism moving towards Derridean deconstruction. Not only is the text dismantled by being shown to be a plurality of coded connotations, but in the process, the reader as a centred 'I' figure is also dismantled: 'This "I" which approaches the text is already a plurality of other texts, of codes which are infinite or, more precisely, lost (whose origin is lost)'. Subjectivity is a construction since it is only a 'deceptive plenitude . . . merely the wake of all the codes which constitute me'. However, Barthes's claim that the 'readerly' text is the product of five codes of reading which organise its intelligibility is something of a return to a more structuralist form of narratology: the *proairetic* code controls the reader's construction of plot; the *hermeneutic* code presents the reader with a question or a problem or an enigma which gives the plot its momentum; the *semic* code is concerned with characteristics, such as psychological traits; the *symbolic* code is concerned with the organisation of symbolic meanings; the *referential* code consists of references in the text to cultural phenomena. However, there is an element of playfulness in Barthes's presentation of these codes, which distances his approach from orthodox structuralism. He does not argue in detail for them or make any scientific claim for them in the manner of other structuralist critics who believe that literary criticism should aspire to a kind of scientific objectivity.

Yet to discuss literary texts in terms of codes is clearly an implicit attack on the kind of criticism that sees literature as being above ideology and having transcendental powers. A code, such as morse code or the barcodes one finds on items in supermarkets, triggers meaning mechanically and automatically and for Barthes writing as *écrivance* does the same. Literary texts such as the novels of Balzac and other realists may be more complex in that a multiplicity of codes are at work but essentially a similar mechanical generation of meaning operates, with the codes triggering certain effects in the reader's mind. And more is at stake here than just reading. Such texts are responsible for constructing the reader's view of reality, but Barthes's critical aim is to demystify the realist literary text and its claim to offer a true representation of reality. For Barthes what is being represented is only a 'reality effect', the title of another of his essays: in *S/Z* the aim is to show in detail, by dividing a text into numbered *lexias* or units of meaning and discussing each of them in turn, how this reality effect is produced by an interplay of codes.

One might compare Barthes's five codes to Kant's categories of mind which order our understanding of the world. For Kant any reality beyond the forms of our consciousness and categories of mind, such as quality and causation, is unknowable but without such categories our relation to the world would just be a chaos of sensations. But whereas Kant believes that his categories are intrinsic to the mind, Barthes suggests that codes of reading are socially constructed; therefore one is not necessarily condemned to accept such codes. It is possible for the 'readerly' to be replaced by the 'writerly'. Since the 'writerly' text does not operate in terms of a limited number of codes, it has the potential to allow the reader to escape from a reality determined in advance by codes rooted in ideology and potentially to create a new reality.

Clearly there was an implicit revolutionary aspect in a political sense to Barthes's structuralist criticism and this made his work very influential with certain British critics. Stephen Heath was one of the first critics to write a study of Barthes and in a later book on the *nouveau roman*, which Barthes had supported for its implicit attack on conventional realism, Heath argues that the realist novel is readable because it 'is relayed by a series of codes and conventions, by the text of the already known and written: that work is readable, therefore, which is cast within their horizon, which repeats them in their naturalized transparence' (Heath, 1972, 21), and whereas Barthes selects Balzac as his exemplary realist, Heath selects George Eliot: 'Thus George Eliot, for example, can offer her novels naturally as an attempt to "give a faithful account of men and things as they have mirrored themselves in my mind". This is the same kind of "innocence" that was encountered in Balzac's description of the *Comédie Humaine* as "visual dictation"'(Heath, 1972, 20).

These ideas were further developed by Colin MacCabe in a study of James Joyce. Joyce for MacCabe represents writing aspiring towards the 'writerly' while the 'readerly' text is again represented by George Eliot. MacCabe uses a phrase which was to become very influential in the work of British critics who were influenced by Barthes. Discussing narration and the use of inverted commas to separate characters' speech from the discourse of the narrator, MacCabe argues that this creates a hierarchy of discourses with the narration functioning as a metalanguage which 'refuses to acknowledge its own status as writing' and 'functions simply as a window on reality. This relationship between discourses can be taken as the defining feature of *the classic realist text*' (MacCabe, 1978, 15).

Other British critics interpreted Barthes's critical ideas in relation to realism in more directly political terms. In a discussion of *S/Z* in their book *Language and Materialism*, Rosalind Coward and John Ellis write that 'realism stresses the product and not the production. It represses production in the same way that the mechanism of the market, of general exchangeability, represses production in capitalist society' (Coward and Ellis, 1977, 46). The idea of 'the classic realist text' was particularly fundamental to Catherine Belsey's influential book, *Critical Practice*, first published in 1980. She states that 'Classic realism ... is what Barthes in *S/Z* defines as the readable (*lisible*), the dominant literary form of the nineteenth-century, no longer "pertinent" in the twentieth' (Belsey, 1980, 73), and she sees it as no accident that 'classic realism' is the dominant form during the period of industrial capitalism. But though Belsey draws on Barthes to declare that the 'readable text is merchandize to be consumed' (Belsey, 1980, 105), again linking 'classic realism' with capitalism, she recognises that *S/Z* is a very different kind of critical text from her own *Critical Practice*. Rather it is 'itself a polyphonic critical text' and 'impossible to summarize adequately, to reduce to systematic accessibility'; it is 'at once frustrating and exhilarating . . . it would almost certainly not be possible (or useful) to attempt a wholesale imitation of its critical method(s)' (Belsey, 1980, 105–6).

This brings out a distinction between Barthes and his British followers. Although ideas are important to Barthes, he seems more aware than critics like Belsey of a potential contradiction in attacking the 'readerly' text or 'classic realism' but at the same time using a form of critical discourse that is itself 'readerly'. For Barthes, 'writerly' language in itself is political: by refusing to conform to 'readerly' conventions that assume that language should be transparent in its meaning and paraphraseable one is undermining the 'readerly' not just at the level of ideas but at the deeper level of form.

Although Barthes's structuralist writings were massively influential on British critics, they were less well received by American criticism. When Barthes gave a paper entitled 'To Write: An Intransitive Verb?' at the Johns Hopkins conference on structuralism in 1966, there was a question and answer session following the paper. Paul de Man, who was later to become the major figure in American deconstruction, was scathing in his criticism both of Barthes's type of structuralist analysis and of his conception of literary history. He attacks Barthes in particular for promoting 'an optimistic historical myth', one that 'represents historical progress and extremely optimistic possibilities for the history of thought'. Barthes's stylistic analyses do not, de Man claims, 'show any progress over those of the Formalists, Russian or American, who used empirical methods, through neither the vocabulary nor the conceptual frame you use'. As regards literary history 'you say things that are false within a typically French myth'. Whereas Barthes places writing since Mallarmé, particularly the *nouveau roman*, in opposition to Romantic writing as regards the treatment of the ego, de Man asserts that Barthes is simply wrong:

> In the romantic autobiography, or, well before that, in the seventeenth-century story, this same complication of the ego (*moi*) is found, not only unconsciously, but explicitly and thematically treated, in a much more complex way than in the contemporary novel. I don't want to continue this development; it is simply to indicate that you distort history *because* you need a historical myth of progress to justify a method which is not yet able to justify itself by results. (Macksey, 1972, 150)

Barthes's reply was interesting. Although he was conventionally thought of as being a demythologiser because of his book *Mythologies*, he states that

> I never succeed in defining literary history independently of what time has added to it. In other words I always give it a mythical dimension. For me,

> Romanticism includes everything that has been said about Romanticism. Consequently, the historical past acts as a sort of psychoanalysis. For me the historical past is a sort of gluey matter for which I feel an inauthentic shame from which I try to detach myself by living my present as a sort of combat or violence against this mythical time immediately behind me. When I see something that might have happened fifty years ago, for me it already has a mythical dimension. (Macksey, 1972, 150–1)

This suggests that Barthes's anti-empiricism goes all the way down, as it were. He is not concerned about the 'empirical facts' of history; these are always in any case distorted by the 'mythical dimension'. Again the driving force of his writing is to create change and if this requires what de Man sees as 'a historical myth of progress', then so be it. De Man, in contrast, believes that one should try to separate fact and myth and is sceptical about the possibility of progress, both in life and literature.

De Man's main objection to Barthes is that his myth of progress leads to a distortion of literary history, with modernist writing being elevated above the literature of earlier periods. Barthes's criticism also operates with oppositions between *écriture* and *écrivance* and 'writerly' and 'readerly' and this makes him vulnerable to a Derridean criticism that deconstructs such oppositions. De Man in his later career was the leading theorist among the Yale deconstructionists and one of his ex-students, Barbara Johnson, subjected Barthes's *S/Z* to a deconstructive analysis which sets out to show that Barthes's attempt to confine Balzac's *Sarrasine* to the category of the 'readerly' becomes entangled in contradictions.

The plot of *Sarrasine* centres on the passion of the sculptor Sarrasine for an opera singer, La Zambinella, but he is ignorant of the fact that *castrati* – castrated men – sang the soprana parts on the Italian operatic stage, and he eventually discovers that La Zambinella, whom he had considered to possess a perfect female body, had been born a man. Johnson uses this collapse of oppositions within the story to undermine Barthes's opposition between the 'writerly' and the 'readerly' text. Barthes's distinction is made up of a difference *between*, but like the difference between male and female in the text of *Sarrasine*, this collapses into a difference *within*, since Johnson argues that the qualities Barthes associated with the 'writerly' are evident in the very text he has used to exemplify the 'readerly': 'Like the readerly text, Sarrasine's deluded image of La Zambinella is a glorification of perfect unity and wholeness ... But like the writerly text, Zambinella is actually fragmented, unnatural and sexually undecidable' (Johnson, 1980, 8). Instead of the text thematising the 'writerly-readerly' opposition, the text itself shows an awareness of the fact that such oppositions cannot be sustained since Sarrasine, 'In thinking that he knows where difference is located – between the sexes – he is blind to a difference that cannot be situated between, but only within' (Johnson, 1980, 10). It is the text itself which 'demystifies the logocentric blindness' of Sarrasine's conception of

La Zambinella so that Balzac's text has already deconstructed the most basic of oppositions: that between male and female: 'Balzac has already in a sense done Barthes's work for him. The readerly text is itself nothing other than a deconstruction of the readerly text.' The text 'does not simply reverse the hierarchy between readerly and writerly by substituting the truth of castration for the delusion of wholeness; it deconstructs the very possibility of naming the difference' (Johnson, 1980, 10–11).

De Manian deconstruction thus attempts to outflank Barthes, the anti-positivist, by demonstrating that in operating with oppositions that are open to deconstruction, he is complicit with positivist thinking which is also dominated by similar value-laden oppositions. However, Johnson perhaps does not give sufficient credit to the playful nature of a text such as *S/Z*. As mentioned earlier, Barthes makes no scientific claims for his codes and he would not be surprised, I think, by the fact that the 'writerly–readerly' opposition could not be made hard and fast. Though differences may collapse into each other when subjected to deconstructive scrutiny this does not mean that one can operate without them, even if one has to qualify certain terms by writing 'under erasure' in brackets after them. De Man as an extreme sceptic shared none of Barthes's political goals so that the kind of criticism he favoured was free to take deconstruction to its extremity, concluding notoriously that 'reading is impossible'. Barthes, in contrast, wants reading to make a difference even if that involves making use of myth and oppositions which may be vulnerable to the rigours of deconstructive logic.

Roland Barthes was a critic who never stood still. As with such modernist artists as Picasso one has to talk of his work as falling into different phases. He can never be securely pinned down though the term 'structuralist' perhaps has greater force than any other that could be applied to him. But his structuralism interacted with his commitment to modernism, his concern with the politics of writing and reading, his refusal to accept the artist–critic division, his aware-ness of the work of poststructuralists such as Derrida. All of Barthes's critical phases continue to be influential and this makes him one of the major critics of the latter half of the twentieth century.

1.1

FROM SCIENCE TO LITERATURE

Roland Barthes

'Man cannot speak his thought without thinking his speech.'

— BONALD

French university faculties possess an official list of the social and human sciences which constitute the object of a recognized instruction, thereby necessarily limiting the specialty of the diplomas they confer: you can be a doctor of aesthetics, of psychology, of sociology – not of heraldry, of semantics, of victimology. Thereby the institution directly determines the nature of human knowledge, imposing its modes of division and of classification, just as a language, by its 'obligatory rubrics' (and not only by its exclusions), compels us to think in a certain way. In other words, what defines *science* (the word will henceforth be used, in this text, to refer to all the social and human sciences) is neither its content (which is often ill defined and labile) nor its method (which varies from one science to the next: what do the science of history and that of experimental psychology have in common?), nor its morality (neither seriousness nor rigor is the property of science), nor its mode of communication (science is printed in books, like everything else), but only its *status*, i.e. its social determination: the object of science is any material society deems worthy of being transmitted. In a word, science is what is taught.

Literature has all the secondary characteristics of science, i.e. all the attributes which do not define it. Its contents are precisely those of science: there is certainly not a single scientific matter which has not at some moment

Extract from Roland Barthes, *The Rustle of Language*, trans. Richard Howard (University of California Press, 1989), pp. 3–10.

been treated by universal literature: the world of the work is a total world, in which all (social, psychological, historical) knowledge takes place, so that for us literature has that grand cosmogonic unity which so delighted the ancient Greeks but which the compartmentalized state of our sciences denies us today. Further, like science, literature is methodical: it has its programs of research, which vary according to schools and periods (like those of science, moreover), its rules of investigation, sometimes even its experimental pretensions. Like science, literature has its morality, a certain way of extracting its rules of procedure from the image it assumes of its being, and consequently of submitting its enterprises to a certain absolute spirit.

One last feature unites science and literature, but this feature is also the one which divides them more certainly than any other difference: both are discourses (which was well expressed by the idea of the ancient *logos*), but science and literature do not assume – do not profess – the language which constitutes them in the same way. For science, language is merely an instrument, which it chooses to make as transparent, as neutral as possible, subjugated to scientific matters (operations, hypotheses, results), which are said to exist outside it and to precede it: on one side and *first of all*, the contents of the scientific message, which are everything; and on the other and *afterwards*, the verbal form entrusted with expressing these contents, which is nothing. It is no coincidence if, since the sixteenth century, the combined rise of empiricism, of rationalism, and of religious evidence (with the Reformation), i.e. of the scientific spirit (in the very broad sense of the term), has been accompanied by a regression of the autonomy of language, henceforth relegated to the status of 'instrument' or of 'fine style', whereas in the Middle Ages human culture, as interpreted by the *Septenium*, shared almost equally the secrets of language and those of nature.

For literature, on the contrary – at least for that literature which has issued from classicism and from humanism – language can no longer be the convenient instrument or the sumptuous decor of a social, emotional or poetic 'reality' which preexists it and which it is responsible, in a subsidiary way, for expressing, provided it abides by a few rules of style: no, language is the *being* of literature, its very world: all literature is contained in the act of writing, and no longer in that of 'thinking', of 'painting', of 'recounting', of 'feeling'. Technically, according to Roman Jakobson's definition, the 'poetic' (i.e. the literary) designates that type of message which takes for object its own form, and not its contents. Ethically, it is solely by its passage through language that literature pursues the disturbance of the essential concepts of our culture, 'reality' chief among them. Politically, it is by professing (and illustrating) that no language is innocent, it is by employing what might be called an 'integral language' that literature is revolutionary. Literature thus is alone today in bearing the entire responsibility for language; for though science needs language, it is not, like literature, *within* language; science is taught, i.e. it makes itself known; literature fulfills more than it transmits itself (only its history is taught). Science speaks itself; literature writes itself; science is led by the voice, literature follows the hand; it is not the same body, and hence the same desire, which is behind the one and the other.

Bearing essentially on a certain way of taking language – in the former case dodged and in the latter assumed – the opposition between science and literature is of particular importance to structuralism. Of course this word, generally imposed from outside, actually overlaps very diverse, sometimes divergent, sometimes even hostile enterprises, and no one can claim the privilege of speaking in its name; the author of these lines makes no such claim; he merely retains the most particular and consequently the most pertinent version of contemporary structuralism, meaning by that name a certain mode of analysis of cultural works, insofar as this mode is inspired by the methods of contemporary linguistics. Thus, itself resulting from a linguistic model, structuralism finds in literature, the work of language, an object much more than affinitary: homogeneous to itself. This coincidence does not exclude a certain embarrassment, even a certain laceration, depending on whether structuralism means to keep the distance of a science in relation to its object, or whether, on the contrary, it is willing to compromise and to spoil the analysis it wields in that infinitude of language of which literature is today the conduit – in a word, depending on whether it seeks to be science or writing.

As science, structuralism 'finds itself', one might say, on every level of the literary work. First of all, on the level of contents, or more exactly, on the level of the form of contents, since structuralism seeks to establish the 'language' of the stories told, their articulations, their units, the logic which links some to others – in short, the general mythology in which each literary work participates. Next, on the level of the forms of discourse: structuralism, by virtue of its method, pays special attention to classifications, orders, arrangements; its essential object is taxonomy, or the distributive model inevitably established by any human work, institution, or book, for there is no culture without classification; now discourse, or ensemble of words superior to the sentence, has its forms of organization; it too is a classification, and a signifying one; on this point, literary structuralism has a glamorous ancestor, one whose historical role is in general underestimated or discredited for ideological reasons: Rhetoric, grandiose effort of an entire culture to analyze and classify the forms of speech, to render the world of language intelligible. Finally, on the level of words: the sentence has not only a literal or denoted meaning; it is crammed with supplementary significations: since it is at once a cultural reference, a rhetorical model, a deliberate ambiguity of the speech-act, and a simple unit of denotation, the 'literary' word has the depth of a space, and this space is the field of structural analysis itself, whose project is much greater than that of the old stylistics, entirely based as it was on an erroneous idea of 'expressivity'. On all its levels – that of the argument, that of discourse, that of the words – the literary work thereby offers structuralism the image of a structure perfectly homological (present-day investigations tend to prove this) to the structure of language itself; derived from linguistics, structuralism encounters in literature an object which is itself derived from language. Henceforth, it will be understood that structuralism may attempt to found a science of literature, or more exactly a linguistics of discourse, whose object is the 'language' of literary forms, apprehended on many levels: a new project, for hitherto literature has been approached 'scientifically' only in a very marginal fashion – by the history of works, or of authors, or of schools, or of texts (philology).

New as it may be, this project is nonetheless not satisfactory – or at least not sufficient. It leaves untouched the dilemma I mentioned at the beginning, one that is allegorically suggested by the opposition between science and literature, insofar as literature assumes its own language – under the name of writing – and science avoids it, feigning to regard it as purely instrumental. In a word, structuralism will never be anything but one more 'science' (several of these are born every century, some quite ephemeral), if it cannot make its central enterprise the very subversion of scientific language, i.e. cannot 'write itself': how can it fail to call into question the very language by which it knows language? Structuralism's logical extension can only be to join literature no longer as 'object' of analysis but as activity of writing, to abolish the distinction, born of logic, which makes the work into a language-object and science into a meta-language, and thereby to risk the illusory privilege attached by science to the ownership of a slave language.

It remains therefore for the structuralist to transform himself into a 'writer', not in order to profess or to practice 'style', but in order to recognize the crucial problems of any speech-act, once it is no longer swathed in the kindly cloud of strictly *realist* illusions which make language the simple medium of thought. This transformation – still rather theoretical, it must be admitted – requires a certain number of clarifications – or acknowledgments. First of all, the relations of subjectivity and objectivity – or, to put it another way, the subject's place in his work – can no longer be conceived as in the palmy days of positivist science. Objectivity and rigor, attributes of the scholar which we still hear so much about, are essentially preparatory virtues, necessary to the work's moment, and as such there is no reason to mistrust them or to abandon them; but these virtues cannot be transferred to discourse, except by a kind of hocus-pocus, a purely metonymic procedure which identifies *precaution* with its discursive effect. Every speech-act supposes its own subject, whether this subject expresses himself in an apparently direct fashion, by saying *I*, or indirect, by designating himself as *he*, or in no fashion at all, by resorting to impersonal turns of speech; what is in question here are purely grammatical stratagems, simply varying how the subject constitutes himself in discourse, i.e. gives himself, theatrically or fantasmatically, to others; hence they all designate forms of the image-repertoire. Of these forms, the most specious is the privative form, precisely the one usually employed in scientific discourse, from which the scholar excludes himself in a concern for objectivity; yet what is excluded is never anything but the 'person' (psychological, emotional, biographical), not the subject; moreover, this subject is filled, so to speak, with the very exclusion it so spectacularly imposes upon its person, so that objectivity, on the level of discourse – an inevitable level, we must not forget – is an image-repertoire like any other. In truth, only an integral formalization of scientific discourse (that of the human sciences, of course, for in the case of the other sciences this has already been largely achieved) could spare science the risks of the image-repertoire – unless, of course, it consents to employ this image-repertoire *with full knowledge*, a knowledge which can be achieved only in writing: only writing has occasion to dispel the bad faith attached to every language unaware of its own existence.

Again, only writing – and this is a first approach to its definition – effectuates language in its totality. To resort to scientific discourse as to an instrument of thought is to postulate that a neutral state of language exists, from which would branch off, like so many gaps and ornaments, a certain number of special languages, such as the literary language or the poetic language; this neutral state would be, it is assumed, the code of reference for all the 'eccentric' languages which would be only so many sub-codes; by identifying itself with this referential code, basis of all normality, scientific discourse arrogates to itself the very authority which writing must contest; the notion of 'writing' implies in effect the idea that language is a vast system of which no single code is privileged – or, one may say, central – and of which the departments are in a relation of 'fluctuating hierarchy'. Scientific discourse believes it is a superior code; writing seeks to be a total code, including its own forces of destruction. It follows that only writing can break the theological image imposed by science, can reject the paternal terror spread by the abusive 'truth' of contents and reasonings, can open to research the complete space of language, with its logical subversions, the mixing of its codes, with its slippages, its dialogues, its parodies; only writing can set in opposition to the savant's assurance – insofar as he 'expresses' his science – what Lautréamont called the writer's 'modesty'.

Last, between science and writing, there is a third margin, which science must reconquer: that of *pleasure*. In a civilization inured by monotheism to the idea of Transgression, where every value is the product of a punishment, this word has an unfortunate resonance: there is something light, trivial, partial about it. Coleridge said: 'A poem is that species of composition which is opposed to works by science, by purposing, for its immediate object, pleasure, not truth' – an ambiguous declaration, for if it assumes the 'erotic' nature of the poem (of literature), it continues to assign it a special and guarded canton, distinct from the major territory of truth. 'Pleasure', however – we admit this more readily nowadays – implies an experience much wider, more significant than the simple satisfaction of 'taste'. Now, the pleasure of language has never been seriously considered; the old Rhetoric had, in its fashion, some idea of it when it set up a special genre of discourse dedicated to spectacle and to admiration, the *epidictic*; but classical art wrapped the *pleasing* which it claimed as its law (Racine: 'The first rule is to please …') in all the constraints of the 'natural'; only the baroque, a literary experiment which has never been more than tolerated by our societies, at least by French society, dared some exploration of what might be called the Eros of language. Scientific discourse is remote from this; for if it accepted the notion, it would have to renounce all the privileges with which the social institution surrounds it and agree to return to that 'literary life' Baudelaire calls, apropos of Poe, 'the sole element in which certain *déclassés* can breathe.'

Mutation of consciousness, of structure, and of the purposes of scientific discourse – that is what must be demanded today, precisely where the flourishing, constituted human sciences seem to leave less and less room for a literature commonly accused of unreality and inhumanity. But precisely: the role of literature is to *represent* actively to the scientific institution just what it rejects, i.e. the sovereignty of language. And structuralism should be in a good position to provoke this scandal; for, intensely conscious of the linguistic nature of human works, only structuralism today can reopen the problem of the linguistic status of science; having language – all languages – for object, it has very quickly come to define itself as our culture's meta-language. This stage, however, must be transcended, for the opposition of language-objects and their meta-language remains ultimately subject to the paternal model of a science without language. The task facing structural discourse is to make itself entirely homogeneous to its object; this task can be accomplished by only two methods, each as radical as the other: either by an exhaustive formalization, or else by an integral writing. In this second hypothesis (which we are defending here), science will become literature, insofar as literature – subject, moreover, to a growing collapse of traditional genres (poem, narrative, criticism, essay) – is already, has always been, science; for what the human sciences are discovering today, in whatever realm: sociological, psychological, psychiatric, linguistic, etc., literature has always known; the only difference is that literature has not *said* what it knows, it has *written* it. Confronting this integral truth of writing, the 'human sciences', belatedly constituted in the wake of bourgeois positivism, appear as the technical alibis our society uses to maintain the fiction of a theological truth, superbly – abusively – disengaged from language.

1.2

FROM *S/Z*

Roland Barthes

I. EVALUATION

There are said to be certain Buddhists whose ascetic practices enable them to see a whole landscape in a bean. Precisely what the first analysts of narrative were attempting: to see all the world's stories (and there have been ever so many) within a single structure: we shall, they thought, extract from each tale its model, then out of these models we shall make a great narrative structure, which we shall reapply (for verification) to any one narrative: a task as exhausting (ninety-nine percent perspiration, as the saying goes) as it is ultimately undesirable, for the text thereby loses its difference. This difference is not, obviously, some complete, irreducible quality (according to a mythic view of literary creation), it is not what designates the individuality of each text, what names, signs, finishes off each work with a flourish; on the contrary, it is a difference which does not stop and which is articulated upon the infinity of texts, of languages, of systems: a difference of which each text is the return. A choice must then be made: either to place all texts in a demonstrative oscillation, equalizing them under the scrutiny of an in-different science, forcing them to rejoin, inductively, the Copy from which we will then make them derive; or else to restore each text, not to its individuality, but to its function, making it cohere, even before we talk about it, by the infinite paradigm of difference, subjecting it from the outset to a basic typology, to an evaluation. How then posit the value of a text? How establish a basic

Extracts from Roland Barthes, *S/Z*, trans. Richard Miller (Farrer, Strauss, and Giroux, 1974), pp. 3–16.

typology of texts? The primary evaluation of all texts can come neither from science, for science does not evaluate, nor from ideology, for the ideological value of a text (moral, aesthetic, political, alethiological) is a value of representation, not of production (ideology 'reflects', it does not do work). Our evaluation can be linked only to a practice, and this practice is that of writing. On the one hand, there is what it is possible to write, and on the other, what it is no longer possible to write: what is within the practice of the writer and what has left it: which texts would I consent to write (to re-write), to desire, to put forth as a force in this world of mine? What evaluation finds is precisely this value: what can be written (rewritten) today: the *writerly*. Why is the writerly our value? Because the goal of literary work (of literature as work) is to make the reader no longer a consumer, but a producer of the text. Our literature is characterized by the pitiless divorce which the literary institution maintains between the producer of the text and its user, between its owner and its customer, between its author and its reader. This reader is thereby plunged into a kind of idleness – he is intransitive; he is, in short, *serious:* instead of functioning himself, instead of gaining access to the magic of the signifier, to the pleasure of writing, he is left with no more than the poor freedom either to accept or reject the text: reading is nothing more than a *referendum.* Opposite the writerly text, then, is its countervalue, its negative, reactive value: what can be read, but not written: the *readerly.* We call any readerly text a classic text.

II. INTERPRETATION

There may be nothing to say about writerly texts. First of all, where can we find them? Certainly not in reading (or at least very rarely: by accident, fleetingly, obliquely in certain limit-works): the writerly text is not a thing, we would have a hard time finding it in a bookstore. Further, its model being a productive (and no longer a representative) one, it demolishes any criticism which, once produced, would mix with it: to rewrite the writerly text would consist only in disseminating it, in dispersing it within the field of infinite difference. The writerly text is a perpetual present, upon which no *consequent* language (which would inevitably make it past) can be superimposed; the writerly text is *ourselves writing*, before the infinite play of the world (the world as function) is traversed, intersected, stopped, plasticized by some singular system (Ideology, Genus, Criticism) which reduces the plurality of entrances, the opening of networks, the infinity of languages. The writerly is the novelistic without the novel, poetry without the poem, the essay without the dissertation, writing without style, production without product, structuration without structure. But the readerly texts? They are products (and not productions), they make up the enormous mass of our literature. How differentiate this mass once again? Here, we require a second operation, consequent upon the evaluation which has separated the texts, more delicate than that evaluation, based upon the appreciation of a certain quantity – of the *more or less* each text can mobilize.

This new operation is *interpretation* (in the Nietzschean sense of the word). To interpret a text is not to give it a (more or less justified, more or less free) meaning, but on the contrary to appreciate what *plural* constitutes it. Let us first posit the image of a triumphant plural, unimpoverished by any constraint of representation (of imitation). In this ideal text, the networks are many and interact, without any one of them being able to surpass the rest; this text is a galaxy of signifiers, not a structure of signifieds; it has no beginning; it is reversible; we gain access to it by several entrances, none of which can be authoritatively declared to be the main one; the codes it mobilizes extend *as far as the eye can reach*, they are indeterminable (meaning here is never subject to a principle of determination, unless by throwing dice); the systems of meaning can take over this absolutely plural text, but their number is never closed, based as it is on the infinity of language. The interpretation demanded by a specific text, in its plurality, is in no way liberal: it is not a question of conceding some meanings, of magnanimously acknowledging that each one has its share of truth; it is a question, against all in-difference, of asserting the very existence of plurality, which is not that of the true, the probable, or even the possible. This necessary assertion is difficult, however, for as nothing exists outside the text, there is never a *whole* of the text (which would by reversion form an internal order, a reconciliation of complementary parts, under the paternal eye of the representative Model): the text must simultaneously be distinguished from its exterior and from its totality. All of which comes down to saying that for the plural text, there cannot be a narrative structure, a grammar, or a logic; thus, if one or another of these are sometimes permitted to come forward, it is *in proportion* (giving this expression its full quantitative value) as we are dealing with incompletely plural texts, texts whose plural is more or less parsimonious.

III. Connotation: Against

For these moderately plural (i.e. merely polysemous) texts, there exists an average appreciator which can grasp only a certain median portion of the plural, an instrument at once too delicate and too vague to be applied to univocal texts, and too poor to be applied to multivalent texts, which are reversible and frankly indeterminable (integrally plural texts). This *modest* instrument is connotation. For Hjelmslev, who has defined it, connotation is a secondary meaning, whose signifier is itself constituted by a sign or system of primary signification, which is denotation: if E is the expression, C the content, and R the relation of the two which establishes the sign, the formula for the connotation is: (ERC) R C. Doubtless because it has not been limited, subjected to a typology of texts, connotation has not had a good press. Some (the philologists, let us say), declaring every text to be univocal, possessing a true, canonical meaning, banish the simultaneous, secondary meanings to the void of critical lucubrations. On the other hand, others (the semiologists, let us say) contest the hierarchy of denotated and connotated; language, they say, the raw material of denotation, with its dictionary and its syntax, is a system like any other; there is no reason to make this system the privileged one, to make it the locus and the norm of a primary, original meaning, the scale for all associated meanings; if we base denotation on truth, on objectivity, on law, it is because we are still in awe of the prestige of linguistics, which, until today, has been reducing language to the sentence and its lexical and syntactical components; now the endeavor of this hierarchy is a serious one: it is to return to the closure of Western discourse (scientific, critical or philosophical), to its centralized organization, to arrange all the meanings of a text in a circle around the hearth of denotation (the hearth: center, guardian, refuge, light of truth).

IV. CONNOTATION: FOR, EVEN SO

This criticism of connotation is only half fair; it does not take into account the typology of the texts (this typology is basic: no text exists without being classified according to its value); for if there are readerly texts, committed to the closure system of the West, produced according to the goals of this system, devoted to the law of the Signified, they must have a particular system of meaning, and this meaning is based on connotation. Hence, to deny connotation altogether is to abolish the differential *value* of the texts, to refuse to define the specific apparatus (both poetic and critical) for the readerly texts – it is to make the limited text equal to the limit-text, to deprive oneself of a typological instrument. Connotation is the way into the polysemy of the classic text, to that limited plural on which the classic text is based (it is not certain that there are connotations in the modern text). Connotation must therefore be rescued from its double contestation and kept as the namable, computable trace of a *certain* plural of the text (that limited plural of the classic text). Then, what is a connotation? Definitionally, it is a determination, a relation, an anaphora, a feature which has the power to relate itself to anterior, ulterior, or exterior mentions, to other sites of the text (or of another text): we must in no way restrain this relating, which can be given various names (*function* or *index*, for example), except that we must not confuse connotation with association of ideas: the latter refers to the system of a subject; connotation is a correlation immanent in the text, in the texts; or again, one may say that it is an association made by the text-as-subject within its own system. Topically, connotations are meanings which are neither in the dictionary nor in the grammar of the language in which a text is written (this is, of course, a shaky definition: the dictionary can be expanded, the grammar can be modified). Analytically, connotation is determined by two spaces: a sequential space, a series of orders, a space subject to the successivity of sentences, in which meaning proliferates by layering; and an agglomerative space, certain areas of the text correlating other meanings outside the material text and, with them, forming 'nebulae' of signifieds. Topologically, connotation makes possible a (limited) dissemination of meanings, spread like gold dust on the apparent surface of the text (meaning is golden). Semiologically, each connotation is the starting point of a code (which will never be reconstituted), the articulation of a voice which is woven into the text. Dynamically, it is a subjugation which the text must undergo, it is the possibility of this subjugation (meaning is a force). Historically, by inducing meanings that are apparently recoverable (even if they are not lexical), connotation establishes a (dated) Literature of the Signified. Functionally, connotation, releasing the double meaning on principle, corrupts the purity of communication: it is a deliberate 'static', painstakingly elaborated, introduced into the fictive dialogue between author and reader, in short, a countercommunication (Literature is an intentional cacography.) Structurally, the existence of two supposedly different systems – denotation and connotation – enables the text to operate like a game, each system referring to the other according to the requirements of a certain *illusion*. Ideologically, finally, this game has the advantage of affording the classic text a certain *innocence*: of the two systems, denotative and connotative, one turns back on itself and indicates its own existence: the system of denotation; denotation is not the first meaning, but pretends to be so; under this illusion, it is ultimately no more than the *last* of the connotations (the one which seems both to establish and to close the reading), the superior myth by which the text pretends to return to the nature of language, to language as nature: doesn't a sentence, whatever meaning it releases, subsequent to its utterance, it would seem, appear to be telling us something simple, literal, primitive: something *true*, in relation to which all the rest (which comes *afterwards, on top*) is literature? This is why, if we want to go along with the classic text, we must keep denotation, the old deity, watchful, cunning, theatrical, foreordained to *represent* the collective innocence of language.

V. READING, FORGETTING

I read the text. This statement, consonant with the 'genius' of the language (subject, verb, complement), is not always true. The more plural the text, the less it is written before I read it; I do not make it undergo a predicative operation, consequent upon its being, an operation known as *reading*, and I is not an innocent subject, anterior to the text, one which will subsequently deal with the text as it would an object to dismantle or a site to occupy. This 'I' which approaches the text is already itself a plurality of other texts, of codes which are infinite or, more precisely, lost (whose origin is lost). *Objectivity* and *subjectivity* are of course forces which can take over the text, but they are forces which have no affinity with it. Subjectivity is a plenary image, with which I may be thought to encumber the text, but whose deceptive plenitude is merely the wake of all the codes which constitute me, so that my subjectivity has ultimately the generality of stereotypes. Objectivity is the same type of replenishment: it is an imaginary system like the rest (except that here the castrating gesture is more fiercely characterized), an image which serves to name me advantageously, to make myself known, 'misknown', even to myself. Reading involves risks of objectivity or subjectivity (both are imaginary) only insofar as we define the text as an expressive object (presented for our own expression), sublimated under a morality of truth, in one instance laxist; in the other, ascetic. Yet reading is not a parasitical act, the reactive complement of a writing which we endow with all the glamour of creation and anteriority. It is a form of work (which is why it would be better to speak of a lexeological act – even a lexeographical act, since I write my reading), and the method of this work is topological: I am not hidden within the text, I am simply irrecoverable from it: my task is to move, to shift systems whose perspective ends neither at the text nor at the 'I': in operational terms, the meanings I find are established not by 'me' or by others, but by their *systematic* mark: there is no other *proof* of a reading than the quality and endurance of its systematics; in other words: than its functioning. To read, in fact, is a labor of language. To read is to find meanings, and to find meanings is to name them; but these named meanings are swept toward other names; names call to each other, reassemble, and their grouping calls for further naming: I name, I unname, I rename: so the text passes: it is a nomination in the course of becoming, a tireless approximation, a metonymic labor. – With regard to the plural text, forgetting a meaning cannot therefore be seen as a fault. Forgetting in relation to what? What is the *sum* of the text? Meanings can indeed be forgotten, but only if we have chosen to bring to bear upon the text a singular scrutiny. Yet reading does not consist in stopping the chain of systems, in establishing a truth, a legality of the text, and consequently in leading its reader into 'errors'; it consists in coupling these systems, not according to their finite quantity, but according to their plurality (which is a being, not a discounting): I pass, I intersect, I articulate, I release, I do not count. Forgetting meanings is not a matter for excuses, an unfortunate defect in performance; it is an affirmative value, a way of asserting the irresponsibility of the text, the pluralism of systems (if I closed their list, I would inevitably reconstitute a singular, theological meaning): it is precisely because I forget that I read.

VI. STEP BY STEP

If we want to remain attentive to the plural of a text (however limited it may be), we must renounce structuring this text in large masses, as was done by classical rhetoric and by secondary-school explication: no *construction* of the text: everything signifies ceaselessly and several times, but without being delegated to a great final ensemble, to an ultimate structure. Whence the idea, and so to speak the necessity, of a gradual analysis of a single text. Whence, it would seem, several implications and several advantages. The commentary on a single text is not a contingent activity, assigned the reassuring alibi of the 'concrete': the single text is valid for all the texts of literature, not in that it represents them (abstracts and equalizes them), but in that literature itself is never anything but a single text: the one text is not an (inductive) access to a Model, but entrance into a network with a thousand entrances; to take this entrance is to aim, ultimately, not at a legal structure of norms and departures, a narrative or poetic Law, but at a perspective (of fragments, of voices from other texts, other codes), whose vanishing point is nonetheless ceaselessly pushed back, mysteriously opened: each (single) text is the very theory (and not the mere example) of this vanishing, of this difference which indefinitely returns, insubmissive. Further, to study this text down to the last detail is to take up the structural analysis of narrative where it has been left till now: at the major structures; it is to assume the power (the time, the elbow room) of working back along the threads of meanings, of abandoning no site of the signifier without endeavoring to ascertain the code or codes of which this site is perhaps the starting point (or the goal); it is (at least we may hope as much, and work to this end) to substitute for the simple representative model another model, whose very gradualness would guarantee what may be productive in the classic text; for the *step-by-step* method, through its very slowness and dispersion, avoids penetrating, reversing the tutor text, giving an internal image of it: it is never anything but the *decomposition* (in the cinematographic sense) of the work of reading: a *slow motion*, so to speak, neither wholly image nor wholly analysis; it is, finally, in the very writing of the commentary, a systematic use of digression (a form ill-accommodated by the discourse of knowledge) and thereby a way of observing the reversibility of the structures from which the text is woven; of course, the classic text is incompletely reversible (it is modestly plural): the reading of this text occurs within a necessary order, which the gradual analysis will make precisely its order of writing; but the step-by-step commentary is of necessity a renewal of the entrances to the text, it avoids structuring the text *excessively*, avoids giving it that additional structure which would come from a dissertation and would close it: it stars the text, instead of assembling it.

VII. THE STARRED TEXT

We shall therefore star the text, separating, in the manner of a minor earthquake, the blocks of signification of which reading grasps only the smooth surface, imperceptibly soldered by the movement of sentences, the flowing discourse of narration, the 'naturalness' of ordinary language. The tutor signifier will be cut up into a series of brief, contiguous fragments, which we shall call *lexias*, since they are units of reading. This cutting up, admittedly, will be arbitrary in the extreme; it will imply no methodological responsibility, since it will bear on the signifier, whereas the proposed analysis bears solely on the signified. The lexia will include sometimes a few words, sometimes several sentences; it will be a matter of convenience: it will suffice that the lexia be the best possible space in which we can observe meanings; its dimension, empirically determined, estimated, will depend on the density of connotations, variable according to the moments of the text: all we require is that each lexia should have at most three or four meanings to be enumerated. The text, in its mass, is comparable to a sky, at once flat and smooth, deep, without edges and without landmarks; like the soothsayer drawing on it with the tip of his staff an imaginary rectangle wherein to consult, according to certain principles, the flight of birds, the commentator traces through the text certain zones of reading, in order to observe therein the migration of meanings, the outcropping of codes, the passage of citations. The lexia is only the wrapping of a semantic volume, the crest line of the plural text, arranged like a berm of possible (but controlled, attested to by a systematic reading) meanings under the flux of discourse: the lexia and its units will thereby form a kind of polyhedron faceted by the word, the group of words, the sentence or the paragraph, i.e. with the language which is its 'natural' excipient.

VIII. THE BROKEN TEXT

What will be noted is, across these artificial articulations, the shifting and repetition of the signifieds. Discerning these signifieds systematically for each lexia does not aim at establishing the truth of the text (its profound, strategic structure), but its plurality (however parsimonious); the units of meaning (the connotations), strung out separately for each lexia, will not then be regrouped, provided with a metameaning which would be the ultimate construction to be given them (we shall merely reconnect, as an appendix, certain sequences which might have become lost in the unraveling of the tutor text). We shall not set forth the criticism of a text, or a criticism of *this* text; we shall propose the semantic substance (divided but not distributed) of several kinds of criticism (psychological, psychoanalytical, thematic, historical, structural); it will then be up to each kind of criticism (if it should so desire) to come into play, to make its voice heard, which is the hearing of one of the voices of the text. What we seek is to sketch the stereographic space of writing (which will here be a classic, readerly writing). The commentary, based on the affirmation of the plural, cannot therefore work with 'respect' to the text; the tutor text will ceaselessly be broken, interrupted without any regard for its natural divisions (syntactical, rhetorical, anecdotic); inventory, explanation and digression may deter any observation of suspense, may even separate verb and complement, noun and attribute; the work of the commentary, once it is separated from any ideology of totality, consists precisely in *manhandling* the text, *interrupting* it. What is thereby denied is not the *quality* of the text (here incomparable) but its 'naturalness'.

IX. HOW MANY READINGS?

We must further accept one last freedom: that of reading the text as if it had already been read. Those who like a good story may certainly turn to the end of the book and read the tutor text first; it is given as an appendix in its purity and continuity, as it came from the printer, in short, as we habitually read it. But for those of us who are trying to establish a plural, we cannot stop this plural at the gates of reading: the reading must also be plural, that is, without order of entrance: the 'first' version of a reading must be able to be its last, as though the text were reconstituted in order to achieve its artifice of continuity, the signifier then being provided with an additional feature: shifting. Rereading, an operation contrary to the commercial and ideological habits of our society, which would have us 'throw away' the story once it has been consumed ('devoured'), so that we can then move on to another story, buy another book, and which is tolerated only in certain marginal categories of readers (children, old people and professors), rereading is here suggested at the outset, for it alone saves the text from repetition (those who fail to reread are obliged to read the same story everywhere), multiplies it in its variety and its plurality: rereading draws the text out of its internal chronology ('this happens *before* or *after* that') and recaptures a mythic time (without *before* or *after*); it contests the claim which would have us believe that the first reading is a primary, naïve, phenomenal reading which we will only, afterwards, have to 'explicate', to intellectualize (as if there were a beginning of reading, as if everything were not already read: there is no *first* reading, even if the text is concerned to give us that illusion by several operations of *suspense*, artifices more spectacular than persuasive); rereading is no longer consumption, but play (that play which is the return of the different). If then, a deliberate contradiction in terms, we *immediately* reread the text, it is in order to obtain, as though under the effect of a drug (that of recommencement, of difference), not the *real* text, but a plural text: the same and new.

X. SARRASINE

The text I have chosen (Why? All I know is that for some time I have wanted to make a complete analysis of a short text and that the Balzac story was brought to my attention by an article by Jean Reboul (1967), who in turn is supposed to have been inspired by Georges Bataille's reference; and thus I was caught up in this 'series' whose scope I was to discover by means of the text itself) is Balzac's *Sarrasine*.

(1) SARRASINE ★ The title raises a question: *What is Sarrasine?* A noun? A name? A thing? A man? A woman? This question will not be answered until much later, by the biography of the sculptor named Sarrasine. Let us designate as *hermeneutic code* (HER) all the units whose function it is to articulate in various ways a question, its response, and the variety of chance events which can either formulate the question or delay its answer; or even, constitute an enigma and lead to its solution. Thus, the title *Sarrasine* initiates the first step in a sequence which will not be completed until No. 153 (HER. Enigma 1 – the story will contain others –: question). ★★ The word *Sarrasine* has an additional connotation, that of femininity, which will be obvious to any French-speaking person, since that language automatically takes the final 'e' as a specifically feminine linguistic property, particularly in the case of a proper name whose masculine form (*Sarrazin*) exists in French onomastics. Femininity (connoted) is a signifier which will occur in several places in the text; it is a shifting element which can combine with other similar elements to create characters, ambiances, shapes, and symbols. Although every unit we mention here will be a signifier, this one is of a very special type: it is the signifier par excellence because of its connotation, in the usual meaning of the term. We shall call this element a signifier (without going into further detail), or a *seme* (semantically, the seme is the unit of the signifier), and we shall indicate these

units by the abbreviation SEM, designating each time by an approximate word the connotative signifier referred to in the lexia (SEM. Femininity).

(2) *I was deep in one of those daydreams* ★ There will be nothing wayward about the daydream introduced here: it will be solidly constructed along the most familiar rhetorical lines, in a series of antitheses: garden and salon, life and death, cold and heat, outside and interior. The lexia thus lays the groundwork, in introductory form, for a vast symbolic structure, since it can lend itself to many substitutions, variations, which will lead us from the garden to the castrato, from the salon to the girl with whom the narrator is in love, by way of the mysterious old man, the full-bosomed Mme de Lanty, or Vien's moonlit Adonis. Thus, on the symbolic level, an immense province appears, the province of the antithesis, of which this forms the first unit, linking at the start its two adversative terms (A/B) in the word *daydream*. (We shall mark all the units in this symbolic area with the letters SYM. Here – SYM. Antithesis: AB.) ★★ The state of absorption formulated here (*I was deep in . . .*) already implies (at least in 'readerly' discourse) some event which will bring it to an end (. . . *when I was roused by a conversation . . .* No. 14). Such sequences imply a logic in human behavior. In Aristotelian terms, in which *praxis* is linked to *proairesis*, or the ability rationally to determine the result of an action, we shall name this code of actions and behavior *proairetic* (in narrative, however, the discourse, rather than the characters, determines the action). This code of actions will be abbreviated ACT; furthermore, since these actions produce effects, each effect will have a generic name giving a kind of title to the sequence, and we shall number each of the terms which constitute it, as they appear (ACT. 'To be deep in': 1: to be absorbed).

(3) *which overtake even the shallowest of men, in the midst of the most tumultuous parties.* ★ The fact 'there is a party' (given here obliquely), soon to be followed by further data (a private house in the Faubourg Saint-Honoré), forms a pertinent signifier: the wealth of the Lanty family (SEM. Wealth). ★★ The phrase is a conversion of what might easily be a real proverb: '*Tumultuous parties: deep daydreams.*' The statement is made in a collective and anonymous voice originating in traditional human experience. Thus, the unit has been formed by a gnomic code, and this code is one of the numerous codes of knowledge or wisdom to which the text continually refers; we shall call them in a very general way *cultural codes* (even though, of course, all codes are cultural), or rather, since they afford the discourse a basis in scientific or moral authority, we shall call them reference codes (REF. Gnomic code).

XI. THE FIVE CODES

As chance would have it (but what is chance?), the first three lexias – the title and the first sentence of the story – have already provided us with the five major codes under which all the textual signifiers can be grouped: without straining a point, there will be no other codes throughout the story but these five, and each and every lexia will fall under one of these five codes. Let us sum them up in order of their appearance, without trying to put them in any order of importance. Under the hermeneutic code, we list the various (formal) terms by which an enigma can be distinguished, suggested, formulated, held in suspense, and finally disclosed (these terms will not always occur, they will often be repeated; they will not appear in any fixed order). As for the semes, we merely indicate them – without, in other words, trying either to link them to a character (or a place or an object) or to arrange them in some order so that they form a single thematic grouping; we allow them the instability, the dispersion, characteristic of motes of dust, flickers of meaning. Moreover, we shall refrain from structuring the symbolic grouping; this is the place for multivalence and for reversibility; the main task is always to demonstrate that this field can be entered from any number of points, thereby making depth and secrecy problematic. Actions (terms of the proairetic code) can fall into various sequences which should be indicated merely by listing them, since the proairetic sequence is never more than the result of an artifice of reading: whoever reads the text amasses certain data under some generic titles for actions (*stroll, murder, rendezvous*), and this title embodies the sequence; the sequence exists when and because it can be given a name, it unfolds as this process of naming takes place, as a title is sought or confirmed; its basis is therefore more empirical than rational, and it is useless to attempt to force it into a statutory order; its only logic is that of the 'already-done' or 'already-read' – whence the variety of sequences (some trivial, some melodramatic) and the variety of terms (numerous or few); here again, we shall not attempt to put them into any order. Indicating them (externally and internally) will suffice to demonstrate the plural meaning entangled in them. Lastly, the cultural codes are references to a science or a body of knowledge; in drawing attention to them, we merely indicate the type of knowledge (physical, physiological, medical, psychological, literary, historical, etc.) referred to, without going so far as to construct (or reconstruct) the culture they express.

XII. THE WEAVING OF VOICES

The five codes create a kind of network, a topos through which the entire text passes (or rather, in passing, becomes text). Thus, if we make no effort to structure each code, or the five codes among themselves, we do so deliberately, in order to assume the multivalence of the text, its partial reversibility. We are, in fact, concerned not to manifest a structure but to produce a structuration. The blanks and looseness of the analysis will be like footprints marking the escape of the text; for if the text is subject to some form, this form is not unitary, architectonic, finite: it is the fragment, the shards, the broken or obliterated network – all the movements and inflections of a vast 'dissolve', which permits both overlapping and loss of messages. Hence we use *Code* here not in the sense of a list, a paradigm that must be reconstituted. The code is a perspective of quotations, a mirage of structures; we know only its departures and returns; the units which have resulted from it (those we inventory) are themselves, always, ventures out of the text, the mark, the sign of a virtual digression toward the remainder of a catalogue (*The Kidnapping* refers to every kidnapping ever written); they are so many fragments of something that has always been *already* read, seen, done, experienced; the code is the wake of that *already*. Referring to what has been written, i.e. to the Book (of culture, of life, of life as culture), it makes the text into a prospectus of this Book. Or again: each code is one of the forces that can take over the text (of which the text is the network), one of the voices out of which the text is woven. Alongside each utterance, one might say that off-stage voices can be heard: they are the codes: in their interweaving, these voices (whose origin is 'lost' in the vast perspective of the *already-written*) de-originate the utterance: the convergence of the voices (of the codes) becomes *writing*, a stereographic space where the five codes, the five voices, intersect: the Voice of Empirics (the proairetisms), the Voice of the Person (the semes), the Voice of Science (the cultural codes), the Voice of Truth (the hermeneutisms), the Voice of Symbol.

ANNOTATED BIBLIOGRAPHY

Barthes, Roland. *Writing Degree Zero*, trans. Annette Lavers and Colin Smith. London, 1967.

Barthes's first book published in 1953 and one which formulates some of the preoccupations that recur throughout his writings. It establishes him as a writer and critic whose fundamental sympathies are with the modernist movement in art. Barthes focuses on classical French writing (*écriture classique*), a way of writing that was so powerful that it was not seen as a particular literary style but merely as a reflection of reality, natural and innocent. He particularly attacks the appropriation of this style by the bourgeoisie in the nineteenth century when it became encoded with bourgeois values and he supports twentieth-century writing which resists it by apparently being devoid of style.

Barthes, Roland. *Mythologies*, trans. Annette Lavers. London, 1972.

Barthes's most popular book and one which showed that structuralism was not an opaque methodology that was relevant only to such fields as social anthropology and literary criticism but could be applied to virtually every cultural area, both low and high. The book also showed how structuralist criticism could operate as political critique. The discussion of myth as a second-order semiotic system is particularly important.

Barthes, Roland. *Criticism and Truth*, trans. Katrine Pilcher Keuneman. London, 1987.

Barthes's response to an attack on him by a traditional French academic critic, Raymond Picard. Picard scathingly criticised Barthes's book *Sur Racine*, which made use of psychoanalysis and marxism, and accused it of intellectual irresponsibility when compared with objective, historically-based academic criticism. Barthes argues against Picard that traditional academic criticism is not ideologically innocent, that literature has an inherent plurality and cannot be pinned down to a restricted set of meanings.

Culler, Jonathan. *Structuralist Poetics: Structuralism, Linguistics and the Study of Literature*. London, 1975.

Still probably the best general study of structuralism. Particularly useful on the relationship between structuralism and linguistic theory. Full discussions of Jakobson, Barthes, Greimas, Todorov, Genette and other significant critics and theorists. Culler's belief that one can construct 'a poetics which stands to literature as linguistics stands to language' is more controversial.

Macksey, Richard (with Eugenio Donato), ed. *The Structuralist Controversy: The Languages of Criticism and the Sciences of Man.* Baltimore, MD, 1972.

The proceedings of a conference in 1966 at which most noted structuralists spoke, including Barthes, Todorov and Lacan. Also contains Derrida's essay, 'Structure, Sign, and Play in the Discourse of the Human Sciences', a major critique of structuralism and arguably the beginning of poststructuralism. An interesting feature of the volume is that it reproduces the discussions that followed the delivery of papers. Thus Barthes's paper, 'To Write: An Intransitive Verb?', is followed by contributions from Todorov, de Man and Derrida, among others.

SUPPLEMENTARY BIBLIOGRAPHY

Barthes, Roland. *Elements of Semiology*, trans. Annette Lavers and Colin Smith. London, 1967.
————. *Critical Essays*, trans. Richard Howard. Evanston, IL, 1972.
————. *The Pleasure of the Text*, trans. Richard Miller. London, 1976.
————. *The Rustle of Language*, trans. Richard Howard. Berkeley, CA, 1989.
————. *Image, Music, Text*, trans. Stephen Heath. London, 1977.
————. *The Grain of the Voice: Interviews, 1962–1980*. Berkeley, CA, 1991.
Belsey, Catherine. *Critical Practice*. London, 1980.
Coward, Rosalind and Ellis, John. *Language and Materialism: Developments in Semiology and the Theory of the Subject*. London, 1977.
Culler, Jonathan. *Saussure*. London, 1976.
————. *Barthes*. London, 1983.
Ehrmann, Jacques, ed. *Structuralism*. New York, 1970.
Gadet, Françoise. *Saussure and Contemporary Culture*, trans. Gregory Elliott. London, 1989.
Genette, Gérard. *Narrative Discourse: An Essay on Method*, trans. Jane Lewin. Ithaca, NY, 1980.
Harland, Richard. *Superstructuralism: The Philosophy of Structuralism and Post-Structuralism*. London, 1987.
Hawkes, Terence. *Structuralism and Criticism*. London, 1977.
Heath, Stephen. *The Nouveau Roman: A Study in the Practice of Writing*. London, 1972.
Jackson, Leonard. *The Poverty of Structuralism: Literature and Structuralist Theory*. London, 1991.
Jameson, Fredric. *The Prison House of Language: A Critical Account of Structuralism and Russian Formalism*. Princeton, NJ, 1972.
Johnson, Barbara. *The Critical Difference: Essays in the Contemporary Rhetoric of Reading*. Baltimore, MD, 1980.
Lavers, Annette. *Roland Barthes: Structuralism and After*. London, 1982.
Lévi-Strauss. Claude. *Structural Anthropology*, trans. Claire Jacobson and Brooke Grundfest Schoepf. New York, 1963.

Lodge, David. *Working with Structuralism: Essays and Reviews on Nineteenth- and Twentieth-Century Literature*. London, 1981.

MacCabe, Colin. *James Joyce and the Revolution of the Word*. London, 1978.

Miller, Joan. *French Structuralism: A Multidisciplinary Bibliography*. New York, 1981.

Moriarty, Michael. *Roland Barthes*. Cambridge, 1991.

Riffaterre, Michael. *Essais de stylistique structurale*. Paris, 1971.

Robey, David, ed. *Structuralism: An Introduction*. Oxford, 1973.

Saussure, Ferdinand de. *Course in General Linguistics*, trans. Roy Harris. London, 1983.

Scholes, Robert. *Structuralism in Literature: An Introduction*. New Haven, CT, 1974.

Sebeok, Thomas A., ed. *Style in Language*. Cambridge, MA, 1960.

Sontag, Susan, ed. *A Barthes Reader*. London, 1982.

Sturrock, John, ed. *Structuralism and Since: From Lévi-Strauss to Derrida*. Oxford, 1979.

Thody, Philip. *Roland Barthes: A Conservative Estimate*. London, 1977.

Todorov, Tzvetan. *The Fantastic: A Structural Approach to a Literary Genre*, trans. Richard Howard. Ithaca, NY, 1975.

———. *The Poetics of Prose*. Trans. Richard Howard. Ithaca, NY, 1977.

———. *Introduction to Poetics*, trans. Richard Howard. Brighton, 1981.

Wiseman, Mary B. *The Ecstasies of Roland Barthes*. London, 1989.

PART 2
FEMINISM

INTRODUCTION: WILL THE REAL FEMINIST THEORY PLEASE STAND UP?

Ruth Robbins

The answer to this titular question is of course no, because it is not a unified theory with a single corpus of work that has to be read before you can begin: there is no feminist Marx or Freud whose oeuvre defines feminism as theory and methodology. This fact is the strength and the frustration of feminism. It is part also of its politics since one of the things that feminism resists is what might be called the 'authorized version', the ready-made responses to texts and life. Feminism is adaptable to different contexts because it has very few assumptions about the nature of its own enterprise, and about the textual and political outcomes it pursues. This means that anyone can do 'it', and can do 'it' to any text. But there's relatively little agreement about what kind of 'it' you should be trying to do. Rather, feminist theory can best be understood as an ongoing series of interventions in reading practices, interventions that pursue a politics of reading, and that also assume that reading practices can make a difference to our experience of the world.

In very broad terms, I would identify as feminist any literary theory and practice which bases itself on the following three things.

1. The first proposition is that a feminist literary theory assumes some relationship between words and the world – between texts and the reality from which they arise and in which they are read. The relationship is never transparent, but that doesn't mean that it isn't there. Feminist theory assumes that Literature is not some transcendent space in which the contingencies of everyday life are somehow elided or absent. Literature, in literate cultures, is part of reality. It reflects the real (though the mirror is generally somewhat distorting); it creates the real (through getting us to believe in its fictional

worlds and by suggesting that we might behave in particular ways); and it offers us alternatives to the real (through critiques of reality as we live it, or through imagining alternative modes of being as in fantasies, utopias, dystopias and science fictions). The text is produced out of a specific reality, and it bears the marks of its time, place, and mode of production. It is to be understood as relating to historic and geographic specificity, both at the moment at which it is first produced, and at the moments when it is reproduced by our readings of it. These principles align feminist literary theory to both Marxist and historicist/materialist approaches.

2. The second proposition is that the relationships between texts and worlds are necessarily political in the broad sense of having to do with power. Texts can be coercive, representing and encoding proper behaviour and proper structures of belief. Texts can also be subversive, attacking dominant modes of understanding and offering alternative ways of living and thinking. If texts are related to the world, texts can change the world. At the heart of feminist literary theory, therefore, is a will to political agency – reading in a particular way, writing about what one has read with this in mind, these things can make a difference. Again, the potential links with Marxist approaches to literature are clear.

3. The third proposition is perhaps the most important. What all feminist theories share is a focus on women. That bald statement conceals a multitude of possibilities, not least because the collective noun 'women' disguises the many differences between women, and the differences in individual women at different times in a single life. Eve has many faces. The focus on women, however, constitutes feminism's main impetus. If Marxists argue that economic conditions dependent on competition and oppression form human subjects, feminism suggests that women are troubled by other structures of oppression as well. Among those structures, feminist theories identify social deprivations specific to women (poor access to education and well-paid work); physiological oppression or the oppression of the body by virtue of its femaleness (the fact that bearing children and the rearing of them is largely 'women's work', or the fact that women are physically less powerful than men, and can be subjected to violence and rape); cultural oppression (in which women are devalued into cultural objects, rather than valued as subjects); and psychological oppression (where women are denied masculine status, and often believe in their own inferiority, because they lack masculine bodies and minds). The name given to the intersections of these structures is patriarchy – the rule of the father – and feminist theory identifies patriarchy at work in the home, in the state, the church or other religious systems, the law, education systems, the workplace, in culture at large, and even in women themselves since they often internalize the values which they are fed by such powerful institutions. Both Marxism and psychoanalysis speak also of these structures: but feminism concentrates on their effects on women, arguing that any structure of oppression

generally rebounds more strongly on women than on men. That is not to say that in white western society a black working man is less oppressed than a white middle-class woman; but it does tend to suggest that a black working woman is likely to be more oppressed than her black male counterpart. Feminist politics seeks to uncover and to change these structural inequalities. A feminist practice of literary theory might be one of the tools by which discovery and transformation could come about: reading, thinking, criticising, writing are all forms of action that underpin oppressions and might be made to serve the undoing of oppression. Feminism is aligned therefore with the theories that account for many kinds of inequalities – with psychoanalysis, with black theories, postcolonial theories, and with lesbian and gay (or queer) theories.

Feminism is an idealist position but remains always in touch with the knowledge that the real (by definition) is not ideal, that it should change, and that it could change if we could think a way through to enacting the necessary revolutions.

One of the dangers of writing a 'history' of feminist theory is that history is an ideological narrative, operating by exclusion, as all narratives necessarily do. The temptation is to write a history that begins at a specific point, 1968, say, when Mary Ellmann published *Thinking About Women*, or 1949 when Simone de Beauvoir published *The Second Sex*, and to argue that subsequent developments in feminist theories constitute a story of progress from naive, simplistic beginnings to our current state of sophisticated knowingness. The issues I'm going briefly to outline do not, however, make such a progressive narrative as much as they imply a series of ongoing interventions. Feminist theory is not prescriptive. It doesn't tell its readers/practitioners what to do, say, think, read. Rather it offers possibilities of approach, things you *might* do, say, think, read, if you find it appropriate and helpful. The only prescription is that feminist theories must never forget to be politicised in the joy of reading texts differently. They must always offer some commitment to reality, to real women's lives.

Feminist literary theory began by looking at the images of women in literary texts. The texts were largely male-authored, and the women in them were generally stereotypically represented either as ideal (virginal, beautiful, passive, dependent, nurturing) or monstrous (whorish, sexually voracious, independent and dangerous). What was drawn from these images were two sets of conclusions. First, male writers wrote unrealistically (badly) about women; second, male writers produced and reproduced these images to enforce their own ideals of femininity on women. There were honourable exceptions, but they were few and far between.

This has seemed to many commentators to be a simplistic approach to the literary text. It assumes transparent connections between image and reality and between the writer's sex and his/her attitudes; and it ignores the 'literariness', the textuality, of the text. But before it is dismissed too easily, what underpins this approach is a revolutionary assumption – that the reader of the text is a woman, not a man. It mounts a gentle, and not always explicit, but still significant attack on the universalising tendency of criticism to assume male readers. On the other hand, there are limitations to such an approach, not least in the fact that 'images of women' criticism notices an oppression but does not set out to change it by offering an alternative to the stereotypes of which it disapproves.

The next phase of feminist criticism, then, moved towards the consideration of women as producers of texts as well as consumers of them: the focus shifted towards what Elaine Showalter ([1979] 1986) named 'gynocritics', or the issue of the woman as writer. This did not mean the end of images of women. Women writers, after all, also write about female characters in their fictional texts, and represent women in poetry and drama too. But the shift to the consideration of the woman writer was significant for several reasons. It is an historicist and materialist approach which considers the practical issue of writing for women – their relationships with education (did they have any?), with publishers (were they paid as men were?), with reviewers (are women treated the same as men in criticism?), with spaces to write in (what Virginia Woolf termed 'a room of one's own') and with language itself. This was a revolution in the academy, especially in terms of thinking about how the literary text might be valued by a given culture. It demanded a rewriting of the canon of literature to include voices that were excluded by the assumptions that the 'great' text transcended its conditions of production and reception (conditions that include the femaleness or otherwise of writers and readers). It demonstrated structural inequalities between male and female writers, their opportunities to write and their critical reception; and it suggested that literary value could legitimately be located elsewhere than male-dominated tradition had placed it. It also suggested new places to look for literature, and a project of rediscovery was inaugurated to find the women writers who had become hidden from literary history, to republish their works, to edit them in scholarly editions and to make a female tradition of literature to set beside the so-called 'great' tradition of great men.

There have been criticisms of this phase too. For one thing, the concentration on the woman as writer, like 'images of women' criticism, is liable to gloss over textuality. For another, as Toril Moi (1985) put it, female scholarship might be ultimately sterile, leading to an impasse when the scholars ran out of texts to rediscover. There was the fear that this kind of feminist activity still excluded large numbers of women – the vast numbers who couldn't read or write, for example – and risked constructing a very partial history of female subjectivity through literature, a history of privileged, mostly white, mostly middle- and upper-class women. Finally, some suggested that gynocritics risked essentialism, that is risked mixing up biology with culture in the assumption that the only 'authentic' representations of women would come from women themselves, a view attacked as dangerously naive, and as playing into the hands of patriarchy by seeing sex and gender as the same thing.

Writing after these revolutionary changes, it's easy to take them for granted, to assume that there are editions of Mary Wollstonecraft or Elizabeth Barrett Browning, that I can read collections of 'forgotten' women writers and have my readings taken seriously as a legitimate academic exercise. But we shouldn't forget that it's not that long ago that Barrett-Browning and Wollstonecraft were out of print and unavailable, and that reading them wasn't quite respectable. And if I don't quite believe in a separatist account of a tradition of women's writing, gynocritics at least provides the tools to find it if it's there.

Like 'images of women', the gynocritical phase is ongoing. The questions about women reading and women writing have not all been answered, and it's still worth revisiting the pioneering works of Moers (1977), Showalter (1977), Gilbert and Gubar (1979) et al. because the arguments were not naive. There is a dialogue that contemporary feminist theorists continue to have with the past, so that we are not condemned merely to repeat feminist literary history because we don't know it.

From the early 1980s another phase of feminist theory is discernible in the English-speaking academy as some of the important texts of French feminism were translated for the first time, especially the writings of Hélène Cixous, Luce Irigaray and Julia Kristeva. These writers are profoundly influenced by the discourse of Lacanian psychoanalysis, by linguistic theory, and by post-structuralist accounts of language and human subjectivity. Irigaray and Kristeva take very seriously Lacan's idea that rather than the subject speaking language, language in fact speaks the subject (you cannot say 'I' without language, you cannot have a concept of selfhood without words). They concentrate therefore on linguistic formations, and on their psychic effects on speaking subjects, motivated in part by the fact that the French language is heavily gender-inflected. The subjects are not always women. But women may well have a different response to a language which defines them in psycho-analytic terms as 'lack' and 'other', and which is the language which shores up the patriarchal law of the father. They seek, then, the gaps and fissures of language into which the displaced feminised (though not always female) subject may insert her/himself. Kristeva (1986), for example, coins a new meaning for the word 'semiotic', meaning the disruptions of language, its silences, elisions, ellipses, its rhythms and sounds, as a space for feminine language. And Cixous (1981) undoes a lot of assumptions about propriety in language, deliberately confusing the distinctions between academic and poetic writing in what she calls *écriture féminine*. Where gynocritics insisted on a mimetic relationship between literature and reality, to the extent that it could not properly account for the textuality of avant-garde writing by women, the writings of Cixous and Kristeva, in their very different ways, provide tools for thinking about experimental writing, whatever the gender of the writer.

There have been many very serious attacks on what is thought of in English-speaking countries as the French approach, especially in Britain where there is a strong resistance to a theoretical model which appears not to be explicitly aligned to a politics of change. Some disapprove also of the inherent difficulty of the works of these theorists, and of their alignment to Lacan, whose relationship with feminism was tenuous to say the least. But in France, psychoanalysis has generally been understood as a political movement, which describes oppression and repression as linked phenomena, signalled in the name of one of the most significant Francophone feminist groupings, Psychanalyse et Politique [Psychoanalysis and Politics]. The dissemination of Lacanian psychoanalysis as a positive tool for feminist theorists by writers such as Rose (1986) and Mitchell (1974) has led to linguistic and psychoanalytic theory forming the basis of much of the most important recent work in the field.

More recently still, from the late 1980s and early 1990s, feminist theory has started to engage with its own inherent essentialism by revisiting the question: what is a woman? Judith Butler (1990, 1993) and Diana Fuss (1989) have eschewed the commonsense biologist position that we all 'know' what a woman (or what a man) is. They argue instead that sex as much as gender is culturally constructed, and that sexual identity is a kind of masquerade or performance. Thus, the reading of texts is itself a performance that calls further into question the authenticity of readers and writers who are always performing multiple identities. Their arguments arise in part from the alignment of feminist thinking with queer theory, in which sexuality rather than sex is the basis of the argument. And since sexuality is learned behaviour rather than a biological 'given', and since sexuality is performative rather than just 'there', the theory leads to the practice of a playful politics of identity that undermines the idea of essence, including the strategic essentialisms that feminist criticism used in order to argue for women's writing. It has, therefore, produced some quite hostile responses (see, for example Ward-Jouve, 1998) because it appears to undo some of the earlier political assumptions about women as a group who are oppressed because they are women.

The multiplicity of ideas that inform feminism means that there is no simple answer to the question of what a feminist critique seeks to do to a text. Feminism is a magpie theory that steals and borrows from other models of criticism, and can therefore be a liberatingly eclectic response to textual formations. It does not consist of repeated critical gestures. It begins with reading carefully and suspiciously. Textual signs act as symptoms, sometimes leading to diagnoses where patriarchy shows its marks as an oppressive disease, sometimes focusing rather on the fissures and gaps that the text opens up in the seemingly closed body of patriarchal discourses. Texts are often related to contexts – the contexts of production, the contexts of consumption, the wider cultural contexts which the text at once reproduces and (potentially) undermines. Texts are related to language practices, and the contradictions of different discourses are pursued to their logical conclusions, implying a relationship between feminism and poststructuralist theories and praxes. And it's not just to do with reading for signs of female oppression: there's enough of that around to make a feminist practice that concentrated solely on women's unhappy lives a very depressing thing to do. It's also a question of what writers do with oppression, how they combat it, and how they enable their readers to rethink and remake their own worlds. Hence my insistence on the relationship between words and worlds in feminist practice. Nor does a feminist theory have to concentrate solely on writing by women. If it works as a critical model, it has to be able to account for the constructedness of masculinity as well as of femininity.

Feminism has felt like a threat to a male-dominated academy because it has taken some of the key assumptions of criticism and subjected them to a critique in their turn. It raises questions about what is meant by literary value, and the literary tradition. It has opened up aesthetic judgements to types of writing dismissed by earlier critics as ephemeral, unimportant, trivial or just plain 'bad'. Feminist theory asks about how these judgements came to be made, who made them, and why? As well as approaching 'literary' texts, it also evaluates critical approaches. It has helped to remake the definition of what literature is in university study over the last twenty-five years. And it should continue that process, in alignment with other groups who have been displaced by a particular narrow notion of what is meant by good writing.

So: I can't tell you exactly how to do 'it', and I wouldn't want to say that there's only one way to do it. I am anxious to avoid a mechanistic criticism that operates by merely listing certain structures of oppression (economic, sex-based, gender-based, class-based, race-based) and seeking them out in all texts. And I suggest that not all modes of theory work equally well for all writing: Cixous and Jane Austen are not an immediately obvious pairing, and while it would be possible to read Austen in the light of Cixous, a reading of this kind would probably inflict damage on both of them, for no real benefit. On the other hand, Butler's theory of gender performance probably could speak to Austen, as could the more traditional 'images' critique, or the arguments of feminist scholarship, and an approach focusing on the conditions of production and reception of her texts. Feminist theory is about the choices you make. Those choices include the kind of critique you want to make, but also the kinds of text you choose to discuss: that choice can also be a feminist choice.

The three texts of feminist theory and practice gathered here are not intended as a catalogue of the only ways to do feminism. Rather, they represent different strands which might be characterised as: feminist reading against the grain, lesbian-feminist textual exploration and as the performance of the feminist scholar.

Claire Kahane's essay, 'Medusa's Voice: Male Hysteria in *The Bostonians*' is in some ways the most traditional feminist approach of the texts gathered here. It takes a male-authored canonical text by a very canonical author (Henry James was, after all, part of Leavis's *Great Tradition*) and reads it against the very assumptions that made the text canonical. Those assumptions include the idea that the text is a coherent whole that makes sense consistently, that the text contains the voice of reason, and that the voice of reason is male/masculine; they would also suggest that the text is somehow 'timeless', transcending its own conditions of production and consumption. In opposition to those assumptions, Kahane argues that *The Bostonians* is rather contradictory and incoherent, hysterical rather than rational, and that it is profoundly implicated in the history of its own era (the 1880s) and its own place (the United States). She suggests that the text dramatizes the links between apparently oppositional terms, first the realms of the sexual and the political, and then the oppositions of female and male, speech and writing, North and South (in a reference to the alignments of the American Civil War), fluidity and solidity. In each of these oppositions, the privileged or victorious term would usually be the second – and that, indeed, is James's apparent assumption in the novel. But careful reading, Kahane argues, shows that the oppositions are not separate. Instead they flow into each other with a radically destabilising effect that unsettles not only the oppositions themselves as they appear within the text, but also the critical judgement of James's novel that places its value in terms of consistency and coherence. She suggests further that this fluidity of difference within the novel was not in the control of the writer, who thought he was saying one thing explicitly, but who can be shown to have been saying something quite different in the fissures of his text.

Kahane's method combines historical research, psychoanalytic theory and close textual reading. She offers a series of contexts for the text: James's return to the US in 1883; his consequent exposure to Bostonian feminist agitation for female suffrage; the figure of the American feminist, Elizabeth Peabody, caricatured as Miss Birdseye in the novel; the context of cultural stereotypes about the potency of spoken language; and the context offered by Kahane's book as a whole about the unfeminine nature of the voice as an oratorical tool, understood as unfeminine because it undoes the stereotype of the silent and private woman which was current in British and American culture of the period. Following Freud, she defines hysteria as the fear of femininity. And then by close reading, she suggests that James's text exposes a hysterical fear of the feminine in its multiple disjunctions between what is explicitly stated and the manner in which it is said. The violence of the novel's climactic scene, in which Basil Ransom abducts Verena Tarrant into marriage, is thus to be understood as a hysterical textual symptom: Basil – and by extension, the novel as a whole, perhaps even James himself, and also the critical tradition which supports the novel as a transcendent, timeless literary artifact – fears femininity and responds to that fear by hysterical action, silencing a woman's voice. The reading becomes then a metaphor for the position of women in western culture, enacting a political relationship between word and world.

In a very different way, Terry Castle's essay might also be understood as a piece of traditional feminist criticism, though it is doing feminist criticism 'differently' in that its focus is on the figure of the lesbian in fiction, and on defining a lesbian mode in fiction. Earlier feminists, with a heterosexual blindness to alternative sexualities, had wondered in the 1970s and 1980s about a female tradition and about whether there were inherent differences between men's and women's writing. Castle asks the feminist question differently – not what is women's fiction, but what is lesbian fiction, does it exist? She is responding to the invisibility of lesbians in culture (hence the title of her book, *The Apparitional Lesbian*); this invisibility, she suggests, is not just a simple and obvious effect of patriarchy, but has been compounded by the refusals of straight feminists and queer theorists interested in gay men properly to imagine the lesbian as a significant figure. The ghost in this essay is Eve Sedgwick's book *Between Men* (1985), which suggests that desire is generally to be figured as a male–male bonding, triangulated through the female other; Sedgwick does not imagine a powerful female desire, either for men, or for other women.

It is to redress this inequity that Castle turns to Sylvia Townsend Warner. This is in part an act of feminist recuperation; Townsend Warner is not a well-known canonical writer, and her works are 'under-read'. Much of the essay is therefore taken up with a plot summary, so that the unknown text can become vicariously known to the reader. But this is also a strategy for drawing out the structures of the novel in order to rewrite the male homosocial triangle with a model of lesbian desire in its place. The 'counterplot' of lesbian desire also does service as a critique of several canonical nineteenth-century texts, novels by Dickens, the Brontës, George Eliot, Scott, Balzac, Hugo and Flaubert, whose characters and plots are Townsend Warner's own ghosts for *Summer Will Show*, in a neatly ironic reversal of the 'usual' stories of literary value and of sexual satisfaction.

Castle's interpretation of Townsend Warner is at once playful and serious. She uses her example to draw a large conclusion about a definition of lesbian fiction which is structural rather than merely biographical. She suggests defining characteristics might include the elements of fantasy and stylisation which resist 'realism' since realism is where male homosociality is valued. She also suggests elements of parody and satire in relation to more canonical texts, taking their situations and rewriting them, for example. And she argues that these elements are political because they unsettle realism as a version of the real that holds true for everyone. These are the methods and ideas of a traditional feminist approach placed at the service of radical lesbian interpretation. Making lesbian women visible to a heterosexual culture that does not want to see them combines aesthetics and politics through criticism.

Although Mary Lydon's essay is the oldest of these three pieces, it is also the most radical attack on traditional modes of male-defined academic scholarship, especially in terms of its vivacious style. The essay also eschews the usual process of argument – hypothesis, evidence, conclusion – and operates instead as the performance of a critical position. Commenting on the essay in a later text on Duchamp, Lydon says that the essay was an experiment in a 'kind of exemplary transvestism which, by scrambling the inscription of assigned sexual roles, would provide access to the full range of human activity' (Lydon, 1995, 135). The essay acts as a model of how one might read differently, and of how such different readings make critical spaces for those usually excluded from academy, including women.

Instead of seeing poststructuralist ideas as a problem for feminism because of their refusal of an absolutist category of the real that sometimes appears apolitical, Lydon acts the magpie, borrowing from theoretical models whenever they seem useful. The essay was originally produced for a conference on autobiography, that mode of writing in which sincerity and authenticity are the supposed goals of writing. The title arises then from the autobiographical fact that Lydon is a mother; but by thinking through the effects of wordplay in puns and researching the etymologies of words, the essay deals not in an essentialist or biologistic identity (mothers) but in 'the staging of the self', or the figuring of the self as other. Because the mother is, in some sense, the figure of the eternal feminine, both nurturing and monstrous, encompassing oppositions, the essay explores juxtaposed oppositions and developments. Beginning with Leonardo's Mona Lisa and Walter Pater's description of it as both monstrous and perfect, Lydon moves to Marcel Duchamp's 'daring art', which took this iconic figure and drew a moustache and beard on it, rendering it as parody, as monster, as homage and as a figure of sexual indeterminacy. It is in the light of Mona Lisa's transvestism that Lydon goes on to read Duchamp's own transvestite appearance as Rose Sélavy, a name which inscribes not single essence (not female because attached to a biological male, for example), but performance and multiplicity.

Oscar Wilde, with the whom the essay begins, reappears in relation to his mother, a woman who had much to say about the relationships between clothes, meaning and thought, and whose pronouncements seem to imply that language acts as a disguise rather more than it expresses essential selfhood. Similarly, the figure of Colette, who shares her father's name and fulfils his unfulfilled ambition to become a writer, is disguised by the language of her name, dresses herself as it were in a name that is both feminine (the diminutive -ette form signals that) and masculine because it belongs to her father.

The point of all these substitutions and disguises is to undo two types of identity. First, the essay attacks sexual identity as a given, and insists that sex is a disguise – in clothes and in language – in which you can dress up at will, that identity is in fact a choice. Implicitly, following on from this, the essay also unsettles the coherent, sincere, authentic, reasonable voice of criticism by pointing out through its style that this too is a disguise rather than an essence. You don't get objective criticism from writers who are wearing the mask of objectivity: you just get the masquerade of objectivity, and there might be more interesting types of performance to try out. It is an eclectic essay that shows the political importance for feminism of playing roles well, but which also insists that we know that it is 'just' playing, and that we might choose roles quite (m/)other from the ones that have already been inscribed.

2.1

MEDUSA'S VOICE:
MALE HYSTERIA IN
THE BOSTONIANS

Claire Kahane

> A voice, a human voice is what we want.
> – Olive Chancellor, in *The Bostonians*

In his article 'Medusa's Head: Male Hysteria under Political Pressure', Neil Hertz discusses what he calls 'a recurrent turn of mind: the representation of what would seem to be a political threat as if it were a sexual threat' (1983, 27). Hertz introduces his discussion with reference to a dramatic scene of Freud's in which Freud simulates the terror of the little boy discovering that his mother has no penis, and then adds, 'In later life grown men may experience a similar panic, perhaps when the cry goes up that throne and altar are in danger' (27). *The Bostonians* is Henry James' representation of that panic, both sexual and political. Such panic is not confined within the borders of the tale, however, for like his conservative hero Basil Ransom, James' narrator also evinces alarm at the feminist challenge to male privilege, an alarm especially provoked by the figure of the feminist orator.

The tradition of oratory, classically a male tradition, had been revived on the nineteenth-century American political scene, in great part through the expansive rhetoric of Jacksonian discourse – optimistic, hyperbolic, and incredibly egoistic in its taking of the measure of the world by the self. Not surprisingly, the appropriation of that ego by a woman speaking with a female voice of political rights and equality was experienced as a particularly radical gesture ... The 1867 New York Constitutional Convention rejected suffrage as an innovation

Extract from Claire Kahane, *Passions of the Voice: Hysteria, Narrative, and the Figure of the Speaking Woman 1850–1915* (Johns Hopkins University Press, 1995), pp. 64–79.

'so revolutionary and sweeping, so openly at war with a distribution of duties and functions between the sexes as venerable and pervading as government itself, and involving transformations so radical in social and domestic life' that it demanded vigilant defeat (Dubois, 1975, 68). Moreover ... in speaking from the platform – the height of immodesty – and calling for women's political rights, the woman orator not only appropriated a male political province, but in her very self-exhibition challenged the sexual pieties of her audience.

The Bostonians is an exemplary representation of that double-barreled challenge; it is exemplary also in its representation of narrative ambivalence, manifesting in its symptomatic discourse an anxiety about the boundaries of desire and identification that it cannot speak directly. Alfred Habegger's (1990) observations on the narrator of The Bostonians provide strong support for a reading of James' hysterical voice. Not only does James' narrator speak out far more often in The Bostonians than in James' other narratives, but 'the contradiction between [the narrator's] calm overview and his brittle, nervous, punctuated sneers' (189) as well as the narrator's frequent use of parentheses that 'function as intrusive markers of another voice speaking through an already intrusive first person narrator' (182–3) – all indicate an essential splitting of the voice of the text. As Habegger succinctly points out, the contradictions and inconsistencies of the narrator 'warn us that in some way the authorial identity is gravely at risk' (189). That risk, I argue, is provoked by authorial ambivalence about feminism and the figure of the speaking woman.

The textual ambivalence of The Bostonians is externally reflected in the critical debate it has elicited about James' representation of the women's movement. Sara de Saussure Davis (1978), for example, argues that James was extremely well informed about the feminist issues of the period; on the other hand, Habegger (1990) demonstrates with equal fervor that the novel is full of historical inaccuracies.[1] Critics also have been at odds in their judgment of James' feminist sympathics, some seeing in the sexist male protagonist a critique of masculine ruthlessness and a vindication of feminism (Habegger, 1990, 26), others judging the hero as inevitably but sensitively bringing the heroine into a heterosexuality far more preferable than her feminist relationships (Brodhead, 1986, 153). What these contrasting positions again suggest is an equivocal narrative voice that implicates the reader as well as the author in its ambivalent point of view.

James described The Bostonians as 'an episode connected with the *so called "woman's movement"*' (italics mine), a subject that profoundly engaged him by 1883, when he wrote these words to his publisher. Having returned to America in 1881 to settle his late father's estate, James had taken up temporary residence with his sister Alice in Boston while she recovered from a severe hysterical attack. Thus, he observed at close quarters both the political controversy over women's suffrage that dominated the Boston social scene of the 1880s and, through Alice's friendship with Katherine Loring, the evolving patterns of female intimacy in American culture, 'those friendships between women that are so common in New England' ... Inspired by his observations to write 'a very American tale ... characteristic of our social conditions', in a revealing early comment about his prospective novel, James described its most salient features as 'the situation of women, the decline of the sentiment of sex, the agitation on their behalf' (*Notebooks*, 1947, 46). The bracketing of 'the decline in the sentiment of sex' by feminist 'agitation' and 'the situation of women' syntactically conveys precisely the unspoken nature of James' concern, for his very sentence structure envisions a kind of impending doom of aphanisis, a loss of desire, of the sentiment of sex itself.

The ostensible plot concerns the struggle between two blatantly antithetical figures – Olive Chancellor, a New England feminist tormented by her inability to speak in public, and her Southern cousin, the conservative masculinist Basil Ransom, an aspiring political writer – for the love and possession of Verena Tarrant, a young ingenue gifted with a politically seductive speaking voice. Significantly, Verena assumes no agency for her speech; rather, she is a vessel, a medium inspired by her father's laying on of hands to speak a text that passes through her in a voice that captivates her audience. Yet if James constitutes her entrance into the novel as an object rather than a subject of speech, he accords her voice a fetishistic power that everyone desires. Marveling at Verena's voice – 'What a power' (James, 1976, 76) – Olive would appropriate it for the public cause of women's rights to which she is passionately committed; Basil, described as 'a representative of his sex' (4), desires it for his private pleasure. James represents their conflict as the ultimate civil war, the battle between male chauvinist and female avenger for the power of the voice with all its accrued cultural privileges.

Yet while their clash of difference to determine cultural authority is the novel's primary structuring trope, at the same time James refuses the victory to either side. North and South, freedom and slavery, speech and writing, the tongue and the touch, public and private – the novel repeatedly sets up these cultural oppositions, binds them to the difference between masculine and feminine, and then provocatively flirts with their collapse. In its oscillating movement, *The Bostonians* would seem to support the precocious vision of Margaret Fuller that while 'male and female represented two sides of a great radical dualism ... in fact they are perpetually passing into one another. Fluid hardens into solid, solid rushes to fluid, there is no wholly masculine man, no purely feminine woman' (Fuller, 1985, 301–2). Similarly, James' text both institutes a radically dualistic structure and insistently shows the boundaries of difference to be permeable.

What is most notable in this regard, however, is that at those moments when difference does seem to collapse, the narrative flow is suddenly disrupted by a digression, an eruption of rage, a bizarrely inappropriate commentary. Listen for a moment to the sound of this passage in which Basil reveals his desire 'to save' his sex, and when asked by Verena, 'To save it from what?' replies:

> From the most damnable feminization! I am so far from thinking, as you set forth the other night, that there is not enough woman in our general life, that it has long been pressed home to me that there is a great deal too much. The whole generation is womanized; the masculine tone is passing out of the world; it's a feminine, a nervous, hysterical, chattering, canting age, an age of hollow phrases and false delicacy and exaggerated solicitudes and coddled sensibilities, which if we don't soon look out, will usher in the reign of mediocrity of the feeblest and flattest and the most pretentious that has ever been. The masculine character, the ability to dare and endure, to know and yet not fear reality, to look the world in the face and take it for what it is – a very queer and partly very base mixture – that is what I want to preserve, or rather as I may say, to recover; and I must tell you that I don't the least care what becomes of you ladies while I make the attempt! (318)

The exclamation points, the syntax of accumulation and release, the breathless, pauseless sentences that amass signifiers of rage – this is a frenzied, hysterical utterance not inappropriate in a character who is so avowedly disgusted by feminism as Basil Ransom. Yet James' narrator tells us that 'the poor fellow delivered himself of these narrow notions with low, soft earnestness ... that it was articulated in (a) calm, severe way, in which no allowance was to be made for hyperbole' (318). This disjunction between the textual effect of Ransom's voice and the narrative commentary on it, a commentary that seems without irony, marks the narrator's ambivalent investment in his hero.

In 'The Relation of the Poet to Daydreaming', Freud had remarked of romantic fantasies: 'They all have a hero who is the center of interest, for whom the author tries to win our sympathy by every possible means, and whom he places under the protection of a special providence' (1908 [1959], SE, 9: 50); this hero represents 'His Majesty the Ego, the hero of all daydreams and all novels' (51). Ransom is surprisingly close to that figure in *The Bostonians*. As the principal deictic center of the novel and one whose utterances often echo those of Henry James Sr, Ransom is set apart from the more consistently ridiculed characters, his elitist pronouncements rendered with more sympathy than irony. Like Freud with Herr K., James seems to think Ransom extremely prepossessing, for only Olive Chancellor actively dislikes him, and that dislike is depicted as hysterical, a consequence of her fear of men and her rivalrous desire to possess Verena. Thus, although at various points in the novel James' narrator intervenes to dissociate his opinions from Ransom's, as when he alludes to the brutal impulses underlying Ransom's male code of chivalry and his sadistically toned relation to women, those very interventions indicate a textual confusion between Ransom and the narrator, and by implication, between Ransom and James.

The most blatant coincidence between Ransom and the narrator is their use of ridicule. Just as Ransom in the novel is made to laugh whenever he is confronted with a feminist challenge to his masculinist assumptions, so the narrator ridicules and satirizes the feminists, primarily by representing female authority as absurd or self-serving. It is perhaps significant that the figure subject to the greatest ridicule, Miss Birdseye, the pathetically ineffectual feminist of the transcendentalist generation, is also the figure who elicits the only other blatantly hysterical outburst in the text, uttered by the narrator himself rather than by his ambivalently depicted surrogate. In fact, the portrait of Miss Birdseye, who resembled Elizabeth Peabody in certain habits of being, is drawn with so much overt ridicule that after reading the manuscript, William James cautioned his brother about causing her public embarrassment (Strouse, 1990, 249).

The narrator first deprecates Miss Birdseye by constructing an allusive analogy between her and her 'common residence':

> Number 756 was the common residence of several persons among whom there prevailed much vagueness of boundary ... Many of them went about with satchels and reticules, for which they were always looking for places of deposit. What completed the character of this interior was Miss Birdseye's own apartment, in which her guests presently made their way, and where they were joined by various other members of the good lady's circle. Indeed, it completed Miss Birdseye herself, if anything could be said to render that office to this essentially formless old woman, who had no more outline than a bundle of hay. But the barrenness of her long, loose, empty parlor (it was shaped exactly like Miss Chancellor's) told that she had never had any needs but moral needs. (27–8)

The house with its vague boundaries, the satchels and reticules that cannot find their proper place, the 'long, loose, empty parlor, shaped exactly like Miss Chancellor's' – this description figures a disordered body, sexless and barren. It is followed by an interpolation comparable in its rage only to Basil Ransom's outburst. Having remarked on her belonging to the Short Skirts League, in a disparaging comparison that familiarly analogizes feminism to sexual exhibitionism, the narrator suddenly erupts venomously:

> This did not prevent her being a confused, entangled, inconsequent, discursive old woman whose charity began at home and ended nowhere, whose credulity kept pace with it, and who knew less about her fellow-creatures, if possible, after fifty years of humanitary zeal, than on the day she had gone into the field to testify against the iniquity of most arrangements. (26)

Why this surprising narrative intrusion of rage? Described as totally lacking in knowledge of the real, Miss Birdseye seems a representation of transcendental excess: she opens her house to everyone, gives succor indiscriminately to Negroes and refugees – and James fumes, as in this shrill and at times incoherent passage that begins, significantly, with a reference to her ineffectual talk:

> She talked continually, in a voice of which the spring seemed broken, like that of an over-worked bell-wire; and when Miss Chancellor explained that she had brought Mr. Ransom because he was so anxious to meet Mrs. Farrinder, she gave the young man a delicate, dirty, democratic little hand, looking at him kindly, as she could not help doing, but without the smallest discrimination as against others who might not have the good fortune (which involved, possibly, an injustice) to be present on such an interesting occasion. (26)

The narrator's irritation with her impotent talk is joined to an insidious little trio of signifiers – delicate, dirty, democratic – to give us James' moral sensibility at its crudest. A precursor to the xenophobia of such modernist writers as Eliot and Pound, who seemed especially to fear contamination by the immigrant hordes, it marks again the novel's concern with boundaries, with a violation that comes from being too 'open' and identified as feminine. Through such images as the short skirt and the delicate, dirty, democratic hand, James transforms a political threat into a physical and sexual one in the kind of hysterical slippage that pervades the narrative voice.

While the text is saturated with images of fetishized hands – the hands of the feminists are 'cold and limp'; their judgment is 'like a soft hand' – the primary fetish object of the novel is not the hand but the voice. Each of the characters is in some essential way defined by a relation to the speaking voice, a relation that also marks their sexual positionality as phallic or castrated. Mrs Tarrant, Verena's mother, descended from a line of public speakers, is humiliated by her husband's inability to speak, and although he has proved his 'eloquence of the hand', her family 'had never set much store on manual activity; they believed in the influence of the lips' (70). The speech of the unctuous journalist Matthew Pardon is replete with sentences 'imperfectly formed' and punctuated by such effete exclamations such as 'Goodness gracious' and 'Mercy on us' (116). Drawing a broad picture of the effeminacy of Pardon, James conjures up conventionally stereotypical features attributed to the male hysteric through the markers of speech:

> He talked very quickly and softly, with words, and even sentences, imperfectly formed; there was a certain amiable flatness in his tone, and he abounded in exclamations – 'Goodness gracious!' and 'Mercy on us!' – not much in use among the sex whose profanity is apt to be coarse. He had small fair features, remarkably neat, and pretty eyes, and a moustache that he caressed ... His friends knew that in spite of his delicacy and his prattle he was what they called a live man. (116)

Like Ransom, who characterizes the age as 'too talkative' – 'talk' being an emptying out of the power of speech – James constructs the novel as full of chatter, of women's talk. Mrs Luna, her name evoking the symbolic link between femaleness and lunacy, is represented as 'a woman of many words', guilty of a verbal incontinence that is in stark contrast to the controlled and balanced speech of Basil, who 'could hold his tongue' and not be 'drawn into an undue expenditure of speech' (182). Interestingly, in an age described as 'too talkative' by Carlyle, Ransom's favorite writer, and by Ransom himself, holding one's tongue becomes a masculine attribute. Olive's voice recurrently performs a breathlessness that the text subtly caricatures: 'I can't talk to those people, I can't' (34); 'I want to give myself up to others; I want to know everything that lies beneath and out of sight, don't you know? I want to enter into lives of women who are lonely, who are piteous. I want to be near them to help them. I want to do something – oh, I should so like to speak!' (34–5).

Marking potency or its lack through the voice of his characters, James implicitly criticizes the increasing flatulence of American discourse and explicitly associates it with a feminization of culture. At the same time, it seems clear that he is concerned with his own potency as a writer, a concern that might have been exacerbated by the fact that his own style could be characterized as feminine. If we recall that in hysteria what is repudiated is femininity, James' narrator reveals himself as increasingly hysterical in his shrill caricatures of female influence on cultural productions and especially on writing.

In this context it is not surprising that Basil, the writer – nominated even by his enemy Olive Chancellor as the 'real man' and by the narrator as 'the most important personage in my narrative' as well as 'a representative of his sex' (4) – is brought in to do battle with this effete company. Ransom is described at his entrance in flagrantly phallic terms:

> he was very long . . . and even looked a little hard and discouraging, like a column of figures . . . a head to be seen above the level of a crowd on some judicial bench or political platform . . . His forehead was high and broad, and his thick black hair perfectly straight and glossy, and *without any division*, rolled back from it in a leonine manner. (4)

Yet after presenting this accumulation of unmistakably masculine signifiers, so that Ransom – grim and hard – is an image of the Law, the One 'without any division,' James remarks that 'if we are readers who like a complete image, who read with the senses as well as with the reason' (5) – and senses and reason are gender-coded – then we are entreated not to forget the feminine components of this phallic being, which James locates in his speaking voice. Ransom 'prolonged his consonants and swallowed his vowels, . . . he was *guilty* of elisions and interpolations which were equally unexpected, and . . . his discourse was pervaded by something sultry and vast, something almost African in its rich, basking tone, something that suggested the teeming expanse of the cotton field' (5). Playing on the same geopsychological dichotomy that Tocqueville first introduced and Henry Adams exploits in the *Education* – the warm, earthly, sensual South represents the 'feminine' principle, while the North, judicial and cold, is 'masculine' – James shows the integrity of his judicial erectness riven by a suspiciously sensual voice that is identified with the feminine.

Indeed, Ransom's Southern drawl reveals itself guilty through the voice, its guilt signified by the interpolations and elisions that are the textual signs of repression. What is it guilty of? James remarks on the 'African' warmth that has infused the voice of the South, insinuating a guilty intercourse, a hidden history that has resulted in the 'curious feminine softness with which Southern gentlemen enunciate' (5). In this passage of allusive innuendo James suggests a history of sexual transgression in the 'teeming cotton fields', a miscegenation embodied in the voice. Although James had originally thought to make his hero a Westerner, by writing him as a Southerner he could use the drawl – the voice of an already violated South – not only to identify an erotic component of the male hero that makes Ransom attractively vulnerable, but to allude to a past history of sexual violation in both North and South that will continue to resonate in the text. Through a number of such sexual allusions to a past transgression, the narrator points to an inaccessible scene of origin for each character's relation to the voice and makes it suspect.

Olive Chancellor, the feminist reformer who is Ransom's antagonist, is given the most neurotic relation to speech. Articulate in private but voiceless in public, Olive is described as morbidly obsessed with the unhappiness of women on the one hand, and enraged at men on the other:

> The voice of their silent suffering was always in her ears, the ocean of tears that they had shed from the beginning of time seemed to pour through her own eyes ... Uncounted millions had lived only to be tortured, to be crucified ... The just revolution ... must triumph, it must sweep everything before it; it must exact from the other, the brutal, bloodstained, ravening race, the last particle of expiation. (35–6)

In this double identification with both victim and avenger, Olive desires to be a martyr-savior in the tradition of Christ, one who, like Nightingale's Cassandra, would save through the power of her complaint: 'I want to give myself up to others; I want to know everything that lies beneath and out of sight ... I want to enter into the lives of women who are lonely, who are piteous. I want to be near to them – to help them' (34).

Not only does this sentimentalizing diction undermine Olive's relation to feminism, but her morbid longing for martyrdom, for an erotic merger with women victims, her flirtation with the romance of suffering, and above all, her inability to give voice to her desire, which defines her as a hysteric, are made the suspect source of feminist agitation more generally: 'It proved nothing of any importance with regard to Miss Chancellor, to say that she was morbid; any sufficient account of her would lie very much to the rear of that. Why was she morbid, and why was her morbidness typical? Ransom might have exulted if he had gone back far enough to explain that mystery' (11). In a sense the novel is James' representation of that mystery, constructed through the indirect modes of insinuation and allusion. Why might Ransom have exulted? And how far back would Ransom have to go to explain that mystery? How far back does

James go? In this remark, the narrator implies a psychohistory to Olive's morbidity, which he coyly supplies through the textual innuendo of an erotically tendentious discourse.

James' image of morbidity is a woman crying, a recurrent figure in the text that is attached to each of the three central characters; the image connects each to a scene of suffering and a relation to the voice. It appears not only in Olive's obsessive vision of an ocean of women's tears to which she would give voice, but also in 'the desire of Ransom's heart' to protect the South, figured as a violated woman, by holding his tongue. It most strikingly occurs in Verena's perception of Olive herself on their first meeting: 'she looked as if she had been crying (Verena recognized that look quickly, she had seen it so much)' (73). What does this parenthesis signify? Where has she seen it so much? Again, while the text tells us nothing directly, it leads us to speculate on this parenthesis, indeed, within the context of the novel, leads us to imagine, as Olive has, a commonality of women's experience as victims of male abuse. And if Verena so quickly recognizes that look, it also insinuates a scene of a woman crying into her own family history, casting suspicion on her father as well.

James' narrator links Selah to the Oneida community of free love, 'a community of long-haired men and short-haired women' (68) who have confused the forms of gender and have broken the laws of marriage and the family on which they depend, by giving the Father free access to all the women, by therefore symbolically instituting incest. Although Verena herself touts 'free union', thus identifying with her father's beliefs, the narrator continually insinuates that Selah's sexual behavior has caused his wife suffering, that 'the poor woman had a great deal, matrimonially, to put up with' (69). Past scenes of female suffering as a result of male sexual transgression are thus implied by the narrator as well as imagined by Olive. Dr Prance, remarking that if Selah were a little more dry, it might be better for him, doesn't 'want him to be laying his hands on any of her folk; it was all done with the hands, what wasn't done with the tongue' (42). The sycophantic Matthew Pardon, who has Selah's permission to 'handle' his daughter, wants Verena 'to "shed" her father altogether; she didn't want him pawing round her that way before she began' (121).

Perhaps the most outrageously eroticized description of Tarrant is his relation to the newspaper offices and vestibules of hotels, the centers of worldly power to which he desires access. Although the passage satirizes Selah's avid desire for publicity, his social pandering is made more repulsive by its erotic overtones:

> he ... had a general sense that such places were national nerve-centres, and that the more one looked in, the more one was 'on the spot.' The *penetralia* of the daily press were, however, still more fascinating, and the fact that they were less accessible, that here he found barriers in his path, only added to the zest of forcing an entrance ... He was always trying to find out what was 'going in'; he would have liked to go in himself, bodily, and failing in this, he hoped to get advertisements inserted gratis. (99)

Casting suspicion on the father through a familiar trope – 'forcing an entrance' – which in the Dora case signified rape, James also introduces a level of suspicion into Verena's vocal transports that continues to function when Olive assumes Selah's role as the kindling agent of Verena's impassioned speech. In short, through a rhetoric of sexual innuendo, Selah is depicted not only as a suspect father and husband, but also as an interloper who threatens the boundaries of family and class, if not of sexual positionality itself.

Olive wants the power of the voice to unveil the father's guilt and the daughter's suffering; Basil wants to keep the secret, to hold his tongue; James' narrator positions himself in between. As James tells us, Basil's 'heart's desire' is 'to be quiet about the Southern land, not to touch her with vulgar hands, to leave her alone with her sounds and her memories, not prating in the market-place either of her troubles or her hopes' (48). To be quiet and not to touch – these prohibitions on the voice and the hand are also narrative prohibitions on revealing the sadomasochistic ground of sexual relations that James' narrator both uncovers and covers over in a recurrent and classically hysterical act of playing secrets through textual allusion.

Perhaps the most revealing secret moment of the text, however, concerns a different aspect of Basil's desire: he is aroused not by Verena's image – 'her exhibition is not exciting' (57) – but by her voice. At the same time, Basil is particularly disturbed that her voice is elicited by her father's touch; he resents 'Tarrant's grotesque manipulations ... as much as if he himself had felt their touch ... They made him nervous, they made him angry' (57). In this surprising textual revelation of Basil's nervousness, James points to Basil's own hysterical identification with Verena, his own fear of being handled, being manipulated, being objectified by the carpetbagging Selah, his apprehension intensified by being a conquered and violated Southerner. Although the narrator quickly covers over this moment of anxiety, Basil as listener remains vulnerable to and therefore defensively derisive of Verena's speech, which, as we are given it, is certainly seductive: Verena 'pours into the ears of those who still hold out, who stiffen their necks and repeat hard, empty formulas, which are as dry as a broken gourd', a feminist vision of enlightened self-interest, of relations based on 'generosity, tenderness, sympathy where there is now only brute force and sordid rivalry' (255).

In this gendered contrast of social relations, Verena's speech again accuses the father/man and idealizes the mother/woman of a past scene. Obliterating the words as signifiers, Basil persistently hears only the music of her voice, the erotics of the voice, the voice of the nightingale. She can sing but not signify; she can give pleasure but not 'mean'. Thinking that 'she speechifies as a bird sings' (216), 'I don't listen to your ideas,' he tells her. 'I listen to your voice' (316). Like Philomela, Verena also will be silenced in the presence of Basil, will be abducted by him in a climax that resonates both etymologically and psychologically as a rape, and which turns her, too, literally into a crying woman. For it is this prophetic image of a woman crying that reappears at the novel's conclusion, an image of Verena's future as a wife that reiterates the image from the past: 'It is to be feared that with the union, so far from brilliant into which she was about to enter, these [tears] were not the last she was destined to shed' (426).

At the same time that the text suggests that marriage itself as a patriarchal institution produces tears, as if Nature herself demands only this brutal patriarchal plot, requires the ransom of heterosexuality to maintain human culture, the narrative moves inexorably to take Verena from the woman and give her to the man by reversing in a series of confrontations the place and proprietorship of the speaking voice. Thus, the narrator portrays the inexplicable effects of Basil's voice on Verena even though she would reject what it says: 'Strange I call the nature of her reflections, for they softly battled with each other as she listened ... to his deep, sweet, distinct voice, expressing montstrous opinions with exotic cadences and mild, familiar laughs' (313). The voice of Nature itself enters the text as Basil's agent when Olive wanders around Washington Square contemplating Verena's future:

> The trees and grass-plats had begun to bud and sprout, the fountains splashed in the sunshine, the children of the quarter, both the dingier types from the south side, who played games that required much chalking of the paved walks, and much sprawling and crouching there, under the feet of passers, and the little curled and feathered people who drove their hoops under the eyes of French nursemaids – all the infant population filled the vernal air with small sounds which had a crude, tender quality, like the leaves and the thin herbage. (300)

This representation of the sounds of the air – crude, tender – made by the infant population signifies a Nature that requires Verena's complicity in her abduction. And it is presented as a sharp contrast to the topography of the southern cape, the feminist enclave to which Olive takes Verena in an effort to elude Basil:

> The ripeness of summer lay upon the land, and yet there was nothing in the country Basil Ransom traversed that seemed susceptible of maturity; nothing but the apples in the little tough, dense orchards, which gave a suggestion of sour fruition here and there, and the tall, bright goldenrod at the bottom of the bare stone dykes. (329)

In the midst of this highly allusive suggestion of 'sour fruition' and 'bare stone dykes' at Marmion, Basil – finally authorized to be legitimate hero by having had a piece of *writing* accepted for publication – converts Verena's desire to his own. Although he tells her, 'It's not to make you suffer ... I don't want to say anything that will hurt you,' as she entreats him 'to spare her', the text emphasizes his rhetoric of attack and conquer: 'a quick sense of elation and success began to throb in his heart, for it told him ... that she was afraid of him, that she had ceased to trust herself, that the way he had read her nature was the right way (she was tremendously open to attack, she was meant for love, she was meant for him)' (349). Basil's words of masculine attack and feminine suffering confirm Olive's earlier prophetic but impotent admonitions:

> the words he had spoken to her ... about her genuine vocation, as distinguished from the hollow and factitious ideal with which her family and her association with Olive Chancellor had saddled her – these words the most effective and penetrating he had uttered, had sunk into her soul and worked and fermented there ... The truth had changed sides; the radiant image began to look at her from Basil Ransom's expressive eyes: it was always passion, but now the object was other. (365)

From this point to the climax of the novel, Basil's actual abduction of Verena, his words are supported by the narrator's own violent discursive manipulations, which move the plot to its 'natural' oedipal conclusion: Verena's voice will be made to 'lubricate' her private life rather than 'gush out at a fixed hour' (370–1). In a muddled sequence of internal contradictions, the narrative voice redefines her relation to Olive and feminism as 'a desire to please others', her relation to Basil as 'a push to please herself' (367); at the same time, it insists that this reconstitution of her desire is precisely not what her fate is to be. Rather, yielding her desire to Basil's, unable to resist the languor of objectification, Verena becomes Basil's possession, her recognition of this capitulation described as 'a kind of shame' (392). Although there is one final attempt at rescue by Olive, who keeps Verena isolated until she can speak in a climactic moment of feminist oratory at the Music Hall, Basil ultimately wins what Olive has called their 'war to the knife' (364) for Verena. In a concluding scene almost surreal in its representation of tensions and contradictions, and an increasingly libidinized diction, the howling and thumping of the mob waiting in the auditorium to hear Verena (but in the novel's wings) – that fearsome mob anxiously reproduced in countless fictional scenes of revolution – sound as a counterpoint to the offstage scene, 'behind the scenes of the world' where the novel's climax is enacted. Verena shrieks for Olive as Basil wrenches her away 'by muscular force' but is also glad to be taken. As Basil leads the weeping girl away, the narrator remarks in perhaps the most subversive ending to a heterosexual marriage plot a sentence worth repeating, 'It is to be feared that with the union, so far from brilliant into which she was about to enter, these were not the last [tears] she was destined to shed' (426).

This final turn of the screw both returns the wandering heroine to the marriage plot and sustains the ubiquitous figure of the crying woman as a figure of closure. This closure is also undermined, however, for there is another final scene, one that we can only hear, since it takes place on stage while the reader is behind the scenes. At the same time that Verena is abducted into private service, Olive enters the public arena; she goes on stage in Verena's place, expecting to be hooted and insulted, 'seeing fierce expiation in exposure to the mob' (425). James likens Olive to 'a feminine firebrand of Paris revolutions, erect on a barricade, or even the sacrificial figure of Hypatia, whirled through the furious mob of Alexandria … offering herself to be trampled to death and torn to pieces' (425). Although this discourse points again to Olive's 'morbid' desire for martyrdom, James does not gratify this desire in the text. At the climax of the novel, the crowd falls silent, leaving open the possibility of an alternative ending to the story of feminine desire, an open ending through which James' own hysterico-political ambivalence could be given play. Olive as a potential 'feminine firebrand' becomes a potential virile feminist like Hertz's revolutionary woman on the barricades, and we are left wondering if Olive will be able to speak, if she can voice herself and the women she would rescue into the circle of privilege and power.

Finally, then, it is Olive who emerges as the figure of tragic and heroic loss, the real interest of the novel, the enigmatic subject to be explored. The character who will never marry, whose most passionate relations are with her own sex, Olive not only recalls Alice James but also ultimately figures James' own problematic desire. Like Freud with Dora, James had to identify with his subject to investigate the sources of her morbidity and constitute this subject in language. Judging from the lability of his narrative voice, that identification led him to his own hysterical drama, constituted by a fantasy of violation that equates speaking with potency and silence with being raped or castrated.

NOTE

1. Habegger claims that James' 'critique derives from a censored vision of antebellum reformers' and is not reliable about 'the Gilded Age' (1990, 226–7).

2.2

SYLVIA TOWNSEND WARNER
AND THE COUNTERPLOT
OF LESBIAN FICTION

Terry Castle

What is a lesbian fiction? ... To theorize about female–female desire, I would like to suggest, is precisely to envision the taking apart of [the] supposedly intractable patriarchal structure [discussed by Eve Kosofsky Sedgwick in her study of male homosocial desire, *Between Men: English Literature and Male Homosocial Desire* (1985)].

... Are there any contemporary novels that undo the seemingly compulsory plot of male homosocial desire? ... The work I have in mind is Sylvia Townsend Warner's 1936 *Summer Will Show*, a historical fiction set in rural Dorset and Paris during the revolution of 1848. What makes this novel paradigmatically 'lesbian', in my view, is not simply that it depicts a sexual relationship between two women, but that it so clearly, indeed almost schematically, figures this relationship as a breakup of the ... male–female–male erotic triangle [described by Sedgwick]. As I shall try to demonstrate in what follows, it is exactly this kind of subverted triangulation, or erotic 'counter-plotting', that is in fact characteristic of lesbian novels in general.

Summer Will Show is not, I realize, a well-known piece of fiction – indeed quite the opposite. Even among Townsend Warner devotees it is still a relatively unfamiliar work, despite a Virago reprint in 1987 ... While not entirely an *un*read work of modern English fiction, *Summer Will Show* is at the very least an *under*read one.

... some of the resistance the work has met with must also have to do, one suspects, with its love story, which challenges so spectacularly the rigidly

Extract from Terry Castle, *The Apparitional Lesbian: Female Homosexuality and Modern Culture* (Columbia University Press, 1993), pp. 66–91.

heterosexual conventions of classic English and American fiction. This story begins deceptively simply, in a seemingly recognizable literary landscape: that of nineteenth-century fiction itself. The tall, fair-haired heroine, Sophia Willoughby, is the only daughter of wealthy landed gentry in Dorset, the heiress of Blandamer House (in which she resides), and the wife of a feckless husband, Frederick, who, after marrying her for her money and fathering her two small children, has abandoned her and taken a mistress in Paris. At the start of the novel, Sophia is walking with her children, a boy and a girl, on a hot summer's day to the limekiln on the estate, in the hope that by subjecting them to a traditional remedy – limekiln fumes – she can cure them of the whooping cough they have both contracted.

Already in these opening pages, given over to Sophia's reveries on the way to the limekiln, we have a sense of her proud, powerful, yet troubled nature: like another Gwendolen Harleth or even a new Emma Bovary, she broods over her unhappy marriage and yearns ambiguously for 'something decisive', a new kind of fulfilment, some 'moment when she should exercise her authority' (11). While devoted to her children, she also feels constricted by them and infuriated at her husband for leaving them entirely to her care. As for Frederick himself, she harbours no lingering romantic illusions there, only 'icy disdain', mixed with a sense of sexual grievance. It is not so much that she is jealous – their marriage has been devoid of passion – but that she resents his freedom and his predictably chosen 'bohemian' mistress:

> For even to Dorset the name of Minna Lemuel had made its way. Had the husband of Mrs. Willoughby chosen no other end than to be scandalous, he could not have chosen better. A byword, half actress, half strumpet; a Jewess; a nonsensical creature bedizened with airs of prophecy, who trailed across Europe with a tag-rag of poets, revolutionaries, musicians and circus-riders snuffing at her heels, like an escaped bitch with a procession of mongrels after her; and ugly; and old, as old as Frederick or older – this was the woman whom Frederick had elected to fall in love with, joining in the tag-rag procession, and not even king in that outrageous court, not even able to dismiss the mongrels, and take the creature into keeping. (31)

At the same time, however, Sophia feels an odd gratitude to the other woman: thanks to Minna, Sophia reminds herself, she is 'a mother, and a landowner; but fortunately, she need no longer be counted among the wives' (20).

All this is to change as a result of the limekiln visit itself. With Sophia looking on, the limekiln keeper – a silent, frightening-looking man with sores on his arms – suspends each of the children over the kiln. Though terrified, they inhale the fumes and Sophia takes them home. In the next few weeks, her attention is distracted by the arrival of her nephew Caspar, the illegitimate mulatto child of an uncle in the West Indies. At her uncle's request, she takes Caspar to Cornwall to place him in a boarding school. Returning home, she finds her own children mortally ill: the limekiln keeper was in fact carrying smallpox and has infected both children. Sophia delays writing to her husband to inform him; yet Frederick comes anyway, having been recalled by a letter written by the doctor who is attending the children.

At once Sophia senses a subtle change in her husband, a mystifying new refinement, which she attributes – balefully, yet also with growing curiosity – to the influence of his unseen mistress. Listening to him repeat the words '*Ma fleur*' over his dying daughter's sickbed, it seems to Sophia as if a stranger were speaking through him: someone possessed of 'a deep sophistication in sorrow'. The intrusive cadence, she reminds herself angrily, must be copied from 'that Minna's Jewish contralto'. Yet afterward, when both of the children are dead and Frederick has gone back to Paris, Sophia finds herself haunted by a memory of the voice – one that seems, 'according to her mood, an enigma, a nettle-sting, a caress' (83).

With the death of Sophia's children, the crucial action of the novel commences. Distraught, grief-stricken, yet also peculiarly obsessed with her husband's other life, Sophia decides to seek him out in Paris, for the purpose (she tells herself) of forcing him to give her more children. Yet, as if driven by more mysterious urgings, she finds herself, on the very evening of her arrival, at the apartment on the Rue de la Carabine where Minna holds her salon. Entering the apartment unobserved, Sophia joins the crowd of guests (including Frederick himself) who are listening to their hostess tell a story.

The story, which is presented as an embedded narrative, is a hypnotic account of Minna's childhood in Eastern Europe – of the pogrom in which her parents were killed, of her own escape from the murderers, and of her eventual rescue by a vagrant musician. The experience of persecution has made her an artist, a storyteller, a romantic visionary and a political revolutionary. As Sophia listens, seemingly mesmerized by the Jewish woman's charismatic 'siren voice', she forgets entirely about Frederick and the putative reason why she has come. Suddenly, the tale is interrupted – barricades are being put up outside in the streets; the first skirmishes of what will become the February Revolution are about to begin. Minna's listeners, mainly artists and intellectuals who support the revolt, depart, along with Frederick, who has not yet seen his wife. And Sophia, still as if under a spell, finds herself alone in the room with Minna.

She is utterly, heart-stoppingly, captivated. Not by Minna's beauty – for Frederick's mistress is a small, dark, and sallow woman, with 'a slowly flickering glance' and 'large supple hands' that seem to 'caress themselves together in the very gesture of her thought' (127). Yet something in this very look, 'sombre and attentive', alive with tenderness and recognition, ineluctably draws Sophia to her. ('I cannot understand,' Sophia finds herself thinking, 'what Frederick could see in you. But *I* can see a great deal' (154).) Minna in turn seems equally delighted with her lover's wife. Together they look out on the barricades: Frederick is below and now sees Sophia; he is piqued when she refuses his offer of a cab. Minna also ignores him, so he leaves. Minna then confides in Sophia her hopes for the success of the insurrection. Sophia, entranced yet also exhausted, falls asleep on Minna's sofa. When she awakens the next day, her hostess is sitting beside her. Inspired by the strange 'ardour' of the Jewish woman's attention, the normally reticent Sophia suddenly finds herself overcome by an urge to recount the story of *her* own life. As if freed from an invisible bondage, she finds herself talking for hours. When Frederick returns that afternoon, he is momentarily 'felled' to discover his wife and mistress 'seated together on the pink sofa, knit into this fathomless intimacy, and turning from it to entertain him with an identical patient politeness.' For 'neither woman, absorbed in this extraordinary colloquy, had expressed by word or sign the slightest consciousness that there was anything unusual about it' (157).

Nor, might it be said, does Townsend Warner. The attraction between Sophia and Minna is treated, if anything, as a perfectly natural elaboration of the wife–mistress situation. The two women, it is true, separate for several weeks, in part because Sophia is afraid of the depth – and complication – of her new attachment. While the political turmoil in the city grows, she stays with her wealthy, superannuated French aunt, Léocadie, who tries to reconcile her with Frederick. Yet she is drawn back into Minna's orbit soon enough, when she hears that Minna has given away almost all of her money to the striking workers and is destitute. Outraged with Frederick for 'casting off' his mistress (which is how Sophia describes the situation to herself), she determines to fulfill his 'obligations' herself. She returns to the now-shabby apartment on the Rue de la Carabine, and finding Minna weak with cold and hunger, decides to stay and care for her. As her absorption in the other woman grows – and is reciprocated – Sophia gradually feels her old identity, that of the heiress of Blandamer, slipping away. As if 'by some extraordinary enchantment', she is inexorably caught up in Minna's world and in the revolutionary activity in which Minna is involved.

Meanwhile Frederick, incensed by the alliance between his wife and his (now) ex-mistress, cuts off Sophia's allowance in order to force her to return to him. Yet his machinations serve only to intensify – indeed to eroticize – the intimacy between the two women. When Sophia tells her friend that Frederick has told the bank not to honor her signature 'as he is entitled to do being my husband', they suddenly comprehend their desire for what it is:

'You will stay? You must, if only to gall him.'
'I don't think that much of a reason.'
'But you will stay?'
'I will stay if you wish it.'
It seemed to her that the words fell cold and glum as ice-pellets. Only beneath the crust of thought did her being assent as by right to that flush of pleasure, that triumphant cry.

'But of course,' said Minna a few hours later, thoughtfully licking the last oyster shell, 'we must be practical.' (274)

Townsend Warner, to be sure, renders the scene of their passionate coming together elliptically – with only a cry (and an oyster) to suggest the moment of consummation – yet the meaning is clear: Sophia has severed all ties with the past – with her husband, her class, and with sexual convention itself.

In the final section of the novel, spring gives way to summer; the popular insurrection, dormant for several months, flares once again. Inspired by her new-found love for Minna, Sophia throws herself into political activity, becoming a courier for a group of communists who are collecting weapons in preparation for open civil war. Her last contact with her husband comes about when her nephew Caspar suddenly turns up in Paris, alienated and sullen, having run away from the school in Cornwall: Sophia is forced to ask Frederick for money to pay for the youth's schooling in Paris. Without her knowledge, Frederick, who now cynically supports the government, instead buys Caspar a place in the Gardes Mobiles, the force opposing the now imminent June rebellion.

Returning from one of her courier missions, Sophia finds that street fighting has begun in the neighbourhood around the Rue de la Carabine. Minna is already on the barricades. Together they join in the battle, loading and reloading the workers' rifles. The Gardes Mobiles launch an attack on the barricade and Sophia, to her surprise, recognizes Caspar in their midst. He plunges a bayonet into Minna, who falls, apparently mortally wounded. Sophia shoots Caspar in retaliation, but is herself captured and taken away with some other prisoners to be executed, only to be freed the next day because she is a woman. She searches frantically for Minna but cannot discover if she is alive or dead. The revolt has been put down and the workers' hopes seemingly destroyed. Returning to Minna's apartment, yet still harboring a hope that her lover will return, Sophia opens one of the pamphlets that she had been delivering the previous day. It is Marx's *Communist Manifesto*. As she settles down to read – exhausted but also arrested by its powerful opening words – the novel comes ambiguously to an end.

I will return to this somewhat curious denouement in a moment: I would like to draw attention first to the more obviously revisionist aspects of Townsend Warner's narrative. For *Summer Will Show* ... is a work obsessed with 'revising' on a number of counts. In the most literal sense the novel is a kind of revisionist fantasia: in recounting the story of her pseudo-Victorian heroine, Sophia Willoughby, Townsend Warner constantly pastiches – yet also rewrites – Victorian fiction itself ...

But it is not only English fiction that Townsend Warner is rewriting in *Summer Will Show* ... Berlioz is certainly there, but so too are the French novelists. The scenes at Minna's Parisian salon have the flavour of Staël and Hugo as well as of Stendhal and Balzac; Sophia's right-wing aunt Léocadie, along with her egregious confessor Père Hyacinthe, are straight out of *La Comédie humaine*. But it is Flaubert, obviously, and *his* novel of 1848, that Townsend Warner is most deeply conscious of displacing. Anyone who doubts the subterranean importance of *L'Éducation sentimentale* to *Summer Will Show* need only consider the name Frédéric – or Frederick – and the parodistic relationship that exists between Flaubert's antihero, Frédéric Moreau, and Townsend Warner's comic villain, Frederick Willoughby.

To invoke Flaubert's masterpiece, however, is also to return – with a vengeance – to the Sedgwickian issue of erotic triangulation. For what is *L'Éducation sentimentale* if not a classic work, in Sedgwick's terms, of male homosocial bonding? Flaubert's Frédéric, we recall, acts out his emotional obsession with his friend Arnoux by falling in love first with Arnoux's wife, then with his mistress. Townsend Warner's Frederick, by contrast, not only has no male friend, his wife and his mistress fall in love with each other. In the very act of revising Flaubert – of substituting her own profoundly 'anticanonical' fiction in place of his own – Townsend Warner also revises the plot of male homosocial desire. Indeed, all of her revisionist gestures can, I think, be linked with this same imaginative impulse: the desire to plot against the seemingly indestructible heterosexual narrative of classic European fiction.

This work of counterplotting can best be figured ... as a kind of dismantling or displacement of the male homosocial triangle itself ... at the beginning of *Summer Will Show* ... Sophia is more or less mired in the 'in between' position that patriarchal society demands of her. As the only heiress of Blandamer, 'the point advancing on the future, as it were, of that magnificent triangle in which Mr. and Mrs. Aspen of Blandamer House, Dorset, England, made up the other two apices' (3), she has functioned, we are led to deduce, as the social mediator between her own father, who has been forced to give her up in marriage in order to perpetuate the Aspen family line, and Frederick, the son-in-law, who has enriched himself by allying himself with the Aspen patrimony.

Yet instabilities in this classic male–female–male triad soon become apparent. The deaths of Sophia's children are the first sign of a generalized weakening of male homosocial bonds; these deaths, we realize, are not just a transforming loss for Sophia, but for Frederick also, who loses, through them, his only remaining biological and symbolic connection to Sophia's dead father, his partner in the novel's original homosocial triangle. Significantly, perhaps, it is the son who is the first of the children to die: in a way that prefigures the symbolic action of the novel as a whole, the patrilineal triangle of father–mother–son here disappears, leaving only a female–male–female triangle, composed of Sophia, Frederick, and their daughter. Even at this early stage, one might argue, Townsend Warner represents the female-dominant triangle as 'stronger', or in some sense more durable, than the male-dominant one.

Yet other episodes in the first part of the novel suggest a disintegration of male homosocial structures. When Sophia delays writing to Frederick during the children's illness, her doctor, thinking the absence of her husband a scandal, writes to him without her knowledge. The letter is intercepted by the doctor's young wife, who brings it to Sophia and offers to destroy it. 'Why should all this be done behind your back?' exclaims the outraged Mrs Hervey, 'what right have they to interfere, to discuss and plot, and settle what they think best to be done? As if, whatever happened, you could not stand alone, and judge for yourself! As if you needed a man!'(72). Admittedly, Sophia decides in the end to let the letter be sent, but the intimation here of an almost conspiratorial bonding between the two women – against *both* of their husbands – directly foreshadows the more powerful bonding of Sophia with Minna. And as will be true later, a strong current of erotic feeling runs between the two women. 'She might be in love with me,' Sophia thinks after Mrs Hervey 'awkwardly' embraces her during one of their first meetings. Now, as she looks at the letter 'lying so calmly' on Mrs Hervey's lap, it suddenly seems only a pretext: 'some other motive, violent and unexperienced as the emotions of youth, trembled undeclared between them.' Later, they walk hand in hand in a thunderstorm, and Sophia briefly entertains a fancy of going on a European tour with Mrs Hervey – large-eyed and delighted and clutching a box of watercolour paints' – at her side (78).

With the love affair between Sophia and Minna, one might say that the male homosocial triad reaches its point of maximum destabilization and collapses altogether. In its place appears a new configuration, the triad of *female* homosocial desire. For Frederick, obviously, is now forced into the position of the subject term, the one 'in between', the odd one out – the one, indeed, who can be patronized. Sophia and Minna do just this during their first supper together, following the memorable colloquy on the pink sofa. Sophia takes it upon herself to order the wine, a discreetly masculine gesture that inspires Minna to remark, 'How much I like being with English people! They manage everything so quietly and so well.' Sophia, catching her drift, instantly rejoins, 'And am I as good as Frederick?' 'You are much better,' Minna replies. After a short meditation on Frederick's shortcomings, the two women subside into complacent amity. 'Poor Frederick!' says one. 'Poor Frederick!' says the other (161–2).

We might call this the comedy of female–female desire: as two women come together, the man who has brought them together seems oddly reduced, transformed into a figure of fun. Later he will drop out of sight altogether – which is another way of saying that in every lesbian relationship there is a man who has been sacrificed. Townsend Warner will call attention to this 'disappearing man' phenomenon at numerous points, sometimes in a powerfully literal way. When Sophia returns, for example, to the Rue de la Carabine to help the poverty-stricken Minna, only to find her lying chilled and unconscious on the floor, she immediately lies down to warm her, in 'a desperate calculated caress'. Yet this first, soon-to-be eroticized act of lying down with Minna also triggers a reverie – on the strangeness of the season that has brought them together, on the vast distance each has traversed to arrive at this moment, and on the man 'between them' who is of course not there:

It was spring, she remembered. In another month the irises would be coming into flower. But now it was April, the cheat month, when the deadliest frosts might fall, when snow might cover the earth, lying hard and authentic on the English acres as it lay over the wastes of Lithuania. There, in one direction, was Blandamer, familiar as a bed; and there, in another was Lithuania, the unknown, where a Jewish child had watched the cranes fly over, and had stood beside the breaking river. And here, in Paris lay Sophia Willoughby, lying on the floor in the draughty passage-way between bedroom and dressing-closet, her body pressed against the body of her husband's mistress. (251)

The intimacy, here and later, is precisely the intimacy enjoined by the breakup of monolithic structures, indeed, by the breakup of triangulation itself. For what Sophia and Minna discover, even as they muse over 'poor Frederick', is that they need him no longer: in the draughty passageway leading to a bedroom, the very shape of desire is 'pressed' out of shape, becoming dyadic, impassioned, lesbian.

What is particularly satisfying about Townsend Warner's plotting here is that it illustrates so neatly – indeed so trigonometrically – what we might take to be the underlying principle of lesbian narrative itself: namely, that for female bonding to 'take', as it were, to metamorphose into explicit sexual desire, male bonding must be suppressed ... Townsend Warner's Frederick has no boyhood friend, no father, no father-in-law, no son, no gang, *no novelist on his side* to help him retriangulate his relationship with his wife – or for that matter, with his mistress either. To put it axiomatically: in the absence of male homosocial desire, lesbian desire emerges.

Can such a principle help us to theorize in more general ways about lesbian fiction? Obviously, I think it can. It allows us to identify first of all two basic mimetic contexts in which, in realistic writing, plots of lesbian desire are most likely to flourish: the world of schooling and adolescence (the world of premarital relations) and the world of divorce, widowhood and separation (the world of postmarital relations). In each of these mimetic contexts, male erotic triangulation is either conspicuously absent or under assault. In the classically gynocentric setting of the girls' school, for example, male characters are generally isolated or missing altogether: hence the powerfully female homosocial/homosexual plots of Colette's *Claudine à l'école*, Clemence Dane's *Regiment of Women*, Dorothy Strachey's *Olivia*, Antonia White's *Frost in May*, Christa Winsloe's *The Child Manuela* (on which the film *Mädchen in Uniform* is based), Lillian Hellman's *The Children's Hour*, Muriel Spark's *The Prime of Miss Jean Brodie*, Catharine Stimpson's *Class Notes* or more recently, Jeanette Winterson's *Oranges Are Not the Only Fruit*, in which the juvenile heroine woos her first love while attending a female Bible study group.

Yet the figure of male homosociality is even more pitilessly compromised in novels of postmarital experience. In the novel of adolescence, it is true, male homosocial desire often reasserts itself, belatedly, at the end of the fiction: the central lesbian bond may be undermined or broken up, usually by having one of the principals die (as in *The Child Manuela* or *The Children's Hour*), get married (as in *Oranges Are Not the Only Fruit*), or reconcile herself in some other way with the erotic and social world of men (as in *Claudine à l'école* or *The Prime of Miss Jean Brodie*). We might call this 'dysphoric' lesbian counter-plotting. To the extent that it depicts female homosexual desire as a finite phenomenon – a temporary phase in a larger pattern of heterosexual *Bildung* – the lesbian novel of adolescence is almost always dysphoric in tendency.[1]

In postmarital lesbian fiction, however, male homosocial bonds are generally presented – from the outset – as debilitated to the point of unrecuperability. Typically in such novels, it is the very failure of the heroine's marriage or heterosexual love affair that functions as the pretext for her conversion to homosexual desire. This conversion is radical and irreversible: once she discovers (usually ecstatically) her passion for women, there is no going back. We might call this 'euphoric' lesbian counterplotting: it is an essentially comic, even utopian plot pattern. A new world is imagined in which male bonding has no place ...

With its insouciant, sometimes coruscating satire on male bonding, *Summer Will Show* typifies the postmarital or conversion fiction: its energies are primarily comic and visionary. It is a novel of liberation. As Minna says to Sophia at one point: 'You have run away ... You'll never go back now, you know. I've encouraged a quantity of people to run away, but I have never seen any one so decisively escaped as you' (217). Yet is this the whole story? Given that the novel concludes with Minna herself apparently slain on the barricades, a victim of Caspar (who in turn is the pawn of Frederick), how complete, finally, is what I am calling, perhaps too exuberantly, its 'undoing' of the classic male homosocial plot?

That the ending of *Summer Will Show* poses a problem cannot be denied ... Granted, Minna seems to be dead (during the onslaught on the barricade Sophia sees Caspar's bayonet 'jerk' in Minna's breast), yet, in a curious turnabout in the novel's final pages, Townsend Warner goes out of her way – seemingly gratuitously – to hint that she may in fact still be alive. Though unsuccessful, Sophia's attempts to locate Minna's body raise the possibility that her lover has survived: a witness to the scene on the barricades, Madam Guy, concedes that Minna was indeed alive when she was dragged away by soldiers; her daughter confirms it (397–8). Later visits to 'all the places where enquiries might be made' turn up nothing, but the man who accompanies Sophia reminds her that the officials in charge may be misleading her on purpose – the implication being that her friend may in fact be held prisoner somewhere (399). The ambiguity is hardly resolved even at the last. When Sophia returns to Minna's apartment and takes up the *Communist Manifesto*, her peculiarly composed attitude seems as much one of waiting as of tragic desolation: far from being traumatized by seeing 'the wine that Minna had left for her' or Minna's slippers on the floor, she merely sits down to read, as though Minna were at any moment about to return.

The utopian tract she peruses in turn hints symbolically at the thematics of return: if we take seriously the analogy that Townsend Warner has made throughout the novel between her heroine's political and sexual transformation, the inspiriting presence of the *Manifesto* here, with its promise of revolutionary hope resurrected, may also portend another kind of resurrection – that of Minna herself.

The novelist here seems to test how much implausibility we are willing to accept – for according to even the loosest standard of probability (such as might hold, say, in Victorian fiction) the possibility that Minna should survive her bayoneting by Caspar, an event which itself already strains credibility, must appear fanciful in the extreme. Yet it cannot be denied that Townsend Warner herself seems drawn back to the idea – almost, one feels, because it *is* incredible. Having offered us a plausible (or semiplausible) ending, she now hints, seemingly capriciously, at a far more unlikely plot turn, as if perversely determined to revert to the most fantastical kind of closure imaginable.

Without attempting to diminish any of the ambiguity here, I think Warner's restaging of her conclusion – this apparent inability to let go of the possibility of euphoric resolution however improbable such a resolution must seem – can tell us something useful, once again, about lesbian fiction. By its very nature lesbian fiction has – and can only have – a profoundly attenuated relationship with what we think of, stereotypically, as narrative verisimilitude, plausibility or 'truth to life'. Precisely because it is motivated by a yearning for that which is, in a cultural sense, implausible – the subversion of male homosocial desire – lesbian fiction characteristically exhibits, even as it masquerades as 'realistic' in surface detail, a strongly fantastical, allegorical or utopian tendency. The more insistently it gravitates toward euphoric resolution, moreover, the more implausible – in every way – it may seem.

The problem with Townsend Warner's novel – if in fact it is a problem – is not so much that it forfeits plausibility at the end but that it forfeits it from the start. There is nothing remotely believable about Sophia Willoughby's transformation from 'heiress of Blandamer' into lover of her husband's mistress and communist revolutionary, if by 'believability' we mean conformity with the established mimetic conventions of canonical English and American fiction. The novelist herself seems aware of this, and without ever entirely abandoning the framing pretense of historicity (the references to real people and events, the 'Berliozian' local color), often hints at the artificial, 'as if' or hypothetical nature of the world her characters inhabit. Metaphorically speaking, everything in the novel has a slightly suspect, theatrical, even phantasmagorical air. Revolutionary Paris resembles a stage set: the rebels near Minna's house are arrayed like 'comic opera bandits' (177), a bloody skirmish in the streets is a 'clinching raree-show' (171). Trying to convince her to return to her husband, Sophia's aunt Léocadie becomes a 'ballerina', with Frederick 'the suave athletic partner, respectfully leading her round by one leg as she quivered on the tip-toe of the other' (203). Elsewhere Frederick is a 'tenor' plotting with the 'basso'

Père Hyacinthe (192). The captivating Minna, in turn, is a 'gifted tragedy actress' (217), a 'play-acting Shylock' (212) or someone 'in a charade' (268). Sometimes Minna leaves the human realm altogether, metamorphosing into something from fairy tale or myth – a 'Medusa', a 'herb-wife', a 'siren', a 'sorceress' – or a creature out of beast fable or Grandville cartoon. She is a 'macaw', Sophia thinks, a 'parrot', 'some purple-plumaged bird of prey, her hooked nose impending', or perhaps the 'sleekest' of cats (326). Her passion for Minna, Sophia concludes, is like the poet's – 'of a birth as rare / As 'tis of object strange and high ... begotten by despair / Upon impossibility' (289).

These built-in intimations of artifice and romance, of delight and high fakery, present on almost every page of *Summer Will Show* work against the superficial historicism of the narrative, pushing it inexorably towards the fantastic. Of course a hankering after the fantastic is present elsewhere in Townsend Warner's writing: *Lolly Willowes* ... begins as a seemingly straight-forward tale about a spinster in an ordinary English village, but swerves abruptly into the marvellous when the spinster joins a coven of witches led by the Devil. Indeed the development of Townsend Warner's writing career as a whole suggests a progressive shifting away from realism toward the explicitly antimimetic modes of allegory and fable: in her last published stories, collected in *Kingdoms of Elfin*, she dispensed with human subjects entirely, choosing to commemorate instead the delicate passions of a race of elves.

Yet the fantastical element in *Summer Will Show* is not, I think, simply a matter of authorial idiosyncrasy. Other lesbian novels display the same oscillation between realistic and fabulous modes. One need only think ... of *Orlando* or *Nightwood*, or, indeed, of Joanna Russ's *The Female Man*, Elizabeth Jolley's *Miss Peabody's Inheritance*, Lois Gould's *A Sea-Change*, Sarah Schulman's *After Delores*, Margaret Erhart's *Unusual Company*, Michelle Cliff's *No Telephone to Heaven* or any of Jeanette Winterson's recent novels, to see how symptomatically lesbian fiction resists any simple recuperation as 'realistic'. Even as it gestures back at a supposedly familiar world of human experience, it almost invariably stylizes and estranges it – by presenting it parodistically, euphuistically, or in some other rhetorically heightened, distorted, fragmented or phantasmagoric way ...

What then *is* a lesbian fiction? ... Such a fiction will be, both in the ordinary and in a more elaborate sense, noncanonical. Like Townsend Warner's novel itself, the typical lesbian fiction is likely to be an underread, even unknown, text – and certainly an underappreciated one. It is likely to stand in a satirical, inverted or parodic relationship to more famous novels of the past – which is to say that it will exhibit an ambition to displace the so-called canonical works that have preceded it. In the case of *Summer Will Show*, Townsend Warner's numerous literary parodies – of Flaubert, Eliot, Brontë, Dickens and the rest – suggest a wish to displace, in particular, the supreme texts of nineteenth-century realism, as if to infiltrate her own fiction among them as a kind of subversive, inflammatory, pseudo-canonical substitute.

... the archetypal lesbian fiction decanonizes, so to speak, the canonical structure of desire itself. Insofar as it documents a world in which men are 'between women' rather than vice versa, it is an insult to the conventional geometries of fictional eros. It dismantles the real, as it were, in a search for the not-yet-real, something unpredicted and unpredictable. It is an assault on the banal: a retriangulating of triangles. As a consequence, it often looks odd, fantastical, implausible, 'not there' – utopian in aspiration if not design. It is, in a word, imaginative. This is why, perhaps, like lesbian desire itself, it is still difficult for us to acknowledge – even when ... it is so palpably, so plainly, there.

NOTE

1. I borrow the euphoric/dysphoric distinction from Nancy K. Miller, who in *The Heroine's Text* uses the terms to refer to the two kinds of narrative 'destiny' stereotypically available to the heroines of eighteenth- and nineteenth-century fiction. A euphoric plot, Miller argues, ends with the heroine's marriage, a dysphoric plot with her death or alienation from society. That the terms undergo a dramatic reversal in meaning when applied to lesbian fiction should be obvious: from a lesbian viewpoint, marriage can only be dysphoric in its implications; even death or alienation – if only in a metaphoric sense – may seem preferable.

2.3

MYSELF AND M/OTHERS: COLETTE, WILDE AND DUCHAMP

Mary Lydon

> *Jack:* Her mother is perfectly unbearable. Never met such a Gorgon . . .
> I don't really know what a Gorgon is like, but I am quite sure
> that Lady Bracknell is one. In any case, she is a monster, without
> being a myth, which is rather unfair . . . I beg your pardon, Algy, I
> suppose I shouldn't talk about your own aunt in that way before
> you.
>
> *Algernon:* My dear boy, I love hearing my relations abused. It is the only
> thing that makes me put up with them at all. Relations are
> simply a tedious pack of people, who haven't got the knowledge
> of how to live, nor the smallest instinct about when to die . . .
>
> *Jack:* You don't think there is any chance of Gwendolen becoming like
> her mother in about a hundred and fifty years, do you, Algy?
>
> *Algernon:* All women become like their mothers. That is their tragedy. No
> man does. That's his.
>
> *Jack:* Is that clever?
>
> *Algernon:* It is perfectly phrased and quite as true as any observation in
> civilised life should be.
>
> — Oscar Wilde, *The Importance of Being Earnest*

That the epigraph should be Wilde gives me pleasure whetted by *The Importance of Being Earnest*, which enjoins us (with what brilliant economy) to take the signifier seriously. Indeed, in the wake of Wilde, it is tempting to invert Derrida's prescription, to say that it is style, rather than women (myself, m/others), which will be my subject: parody, rather than tragedy, my genre.[1] As Wilde would have it, let truth become 'a matter of style.' It remains for us to

Extract from Mary Lydon, *Skirting the Issue: Essays in Literary Theory* (University of Wisconsin Press, 1995), pp. 42–51.

wonder, however, with Derrida, whether 'that doesn't really amount to the same thing – or is it to the other' (Derrida, 1979, 37).

Thus the slash in my title would be an effect of style 'which perforates even as it parries,' a phallic mark, inscribing 'the irritating void of a hiatus' in my relation to mothers (Derrida, 1979, 41).[2] It would attempt to change the subject (*stilum vertere*), to inaugurate a stereoscopic (double) vision, to take up the position of the viewer/voyeur before Marcel Duchamp's *Etant donnés*, who, eyes trained through twin peepholes on the naked female body on the other side of the door, is at once implicated in and separated from the given, the data, the woman.

If mothers are monstrous, as Wilde suggests, I would be Perseus, apparently, cutting off the Gorgon's head, so that Pegasus, the poet's steed, might spring from her blood and carry me away. For what is the significance of that slash, isolating the letter *M*, initial letter of *myself, Mary, mother*; if not decapitation? It is one of those deconstructions described by Derrida as 'practical re-stagings of all the false starts, beginnings, incipits, exergues, titles, fictive practices etc.', designed, as Mallarmé suggests, 'to expose our Lady and patroness, to show her dehiscence', a word for which Derrida provides this gloss: 'As in the realm of botany, from which it draws its metaphorical value, this word marks emphatically that the divided opening, in the growth of a plant, is also what, in a positive sense, makes production, reproduction, development possible' (Derrida, 1972, 62; Mallarmé, 1945, 383; Derrida, 1977, 197). Like a seedpod, *mother* explodes into *others*, and a space is cleared for the staging of the self: *M* is for *mask* and *masquerade*. The language is, appropriately, flowery. Just as it is the style which in the flower bears the stigma of femininity, so too in this text.

M is also for Mona Lisa, emblem of enigmatic womanhood, object of the father's, that is to say Walter Pater's, desire. He describes her thus:

> The presence that rose thus so strangely beside the waters is expressive of what in the ways of a thousand years man had come to desire ... and the eyelids are a little weary. It is a beauty wrought out from within upon the flesh, the deposit, little cell by cell, of strange thoughts and fantastic reveries and exquisite passions ... All the thoughts and experience of the world have etched and moulded there in that which they have of power to refine and make expressive the outward form, the animalism of Greece, the lust of Rome, the reverie of the middle age with its spiritual ambition and imaginative loves, the return of the Pagan world, the sins of the Borgias. She is older than the rocks among which she sits; like the vampire, she has been dead many times, and learned the secrets of the grave; and has been a diver in deep seas, and keeps their fallen day about her; and trafficked for strange webs with Eastern merchants; and as Leda, was the mother of Helen of Troy, and as Saint Anne, the mother of Mary; and all this had been to her but as the sound of lyres and flutes, and lives

only in the delicacy with which it has moulded the changing lineaments and tinged the eyelids and the hands. (Pater, 1973, 124–5)

Which of us would not be tempted to assume this role, this mask? To don the veils of Nietzsche's woman as truth, *actio in distans* (action at a distance), the dance (*Tanz*) of the seven veils?[3] But such a prescription for woman and motherhood is suspiciously like a paternal placebo. It takes a wily physician, Marcel Duchamp (M. D.), to provide a real pharmakon: the impropriety of the false beard and mustache and the inscription, *L.H.O.O.Q.*, which gives us the sex-role stereotype to look at and to read (Lisa may be read in French as *Lis-ça*, read that), turning it into a joke (the French name for the painting is *La Joconde*) in a dazzling free play of linguistic and sexual difference.[4]

Barbe et moustache (French for 'beard and mustache') gives us *barb*, the point or style of Rrose Sélavy, Duchamp's female alter ego, with her false air (hair) marcelled, of course. (The letter *r* is pronounced 'air' in French.) The bearded lady, *La Joconde*, and the man in women's clothes and wig evoke Nietzsche's 'pervasive strategy of intersubstituting opposites', while our de-layed reaction, relayed through letters après coup, suggests Derrida's *différance* (deferment/difference). '*water writes always* in plural' is the title of Octavio Paz's essay on Duchamp (Paz, 1973, 144–58). In 'The Ends of Man' Derrida writes: 'As Nietzsche said, it is perhaps a change of style that we need; Nietzsche has reminded us that, if there is style, it must be plural' (Derrida, 1969, 57). One of the most advanced aspects of Duchamp's art was his way of pluralizing style, displaying in the process the male and female roles as ready-mades.

This play on sexual difference was facilitated by, if not indeed founded on, separation from the mother, on Duchamp's status as a *transatlantique*, plying between America and France. Inaugurated by wordplay, bilingualism and bi-sexuality are interlaced, the separation from the mother tongue and motherland, France (celebrated in poetry as *mère des arts*, mother of the arts), makes space for the style of Rrose Sélavy, for her finery (*parure*) and her appearance (*paraître*).

From the *art osé* (daring art) of the blooming Rrose Sélavy, whose name may also be read as 'Eros c'est la vie' (Eros is life), to Oscar Wilde's green carnation may not be too erratic a step. 'One should be a work of art or wear a work of art,' Wilde declared, and his practice of style embraced both the sartorial and the rhetorical. It is doubtful if his *art osé* would have flourished but for the distance he established between himself and Mother Ireland, a figure whom his own mother, who wrote fiercely patriotic poetry under the nom de plume of Speranza, did much to embody. It is significant, perhaps, that the only mother to figure prominently in any of Wilde's plays has the title role in *A Woman of No Importance*, a fact which may be interpreted as wish-fulfillment on his part, since Lady Wilde appears to have preempted his position as an arbiter of style. Here is what she has to say about dress:

Dress ought to express a moral purpose. It symbolises the intellect ... The literary garb should be free, untramelled and unswathed, and fastened only with a girdle or brooch. No stiff corselet should ever depress the full impulses of a passionate heart. There should be no false coils upon the head to weight upon the hair, no fuzzy bush on the brow to heat the temples and mar the cool logic of some grand deep thought [pace Marcel Duchamp]. The fewer frills, cuffs, and cascades of lace the better … Nothing to mind, nothing to care about, no bondage through fashion or vanity, either of soul or body, should be the law of dress for literary women. Certainly no inspiration could have come to the Pythia had she worn a corselet and hoop.

A woman should study her own personality. She should consider well what she means to be – a superb Juno, a seductive Aphrodite, a blooming Hebe, or a Pallas Athene. When the style that suits her best – whether for homage or love – is discovered, let her keep to it. As the symbol of her higher self, unchanged by frivolous mutilations of fashion, dress then attains a moral significance and becomes the esoteric expression of the wearer's spiritual nature. (Wyndham, 1951, 79–80)

Lady Wilde pronounced with equal authority on rhetorical style:

Epigram is always better than argument … and paradox is the very essence of social wit and brilliancy. The unexpected, the strange combination of opposites, the daring subversion of some ancient platitudes, are all keen social weapons. But only assured celebrity makes society pardon originality, for people generally resent being lifted out of their old grooves … Women especially should be aware of originality … clever women should be vigilant to tone down their conversation to the regulation pattern … As for insignificant people, they should say what they are expected to say. (Wyndham, 1951, 81)

The tone of these pronouncements is unmistakable. It might be pure Lady Bracknell – for Oscar Wilde. If this does not exactly amount to the same thing, the distinct resemblance adds nuance, at least, to Oscar's statement about men and their mothers.

Clearly, the Wilde family home at 1 Merrion Square, Dublin, was ruled by the imposing person (she was over six feet tall) of Lady Jane Wilde. Her husband, Sir William, described by one observer as 'a miserable-looking little creature, who apparently unshorn and unkempt, looked as if he had been rolling in the dust', must have faded into insignificance beside his Junoesque wife. Emblematic of his eclipse was the court action in December 1864, which was listed as 'Travers v. Wilde and Another' (Wyndham, 1951, 83). The Wilde in question was Lady Wilde; Another (who never took the stand) was her husband. This circumstance sheds an uncanny light on their son's litigiousness in 1895, when he sued the marquess of Queensberry (he of the rules) for libel and was himself tried and subsequently convicted of homosexuality, then a crime. The cause of the initial libel action had been an open card left by the marquess at Wilde's club, addressed to 'Oscar Wilde posing as a somdomite [*sic*]' (Jullian, 1969, 314). It is tempting to conjecture that Wilde may have prosecuted on the grounds of that redundant *m*, a fault of style, unless, of course, he resented the implication that he was not being earnest. Be that as it may, fathers fare worse, if anything, than mothers in Wilde's work: the hero of *The Importance of Being Earnest* has lost both parents (Lady Bracknell calls it 'carelessness') and seems to originate in a handbag.

It is Oscar Wilde's particular version of 'family romance' and his apparently unconscious desire to engender himself that leads me to the third panel of my triptych of 'others', the novelist Colette, who would certainly have agreed with Wilde's aphorism that 'it is only shallow people who do not judge by appearances. The mystery of the world is the visible, not the invisible.'

From a letter written to Colette by her mother, 'I shall snip out the bits and pieces of [another] erratic exergue' (Derrida, 1979, 35). 'When I returned from the two or three short trips I made to Paris ... I found my dear Colette a shadow ... and hardly eating. Ah! what a child!' (Colette, 1966, 59). Reading this, our ears resound with the quintessentially maternal text: 'Eat, my child, eat!' Our recognition is facilitated by the context, the legendary mother–daughter relation which Colette's autobiographical works have so richly celebrated. But the letter, though addressed to the daughter, is not about her, but about her father. Let me restore what my ellipses suppressed: 'When I returned from the two or three short trips I made to Paris to see you ... I found my dear Colette a shadow of himself and hardly eating. Ah! what a child! What a pity he should have loved me so much! It was his love for me that destroyed, one after another, all those splendid abilities he had for literature and the sciences. He preferred to think only of me, to torment himself for me, and that was what I found inexcusable. So great a love! What frivolity!'

The ease with which I could effect my perverse reading in English (*le vice anglais?*) directs the gaze to that nodal point in this text, the name Colette. Offering itself to be read as a girl's name in the first version, it is problematized by the contiguity of the masculine pronoun in the second ('I found my dear Colette a shadow of himself'), the effect of which, indeed, is to render both noun and pronoun undecidable, unreadable. It is only the knowledge that Colette's mother always addressed her husband by his surname (the novelist records her mother's voice in *La Maison de Claudine* 'calling my father, as always, by his surname: "Oh, Colette! Colette!"') that allows us to read the name as a family one, therefore masculine, in the second version (Colette, 1953, 46).

But Le Capitaine, as he was known to everyone else, had a special name for his wife too, and their daughter writes of 'the infallibility of her whom only one person in the world – my father – called "Sido".' Only one person in the world until 1928, that is. With the publication of *La Naissance du jour*, Colette lays claim to both parental names, declaring that 'both legally and familiarly, as well as in my books, I now have only one name, which is my own,' and calling her mother Sido without quotation marks (Colette, 1966, 6, xvi).

In the interval between the initial irruption of the Name-of-the-Father and this forceful reappropriation of it, Colette had legally become Colette Gauthier-Villars, the wife of the notorious Willy. Curiously, her husband, in contrast to her father, was universally known by a single masculine first name. It appeared on the cover of the early Claudine novels which his wife had produced on his demand, a situation which led him to inform her that he was Colette and she was Claudine, he the author-father, she the fiction-daughter. Her first gesture of independence toward him consisted in publishing *Dialogue des Bêtes* in 1904 under the name of Colette Willy. As Colette Gauthier-Villars she would have been barely recognizable, even to her mother, who still called her by the pet name of Minet-Chéri (Colette, 1966, 58). This epithet combines in a striking tautology the name of Colette's most celebrated male character, Chéri, lover of the aging Léa, and the word *minet*, one sense of which is 'a fashionable dashing young man'. It would not be extravagant to suggest, I think, in light of this onomastic legerdemain, that Colette's writings might be an endless reinscription of the family name(s).

But to return to Sido's letter: 'Ah! what a child!' she exclaims of her husband, in the jubilatory affirmation of motherhood, so often celebrated by her daughter (whom she described as her 'masterpiece'), which recalls irresistibly, in this instance, Freud's remark that 'even a marriage is not made secure until the wife has succeeded in making her husband her child as well and in acting as a mother to him' (Freud, SE 22: 133–4). This 'flutter of jubilant activity' is, however, contaminated by 'paranoiac knowledge' (Lacan, 1977, 1–7). 'What a pity he should have loved me so much! It was his love for me that destroyed, one after another, all those splendid abilities he had for literature and the sciences.' The description would seem entirely consistent with the imaginary dual relation between mother and child, that 'desperate paradise ... in which feeling becomes, in its intensity, destructive of the other' (Mehlman, 1974, 25). Thus are Le Capitaine's 'splendid abilities ... for literature and the sciences' destroyed.

Her father's arrested development was not revealed to Colette until after his death. She writes:

> I can still see, on one of the highest shelves of the library, a row of volumes bound in boards, with black linen spines. The firmness of the boards, so smoothly covered in marbled paper, bore witness to my father's manual dexterity. But the titles, handwritten in Gothic lettering, never tempted me, more especially since the blackrimmed labels bore no author's name. I quote from memory: *My Campaigns, The Lessons of '70, The Geodesy of Geodesies, Elegant Algebra, Marshall Mac-Mahon seen by a Fellow Soldier, From Village to Parliament, Zouave Songs* (in verse) ... I forget the rest.
>
> When my father died, the library became a bedroom and the books left their shelves.

'Just come and see,' my elder brother called one day. In his silent way, he was moving the books himself, sorting and opening them in search of a smell of damp-stained paper, of that embalmed mildew from which a vanished childhood rises up, or the pressed petal of a tulip still marbled like a tree agate.

'Just come and see!'

The dozen volumes bound in boards revealed to us their secret, a secret so long disdained by us, accessible though it was. Two hundred, three hundred, one hundred and fifty pages to a volume; beautiful cream-laid paper, or thick 'foolscap' carefully trimmed, hundreds and hundreds of blank pages. Imaginary works, the mirage of a writer's career.

There were so many of these virgin pages, spared through timidity or listlessness, that we never saw the end of them. My brother wrote his prescriptions on them, my mother covered her pots of jam with them, her granddaughters tore out the leaves for scribbling, but we never exhausted those cream-laid notebooks, his invisible 'works.' All the same, my mother exerted herself to that end with a sort of fever of destruction: 'You don't mean to say there are still some left? I must have some for cutlet frills. I must have some to line my little drawers with . . .' And this, not in mockery, but out of piercing regret and the painful desire to blot out this proof of incapacity.

At the time when I was beginning to write, I too drew on this spiritual legacy. Was that where I got my extravagant taste for writing on smooth sheets of fine paper, without the least regard for economy? I dared to cover with my large round handwriting the invisible cursive script, perceptible to only one person in the world, like a shining tracery which carried to a triumphant conclusion the single page lovingly completed and signed, the page that bore the dedication:

> To my dear soul,
> Her faithful husband
> JULES-JOSEPH
> COLETTE

(Colette, 1966, 59–61)

What can one add to this that does not seem hopelessly pedantic? Nothing, perhaps, except that Colette's reminiscences were prompted, she tells us, by a visit to a spiritualist, Madame B., who told her that the spirit of an old man was sitting behind her.

'He's very much taken up with you at present.'

'Why at present?'

'Because you represent what he would so much have liked to be when he was on earth. You are exactly what he longed to be. But he himself was never able.' (Colette, 1953, 194)

How did Colette fille succeed where Colette père had failed? By escaping from the desperate paradise of Saint-Sauveur, from Sido's house, as it is identified in Colette's hand on the margin of a photograph, the name 'Sido' in quotation marks. For those quotation marks to disappear, the house had to be transformed first into Claudine's (*La Maison de Claudine*) by the intervention of a third term, Colette's husband, Willy. Through his mediation Colette separated herself from her mother, reappropriated the Name-of-the-Father, in a sense became her father and acquired the right to his name for the mother, and became her mother as well, since she was customarily addressed as Madame Colette. Lacan's gloss on the verb 'to separate,' *séparer* in French, *separare* in Latin, might usefully be invoked here:

> *Separare*, to separate – I would point out at once the equivocation of the *se parare*, of the *se parer*, in all the fluctuating meanings it has in French. It means not only to dress oneself, but also to defend oneself, to provide oneself with what one needs to be on one's guard, and I will go further still, and Latinists will bear me out, to the *se parere*, the *s'engendrer*, the to be engendered which is involved here. How, at this level, has the subject to procure himself? For that is the origin of the word that designates in Latin *to engender*. It is juridical, as indeed, curiously enough, are all words in Indo-European that designate *to put into the world*. The word *parturition* itself originates in a word which, in its root, simply means to procure a child from the husband – a juridical and, it should be said, a social operation. (Lacan, 1978, 214)

The symbolic meaning of *m/other*, the nature of my biographical desire, now comes to light. It is to separate myself from the mother, not only from the insatiable phallic mother but also from the mother in myself, as my sexuality, the real of my body, continually tends to restore the lost object, the mother, to me willy-nilly. In contradistinction to a feminist position which would privilege an archaic, autoerotic pre-Oedipal feminine sexuality, it is my desire to distance myself from the 'dark continent' which is femininity. My sexuality would be 'extraterritorial', 'reconstructed in a field which goes beyond sex'. I would aspire to the condition of the true woman, the 'femme' woman described by Michèle Montrelay as 'having forgotten her femininity', having escaped from what Mary Wollstonecraft called 'the consciousness of being always female which degrades our sex' (Montrelay, 1978, 94; Wollstonecraft, cit. Olsen, 1979, 43). Such a forgetting of femininity (or at least of an archaic femininity) would constitute the symbolic castration which would permit its representation, the inscription of the phallic mark, *m/others*, which constitutes my desire.

Marcel Duchamp, Oscar Wilde and Colette represent different stages in my forgetting, each representing a variation on the themes of being engendered, the subject procuring himself or herself as subject, style as dress and address, instrument of defense or inscription, 'perforating as it parries'. They are milestones on my excursion into the extraterritorial.

This risky forgetting of femininity may have a parallel in Nietzsche's active forgetting, his desire, in Gayatri Spivak's words, 'to know and then actively to forget, convincingly to offer in his text his own misreading' (Spivak, 1978, xxxviii). Thus it is not the image of woman, as myself and/or mother that concerns me, but femininity as masquerade. It is in my disguises that I inscribe myself. As someone (I forget who) has written, 'Beyond the mythology of the signature, beyond the theology of the author, one's biographical desire gets inscribed in the text and it leaves an irreducible mark that is also irreducibly plural.'

For the desperate paradise of a specular relation with the image of woman, for the 'frivolity' of that love which Sido found 'inexcusable', I would substitute frivolity of another kind, which is not to trivialize the subject: 'I do not know any other way', writes Nietzsche, 'of associating with great tasks than *play*' (Nietzsche, cit. Spivak, 1978, xxx).

NOTES

1. I believe the publication of this essay in 1981 marked the first appearance in print of the coinage *m/others*, which has since become a commonplace of feminist criticism. A great deal has been published on Colette and autobiography since 'Myself and M/Others' appeared, notably works by Nancy K. Miller, Jerry Aline Flieger and Lynn Huffer. 'Myself and M/Others' nonetheless inaugurated, I believe, a certain kind of reflection on Colette and on the question of autobiography; that is why I decided to include it here [in *Skirting the Issue: Essays in Literary Theory*, JW].
2. [Jeffrey] Mehlman, commenting on the systematic suppression of dieresis in Leiris' autobiographical text *Biffures* (where *Moïse*, for example, becomes *Moisse*), borrows the phrase 'le vide irritant d'un hiatus' to describe the effect dieresis produces – its graphic function. In *Biffures*, Mehlman argues, this graphic function would be homologous to that of the 'third term' constituted by what Lacan calls the Name-of-the-Father in the mother-child dyad.
3. 'The magic and most powerful effect of women is, in philosophical language, action at a distance, *actio in distans*; but this requires first of all and above all *distance*' (Nietzsche, 1974, 124). Commenting on this passage from Nietzsche in *Spurs*, Derrida quotes the German: '*Dazu gehört aber, zuerst und für allem* – Distanz!' Playing on the word *Distanz*, whose second syllable evokes *Tanz*, or dance, he asks, 'what is the opening step of that Dis-Tanz?' (Derrida, 1979a, 46–7).
4. I am indebted for this part of the discussion to George H. Bauer, 'Duchamp, Delay, and Overlay' (1978, 63–8).

ANNOTATED BIBLIOGRAPHY

Ellmann, Mary. *Thinking About Women*. New York, 1968.

A founding text of literary feminism, Ellmann's method is an 'images of women' critique, but it works on assumptions that are still current and appropriate in literary theory. Her interest is 'women as *words* – as the words they pull out of mouths' (xv). She argues that words make realities, and that the judgements of women in literature (as writers or characters) depend on the layers of meaning that go with certain words. She also identifies and analyses nine stereotypes of femininity, demonstrates the inconsistency of thinking through stereotypes, and implies that these literary representations have real effects.

Felski, Rita. *Beyond Feminist Aesthetics: Feminist Literature and Social Change*. London, 1989.

Felski's book draws together Francophone and Anglophone traditions of feminist theory to argue that an adequate feminist account of women's writing requires Marxist-materialist explanations combined with psychoanalytic and linguistic models. She concentrates on contemporary 'realist' writing largely by European women in order to resist too easy a withdrawal from materialist feminism such as French theory appears to threaten. But the book does not resist psychoanalysis, postmodernism or linguistics; rather it seeks a broad, inclusive framework for theory and practice.

Gilbert, Sandra M. and Gubar, Susan. *The Madwoman the Attic: The Woman Writer and the Nineteenth-Century Literary Imagination*. New Haven, CT, 1979.

A classic of early feminist practice, this book considers the material and the psychological position of women writers in the nineteenth century. It argues that anger and madness are the displaced subtexts of women's writing, and that these themes are a direct result of social constraints on women. It discusses the 'canonical' writers of the female literary tradition (Austen, the Brontës, Eliot, Rossetti and Dickinson); but they also place these writers into the larger contexts of the male tradition and the relatively unknown tradition of the so-called 'minor' women writers. For a revision of their ideas, see Armstrong's *Desire and Domestic Fiction*.

Poovey, Mary. *Uneven Developments: The Ideological Work of Gender in Mid-Victorian England*. London, 1989.

A development of the practice of Gilbert and Gubar's book, Poovey provides a rigorous historical analysis of gender relations in mid-Victorian England, and analyses the relationships between legal, statistical and medico-moral discourses and literary writing by both men and women. It includes sophisticated contextual discussions of the life and work of Caroline Norton, *David Coppefield, Jane Eyre* and the figure of Florence Nightingale, examining the matrix of discourses, a hidden history of ideological formations, that reproduced 'uneven' gender relations.

Spelman, Elizabeth V. *Inessential Woman: Problems of Exclusion in Feminist Thought*. London, 1988.

Spelman's book was one of the first to call into question the strategic essentialism of feminism – the view that all women share common experience. In readings of Greek philosophy, the writings of de Beauvoir and Chodorow, and discussions of race and language, she demonstrates that the inclusion of all women in the category of 'Woman' is actually a process of exclusion. While not strictly a book about literature, Spelman's insights have been influential in feminist literary theory undoing a politically naive position about the ahistorical, trans-racial and cross-class vision of women's oppressions.

SUPPLEMENTARY BIBLIOGRAPHY

Armstrong, Nancy. *Desire and Domestic Fiction: A Political History of the Novel*. Oxford, 1987.

Beauvoir, Simone de. *The Second Sex*, trans. H. M. Parshley. Harmondsworth, 1972.

Beer, Gillian. *Reader I Married Him: A Study of the Women Characters of Jane Austen, Charlotte Brontë, Elizabeth Gaskell and George Eliot*. London, 1974.

————. *Gender Trouble: Feminism and the Subversion of Identity*. London, 1990.

Butler, Judith. *Gender Trouble*. New York, 1990.

————. *Bodies that Matter: On the Discursive Limits of 'Sex'*. London, 1993.

Castle, Terry. *The Apparitional Lesbian: Female Sexuality and Modern Culture*. New York, 1993.

————. *The Hélène Cixous Reader*, ed. Susan Sellers. New York, 1994.

Cixous, Hélène. 'The Laugh of the Medusa', in *New French Feminisms: An Anthology*, eds Elaine Marks and Isabelle de Courtrivon. Hemel Hempstead, 1981.

Cixous, Hélène and Clément, Cathérine. *The Newly Born Woman*, trans. Betsy Wing. Minneapolis, MN, 1986.

Elam, Diane. *Feminism and Deconstruction: Ms en Abyme*. London, 1994.

Faderman, Lillian. *Surpassing the Love of Men: Romantic Friendship and Love between Women from the Renaissance to the Present*. London, 1985.

Felski, Rita. *The Gender of Modernity*. Cambridge, MA, 1995.

Fuss, Diana, *Essentially Speaking: Feminism, Nature and Difference*. New York, 1989.

Gallop, Jane. *The Daughter's Seduction: Feminism and Psychoanalysis*. Ithaca, NY, 1982.

Gilbert, Sandra M. and Gubar Susan, *No Man's Land: The Place of the Woman Writer in the Twentieth Century*, 3 vol: Vol. 1, *The War of the Words*; Vol. 2, *Sexchanges*; Vol. 3, *Letters from the Front*. New Haven, CT 1987–94.

Greene, Gayle, and Coppélia Kahn, eds. *Making a Difference: Feminist Literary Criticism*. London, 1985.

hooks, bel. *Ain't I a Woman? Black Women and Feminism*. London, 1982.

Irigaray, Luce. *This Sex Which is Not One*, trans. Catherine Porter with Carolyn Burke. Ithaca, NY, 1985.

————. *The Speculum of the Other Woman*, trans. Gillian C. Gill. Ithaca, NY, 1985.

————. *The Irigaray Reader*, ed. Margaret Whitford. Cambridge, MA, 1991.

Jacobus, Mary, ed. *Women Writing and Writing About Women*. London, 1979.

Kahane, Claire. *Passions of the Voice: Hysteria, Narrative and the Figure of the Speaking Woman, 1850–1915*. Baltimore, MD, 1995.

Kaplan, Cora. *Seachanges: Culture and Feminism*. London, 1986.

Kristeva, Julia. *The Kristeva Reader*, ed. Toril Moi. Oxford, 1986.

Lydon, Mary. *Skirting the Issue: Essays in Literary Theory*. Madison, WI, 1995.

Marks, Elaine and de Coutivron, Isabelle, eds. *New French Feminisms: An Anthology*. Hemel Hempstead, 1981.

Mitchell, Juliet. *Psychoanalysis and Feminism*. Harmondsworth, 1974.

Moers, Ellen. *Literary Women: The Great Writers*. London, 1977.

Moi, Toril. *Sexual/Textual Politics: Feminist Literary Theory*. London, 1985.

————, ed. *French Feminist Thought*. Oxford and New York, 1987.

Munt, Sally, ed. *New Lesbian Criticism: Literary and Cultural Readings*. Hemel Hempstead, 1992.

Rose, Jacqueline. *Sexuality the Field of Vision*. London, 1986.

Showalter, Elaine. *A Literature of Their Own*. London, 1977.

————. *A Literature of their Own: British Women Novelists from Brontë to Lessing*. London, 1982.

————, ed. *The New Feminist Criticism: Essays on Women, Literature and Theory*. London, 1986.

Ward-Jouve, Nicole. *Female Genesis: Creativity, Self and Gender*. Cambridge, 1998.

Weedon, Chris. *Feminist Practice and Poststructuralist Theory*. Oxford, 1987.

PART 3
MARXIST LITERARY THEORIES

INTRODUCTION:
THE POLITICS OF LITERATURE

Moyra Haslett

> No doubt we shall soon see Marxist criticism comfortably wedged between Freudian and mythological approaches to literature, as yet one more stimulating academic 'approach', one more well-tilled field for students to tramp.
>
> (Eagleton, 1976, vii)

We might think of marxist literary theories as a political rather than a literary choice. Marxist theories are adopted by many academic disciplines and are marked by a high degree of internal debate, but despite their differences they share common goals and commitments. It is the marxist conviction of the interrelationship of word and world, of theory and practice, and of the inequities of the capitalist system in its various forms that makes it more than fashionable. So that, notwithstanding the ways in which marxism has both informed and been informed by other theoretical perspectives, marxism is impoverished as a theory if it is thought of as just one option within many. This conviction has made marxism unpopular, an identification which increasingly fewer theorists are prepared to make. Marxist theory is so pious, so humourless, so out-of-date, its detractors claim. But marxist literary theories – like feminism and postcolonialism, those theories which also define themselves as both a theoretical and political practice – continue to ask the most challenging questions within the discipline of literary study: what is the relation between literature and society? does literary value exist and if so in what? what is the relation between my study and the lives of others outside of the academy? Few marxist theories today would claim to reveal absolute truths, but they do assert a *situated* argument of what is true or false, for that specific historical moment. For example, marxism argues that all viewpoints are socially determined, but that does not entail that all viewpoints are equal in value. A prisoner is more likely to recognise the oppressive nature of a particular juridicial system than a judge. (In classical Marxist terms, the working classes will recognise the injustices of capitalism rather than the capitalists.) All marxist theories continue to assert that certain inequities – such as class exploitation and poverty – will always be 'wrong', and marxist literary theories continue to assert that these issues are not unrelated to literature. Marxism is thus both a political movement and a form of intellectual resistance. Most commentators today – Marxist and non-marxist – would agree that the end of the twentieth century has been marked in the West as a time of political quietism. Marxist commentators warn that we are in danger of forgetting not just how to act but how to think in resistance to capitalism.

Marxist literary theories inevitably refer us to the writings of Karl Marx, the first major critic of capitalism as a system. Writing out of and within the experience of capitalism in the mid-nineteenth century, Marx's work bears the traces of its own context and tells us something of our own. Undoubtedly, much of Marx's work has dated: the working classes no longer seem likely to be in the vanguard of revolution, at least in the industrial West, and the activism of feminists, anti-racist movements and gay people reminds us that Marx's work contains as many silences and blind spots as we can read in, say, Jane Austen's exclusive focus on the gentry. But capitalism continues to have the same kinds of consequences as it did in the nineteenth century. We still have a wide gulf between the richest and the poorest of our society, many people still find their work unrewarding and repetitive, we are witnessing the growth of the working poor, of an 'underclass', of homelessness, slave labour, and insecure and part-time labour. That Marx's writings bear the imprint of their own time is as unimportant to contemporary marxist theorists as the collapse of the Soviet Union and the economic changes within Chinese society. The theories of western marxism, and especially its cultural theories, have been marked by their divergence from rather than fidelity to communist dogma and the most deterministic readings of Marx, identified with Engels and Lenin. And Marx's works have been retranslated, variously interpreted and critiqued within marxism. (In the extract reprinted here, for example, Eagleton criticises Marx's celebration of the 'eternal charm' of ancient Greek art in *Grundrisse*.) For this reason I have refused the traditional capital 'M' in my writings on marxist theory, since marxist theories are, on closer inspection, much more diverse than the idea of fidelity to a founding father would suggest.

The interviews which the editors of *New Left Review* conducted with Raymond Williams in 1979 reveal something of the debates *within* and *between* marxisms. Williams is a tremendously influential and signficant figure within marxist literary theory, but his importance is due as much to his arguments with orthodox 'Marxism' as it is to any fidelity to marxist precepts. Thus, long before 'postmarxism' was discussed, or postmodernism repudiated 'grand narratives', many marxist theorists were already repudiating marxist teleologies, or what Williams calls 'formulas'. In the extracts included here Williams rejects the kind of marxism which confidently knows what the next epoch of history has in store, and objects to the implicit celebration in speaking of a 'mastery' of nature. In his quarrel with certain forms of marxism, Williams demonstrated that it was possible to remain marxist and still disagree with received orthodoxies.

Despite their diversity, marxist cultural theories, however, do share common characteristics and commitments. First and most fundamental of these is the refusal to separate art from society. Even those aestheticist artworks which attempt or claim to resist context – abstract painting, a Mills & Boon romance, Lewis Carroll's 'nonsense' poem 'Jabberwocky', the aestheticism associated with Walter Pater and Oscar Wilde, improvisatory jazz – are social for they are all created and received in concrete contexts. In all marxist readings, art is interpreted as a material practice, perhaps because it relies upon a 'technology' (the pen, the printing press), is concretely realised in situations which themselves are material (the folkballad sung in a bar or courtly masque performed for royalty) or is bought and sold like other commodities (and is thus subject to such factors as sponsorship, marketing, financing, production and distribution). One marxist reading of ostensibly aestheticist artworks, such as those suggested above, argues that aestheticism is itself an attempt to disguise their very implication in the kinds of commercial concerns which they so disdain. The attempt to escape from commercialism is still a response to that same commercialism. Indeed, marxist writers such as Raymond Williams and Terry Eagleton have argued that art began to perceive and represent itself as 'outside' of society only in the late eighteenth century, the very time in which art was becoming increasingly commodified. At the level of the producer of art – the novelist, folksinger, cartoonist – art is also already social, since the artwork is created by an individual with a class, gender and racial identity, and whose fashioning of the artwork is determined by such factors as education and affluence. In place of the author as expressive genius, whose intrinsic talents means that he or she transcends her own time and place, we have the author as producer who is inevitably part of his or her own context. At the level of the word too, art is social, since language is a social convention rather than a merely individual one (as Vološinov argues contra Saussure). Marxist literary theories thus attempt to situate the artwork within a total context, an ambitious project which will always be an aspiration rather than a necessarily completed task. (Williams' continual gestures towards greater complexity are exemplary here.)

Marxist theories are then distinguished from other approaches in the way in which they prioritise the materiality of culture, the way in which it is produced, distributed and received as a concrete and social practice. For marxist theorists the economic mode of society is crucial here because it is the economic system which frequently – though not always – determines how art will be so constructed. The relationship between the economic and the literary is both the central concern of marxism and the subject of its most heated debates. Williams wrote of how the economic determines a 'whole way of life' and that non-economic (in marxist terms superstructural) forces, such as literature, should be related to this rather than to the economic element alone. In practice, indeed, no separation between spheres is possible: the 'economic' sphere includes the social relations of people, and the 'literary' is marketed and bought like any other product. The theoretical persistence with which marxist theories situate the artwork within society is also a political resistance to the ways in which capitalism separates the social and the individual, culminates in the division of labour and specialises spheres of human activity. So that while marxist approaches to literature attempt to describe and understand this splitting of aesthetics and society, they are also attempts to rectify this splitting, to change it.

Within these parameters, marxist approaches to literature are surprisingly varied, and there is no programmatic way of 'applying' marxist ideas. Of course, marxist critics will continue to discuss such issues as class struggle, commodification, the alienation of labour and so on, but these shared concerns have not entailed that marxist readings are always identical in approach, or even that their conclusions will be the same. Literature might be seen to reflect life under capitalism: for example, in arguing that modernist art portrays and even exacerbates the individual's solipsism and isolation (Lukács) or that art is split between elitist 'high' art and popular 'low' art (cultural studies theorists, such as Bourdieu). Alternatively, however, literature might be seen as opposing the ill-effects of capitalism: specifically artistic traditions may be 'relatively' free of economic determination so that this relative autonomy permits art to critique capitalist relations (Adorno), or that art alone resists appropriation by the market (Bürger on Cubism and avant-garde art); or that new technologies make a collective imagination possible (Benjamin on photography, newspapers and cinema). Marxist approaches to literature are thus attempts both to articulate the relationship between literature and society and to call the separation which this implies into question. Pragmatically, we may have to separate art and society in order to explain their relation, but simultaneously we need to resist this separation by remembering that art is *part of* society. The theoretical complexity involved in this double manoeuvre has often been overlooked, as marxist theorists have been accused of 'reducing' literature to a passive reflection of society, rather than seeing literature as fully implicated within society.

That thought itself is also socially determined, and that this makes the relationship between art and its contexts more complex still, is explored in marxist analyses of ideology. Ideology might be described as the material production of ideas, values and beliefs. This description, however, fails to address the way in which values and beliefs are often conflictual and are overdetermined by power relations. Certain classes and groups of people are able to influence and even manipulate more than others and to disguise the ways in which their values are inherently self-interested. It is in the interest of free-marketeers, for example, that they persuade us that the 'free market' is synonymous with choice. In practice, however, free choice is a myth, since we are limited by what we can afford and what is available. 'Best-selling' lists of books, for example, are commonly accepted as those books which people most want to read. But this implies that people are 'free' to read, or indeed buy, any book they please. The desire for reading, however, is influenced by other factors: suggestive advertising, price, availability, education, peer experience (we read what others read) and, relatedly, class, gender or racial identity. The demand for books is related to what publishers and booksellers make available and how they make it available. Depending on your ideological viewpoint, then, the lists of best-selling books signal popular 'free' choice or mystify the concept of 'choice'. And in an era of global, multinational capitalism, the first ideological stance is the more powerful.

Many of the most significant marxist theories have discussed the ways in which literature permits us to perceive the ideology of its context. When the country-house poems of the seventeenth century (such as Ben Jonson's *Penshurst* and *To Sir Robert Wroth* and Thomas Carew's *To Saxham*) praise the great estates of England, one of their conventions is to describe the way in which nature bestows its plenty upon the lord's dinner table. Nature itself honours the aristocracy. But this conventional poetic hyperbole disguises human labour. It omits the labourers, whose toil in the gardens and fields permits the estate to 'yield' its abundance. That Jonson and Carew were dependent upon the patronage of such lords reveals the way in which their idealised, arcadian representation of the English country house is an accommodation with the feudal relations which sustain their own lives. The dissimulation within the poems helps to legitimate the interests of the English ruling class (see Williams, 1973).

Literary texts, however, do not always reflect ideology in such an obvious manner, nor is ideology always simply a matter of the imposition of a set of erroneous beliefs ('false consciousness'). Definitions of ideology as a form of 'false consciousness' suggest that ideology is always imposed by the ruling classes. These definitions appear to doom the underclasses to subjection, to being dupes in believing that which is against their own interests. But accepting the imposition of beliefs 'from above' may be in the underclasses' *own* interests too: self-deception might make life more tolerable, so that, rather than their beliefs being at odds with their interests, they have conflicting kinds of interests. Gramsci was the first marxist to theorise the ways in which people collude in or consent to prevailing ideological values. Election campaigns are one place we might look for contemporary ideological formations. Here we can see what is appealing, and what is considered as a campaign blunder, and the ways in which they tap important aspects of ideological power relations in complex societies. Neither are these values always negative. In the analogy of best-selling books discussed above, for example, readers who clamour for romantic fiction may not merely have been fooled into buying by, say, Mills & Boon's marketing machine or because it is seen to be a 'feminine' type of reading. They may also *want* to read such books, and their desire to do so may be quite legitimate.

Gramsci's reworking of ideology as a consensual formation was an attempt to explain why Italian workers failed to seize power in the years following the First World War, when it had appeared that all the 'objective' material conditions for a worker's revolution were in place. Marxist analyses of ideology thus became ways of explaining capitalism's continued existence, and of understanding the ways in which we accept its system. Althusser's writings in the 1970s were influenced by the translations of Gramsci's work just becoming available. Althusser's twist on Gramsci's own theories of ideology was to argue that our acceptance of capitalism is achieved at an unconscious level, and that there is a contradiction between the ways in which we think of our position within society and the ways in which we really live it. In Althusser's famous phrase: 'Ideology represents the imaginary relationship of individuals to their real conditions of existence' (1984, 36). This means that our identity is consituted within ideology, so that ideology is not only a matter of performing but also of living in ideology. This theory might appear to be the very opposite of an emancipatory theory: if we live in ideology, how can we ever come to know it, since no 'outside' of ideology is possible? For Althusser knowledge of ideology is possible through theory-as-science and through art. And this latter argument was developed in the 1970s by Macherey and Eagleton. Literature, they argued, could make ideology visible, for in giving ideology a form, literature foregrounds its typical contradictions. A 'symptomatic' reading could thus read the gaps, inconsistencies and limits of a text, as Freud has suggested we might read dreams and slips of the tongue so as to reveal the traces of what they repress. In the excerpt included here, for example, Eagleton argues that the 'rustic' and 'educated' languages of Thomas Hardy's novels are incommensurable for his critics, who fail to see that this 'inconsistency' reveals the ideological nature of our definitions of 'literature' itself.

Eagleton's example here illustrates how he has resisted the latent formalism in Macherey's original work. In arguing that literature puts ideology into contradiction through literary form, Macherey's theory suggested that all literary texts are subversive. But this is to essentialise a definition of 'Literature', and to forget that such a definition itself might constitute an ideology. In Macherey's early writings, the literary text, instead of being considered in its particularity (in its historical, social, economic, ideological, technological or institutional matrices), becomes a manifestation of the invariant structure which is 'Literature'. In his later work, Macherey revised his writings on literature, influenced by Renée Balibar's study of the use of literature in the French educational system, *Les Français fictifs* (1974). 'Literature' in nineteenth- and twentieth-century France is defined according to how it is constructed within the classroom and there moulded according to the ways in which language itself is taught. While this extract demonstrates Eagleton's familiarity with Balibar's work, his own work might also be aligned with the British tradition of cultural materialism, which focuses on contemporary contexts for historical texts. For example, in the opening of the extract, Eagleton argues that a literary text is not inherently conservative or radical, ideological or oppositional, but is so only in relation to its contexts. And because its contexts of reception change, the literary text does not remain the same throughout the history of its reception. No text can be immutably either 'ideological' or 'oppositional' because such judgements will always be determined by other relations which are constantly changing. If the film versions of Jane Austen today portray a conservative, nostalgic image of rural England, it is not so much a matter of the intrinsic conservatism of Austen's work as that the conservative aspects of her own society are still with us. Britain in the 1990s is still a society deeply divided according to class and one in which the countryside alliance of large landowners and landed gentry continues to exercise wide influence. In Eagleton's example, the reception of the novels of Thomas Hardy can tell us much about twentieth-century values, since many readings illustrate their own concerns rather than that of late Victorian society. And we can see from this genealogy of Hardy criticism that the definition of 'literature' itself is constantly changing.

In the excerpts included here, we can see the interviewers of *New Left Review* task Williams with treating 'literature' as an ideology. Williams admits that this is a problem, and his response – that he was writing against a received idea of 'Literature' which needed to be resisted – is an answer which, hopefully, will not be so pertinent for future generations of academics and students. The theoretical approaches of marxism, feminism, postcolonialism, new historicism and cultural studies have all questioned traditional definitions of what we should study and research, though, as yet, 'canonical' Literature maintains its dominance and the question of literary 'value' remains contentious. Williams argues that it would be naive to think that we could eradicate judgement, so that the best we can do is to continue to judge but to reveal as much as possible the way in which that judgement is situated. We should recognise and recontextualise as much as possible our own and others' judgements. In Williams' words, we should try: 'To seek the maximum disclosure of the circumstances of judgment, which would allow someone else to dissociate himself [*sic*] from it; but then openly and not by a presumptive category'. This too may be a limited response to the problem of literary value, but it is also the most attractive and disarming. For marxism – like feminism and postcolonialism – wears its commitment openly, and does not hide behind the pretence of impartiality.

For critics of marxist literary theories, it is this very commitment, however, which makes their readings suspect. A common accusation of marxist approaches to literature is that they are insufficiently attentive to the form of literature. (In the convenient opposition of formalism and marxism, the first pays undue attention to form at the expense of context, the second to context at the expense of form.) One marxist critic who has explicitly addressed this question, and through specific readings of literary texts, is Fredric Jameson in *The Political Unconscious*. Jameson's principle argument in this work is that narrative provides complex resolutions to the more basic contradictions of history. In his readings of Conrad, for example, the literary modes of impressionism and romance are seen as recourses against the rationalization and reification of nineteenth-century capitalist society. Conrad's use of the sense perceptions of impressionism can be understood as both a consequence of this transition and a strategy by which his novels resist it. In the style's foregrounding of the senses, reality is turned into image. This is an embodiment of reification, but it also projects beyond it. So that the literary text in its potential to resolve real contradictions on the level of symbol is both a figure of ideology in Althusser's sense and also an emancipatory ideal. Literature transcends the real, even if only symbolically.

Jameson's discussion of the ways in which narrative is a 'socially symbolic act' also demonstrates how marxist readings need not read literature merely as a reflection of its particular context. It is not a matter of learning something of the historical context and then reading the text off against that as a form of 'background', as the historicist approaches to Shakespeare of, for example, Dover Wilson and Tillyard tended to do. Rather history is read in the *formal* fissures and contradictions within a text. Jane Austen's novels, for example, notoriously do not refer to the French Revolution, Enclosure Acts or Luddite agitations which constitute the history we associate with the Romantic period. Yet her novels do dramatise the tensions between a precapitalist, feudal order in which status hierarchies are strictly maintained and a capitalist order in which social mobility is more possible through 'merit'. These tensions are embodied in the figure of Mr Knightley in *Emma*. He criticises Emma's attempts to raise Harriet Smith 'out of' her station and his estate of Donwell Abbey represents the fixed, stable, stratified and coherent order associated with this vision of society as inherently hierarchical. Yet Knightley is also a figure of the agrarian capitalist, who spends the little spare money he has frugally and who sensibly reinvests his profits in the farm. He prefers looking over his accounts than dancing and recognises in his tenant Robert Martin a man who shares his own values, despite their differences in rank. The character of Knightley, then, can symbolically resolve the determinate contradictions which are registered within the novel. He combines the elegance and refinement of the natural aristocrat with the moral, capitalist virtues of industry and thrift. And this symbolic act is possible within Austen's notorious limit of '3 or 4 families in a country village', what Jameson would call narrative's 'strategy of containment'.

Austen's novels are then thoroughly 'historical', since, like all narratives, their ultimate horizon, their political unconscious is History itself. Jameson refutes the idea that this historical subtext is 'extrinsic' to the work, something which he, not the text, brings to bear upon it. Instead his 'formal' analysis is defined as 'contextual', a definition we think of as paradoxical only because such theoretical strategies have tended to be situated as oppositional to one another. Formal patterns in the work are read as symbolic enactments of the social within the formal (Jameson, 1983, 77). Jameson's readings are thus attempts to combine heuristic with deductive procedures. His initial approach to the work is an immanent description of its formal and structural properties. It is deductive insofar as its hunt for formal contradictions is motivated by its aim of transcending the purely formalistic, its ultimate intention of relating these contradictions to history as the subtext of the work. And such contradictions will enable a political analysis, in its widest sense.

Jameson's reconciliation of formal with contextual concerns is not the only synthesis within his work, however. The way in which it unites diverse, and often antithetical, theoretical influences is the most controversial synthesis from a marxist perspective. Indeed much of the diversity of marxist approaches alluded to at the beginning of this introduction can be traced through his work. Jameson draws upon such marxist theorists as Althusser and Macherey (structuralist marxists) and Sartre and Lukács (Hegelian marxists), and combines their approaches with those of psychoanalysis, structuralism and poststructuralism. That Hegelian and structuralist marxisms are antithetical does not unduly trouble Jameson. (Hegelian marxisms position history as the dominant form of totalisation – Sartre, for example, prioritises History as the totalisation of individual agency in which consciousness is the basis of that totality. Structural marxisms decentre the idea of totality, for example in Althusser's theory of overdetermination and his argument that history is a process without a subject.) In part this unabashed eclecticism is the attraction of Jameson's theory. But it also makes his work problematic from a marxist perspective. Jameson's synthesis of antithetical marxisms and his emphasis upon social *totality* as a standard of judgement for the literary text are both 'Hegelian' manoeuvres. In subsuming all other approaches within marxism, Jameson's theory parallels Hegel's view of history as the unfolding of progressive stages in which new ideas and cultural forms develop by 'sublating' older ones, that is by simultaneously adopting and transcending them, reconciling and preserving them. So too in Jameson's writings, no theory, however 'partial', cannot be usefully assimilated. In Bhaskar's discussion of dialectics, we can see obvious parallels between Hegel and Jameson's approach: 'For Hegel truth is the whole and error lies in one-sidedness, incompleteness and abstraction; it can be recognized by the contradictions it generates and remedied through their incorporation in fuller, richer, more concrete conceptual forms' (in Bottomore et al, 1991, 144). Yet the suspicion remains, as Eagleton has argued, that Jameson is able to assimilate competing theories only because his analysis remains on the level of pure theory, suggesting, to put it in its crudest terms, that we need only see the 'whole' in order to put the world to rights.

The excerpts chosen here thus rehearse something of the debates within marxism: Eagleton argues that 'Literature' is an inherently ideological construct, so that we should be alert to the ways in which we might participate in such formations. Williams argues that literature need not be *inherently* ideological, but that its modern forms have been 'compromised' by increasing specialisation. Jameson refuses to condemn literature as ultimately ideological, by tracing the ways in which all ideologies are simultaneously, potentially utopian. That the more structuralist marxisms associated with Eagleton and Hall in Britain have been less popular among American marxist theorists reveals the absence of a grassroots marxism in America since the McCarthy era. Yet as the selections from new historicism, cultural studies, postmodernism and feminism in this anthology suggest, marxism's presence can be traced in the formation and critical practices of other theories. In the 1990s gender, sexuality and race have become the more popular sites for political praxis, and this is reflected in current theories and in the academic study of literature. While the greater part of Williams' work remained impervious to such debates, Eagleton and Jameson offer alternative modes of engaging with these challenges today: Eagleton's refusal to jettison the claims of class and economic inequalities, Jameson's attempt to conflate what others claim are irreconcilable. Jameson's generosity is the more attractive in theoretical terms, but Eagleton's principled position is the more necessary as a form of political resistance.

Unfortunately, the publishers withheld the right to republish from Fredric Jameson's *The Political Unconscious* (London: Routledge, 1983 – see pp. 206–80).

3.1

FROM *TOWARDS A REVOLUTIONARY CRITICISM*

Terry Eagleton

. . .

. . . A 'knowledge' of the text – one able to reconstruct the conflicts and dis-
positions of its specific historical codes – is often possible; it is just that it is not
necessarily the most important thing to do. For what will not be possible will be
to 'read off' from such analysis the multiple destinations of the text, the ways it
will be constructed in particular conjunctures; and these, precisely, are the
primary sites of political intervention. In his lengthy study of Goethe's *Elective
Affinities*, Benjamin names historical analysis 'commentary' and contemporary
reconstruction 'criticism'; each, he considers, is empty without the other.

It could be claimed, indeed, that what constitutes a product as 'literary' is
exactly this contextual mobility. Pieces of writing became 'literary' not chiefly
by virtue of their inherent properties, for much that is called 'literature' lacks the
estranging devices characteristic of 'poetic' discourse, and there is no piece of
writing on which such estranging operations are not in principle possible. The
'literary', rather, is whatever is detached by a certain hermeneutic practice from
its pragmatic context and subjected to a generalizing reinscription. Since such
reinscription is always a particular gesture within determinate ideologies,
'literature' itself is always an ideological construct. What counts as a 'literary'
text is a matter of ideological definition; it is perfectly possible for a piece of
writing to move from a 'literary' to a non-literary' register and back in the

Extract from Terry Eagleton, *Walter Benjamin or, Towards a Revolutionary Criticism* (Verso,
1985), pp. 122–30.

course of its historical career. Some texts are born literary, some achieve literariness, and others have literariness thrust upon them. Breeding may in this respect count for a good deal more than birth. 'Seventeenth-century English literature', for example, customarily includes the theatre scripts of Shakespeare and Jonson, the essays of Bacon, the sermons of Donne, the historiography of Clarendon, perhaps the philosophy of Locke, the poetry of Marvell, the spiritual autobiography of Bunyan, and whatever it was that Sir Thomas Browne wrote. It would defy the best-trained taxonomist to say what all of these pieces of writing have in common. For it is certainly not a question of an 'objective' classification such as a 'fact/fiction' dichotomy. What all of these writings have in common is that they are *written*. 'Written', of course, in the sense of *well* written: 'fine writing'. 'Fine', that is to say, for anyone acquainted with what constitutes 'fine writing'. Which is to say, those who write 'finely' of such writing. But there remains the problem of what happens when few people or none find any of the writings just listed fine any more. Do they continue to be 'literature', only, as it were, 'bad fine writing'? Could such an event occur in any case, short of some utter spiritual catastrophe? Will Shakespeare continue to be 'great' if, given a radical enough historical mutation, people cease in Brecht's fine crude phrase to 'get anything out of him'? Is it possible that if we discovered a little more of what ancient Greek tragedy was 'really' about, we would stop liking it? Marx asks himself in the Introduction to the *Grundrisse* why it is that such ancient art continues to exercise an 'eternal charm'; but how do we know that it will? In what sense was it 'art' for the ancient Greeks in the first place?

If 'literature' is that writing which in some sense generalizes its propositions beyond a pragmatic context, or which is induced to do so by the operations of a particular reading, then we have an instant clue to its undeniable ideological power. For in the very act of such generalizing, 'literature' invests its propositions with peculiarly 'concrete' force; and there is no more effective ideological device than such a coupling. If the very form of a Burns poem intimates that it is of supreme indifference whether the author did indeed have a love who struck him as resembling a red rose, then it must be that all women are a little like that. One might risk saying, indeed, that in this sense the 'aesthetic' is the starkest paradigm of the ideological that we possess. For what is perhaps most slippery about ideological discourse is that, while appearing to describe a real object, it leads us inexorably back to the 'emotive'. Ideological propositions seem to be referential, descriptive of states of affairs, and indeed frequently are so; but it is possible to decode their 'pseudo-' or 'virtual' propositions into certain more fundamental 'emotive' enunciations. Ideological language is the language of wishing, cursing, fearing, denigrating, celebrating and so on. Any apparently 'constative' enunciation, such as 'The Irish are inferior to the English', is fully intelligible only in the light of some such 'performative' as 'I wish they would go back home'. This is not to claim that *every* proposition of ideological discourse has its emotive equivalent, any more than every piece of a dream-text may be unravelled to its attendant referent. There will be statements in the discourse that genuinely are referential, that may be either verified or falsified, and to do so is politically important. What should be recognized, however, is that the cognitive structure of ideological discourse is subordinate to its emotive structure – that such cognitions or miscognitions as it contains are on the whole articulated in accordance with the demands, the field of discursive play, of the emotive 'intentionality' it embodies. I say 'on the whole', because to say otherwise would be to mistake the homogenizing impulse of ideology for an achieved homogeneity – to ignore, in short, its contradictions, the points at which, for example, a contradiction between the cognitive and the emotive may provide a fissure for the levers of deconstruction.

If what is in question, then, is a form of discourse that while always apparently referential and sometimes genuinely so, nevertheless reveals itself to theoretical inquiry as a complex encodement of certain 'lived' relations to the real that may be neither verified nor falsified, what more exemplary model could there be to hand than 'literary' discourse itself? Like all ideology, literary texts frequently involve cognitive propositions, but they are not in business for that. When a novel tells us what the capital of France is, it is not of course to enforce a geographical truth; it is either to obliquely signal a fact about the nature of its discourse ('this is realism'), or to marshal a local 'support' for a particular set of emotive enunciations. If that local unit of discourse is falsifiable, the enunciation as a whole is not. In realist literature, the emotive level is slid under the pseudo-referential; and to this extent such literature resembles nothing quite so much as the workings of more quotidian forms of ideological language.

What they say of jokes is true of literature too: it's the way you tell it that matters. Indeed the fact that such speech-acts as jokes do, epistemologically speaking, precisely what I have described 'literature' as doing warns us that such operations are not exclusively definitive of the 'literary' – that the 'literary' cannot be exclusively epistemologically defined. Since jokes are not primarily intended to communicate information, they have leisure to flaunt and foreground their 'form' – a fictionalizing crucial to their pleasurable effects. Such foregrounding may draw us libidinally deeper into the joke, endorsing its ideological 'world'; but it may also raise the joke's own freedom from direct reference to the second power, liberating us in turn into a pleasurable appreciation of its flagrant constructedness, its emancipatory powers to digress, embroider and self-proliferate. In this, it can be seen to resemble the 'modernist' text. If all 'literary' texts are parodies of speech-acts, then the modernist text might be said to be a parody of a parody. When Samuel Beckett concludes *Molloy* by telling us: 'It is midnight. The rain is beating on the windows. It was not midnight. It was not raining', he brazenly reveals the virtuality of his enunciation, exposes the text as a machine for producing pseudo-statements. It is in such doubling of the text, such raising of the parody to the second power, that 'literary' works may perform productive operations upon the ideological. For if an English chauvinist were able to say: 'The Irish are inferior to the English. The Irish are not inferior to the English', it would not merely be a matter of adopting another position: it would be a question of discovering something of the nature of positionality itself, its production of a closure constantly threatened by the heterogeneity of language.[1]

The aesthetic as contextually mobile: Benjamin is fully aware that the appropriation of artefacts is a process of struggle – that texts are arenas where battle is engaged, products to be wrested if possible from the grip of history and inserted instead into the matrix of tradition. To do so will mean contesting those productions of the artefact that are the work of bourgeois ideology. Let us take, as an example of such ideological production, the critical treatment of Thomas Hardy.

The name 'Thomas Hardy', like that of any other literary producer, signifies a particular ideological and biographical formation; but it also signifies the process whereby a certain set of texts are grouped, constructed, and endowed with the 'coherency' of a 'readable' *oeuvre*. 'Thomas Hardy' denotes that set of ideological practices through which certain texts, by virtue of their changing, contradictory modes of insertion into the dominant 'cultural' and pedagogical apparatuses, are processed, 'corrected' and reconstituted so that a home may be found for them within a literary 'tradition' that is always the 'imaginary' unity of the present. But this, in Hardy's case, has been a process of struggle, outrage and exasperation. He is a major realist, the creator of 'memorable' scenes and characters; yet he can be scandalously nonchalant about the 'purity' of orthodox verisimilitude, risking 'coincidence' and 'improbability'. With blunt disregard for formal consistency, he is ready to articulate form upon form – to mingle realist narration, classical tragedy, folk-fable, melodrama, 'philosophical' discourse, social commentary, and by doing so to betray the laborious constructedness of literary production. He is, acceptably enough for a Victorian, something of a 'sage'; yet his fictional meditations assume the offensively palpable form of 'ideas', obtrusive notions too little 'naturalized' by fictional device. He seems, gratifyingly enough, a novelist of the 'human condition'; yet the supposedly dour, fatalistic bent of his art, its refusal to repress the tragic, has had a profoundly unnerving effect upon the dominant critical ideologies, which must be rationalized as 'temperamental gloom' or a home-spun *fin-de-siècle* pessimism. His 'clumsy' provincialism and 'bucolic' quaintness are tolerable features of a 'peasant' novelist; but these elements are too subtly intertwined with a more sophisticated artistry and lack of rustic 'geniality' to permit a confident placing of him as a literary Hodge.

A predominant critical strategy has therefore been simply to write him out. Henry James's elegant patronage ('the good little Thomas Hardy') finds its echo in F. R. Leavis and *Scrutiny*, who expel Hardy from the 'great tradition' of nineteenth-century realism. More generally, Hardy criticism may be seen to have developed through four distinct stages, all of which may be permuted in the work of any particular critic. Hegemonic in Hardy's own lifetime was the image of him as anthropologist of Wessex – the charming supplier of rural idylls who sometimes grew a little too big for his literary boots. After the publication of *The Dynasts*, a new critical phase was initiated: Hardy was now, in G. K. Chesterton's notorious comment, 'the village atheist brooding and blaspheming over the village idiot', the melancholic purveyor of late nineteenth-century nihilism. This view, conveniently distancing as it was, on the whole dominated the earlier decades of the century; but throughout the forties and fifties, Hardy's reputation was more or less in decline. An Anglo-Saxon criticism increasingly controlled by formalist, organicist and anti-theoretical assumptions ('New Criticism' in the United States, *Scrutiny* in England) could make no accommodation for Hardy's texts; R. P. Blackmur insisted in 1940 that Hardy's sensibility was irreparably violated by ideas (1940). From the late forties onwards, however, there was a notable shift towards a more 'sociological' reading of Hardy. In 1954, an influential study by Douglas Brown focused sentimentally upon the conflict between rural 'warmth' and urban invasion (1954); and four years later John Holloway was reflecting upon Hardy's 'vision of the passing of the old rhythmic order of rural England' (1960). Safely defused by such mythologies, Hardy could now for the first time merit the attention of critics more preoccupied with colour imagery than with the Corn Laws or the Immanent Will; and the sixties and seventies witnessed a stealthy recuperation of his texts by formalist criticism. Hardy has been phenomenologized, Freudianized, biographized, and claimed as the true guardian of 'English' liberal-democratic decencies against the primitivist extremism of emigré modernists.

From the beginning, however, the true scandal of Hardy has been his *language*. If there is one point on which bourgeois criticism has been virtually unanimous, it is that Hardy, regrettably, was really unable to *write*. Since this is rather a major disadvantage for a novelist, it is not surprising that criticism has found such difficulties with his work. Confronted with the 'unrealistic' utterances of his 'rustics' and his irritating 'oddities of style', criticism has been able to do little more than inscribe a 'Could do better' in the margins of Hardy's texts. The *Athenaeum* of 1874, reviewing *Far From the Madding Crowd*, complained that Hardy inserted into the mouths of his labourers 'expressions which we simply cannot believe possible from the illiterate clods whom he describes'. A reviewer of *The Return of the Native*, who protested *en passant* about the 'low social position of the characters', found that Hardy's characters talked as no people had ever talked before: 'The language of his peasants may be Elizabethan, but it can hardly be Victorian'. If the language of the 'peasants' was odd, that of their author was even odder. Again and again, Hardy has been berated for his maladroit, 'pretentious' use of latinisms, neologisms, 'clumsy and inelegant metaphors', technical 'jargon' and philosophical terms. On the one hand, criticism is exasperated by Hardy's apparent inability to write *properly*; on the other hand, it sneers at such attempts as the bumptiousness of a low-bred literary upstart. *Scrutiny* in 1934 bemoaned his 'clumsy aiming at impressiveness'; a doughty defender like Douglas Brown nonetheless finds his prose 'unserviceable, even shoddy'; and David Lodge informs us that 'we are, while reading him, tantalized by a sense of greatness not quite achieved'.

The ideological secret of these irritabilities is clear. Early Hardy criticism passionately desires that he should be a categorizable chronicler of bumpkins, and protests when such 'rustic realism' is vitiated; later criticism desires to take Hardy seriously as a major novelist, but is forced to acknowledge that, as an 'autodidact', he was never quite up to it. What is repressed in both cases is the fact that the significance of Hardy's writing lies precisely in the *contradictory* constitution of his linguistic practice. The ideological effectivity of his fiction inheres neither in 'rustic' nor 'educated' writing, but in the ceaseless play and tension between the two modes. In this sense, he is a peculiarly interesting illustration of that literary-ideological process that has been analysed in the work of Renée Balibar (1974) 'Literature', Balibar argues, is a crucial part of that process whereby, within the 'cultural' and pedagogical apparatuses, ideologically potent contradictions within a common language (in the case of post-revolutionary France, *'français ordinaire'* and *'français littéraire'*) are constituted and reproduced. The 'literary' is an ensemble of linguistic practices, inscribed in certain institutions, that produce appropriate 'fictional' and ideo-logical effects, and in doing so contribute to the maintenance of linguistic class-divisions. Limited though such an analysis is by its residual 'sociologism', and fragile though it may be when exported from the specific pedagogical condi-tions of bourgeois France, it nevertheless has a marked applicability to Hardy. It is not a question of whether Hardy wrote 'well' or 'badly'; it is rather a question of the ideological disarray that his fictions, consciously or not, are bound to produce within a criticism implacably committed to the 'literary' as yardstick of maturely civilized consciousness. This is not to suggest that the question of the aesthetic effects of Hardy's texts can be reduced to the question of their ideological impact; that a text may embarass a dominant ideology is by no means the criterion of its aesthetic effectivity, though it may be a component of it. But in Hardy's case, these two issues are imbricated with a peculiar closeness.

The only critic who has understood this fact is, characteristically, Raymond Williams, who finds in the very letter of Hardy's texts the social and ideological crisis that they are constructed to negotiate (1970, 106f.) Williams, indeed, has been one of the most powerfully demystifying of Hardy critics, brilliantly demolishing the banal mythology of a 'timeless peasantry' dislocated by 'external' social change. But his text, symptomatically, has had little general influence; and the same may be said of Roy Morrell's masterly study (1965) which tackled and defeated several decades of belief that Hardy was a 'fatalist'. Despite these interventions, criticism remains worried by the precise status of Hardy's 'realism'; and it is not difficult to see why. For the contradictory nature of his textual practice cannot but throw into embarrassing relief those ideologically diverse constituents of fiction that it is precisely fiction's task to conceal; it is by 'not writing properly' that he lays bare the device.

Whether Thomas Hardy can be wrested from history and inserted into tradition – whether it is *worth* doing so – is not a question that can be historically preempted. It remains to be seen. 'Much of the greatness of [Proust's] work', writes Benjamin, 'will remain inaccessible or undiscovered until the [bourgeois] class has revealed its most pronounced features in the final struggle' (Benjamin, 1973, 212). For Benjamin, we are not yet capable of reading Proust; only the final political combat will produce the conditions for his significant reception. It is the proletariat who will render Proust readable, even if they may later find no use for him. Benjamin's anti-historicism is equally hostile to the teleology of a Lukács and the cultural ultra-leftism of some of the Futurists and Proletkultists. It is neither the case that Sophocles will inevitably be valuable for socialism, nor that he will inevitably not be; such opposed dogmatic idealisms merely suppress the complex practice of cultural revolution. Benjamin, to be sure, is the voracious snapper-up of unconsidered trifles who believes that 'nothing that has ever happened should be regarded as lost for history' (Benjamin, 1973, 256); Sophocles must be collected, because he may always come in handy when you least expect it. But he always may not: for 'only a redeemed mankind receives the fullness of its past – which is to say, only for a redeemed mankind has its past become citable in all its moments' (Benjamin, 1973, 256). Only on Judgment Day will Sophocles and Sholokov be narratable within a single text; until then, which is to say forever, a proletarian criticism will reject, rewrite, forget and retrieve. And the Proust whose texts socialism shall recompose will not be the Proust consumed in the salons; no value is extended to the masses without being thereby transformed.

NOTE

1. It would, however, be a purely formalist account of the ideological to see it merely in terms of 'closure' against 'heterogeneity', 'work' against 'text'. For 'textual' devices of slippage, displacement, condensation and so on are themselves vital to the operations of ideological discourse. See my 'Text, Ideology, Realism' (1980, 149–73).

3.2

MARXISM AND LITERATURE

Raymond Williams

. . .

There is a very striking change of overall stance in the book. We have taxed you with bending over backwards in Culture and Society *to make concessions towards very conservative figures, in a kind of political displacement to the right.* Marxism and Literature, *on the other hand, appears at times to veer towards a radicalism of the ultra-left. For one theme of the work is a frontal assault on the very idea of literature as such. In effect, you denounce it as an elitist elevation of certain forms of writing to a special status – the 'literary', a category which you say possesses the same kind of reactionary spell today as that of the 'divine' in feudal society. Now this line of argument provokes a number of resistances. One is certainly that while you seek to sweep away the concept of literature, you want to preserve the idea of culture. Yet culture, as we pointed out earlier, is genuinely vulnerable to charges of ambiguity and redundancy – what does it connote that 'society' or 'art' do not? – in a much more obvious way. Even so, there are good reasons for retaining it in a materialist vocabulary. A fortiori there seem to be many for keeping some notion of literature. Your fundamental argument seems to be that there exists a complete continuum of creative practices of communication. Therefore, since all forms of writing are by definition creative, it is reactionary and exclusivist to privilege some as literary, thereby tacitly or explicitly devaluing others. But*

Extract from Raymond Williams, *Politics and Letters: Interviews by the New Left Review* (Verso, 1981), pp. 324–58.

why is it necessary to attach such connotations of privilege and repression to the concept of literature as a specialized category of writing? Specialization is not necessarily domination. Why is the traditional criterion of aesthetic function inadequate to delimit the field of the literary? Doesn't your current position, if it were strictly maintained, lead to a complete relativism in which it becomes effectively impossible to discriminate between different forms of writing or types of work at all?

Well this is difficult. What I would hope will happen is that after the ground has been cleared of the received idea of literature, it will be possible to find certain new concepts which would allow for special emphases. Otherwise there is obviously a danger of relativism or miscellaneity, of which I am very conscious. That will have to be done – it will be a necessary stage. Even with the category of the aesthetic, I say it is wholly necessary to reject the notion of aesthetics as the special province of a certain kind of response, but we cannot rule out the possibility of discovering certain permanent configurations of a theoretical kind which answer to it – as we certainly don't rule out conjunctural configurations of a historical kind in which the category effectively obtained. In the case of literature, it was a movement of insight and surprise to discover the historical shift in the meaning of the term. There would be absolutely no need to reject the concept of literature – at least in this way – if it still meant what it did in the 18th century: a group of written works of a certain level of seriousness, capable of sustaining an attention that others could not. But from the 19th century onwards, the definition of literature has rested on an ever firmer separation between imagination and reality, fiction and fact, writing to create an artistic whole and writing in all its other functions. This increasing specialization had two effects. First, the forms of writing which were described as creative or artistic or imaginative were secluded from the kinds of correlation with social reality which in principle were always there – they were constituted as a reserved area. Secondly, all kinds of writing which didn't possess this label offered themselves as writing the real in ways which prevented any examination of their processes of production and composition, which were actually quite cognate with the processes of composition inside the reserved area which was called literary. In fact, it may be as important to establish the existence of a convention – one might even still like to call it a literary convention – within a scientific paper, as it is to trace a convention in a work which has been singled out as literary. Our own time is a bad one for literature in the traditional sense. There is an extreme confidence in other kinds of writing, as against those forms we have been accustomed to call literary. I am well aware that in attacking the concept of literature, there is a danger of demoralizing the situation even further. The reason my attack was nevertheless so radical was that I had decided, from within the tradition of literary criticism itself, that its categories of literature and of criticism were so deeply compromised that they had to be challenged *in toto*. It was necessary to show that all kinds of writing produce meaning and value – to use that shorthand again – by modes of composition and deep conventions of stance or focus. The mistaken assumptions which lie hidden in the old concepts have to be cleared away for us to be able to begin searching again for a more tenable set of emphases within the range of writing practices – I agree that you could not go on with an undifferentiated range. On the other hand it seems to me that from now on we have to accept it as a true range, without any categorical division between what is done on one side of a line and what is done on the other.

. . .

You have argued that in lieu of the traditional practices of criticism, literary studies today should take the form of a dual movement – tracing back any given writing to its material and historical conditions of production, on the one hand, and then tracing back our own social and historical conditions of response to it, on the other hand. You are presumably suggesting that if we effect that double process we will arrive at new evaluations of writers and works. Could you give a concrete example? You have spoken of the case of Milton, in its way a cause célèbre, *but it lacks sufficient force: for it is something of a myth that Milton was ever completely dismissed before the war – Eliot himself backtracked very quickly, while after the war the revalua-tion of Milton came from so many diverse ideological horizons – from Christopher Hill to Christopher Ricks. A much more powerful case is your own analysis of the country-house poems in* The Country and the City. *There you delve back into the precise connections between poet and patron, the actual history of the houses that were the object of the poems, the conventions that governed their writing – in general the whole relationship of the poetic constructs to the real conditions of their own production. At the same time, not on the same pages but in the same book, you set out to the reader very clearly your own personal and social position as an interpreter or reader of these texts, as the grandson of an agricultural labourer, as a committed socialist. The only final element which is absent from the book is any actual evaluation of the texts themselves, from which you seem in a certain sense to abstain. Yet would not the total act of a post-criticism, if one could put it like that, also involve some kind of evaluation at the end of this dual process?*

I think it would, although I am not sure whether evaluation is quite the right word for it. You could say that while the first process is intrinsically common, subject to intellectual checks by others if correctly done, the second is necessarily personal, a declaration of interest, and therefore completely vari-able since everyone is initially in a different situation, although we should not forget the true common modes, beyond that, of class affiliation. That is a difficulty, but the movement towards declaration of situation is nevertheless crucial, given the successive mystifications of the trained reader or the informed critic or the cultivated gentleman. It does not have to lead to relativism, because the active valuations to emerge from the whole process would not be connected with those elements of one's own situation which are really just biographical idiosyncrasies that issue into personal preferences – my reaction to Herrick's poem, which I dislike so much for reasons I mention in *The Country and the City*, would be an example; they would instead be related to those which associated one with others in certain more general acts of valuation. In other words, one should be able to distinguish kinds of valuation which are crucial to communicate to others, and preferences of style which one expresses all the time but are not of real importance to anyone else, however significant they may be to oneself. The latter do not command interest at the centre of a major area of discourse, although one kind of criticism has tried to promote them as such – something the best criticism has always attempted to overcome, but sometimes by elevating personal preference via certain suppressions to what is apparently an impersonal judgment. Serious acts of valuation, by contrast, are those which have a wider continuity of effect as an active process. They are modes of standing towards a particular form, which show it in a different light that affects not just some way in which we react to it, but some way in which we live. So many past cultural forms exert an active pressure on the way people judge and act, as they derive formulations from very powerful art which they value as great works, that this process of common and communicable valuation is crucial.

Your reader gets the definite impression that of the first three poems you discuss at length in The Country and the City, *respectively by Jonson, Carew and Marvell, you have a marked preference for Marvell's, although in some respects it represents a more astonishing social mystification than either of the other two, as you show from the career of the family to whom it was addressed – the subsequent marriage of Fairfax's daughter to Buckingham. Is that the sort of evaluation you want to withdraw importance from?*

That's the type of case. There judgment can never go beyond terms of relative power or range within a form. Often a work is clearly very powerful in this sense, but precisely that evaluation may then necessarily involve a more severe general consideration. What I am rejecting is the notion of valuation without the development of either of the two situating processes – that which has come to be encapsulated as criticism. Today it has become divorced even from the historical models to which it used to be attached. A renaissance epitaph will be condemned by a student simply because its language is unfamiliar, 'stilted'. Criticism of that sort is a licence for trivial ignorance and complacency. In fairness to practical criticism, this is the sort of reaction it would have hated when it was still a live force. But if you erect 'my first-hand response' into a criterion of judgment, it is very difficult to exclude such responses on grounds of principle – all that can be said is you've got a very clumsy first hand . . . This is now the typical emphasis of a consumer society – the idea that the whole purpose of human production in all its range over history is to bring successive objects before someone who has the sovereign rights of the consumer to pick them over to see whether he likes them or not. That now masquerades as an intellectual activity. Of course this is not the whole history of criticism, but within the tendency in the English-speaking world that I isolated earlier there was a certain inevitability in the descent towards a trivialism of preference, or towards a technicism which ends in no judgments of any kind – a simple technical recomposition of the text.

In their theses on formalism, Jakobson and Tynyanov argued that the category of the contemporary properly includes any work that is active in a given period – so that while one might say, for example, that Naomi Mitchison is not a contemporary novelist, there is a sense in which the works of Shakespeare are contemporary since they continue to play a vital role, if of a complex kind, in the culture of late 20th-century Britain. If that were so, it would seem to raise a problem for any approach to literature which concentrates on its conditions of production. For works can outlive the moment of their production; they not only come into being in history, they acquire a history of their own over time, although not necessarily a continuous one. In that respect it could be said that John Donne scarcely existed in the 19th century, but had a very powerful existence in literary culture in the early 20th century. The emergence of powerfully organized literary studies in this century has compounded the problem, increasing – to use your terms – the volume of the archaic as distinct from the residual within contemporary culture and often assisting the residual and other forms in complex ways to survive. How would you accommodate this phenomenon in your theory of written productions?

Certainly the process of returning a work to its conditions of production could be understood in too narrow a sense. This is very important to clarify. We do not now read Shakespeare, we read editions of Shakespeare and this not just in the technical sense of when the pages were printed, but in a very much more substantial sense of the reproduction of the text in a quite different culture. I would certainly regard the conditions of production of a classic author who is continually re-introduced and widely read in every period as including that process of re-introduction. The case of Shakespeare is a particularly strong one, because of the highly variable ways he has been read and in which his plays have been staged. There is a history of production in Shakespeare which is distinct from that of the original innovating individual writer. Another ex-ample would be Horace's famous ode, *Beatus Ille*, which was reproduced in different forms in various successive phases of the revival of classical culture, characteristically often omitting the last line and therefore the social situation in which it was written, and therefore the whole meaning of the ode. Transla-tions, of course, pose this problem especially acutely, as I discovered in working through different editions of Ibsen. The conditions of production thus always include the conditions of making a text contemporary: to forget this would be to fall into a mere sociologism of the originating condition. All the forces which keep the text current are among its conditions of production.

There still seems to be an important dilemma posed by the possibility of contradictions between what you call a socially communicable valuation of the art of the past and other potential sorts of valuation. We could perhaps focus this most clearly by taking not literature but architecture. For architecture is peculiar among the arts in that, unlike painting or writing, its production typically involves large amounts of wealth, and exploitation of labour on a large scale. This is true of the bulk of what is regarded as fine architecture today, which is of course not exhaustive of other forms of building. Successive dominant styles of architecture have been connected much more closely and directly with the material privileges of the ruling order than literature or painting. It is therefore appropriate that one of the most powerful single paragraphs in The Country and the City *should be devoted, not to the country-house poems, but to the country houses themselves. You write: 'It is fashionable to admire these extraordinarily numerous houses: the extended manors, the neo-classical mansions, that lie so close in rural Britain. People still pass from village to village, guidebook in hand, to see the next and yet the next example, to look at the stones and the furniture. But stand at any point and look at that land. Think it through as labour and see how long and systematic the exploitation and seizure must have been, to rear that many houses, on that scale. See by contrast what any ancient isolated farm, in uncounted generations of labour, has managed to become, by the efforts of any single real family, however prolonged. Then turn and look at what these other "families", these systematic owners, have accumulated and arrogantly declared. It isn't only that you know, looking at the land and then at the house, how much robbery and fraud there must have been, for so long, to produce that degree of disparity, that barbarous disproportion of scale. The working farms and cottages are so small beside them: what men really raise, by their own efforts or by such portion as is left to them, in the ordinary scale of human achievement. What these "great" houses do is to break that scale, by an act of will corresponding to their real and systematic exploitation of others' (Williams, 1975, 105–6). This is an extraordinarily moving passage. Here the summons to the reader to look at actual conditions of production, in a much more gross and tangible sense than anything we have discussed up to now, is brought home with tremendous force. These conditions of production, you rightly point out, include not only the economic expropriation of land and exploitation of labour, but also the cultural will to inscribe domination, command and distance in the very scale and shape of the buildings themselves.*

Now there is a striking contrast to this passage in another paragraph of the book, which forms a kind of pendant to it. You quote the lines from The Prelude *in which Wordsworth looks out from Westminster Bridge and admires the 'ships, towers, domes, theatres and temples', 'all bright and glittering in the smokeless air'. You then say, 'I have felt [the same pulse of recognition] again and again: the great buildings of civilization; the meeting-places; the libraries and theatres; the towers and domes; and often more moving than these, the houses, the streets ... I find I do not say, "There is your city, your great bourgeois monument, your towering structure of this still precarious civilization", or I do not say only that; I say also, "This is what men have built, so often magnificently, and is not everything then possible?"' (Williams, 1975, 5–6). Here is the completely opposite response. But in fact historically the architects and patrons of the towers and domes in the city were very often the same people who designed and constructed the mansions in the country. Wren, Gibbs, Hawksmoor, Kent built country-seats as well as churches, magnate villas as well as libraries or law-courts or universitity colleges. The wealth that financed all these edifices was equally extracted from the direct producers. The towers and domes, they too raised on a higher than human scale, were also designed to impress and overawe. You compare the size of the larger country houses with what any one real family could do on its own, and the point is absolutely telling and truthful; but the great buildings of a large city are also moving just because so many people worked to erect them, amidst duress and exploitation, sometimes across many generations. You would not think of calling St Paul's or King's College barbarous. However difficult it may be to reconcile the two, the direct intention of superordination and command appears to have been inseparably linked to the capacity to create proportions and order of beauty. The conflict in your responses illustrates the contradiction perfectly. Shouldn't a materialist aesthetic theory be able to address itself to this problem?*

It is best, I think, to admit the contradiction. I was writing from strongly felt responses in both cases and the result does raise a theoretical problem. I can go some of the way to resolving it by a distinction between public buildings and private ones. But I know there are complications with that, since there are private buildings which have been converted to public purposes and certain public buildings have reverted to private use. But the more serious question is: how far would the perfectly legitimate criterion of public power and public access on the one hand and private power by command on the other – how far would that take one? Could one work it through to actual differences in message of a quite physical kind? I think one could go some of the way. I wish I could say that one could go all the way. I have very complex feelings in cathedrals, for example, which really do induce awe and reverence in me, which are at once disturbed by some battle honour or flag or the terms of some tablet which make me very aware of what kind of awed reverence the setting is intended to induce. If I've felt both ways about cathedrals, I've on the whole always felt only one way about castles. But even there, I did once find myself admiring a pre-Norman Welsh castle, thinking that it was strong as the rocks out of which it came, and then suddenly realizing – My God, what am I saying? When I look at implanted English castles like Harlech or Caernarfon I hate every fine stone. The fact is that it is very different when you think of a building as somewhere we can go, or as somewhere where our enemies go and from which they control us. I suppose a Norman might have a reverse judgment on these castles. But that would still be consonant with my general position, to seek the maximum disclosure of the circumstances of judgment, which would allow someone else to dissociate himself from it; but then openly and not by a presumptive category.

So far as country houses are concerned, one would have to be quite sure that one is able, in a way that Richards showed to be very difficult with sounds in poetry, to isolate purely physical features of the building – qualities of proportion, character of the stone, geographical position – from not just its own original intention and function, but also what your eyes are quite aware of when you're looking at it: the social impulses which people bring to saying that this is a beautiful building. I really do feel confident in replying, most of them are not beautiful *houses* – you're looking at them as beautiful houses as a way of being deferential to them as mansions. But then I have a difficulty about other buildings on eminences, like the Parthenon. For there are certain qualities in the Parthenon which are quite clearly drawing on the same sensory pull. I find it even more difficult when I take the problem across to very strong aesthetic feelings which I have about land, actually stronger about land than about buildings. I don't fully understand them, partly because I've never had any training in this kind of visual discrimination. In the case of literary works, where I would be able to go further in precise analysis, I think I could generally show that in the end the whole form – for example, panegyric heroic poetry, a particularly powerful mode that arouses strongly conflicting responses in me – has these aesthetic qualities because it has those purposes.

Couldn't the logic of what you are saying be summarized in a proposition that perhaps you initially wanted to deny: that the category of the aesthetic has to be retained as something separate from what otherwise would be a moral, social or political response to a work, and that there may even be a tension between them – which is where the real rub occurs?

The tension is certainly where the difficulty occurs. I don't at all want to deny the experiences you call aesthetic. It is a major human gain to attend with complete precision, often without any other consideration, to the way someone has shaped a stone or uttered a musical note. To deny that would be to cancel so much of human culture that it would be comical. But I think we need a much more specific analysis of the situations, the occasions, the signals which release that response, that kind of attention. I am absolutely unwilling to concede to any predetermined class of objects an unworked priority or to take all the signals as equally valid. We need a very complex typology of occasions and cues, which I think is quite practicable, although it will inevitably be partial. One would then have to look at the situations and occasions in which those signals and cues conflict with other systems which it is really very important not to cede. It is crucial that we resist the categorical predetermination of them as a reserved area, and the extreme training against taking these experiences back out and putting them in relation to other value systems. No doubt in various judgments one will be caught out saying – I really do find this working on me, although I hate the fact that it does so. By really exploring that contradiction, I may find out something about myself and others. That's probably as far as I can tell.

Your commitment to a resumption of the realist project raises the question of the relation of your work to that of Lukács – with whom you have been compared, most recently by Terry Eagleton. There are obvious similarities between your literary positions and the critical realism advocated by Lukács, including your respective critiques of naturalism or even of metaphysical modernism. At the same time, your judgments of writers of this century have often differed quite sharply – most evidently in the theatre, where you have praised Brecht or Beckett in ways quite foreign to Lukács. What is your own view of these affinities and divergencies?

I feel very close in approach to Lukács over the realist novel, although our accounts are not the same when you come right down to it. Lukács's characterization of the essential movement of the realist novel in the 19th century as the discovery by the dramatic hero of the limits of an unjust society, although a very important version, is based much more largely on French and some Russian fiction than on the European novel as a whole. I feel that if I had put this to him he would not have said: you are thinking in quite different theoretical terms, but: well, what are the other models? We would have argued in the same terms, but I think arrived at different conclusions. When, however, we come to the 20th century, there is a radical divergence. For Lukács, although it is difficult to talk about him in a unitary way because his positions varied so much over the decades, did have – much more strongly than I have ever had; for this was the main reason for my distance from Marxist literary criticism for so long – the notion of a pre-existent social reality with which the literary model can be compared. In however sophisticated a form, this remained a constant premise of his thinking, which was a major barrier when he came to consider the modernists. For a novel by Joyce or Kafka is not self-evidently interpretable in terms of a novel by Stendhal or Maupassant. I think that this was where for a generation a certain mainstream of Marxism stuck. All it could assume as the social reality to which that kind of fiction corresponded was a certain state of alienation which it described as decadence. Even now when these works are being recovered in the socialist countries, it is on the basis that there was a condition of class fragmentation and indifference in the actual society which demanded new forms. You cannot usefully follow that road. It is too negative, but more crucially it idealizes 19th century capitalist society, by assumption.

So my accounts and those of Lukács could be very similar for a type of literature in which the question – how does this fiction compare with otherwise observable (a phrase one can settle upon rather than pre-existent) social reality – seems unproblematic. The realist novel of the 19th century does not make it *essential* to clarify the differences between the otherwise observable and the pre-existent. They can appear virtually identical. But once you move to 20th-century fiction, the substantial theoretical divergence between them becomes critical. I have never been concerned to defend realism in the historically reactionary sense that Lukács gave it or that those who are now attacking realism limit it to. My argument for realism has always been that it is a certain perception of reality and a certain awareness of interrelationships, not that it carries a certain mode of composition with it, nor that it has a second-order relation to a pre-existing reality. There is, in the end, that major theoretical difference, which happened not to be so important in the case of 19th-century realism, but which became very important in the 20th-century novel.

You define your present theoretical position in Marxism and Literature *as a cultural materialism. You argue, in effect, that Marxism has traditionally suffered not so much from an excess but from a deficit of materialism, because in practice its distinction between base and superstructure has tended to etherealize the activities of the superstructure, depriving them of their effective materiality by comparison with those of the base. Throughout your own work, you have always brought out the technical, physical, material conditions of any communicative practice that you have discussed.* Marxism and Literature, *however, contains the first full statement of this emphasis, which is now eloquently foregrounded. You write, for example: 'What is most often suppressed [by the conventional Marxist notion of economic production] is the direct material production of "politics". Yet any ruling class devotes a significant part of material production to establishing a political order. The social and political order which maintains a capitalist market, like the social and political struggles which created it, is necessarily material production. From castles and palaces and churches to prisons and work-houses and schools; from weapons of war to a controlled press: any ruling class, in variable ways though always materially, produces a social and political order. These are never superstructural activities ... The complexity of this process is especially remarkable in advanced capitalist societies, where it is wholly beside the point to isolate "production" and "industry" from the comparably material production of "defence", "law and order", "welfare", "entertainment" and "public opinion". In failing to grasp the material character of the production of a social and political order, this specialized (and bourgeois) materialism failed also, but even more conspicuously, to understand the material character of the produc-*

tion of a cultural order. The concept of the "superstructure" was then not a reduction but an evasion' (Williams, 1977, 93). Rejecting the whole distinction between base and superstructure, you speak throughout the book of 'a single and indissoluble real process' simultaneously integrating economic, social, political and cultural activities.

Now you are certainly right to emphasize the dangers of an idealist account of culture as a sphere of intangible notions and values, and to point out that any culture is composed of real, physical processes of communication and reproduction. But can we really say that it is therefore 'wholly beside the point to isolate production and industry from welfare, entertainment and public opinion'? We earlier criticized your tendency to miss the importance of causal hierarchies in historical analysis, in which far from being beside the point, it is absolutely essential to be able to isolate the forces which have a superior capacity to induce large-scale social change; and argued that in your previous writings you were inclined to overlook the fact that economic production permits cultural production in a way which is not symmetrically true of the relation of cultural production to economic production. Your latest emphasis now seems to produce a new circularity in which all elements of the social order are equal because they are all material. But actually that is not the case: if you like, some forms of matter are more materially effective than others. In your example, you say that a political order is necessarily a material produc-tion – of palaces, churches, prisons and schools. But of course it is not the buildings which themselves constitute a political system; it is the uniformed or civil agents of the ruling order who operate them that define their function. Law-courts or prisons are dispensable sites of a capitalist legal system – in emergencies, tribunals have been held in the open air, prisoners incarcerated in ships or hotels. The same is obviously not true of the great factories and machine-complexes of an industrial economy. After a revolution, prisons have been converted without difficulty into schools, as happened in Cuba: could steel mills become law-courts? To put it another way, you speak of weapons of war and a controlled press, but you forget that these depend on primary industrial processes, of which they are later products. You should have no difficulty in registering that point, but it seems to get lost in the keenness of your polemic against analytic over-separation of the range of processes within any social totality to the point where there is a deleterious abstraction and reification of them. But after all, there must be few people who believe that the real world is divided up in such a way that all the objects which belong to the economy are in one space, all those involved in politics in another space, and those in culture in yet another space.

By contrast with your emphasis in Marxism and Literature, *there are two significant passages in earlier works whose import seems much more right. One of them is interestingly in* Culture and Society, *generally a much less materialist work than* Marxism and Literature. *You criticize Richards's idea of literature as a training ground for life, which you say is servile. Then you write:*

'Great literature is indeed enriching, liberating and refining, but man is always and everywhere more than a reader, has indeed to be a great deal else before he can even become an adequate reader' (Williams, 1961, 245). There is an idea of primacy here which you normally reject. Elsewhere, in a memorable passage of your discussion of The Return of the Native, *you comment in* The English Novel: *'It is the process also in which culture and affluence come to be recognized as alternative aims, at whatever cost to both, and the wry recognition that the latter will always be the first choice, in any real history' (Williams, 1970, 104). Here again, you acknowledge an order of material priority which you seem otherwise reluctant to concede. Would you be willing to accept these sentences as corrections of your argument in* Marxism and Literature?

This is very interesting. There is certainly a need for clarification because I haven't found myself disagreeing with your critique, which means that I must have been wrong in my formulations, or I must have been misunderstood. I was trying to say something very much against the grain of two traditions, one which has totally spiritualized cultural production, the other which has relegated it to secondary status. My aim was to emphasize that cultural practices are forms of material production, and that until this is understood it is impossible to think about them in their real social relations – there can only ever be a second order of correlation. But, of course, it is true that there are forms of material production which always and everywhere precede all other forms. I am very glad to make that clarification – it doesn't seem to me like a concession. What one then has to say is that these forms of production are really very basic indeed; they are the production of food, the production of shelter, and the production of the means of producing food and shelter – an extended range which is still related to the absolutely necessary conditions of sustaining life. The enormous theoretical shift introduced by classical Marxism – in saying *these* are the primary productive activities – was of the most fundamental importance. Very often today, however, there is a slide from this pattern of activities to the structure of a late capitalist economy, as if everything which occurred in contemporary industry or agriculture were forms of production self-evidently related to primary need, as opposed for example to writing novels or painting pictures. I think in moments of polemic I've tended simply to reverse the emphasis, which is wrong. But what I was reacting against was the characteristic use of phrases like 'the linchpin of the British economy is the car industry'. There is no sense in which the car industry is primary production for the maintenance of human life in the same sense as the production of food or shelter or building materials. It is not even the primary answer to the need for mobility, since there are other forms of transport that are less socially differentiated. At the same time, within strictly industrial output itself, a great deal is now produced that has to do with relative social position or indeed with entertainment or leisure. Now this is where it would have been very much better to have argued my case historically. The economy Marx described was much more directly related to satisfying, or rather failing to satisfy, basic human needs than the economy of advanced capitalism. By the time you have got to the point when an EMI factory producing discs is industrial production, whereas somebody elsewhere writing music or making an instrument is at most on the outskirts of production, the whole question of the classification of activities has become very difficult. Even taking a received classification, the distribution of employment between primary, secondary and tertiary sectors is now without precedent. Precisely because of great advances in the productivity of labour, the necessities that are essential for the sustenance of human life at all – naturally in variable forms: different kinds of food, different kinds of shelter and so on – are today a much smaller part of even industrial production than ever before; once you move outside it, you are into an area which is to my mind indisputably political and cultural in a broader sense, in that the pattern of investment and output is so clearly determined by the nature of the whole social order. The proportion of primary production in the traditional sense is now so small that we could seriously mislead ourselves about the contemporary economy and even about causal relations, where I think you made the strongest point, if we simply retained the classical definition. This involves a correction both to the way in which I put the problem and the way in which you put it, because you were saying that I should have looked at it historically and you were right, but I am saying that if you looked at it historically you would not come out with the formulation quite as you put it.

This certainly meets the general objection. But perhaps you still have a tendency to look at the contemporary capitalist economy too quantitatively – although even there, while it is undeniable that in a country like England the number of people working in primary production in a traditional sense is much more limited than in the past, you should not forget the invisible producers overseas assuring the import needs of the society. Much more important, however, is the qualitative weight and role of respective forms of production within any given economy. It is very difficult, of course, to demonstrate the relative causal efficacy of different sectors of activity, since no society affords us the experimental conditions of a laboratory. But an approximate index of causal hierarchy is provided if we compare the effects of a suspension of each activity. Even a bourgeois liberal will admit, on reflection, that if all novelists stopped writing for a year in England, the results would scarcely be of the same order as if all car workers halted their labour. To take a more relevant example for your argument, a complete cessation of the main communications industries – television, radio and press – would serious affect the life of any modern capitalist society: but its effects would not be comparable to major strikes in the docks, mines or power stations. The workers in these industries have the capacity to disrupt the whole fabric of social life, so decisive is the importance of their productive activity. It is at moments like the miners' strike of 1974 that we can see the reality of the hidden causal relations Marx called the determination in the last instance by the economy.

Let me more or less agree with that, and then bring in another consideration. I see no difficulty at all in setting and where necessary revising (because I think historically there would be need for revisions) a relative hierarchy of different kinds of production as suppliers of social needs and therefore as available historical causes. Indeed one of the main distortions of capitalism is precisely its confusion of that hierarchy even in changing human historical terms – it never gets that right for long. I am very willing to concede these questions of hierarchical cause and effect. But I would not be willing to say that at the top of the hierarchy is productive industry, then come political institutions or means of mass communication, and then below them the cultural activities of philosophers or novelists. Not that there wouldn't always be a certain scale of that kind, but it is increasingly in the nature of the modern capitalist economy that there is a slide in the first bracket from indispensable needs to the dispensable conditions of reproduction of this order or of the ability to maintain life within it, for we can imagine certain breakdowns to which human beings could make adaptations of a very difficult kind by living in different ways. The hierarchies, while in general following a line from activities which answer to basic physical needs down through to those of which you at least can state negatively that if they were not performed, human life would not be immediately threatened, are not immutable. After all, stoppages of electrical power or oil would now make life impossible in the very short term, yet it is obvious enough historically that our society didn't possess them until recently, yet life could be sustained by other methods. To take another example: there have been some estimates that over half the employed population of the United States, the most advanced capitalist country, is now involved in various kinds of information handling and parcelling. If that were so, an information strike would call the maintenance of human life *in that social order* very quickly into question. Modern industrial communities are in that sense much more at risk in terms of their primary needs than much less productive societies of the past; they could theoretically and after long dislocation get out of such crises, but the amount of suffering involved would be comparable to the suffering of the famine or the cyclone.

In this sense, the hierarchy of productions is itself determined within a cultural order which is by no means separable as an independent sphere in which people wonder about the ultimate concerns of life. It is qualitatively different to live in an economy in which there is major industrial production of opinion and entertainment from a society in which beliefs were taught by priests or scribes. At every point where determinations of need are being fought out, the cultural order is crucially involved. A typical day-to-day example of social-democratic argument from the 1950s, which we now hear in every government campaign, across the whole spread of bourgeois politics, is that we must first invest in essential production, and then we can have all these other things you want, like schools and hospitals. What are isolated as priorities are in no sense as a sum more essential than schools or hospitals – indeed hospitals (one needs to be reminded of the fact) should be bracketed in any developed society in the primary category of activities maintaining human life, not all that far behind food. What is still described in capitalist terms as essential production actually means profitable commodity production in the narrow sense: everything else is then superstructural to it in a kind of caricature of an oversimplified Marxism. What I would like to see is the vocabulary of the dominant, emergent and subordinate applied to the historically, although never absolutely, changing character of the whole range of processes, and once we start by agreeing that they are all social-material, I think we are in a position to do this. I'm not saying I have done it: I certainly have not. But if I could help to provoke its doing, that would be a contribution.

Discussing the problem of determination, you criticize the notion that determination is only limitation – you argue that this is effectively the bourgeois idea of society as a system of constraints on a putatively pre-social individual. You insist that determination is not only limitation, 'it is also pressure', and then you write: 'It is always also a constitutive process with very powerful pressures which are both expressed in political, economic and cultural formations and, to take the full weight of 'constitutive', are internalized and become "individual wills"' (Williams, 1977, 87). Is the term 'constitutive' really given its whole conceptual weight here? For the individual/society opposition is not superseded by adding pressure to limitation, since pressure as much as limitation is a process externally imposed on someone. So even in the modified formulation which is glossed by the very strong and correct term 'constitutive', the actual promise of 'constitutive' is not attained in the notion of pressure and limitation. Isn't there a residual element of the individual/society opposition left here?

That may be fair. I think it is important to distinguish two levels in this matter. There is the fundamental level where limitations and pressures arise long before the individual could be adequately conscious of them. This level forms the true social constitution of those individuals; internalization would not be a conscious process – it would be something that was never separable from the realization of the individual person – it would already have happened. But we also have to consider the question of limitation and pressure as these go on through adult life, at a level which is other than constitutive. There are formations which direct, or in their disintegration block, certain developments, and these are typically felt as limitations or as pressures. It is probably an improvement to stipulate that quantitatively the larger part of determination is always at the level of constitution, where to talk of internalization is misleading because there is no sense there in which you can separate the social from the individual, it is simply a whole process. But by the time someone is a conscious individual, even capable of consciously reviewing elements of his own constitution, doors can be opened or closed; pressures be exerted or resisted; limitations encountered or overcome. I would very much want to keep that active continuing process at a level that is not constitutive, because the danger of current theories which tend to inflect the notion of determination towards that of reproduction is that they underestimate the amount of adult choice that exists – which should not be thought of simply in individual, voluntarist terms, but much more in terms of the availability and persistence of alternative formations.

The intellectual difficulty of any concept of determination is that, on the one hand, it has got to have a certain unity and stability and rigour – it should not be allowed to slide towards a rule of thumb which has constantly to be qualified in the way that, say, all vulgar Marxist notions have to be in practice. On the other hand it must be able to account for the objective fact of alternatives in individual lives, in natural histories, in the whole of world history in fact. In your reply, you seem to be describing in a generalizing way an individual experience as a matter of empirical record, rather than seeking a theoretical definition that would account for that experience of choice, alternatives, or missed turnings. Against the way you've put it, one might make the schematic suggestion, which may begin to meet the two divergent strands of the intellectual problem, that determination can indeed be construed in the strongest possible sense, which is of not only reproduction but production, production and reproduction, but because of the nature of the mode of production, it is always a production of contradiction.

Yes, in general I agree. It is the point I was trying to make about the real nature of 'the base'.

ANNOTATED BIBLIOGRAPHY

Eagleton, Terry. *The Eagleton Reader*, ed. Stephen Regan. Oxford, 1998.
This anthology reproduces work from throughout Eagleton's career, and thus demonstrates something of the shifts in British Marxist theories over the last thirty years: from early work inspired largely by Williams, through the structuralist Marxism of the 1970s and early 1980s, to the critiques of postmodernism and the exploration of Irish postcoloniality of the 1990s. The writings include theoretical reflections as well as particular readings of literary texts. Regan's introduction and notes to each essay provide a useful commentary on Eagleton's work, if not a particularly critical one.

Eagleton, Terry and Milne, Drew eds. *Marxist Literary Theory: A Reader*. Oxford, 1996.
Both this and Mulhern's (below) are good places to start, as their anthologised essays reflect the diversity of Marxist approaches to literature. Eagleton's and Milne's anthology has the broader historical range: from seminal extracts from Marx and Engels to Callinocos' polemic against postmodernism (1989). Excerpts from theorists now seen as problematically 'vulgar' Marxists (such as Caudwell and Goldmann) can be usefully contrasted with later structuralist Marxisms, and Marxist-feminist and post-colonial approaches illustrate the increasingly hybrid nature of Marxist theories.

Mulhern, Francis. *Contemporary Marxist Literary Criticism*. Harlow, 1992.
Mulhern's anthology is an important supplement to that of Eagleton and Milne, as its more limited focus permits the inclusion of more contemporary and specialised topics: issues of gender (Cora Kaplan) and empire (Said) are again included, but so too are discussions of popular culture (Bennett and Denning), the avant-garde (Bürger) and film theory (Stephen Heath). Mulhern's introduction situates these readings within a discussion of the evolution of Marxist literary criticism and reviews the state of Marxist theory the early 1990s.

Williams, Raymond. *Marxism and Literature*. Oxford, 1977.
This is the first book in which Williams explicitly identified his practice with Marxism, but its value is primarily its ability to discuss complex and subtle theories clearly. In the first section there is a focus on the historical development of the key terms culture, language, literature and ideology; in the second Williams questions and

redefines key Marxist concepts such as 'base and superstructure' and 'determination', and elaborates his most influential theory – of the 'dominant, residual and emergent' ideologies of society; in the final section Williams turns to literature as a material practice (the social character of signs, notations and conventions, for example) and concludes with the questions of commitment and creative practice.

Williams, Raymond. *Politics and Letters: Interviews with New Left Review*. London, 1981.

Through the mode of interviews, this book allows us to see both the divergences between Marxist perspectives (between Williams and his interviewers from the *New Left Review*) and Williams' own revisions of his earlier work. There are substantial interviews on each of his published books, as well as biographical and political discussions, and all are highly accessible and lively.

SUPPLEMENTARY BIBLIOGRAPHY

Adorno, T. et al. *Aesthetics and Politics*. London, 1980.

Althusser, Louis. *Lenin and Philosophy and Other Essays*, trans. Ben Brewster. London, 1971.

————. *Essays on Ideology*, trans. Ben Brewster. London, 1984.

Barrell, John. *Poetry, Language and Politics*. Manchester, 1998.

Barrett, Michèle. *The Politics of Truth: from Marx to Foucault*. Oxford, 1991.

Belsey, Catherine. *Critical Practice*. London, 1980.

Bennett, Tony et al., eds. *Culture, Ideology and Social Process: A Reader*. Milton Keynes, 1981.

Benton, Ted. *The Rise and Fall of Structuralist Marxism*. London, 1984.

Bewes, Timothy. *Cynicism and Postmodernity*. London, 1997.

Bottomore, Tom et al., eds. *A Dictionary of Marxist Thought*. Oxford, 1991.

Brantlinger, Patrick. *Fictions of State: Culture and Credit in Britain, 1694–1994*. Ithaca, NY, 1996.

Brown, Laura. *Alexander Pope*. Oxford, 1985.

————. *Women and Ideology in Early Eighteenth-Century English Literature*. Ithaca, NY, 1993.

Coole, Diana. 'Is class a difference that makes a difference?' *Radical Philosophy*, 77, May/June 1996.

Eagleton, Terry. *Marxism and Literary Criticism*. London, 1976.

————. *Walter Benjamin: or Towards a Revolutionary Criticism*. London, 1981.

Felski, Rita. *Beyond Feminist Aesthetics: Feminist Literature and Social Change*. London, 1989.

Gagnier, Regenia. *Idylls of the Marketplace: Oscar Wilde and the Victorian Public*. Aldershot, 1987.

Hawkes, David. *Ideology*. London, 1996.

Jameson, Fredric. *The Political Unconscious: Narrative as a Socially Symbolic Act*. London, 1983.

Janowitz, Anne. *Lyric and Labour in the Romantic Tradition*. Cambridge, 1998.

Johnson, Pauline. *Marxist Aesthetics*. London, 1984.

Landry, Donna. *The Muses of Resistance: Laboring-Class Women's Poetry in Britain, 1739–1796.* Cambridge, 1990.

Levinson, Marjorie. *Wordsworth's Great Period Poems.* Cambridge, 1986.

Lovell, Terry. *Consuming Fiction.* London, 1987.

Macherey, Pierre. *A Theory of Literary Production*, trans. Geoffrey Wall. London, 1978.

Milner, Andrew. *Literature, Culture and Society.* London, 1996.

Sim, Stuart, ed. *Post-Marxism.* Edinburgh, 1998.

Simpson, David, ed. *Subject to History: Ideology, Class, Gender.* Ithaca, NY, 1991.

Sprinker, Michael. *History and Ideology. Proust:* A la récherche du temps perdu *and the Third French Republic.* London, 1998.

Williams, Raymond. *The Country and the City.* London, 1973.

———. *Keywords.* Fontana, 1983.

Wood, Ellen Meiksins and Foster, John Bellamy, eds. *Defense of History: Marxism and the Postmodern Agenda.* New York, 1997.

PART 4
READER-RESPONSE THEORIES

INTRODUCTION:
THERE IS NO SUCH THING AS
READER-RESPONSE THEORY

Martin McQuillan

READERS

In the end most of the questions we ask in the name of Literary Theory come down to the difficulties of reading. One of the obvious places to start from in trying to answer such questions is the role of the reader. As a student or critic of Literature this is what you are: a reader. If Literary Theory destabilises assumptions about the experience of the Literary then it is quite right that Theory should interrogate what comes 'naturally' to Literature, namely the reading process. Without reading or readers there would be no such thing as Literature. Books which are not read are merely ornaments on a shelf made from paper and ink. They might as well be used as paperweights or doorstops and certainly cannot be said to constitute the Literary.

A text only becomes meaningful when it is read, when a reader interacts with the words on the page to produce meaning. What we call reading is an active participation on the part of the reader to construct meaning from a piece of writing. Reading is therefore something which the reader has a role in and something which takes place over a period of time. It is only when the reader actually reads (actively participates in the construction of meaning) that a text might be said to exist. You will notice the fine distinction we are making here between the terms 'book' or 'piece of writing' and 'text'. This will be a distinction familiar to you from your understanding of Structuralism. 'Text' is the name given to the interaction between reader and writing which produces meaning. A text is the temporal experience of reading which actualises meaning, the experience of which is specific to each individual reader. We might speak of the novel *Pride and Prejudice* but the novel only becomes a 'text' when it is read by a reader.

Accordingly, every reader will have his/her own experiences of a 'text'. I might read *Pride and Prejudice* and think it a witty satire on social manners, you might read *Pride and Prejudice* and find it a piece of reactionary propaganda which supports the subordination of women. While we could both be correct in our readings (or we could both be wrong) certainly our experiences of the text are different. The experience of the text is not solely constituted by the hour we spend in the library or on the tube reading. A reading of a text is as complex as the person who reads. The meanings that you as a reader will produce in relation to a text are affected by all the things which make you up as a person. The actual time spent reading is important but your experience of reading will also be informed by the experiences you bring to that moment of reading.

For example, the way you read is influenced by your gender (often women and men read differently). This does not just mean that women read in the garden using a treasured postcard as a bookmark while men read in the toilet using a half-eaten sandwich to mark their page. Rather, it means that the experiences which have informed you as a person and which have conditioned you socially in certain codes of masculinity and/or femininity will effect the way you respond to a piece of writing. As a post-Spice Girls woman of the early twenty-first century you might find the predicament of the Bennett sisters in *Pride and Prejudice* disturbing if not altogether alien. However, a reader in 1950s Britain with its much stricter social conventions might find Elizabeth Bennett's circumstances reassuringly (and disturbingly) familiar. Indeed, a reader from a society with altogether different ideas about the situation of women may even find the novel licentious.

It is not simply that women read in a different way from men. Certainly all women do not read in the same way. Rather the positions that are open to men and women as readers may vary within the same textual experiences. Further-more, a text may set itself up as offering different readerly positions to men and women. For example, it would be perfectly possible for a male and female reader to both read *Pride and Prejudice* as an ideological support to patriarchy (or as a social satire) but the text itself offers different positions to the male and female reader in relation to the plot and characters. Remember the D'Arcy mania which swept Britain following the recent BBC adaptation of this novel. The text encourages the heterosexual female reader to collude with the romantic fantasy that Elizabeth had got her man through true love. The male reader is encouraged to identify with D'Arcy as the strong and (mostly) silent type who wins his girl through integrity and speaking his mind. These positions offered to the reader depend upon conventional ideas about masculinity and femininity and also help to perpetuate those ideas. However, it is always possible to read against the positions offered by a text. We might say that Elizabeth gets D'Arcy not by the miracle of true love but because she plays the marriage market of Regency England better than any of the other women. She gets D'Arcy, the house and the money not because she will only marry for love but because she is the most desirable commodity on the marriage market and will make D'Arcy (the man with most consumer power) the best wife.

In certain respects the various theoretical positions of Feminism, Postcolonialism, Marxism, and Queer Theory are really only inflections of this interrogation of the role of the reader. These readings of *Pride and Prejudice* depend upon the ways we might read as a wo/man. Feminism is a process of reading by women in order to question the representation and construction of femininity by a text so as to ask whether that construction is an adequate response to the experiences of women as readers and thereby challenge such constructions. The text might offer us the consoling love story but we chose to read against that position. However, the gender of a reader is not the only experience s/he brings to a text. The position a reader occupies in relation to a text will also be influenced by their race and their class (as well as their sexuality, age, education, environment and so forth). A working-class reader may offer a different reading from a middle-class reader and it is not necessarily the case that it will be the working-class reader who sees Jane Austen's novel as a portrait of bourgeois normality to the exclusion of the proletariat as a class. A black woman may produce a different reading of *Pride and Prejudice* than a white woman. She could ask why she was being offered this text as a canonical representation of the nineteenth century rather than the autobiography of an enslaved woman such as Mary Prince. In this way the role of the reader is informed by present historical circumstances as well as the reading positions offered by the text.

Literary Theory enables us to read against the grain of the positions offered to us as readers by a text. This is what we mean by critical thinking or critical theory, to read carefully with and against the assumptions and values a text offers to us as natural or normal. In so doing a critical reader should not come to the text with their own set of presuppositions about what the text will be about and so close off the possibilities of meaning within the text. Rather the reader ought to be sensitive to the singularity of a text, what makes it unique and what constitutes the individual relation between a particular reader and this particular text. In this way the reader responds to each individual text to produce specific critical readings, rather than take a series of theoretical terms and operations and apply them willy-nilly to a range of different texts. This is the sausage machine type of theory we as readers should always try to avoid: having a preconceived theoretical model into which we pour texts at one end and produce identical predetermined and packaged readings at the other end.

For example, not all postcolonial readings of Jane Austen novels would necessarily question the text's canonical status. A reading of *Persuasion* might respond to the references made to the places visited by the British navy which exclude any mention of the Caribbean or Indian natives living there. When reading *Mansfield Park* we might pay attention to the fact that Sir Thomas makes his money by owning slave plantations in Antigua, while a reading of *Emma* might respond specifically to a short but significant exchange between

Emma and Mr Knightly in which the condition of women in England is compared to the condition of slaves in the colonies. In this last instance a postcolonial reading would necessarily become involved with questions of gender just as any reading of *Mansfield Park* must engage with issues of class and ownership. In fact it is impossible (even if we wanted to) to compartmentalise the discrete approaches offered to us as readers by something like this anthology. In each singular act of reading our critical response will inevitably synthesise the different knowledges we gain from the different approaches we take to a text. For example, there is no such thing as a 'pure' postcolonial reading which took account solely of issues of race and Empire independent from considerations such as gender, class, psychoanalytic constructs of otherness, deconstruction's understanding of knowledge and language, cultural hegemony, history and so forth.

There is then no single theoretical approach to a text. The various knowledges which come under the term Literary Theory are not separated within the act of reading in the way that they are in this anthology for the pedagogical ease of categorisation. Different approaches combine and relate to one another in complex ways and will do so uniquely during each individual act of reading. This is as true for one person reading two different texts by the same author as it is for two people reading the same text. If there were no difference of opinion between readers then there would be no need for critics and no need for you as a reader to attempt to express your response to a text in the form of critical thinking or in a written essay. Criticism then (we might equally use the word reading) is an act of judgement by an individual in the face of a text. This is literally what criticism means, it comes from the Greek word *criticos* meaning to judge. If every critical reading is a judgement in response to a text then it is the difference between judgements made by individual readers which makes criticism possible and is the very condition of a political reading of a text.

It is impossible for there ever to be a purely just judgement which could impose itself without encountering some opposition. The fact that people challenge laws is because these laws are judgements imposed upon them by others who have their own sets of interests to protect. The necessary making of laws is the condition of society, the challenging of those judgements is the possibility of politics. No judgement is ever absolutely correct and is always made from a subjective point of view to the detriment of some person or group. Therefore, criticism can be said to be political because it is an act of judgement which cannot foreclose discussion in the way it would like (my reading is correct and you are wrong) and so has to compete with other critical readings in a strategic network of relations. Thus, it is the singularity of the reader and the singularity of the readings which s/he produces which makes criticism possible and is the conditions of a 'political reading' as such.

Now – and here is the crux of the matter so pay attention – this is not the same thing as saying all readings are equally valid and, as you may have been told, there are no wrong answers in literature. I say this not because there is some innate perfect meaning lying buried in a text waiting to be extracted by a suitably qualified reader. Rather it is because as readers we come to a text not only with our own set of personal experiences to inform our reading but we also come via certain institutional paths and as subjects in history. These two things are related but let's take the first one first.

There has never been an occasion in your life, and there never will be, when you read 'innocently' or 'simply'. Whenever you read you read according to a set of institutional codes and expectations. In the past you may have read for character, theme, plot, setting, description, the author's biography, clever uses of language or what the text had to say about the human condition. None of these things are necessarily 'natural' to reading or could be described as reading 'innocently'. When you read for such things you were following a practice of reading laid down for you by the institution which policed your reading. This may have been a school, a university or media reviews of books, all of which will have guided you as to what to look for in a text, what to expect to be there when you found it, and the sorts of things to say in response to it. You may have been encouraged in the past to say things like 'this is a very effective use of language' or 'this line tells us about the poet's relation to his father' or 'Macbeth is one of the most interesting characters in English Literature'. Effective language is language which means something so that is hardly a valid criticism, if all books were merely the author's biography retold with the names changed there would be no such thing as fiction, and Macbeth was Scottish. It is not that language, biography, character, plot and so forth are not significant things to be interested in when reading, as the section on Structuralism in this anthology has shown language and plot are particularly important. Rather, the point is that when you read for these things in the past you did so not because they were the natural thing to do but because you were trained to do so by the institution in which you practised your reading. It may have been appropriate at 'A' level or 'H'-grade to have talked about character in Macbeth and wholly inappropriate to discuss the symbolic exchange of the phallus in the play.

Texts also change with history. For example, a reader of Shakespeare's *The Merchant of Venice* reading after the holocaust will not approach the play in the same way as a Renaissance reader trained to appreciate the character of the Jew as a comic villain. On the one hand, a Marxist or New Historicist approach would suggest that through reading a reader can gain access to the historical context from which a text emerged. Reading *The Merchant of Venice* would tell us about the circumstances of Shakespeare's historical moment. Knowledge of this history informs the response of an individual reader and places that reader within a historical relation to the text. On the other, and as a radicalisation of this Marxist approach, deconstruction proposes in a memorable phrase that 'there is nothing outside of the text'. This means that even when we think that we are standing outside of a text looking in on it (for example, acceding to the historical circumstances of Renaissance England by reading Shakespeare in the twentieth century) we as readers are already caught up in a network of textual relations which condition our reading. These textual relations include the narratives of identity we bring to the text (e.g. class, gender, sexuality), the institutional rules which guide our reading, and our place in the narrative of history (e.g. being a postcolonial or postmodern reader). This is only half the story though because the text we are reading will be part of, and will have helped shape, that network of textual relations which the reader is in. For example, Shakespeare's writing has played a significant role in the construction of the canon of English literature and so affected ideas about national identity, femininity and masculinity, the exclusion of racial minorities from literature and so on. In other words, when we read a text there is nothing but context.

RESPONSES

This is a dizzying paradox when encountered for the first time but it goes to show that even the most difficult and puzzling aspects of Literary Theory often come down to the question of the reader. My task in this introduction, like the other introductions in this anthology, was to introduce a specific theoretical approach, namely what is called Reader-Response Theory. As you will appreciate from all that has been said above the problem of the reader inflects every aspect of Literary Theory and cannot be set apart from particular theoretical approaches. In this way I would like to suggest that there can be no such thing as a discrete theoretical approach to reading which does not take account of every other section of this anthology and every essay in it. However, as we shall see there is a branch of Literary Theory called Reader-Response Theory which sets out to specifically examine the role of the reader. Such a description of Reader-Response Theory is only true up to a point. For the most part the heterogeneous theoretical approaches sometimes called Reader-Response Theory (sometimes called Reception Theory) are not a unified field of thought. Very often Reader-Response Theory is a catch-all term for a collection of writings about reading (most of which are either opposed or contradictory) which is used more for ease of categorisation than to express the force of a distinctive theoretical approach. It could hardly be otherwise since the idea of the reader is so important to the whole of Literary Theory and crosses over all the boundaries and categories of theory. I am pleased rather than apologetic when I suggest to you that there is no such thing as Reader-Response Theory, if by theory we mean a unified body of knowledge which produces a general set of rules, practices and prescribed formulae which will operate consistently every time.

Reader-Response has been a concern of criticism at least since Plato and Aristotle. In *The Republic* Plato considers the ways in which the reader receives representations (or texts) in the famous parable of the cave in Book IX. In his *Poetics*, Aristotle is concerned with the effects produced on the reader by a tragic drama. Aristotle calls the feelings of pity and fear aroused in the reader (or spectator) of tragedy, catharsis. Nineteenth-century critics like Samuel

Taylor Coleridge and Matthew Arnold were also interested in the responses readers made to texts. In his lectures on Shakespeare, Coleridge identified the reader's active participation in the illusion of fiction as 'willing the voluntary suspension of disbelief', while Arnold's criticism was often concerned with the ways in which reading might affect the individual in order to make them better citizens. This was also an interest of what is frequently called New Criticism. New Criticism was a formalist approach to literary study dominant in Europe and America shortly before and after the Second World War. Most of what is known as Reader-Response Theory is recognised as having been written in response to New Criticism.

As a type of formalism New Criticism emphasised the importance of the words on the page as the primary arbiter of meaning. In this type of criticism the role of the reader is secondary to the text itself which is thought of as an independent and self-contained entity. All meaning resided within the text and it was the task of the reader to uncover what was already there. This is not to say that all New Critics were not interested in the question of the reader. The British critic I. A. Richards pioneered a variety of practical criticism in which he set his students the task of analysing previously unseen poems which had the poets' names removed. Richards observed that different people produced different readings of the same text and often said that they disliked poetry written by the so-called great authors. However, he put this divergence down to the intrinsic ambiguity (and therefore cleverness) of the texts themselves rather than consider the idea that people offered different readings because their own individual experiences informed their production of meaning in different ways. The American critics W. K. Wimsatt and Monroe Beardsley went further to suggest that literary criticism should not be concerned with issues such as the reader, or the author's biography and intentions, or the historical context from which the text emerged. Such matters were extraneous to the fundamentally autonomous text and should be considered an error in reading. Wimsatt and Beardsley called the mediation of the reader's response to a text (as an outside concern) into a piece of criticism the 'affective fallacy'. The way the reader is affected by a text being a false concern, what was important was to pay attention to the form of the text. Such insistence did not always fit easily within the work of a New Critic like F. R. Leavis who shared Arnold's assumptions about the improving effects of great works of literature.

The dominance of New Criticism in the Anglo-American academy began to be challenged in the late 1960s by different groups of critics interested in the question of the reader. Structuralism in its French and later Anglo-American forms displaced the importance traditionally focused on the author as producer of meaning in New Criticism. In an extraordinarily powerful and influential essay 'The Death of the Author' the French critic Roland Barthes stressed the active involvement of the reader in the production of meaning. The Italian structuralist (later novelist) Umberto Eco also emphasised the importance of the reader in opening up the possibilities of interpretation in his book *The Role of the Reader*. Structuralist Narrative Theory (sometimes called Narratology) also added to the debate by identifying different positions available to a listener of a story. The American Narratologist Gerald Prince distinguished between the reader and the narratee, the narratee being the person who a text posits as a listener (for example, the 'you' I have addressed through out this essay). This is not the same thing as the reader, just as the narrator of a story like *Great Expectations* (Pip) is not the same as the author (Charles Dickens). Narratology helped opened up debates about the different positions open to listeners, receivers and readers but not all the Reader-Response Theory which followed it observes the subtle distinction between reader and narratee.

The Reader-Response Theorists (now we are talking about those critics who for ease of categorisation are placed within the canon of disparate texts which is known as Reader-Response Theory) Michael Riffaterre and Jonathan Culler are related to structuralist traditions of reading. Like Wolfgang Iser and Stanley Fish they accept that the meaning of a literary text cannot be separated from the role taken by the reader. Their work responds to New Criticism's insistence that meaning rests in and with the text waiting for a reader to uncover it. Fish along with Culler was one of several Anglo-American critics influenced by ideas in European Continental philosophies during the 1960s and 1970s. Fish's Reader-Response Theory proposes that all readers are part of interpretative communities which train the reader into a shared set of expectations about how a text should be read and what it might mean. Influenced by Culler's later interest in deconstruction Fish concludes that it is the task of the critic to examine the rules and conventions of any interpretative community which determines the outcome of a reading. The importance placed on the reader by Structuralism and Reader-Response Theory at this historical juncture is particularly significant because such an approach to reading challenged the traditional hierarchies of authority in which students were told how to read by teachers who had 'mastered' the text by cracking the author's/text's hidden code of meaning. Stressing the active participation of the reader in producing meaning rather than the importance of the author or teacher was a considerable subversion of authority. No doubt such Reader-Response Theories were shaped by the political spirit of the 1960s and 1970s just as much as they offered intellectual support to intellectual radicals.

Michael Riffaterre's essay in this section, 'Describing Poetic Structures: Two Approaches to Baudelaire's "Les Chats"', is a good example of the crossover between Structuralism (here semiotics) and Formalism. This essay is a criticism of the linguist Roman Jakobson and the anthropologist Claude Lévi-Strauss's reading of a poem by Baudelaire. While Riffaterre shares Jakobson's Formalist view of poetry as a special use of language he argues that the linguistic features identified by Jakobson and Lévi-Strauss could not be perceived even by informed readers and so their account of the poem is invalid because it fails to recognise that literary meaning depends upon the reader's response to the text. Instead Riffaterre proposes a reading of the poem which only takes account of those aspects of the poem which a succession of readers throughout history have responded to. The fact that various readers (including what he calls the 'superreader' such as poets, critics and translators) have responded to these aspects of language shows their significance. However, Riffaterre remains formalist enough to insist that the reader's response is only evidence of the presence of poetic meaning in a text. Meaning remains a property of the words on the page and is not constructed by the reader. The problem for Riffaterre is his inability to explain why the linguistic features noted by Jakobson and Lévi-Strauss are not evidence of poetic meaning.

German *Rezeptionstheorie* [Reception Theory] is only one strand of the many theories of Reader-Response but is often thought of as a metonym for the whole field. It might be useful to think of Reception Theory as a moment in the history of European philosophy's interest in questions of the literary. Like deconstruction, it is informed by the European tradition of philosophical phenomenology which proposes that the object of philosophical investigation is the contents of consciousness. Phenomenology (the study of phenomena) is interested in how phenomena (that which appears) are perceived and understood. The reading process is then an obvious point of departure for such a study. The Reception Theory of German critics like Hans-Robert Jauss and Wolfgang Iser takes its lead from a tradition of German phenomenological interest in literature leading from the philosophers Edmund Husserl and Martin Heidegger to Hans-Georg Gadamar and the Geneva School of phenomenological criticism which included the American J. Hillis Miller (later a significant voice in deconstruction). Gadamar's version of hermeneutics (the science of interpretation) is particularly important for Reception Theory because it stresses that interpretations of literature arise out of a dialogue between past and present readings.

Hans-Robert Jauss's essay, 'The Poetic Text Within the Changes of Horizons of Reading', is another account of a poem by Baudelaire. Like Riffaterre's reading Jauss's description of his moment-by-moment responses to the text as it opens out before him offers him a way of providing a detailed close stylistic analysis like the formalist New Critics while paying attention to the active participation of the reader in the production of meaning. In the second half of this essay we can see the emphasis Jauss places on history in the construction of literary meaning and the conditioning of a reader's response to a text. He argues that while different historical periods may have their own dominant interpretations of a text the meaning of a text lies in the fusion of these different interpretations over time. Similar to Riffaterre's version of different readers picking up on significant points in a poem and thereby singling out these points as constitutive of the poem's meaning, Jauss thinks of literary meaning as a coming together of all the points of interest remarked upon by readers at various historical moments. Once again the problem with such an approach is the difficulty it has in dealing with an idiosyncratic interpretation of a text by a single reader. Wolfgang Iser's essay 'The Imaginary' shows that there is no single predominant philosophical starting point in the history of reader-oriented theories. It follows the fate of the readerly concept of imagination in critical writing by Coleridge and Sartre. Iser's interest is in showing that consciousness is put into play by the undecideability of the imaginary. In this respect Iser's account of readerly consciousness is at odds with other 'subjectivist' response theorists such as Norman Holland and David Bleich who suggest that reading is informed by the autonomous psychology of the reader's unified personality.

While many of the arguments made in these essays may be familiar to you from your reading of other theoretical approaches, and Reader-Response Theory (if such a thing exists) is no longer as significant a theoretical force as it once was, these three texts are still worth reading. Firstly, they are exemplary in their subtle and detailed close reading of texts. Secondly, they show the importance of the reader in the construction of meaning. Thirdly, they are pivotal texts in the development of ideas about the literary and indicate the ways in which the question of the reader has taken up a dominant place in Literary Theory. Fourthly, they are proof that any theoretical category is not a conceptually unified critical position but consists of conflicting knowledges which are influenced by (and influence) other areas of thought.

4.1

DESCRIBING POETIC STRUCTURES: TWO APPROACHES TO BAUDELAIRE'S 'LES CHATS'

Michael Riffaterre

Poetry is language, but it produces effects that language in everyday speech does not consistently produce; a reasonable assumption is that the linguistic analysis of a poem should turn up specific features, and that there is a causal relationship between the presence of these features in the text and our empirical feeling that we have before us a poem. The act of communication – the sending of a message from speaker to addressee – is conditioned by the need it fills: the verbal structure of the message depends upon which factor of communication is focused on. In everyday language, used for practical purposes, the focus is usually upon the situational context, the mental or physical reality referred to; sometimes the focus is upon the code used in transmitting the message, that is, upon language itself, if there seems to be some block in the addressee's understanding, and so forth. In the case of verbal art, the focus is upon the message as an end in itself, not just as a means, upon its form as a permanent, unchangeable monument, forever independent of external conditions. The naked eye attributes this enduring, attention-getting quality to a higher unity and more intricate texture: the poem follows more rules (e.g. meter, lexical restrictions, etc.) and displays more conspicuous interrelationships between its constitutive elements than do casual utterances.

For these features Roman Jakobson has proposed a general formula. Selection and combination are the two basic ordering principles of speech. Selection is based upon equivalence (metaphoric relationship), either similarity or

Extract from *Yale French Studies*, 36–7 (1966), pp. 26–39.

dissimilarity; the speaker designates his topic (subject) by choosing one among various available synonyms and then says what he has to say about it (predicate) by another selection from another set of interchangeable words (paradigm). The combining of these words, that is, their contiguity, produces a sentence. Jakobson defines a poetic structure as one characterized by the projection of the principle of equivalence from the axis of selection to the axis of combination. (Jakobson, 1960, 350–77, esp. 358ff.). For instance, words are combined into rhythmic, alliterative, and rhymic sequences because of their equivalence in sound, and this inevitably establishes semantic equations between these words; their respective meanings are consequently perceived as related by similarity (hence a metaphor or simile) or dissimilarity (hence an antithesis).

Which is to say that the recurrence of equivalent forms, *parallelism*, is the basic relationship underlying poetry. Of course, since language is a system made up of several levels superimposed one on top of the other (phonetic, phonological, syntactical, semantic, etc.), parallelism manifests itself on any level: so then, a poem is a verbal sequence wherein the same relations between constituents are repeated at various levels and the same story is told in several ways at the same time and at several times in the same way. This can be usefully restated in structural terms once we have called to mind basic definitions: a structure is a system made up of several elements, none of which can undergo a change without effecting changes in all the other elements; thus the system is what mathematicians call an invariant; transformations within it produce a group of models of the same type (that is, mechanically interconvertible shapes), or variants. The invariant, of course, is an abstraction arrived at by defining what remains intact in the face of these conversions; therefore we are able to observe a structure only in the shape of one or another variant. We are now ready to agree with Claude Lévi-Strauss that a poem is a structure containing within itself its variants ordered on the vertical axis of the different linguistic levels. It is thus possible to describe the poem in isolation, so that we need not explain its singularity by dragging in hard-to-define concepts like non-grammaticalness or departure from the norm. Comparison of variants, prerequisite to analysis, is accomplished by simply scanning the text at its various linguistic levels one after the other.

Such is the approach tried out by Jakobson and Lévi-Strauss on 'Les Chats', a sonnet of Baudelaire's, and with extraordinary thoroughness. (Jakobson and Lévi-Strauss, 1962, 5–21). They modestly declare that they are interested only in describing what the poem is made of. Nevertheless they do draw conclusions as to the meaning of the poem and try to relate it to the esthetics and even the psyche of the poet, purlieu of literary scholars. This raises a question: how are we to pass from description to judgment – that is, from a study of the text to a study of its effect upon the reader? The sonnet is a good occasion for such discussion, for critics generally downgrade the poem (*Fleurs du Mal*, LXVI), a product of Baudelaire's early period (1847), and find it less Baudelairean than most of the others. But the poet did not feel that way about it: he thought it good enough to publish in the feuilleton of a friend, in hopes of drumming up some interest; then he selected it for a preview of his abortive *Limbes* (1851); finally, he thought it worth keeping in the editions of the *Fleurs* that he was able to prepare himself. If structuralism can help determine who is right here, we shall have tested its practical workability in matters of literary criticism.

Far more important, however, is the question as to whether unmodified structural linguistics is relevant at all to the analysis of poetry. The author's method is based on the assumption that any structural system they are able to define in the poem is necessarily a poetic structure. Can we not suppose, on the contrary, that the poem may contain certain structures that play no part in its function and effect as a literary work of art, and that there may be no way for structural linguistics to distinguish between these unmarked structures and those that are literarily active? Conversely, there may well be strictly poetic structures that cannot be recognized as such by an analysis not geared to the specificity of poetic language.

'Les Chats'

[1]Les amoureux fervents et les savants austères
[2]Aiment également, dans leur mûre saison,
[3]Les chats puissants et doux, orgueil de la maison,
[4]Qui comme eux sont frileux et comme eux sédentaires.

[5]Amis de la science et de la volupté,
[6]Ils cherchent le silence et l'horreur des ténèbres;
[7]L'Erèbe les eût pris pour ses coursiers funèbres,
[8]S'ils pouvaient au servage incliner leur fierté.

[9]Ils prennent en songeant les nobles attitudes
[10]Des grands sphinx allongés au fond des solitudes,
[11]Qui semblent s'endormir dans un rêve sans fin;

[12]Leurs reins féconds sont pleins d'étincelles magiques,
[13]Et des parcelles d'or, ainsi qu'un sable fin,
[14]Etoilent vaguement leurs prunelles mystiques.[1]

Jakobson and Lévi-Strauss submit the text to scannings of its meter, sound texture, grammar, and meaning; they are thus able to collect several sets of the equivalent signs that actualize the sonnet's structure. Let me describe briefly the systems thus obtained, with a sampling of the variants comparatively studied in order to establish these systems. My aim here is only to show how the authors' analysis is carried through. The most significant of their arguments omitted here will be taken up in my discussion of the validity of their approach.

Jakobson and Lévi-Strauss recognize the following complementary or intersecting structures:

1. a *tripartite division* into: *quatrain I*, which represents the cats as passive creatures, observed by outsiders, lovers and scholars; *quatrain II*, where the cats are active but, again, seen as such from the outside, by the powers of

darkness; the latter, also seen from outside, are active: they have designs on the cats and are frustrated by the independence of the little beasts; *sestet*, which gives us an inside view of the cat life-style: their attitude may be passive, but they assume that attitude actively. Thus is the active–passive opposition reconciled, or perhaps nullified, and the circle of the sonnet closes.

This tripartite structure is defined by two equivalent models: one grammatical, formed by three complex 'sentences' delimited by periods, and further defined by an arithmetic progression in the number of their independent clauses and personal verbal forms (as distinct from forms in the infinitive or participle); one metric (the rhyme systems unify the tercets into a sestet while separating it from the quatrains). These two models are further bound together by the relationship between rhyme and categories: every feminine rhyme coincides with a plural ending, every masculine one with a singular.

2. a *bipartite division* that opposes the octet and the sestet. In the *octet* the cats are seen from an outside observer's point of view and are imprisoned within time and space ([2]*saison* and [3]*maison*, which rhyme and meaning make equivalent). In the *sestet* both viewpoint and space-time limits drop away: the desert bursts the house wide open; the eternity of [11]*dans un rêve sans fin* annuls [2]*dans leur mûre saison*: in this case the equivalence is an antinomy and is formally established by the parallelism of the *dans* constructions, the only two in the poem. This overall opposition combines with two secondary ones: *quatrain I tercet I* ([3]*maison:* [10]*solitudes:* [2]*saison:* [11]*sans fin*) and *quatrain II tercet II* (cats in darkness vs. cats radiating light).

To take only one of these secondary oppositions: in *quatrain II tercet II*, on the one hand, [12]*Leurs reins féconds sont pleins* is synonymous with [5]*Amis . . . de la volupté* (16), and one of the subjects in the quatrain and three subjects in the tercet all alike designate inanimate things; on the other hand, the antinomy of darkness and light is backed up by corresponding sets of equatable items: [7]*Erèbe* and [6]*ténèbres* echo each other in meaning and in sound, as do [12]*étin*CELLES, [13]*par*CELLES *d'or* and [14]*prun*ELLES.

3. a chiasma-like division linking *quatrain I* and *tercet II*, where the cats function as objects ([3]*chats,* [12,14]*Leurs*) and, on the other hand, *quatrain II* and *tercet I*, where they are subjects. The *quatrain I–tercet II* coupling, to which I shall limit this summary, contains the following formal equivalences: both stanzas have more adjectives than the internal strophes; the first and last verbs are both modified by rhyming adverbs ([2]*Aiment également;* [14]*Etoilent vaguement*); these are the only two stanzas made up of sentences with two subjects for one verb and one object, each subject and object being modified by one adjective, etc. A semantic relationship underlies these formal features: in *quatrain I* a metonymic relationship between the animals and their worshippers (i.e. cats and people live in the same house) generates a metaphoric similarity ([4]*comme eux* twice repeated); the same thing in *tercet II*, where a synecdochic (*pars pro toto*) description of the cats, using different parts of their body, permits their metaphoric identification with the cosmos, or so say the two analysts.

These three systems fit one inside the other and together make of the sonnet a 'closed' structure, but they coexist with a *fourth system* that makes the poem an open-ended structure which develops dynamically from the first line to the last: two equal *sestets* (1. 1–6 and 9–14), separated by a *distich*. Of the four structures, this last is the one most at variance with the stanza and rhyme architecture that defines the sonnet as a genre: the aberrant distich presents features that do not occur anywhere else, against a background of features that occur only elsewhere in the poem, some of them related to those of the distich by antonymy (every single subject–verb group is plural except for [7]*L'Erèbe les eût pris*; against the rule followed throughout the rest of the poem, [7]*funèbres –* [8]*fierté* alliterate, etc.). Now Jakobson and Lévi-Strauss regard this distich as a transition: the pseudo-sestet describes objectively a factual situation of the real world; two opposite human categories, sensual and intellectual, are reconciled through their identification with the animal endowed with the diametric traits of both types of men; these traits in turn explain the cats' love for silence and darkness – a predilection that exposes them to temptation. Erebus threatens to confine them to their animal nature by taming them; we are relieved to see him fail. This episode, translated in terms of parallelism, should be seen not just as another antonymy but as 'l'unique équivalence rejetée' (14).

Nevertheless, this rejection has its positive effect: an equivalence with the sphinx can substitute for it. The sphinx, with a human head on an animal body, transposes into myth the identification between real cats and people. Also, the monsters' motionless daydreaming and the cats' sedentariness (likewise characteristic of the human types they symbolize) are synonymous; and the way the cats ape the sphinxes is a new equivalence stated simultaneously at the grammatical level, in the narrative (it is [9]*en songeant* that they look like the [10]*sphinx allongés*), at the morphological level (*allongés* and *songeant* are the only participles in the text) and at the sound level the two verbs are related by paronomasia. The second *sestet* is devoted to the deepening mystery of this *miracle des chats* (15). *Tercet I* still sustains the ambiguity: it is difficult to decide whether cats and sphinxes are linked merely to magnify the image of the cats stylistically, or whether we have here the description of actual similarity, the racial bond between the household sphinx and the desert cat. In *tercet II*, however, substitution of parts of his body for the whole cat dissolves the beast into particles of matter, and the final identification associates these particles with desert sands and transmutes them into stars: the fusion of cats and cosmos has been accomplished. This apotheosis to infinity does not exclude a circular structure from the text. The authors believe there is a parallelism between *tercet II* and line 1, the myth being seen as a variant on a universal scale of the 'constricting' union, inward-turning, when the lover folds his love into his arms, and of the expansive union, outward-turning, when the scholar takes the universe in his embrace; similarly, cats either interiorize the universe, or else they spread themselves out beyond the bounds of time and space (20).

From all the foregoing, we can at least draw the conclusion that these mutually combinatory and complementary structures interplay in a way unique. The poem is like a microcosm, with its own system of references and analogies. We have an absolutely convincing demonstration of the extraordinary concatenation of correspondences that holds together the parts of speech.

THE IRRELEVANCE OF GRAMMAR

But there is no telling which of these systems of correspondences contribute to the poetry of the text. And there is much to be said about the systems that do not.

The divisions proposed explain a good deal of the tension between symmetrical and asymmetrical rhymes and the grammar arrangements upon which the composition of the sonnet rests. The first division is beyond criticism; the second is well substantiated, since it hinges on an articulation (the octet–sestet boundary) which corresponds to a change so sharp that it prompted postulation of the fourth division. Divisions three and four, especially the last, make use of constituents that cannot possibly be perceived by the reader; these constituents must therefore remain alien to the poetic structure, which is supposed to emphasize the form of the message, to make it more 'visible', more compelling.

Equivalences established on the basis of purely syntactic similarities would seem particularly dubious – for instance, the parallelism pointed to between the relative clauses of lines 4 and 11: this last allegedly draws the 'contour of an imaginary quatrain, a make-believe homologue of the first quatrain' (13). At most, this might be conceivable if the clauses appeared against an empty or uniform context; not in an actual sonnet, whose continual variation of verbal shapes makes a marked contrast necessary in order to impose perception. Even there, the parallelism from one line to another can be superseded by a stronger relation within one of the two lines involved. This happens in the case of the equation urged by Jakobson and Lévi-Strauss between [4]*Qui comme eux sont frileux* and [12]*Leurs reins féconds sont pleins*, on account of their syntactic parallelism and their internal rhymes. In context the difference outweighs the similarities: an internal rhyme like [5]*Science*–[6]*silence* is obvious, and so is *eux–frileux*, because identical stresses 'confirm' them; but a natural reading of line 12 will have to take into account the tight unity of *Leurs reins féconds*, which demands a pause after *féconds*, the normal caesura disappearing almost because *pleins* cannot be severed from *d'étincelles; pleins* is enclitic, which practically cancels out the rhyme. Suppose we read without regard for meaning or grammar: the rhyme resuscitates, but any responsion to the rhyme in line 4 still appears purely theoretical, for *comme eux sont frileux* is homologous only to *comme eux sédentaires* and is not free to connect elsewhere. For the significant rhyme system, the one that organizes the rhythm and 'illustrates' the meaning, is the homophony under equal stress of *comme eux* repeated twice. The *frileux* rhyme is a secondary modulation: it 'makes believe' that the line ends at the caesura,[2] thus getting the rhythm off to a fresh start and making the 'unexpected' repetition all the more striking; the fact that it rhymes with *comme eux* lays emphasis upon *sédentaires* by contrast – a second *comme eux* led the reader's subconscious sense of balance to expect a second rhyme, and the expectation is beautifully frustrated. We did find a parallelism anyway, but the remoter one has lost the contest, and this suffices to make homologue-collecting an unreliable tool. Extensive similarities at one level are no proof of correspondence: a parallelism is seen between *quatrain I* and *tercet II*, based upon the equivalence of two subjects ([1]*Les amoureux fervents, les savants austères/*[3]*des parcelles d'or, un sable fin*), one verb with rhyming adverb ([2]*Aiment également/*[14]*Etoilent vaguement*), one adjective-noun object ([3]*Les chats puissants et doux/*[14]*leurs prunelles mystiques*) in identical sequence (9). But, in any verse structure, I do not see how two variants can be equivalent if the positions of their components are not homologous: meter lends significance to the space occupied by the sentence. The relation of object to verb in line 14 is not the same as in *quatrain I*, since the quatrain keeps them apart with parentheses and enjambement, whereas the *tercet* unites them. Hence inevitably a difference in emphasis and a shift in respective positions within the line. Furthermore, the equation of the subjects is all askew: the components are alike, and we could link *amoureux fervents* vertically with *parcelles d'or* or diagonally with *sable fin*; but the systems they enter are not comparable, for *sable fin* does not stand in the same relation to *parcelles d'or* as *savants* does to *amoureux*. These last two are opposite equals, and their contiguity expresses their polarity; but the contiguity of *parcelles* and *sable* simply repeats twice the same meaning, *ainsi que* indicating a metaphorical relation. *Ainsi que* and *et* may have the same virtual function in language and be classifed alike: but not here, where they are neither synonymous nor antonymous. The parallelism suggested by grammar remains virtual because it has no homologue in the meter or in the semantic system.

No segmentation can be pertinent that yields, indifferently, units that *are* part of the poetic structure, and neutral ones that are not. The weak point of the method is indeed the categories used. There is a revealing instance where Jakobson and Lévi-Strauss take literally the technical meaning of *feminine* as used in metrics and grammar and endow the formal feminine categories with esthetic and even ethical values. They are trying to prove a sexual ambiguity in the poem, the motif of the androgyne, and they find some evidence in the 'paradoxical choice of feminine substantives as masculine rhymes' (21). True, the gender of French nouns does orient the associations they trigger: this kind of effect is conceivable with words that signify concrete objects or even abstract concepts, as long as they can be humanized or personified – for example, [5]*volupté*, which is more female than *plaisir* would be. It hardly holds, however, in the case of purely technical terminology, where *masculine* means merely 'ending on a fully pronounced syllable' and *feminine* merely 'ending on an unstressed syllable' (especially where one need not even be aware of these conventions in order to perceive an alternance). By stretching this to the limit, we may discover cases where the feminine rhyme does evoke some such associations because it coincides with the specific feminine gender ending; it is altogether unlikely with masculine rhymes, which do not offer any similar concurrence. Only technicians would think of it (they have thought of it); metalinguistic rationalization of this sort betrays how easily the wariest of analysts slips into a belief in the intrinsic explanatory worth of purely descriptive terms.

The two critics obviously assume that the definition of categories used to collect data is also valid to explain their function in the poetic structure – that linguistic oppositions, for example, automatically entail stylistic differences. The role of liquid phonemes in the sonnet's sound texture, for example, is declared to be significant: *quatrain II* is certainly characterized by noticeable variations, since this is a stanza where the phonetic dominance shifts from nasal vowels (only 3) to liquid consonants (24); extreme variations cannot fail of their effect. There is, however, a linguistic opposition between /l/ and /r/, particularly marked in French, and this is frequently exploited in poetry in a manner consistent with the phonetic nature of the opposing features. A slight regression of /r/ before /l/ in the *tercets* is interpreted as 'eloquently accompanying the passage from the empirical feline to his mythic transfigurations' (12). But no one is likely to believe that there is any significance in a difference as imperceptible as that between fourteen /l/ and eleven /r/, especially when *tercet II*, with /l/ enjoying a majority of two, begins with an /r/ cluster (*Leurs reins*) which will surely catch the eye and ear sooner than an inequality attenuated by distribution along the lines. If we look only for sharp changes, then the drop in the number of liquids from *quatrain II* to *tercet I* affects both contenders equally, /l/ ending on top by one point; the one smashing victory of /l/ over /r/ – three to nothing – occurs in line 5 *before* the transfiguration; in quatrain II, which is also the only place where brutal variations can be found, the liquids go hand in hand for the whole stanza, rejoicing at the peak of their power. Since liquids as a group do appear significant, the authors assume that every essential linguistic feature of the group must also be significant. The fact is, however, that it does not work out that way: the liquids are significant only as a group; their oppositions, *within* the group, though they are actualized and play their part in the linguistic structure, are not actualized in the style.

Conversely, the analytical categories applied can pull together under one label phenomena which are in fact totally different from one another in the poetic structure. A case in point is the plural. Jakobson and Lévi-Strauss rightly note its high frequency and its concurrence with important elements. Because a single grammatical category is applicable to every line of the poem, they see it as a key to the understanding of the sonnet; they quote a pronouncement of the poet that seems to give symbolic meaning to the plural: *Multitude, solitude: termes égaux et convertibles par le poète actif et fécond.* Better still, the authors see this mutual 'convertibility' symbolized in [10]*solitudes*, where 'solitude' as the word itself and 'multitude' as the morpheme -*s* enjoy togetherness. This argument recalls their confusion of femaleness and feminine gender; they seem to assume that there is always a basic relationship between actual plurality (and what it symbolizes in Baudelaire's eyes) and plural morphemes. Needless to say, there are many exceptions to that general rule – and what is more, one of them occurs right here: [6]*ténèbres* is a conventional, meaningless plural; let us skip it, and also its rhyme companion [7]*funèbres*. We should probably discount all descriptive plurals, since they are dictated by nature and not the poet's choice: *mystiques* would drop out, cats having two *prunelles*, and also *reins*. We can keep *chats* and their human counterparts: collective singulars being available for groups, the plural may well have meaning. But *solitudes*, the pretext for this philosophical foray, will have to go: it is no paradox at all, just a hyperbole, a cliché where *solitudes* means 'desert' – an emphatic plural stemming from the Latin. Baudelaire's quotation may apply elsewhere, certainly not here, and no interpretation of the sonnet can be drawn from it. The authors' mistake is understandable. In their search for a plural structure, they needed a unifying factor. The text yielded no sign that the data could be related, yet their common label demanded that they be so related. Faced with this dilemma, the authors must have gladly seized upon the coincidence between *solitudes* and Baudelaire's aphorism: the poet's mental obsession provided just the invariant required. Had all plural forms not been brought under the one label, there would have been no compulsion to find, at all costs, an equivalence value for every plural form.

But among these data lumped together because of their morphological similarity, there is a group of plurals set apart from the others because of their distribution: that is the plural feminine rhymes. These do form a stylistic structure, because their -*s* endings make the rhyme 'richer' for the eye by increasing the number of its repeated components. In [1,4]*austères–sédentaires*, for instance, the *s* reinforces the visual similarity and offsets the spelling vagaries that spoil the transcription of /ε/. The way in which the -*s* is related to and functions in the rhyme system has nothing to do with its simultaneous function in the singular–plural opposition, where it carries a meaning: in the rhyme it works only as an eye-catcher. The interrelations of the -*s* rhymes within the conventional rhyme system are what gives them significance. Poetic convention demands, first, that the rhymes of the sonnet should form an invariable pattern alternating feminine and masculine rhymes; second, that this invariant alternation be combined with sound variants within each alternating series. The visual and aural implementation of the variant is constantly reinforced and constantly compels attention, thus strongly individualizing each stanza; this depends entirely upon the poet's creative fancy. The implementation of the invariant, on the contrary, is normally limited to the compulsory masculine–feminine alternation. By adding -*s* to the -*e*, Baudelaire personalizes, so to speak, what was an automatism, reemphasizes the opposition for the eye. A second constant element in the system of the sonnet as a whole gives more weight to the unifying factor in the rhymes, which more effectively countervails the centrifugal tendencies of each stanza to form an independent unit. Every line affected by this addition is thereby made to look longer, and the fact that such a line ends the sonnet contributes to its unity by emphasizing the final item and therefore the reader's consciousness of a terminal accord; since the word thus underlined happens to be *mystiques*, the combination of meaning and visual emphasis, accompanying it like an upbeat, make the end of the poem a point of departure for reverie and wonder. Jakobson and Lévi-Strauss point out that the feminine rhyme is orally actualized, despite the total disappearance of the unstressed end syllable in modern pronunciation, by the presence of a postvocalic sounded consonant in the rhyming syllable, and they remark, indeed, that this coincides with plural morphemes (7, 11); but they see the plural as a parallel to the postvocalic consonant, that is, reinforcing each rhyme pair, separately, since that consonant varies and therefore structures only the stanza in which it occurs (/r, br, d, k/). In fact, the invariable -*s* creates a frame that tightens the whole sonnet. This structure would not be overlooked if the term chosen did not also cover forms that are grammatically identical but stylistically foreign to these -*s* rhymes; [1]*amoureux*, [4]*doux*, [10]*sphinx* would not further obscure the operation of the -*s* ending; grammatical equivalence would not be equated with stylistic equivalence.

What I have just said should not be construed as a rejection of the principle of equivalence: similarity in dissimilarity, dissimilarity in similarity, are apparent at all levels. But it seems evident that its pertinence cannot be shown by using grammatical terminology, or any preconceived, aprioristic frame. R. Jakobson chose grammar units to make this exegesis and many others because grammar is the natural geometry of language which superimposes abstract, relational systems upon the concrete, lexical material: hence grammar furnishes the analyst with ready-made structural units. All parts of speech, in fact, may function in parallelism and contrasts; the importance of pronouns, long neglected by style analysts – pronouns, are, precisely, typical relational units – comes out clearly in the first division of the poem. Jakobson seems to think that any reiteration and contrast of a grammatical concept makes it a poetic device, that the interrelationship of meter, morphological classes and syntactic construction actualizes the structure and creates the poetic effect (Jakobson, 1961, 398ff., esp. 403 and 408–9). There is no doubt that a linguistic actualization does take place, but the question remains: are the linguistic and poetic actualizations coextensive?

The sonnet is rebuilt by the two critics into a 'superpoem', inaccessible to the normal reader, and yet the structures described do not explain what establishes contact between poetry and reader. No grammatical analysis of a poem can give us more than the grammar of the poem.

THE POEM AS RESPONSE

The literary scholar, especially of the humanist stripe, has always assumed that grammar failed because it was incomplete, that the narrow, rigorous methods of the *esprit de géométrie* could never catch the subtle, indefinable *je ne sais quoi* that poetry is supposed to be made of. In fact the opposite is true: the linguist sees all the data, and that is precisely the reason he was prone, especially in pre-structuralist times, to define a poetic utterance as abnormal, as language plus something else. The whole idea of structure, of course, is that within the body of the text all parts are bound together and that stylistically neutral components and active ones are interrelated in the same way as the marked and unmarked poles of any opposition. Our only solution is to observe and rearrange the data from a different angle. A proper consideration of the nature of the poetic phenomenon will give us the vantage point required.

First of all, the poetic phenomenon, being linguistic, is not simply the message, the poem, but the whole act of communication. This is a very special act, however, for the speaker – the poet – is not present; any attempt to bring him back only produces interference, because what we know of him we know from history, it is knowledge external to the message, or else we have found it out by rationalizing and distorting the message. The message and the addressee – the reader – are indeed the only factors involved in this communication whose presence is necessary. As for the other factors – language (code), non-verbal context, means of keeping open the channel – the appropriate language of reference is selected from the message, the context is reconstituted from the message, contact is assured by the control the message has over the reader's attention, and depends upon the degree of that control. These special duties, and the esthetic emphasis characteristic of poetry demand that the message possess features corresponding to those functions. The characteristic common to such devices must be that they are designed to draw responses from the reader – despite any wanderings of his attention, despite the evolution of the code, despite the changes in esthetic fashion.

The pertinent segmentation of the poem must therefore be based on these responses: they pinpoint in the verbal sequence the location of the devices that trigger them. Since literary criticism aims at informing and improving such responses, we seem to have a vicious circle. It is only apparent, however, for what is blurred in a response is its content, the subjective interpretation of that response, which depends on elements exterior to the act of communication. The response itself testifies objectively to the actuality of a contact. Thus two precautions absolutely must be taken: (1) empty the response of its content; I can then use all forms of reaction to the text – idiosyncrasy-oriented responses (positive or negative according to the reader's culture, era, esthetics, personality) and goal-oriented responses (those of the reader with nonliterary intent, who may be using the poem as a historical document, for purposes of linguistic analysis, etc.: such a reader will rationalize his responses to fit into his sphere of interest and its technical terminology); (2) multiply the response, to guard against physical interference with contact, such as the reader's fatigue or the evolving of the language since the time the poem was encoded.

This tool of analysis, this 'superreader', in no way distorts the special act of communication under study: It simply explores that act more thoroughly by performing it over and over again. It has the enormous advantage of following exactly the normal reading process, of perceiving the poem as its linguistic shape dictates, along the sentence, starting at the beginning (whereas many critics use the end to comment on the start, and so destroy suspense; or else they use diagrams that modify the balance of the text's natural emphasis system – the chiasma-like division in the Jakobson and Lévi-Strauss analysis, or what they call diagonal or vertical correspondences); it has the advantage of screening pertinent structures and only pertinent structures. My superreader for 'Les Chats' is composed of: to a limited extent, Baudelaire (correction of line 8, placing the sonnet in the ensemble of the collection); Gautier (his long paraphrasis of the sonnet, in his preface to the third edition of the *Fleurs*), and Laforgue (some echoes in *Sanglot de la Terre*, 'La Première Nuit'); the translations of W. Fowlie, F. L. Freedman and F. Duke; as many critics as I could find, the more useful being those whose reason for picking out a line had nothing to do with the sonnet; Jakobson and Lévi-Strauss for those points in the text where they deviate from their method (when they are being faithful, their analysis scans everything with even hand and is therefore misleading); Larousse's *Dictionnaire du XIXème Siècle* for the entries which quote the sonnet; philological or textbook footnotes; informants such as students of mine and other souls whom fate has thrown my way.

Each point of the text that holds up the superreader is tentatively considered a component of the poetic structure. Experience indicates that such units are always pointed out by a number of informants who usually give divergent rationalizations. These units consist of lexical elements of the sentence interrelated by their contrasting characteristics. They also appear to be linked to one another by relations of opposition. The contrasts they create is what forces them upon the reader's attention; these contrasts result from their unpredictability within the context. This unpredictability is made possible by the fact that at every point in a sentence, the grammatical restrictions limiting the choice of the next word permit a certain degree of predictability. Predictability increases as the number of levels involved and the number of restrictions increase, which happens with any kind of recurrence, like parallelism in general and meter in particular – and where predictability increases, so does the effect of an unpredicted element ...

[In the lengthy and detailed analysis that follows, Riffaterre uses the first person plural ('we' 'us'), the third person singular ('the reader'), and impersonal constructions ('it is now clear that') to refer to the reactions of a reader – presumably the superreader – moving through the poem line by line. To give a sense of the method and of the flavor of the analysis, I quote here a typical paragraph. – *ed.*]

At this point, however, the importance of *frileux* and *sédentaires* gives by flashback a new orientation to our sense of the quatrain. The repeated identification *comme eux ... comme eux* clinches the demonstration of identity between cats and their human counterparts. In this culminating phrase we might have expected adjectives in keeping with those that preceded, all laudatory; we might even have expected a climaxing allusion to certain glorious qualities common to both parties. Instead we get the mediocrity of *frileux* and *sédentaires* – a comic letdown; all the more galling because these are every bit as true as the preceding adjectives, though they ruin the image that has been built up. *Frileux* is fussy and oldmaidish; Baudelaire used it effectively in a parodic self-portrait, the satirical 'Spleen I': *d'un fantôme frileux*. *Séden-taire* conjures up the image of the constipated stay-at-home, epitome of the unwholesome bourgeois. The reader takes in this surprise but has in mind the whole quatrain, so that *orgueil de la maison* still sounds complimentary, with perhaps a touch of parody in the *maison*, which narrowly limits the sphere of the fame, the scope of the glory: even thus does La Fontaine's fox cut his blandishments to the measure of the crow when he crowns him *phénix de ces bois* – but keeps the eyrie of the immortal bird in the neighborhood. Similarly, *mûre saison*, a conventional poetic substitute for *l'âge mûr*, may now be felt as a bit too elegiac, whereas without the twist in line 4 it would simply be the expected ornamental phrase needed to beautify everyday reality. Scholars, in the context and on the level of *amoureux*, are in danger of losing their dignity: their austere mien no longer impresses us, now that we see them as chilly homebodies. *Amoureux* is not, like *amants*, confined to serious or tragic contexts: the shock wave from line 4 destroys the synonymity with *amants* and actualizes the depreciatory or condescending connotations: nineteenth-century dictionaries rank *amoureux* below *amants*; *amoureux*, not *amants*, is the core of many mocking phrases like *amoureux transi*; and Baudelaire uses it elsewhere only to deride lovers (in the burlesque 'La Lune offensée' their silly irresponsibility *sur leurs grabats prospères*; in 'Hymne à la Beauté' where the irony is all his, as a comparison with the source makes clear their ungainly bed gymnastics: *L'amoureux pantelant incliné sur sa belle*; whereas his *amants* are never equivocal, always poetic) ...

NOTES

1.   Cats
    Fervent lovers and austere sages
    Love equally, in their season of ripeness,
    Cats, powerful and soft, pride of the household,
    Who, like them are easily chilled and like them sedentary.

    Friends of knowledge and of sensual pleasure,
    They seek out silence and the awfulness of shadows;
    Erebus would have taken them as funereal coursers,
    If they could bend their pride to servitude.

    They assume, in their musings, the noble attitudes
    Of great sphinxes stretched in the depth of solitudes,
    Who seem to fall asleep in an endless dream;

    Their fecund flanks are full of magic sparks,
    And golden particles, like fine sand,
    Bespangle dimly their mystical pupils
                        Trans. Jane Tompkins and Catherine Macksey
2. This structural role of the break is well documented: Malherbe condemned internal rhymes precisely because they had such effects.

4.2

THE POETIC TEXT WITHIN THE CHANGE OF HORIZONS OF READING: THE EXAMPLE OF BAUDELAIRE'S 'SPLEEN II'

Hans-Robert Jauss

. . .

II. THE PROGRESSIVE HORIZON OF AESTHETIC PERCEPTION
(A HERMENEUTIC RECONSTRUCTION OF THE FIRST READING)

Spleen

J'ai plus de souvenirs que si j'avais mille ans.

Un gros meuble à tiroirs encombré de bilans,
De vers, de billets doux, de procès, de romances,
Avec de lourds cheveux roulés dans des quittances,
Cache moins de secrets que mon triste cerveau.
6 C'est une pyramide, un immense caveau,
Qui contient plus de morts que la fosse commune.
– Je suis un cimetière abhorré de la lune,
Où, comme des remords, se traînent de longs vers
Qui s'acharnent toujours sur mes morts les plus chers.
Je suis un vieux boudoir plein de roses fanées,
12 Où gît tout un fouillis de modes surannées,
Où les pastels plaintifs et les pâles Boucher,
Seuls, respirent l'odeur d'un flacon débouché.

Rien n'égale en longueur les boiteuses journées,
Quand sous les lourds flocons des neigeuses années
L'ennui, fruit de la morne incuriosité,

Extract from Hans-Robert Jauss, *Toward an Aesthetic of Reception* (University of Minnesota Press, 1982), pp. 139–218.

18 Prend les proportions de l'immortalité.
  – Désormais tu n'es plus, ô matière vivante!
  Qu'un granit entouré d'une vague épouvante,
  Assoupi dans le fond d'un Sahara brumeux!
  Un vieux sphinx ignoré du monde insoucieux
  Oublié sur la carte, et dont l'humeur farouche
24 Ne chante qu'aux rayons du soleil qui se couche.

'Spleen': A poem that announces itself with this title poses several initial questions for the contemporary reader. What does *spleen* mean, and what can the word mean precisely as the title to a poem? Does it hint at a condition like depression, or only at the eccentric mood of one person? Will someone speak of himself here, of the world, including our world, or only of his own? (... the indented passages represent the commentary of my 'historical reader of the present.')

> For the reader of our present time, the title 'Spleen' discloses the horizon of an open, largely still-indeterminate expectation and, with this, initiates the suspense of a word's meaning that can only be clarified through the reading of the poem. For in today's German usage (and in French as well), 'spleen' has sunk to the trivial significance of a 'tick', a 'fixed idea'; it scarcely still allows one to suspect what sort of aura of singularity could be fitting for a person who presented his 'spleen' as an attitude of wanting to be different in the face of his world. Felt as an anachronism, and allowing one to forget its original significance, the word may still recall connotations of depression (as Stefan George translated it) or of an eccentric mood for the educated reader – connotations of a consciously adopted attitude, to distinguish it from the natural characteristics of a person. The average reader can scarcely understand more by the 'spleen' of a fellow person than a behavioral tick that remains fundamentally harmless, that does not hurt anyone else, and that can express itself in a fixed idea that, for the person concerned, obviously determines his relationship to the world as a whole in a monomaniacal way. This everyday significance returns the placement of the word in the title to the condition of the mysterious – thanks to the expectation, established by all lyric poetry, that in the medium of poetry the everyday and the occasional can take on a new and deeper significance, or recover an older, forgotten meaning.

'J'ai plus de souvenirs que si j'avais mille ans' (I. 1): The voice of an unknown 'I' speaks into the space of the expectation awakened by the title word of 'Spleen'. It names itself already with the first word, and with the first line it strikes a tone that surprises the reader through the overpowering claim 'to possess more memories than a life of a thousand years could comprehend.' The word-sequence as well as the rhythm of this first line, separated off like a preamble, heightens the general impression that the realm evoked by the memories stretches into the immeasurable. The comparative phrase, 'More memories than', is redeemed in the second half of the line through the unexpectedly high number, 'thousand'; and yet precisely this weighty magnitude (with the connotation of 'millenium') is, in its naming, already surpassed, the number extending into the limitless through the preceding 'plus de'. Read as a line of verse, the following accents may be noted:[1] *J'ai plus de šouvenīrs que ši j'avais mille ans*: also noted is a rhythm that in the first half-line works harmonically with the regular ('pseudoiambic') sequence of weakly and strongly accented syllables, but that in the second half-line works in a troublesome way with the main accents suspended and bumping up next to one another through the four unaccented syllables.

> The accents on the 'strong words' *souvenirs, mille* and *ans* could be supplemented through secondary verse accents: in the first half-line, on *plus* in the second syllable (to bridge the large distance to the sixth syllable with the main accent), and possibly also on the fourth syllable, But in the second half-line the first four syllables can, on grammatical grounds, scarcely support an accent, so that special weight falls on the last two words suspended through the four unaccented syllables.

With *mille*, the reader can scarcely miss hearing the echo of the main-accented *ī* of *souvenīrs*, which it's placement before the middle caesura accents even more, so that the repeating vowel renders even more conspicuous the delimitation of the memories to the number thousand and 'more than a thousand', as well as the reversal of the harmony of the first half-line in the disproportion of the second.

> Symmetry and asymmetry are peculiarly enfolded in the first line. With the middle caesura, which seeks to guarantee metrically the equivalence of the two half-lines, Baudelaire compositionally opened the symmetrical construction of the classical alexandrine onto the asymmetry of the immeasurable: a phonetic preponderance of the *ī*-sound in the second half-line, which reinforces the meaning (*souvenīrs*, highlighted through the final position of the syllable before the caesura, as opposed to a twofold repetition of the *ī* in *ši* and *mille*), corresponds to the semantic surpassing of *mille ans* through the *plus de* in the first half-line, so that the hyperbolic number 'thousand' – phonetically announced as the peak of the *i*-series – becomes the counterpoint to *souvenirs*. But as one retrospectively recognizes, *spleen* (through the long *ī*) also already belongs to this signifying series of sounds, so that between the title word and the first line equivalence of significance is suggested that recalls the reader's suspended questions at the outset, and allows one to concretize them anew.

If the first line already states something about the *spleen* of the 'I' who speaks, is it a condition of the greatest happiness or the deepest suffering? Is it self-presumption or doubt that speaks out of it? Does a boldness encroach here, or an agony predominate?

Lines 2–5: The reading of the lines following the first comes to a halt after line five.

> The halt is syntactically marked by the end of the sentence; in the ongoing continuation of the reading as well, the ends of sentences will provide the most obvious subdivisions within the two unequal strophes of the poem.

The beginning of line two, 'Un gros meuble à tiroirs,' is transitionless, and through a motivation that is at first unrecognizable, it arouses the tension of wondering whether and how the description of a dressing or writing table – extending ever further through three lines – might then hang together with the initial leading theme of the memories of the speaking 'I' that is struck up in line one. This tension only resolves itself – and explosively, as it were – at the end of line five with the long-delayed figure of a scarcely awaited comparison: 'Cache moins de secrets que mon triste cerveau.'

> The tension produced by the structure of this verse construction allows one to grasp once again the expectation of lyric consistency that is essential for aesthetic perception. Here everything works together in the grammatical and phonetic organization to allow the shocking resolution of the thematic expectation posed with 'un gros meuble' to appear as a decisive contrast: the surpassing constructed once again in a comparative 'moins de secrets que' (after the 'plus de' of l.1), and the fall from the stylistic heights and thing-filled plenitude of the bureau into the prosaic character of the technical medical term *cerveau* that is also already announced phonetically and then, as it were, exploded through a doubled series of *s*-alliterations and consonantal *r*-connections (*secrets ... triste ... cerveau*). One can also speak of an explosive effect of the rhyme-word on the semantic level, where the reversal appears in the middle of the tight combination of adjective and substantive (one would expect 'soul' or 'heart' after the poetic epithet 'sad', and hardly 'brain'!) and is heightened even more through the rhyme. If one follows the chain of rhymes, then through the equivalences of *a* with the transition from the simple to the complex rhymes (from *a* in ll. 3–4), the effect is produced of a steady growth heightened through the homonymy (from *ans–bilans* to *romances–quittances*), which the *o*-rhyme of line five then suddenly disrupts.

With the comparison between writing desk and brain, the reader is offered a solution to the question regarding the connection between the opening line and the next group of verses: isn't the old desk covered with a jumble of mementos also a place of memories, the sum-total of time used up, perhaps even a possession of that 'I' who at the beginning gazed back on an immeasurable plenitude of memories? Is the chaotic state of the desk, with its unfathomed secrets, a sign for how the 'I' possessed of 'spleen' comes upon its plenitude of memories within its remembrance? Does 'Spleen' as the title word mean precisely this view of the mute relics of a past ossified into chaos? Yet opposed to this solution is the fact that, in its comparison, the lyric 'I' also once again already distinguishes itself from the compared term: the 'remembrance' of the bureau conceals fewer secrets than its 'sad brain', so that the disorder of the things in lines 2–4 is a different state of affairs. In lingering with one's first reading, the reader can already gain the impression that prosaic and poetic things contrast charmingly in the mess on the chest of drawers, and that the catalog peaks with the grotesque image of 'locks of hair wrapped in receipts' – in brief, that it is a matter of a 'beautiful disorder'. Toward what might it be leading?

> While the thematic trajectory as a whole allows the recounting of the leftovers of the past to develop symmetrically, the smaller imagistic units constitute symmetrical contrasts, also supported by the metrical system. In all the verses the regular middle caesura creates symmetrical half-lines that give a harmonious sense of division to the recounting of the contents of the chest of drawers. On closer inspection, the recounting itself allows one to recognize a semantic ordering principle: prosaic and poetic objects follow one another with beautiful regularity. In line two the series is begun with 'accounts', upon which 'poems and love letters' follow in line three. The counterweight to these is created after the middle caesura by 'legal briefs', with which 'songs' contrast once again in the same half-line. In the next line, this method of producing a beautiful disorder is driven into a kind of bottleneck: the succession of heterogeneous things turns into their admixture, when 'locks of hair' appear that are rolled up in 'receipts'. Thus the poetic catalog of a past stored up in disorder culminates in the profanation of the beautiful, in a final grotesque image of sentimental love.

'C'est une pyramide, un immense caveau' (ll. 6/7): as if the 'I' that speaks would not itself provide an answer to the implicit question of what its remembrance might then be, if it is to be still more and different than the desk in the comparison, the next pair of lines begins with a provocative utterance on the part of the self that is surprising in its immediacy and that strikes up anew the measured tone of the first line. Once again a movement toward the overly large comes into play that is not satisfied with the image of the pyramid, but that surpasses even the representation of the immense grave through the comparative construction of a further comparison: 'qui contient plus de morts que la fosse commune.' But the sequence of images that carries this movement toward excess also suggests a second line of significance that is striking in its contrast: the far-reaching movement of memory can evidently grasp only what is dead. It culminates in the past-become-stone of the pyramid, and in the heap of bones of the mass grave. Does the decay of memory into a remembrance that contains only what is dead accordingly allow us to understand what 'spleen' can mean for the lyric 'I'?

> The provocative element in the renewed utterance on the part of the self lies not only in the reprise of the apodictic tone of line one, but also in the

concealed synchronization of the newly appearing pair of lines with line five. Here the analysis can make note of the equivalences of the 'strong words' as well as a syntactic countersymmetry between line five and lines six and seven. The strong accent before the ever-preserved middle caesura and at the line-ends establishes a positional ordering of significance of *secrets, pyramide* and *morts* on the one hand, and of *cerveau, caveau* and *fosse commune* on the other. Between the small secrets of the bureau and the large ones of the pyramid, as between the small container of the brain and the large one of the grave, a disproportion arises that sets the development toward the immeasurable into play for a third time (after the memories of line one and the relics of lines two to four). Only with *morts* does the third member of the two lines of significance bring the *tertium comparationis* to light, and then bring about (as previously with *cerveau* of line five in contrast to lines two to four) the fall from the stylistic heights: with *fosse commune* as the final member of the comparison for the abstruse remembrance, the crassest representation of a worthless gravesite destroys the aura that surrounded a pyramid as the most sublime sort of grave. The syntactic parallelism of the opposing comparative formulations *moins de* (l. 5) and *plus de* (l. 7) can serve various functions. It arranges *secrets* and *morts* with one another, so that one can ask oneself whether those secrets of the remembrance were to mean its dead. It heightens once again the movement toward excess through the figures of surpassing. And finally, it serves here as well to distinguish once again the 'I' in its comparisons from the compared elements. To the extent that this view already holds for the comparative formulation *plus de* in the first line, as well as for all of the previous three utterances on the part of the self, the effect of a discontinuous movement arises.

The lyrical 'I' undertakes again and again the attempt to identify itself, in that it poses one comparison after another and then takes them back. Will this movement come to an end, and will the 'I' perhaps arrive at itself?

'Je suis un cimetière abhorré de la lune' (ll. 8–11): a dash is scarcely needed here as a typographical signal that would make the new beginning of the following group of lines unmistakable. For here, where the new line once again – as previously only at the poem's beginning – begins with 'I' as the first word, the self-proclamation takes on the strangest form: 'I am a cemetery abhorred by the moon.' If a certain distance of observation had still been maintained in the series of comparisons of the self with the bureau, pyramid, and mass grave, then the movement now turns into a self-identification that demands of the reader that he step across a threshold into the unreal and the uncanny. The uncanny is rendered most strongly perceptible through the onomatopoetic *abhorré*, which introduces a series of graveyard thoughts that is once again more familiar. The reader, who [the scholarly analyst would point out] is led by the parallel line-openings, and looks back from the graveyard lines to the opening line, can ask himself whether the connection now brought to light might mean that the immeasurable collection of memories of which the 'I' boasted in the first line has now passed into the uncanniness of the Golgotha that the same 'I', after line eight, is or believes it is. Would this mean that the question of what 'Spleen' means for the 'I' that speaks is already answered?

The syntactic parallelism in the strong opening positions of 'J'ai' (l. 1) and 'Je suis' (l. 8) – which highlight the first and fourth sentences in front of the intervening ones through the 'I' as a repeating subject – can hardly be missed. For the syntactic correspondence is furthermore also supported through phonetic equivalences: 'Je suīs un cīmetīère' (l. 8) repeats the signifying *i*-series of line one three times over. Lines nine and ten, with the imagery of the graveyard lyric that has become clichéd for us, would indeed fall into the category of the trivial, were it not that the *or*-syllable of the onomatopoetically uncanny *abhōr̄r̄é* is maintained in *remōr̄ds* (l. 9) and *mōr̄ts* (l. 10), and that the double-meaning of *vers* (worms or verses) gives a grotesque *pointe* to the familiar topos of *vanitas*.

'Je suis un vieux boudoir' (ll. 11–14): The expectation that the attempts of the lyric 'I' to describe his state of mind had come to rest with the 'graveyard of memories' – his expectation is not fulfilled. The unrest that, even in that imagery, had not been thoroughly pacified ('de long vers qui s'acharnent toujours,' ll. 9/10) takes the upper hand once again. As if this 'I', driven by an inexplicable motivation – is it doubt, anxiety or a certain unnamed suffering? – must always seek its identity in a different realm of used-up time, it now reaches out toward a space that conjures up a new parade of memories. It is an old boudoir, with a decor within it that allows one to recall the old bureau; [the scholarly analyst adds that] even the distant but still audible internal rhyme *meuble à tiroir/vieux boudoir* encourages this retrospective comparison. Once again the things take on the shape of a beautiful disorder. But this time they offer not the view of an accidental heap of incompatible elements, but rather conjoin into the harmonious ensemble of an elegant lady's room.

The first impression of a finely tuned harmony, all the more strongly noticeable after the dissonant graveyard verses, arises above all from the effect of two rich rhyme-pairs that contrapuntally maintain the main accent of the vowel *e* in the end-rhyme for eight lines, in a willed monotony that allows for a delicate play with the minimal deviation within the alternation between feminine (*fanēēs/surannēēs*) and masculine (*Bouchēr/débouché*) rhymes. Baudelaire's concept of poetic language – which must correspond to 'the immortal needs for monotony, symmetry and surprise' in man[2] – could scarcely be better illustrated.

On closer examination, the harmony of this beautiful disorder is nonetheless already bathed in the light of decay: the things of the decor are all accompanied by an adjective expressing decline ('roses fanées', 'modes surannées', 'pastels plaintifs', 'pâles Boucher', 'flacon débouché'), and in their solitariness ('seuls, respirent l'odeur d'un flacon débouché') they allow one to feel an emptiness, not to say the disappearance of an occupant (one of the 'dearest dead' of l.10?). Does this mean that the renewed effort by the lyric 'I' to find salvation in a past has once again become lost in an empty world of things decayed within themselves?

> The alliteration of three p's in line thirteen, which then falls to a b, ironizes, as it were, a decrescendo ('Où les pāstels p̄laintifs et les p̄ales B̄oucher') that turns the word play going on between the rhyme-word *Boucher* and *débouché* into the grotesque: the still harmonious representation of the last perfume escaping from the uncorked bottle overturns into the dissonant connotation of a 'decapitated' rococo painter Boucher.

'Rien n'égale en longueur les boiteuses journées' (ll. 15–18): The transition-less beginning of the next group of verses, four lines long, is not only typographically marked through a second large strophic unit, but is also marked through the fact that the 'I' has unexpectedly disappeared (the two preceding sentences began with 'Je suis'). The voice that now begins to speak appears unimplicated in the experience it first portrayed in high lyrical tones, and then, as it were, allowed to appear on stage in personified form and thereafter commented on in a tone of definitional formality. Along with the disappearance of the 'I', the theme of memory also appears to have been exhausted: the *ennui* steps forth not from out of the past, but rather as the shape of an endless present, from out of the 'halting days' and the 'snowed-in years'. Already with the first reading, the staging of its appearance must strike one: in their extraordinary onomatopoetic beauty, the preceding two lines seemed to open onto the view of a winter landscape and did not yet allow one to anticipate that which only the delayed naming of the ennui allows one to perceive – the all-permeating power of that 'gloomy indifference' that before our eyes grows to an infinite size (as also manifest in the monstrous rhyme-pair (*incuriosité/immortalité*). With this movement, whether the answer to the significance of 'Spleen' is to be sought in the appearance of ennui is not the only question that poses itself. There is also the further question of what it might indeed mean that this foreign power evidently raises its head and rules the stage of the world that is, from now on, the present, precisely, at the moment when the 'I' has stepped off that stage and has ceased to speak as a subject.

> With the beginning of this group of verses, the surprising change of subject, level of tone, and temporal dimension is nonetheless provided with a transition and a contrast in that lines fifteen through eighteen immediately continue the rhyme-scheme of the preceding lines eleven through fourteen. Thus the two four-line strophes, equivalently rhymed, constitute a symmetrical whole precisely at the break between the two large strophic units (ll. 2–14, ll. 15–24), a whole that immediately resynchronizes the strophic division, and suggests that one ought to

discover lines of significance in the phonetic equivalences that had remained concealed at first glance. The symmetry of the feminine rhymes establishes a relation between *roses fanées* and *boiteuses journées*, then between *modes surannées* and *neigeuses années*. In the first case, the movement falls from the beauty of the withered roses into the negative temporal experience of the 'halting days'; in the second case the passing character of yesterday's fashions is elevated up to the beautiful monotony of the 'years that are like heavy snowflakes'. The symmetry of the masculine rhymes allows one to expect and to recognize that the second group of four lines, as already with the first (with *Boucher/débouché*), also carries along with it an ironic significance in the background. It manifests itself in the change of tone, when first the two lines of beautiful monotony, so perfect in their onomatopoeia (as well as in the internal rhyme of the preciously placed adjectives *boiteuses/neigeuses*), delay the entrance onto the stage on the part of ennui (through enjambment and syntactic inversion), and then two contrary lines follow that gloss this appearance as if 'painting with concepts'. The appearance is elevated to personification, defined in terms of its origin (*fruit de*) in an allegorizing manner, and described in its effects, all with a display of learned words that fall out of the lyric rhythm through polysyllabic character alone. Along with this, the representation of the endlessly growing *ennui* takes on sensorial and audible form in the return of the ever more significant *i*-series and in the threefold *p*-alliteration ('p̄rend les p̄rop̄ortīons de l'īmmortalité,' l. 18).

The ironization culminates in that most striking rhyme-pair *incuriosité/immortalité*, and leaves behind it the question of whether in the end, if the *incuriosité* has achieved the proportions of *immortalité*, the immortality must not also fall to the 'gloomy indifference.'

'– Désormais tu n'es plus, ô matière vivante!' (ll. 19–24): Here the new beginning of a final group of six lines is so transitionless that it scarcely needs the dash as a typographical signal. *Désormais* turns the preceding scene around into the future, and seems to give the following lines the character of prophetic discourse. Who can speak in such a manner, and with what authority? Who is the 'you' on whom this anonymous judge turns? Is it a matter of a self-address in the pathetic 'you'-form, or does this 'you' mean another person? What does 'matière vivante' mean? Is it man as a living being, opposed to matter; is it a figure in the still unrecognized metamorphoses of the lyric subject; or is it the part of his corporeal appearance that stands opposed to the 'I' in its spiritual existence? But now further surprising metamorphoses seem to fall immediately upon the 'you' itself that is so mysteriously evoked: from out of 'living matter', a granite block appears (the hardest stone, hard like the *k*-sound with which line twenty begins in its enjambment: 'qu'un granit'); from out of the granite block, the old sphinx appears – but now, opposed to the expectation that it would be a silence-made-stone, it begins to sing, although invited by no one since no one knows of it any longer, thereby burdening the reader with the enigma of what it might indeed be singing of with its gesture of wild but sullen fury ('dont l'humeur farouche ne chante'). Along with this final, highly unexpected reshuffling of the role of the lyric subject, the external scene has also changed: in the place of the decor laden with the past, and the external world that was wintered and darkened yet nonetheless still homey, the fear-producing ('entouré d'une vague épouvante') no man's land ('oublié sur la carte') of a desert has appeared, in which only the sun – already setting and evidently indifferent (doesn't 'qui se couche' respond ironically to 'humeur farouche?') – remains to hear the sphinx's song.

The three rhyme-pairs give variation to the semantic contrast of *matière vivante* in such a way that the contradiction between matter and life is continually reformulated up to the end. After *vivante*, there follows – emphasized through the hiatus of the half-accented *e* from *vague* to the main-accented *é* – the pejorative word *épouvante* for the petrifying terror; in response to *brumeux* (dark), which with its connotation of 'misty' still allows one to think of the life-giving element of water, there is the negative composite-word *insoucieux*. The power of negation is phonetically sharpened in line twenty-two through contrastive equivalences: the alliteration of *i* and *in* ('Un vīeux sphīnx īgnoré du monde insoucieux') and the double recurrence of *s* (*s̄phinx . . . in̄s̄oucieux*) have the effect that the rhyme-word – to the extent that it reuses nearly all the phonetic elements of *vieux sphinx* (even the *ö*-sound of the epithet returns in the last syllable) – not only semantically negates the existence of the old sphinx (the sign of negation *in* takes up the sound of *sphinx* and is further strengthened through the morphological equivalence with the prefix of *īgnoré*); it also, as it were, literally refutes it sound by sound. On the syntactic level, the participial constructions of lines twenty through twenty-three, arranged as parallels, rather describe the progressive process of a materialization of the *matière vivante*: the series of past perfect participles *entouré–assoupi–ignoré–publié* increasingly removes the lyric subject from the life-sphere of the shared world. All the more astounding, then, the effect in line twenty-four of the turn around from the ossified condition of the past perfect into the present tense of *chante*. Delayed in the enjambment after *humeur farouche*, the active verb allows one to recognize that the gesture of revolt that was no longer expected actually already began with the adversative *et*. The preceding rhyme-word *far-ouche* has an especially important poetic function in this turnaround. As the third and last representative of life among the rhyme-words (after *vivante* and *brumeux*), it on the one hand deviates with its main-accented vowel from the preceding series of *u*-sounds that, in the words *entōūré-assōūpi-insōūcieux* and finally (the oppositive at the beginning of the same line) *ōūblié*, supports the process of the threatening materialization.

But on the other hand, the final ironic *pointe* is constructed with the highest art: that the sun indifferently 'goes to sleep' on the side of the material world emptied of man, whereas the sphinx gives voice to its final song of revolt on the side of life. '*Qui se couche*' is expressed syntactically (as an uncommon attributive phrase) and rhythmically (as an assymmetrical violation of the middle caesura that is otherwise maintained) in such a way that the semantic *coincidentia oppositorum* in the rhyme-pair *farouche/qui se couche* can be said to explode.

III. The Retrospective Horizon of Interpretive Understanding (The Movement of an Interpretation in the Second Reading)

'I have found the definition of beauty – of my beauty. It is something ardent and sad, something a bit vague, leaving free play to conjecture' (Baudelaire, 1951, 1187). Baudelaire's definition of beauty via an indeterminacy that leaves free play to 'conjecture', while at the same time also already being delimited by the *coincidentia oppositorum* of *ardent* and *triste*, may here serve to begin the second movement of the interpretation. The first movement was to follow the reader's aesthetic perception step by step, until with the last line of the poem, its form – if not necessarily also its meaning – fulfilled itself as a whole for him. To find the still unfulfilled meaning demands, ... the return from the end to the beginning – so that, from the perspective of the achieved whole of the form, the still indeterminate particulars might be illuminated, the series of conjectures clarified in their contexts, and the meaning still left open sought within the harmony of a coherence of meaning. The conjectures of, and questions left open by, the first reading of the 'Spleen' poem allow themselves to be brought formally and thematically into a certain common denominator. The perceiving understanding fell, from verse-group to verse-group, upon gaps in the lyric consistency, upon new beginnings or transitions *ex abrupto*, so that at first an overarching motivation remained imperceptible. Thus one should ask whether a latent principle of unity, recognizable only within the horizon of the second reading, lies in that manifestly fragmentary character of the lyric movement that makes itself felt as much in the irregular units of verse as in the unexpected representatives who stand for the lyric subject. And if the expectation of lyric consistency is fulfilled with the second reading, is the question then also resolved regarding the meaning of the title, the still unknown significance that spleen is supposed to have for the lyric 'I'?

If one looks at the whole of the lyric form, then Baudelaire's poem is unique in that on the one hand the strict norms of the alexandrine are preserved and played upon with virtuosity, and on the other hand the symmetrical law of construction of this classical genre of poetry par excellence is continually violated by an asymmetrical unfolding and retraction of the lyric movement. If one recalls Baudelaire's definition of poetry – that it 'responds with rhythm and rhyme to the immortal needs of man for monotony, symmetry and surprise' (1951, 1363) – then the surprising feature of this 'Spleen' poem lies in the power of the asymmetrical tendency that in the strophic-syntactic units of verse as well as in the boldness of the comparisons and self-identifications increasingly works against the harmonizing system of verse, rhyme and syntactic parallelism, only to be brought to a standstill at the end, as if by command, in the final strophe that shoots across the rest ('– Désormais tu n'es plus, ô matière vivante!'). This manifests itself most strikingly in the irregularly developing length of the seven sentence units.

The lyrical movement passes from the smallest verse-unit (one line, l. 1) to the largest (six lines, ll. 19–24), and within this tensional arc it heightens itself syntactically through a twofold start, as it were. That is, a sentence of four lines (ll. 2–5) follows upon the smallest sentence-unit of line one, whereupon the movement begins anew, this time with a sentence two lines long (ll. 6/7), and then develops asymmetrically according to a formula of acceleration: first three lines (ll. 8–10), then four (ll. 11–14), then four again (ll. 15–18), and finally six (ll. 19–24). The asymmetrical acceleration is itself unconstant: after the steady movement from two to three to four lines (ll. 6–14), the four-line sentence-unit reduplicates itself, so that amidst the impetuously developing asymmetry, a symmetrical structure of twice four lines unexpectedly emerges, which is also bound together most harmoniously through the sameness of the rhymes. The reader can nevertheless afterwards reperceive this configuration in the rhythm of the whole movement, as a reversal of the acceleration into a monotony that seems to grow into the immeasurable. This effect is similarly produced through the rhyme sequence of the fourth and fifth sentence-units, where first the rhyme-pair *vers/chers* follows upon *lune*, then the doubled rhyme on *élée*, which extends itself monotonously upon the twice four rhyme-words. When the asymmetrically developed total movement is then brought to a standstill at the end by the final sentence-unit, once again harmoniously organized in three rhyme-pairs, the whole of the lyric structure confirms what was also to be discovered in its parts from the beginning onward. The first five lines, through the chain of rhymes from *ans–bilans* to *romances–quittances*, already led to the effect of a developing movement that was then suddenly cut through by the explosively prosaic rhyme-word *cerveau*. The formal principle that, as the composite figure of an assymetrical development and a sudden cutting off, organizes the discontinuous total rhythm of the poem – this principle obviously corresponds to a thematic discovery on the part of the first reading: that the lyric 'I' in the course of his self-comparisons continually distinguishes himself from the compared element, and undertakes new attempts at identification. Let us now see whether in the recognized organization, the significance of spleen might also be discovered, which significance seemed to conceal itself from us in the metamorphoses of the lyric 'I' and of the world of things that it evoked.

Through its being set off like a preamble, the first verse awakens the expectation that memory could constitute the principle that establishes the unity of all the evocations, and further, that it could prove to be the origin of the spleen, of that enigmatic state of mind of the 'I' who is speaking. At first the type and manner of the evocations does in fact seem to correspond to this expectation. For remembering here leads neither to the happiness of time refound nor to the melancholy suffering of the 'no longer'. Remembering evidently begins here with a gesture of self-transcendence, which then un-questioningly turns into doubt as the various and always fruitless attempts of the lyric 'I' to refind himself in a past then only present him with the view of a world of things that is emptied of meaning. Within this process, the lyric 'I' as well can no longer remain self-integral in the mode of a self-certain subject. This is indicated above all by the progressive reshuffling of the grammatical person of the subject and its predicates: the *j'ai*, the 'I' that *has* its memory, is followed by the distancing *il* for the first object with which it compares itself; then by a *c'est* that cancels the distance as it compares the subject with the pyramid and grave; and thereafter by a distanceless *je suis* that allows the *comparandum* and *comparatum* to become indistinguishable within an 'I' that is first the cemetery, then the boudoir. With the *il* of the personification, which then comes on the stage as ennui in the enjambment of the *quand*-sentence, the former lyric subject is effectively erased and at the same time the process of memory is broken off. And when the vanished 'I' is finally apostrophized once again in the grammatical person of the *tu*, the lost identity is also apparent in the fact that the 'I' that no longer has or is anything has one last and enduring identification imposed upon it by the anonymous and unrecognizable authority of this apostrophe – the identification with an *il*, the sphinx as third person. Accordingly we can no longer consider memory as the principle that establishes unity; it already succumbs to an obscure power that alienates all the forms of the recalled past times, the same power against which the lyric subject as well evidently cannot maintain the integrity of its consciousness of itself as an 'I' – so that both memory and autonomous subject are at once destroyed. The inexplicable motivation that compels this 'I' to seek its identity in the space of a memory that has become immeasurable, the motivation that immediately allows all of the past life that the subject would grasp, either to disintegrate chaotically or to ossify morbidly – what lies nearer at hand than to recognize this motivation in the power that Baudelaire, with allegorical exaggeration, expressly allows to take the place of the muzzled 'I,' and even names: 'L'ennui, fruit de la morne incuriosité?' If ennui is in fact supposed to be able to uncover the sought-after meaning of spleen, then first of all the 'definition' given it as 'fruit of gloomy indifference' must be taken seriously, must be tested as the key to an interpretation that at this point is not yet to have recourse to whatever the history of the words *spleen* and *ennui* in Baudelaire's usage can tell us.

If one looks back from lines fifteen through eighteen to line one, one can become aware that the ennui enters into the same movement of a development into the immeasurable as memory did at the beginning. With the formulation 'enters into', I intend to call into question the understanding that the ennui also *causes* the movement. For it is precisely this that the syntactic structure of these lines leaves entirely uncertain: the endless present of the 'halting days' that can be compared with nothing, and the ennui that has developed out of the 'snowed-in years' into the immeasurable, are temporally equated by way of the *quand*-phrase. The ennui that allows the beauty of a winter landscape, at first recalled *ex negativo*, to turn into gloomy indifference – is it itself perhaps supposed to be only one among the other views of progressive reification in which the lyric 'I' experiences the loss of its world? In the first go-through, we already noticed that the ennui came forth not from the past, but rather as a figure of monotony from the present, and that it allowed this present to appear to last eternally. The aspect of 'morne incuriosité' thus is also lacking to the evocations of the past that the first line produces. Quite the contrary: what begins with 'J'ai plus de souvenirs que si j'avais mille ans' therefore precisely produces the further attempts at the search for identity, for this 'I' is overpowered by memories that could not become a matter of indifference to it – since it is in terror of not being able to forget but at the same time not being able to rediscover itself in that which is remembered. What in the first reading we could have taken for a gesture of self-presumption, now announces much more a terror in the face of the limitless that opens up with the first comparative ('plus de souvenirs') and returns with the second one ('moins de secrets'). The terror renews itself when the 'I' haphazardly recalls remembered or represented places in a hasty movement, as if it had to seek a halt to a growing emptiness, and yet in everything where it lingers – desk, pyramid, grave, cemetery or boudoir – can always grasp hold only of things from a dead time: emblems of a ceaseless reification that allows the past life to which they refer to become unknowable, and that in the end falls upon the autonomous subject itself.

In this interpretation, the formal discovery coincides with the thematic one: the compositional figure of the asymmetrical development of the rhythmic movement then suddenly being cut off again coincides with the fragmented continuity of an experience of self become ceaseless, in which the lyric 'I' tries again and again in vain to rebuild the collapsed world within the imaginary. With this, the question of what spleen can mean as an experience of the lyric 'I' finds an answer that can be quite simply stated. From now on spleen can take on the meaning of an unexpressed anxiety – the world-anxiety[3] that, as a principle establishing unity, is able to explain the latent origin as well as the manifest consequences of the spleen; the collapse of all ego-centered orientation, according to which space and time open up onto the unencompassable, as well as the vanishing path of the 'I' seeking a halt, who objectifies himself in the relics of his vainly projected world. This hypothesis should first be strengthened by way of an external mode of argumentation, and then tested when we follow the interpretation through to the end.

> In morality as in physics, I have always had the sensation of the abyss [*gouffre*], not only the abyss of sleep, but the abyss of action, dream, memory, desire, sorrow, remorse, beauty, number, etc. I have cultivated my hysteria with pleasure and terror. (Baudelaire, 1951, 1225)

Contained in this famous note in *Mon coeur mis à nu* is the first premonition of the mental illness to which Baudelaire was to succumb four years later. The quoted text has been drawn upon above all for the interpretation of the 'Gouffre' poem, and a noteworthy 'poetics of the fall' has been derived from it that makes the double meaning of *la chute* – theological as well as psycho-analytic – useful for the understanding of Baudelaire's poetry (Milner, 1974, 86–107). But the note can also be read as a commentary that is surprisingly closer textually to our 'Spleen' poem. Then it describes world-anxiety as a break in experience that tends to enter amidst the accomplishments and states of mind of the familiar world, in memory as well as in remorse or desire, in everyday activity as well as in the experience of beauty. One recognizes here without difficulty the stations along the vanishing path of the 'I' in the 'Spleen' poem ('le gouffre du souvenir, de l'action, du beau' in the turn to the past, the present, and the future; *regret* and *remords* are not represented, while *nombre* is to be related to memory, *désir* perhaps to beauty); except that in the poem the abyss of anxiety is objectified not as the undercurrent from a depth, but rather as terror in the face of the limitless, against which the enthralled 'I' can at first still oppose representations of enclosure (the desk, pyramid, grave, cemetery, boudoir) . . .

In its literary representation, anxiety is always anxiety that has already been mastered in the achievement of form through aesthetic sublimation. Just as Baudelaire's poem knows how to bring into language the most extreme alienation of the consciousness that has been overpowered by anxiety, it in fact brings about its own catharsis. As ineluctably as the process of self-alienation progresses into a loss of the world, traces of rebellion are none-theless indicated in the counterimages that are evoked. The recalled spaces of memory are not immediately handed over to chaos and ossification, but rather first take on a form of 'beautiful disorder' before they succumb to the emptiness of meaning. Even in the terrible, the 'I' filled with anxiety discovers unanticipated spectacles of beauty along its escape path. The first reading came upon a poetry of details in the imagery of the bureau's contents, the boudoir, and the wintery ennui, a poetry that can inject itself, as it were, into the catalog of the dead things (most beautifully in 'avec de lourds cheveux roulés dans des quittances'). And even in the fear-inducing no man's land of the 'Sahara brumeux', the highly poetic repertoire of slumbering granite, forgotten sphinx, unheard song and setting sun is offered up in opposition to the space of anxiety presented by the petrification. Finally, in response to 'farouche' as the epithet of savage doubt, 'qui se couche' appears in the final couplet as an ironic gesture, reconciled in rhyme, of decline within beauty. The sphinx, in the evocation of which the 'rêverie pétrifiante' is completed, is the ultimate form of the reification of the lyric 'I', the place-holder of the fallen subject, and the origin of the song, the sublation of terror into poetry – all combined into one.

With what right can one in this manner interpret the sphinx as the last in the series of 'metamorphoses' of the lyric 'I'? Talk of 'metamorphoses' presupposes the representation of organic transformation of a preserved, substantial identity of the subject, and it is therefore not appropriate to the experience of the lyric 'I' in this 'Spleen' poem, an 'I' that precisely loses its substantial identity as a subject step by step. Its path of experience is therefore also not defined through a continuous transformation of forms of the alien world and of one's own person that, even in its fall, would leave the suffering self with the final refuge of an opposing or otherwise excluded standpoint. The path of experience under the spell of spleen is much more conditioned through a discontinuous reversal of the 'I' into a non-'I', of the most proper into the most alien; the boundary between inside and outside collapses, and what was internally sublated can now return from outside as a foreign power in which the 'I' can no longer recognize the alienation of itself.

Baudelaire found in allegory the poetic instrument that first and foremost allows this process of a destruction of the self to be made representable. This 'Spleen' poem brings to view in an exemplary manner the new revival of the allegorical method that had been declared dead. At the beginning, in lines two through five, the classical form of the developed comparison is first still employed, but with the peculiarity that the comparatum ('mon cerveau'), delayed across the three lines, only retrospectively allows the greatly drawn-out comparandum ('un gros meuble') to become recognizable as such. Thus the effect arises that the real external scene of the decor – 'un gros meuble à tiroir,' etc. – unnoticeably reverses into the internal scene: 'cache moins de secrets que mon triste cerveau.' In the next step the classical boundary between comparandum and comparatum is annulled through the fact that the lyric 'I' unnoticeably combines itself with the compared element in the act of comparison: 'Je suis un cimetière ... Je suis un boudoir.' Here one can speak absolutely of allegorical identification (for which no precedent is known to me from the earlier Romance tradition), for with the cancellation of the comparison, the 'I' posits itself as the same as what it is not. The failure of this desperate and powerful attempt at identification immediately introduces a second attempt that demonstrates once again that the 'I' in spleen can no longer master the alien world on its own. For the subsequent step, Baudelaire introduced the personifying allegory. If it traditionally allowed a state of mind such as ennui to come onto the stage in allegorical dignity – as well as to gloss its origin in a pseudo-learned way, and to elevate its effect into the realm of the cosmic – here it attains a new function, namely, to make visible the overpowering of the self through the alien, or (as one may now also put it) the ego through the id. The wintery world that has imperceptibly become the stage on which ennui alone still rules has at the same time excluded the 'I' from the stage, even though the foreign power is nothing other than 'gloomy indifference', than an alienation of itself.

The 'I' excluded from the stage of the world appears distanced in a threefold manner in line nineteen: it has become a 'you' that must cede the central place of the subject to another 'I'; it is exiled out of the present into an unchangeable future beside the world, and it has evidently forfeited its corporeal as well as its spiritual form, since now it is addressed only as 'matière vivante'. Whatever is still living in it will succumb to a materialization that, at the stage of disappearance represented by the granite block, turns, as it were, the 'hard core' of the innermost self toward the outside and threatens the lyric 'I' with total ossification. The apodictic tone of a judgment being handed down and the ironically celebratory address of line nineteen – 'Désormais tu n'es plus, ô matière vivante!' – suggest this interpretation. Does this mean that in the end, the world-anxiety inverts into an anxiety about being judged? In favor of this idea is the possibility of interpreting archetypally the authority of a super-ego that imposes this judgment and remains anonymous: according to Gaston Bachelard, the dream of being petrified can signify terror of God's worth (Bachelard, cit. Garland, 1969, 335). There is even an archetypal meaning for the sphinx: it can stand for the figure of the fallen sovereign, into which the disempowered autonomous subject can be transposed (Durand, cit. Garland, 1969, 335).

Yet the poem precisely does not end in such archetypal symbolism. In its final image, two secular myths – sphinx and pillars of memory – are brought together and employed against the tradition in a new way to prepare for the lyric movement's final reversal. The sphinx normally conceals a truth, especially for him who might solve its riddle, but here it has become a 'remembrance for no one', an allegory of the forgotten. But as the sphinx itself now breaks its petrified silence and begins to sing, the mythological reminder of the statue of memory immediately indicates one final thing, and a first thing for a second time: the last hour of singing, since it sounds here not at dawn but at the setting of the sun; and the rising of beauty into song, which overcomes anxiety and atones for the loss of the 'I'. Thus, at the end the poem leads the reader back to its beginning: through the final form of its subject, which now becomes retrospectively recognizable in the first form (for who may say with greater right than the sphinx, 'j'ai plus de souvenirs que si j'avais mille ans'?), and through the compositional figure of a 'poetry of poetry' that describes its own coming into being (for what is the sphinx to sing about, if not of that which the poem already encompasses?).

NOTES

1. In the following, alliteration or phonetic recurrence is indicated through a raised hyphen.
2. According to the famous definition given in the *Projets de Préface* of 1859/60 (1951, 1363).
3. With 'world-anxiety' [*Weltangst*], I refer to W. Schultz ... (1977, 14ff.) By it I understand that manifestation of anxiety that distinguishes itself from object-related fear, which probably began with the Christian religion, and which perhaps is to be related to the expectation of the Last Judgment, in that it is the singularization of real anxieties into an indeterminate world-anxiety.

4.3

THE IMAGINARY

Wolfgang Iser

...

THE IMAGINATION AS FACULTY (COLERIDGE)

The last significant attempt to grasp the imagination as a faculty was made by Coleridge, though he changed the inherited notion to such an extent that the time-honored faculty concept ceased to be the overarching view of the imagination. Although the much quoted tripartition into 'fancy', 'secondary imagination' and 'primary imagination' was not Coleridge's own, he emphasized that it was his 'object to investigate the seminal principle, and then from the kind to deduce the degree' (Coleridge, 1953, 64). 'Repeated meditations led me first to suspect, (and a more intimate analysis of the human faculties, their appropriate marks, functions, and effects matured my conjecture into full conviction,) that fancy and imagination were two distinct and widely different faculties, instead of being, according to the general belief, either two names with one meaning, or, at furthest, the lower and higher degree of one and the same power' (60f.).

This statement is important insofar as Coleridge did not attempt to develop the principle of differentiation but instead ended the first volume of *Biographia Literaria* with a letter from a friend who, for all his good will toward Coleridge, clearly felt that the explanation of the differences given to him stood the world on its head: *'your opinions and method of argument were not only so new to me, but so directly the reverse of all I had ever been accustomed*

Extract from Wolfgang Iser, *The Fictive and the Imaginary: Charting Literary Anthropology* (Johns Hopkins University Press, 1993), pp. 171–204.

to consider as truth, that even if I had comprehended your premises sufficiently to have admitted them, and had seen the necessity of your conclusions, I should still have been in that state of mind, which ... you have so ingeniously evolved, as the antithesis to that in which a man is, when he makes a bull' (199). Unfortunately, we do not know what these arguments were, but the reaction to them shows that Coleridge's division of the imagination into multiple faculties was regarded as a radical break with tradition.

This is consistent with Coleridge's concept of faculties in general, as can be seen from a remark made in 1818: 'As every faculty, with every the minutest organ of our nature, owes its whole reality and comprehensibility to an existence incomprehensible and groundless, because the ground of all comprehension' (Coleridge, 1863, 242). The groundlessness of every faculty echoes Schelling's statement that 'the ground is, against that for which it is the ground, not existent' (Schelling, 1972, 440). For what is, cannot be of the same quality as the source from which it springs. But this does not mean that the inaccessible ground will be lost sight of or forgotten. For Coleridge it is not even mysterious – as it was still for Hume – for that would mean giving precedence to the intellect as the ultimate referential authority. Furthermore, one can leave a mysterious origin to itself so long as the workings of the faculty can be grasped through experience. But evidently this was not enough for Coleridge. The above-quoted passage continues: 'not without the union of all that is essential in all the functions of our spirit, not without an emotion tranquil from its very intensity, shall we worthily contemplate in the magnitude and integrity of the world that life-ebullient stream which breaks through every momentary embankment, again, indeed, and evermore to embank itself, but within no banks to stagnate or be imprisoned' (Coleridge, 1863, 242 f.).

The stream metaphor makes vivid the groundlessness of the faculties, although it has to be twisted if it is to show what Schelling called 'not existent'. For the stream, precisely because it can be understood only by way of its activity, constantly flows in a double movement: It floods its banks but always 'embanks' itself again. Here we have a play of differences that inscribes the groundlessness of the faculties into their operations. Indeed, the differences are the conditions that enable the faculties to manifest themselves as activities. But since activity only embodies the function of the faculties that the play of difference unfolds, the ground of the faculties clearly lies in neither. This groundlessness is what, in fact, brings the faculties to life. It is therefore little wonder that Coleridge's friend was shocked by the new description of the imagination: *'In short, what I had supposed substances were thinned away into shadows, while everywhere shadows were deepened into substances'* (Coleridge, 1958, 199); for now, as we may deduce, the split faculty is no longer to be viewed as an alliance of faculties as it was by Tetens. Instead, a differentiated spiritual 'basic power' (in Tetens's words) is replaced by difference, which as the indicator of groundlessness so alters the workings and the objectives of the imagination that the world seems to have turned topsy-turvy.

This is the backdrop against which one must see the distinctions that Coleridge does draw in the much-quoted passage dealing with the imagination:

> The IMAGINATION then, I consider either as primary, or secondary. The primary IMAGINATION I hold to be the living Power and prime Agent of all human Perception, and as a repetition in the finite mind of the eternal act of creation in the infinite I AM. The secondary Imagination I consider as an echo of the former, co-existing with the conscious will, yet still as identical with the primary in the *kind* of its agency, and differing only in *degree*, and in the *mode* of its operation. It dissolves, diffuses, dissipates, in order to recreate; or where this process is rendered impossible, yet still at all events it struggles to idealize and to unify. It is essentially *vital*, even as all objects (*as* objects) are essentially fixed and dead.
>
> FANCY, on the contrary, has no other counters to play with, but fixities and definites. The Fancy is indeed no other than a mode of Memory emancipated from the order of time and space; while it is blended with, and modified by that empirical phenomenon of the will, which we express by the word CHOICE. But equally with the ordinary memory the Fancy must receive all its materials ready made from the law of association. (Coleridge, 1958, 202)

This graduated definition of the faculties shows their groundlessness as well as their unfolding by way of different functions. If a faculty originated from a knowable ground, then it would, first and foremost, represent that ground and could not, therefore, ramify into a plurality of activities. But a graduated definition can be made only via contexts whose basic limitlessness allows the multiple faculties to manifest themselves in a limitless number of nuances.

We may assume, then, that this new, graduated definition of the faculties – arising from their groundlessness – was what gave Coleridge's friend such a headache. For initially Coleridge's specific comments on 'primary imagination', 'secondary imagination' and 'fancy' feed off traditions reaching back as far as the Aristotelian concept of *memoria*; indeed, he may well have used them in order to stress the consequences of this graduated definition of the imaginative faculties. If these have no fathomable ground, then their groundlessness cannot be equated with a hidden intentionality. Activities are powered not by the faculties themselves but by the subject in his different attempts to relate to himself and to the world in an equal manner. Within the finite mind the infinity of self-constitution is to be repeated; the conscious will guides the operations of undoing the world of objects in order to enable the subject to re-create it anew in such a way that he will become present to himself; and finally empirical choices – made by fancy – facilitate the combining of data to meet the needs of the situation.

This graduated definition of the imaginative faculties is geared to a theory of the subject that leans heavily on philosophical idealism ... Coleridge avoids a central dilemma of traditional faculty psychology that, in the final analysis, conceived of the imagination as a self-activating potential and hence endowed it with an intentionality it cannot have, because intentionality pertains to consciousness and not to imagination. It is therefore only logical that Coleridge's graduated definition corresponds to an equal differentiation of activating agents, which in their turn represent basic conditions for the constitution of the subject, a process for which the imaginative faculties appear to be indispensable. This close interplay suggests that Coleridge adhered to the concept of the faculties because they embodied man's natural equipment.

The graduated definition fans the imaginary out into a plurality of faculties that require an equally differentiated context in order to render their workings tangible. The 'primary imagination' serves to bring out the contextuality needed to repeat the creative act in the finite mind. If the faculty bore its own ground within itself, then it would not be capable of such an application but would define the subject according to the terms of that ground. Similarly, if the faculty were self-activating, it would no longer lend itself to be channeled into the subject's self-constitution, and would thus remain unavailable to the subject's intentions. But what does it mean to conceive of the subject as the creator of itself by repeating the 'eternal act of creation'? Coleridge says in his essay 'On Poesy or Art':

> Believe me, you must master the essence, the *natura naturans*, which presupposes a bond between nature in the higher sense and the soul of man. The wisdom in nature is distinguished from that in man by the co-instantaneity of the plan and the execution; the thought and the product are one, or are given at once; but there is no reflex act, and hence there is no moral responsibility. In man there is reflexion, freedom, and choice; he is, therefore, the head of the visible creation. In the objects of nature are presented, as in a mirror, all the possible elements, steps, and processes of intellect antecedent to consciousness, and therefore to the full development of the intelligential act; and man's mind is the very focus of all the rays of intellect which are scattered throughout the images of nature. Now so to place these images, totalized, and fitted to the limits of the human mind, as to elicit from, and to superinduce upon, the forms themselves the moral reflexions to which they approximate, to make the external internal, the internal external, to make nature thought, and thought nature, – this is the mystery of genius in the Fine Arts. (Coleridge, 1958, 257f.)

The repetition of the 'eternal act of creation' in the human mind is the main task of the 'primary imagination', in the execution of which it gains its vivid expression. What is repeated changes in the repetition because the purpose for which it is repeated is not an inherent part of it. Consequently, between mind and nature there lies difference that inscribes itself into the repetition. Since plan and execution are simultaneous in nature, nature cannot be conscious of itself, whereas if the human mind tries to repeat the *natura naturans*, there arises difference, which triggers reflecting acts and arouses the mind to consciousness of itself. This indicates the ordinary idealistic interplay between mind and nature. Being initially nature's otherness, the mind eventually detects its own possibilities in the mirror of nature that turns out to be the mind's unconscious. *Natura naturans* therefore entails making nature into mind, and mind into nature – a never-ending process that takes place in the finite mind as the 'eternal I AM' . . . For Coleridge, . . . the imagination is of prime importance because the mind cannot become conscious of itself of its own accord. Consciousness needs something else that in itself has to be groundless so that it will not define the mind according to its own terms.

The to-ing and fro-ing between mind and nature, with the mind being revealed as the interior of nature and nature being revealed as the unconscious mind, shows 'primary imagination' at work. It always solidifies into a product when the play movement issues into an image, for only through images can the mind ascertain that it is a repetition of the *natura naturans*. The image, however, is an offshoot of the oscillation between mind and nature, and consequently arrests the back-and-forth movement. Whenever this happens, the process of self-constitution comes to a standstill, as none of the images issuing from this play movement will ever represent the goal the mind tries to obtain: to be identical to the principle underlying the *natura naturans*.

For this purpose, 'secondary imagination' is required; it differs from the 'primary imagination' only in matters of degree but is nevertheless distinguishable insofar as its actions apply to the world of objects. It is an 'echo' because it decomposes the world of objects and then creates this world anew in such a manner that the hitherto inconceivable structure of consciousness becomes present to the mind. The oscillation through which the imagination unfolds itself takes place between the mind, as it tries to secure its self-constitution, and the data of empirical reality. But when the same oscillation once again comes to a standstill in images, 'secondary imagination' models them differently. On the higher plane, mind and nature were made to reflect each other, whereas here the necessary precondition for form is decomposition. The more specific the achievements demanded of the imagination, the more clearly it reveals itself to be a destructive force. Because of their awareness of its potential, the Romantics were able to channel the destructive aspect of the imagination.

Although imagination is not to be defined in its own terms, or in those of the subject or of the context within which it becomes operative, it must nevertheless be something that precedes both the activating stimulant, the functions exercised, and the impact made, because all of these depend on a presupposed entity that they qualify. How is this entity to be described, if it cannot be the sum of qualities or predicates?

The hallmark of all three faculties activated by the subject is the back-and-forth movement: there is oscillation between mind and nature (primary imagination), between decomposition and recomposition (secondary imagination), and between combination and separation (fancy). This is a basic movement of play that, however, is not to be equated with imagination proper, or with its qualifications and predications; nor does it originate from the activating agent or from the context; instead, it presents the three imaginative faculties in action. Elsewhere in his work, Coleridge comments directly on the particularity of activated imagination: 'As soon as it is fixed on one image, it becomes understanding; but while it is unfixed and wavering between them, attaching itself permanently to none, it is imagination ... The grandest efforts of poetry are where the imagination is called forth, not to produce a distinct form, but a strong working of the mind, still offering what is still repelled, and again creating what is again rejected' (Coleridge, 1967, 103).

'Wavering' is, however, a special kind of oscillation: Instead of being an unstable, and hence fluctuating, connection between poles, it destabilizes the poles themselves. Hence imagination in action does not congeal into any form; rather, its manifestation as back and forth exposes to change everything that is encompassed by the 'wavering'. This includes the world of objects as well as the self-constituting subject. 'Wavering' as the self-presentation of the imagination indicates the presence of the activated imagination as a movement of play. The characteristics of this movement are what Coleridge calls offering and repelling, creating and rejecting, which then allow an ever-increasing differentiation of the interplay between subject and faculties, faculties and context, and finally groundless faculties and attributed predications. The play is constantly threatened by the ambivalence that underlies all oscillation, for the never-ending process is in conflict with the need for a result. Consequently Coleridge goes on repelling what is offered and re-creating what is rejected, so that imagination attains its presence through play. He knows that the 'power of poetry is, by a single word perhaps, *to instil that energy into the mind, which compels the imagination to produce the picture.*' This sentence forms part of his criticism of certain contemporary poets whose work is highly pictorial, 'where all is so dutchified, if I may use the word, by the most minute touches, that the reader naturally asks why words, and not painting, are used?' (Coleridge, 1967, 134 f.). The picture is always a product of the imagination, and so cannot be imagination itself. What Coleridge termed 'wavering' is grasping the imagination at a moment when it turns into a product, or, better still, when it turns into a generative matrix.

To become manifest, imagination requires an external stimulant that, in turn, will be drawn into the play it has triggered. As the faculty is groundless, it cannot shape the subject, and as the subject has no immediate access to its ground, it needs the activation of its imaginative faculties in order to appear before itself. 'The other position,' says Coleridge, 'namely, I AM, cannot so properly be intitled a prejudice. It is groundless indeed; but then in the very idea it precludes all ground, and separated from the immediate consciousness loses its whole sense and import. It is groundless; but only because it is itself the ground of all other certainty' (Coleridge, 1958, 178). It is therefore only logical that the relation between the groundless faculty and the groundless subject, 'a subject which becomes a subject by the act of constructing itself objectively to itself' (Coleridge, 1958, 183), should occur as a movement of play that, as 'wavering', lacks structure.

Self-constitution implies that, at the beginning of this activity, the subject has neither knowledge nor consciousness of itself. I. A. Richards therefore rightly stresses that 'Coleridge's theory of knowing treats knowing as a kind of making, *i.e.* the bringing into being of what is known' (1960, 49). Clearly, then, there can be no precise preconception as to what the subject is aiming at in the course of its self-constitution. It follows that whatever the subject needs to constitute itself may also overwhelm it. Indeed, this might be an additional reason why one faculty splits itself into several, because the subject controls its self-constitution through different contexts within which it activates the faculties in order to make itself present to itself. These contexts in turn not only channel the faculties but also motivate them in their various ways. In *Table Talk*, Coleridge points out that one 'may conceive the difference in kind between the Fancy and the Imagination in this way, that if the check of the senses and the reason were withdrawn, the first would become delirium, and the last mania' (Coleridge, 1917, 309). In this respect one could regard the different contexts as ways through which the subject prevents self-constitution from going out of control.

When the imagination, activated by the subject, becomes operative in the world of objects whose decomposition is to provide the material for new creation, it does not have a free hand but will inevitably be patterned by the context concerned. But since the subject as the activating agent is itself groundless, it, too, will be affected by these patterns. Initially it seemed that the subject only needed to tap its faculty in order to make itself present to itself; in the course of such a process, however, the subject experiences continual modifications. If the imagination appeared at the beginning to be a potential that could be manipulated for whatever purpose, it turns out, when pricked into action, to be a force that may manipulate its manipulator.

This occurs because every form of intentionality, including that of the 'conscious will', is of limited range, and cannot fully control its aim. As a consequence, when the world of objects is dissipated by the imagination, this dissipation will in turn affect the subject that has created it. During activation, the subject embeds its intentionality in the imagination, which thus becomes active. As an 'actant', imagination enables the subject that would like to see itself as its own ground to unfold itself as the endless mirroring of itself. The process is made possible by the asymmetry of the oscillation, which opens up the groundlessness of subject and faculties into an infinite multiplicity of aspects. The movement has to be asymmetrical because the imagination is required to become active, and can succeed in constituting the self only by continually overshooting the stages of the subject during its journey toward itself.

... The imagination is not a self-activating potential, and when it is mobilized by an outside stimulant, it reveals itself as a differentiated play movement described by Coleridge as 'wavering'. Furthermore, imagination is characterized by a duality; since production is preceded by destruction, the idea of *creatio ex nihilo* is revealed to be pure mythology.

Coleridge still spoke of the imagination as a faculty. Even so, the question arises as to whether the description of it as 'groundless' denotes cognitive capitulation in the face of its inaccessibility, or whether it refers to whatever it is that precedes its effects and therefore cannot be identical to them. If it is the latter, then the reference is certainly not to a faculty in the traditional sense of a potential that can be tapped for whatever purposes; instead, the now manifest imagination is revealed as a movement of play that plays with and against the very agent that has mobilized it.

THE IMAGINARY AS ACT (SARTRE)

So long as the imaginary was linked to the subject, it could be regarded as a faculty that, like all the other faculties, appeared to represent the natural equipment of human beings. Even the prevalent concern for the self-constitution of the subject only modified the inherited concept. However, the loss of certainty as regards the ground of the faculties led Coleridge to view the imagination not only as divided but also as an 'actant'. If the imagination enables the subject to grasp itself as the consciousness of an unconscious nature, this interrelationship reveals cybernetic features, feeding back the subject's 'other' as part of the process of its self-grasping.

The nature of a 'faculty' is bound to change when the agent that activates it changes. Coupling the imagination with the self-constituting subject considerably altered the traditional concept of the faculties; but, finally, the classification of the imagination as a faculty became virtually obsolete when it ceased to be linked to the subject. This was the step taken by Sartre in his early book *L'Imaginaire*. He replaced the imagination as a faculty with a multiple manifestation of the imaginary. For Coleridge, the faculty of the imagination was unknowable. The same holds true for Sartre's imaginary, which can be grasped only in stages that lead from what appears to be the 'certain' through the 'probable' to what is considered to be a bare outline of 'imaginary life' – to use the terms of description that Sartre himself regarded as part of phenomenological psychology.

Phenomenologically, the imaginary must be viewed as an act of consciousness. Sartre therefore begins with a statement that his 'book aims to describe the great functions of consciousness to create a world of unrealities or "imagination", and its noetic correlative, the imaginary' (1972, vii). If the imaginary is closely allied to the activities of consciousness, then the categorization of the imagination as a faculty is invalidated. Instead of being an unplumbable attribute of human beings, the imaginary is a mental image that indicates 'only the relation of consciousness to the object; in other words, it means a certain manner in which the object makes its appearance to consciousness, or, if one prefers, a certain way in which consciousness presents an object to itself ... However, in order to avoid all ambiguity, we must repeat at this point that an image is nothing else than a relationship' (1972, 5). The stress laid on the imaginary as being a relation of consciousness to its objects reflects Sartre's phenomenological approach, according to which there is no knowledge of what consciousness is, apart from its relation to objects. The imaginary, then, is a particularly striking form of connection and manifests relations of consciousness to objects as mental images.

To understand the nature of these relations, we must bear in mind that for Sartre perception and ideation embody 'the two main irreducible attitudes of consciousness' (138), with the act of perception directing intentions toward a given object, and the act of imagining involving an object that is '*being grasped as nothing* and *being given-as-absent*' (209). While perception grasps a given object, the mental image links consciousness to an object that is not given and so has to be supplied. There are two basic forms of such objects; either they are absent or they are nonexistent (see 60).

If consciousness is able to posit objects through the act of imagining, it appears 'to itself as being creative, but without positing that what it has created is an object' (14). This qualification is important and needs to be kept in mind. Consciousness controls the object posited as a mental image, but it does not have the same control over its own activity in the course of this positing. It is creative insofar as through its act of ideation it produces something that does not exist or does exist elsewhere; in both cases the object is absent (see 60) and must be put together in such a way that it takes on almost perceivable qualities. These may range from the illusion of having a perception to having a hallucination, which vividly illustrates how consciousness may lose control of its 'creative character', and is thus swallowed up by its own mental images. These images always present their object as '*being given-as-absent*' (209); they can do so only by drawing on memory, knowledge, and given information in order to fashion it. By making the absent present, they bring into being an imaginary object that is '*being grasped as nothing*' (209). The 'nothing', of course, refers to the absence or nonexistence of the object, and this makes it quite different from the dissipation of the world of objects that enabled Coleridge's subject to make itself present to itself through a 'recreative process'.

For Sartre, the negating as a real presence of what can be 'seen' in a mental image makes way for the irreal presence of the absent. The presence of a mental image means that, as part of being caught up in it, we are lifted out of the condition that we were in before. The 'nothing' inherent in the imaginary object becomes 'creative' as it causes an almost total turnabout of our condition, and this turnabout may go so far as to make our present existence unreal.

There is another side to this 'nothing' that is fundamental to approaching the imaginary. The mental image as such is not yet the imaginary itself but a mode of consciousness, while consciousness, in turn, is the necessary backdrop against which the imaginary manifests itself.[1] Sartre also takes this 'nothing' – which is an integral part of the imaginary object – as a means by which consciousness protects itself from being absorbed by the images it has posited.

'Besides, it is because consciousness feels itself but slightly enchained that it posits its object as non-existent. It pretends to see a cat; but since it is aware in spite of all of the origin of the vision, it does not pretend that this correlative exists. Whence this paradox: I really do see something, but what I see *is nothing*. This is the reason why this chained consciousness takes the form of an image: because it does not reach its own end. In the dream the captivity is complete, so the cat is posited as an object' (1972, 55f.). Consciousness is exposed to the danger of being trapped by its projected images because it can exist only as consciousness of something (see 76f., 85). In the act of perception, consciousness can direct itself toward given objects, but in the act of imagining it posits its own object. This means 'that the theme is not added to the image but that it is its most intimate structure' (212). Thus consciousness slides into the mental image and becomes an ideating consciousness, which is clearly different from being a perceiving consciousness. It follows that there is no such thing as consciousness in itself, since consciousness can only be consciousness of what it has made conscious.

This whole process can be observed on various levels. Forming a mental image entails capturing the absent or nonexistent through an analogue that feeds on knowledge, memory, experience, information, desire, and so on. But although these sources play an important role, they have no control over the act of imagining, which springs from a thetic consciousness but simultaneously has repercussions on it. This interaction deforms all the material that goes to make up the mental image, because it has to be adapted to the image and therefore simplified both structurally and visually.

The formation of mental images is necessary not only in order to conjure up the absent or nonexistent but also – and indispensably – for acts of comprehension. Sartre contends that all comprehension is accompanied by symbolic schemata that represent those thoughts that are necessary for the mastery of what is to be undersood. These schemata increase in proportion to the difficulty that comprehension encounters, and the knowledge stored in memory has to be actualized accordingly. 'Knowledge is in some manner a recollection of ideas. It is empty, it implies past and future understanding but is itself not understanding' (118). The symbolic schemata, however, are present only as 'provisional, insufficient, a step to be surpassed' (131), and are discarded if they prove unsuitable for the purpose. They also function as a selective screen, for otherwise thought would be swamped by their recall. The schemata that accompany thought are filters screening out those memories and experiences that are relevant to the matter requiring comprehension. The schemata function as representatives, concretizing the possibilities that thought needs for its acts of comprehension. What they represent is neither thought, nor knowledge, nor memory by itself but, rather, a mixture of them as a means of testing and adjusting thought operations.

Here we have, then, a back-and-forth movement between suitability and unsuitability that enables the imaginary to manifest itself, having been called upon by consciousness. The proliferating change of representatives highlights the presence of the imaginary, insofar as the representative has to be negated whenever it does not tally with the demands of thought. This reversal is a further aspect of the 'nothing' as a component of the mental image that is not exclusively confined to indicating the presence of the absent, or the self-protection of consciousness against its possible captivity, but also indicates the negation of what is inevitably posited through the mental image as an appearance accompanying thought. This negation is essential, because no single schema can represent what thought aims at. Indeed, any attempt at comprehension would have to fail if these representatives – which, as symbolic schemata, merely offer possibilities of orientation – already stood for the thing itself. By manifesting itself as a negation of representatives, the imaginary prevents them from representing thought.

Relations can also be reversed, and the mental images called forth by consciousness may begin to affect consciousness itself – as, for example, in dreams and hypnagogic images. When we are daydreaming or half asleep, the attentiveness of consciousness is reduced; it is still present as is evident from the fleeting configuration of images that come and go, but their sequence is out of control. In such a situation 'the fascinated consciousness . . . yields to the blandishments of the moment and forms an absurd synthesis in conferring a *meaning* on its new image which permits the retention of the unity of thinking' (50).

Two things may be learned from this. First, there is evidently no consciousness without imagemaking, for only through imagemaking is consciousness able to fulfill its intention that is concretized to the degree in which its target becomes determinate. As it seeks to open up this target, what is given must be animated by mental images – not least in order to bridge the difference between intention and object.

Second, because there is no overarching reference to regulate the close relationship between intention and mental image, consciousness will be flooded by its images if attention lapses. But since consciousness posits its own images that contain nothing but what has been put into them, consciousness in such situations will become a prisoner of itself (see 50). To be caught up in one's images means being in the presence of the absent, whose power increases to the degree in which consciousness is absorbed by these images; these will then triumph over the intentionality that first brought them into being.

In dream, the difference between consciousness and its images is canceled out; according to Sartre, 'the dream is the perfect realization of a shut imaginary consciousness, that is, a consciousness for which there is absolutely no exit and towards which no external point of view of any sort is possible' (193). Even if, as Husserl suggests, one can dream oneself into a situation 'in which I dream myself dreaming, or more clearly, in which I dream that I am dreaming,' the dreamed dreams themselves still cannot become perceptible objects from which consciousness could withdraw (Husserl, 1980, 184). For 'fantasy', as Husserl contends, is a modification of consciousness that manifests itself – where it is predominant – as a 'consciousness of non-actuality' (299). Since actuality 'means as much as taking stands' (363), nonactuality is nothing but an 'analogue of pure fantasy (and fixes a concept of imagination, insofar as pure imagination expresses the prevention of actuality)' (363f).

If consciousness can be thrown out of gear by its posited mental images, this is because, as consciousness of something, it is dependent on what it targets. Since pure consciousness would be either empty or groundless, referential contexts emerge whenever consciousness seeks to grasp itself. We get either referential frameworks that are ego-oriented or that are built on the nonexistence of such a concept. If there is only consciousness of something, then consciousness assumes qualities of its targets, in consequence of which we sometimes have a positing consciousness, sometimes an ideating, perceiving, comprehending and realizing consciousness. As an ideating consciousness, it posits its own object, which, contrary to a perceiving consciousness, makes it focus on its own product. Once the absent or nonexistent has become present, intentionality is fulfilled, although at this stage the mental image begins to take effect. While perceiving consciousness controls and is controlled by the objects given to it, the impact of the mental image cannot be so restrained. Indeed, any attempt to model the image will simply bring forth other images that will ramify into a flood of unconnected pictures, for the object of the mental image only expresses a connection of consciousness, and its content will change when the connections change. Thus, if a thetic consciousness changes into an ideational one, it tends to become enthralled by the images posited, which, in turn, begin to hold sway over their own source. We then have a consciousness dependent on its own production. Consciousness, on the other hand, is inconceivable without its positing activity, since otherwise 'it would have to be conceived as completely engulfed in the existent and without the possibility of grasping anything but the existent' (Sartre, 1972, 217). The shrinking of distance between consciousness and its product makes consciousness slide into what it has brought forth.

We may examine the process from two different perspectives, both of which will shed light on how the imaginary is manifested through a positing consciousness. One of these perspectives is described by Sartre himself: Every mental image gives presence to either the absent or the nonexistent, and therefore contains a certain 'nothing', because the presence does not eliminate the absence or give existence to the nonexistent but actually maintains the nonbeing of what appears as presence in the mental image. This 'nothing' has a certain suction effect that the intentionality of consciousness cannot escape.

... consciousness comes to full fruition by luring the imaginary into shape, for consciousness as pure intentionality is empty and the imaginary is unable to posit itself. Sartre's prime concern is not to describe the idea but to understand it as a form that permits the imaginary to be transcendentally reduced for phenomenological purposes. His extensive description of both consciousness and idea is due to the fact that the imaginary can no longer be isolated as a faculty with an existence of its own, independent of consciousness that directs itself to targets in the world. The questions Sartre has to answer are how the imaginary asserts itself through consciousness, and what happens to consciousness when it has to mobilize the imaginary in order to fulfill its intentions. He sees consciousness as always being anchored in the world, the grasping of which governs its intention; consequently, to 'posit an image is to construct an object on the fringe of the whole of reality, which means therefore to hold the real at a distance, to free oneself from it, in a word, to deny it' (Sartre, 1972, 213). 'And if the negation is the unconditioned principle of all imagination, it itself can never be realized except in and by an act of imagination. That which is denied must be imagined' (218). The world is negated in the act of imagining, because all comprehension entails overstepping what is to be comprehended. But in this situation there are no frames of reference for what is to be comprehended, and it is only the act of imagining that opens up the possibility of correlations by means of mental images. Thus the negation of the world is as indispensable for this process as it is ambiguous.

This ambiguity reveals itself in Sartre's wavering over whether consciousness precedes the imaginary or vice versa. If the world has to be negated as a precondition for its comprehension, then the imaginary has no control over consciousness. 'Thus the imaginative act is at once *constitutive, isolating and annihilating*' (210). This means that consciousness, which is always anchored in situations, can only direct itself toward a particular segment of the given world, which must be isolated by negation and reconstituted for comprehension. What, then, triggers the negating impulse? Is it the imaginary, working directly through consciousness? Or is it a realizing consciousness that, by fulfilling its intention, has changed to an ideational consciousness? Sartre seems at times to opt for the second of these, because for him every positing 'of the imaginary will be accompanied by a collapsing of the world' (218). What is unmistakable, however, is that the imaginary can negate only by way of consciousness, because before taking on such a function it is neither knowable or cognizable; it could manifest itself only through consciousness, and would make consciousness itself appear as if it were the negating agent. This being so, negation becomes the salience of the imaginary in the mirror of consciousness. But this might also be taken to mean that the imaginary must enlist the aid of consciousness if it is to make any kind of appearance. In this case negation would be less a precondition for conceiving the world for the purpose of comprehension than a matter of the imaginary being the 'other' of consciousness – an 'other' that can make itself present in consciousness only as negation.

This option also appears to play a role in Sartre's thinking. Toward the end of his book he says, 'So imagination, far from appearing as an accidental characteristic of consciousness, turns out to be an essential and transcendental condition of consciousness' (219). If this is so, negation becomes extremely ambiguous. As a transcendental condition of consciousness the imaginary – by way of the ideating consciousness – 'uses the world as the negated foundation'

(218). But it can also negate the ideating consciousness, as it does in hypnagogic images and dreams, where 'the imaginary world occurs as a world without freedom' (198f.). If the imaginary, even though initially patterned by the intentionality of consciousness, can negate both the world and the ideating consciousness, the question arises whether negation is an inherent quality of the imaginary or only its manifestation as conditioned by consciousness. Since the imaginary, though given in evidential experience, is not knowable, one can focus only on its manifestations. With the imaginary negating in order to promote operations of consciousness, the resultant ambiguity of the negation is unmistakable: On the one hand, the imaginary presents itself as '*something* which is nothingness in relation to the world, and in relation to which the world is nothing' (217); on the other hand, it fascinates consciousness to the point of captivity. Moreover, as we have already seen, a 'nothing' may reveal itself insofar as the absent or nonexistent is present in the mental image but is negated in its real presence, and such distinctions are impossible without an ideational consciousness. The latter channels the imaginary, which it has aroused, and also becomes a backdrop against which the activated imaginary reveals itself to be too ambiguous for consciousness to grasp. Thus negation by the imaginary, once it enters consciousness, splits into various modes of 'nothing', and these in turn show the imaginary to be a modification of consciousness.

To a certain degree this might amount to a conceptual definition of the imaginary. 'Fantasy', says Husserl, 'is through and through modification, and it cannot contain anything other than modification' (1980, 286) ... For fantasy, one should add, has no objects of its own; instead, it manifests itself in consciousness by altering the latter's relation to objects through changing a realizing consciousness into an ideating one. Consciousness needs the imaginary in order to give presence to the nongiven absent, and in the act of imagining, consciousness itself undergoes a modification that inscribes itself into intentionality by splitting it into various modes of positing, perceiving, ideating and realizing. Thus, when Sartre calls the imaginary the transcendental condition of consciousness, this is not because the imaginary actually constitutes consciousness but because, by modifying stances, it makes consciousness operative. Conversely, consciousness is not without influence on the imaginary, because modification presupposes something to be modified, and the latter in turn is bound to affect the modifying operations. The range of modification extends from the negated world to the imprisonment of consciousness through its images in dreams. So long as the imaginary manifests itself as an act negating the world, it remains under the control of a consciousness that has, however, been modified into an ideational consciousness. But when the images take over, consciousness is modified to nonactuality. These are the two extremes of the imaginary as manifested in consciousness.

Regardless of how the relationship is articulated, modification is what tilts the balance between consciousness and the imaginary. Indeed, the imaginary is present in all the tilting operations that direct attitudes of consciousness.

Modification does not bring about irrevocable changes but takes place when consciousness slides into what it has posited, or when attitudes of consciousness are tilted, in movements that articulate various forms of negation and are peculiarly double-edged. They are products, and yet at the same time they are the unstoppable dynamism that produces the products, which in their turn cannot halt the double movement. Products are tailored to meet specific requirements, and these do not disappear completely when consciousness – as in dreams – becomes enthralled by its images. But the sliding and tilting movements are infinite in their scope.

Since this play movement is not without structure, it differs from what Coleridge called 'wavering'. We have seen that the imaginary, as a mental image posited by consciousness, may take effect as a negation of reality or as a modification of consciousness. This gives rise to an interacting relationship that makes it impossible to understand consciousness or the imaginary in isolation. Thetic consciousness that posits the imaginary as mental imagery will slide into its images because it participates in its own processes of production. Thus consciousness that is anchored in the world will be driven beyond the world by what it has posited. Illusions, dreams, daydreams and hallucinations show how consciousness may be overwhelmed by the effects of its productions. Thetic consciousness then changes into a backdrop, permitting its own incipient helplessness to be registered. While the imaginary is posited by consciousness as the mental image, its effect tends to split, paralyze and imprison consciousness. During the act of positing, consciousness slides into the mental image. This, in turn, tilts thetic consciousness into different stances, so that it may change into a realizing, perceiving or ideating consciousness.

As consciousness is bound to participate in its production, even thetic consciousness is nothing but one of the stances into which consciousness is tilted. In consequence, it is as impossible to talk of *the* consciousness as it is of *the* imaginary in itself. Instead, the ensuing play movement of back and forth operative between consciousness and the imaginary makes them interpenetrate to such a degree that tilting and sliding play against one another. Thetic consciousness slides into the idea posited and thus is tilted into kaleidoscopically changing starices that indicate the presence of the imaginary in terms of consciousness. If an imaginary activated by consciousness manifests itself as a play structure by making its activating agent slide into its product and continually tilt the attitudes of consciousness, then its unfathomableness is translated into an endlessness of gaming.

Since in play everything is ready for tilting, playing is not predetermined but, rather, arises out of a basic indeterminacy. As the to-and-fro movement is patterned, sliding and tilting reveal that form has been imposed on the imaginary – a form, however, that also molds the manner in which consciousness is played. The result is the close interrelation between consciousness and the imaginary in a connection whose continual sliding and tilting are unpredictable because play inscribes into it the unpredictability of what first makes the gaming possible.

NOTE

1. ... Sartre considers the image as something 'intermediate between the concept and the perception' (1972, 105).

ANNOTATED BIBLIOGRAPHY

Barthes, Roland. 'The Death of the Author'. *Image-Music-Text*, trans. Stephen Heath. London, 1977.

One of the most important (and shortest – eight pages) pieces of criticism you will ever read. Barthes argues that while the reader is actively involved in the construction of meaning, the author by comparison does not control how meaning is produced in the moment a text is in general circulation. Once a text is being read by readers who interpret it in different ways the author (as a producer of meaning) is effectively dead.

de Man, Paul. *Allegories of Reading: Figural Language in Rousseau, Nietzsche, Rilke, and Proust*. New Haven, CT, 1979.

A difficult but endlessly rewarding account of how reading is figured by the play of language within a text. As such meaning is said to be arbitrary and beyond the control of the reader as well as the author. De Man's version of deconstruction offers a consideration of phenomenology and consciousness beyond Reader-Response Theory's constrained understanding of language. See the entry on this title in Part 6 on Deconstruction and Part 7 on Poststructuralism, below.

Eco, Umberto. *The Role of The Reader: Explorations in the Semiotics of Texts*. Bloomington, IN, 1979.

Like Barthes' later work, Eco makes a distinction between 'writerly' (or closed) texts which limit the possibilities of interpretation and offer a fixed meaning to the reader (e.g. Superman comics or James Bond novels) and 'readerly' (or open) texts which depend upon the active participation of the reader in the production of meaning (e.g. *Finnegans Wake*).

Fish, Stanley. *Is There A Text in This Class? The Authority of Interpretative Communities*. Cambridge, MA, 1980.

All of Fish's Reader-Response essays collected one volume. He argues that any reader is part of a community of readers and their response to a text will be determined by the conventions of reading within which he or she is educated in a given socio-historical context.

Freund, Elizabeth. *The Return of the Reader: Reader-Response Criticism*. London, 1987.

A detailed but concise and accessible account of the canon of texts known as Reader-Response Theory. Starting with I. A. Richards and the New Critics the study goes on to introduce the work of Culler, Fish, Holland and Iser. Freund's introduction relates the question of the reader to other theoretical approaches.

SUPPLEMENTARY BIBLIOGRAPHY

Barthes, Roland. *S/Z*. Trans. Richard Howard. New York, 1974.

Bennett, Andrew, ed. *Readers and Reading*. London, 1995.

Bleich, David. *Subjective Criticism*. Baltimore, MD, 1978.

Brooks, Peter. *Reading for the Plot: Design and Intention in Narrative*. Oxford, 1984.

Crosman, Inge and Suleiman, Susan R., eds. *The Reader in the Text: Essays on Audience and Interpretation*. Princeton, NJ, 1980.

Culler, Jonathan. *On Deconstruction: Theory and Criticism After Structuralism*. Ithaca, NY, 1982.

Docherty, Thomas. *Reading Absent Character: Towards a Theory of Characterization in Fiction*. Oxford, 1983.

Gadamer, Hans-Georg. *Truth and Method*, trans. Garrett Barden and John Cumming. New York, 1975.

Holland, Norman. *5 Readers Reading*. New Haven, CT, 1975.

Holub, Robert C. *Reception Theory: A Critical Introduction*. London, 1984.

Howendahl, Peter Uwe. *The Institution of Criticism*. Ithaca, NY, 1982.

Iser, Wolfgang. *The Implied Reader: Patterns of Communication in Prose Fiction from Bunyan to Beckett*. Baltimore, MD, 1974.

——. *The Act of Reading: A Theory of Aesthetic Response*. Baltimore, MD, 1978.

——. *Prospecting: From Reader-Response to Literary Anthropology*. Baltimore, MD, 1989.

——. *Toward an Aesthetic of Reception*, trans. T. Bahti. Brighton, 1982.

Jauss, Hans-Robert. *Aesthetic Experience and Literary Hermeneutics*. Minneapolis, MN, 1982.

Miller, J. Hillis. *The Ethics of Reading: Kant, de Man, Eliot, Trollope, James, and Benjamin*. New York, 1987.

Orr, Leonard. 'Receptions-aesthetics as a Tool in Literary Criticism and Historiography', *Language Quarterly*, 21: 3/4 (1983).

Prince, Gerald. 'Introduction to the Study of the Narratee', *Poétique*, 14, 1973.

Richards, I. A. *Practical Criticism*. London, 1964.

Riffaterre, Michael. *Semiotics of Poetry*. London, 1978.

Riquelme, John Paul. 'The Ambivalence of Reading', *Diacritics*, 10: 2, 1980.

Scholes, Robert. 'Cognition and the Implied Reader', *Diacritics*, 5: 3, 1975.

Thomas, Brook. 'Reading Wolfgang Iser or Responding to a Theory of Response', *Comparative Literature Studies*, 19, 1982.

Tompkins, Jane P., ed. *Reader-Response Criticism: From Formalism to Post-Structuralism*. Baltimore, MD, 1981.

Weber, Samuel. 'Caught in the Act of Reading', in *Demarcating the Disciplines: Philosophy, Literature, Art*, ed. Samuel Weber. Minneapolis, MN, 1986.

Wimsatt, Jnr, W. K. and Beardsley, Monroe C. 'The Affective Fallacy', rpt. in W. K. Wimsatt, *The Verbal Icon: Studies in the Meaning of Poetry*. London, 1970.

PART 5
PSYCHOANALYTIC CRITICISM

INTRODUCTION: SCREENING THE OTHER

Jill Barker

Both literary criticism and psychoanalysis engage in the interpretation of texts – the former explicates or comments on texts which have been crafted and (usually) published, while the latter uses artlessly spoken texts, which are treated by the analyst as a source of information from the unconscious mind of the speaker and used therapeutically. Both disciplines thus seek for a meaning beyond the immediately apparent context of the text, both seek an enhanced understanding though with different goals. The essays reprinted here correspondingly face in two directions: one towards psychoanalysis, the other towards literature. Stephen Heath subjects a work by Jacques Lacan to a close critical analysis, while James Mellard uses Lacanian theory to scrutinise Virginia Woolf's novel *To the Lighthouse*.

The screen of my title is a pun suggested by Freud's term 'screen memories' (SE, III, 1903) for the memories that conceal significant earlier events: within both the literary text and the discursive text of psychoanalysis, the other is displayed (screened) as in a cinema – at a distance from its origin, and also hidden (screened) from view behind the metaphoric duplicities (sophistries) of language. Yet the qualities of this 'other' are of great importance, since the self is projected into/onto the other and formed in relation to it. The function and significance of the divisions within the subject permeate the two essays excerpted here: in their various ways, both extracts address the fundamental Lacanian concepts of loss, desire and the three 'orders' of the psychic structure as they occur within language.

The 'talking cure' developed by Sigmund Freud (1856–1939) assumed that the patient's stream of unchecked speech ('free association'), especially including reported dreams, could provide the therapist with metaphoric clues to the discords within the unconscious mind which were causing the patient's physical (and therefore psychic) symptoms. For Freud, and for later psychoanalysis generally, mind and body interact closely. Language thus gives a kind of oblique access not just to that area, of the mind which is outside conscious control but also to knowledge which is outside awareness, and especially to events which are lost to memory. Like the screen and like a code it both conceals and reveals the subject, hiding the history of a psychic state in language which, read subtly, narrates the events of the subject's construction. Symptoms in the present are read as a coded repetition of past traumas or frustrations, now repressed from consciousness. The early 'analyses' were narrated by Freud in his case studies, such as 'Dora' ([1901] SE, XVII, 1905) and 'The Wolf Man' (SE, XVII, 1918), while the conceptual bases for the therapy were developed within and alongside those essays in works such as *Jokes and Their Relation to the Unconscious* (SE, VIII, 1905) and *Some Psychical Consequences of the Anatomical Distinction Between the Sexes* (SE, XIX 1925). In publications ranging over more than thirty years, language, narrative and subjectivity are simultaneously both the object of study and the means by which psychoanalysis reaches its objective. The discourse of the unconscious is read with attention to many of the same features that literary critics consider – repetitions, metaphor (condensation) and metonymy (displacement). This textual focus by psychoanalysts has made it an appropriate resource for literary criticism: Wright (1984) and Vice (1996) discuss the similarities at greater length.

A set of more-or-less experimental therapeutic praxes and a collection of theories about the nature of the mind and of language (and their intersection) form the unstable, disputed but nevertheless hugely influential foundation of psychoanalysis. Psychoanalytic theory is itself multiple: Freud's opinions changed during his lifetime, and those theories in turn were taken up with differing emphases by disciples who developed and reinterpreted them: Jungians, Kleinians, ego psychologists, Gestalt theorists, and Lacanians are just a few of the major schools of psychoanalytic thought, each of which deserves study in its own right. All of these multiple sets of ways of reading that constitute 'psychoanalytic literary theory' are concerned with the nature of subjectivity, and with the subject's emotional orientation towards figures from the outside world, reconstituted as aspects of the mental world. Thus reconstructing the world afresh, the subject is at a remove from (an otherwise inaccessible) reality, in ways which resemble Foucauldian concepts of the social construction of meaning as well as feminist 'constructionist' gendering.

Although Freud used literature and his own interpretations of literary texts (notably Sophocles' *Oedipus Rex* and Shakespeare's *Hamlet*, but also E. T. A. Hoffman's 'The Sandman') to elucidate points about the organisation of (and processes within) the unconscious mind, early attempts to apply Freud's theories to literature did not produce particularly sophisticated insights.

For Freud, desire and the loss of the object of desire are crucially bound up with sexuality and gendering and with emotional maturation, and these in turn with the identity of the speaking subject, again generating intersections and interactions between psychoanalytic literary criticism, feminism, structuralism and deconstruction. Psychoanalytic literary theory is involved in a ceaseless set of ramified dialogic exchanges with each of these, as they are with one another, in ways which can be conflictual as much as cooperative. Barthesian theories of the death of the author mesh with structuralist theories of the signifier and of the text as a social product. If there is no longer a clear intentional connection between the writing of a text and the reader's interpretation of that text, it is clear that the early twentieth-century psychoanalytic approach of 'psycho-analysing' the characters, or of interpreting a text as a manifestation of an individual author's subjectivity, is no longer appropriate to a postmodern perception of the detached, contingent nature of textual interpretation. A considerably more sophisticated approach is to view texts as cultural products, containing their own subjectivity which resides in the text itself. It is the text which manifests anxieties, immaturities or neuroses. Literature has been described as doing the dreaming of the culture, and as Freud observed, psychic work takes place in dreams, helping to sort out and to express that which is repressed from the conscious mind. Thus Mellard's reading (5.3 below) is not interested in any psychic investment Virginia Woolf may have in 'her' text, nor in the characters, except as they represent aspects of the text's subjectivity. In considering the transference and counter-transference and its fluidities, psycho-analytic theory is close to Barthes' view of the *scriptible* (Barthes, 1970), where rival discourses discern various meanings within the text, depending on their own agendas. Reader-response theory, too, draws on both structuralist and psychoanalytic assumptions.

The space available precludes discussions of the variety of psychoanalytic schools. This chapter focuses on one of the most substantial and radical rereadings of Freud: that of Jacques Lacan (1901–81), whose school has been most stimulating and productive for literary criticism since the mid-1970s, though Lacan's teaching goes back to the 1930s. Lacan's rereading focused on Freud's texts, which had been generally treated as about the mind and the body, in terms of language and meaning. In seeing that the unconscious is structured like a language, Lacan brought Freud's theories into an area where they could be treated using the concepts of the structural linguists. He thus reclaimed them for the domain of hermeneutics and poststructuralist philoso-phy, while never losing touch with the therapeutic concerns which they also addressed. Lacan's thought was disseminated through the training Seminar for students intending to become clinical psychoanalysts which he conducted from 1954 to 1980 for the French Society of Psychoanalysis. Access to the written version of the seminar was for long occluded, complex and disputed. Power struggles over access to Lacan's notes or to pirate copies of the seminar delayed its publication, the 1954 seminar appearing only in 1975. Further disputes delayed translation of Lacan's allusive and complex prose into English and the massive French *Écrits* appeared in English at less than half the length, as *Écrits: A Selection*. Other translations, notably by Wilden (1981), give access to further sessions of the Seminar. Students will find a guide such as Wright (1984) or Bowie (1991) helpful for exploring Lacan's notoriously obscure writing in greater depth.

Freud had found that human development – the achievement of mature subjectivity – involved the establishment of specific objects of desire and an acceptance of loss as imposed by external constraints. Because desire both seeks its goal and is blocked from its goal, it becomes deflected towards substitute goals (objects). For Freud these objects tend to be read as real, even though the movement from one real object to another reality may be reached via a pun (that is, via language). A classic example is the well known 'glanz auf der Nase' bilingual pun, where a shine on the nose (of the nurse of a German-speaking infant) became an eroticised desire to look at ('glance at') the nose in the English speaking adult. It is this conceptualised image of a substitute object of desire that Lacan calls the *objet petit a* (the small 'o' other, so-called because French for 'other' is 'autre'). Its effects are discussed by Heath (5.2 below). That which opposes the subject's initial desire is the Law of the Father, which is similar to the Other (with a capital O), occasionally rather enchantingly translated as 'the big Other'. One might, only half-jokingly, see the difficulties over publication of Lacan's Seminar as constructing Lacan (himself) in the field of the Other, and his writings as an *objet petit a*. The would-be translators and editors, however, are not unlike a primal horde as they wrangle over the masculine inheritance of the Law of the Father.

The mother is commonly a desired other but, because already claimed by the Father, unattainable to the infant. She becomes symbolised as an object of desire within the unconscious mind by some other term. Processes of condensation and displacement which may be experiential or linguistic or both generate this alternative, screening term, behind which the mother/object is concealed. Recent psychoanalytic theorists indicate this psychic location by the term (m)Other, indicating both the mother (who is the initial desire both of the subject and also of the Father) and the impossibility of that desire – thus the structure of the term 'mother' contains within it the structures of denial and loss: of the necessity for the substitution of an *objet petit a* for the original object of desire. All this is contained in the sign '(m)Other', and discussed by Mellard in the excerpts from his reading of Woolf's *To the Lighthouse* (5.3 below). In accepting the Law of the Father there are gains as well as losses, as the infant moves out of the Imaginary state with its oceanic sense of unity of the self into the Symbolic order where semiotic structures (especially but not exclusively language) are possible. Narratives of this transition as a temporal sequence can give the impression that one model has superseded another, but ideally the three orders are conceptualised as coexisting and even as inter-penetrating one another on occasion. The psyche has different *kinds* of access to the Imaginary and the Symbolic orders, while the Real is outside psychic experiences because exterior to representation of any kind.

It can be argued that Lacan generates a poststructuralist reading of Freud. On the one hand psychoanalysis seems to be intrinsically and originally a structuralist interpretation of the nature of texts, language and the subjectivities within these semiotic systems. In its use of terms of irreducible and mutually defining opposition (subject/object etc.) and its totalising construction of the orders of the Imaginary, the Symbolic and the Real, Lacanian theory is fundamentally structuralist, no matter how far discussion may complicate and sophisticate those terms. Counter-claims are made that the Lacanian view of the Real as outside language and of subjectivity as decentred from an 'essential' self gives it poststructuralist credentials, allowing a participation in (rather than a subjection to) the deconstructive turn. This debate is focused in *The Purloined Poe* (1988) where both Derrida and Johnson see psychoanalysis as subject to the deconstructive turn. Wright (1984) agrees. Žižek (1989) most persuasively sees psychoanalysis as poststructuralist. Lacan refers ambiguously to the 'desire of the Other': most simply, the subject's desire for the Other. The phrase also indicates the insistence by the Law of the Father that it be heard within the Imaginary, an urgency generated by definition because the very existence of the Imaginary poses a barrier for the Other: a moment when/place where it experiences lack and, inevitably linked with lack, desire. Žižek sees that one implication of what he calls 'the lack in the Other' is that an unnameable (and so extra-structural) transcendent term disrupts the apparently closed structure outlined by Lacan's three orders. Discovering such a lack depends on using the 'Other' flexibly, as a subject in its own right, as well as a force outside the subject. Mellard appears to follow Žižek in describing Mr Ramsay as the lacking/desiring Other, when he seeks and is satisfied by Lily Briscoe's approval. But if Lily Briscoe's praise can supply the 'lack in the Other', has it not also named that lack, and so reclaimed it for the structures of an intellectual analysis of the text? This logical paradox focuses a danger perennially hovering over psychoanalytic approaches to literary criticism.

Lacan's strongly visual imagination is manifested in his use of elaborate diagrams which, in purporting to explain, tease the reader with the offer of clarity while actually delivering further obscurity and so a further demand for interpretation. In general these schemata of Lacan's such as the schema L (Lacan, 1977, 193) or schema R (197) are useless without extended additional explanation, thus plunging back into the linguistic condition from which they seem to hold out the possibility of transcendence and escape. Lacan's diction is often also spatio-mathematical: a psychic event may take place 'in the field' of some specified concept, where another writer might say something like 'under the aegis' or 'in the context'. The formulation, while sustaining that sense of physical location which pervades psychoanalytic conceptualisation, additionally invokes both mathematical terminology and the idea of magnetic fields of force. Equally significantly, it recalls Jakobson's structuralist-linguistic discussion of the 'axes' along which metaphor and metonymy move. Freud's divided consciousness becomes for Lacan a linguistic subject, existing in and divided by language. Heath is concerned with the moment of that division and the awareness of 'difference' which constitutes it: gender difference, certainly, but also that which imposes division of the subject from the other: the phallus.

Heath's essay begins with ways in which the relation between the subject and the other involves the gaze, and how the gaze produces conclusions of a deceptive certainty, eliding the degree to which what is seen is already contained within interpretative social structures – the viewer sees that which social structures dictate is there to be seen, in this case sexual difference. Such an argument seriously undermines psychoanalytic perceptions founded in the visual. Freud had already identified the 'scopic drive' and the importance of seeing to infant psychic development (see, for example, 'The Uncanny': SE, XVII, 1919) and had referred to the unconscious mind as 'ein andere Schauplatz' – an alternative theatre-stage). Again, Lacan's most frequently cited essay is 'The Mirror Stage' (Écrits, 1977), a discussion of the infantile misidentification of the self as unified, through viewing its reflection in a mirror. It is at least in part through this interpretative gaze, distinguishing field and ground, that the gazer-subject foreshadows entry into the sense of an arbitrary division from other(s) and an illusory wholeness of self which the Symbolic order, and thus language, constitutes. The theme of reflections, of concealment, of licit and illicit viewings, of *trompe l'œuil*, pervades psychoanalytic literary criticism, and produces an interpretation of the visions in dramas as continuous with verbalised language, both being capable of representing unconscious states metaphorically.

It is therefore not surprising that Lacanian theory was first transmitted to the English-speaking world through the work of film-theorists to whom it offered ways of theorising their medium at an academic and critical level of sophistication. Through the 1970s the journal *Screen* functioned as a critical forum for discussions of contemporary French philosophy and of its development within film theory. With the increasing availability of English translations of Lacan's works, discussions broadened to literary criticism more generally.

From its inception, it was apparent that psychoanalysis was not just problematic, but also productive and inescapable for feminists. Responses vary from as early as Julia Kristeva ('About Chinese Women' (in Moi, 1974), and a large corpus of writing) through Mitchell (1982) and Gallop (1982) to Doane ('Woman's Stake: Filming the Female Body', in Vice, 1996). Stephen Heath, in the article excerpted here, addresses the problems that the Freudian concepts of castration and penis-envy raise for feminism, in a detailed explication of and challenge to Lacan's Seminar XX, which in turn addresses Freud's famous quandary, 'What does woman want?' This is especially important to Freud, whose view of the processes of emotional maturation is unequivocally gendered. Yet that view depends on perceiving woman as lack (of the phallus). For

Lacan the phallus, though still powerfully metaphorised by the penis, has become something transcendent. Heath observes what this means for Lacan when the latter uses visual modes: interpreting such objects as the Bernini statue, or the child's view of sexual organs, observing flaws in Lacan's assumption that seeing and knowing are the same thing. By definition, the entry of the (masculine) subject into the Symbolic order involves a sight of the female as absence (as a lack), in terms of the absence of the phallus. Often it seems that, for Lacan, difference within the subject is precisely the difference between man and woman, and subjectivity depends on locating the woman as other (and within the Other) and the recognition of that lack which constitutes the self. Heath criticises Lacan since, in discussing gender difference, the latter uses discourse which does not locate itself in relation to gender: which, in implicitly believing itself in relation to gender, ignores its own assumptions of authority and masculinity. Heath recognises that Lacan's most significant perceptions place the important area of difference within language, where the subject is constituted. Here the subject's lack is enacted, not in relation to biological detail, but in relation to the *idea* of a plenitude of meaning which language (and the Other) appear to promise but cannot supply. Interestingly, Woolf's text insistently places lack with the masculine and in the Symbolic, and a corresponding excess (or, better, bonus) of presence in the field of the Imaginary as inhabited by Mrs Ramsay.

Heath sees that the symbolising psychic structure put forward by Lacan both depends on, and exists in tension with, that 'essential' physical feature of different genitalia which culture uses to divide masculine from feminine in terms of 'loss'. That particular interpretation is itself a cultural construct, and there are many moments in Lacan's writing where he fails to see this. An insistent return to the physical, without a perception that it too is a cultural construct (a vision), can only destabilise the theory he has built upon it of the mind in the Symbolic order. It is imperative also to reverse the chain of thought and see the phallus as a figure for, or a signifier of, that (undefined) loss which is inherently a part of humanity *as a linguistic entity*. Heath observes that the Foucauldian circumstances to do with power relations which construct a view of the female as a view of lack have been silenced. Hysteria can be seen as a refusal to take up that position of the not-male. Instead, Freudian psycho-analysis sees such symptoms as supporting and confirming its own theoretical structures. Woman is thus not construed as a speaking subject, except when producing the kinds of meaning that psychoanalysis as a dominant discourse has empowered itself to hear and to 'cure': the very meanings that it sees as direct access to the unconscious. Heath suggests that the abstractions of Lacan's linguistic theory might offer solutions to the problematic of an apparent essentialism in much of Freudian and Lacanian discussion, while acknowledging that theorising the relationship between the body and the Symbolic order can lead to a chicken-and-egg situation: either our insertion into language depends on physical difference, or our perception of physical difference stems from our semiotic (linguistic) capacities to understand what we see. Which came first is a political question. As suggested above, one solution is to recognise that even the body is only present to the gaze through the culturally constructed conventions of interpretation – of, in fact, the already – existing Symbolic order.

Mellard takes the idea of subjectivity in the text further, using Woolf's entire text as (a model of) the psychic structures of the subject, and so the characters in it are metaphoric divisions within the subject. Thus Mr Ramsay *is* 'the Other' and the Father of the Symbolic order within the text's psychic structure, with Mrs Ramsay representing the extra-Symbolic, otherwise known as the Imaginary (the historic implications of 'pre-Symbolic' should be avoided – the Imaginary is not located in time), or as the female/the lack. (This reading is to some extent against the grain of Mrs Ramsay's plenitude, noted above, which it copes with as part of the misrecognitions of the Mirror stage). At the same time, however, the characters are open to treatment as 'subjects' in their own right. Mellard can turn to use Mr Ramsay as subject within whose structure Mrs Ramsay functions as *objet petit a*, thus elucidating the multi-directionality of Lacan's phrase 'the desire of the Other'.

Where Heath cites Irigaray and her recognition that the relation between the woman and the mother needs to be explored in the Imaginary, Mellard shows ways in which this might be done, in the conflicted manipulations with which Mrs Ramsay imposes marriage on the younger women, and is opposed by Lily Briscoe's negotiations as an artist within the Imaginary and the Symbolic. Lily must satisfy herself in relation to both orders, through the (m)Other. The Imaginary for Mellard is made up of the distinctive misrecognitions of the Mirror phase: the fantasised sense of wholeness, whose completion takes place through an acceptance of loss/prohibition – in other words, of the Law of the Father. Mellard explicitly places the Imaginary and the Mirror Phase together in the field of the undifferentiated self and the power of the mother, the Imaginary union between infant and (m)Other flourishing pre-linguistically. Unnoticed by Mellard, Mrs Ramsay, however, reveals that the projection of wholeness is onto an other that is already divided and doubting – searching for interpretations even within the Imaginary, as both she and the novel consider her own status as a social and moral being. Mrs Ramsay, as well as Lily, is involved in a balancing act where the Symbolic and the Imaginary cannot just be treated as children to be managed.

Mellard's bivalent text functions in two directions: using Woolf to explain Lacan, and Lacan to explicate Woolf. (The latter is a dangerous, almost reductive, project since he risks finding a final 'truth' in the text, and at times his discourse appears to suggest that it is Woolf who put 'meanings' in the text and not Mellard. If Mellard's search for his own *objet petit a* is illusorily satisfied, we at least should know better than to mimic him.) There is here an example of an enduring difficulty for literary criticism that the reading ends up saying less than the original while implying that it says more. More effective is his use of Woolf to explicate Lacan. Mellard's discussion, largely avoiding gender issues and focusing on the subject in the text, is especially valuable for its acute description of the orders of the Real, the Imaginary and the Symbolic. It weaves that discussion into an interpretation of Virginia Woolf's novel as a narrative of a subjectivity which matures by bringing the three orders into alignment within the field of desire, loss and mourning. Mellard expands Daniel Ferrers' perception that the 'Time Passes' section is an attempt to evade the Symbolic. He perceives the three sections of Woolf's novel as bearing a close relationship with Lacan's three orders of psychic experience, and the narrative sequencing as an enactment of a process of development of (textual) subjectivity through the three orders, to a condition of closure in which a kind of harmony or resolution is achieved.

The first section, 'In the Window', Mellard sees as the Imaginary, involved with elements of the Symbolic. Wright describes the Real as 'the given field of brute existence: ... that to which all reference and action have relevance, but which can only be handled through signifying practices' (Wright, 1984, 110). Like the inhabitants of Plato's cave, we as subjects can only perceive the Real at a remove, through the conceptual, symbolising processes within which it has meaning for us. For Mellard, the Real is imaged by the subject-free section of the novel, 'Time Passes'. The Real of unobserved and therefore uninterpreted decay in the edifice and fittings of the house is mapped against the human measure (and therefore Symbolic structure) of ten years, in a convincing reading which forms an immensely accurate description of the nature of the Lacanian Real.

Mellard necessarily combines his discussion of the passage through the orders with observations of the varieties of otherness which constitute the text's subjectivity. His reading shows how the other is constituted both as the Law of the Father and as the object of desire – how desire is (for) the desire of the Other. This can even take place in the Imaginary-dominated scenes of 'In the Window', where the episode in which Mrs Ramsay responds to Mr Ramsay's need of her, at the same time precipitating an Oedipal crisis for her son James, at the moment when he loses her attention. (This has the force of a castrating impact, as he observes the Law of the Father and the desire of the Other as one and the same thing.) Ten years later in the 'To the Lighthouse' section, James experiences the same desire (in repeating the mother's desire) of/for the Other in his delight at his father's approval of his sailing skill. The *objet petit a* is both the son and Mrs Ramsay: a shifting term, depending on where the subjectivity of the text is located.

Both Mellard and Heath are concerned with the ways in which differences (or divisions) are established in the subject – Mellard's multiple, shifting subjects face the Law of the Father in several guises – first as Mr Ramsay, denying the pleasurable trip to the lighthouse, but also (with Mr Ramsay now as subject) as the absolute loss figured by death. The death of Mrs Ramsay, who has been for so long the desire of the Other, flings the Symbolic order into conflict with the Real, at least until the desire of the Other can be transferred onto alternative objects (such as Lily Briscoe or the fine pair of boots). Imaginary relations cannot resolve difference – in other words, in the realm of the Imaginary, the Oedipal conflict is always continuing; loss is a free-floating anxiety. Even in the Symbolic difference is not so much resolved as rendered bearable. Reconciliation of the subject to the fact of lack – to the deferral of desire – is eased by the assimilation of (and participation in) the Symbolic order – not as an imposition on a subjected passive sufferer, but as a speaking subject, that is as a subject who has some ownership of the Symbolic: a right to be there. Thus, by accommodating mourning the subject comes to be able to occupy the place of the Other, albeit fitfully, and accept the temporary satisfactions of fulfilling the dictum that 'all desire is the desire of the Other'. The conclusion of Mellard's epic journey of textual subjectivity appears to be reassuring: finally, in the section 'To the Lighthouse', the task of mourning for the lost other is accomplished, and the text, by integrating its divisions, accomplishes its own Symbolic order.

There are unresolved difficulties in Mellard's analysis regarding firstly the ways in which the three Lacanian orders exist within one another (if they do), and secondly the modes whereby the sense of priority and closure associated with the 'achievement' of the Symbolic should be understood. These remain to be explored by future readings. Taking up connections between psychoanalysis and narrative theory, Mellard sees narrative as a model of the trajectories of desire, placing the reader in the position of the desiring subject, and the satisfactory conclusion of the narrative as the (achieved) *objet petit a* – that is, the mother in the field of the Imaginary. To see narrative itself as the protracted deferral of desire is to relocate the psychoanalytic discussion of a novel as a philosophical discussion about the nature of the literary text.

5.1

DIFFERENCE

Stephen Heath

I

From *Encore*, Lacan's 1972/73 seminar devoted to 'what Freud expressly left aside, the *Was will das Weib?*, the *What does woman want?*' (1975a, 75); this passage on female pleasure, enjoyment, *jouissance*:

> ... just as with Saint-Teresa – you only have to go and look at the Bernini statue in Rome to understand immediately she's coming, no doubt about it. And what is she enjoying, coming from? It's clear that the essential testimony of the mystics is that of saying they experience it but know nothing about it. These mystical ejaculations are neither idle gossip nor mere verbiage, in fact they're the best thing you can read – note, right at the bottom of the page. *Add to them Jacques Lacan's Ecrits*, a work of the same order. Given which, naturally, you're all going to be convinced I believe in God. I believe in the *jouissance* of the woman in so far as it is *en plus*, something more, on condition you block out that *more* until I've thoroughly explained it. (1975a, 70)

Ignoring the habitual self-presentation, ... , ignoring the assurance of the position of knowledge ... , what is striking in the passage is the certainty in a representation and its vision ... No doubt, not the trace of any difficulty, to see the Bernini statue is to understand at once, is to have one's gaze filled with Saint Teresa's coming, with the *jouissance* of the woman; the statue is adequate, the image it gives enough.

Extract from *Screen*, 19: 3 (1978), pp. 51–112.

Yet who exactly is Lacan addressing? Men? Women? Whose is the certainty he assumes so easily ('you only have to')? The passage is indifferent to such questions, as is Lacan's work generally in the forms of its enunciation: the topic is so often sexual difference but the treatment of that topic has no incidence as the possibility of a problem of sexual difference across the subject of the enunciation and the pattern of address of a discourse, of this discourse; the property of the discourse remains assured, assurance of the relation of Lacan to audience, the imaginary of the *evidence* of the statue. Thus any answer to the questions posed will be in terms of the identification of a discourse that is finally masculine, not because of some conception of theory as male but because in the last resort any discourse which fails to take account of the problem of sexual difference in its enunciation and address will be, within a patriarchal order, precisely indifferent, a reflection of male domination. It might be added, moreover, as a kind of working rule, that where a discourse appeals directly to an image, to an immediacy of seeing, as a point of its argument or demonstration, one can be sure that all difference is being elided, that the unity of some accepted vision is being reproduced.

The something more, the *en plus*, that Lacan sees so readily in the statue as the *jouissance* of the woman makes up for the something less, the absence, that the woman represents, represents in the first instance according to a scenario that is another certainty of seeing. Time and time again, Freud proposes the initiation of the castration complex in women, as it were, at sight: 'little girls ... notice the penis of a brother or playmate, strikingly visible and of large proportions, at once recognise it as the superior counterpart of their own small and inconspicuous organ'; 'A little girl behaves differently. She makes her judgement and her decision in a flash. She has seen it and knows that she is without it and wants to have it'; 'the little girl discovers her own deficiency from seeing a male genital'; etc. (Freud, *SE*, 19: 252; 21: 233). As in the Lacan passage, seeing is understanding, only here it is the understanding of the lack, the condition of the more to which the woman will subsequently be returned by psychoanalysis; the woman sees and knows at once, in a flash, that she has nothing to see. The account effectively operates in a binding tourniquet in which the little girl resolves the hesitations of the little boy who 'when he first catches sight of a girl's genital region ... begins by showing irresolution and lack of interest ... he sees nothing or disavows what he has seen' (Freud, *SE*, 19: 252): the girl is given in analytic theory to know at once the nothing she sees, confirming in that certainty, the certainty of the analytic scenario that premisses the woman as the difference of the man, his term, the nothing to see that the boy is brought to know; the woman does represent the lack to see on her body, acknowledging, as little girl, visibility on the side of the man. Freud refers to the 'strikingly visible', Lacan to the phallus as 'something the symbolic use of which is possible because it can be seen, because it is erect; of what cannot be seen, of what is hidden, there is no possible symbolic use' (Lacan,

1978b, 315). Naturally, given the perspective of visibility established, it is the sex of the woman that is taken as the very instance of the unseeable, the hidden: Freud records his belief that 'probably no male human being is spared the fright of castration at the sight of a female genital' (Freud, *SE*, 21: 154); Lacan talks of 'the pre-eminently original object, the abyss of the female organ from which all life comes forth' (Lacan, 1978b, 196).

The function of castration as the articulation of the subject in difference is brought down to a matter of sight, the articulation of the symbolic to a vision. Where the conception of the symbolic as movement and production of difference, as chain of signifiers in which the subject is effected in division, should forbid the notion of some presence from which difference is then derived; Lacan instates the visible as the condition of symbolic functioning, with the phallus the standard of the visibility required: seeing is from the male organ. The problem, moreover, is maintained, not eased, by the distinction between penis and phallus customarily asserted ... the phallus is a signifier, is not an object, not the penis, but the latter nevertheless is its consistence as symbol, the phallus is said to symbolise the penis which, strikingly visible, is the condition of the symbol ... The penis/phallus distinction-oscillation-relation is symptomatic: on the one hand, psychoanalysis points to the production of subject, unconscious, desire in the symbolic; on the other, it derives that production from the fact of a perceived castration – the woman's lack – in a theory of infantile sexuality; the penis/phallus is the join of the two emphases, the 'privileged signifier of that mark in which the part of the logos comes together with the advent of desire' (Lacan, 1966, 692; 1977, 287)[1] where the privilege can only be founded from a difference in nature *to be seen*; a recognition of lack is given outside of any signifying process as a fact of each individual subject with a return in the symbolic – the phallic function – that ties process to vision. What is at stake and shut off in the logic of the penis/phallus is the history of the subject in as far as that history might include effects of social organisation, and, for example, of patriarchal order. That such a logic may really describe the production of subjectivity in a relation of sexual difference in a patriarchal society is not necessarily in question; that production, however, cannot be inverted – except to reproduce and confirm its established terms – into the fixed point of an origin, the translation of a vision. The vision, any vision, is constructed, not given; appealing to its certainty, psychoanalysis can only repeat the ideological impasse of the natural, the mythical representation of things.

The woman who is there in psychoanalysis, whom it hears, is the hysteric. Hysteria, as is well enough known, has its importance as the very beginning of psychoanalysis: Freud attends Charcot's famous 'lessons' in the Salpêtrière, interests himself in Breuer's experience with Anna O and the 'talking cure', publishes with Breuer the *Studies on Hysteria* ('the starting point of psychoanalysis'), moves back, across the recognition of the importance of the sexual element, from the clinical definition of hysteria accomplished by Charcot to its understanding as a psychological disturbance now posed as an implication of the subject in specific unconscious mental processes; from compression of the ovaries to compression of the brain, the hand pressing on the patient's forehead, to the final analytic situation, only the contact of speech, association, interpretation. It is with the hysteric that psychoanalysis encounters symptom as meaning, the other scene that speaks across the body, a knowledge produced from the subject as effect: 'The hysteric produces knowledge. The hysteric is an effect, as every subject is an effect . . .' The discourse of hysteria is not just a beginning of psychoanalysis, it is, in its forcing of the signifying matter, a fundamental condition. When Lacan identifies four basic positions of discourse, that of the analyst is a quarter of a turn away from that of the hysteric which is its constant attention; analysis is said to be nothing other than the structural introduction of the discourse of the hysteric, the analyst is 'a perfect hysteric, that is, without symptoms' (Lacan, 1976a, 12)[2]. This function of hysteria, the appeal to the discourse of the hysteric, is not as such implicated in any division based on sexual difference and it should be remembered that Charcot and Freud after him insisted on a reappropriation of the disturbance of hysteria outside of its limitation as a female condition . . . Yet, at the same time, hysteria constantly comes back to the woman: already in Freud (the *Studies on Hysteria* are all of women), today in psychoanalysis in the obligatory reference in analytic writing concerned with questions of the female to hysteria; the latter reference is so strong indeed that 'feminine' and 'hysterical' are taken as more or less interchangeable . . .

The success of Freud and psychoanalysis with female hysteria was an understanding of it as a problem of sexual identity in phallic terms: the hysteric is unsure as to being woman or man . . . hers is a body in trouble with language, that forcing of the signifying matter, resisting and accepting simultaneously the given signs, the given order. Listening to the woman as hysteric, psychoanalysis opens and closes the other scene, with the point of closure exactly 'sexual identity', 'sexual difference'; hence, symptomatically, the curious lag of psychoanalysis felt by Freud with regard to femininity, women still the great enigma, the 'dark continent' . . . curious just because of that beginning with hysteria, the cures with women, the attention focused there. When Dora, subject of a case which is published in confirmation of the theses set out in the *Studies on Hysteria* (Freud, SE, 7: 3–122), politely disappears from Freud's sight on the last day of 1900, interrupts her treatment, she breaks with a Freud, with an analysis, caught up in a logic of sexual identity and difference unable to envisage any other economy (thus unable, for example, to engage with what it could only anyway see as her 'homosexuality'). In every sense, psychoanalysis answered to the hysteria it realised as its initial and decisive object: what works is identity, the phallus, that difference, having or not, variations from there, with the woman as other, less and more, falling short and beyond; start from the hysteric, the problem of identity, focus centrally the term of identity with the male as measure, as standard . . . come back to the woman as as yet, as always, unknown ... – the lag is produced by the logic, the woman can only be 'the woman', *different from*. For centuries, hysteria has named an incapacity to take that place, to be the difference, 'the woman'. To explain hysteria by the problem of sexual identity is to miss the struggle in female hysteria against *that* assumption of difference, against *that* identity, is to refind hysteria as a nature of women and not the site of a resistance – nothing to do with an essence – in culture.

...

II

The spectacle of the woman then, the more and the less of *Encore* with its Freudian question as to what woman wants; in the first instance, the main theses of Lacan's answer, how the question works:

(a) *There is no sexual relation*, this being the very reality of psychoanalysis: 'the only basis of analytic discourse is the statement that there is no – that it is impossible to pose – sexual relation' (Lacan, 1975a, 14). No sexual relation does not mean no relation to a sex; on the contrary, this latter relation is precisely what is at stake in the function of castration which is in fact the point of the absence of the former. The division of the subject in the symbolic, in the desire of the Other, is the impossibility of any unity of relation: 'in so far as it is sexual, *jouissance* is phallic, which is to say that it does not relate to the Other as such' (Lacan, 1975a, 14); 'the *jouissance* of the Other taken as a body is always inadequate' (Lacan, 1975a, 131) Male or female, the subject is implicated from and in the phallus, phallic *jouissance*, but differently: there is a male and a female way of failing relation. In other words, the structure of a subject is a division in the symbolic; that division is not the fact of some immediately given sexual difference, men and women are not complementary to one another, two halves that could be joined in union, both are produced in division; the phallus is the term of that production in as much as it functions as the signifier in the articulation of castration; male and female differ in consequence of the phallic function in castration, are in the position of a different relation to phallus and castration; thus there can be no sexual relation, only a relation to phallic *jouissance*, in the woman as in the man.

(b) *The woman is not-all*: 'the woman is defined from a position that I've noted as not-all in respect of phallic *jouissance*' (Lacan, 1975a, 13). The woman cannot really sustain phallic *jouissance*, her relation to the phallus as term of symbolic castration is lacking: 'in her body' she is 'not-all as sexed being', 'the sexed being of these women not-all passes not via the body but via what results from a logical requirement of discourse' (Lacan, 1975a, 15); 'the woman is not-all, there is always something with her which eludes discourse' (Lacan, 1975a, 34). The gist of this is that in as far as the phallus marks the turn of the symbolic representation of the sexual, the woman is not all – not quite, not whole, not completely – in that representation: she misses out on the phallus and misses in the discourse which it organises and which is the relay of her excess, her sexuality.

(c) *Everything revolves round phallic jouissance.* Sexual *jouissance* is phallic, *jouissance* – enjoyment, pleasure – of the organ; it is not a sexual relation, a relation to the Other as such. The order of the symbolic, the phallus being the privileged signifier of that order, causes and limits *jouissance*, the phallic being that limitation, and for both men and women: the woman is caught up in *phallic jouissance* but not-all, there is 'something more', 'a supplementary *jouissance*' (Lacan, 1975a, 68–9); the man sustains phallic *jouissance* which is then the obstacle that prevents him from really enjoying the body of the woman, what he has is 'the enjoyment of the organ' (Lacan, 1975a, 13). Thus, 'the enjoyment of the Other ... is something else again, namely the not-all' (Lacan, 1975a, 26).

(d) *There is a jouissance beyond the phallus which is the jouissance of the woman.* 'When I say that the woman is not-all and that it is for that reason that I cannot say *the* woman, it is precisely because I am raising the question of a jouissance which in regard of everything which serves in the phallic function is of the order of the infinite' (Lacan, 1975a, 94).

(e) *The woman is that which relates to the Other.* Woman *and* Other 'locus of the signifying cause of the subject' (Lacan, 1966, 841), are not-all, more and less than the order of the phallus, radically other: 'The Other is not simply that locus of the stammering of truth ... By her being in the sexual relation, in relation to what can be said of the unconscious, radically the Other, the woman is that which relates to the Other' (Lacan, 1975a, 75). Woman is equivalent to trust, 'at least for the man' (Lacan, 1975a, 108); the questions of the desire of the Other and the desire of the woman are one and the same, the question of the truth: '*What does woman want?* – woman being on the occasion the equivalent of the truth' (Lacan, 1975a, 115).

(f) *Thus (the jouissance of) the woman is in the position of God.* The Other is the only place left 'in which to put the term God' (Lacan, 1975a, 44). Since the Other 'must have some relation to what appears of the other sex' (Lacan, 1975a, 65), 'why not interpret a face of the Other, the God face, as supported by feminine *jouissance*?' (Lacan, 1975a, 71); 'it is in as much as her *jouissance* is radically other that the woman has more relation to God' (Lacan, 1975a, 77); in the *jouissance* of the woman one can mark that 'God has not yet made his exit' (Lacan, 1975a, 78).

'Nothing can be said of the woman' (Lacan, 1975a, 75), but Lacan in *Encore* does nothing but talk of the woman (concerned perhaps to give 'a real consistency to the Women's Movement') (Lacan, 1975a, 69). True, at one level 'the woman' is emptied of any essence, produced in function of a symbolic order, but that function itself is universal, 'the woman part of speaking beings' (Lacan, 1975a, 74) and the woman everywhere returns in her common places – close to unconscious, Other, Truth, and God. To say that the 'the' of 'the woman', 'definite article designating the universal' (Lacan, 1975a, 68), is to be crossed out, barred through, is in no way to challenge the universalisation;

indeed, it is its very renewal, another turn of the screw, the same discourse of the essence continues: 'there is no woman but excluded by the nature of things which is the nature of words ...' (Lacan, 1975a, 68).

When psychoanalysis produces woman, the woman, as not-all, it falls short, remains locked in a static assignation. It is not the woman who is not-all but psychoanalysis, which is what the latter has been so generally unwilling to grasp. Psychoanalysis discovers and ceaselessly fails – in its theory – the unconscious, and that failure is history, the social relations of production, classes, sexes. It is not by chance that Lacan devotes a year's seminar to 'What does woman want?' ... at the very time that 'the woman', as women, is intervening against the given relations, for social transformation, and with a political claim on psychoanalysis in the theoretical constructions and concepts it elaborates.

There is in Lacan's writing the presence of an unquestioned imaginary of the woman. When he expresses his enthusiastic liking for Benoît Jacquot's *L'Assassin musicien*, what strikes him, a bubbling fascination, is the little girl – a little girl is 'a virtual woman, hence a being much more engaged in the real than males' (Lacan, 1975b, 187) – and above all her spontaneity, her naturalness, a real little girl (Lacan, 1976b, 64). Somewhere, for Lacan, the woman is always the exact image of herself, contained such as she is, on the God face of the Other, infinitely unknowable, knowable only as the different, visibly, certainly that. Thus the image of Saint Teresa, the sureness of the religious representation, the woman held as the truth of that view ...

III

Lacan's work is vastly more important than the position he is led to develop, the worst stereotypes he grotesquely rejoins and repeats. That importance, the sense of the 'return to Freud', is the attention given to the constitution of the subject in the symbolic and the relation of the unconscious there, with questions of sexuality posed accordingly ...

Lacan comes back to the relation of sexuality in the symbolic constitution of the subject. Language is the condition of the unconscious, which latter is a concept forged on the trace of what operates to constitute the subject. Caused in language, which is division and representation, the subject is taken up as such in an interminable movement of the signifier, the process of the symbolic, and in a structure of desire, the implication of the subject's experience of division, of lack, in language. Hence the importance of language for psychoanalysis as the site of its object, unconscious desire; to grasp language as the condition of the unconscious is to insist on desire in language and to make the subject the term of a constant construction and representation, outside of the expression of any unity, biological included. 'Analytic discourse allows us to glimpse that it is through language that man is separated, blocked from everything concerning the sexual relation, and that it is thereby that he enters the real, more precisely that he is lacking in this real' (Lacan, 1976a, 120). There is no sexual relation because there is no one, no two together, man and woman given complementarily; language is and recounts a division which constitutes the subject in relation to the Other not to any one, the Other as point of the distribution-circulation of signifiers within which the subject is produced in a structure of desire, 'the desire of man is the desire of the Other' (Lacan, 1966, 693; 1977, 288). Desire passes through, is in relation to the Other, not through or to some 'partner', is a function of the subject in language in its implication of the unconscious: 'The function of desire is a last residuum of the effect of the signifier in the subject' (Lacan, 1973a, 141; 1978, 154).[3]

In order to advance a little further in this context, the following passage may be quoted in which Lacan refers sexuality in the subject to lack and goes on to specify the overlap of two lacks:

> ... what must be done, as man or as woman, the human being has always to learn entirely from the Other ...
>
> That it be the drive, the partial drive, that orientates the human being in the field of sexual fulfilment, that it be the partial drive alone that is the representative in the psyche of the consequences of sexuality, there is the sign that sexuality is represented in the psyche by a relation of the subject that is deduced from something other than sexuality itself. Sexuality is established in the field of the subject by a path that is that of lack.
>
> Two lacks overlap here. The first has to do with the central default around which turns the dialectic of the advent of the subject to its own being in the relation to the Other – by the fact that the subject depends on the signifier and that the signifier is first of all in the field of the Other. This lack takes up the other lack which is the real, initial lack, to be situated at the advent of the living being, that is, in the fact of sexed reproduction. The real lack is what the living being loses, of its portion of living, in reproducing itself through the way of sex. This lack is real because it relates to something real, namely, that the living being, by its being subject to sex, has fallen under the jurisdiction of individual death. (Lacan, 1973a, 186; 1978, 204–5)

Effectively, the passage reformulates the join of the biological and the psychological seen at issue in Freud. On the sexual hinge species, individual and subject, and the hinge is the overlap of the two lacks. The species exists through its individuals who are transitory in the function of its reproduction, the assurance of its continuation; hence 'the presence of sex in the living being is bound up with death' (Lacan, 1973a, 162; 1978, 177). The individual exists as subject in the relations of the symbolic, the human being is a speaking subject, which is the condition of unconscious and desire, the articulation of sexuality for the individual as subject. The biological apparatus is returned –

parasited ... – by the production of the signifier, its representation of the subject, its process of the body. When Lacan stresses the fundamental role of drive, it is exactly as the point of this return ... : 'sexuality comes into play only in the form of partial drives; the drive is precisely that montage by which sexuality participates in the psychical life' (Lacan, 1973a, 160; 1978, 176); 'with regard to the instance of sexuality, all subjects are equal, from the child to the adult: their dealings are solely with what of sexuality passes in the networks of the constitution of subjectivity, in the networks of the signifier; sexuality is realised only through the operation of the drives in so far as they are partial drives, partial with regard to the biological finality of sexuality' (Lacan, 1973a, 161; 1978, 176–7). Drives, then, are 'the echo on the body of the fact of language' (Lacan, 1975c, 8): the frontier between 'the mental and the physical' across the individual is an overlap, joining and disjoining, the partiality of the return, the circuit, of drives out of line with the simple biological finality of sexuality, reproduction; in its subjectivity, caused by language, the individual is excessive with regard to that finality, with the terms of the excess being unconscious, desire, death. What is crucial, in other words, is not the relation between masculine and feminine but that between the living subject and its loss in the sexual cycle of reproduction; 'In this way I explain the essential affinity of every drive with the zone of death, and reconcile the two sides of drive – which at once gives the presence of sexuality in the unconscious and represents, in its essence, death' (Lacan, 1973a, 181; 1978, 199).

It is in this perspective that sexuality is to be understood as the reality of the unconscious: sexuality is not a 'content' of the unconscious but a process, the process of desire – 'in our experience, sexual desire has nothing objectified about it' (Lacan, 1978b, 263). The desire of the subject from its division in the field of the Other, in the symbolic, is the relation of sexuality for the individual subject; desire is that 'nodal point by which the pulsation of the unconscious is linked to sexual reality' (Lacan, 1973a, 141; 1978, 154). Thus it becomes difficult to establish a difference expressible as male unconscious/female unconscious (this is one aspect of Freud's conception of libido – the force of the presence of desire, the dynamic manifestation in mental life of sexual drive – as 'masculine': 'active' in both men and women): the unconscious is the fact of the division of the subject in the symbolic, not of the male from the female; the mechanisms of desire, the dialectic of subject and object, fully engage the bisexual disposition of the individual. Yet to indicate that difficulty is not to suggest a simple indifference, it is to stress only that difference must be specified in respect of the division in the symbolic, of the history of the subject. In psychoanalysis, such specification depends on the phallus, the privileged signifier; the variety of mental structures that overrun the anatomical differ-ence of the sexes has nevertheless a fixed reference, phallic sexual difference.

The joining-disjoining overlap of the biological by the mental as the turn of the subject allows a quite radical conception of sexuality, allows the possibility of a quite other posing of difference. Sexuality is not given in nature but produced; the individual subject is not constructed from sexuality, sexuality is constructed in the history of the subject, with difference a function of that construction not its cause, a function which is not necessarily single (on the contrary) and which, *a fortiori*, is not necessarily the holding of that difference to anatomical difference (phallic singularity). Production, construction in the history of the subject, sexuality engages also from the beginning, *and thereby*, the social relations of production, classes, sexes – an engagement which cannot be, the lesson of psychoanalysis, a reduction but which equally, the lesson of the limiting certainties of psychoanalysis against the effective implications of its theory, cannot be left aside, for later, beyond the enclosure of an analytically defined area.

An example in this context, fairly small but significant. Exploring the idea of the sexual reality of the unconscious, Lacan speculates, with a panoply of supporting references to the study of mitosis, the maturation of sexual cells, chromosomes, and so on, that 'it is through sexual reality that the signifier came into the world' (Lacan, 1973a, 138; 1978, 151). If that speculation is accepted, then the effect, contrary to the fundamental emphases of the psychoanalytic theory developed by Lacan, is to make sexual reality the condition of the symbolic, hence of the unconscious – of which it is thus, finally, as original sexual 'reality', the content. Lacan is close here to Freud's laying down of arms before the ultimate reality of the great enigma of the biological fact of the duality of the sexes (note in both Freud and Lacan the appeal beyond psychoanalysis, to science, the answer that must lie within the province of biology). In the theory, there is no place for sexual reality as foundation, as nature; the reality of sexuality is bound up with the reality of the symbolic construction of the subject – what returns is a history, unconscious desire, not the expression of an origin. That Lacan can nevertheless countenance the idea of the latter, can run analysis back into biology and myth, is symptomatic. The constant limit of the theory is the phallus, the phallic function, and the theorisation of that limit is constantly eluded, held off, and, for example, by collapsing castration into a scenario of vision; to say that it is through sexual reality that the signifier comes into the world is not far from deriving the phallus as privileged signifier from an essence in nature and not from an order of the symbolic – but then the problem, the debate, is precisely there.

IV

It is that problem, that debate, that will now be of concern in connection with the production of sexuality and the question of difference. The body is worked over in the symbolic, is sexed from its passage there, articulation of castration, moment of lack, drama of the subject. The phallus is given as the signifier of lack and the measure of desire, the veritable function of the symbolic: 'the phallus . . . is the signifier of the very loss the subject suffers by the fragmentation of the signifier' (Lacan, 1966, 715); 'the phallus . . . is the signifier destined to designate the whole set of effects of signified, in that the signifier conditions them by its presence as signifier' (Lacan, 1966, 690; 1977, 285); the phallus, in fact, is thus what *makes exchange* (of subject, language, body). The site of castration is the body of the mother, with the father possessor and figure of the phallus, guarantor of the order of the symbolic; 'it is when the father is deficient in one way or another (dead, absent, blind even) that the most serious neuroses are produced' (Lacan, 1949, 317). Mother and infant are two, that is, one, the imaginary possibility of a unity; the third, the father, makes two, assures the phallus as term of division in each individual subject; never the complementarity of two subjects, the division between them, but always the drama of the subject in the field of the Other, the experience of its lack-in-being, its being from lack, the lack of which the phallus is the signifier, inscribing its effects in the unconscious, in the gap between enunciation and enounced, a logic of the subject in the symbolic. That logic is then specified as a dialectic of being and having in which male and female positions can be distinguished: 'One can, simply by reference to the function of the phallus, indicate the structures that will govern the relations between the sexes. Let us say that these relations will turn around a being and a having ... with regard to a signifier, the phallus ...' (Lacan, 1966, 694; 1977, 289).[4] Man and woman are not together in a sexual relation but each separate in the relation of phallic *jouissance*: the man invests the woman as being the phallus, giving what she does not have, denies the function of castration; the woman invests the man as having the phallus, wishing to be the phallus for him, desiring his castration. In short, the phallus as privileged signifier, the constant and final meaning of symbolic exchange, for men and for women.

...

It is true that no sexual revolution will shift dividing lines, the problem is one of social revolution. Privileging the sexual has nothing necessarily liberating about it; on the contrary, the sexual functions only too readily as an instance by development of and reference to which the social guarantees its order outside of any real process of transformation, produces exactly a containing ideology of 'liberation'. It is much the same story as with the inclusion in the theory of the possibility of the idea that 'it is through sexual reality that the signifier came into the world'. Hold to such an idea and difference will easily return as nature, not within the terms of a symbolic production; which is what patriarchy has always asserted, pinning women down to their sex, to a sex: the woman as the difference in nature. The political question is the avoidance of any collapse into that difference (which is to deny any difference, to accept the term of the given order, the interminable same of the phallus). A question, for example, of what from the perspective of that given order can appear as a radical desexualisation, and which is nothing other than the reposing of sexuality in its symbolic and social production. Paradoxically perhaps at first view, this may well be one of the decisive aspects of the insistence as to the extensiveness of women's sexuality: 'the woman has sexes all over' (Irigaray, 1977, 28) ... Which is to say that in current ideological struggle it is not enough to assert in opposition women's relation to a non-genital, 'dispersed' sexuality, since such an emphasis (more-over close to Freud, who can talk of a feminine sexuality 'dispersed over the body from head to foot': Freud, SE, 12: 33) is a powerful representation of woman from within, and as part of, the existing oppression, woman as a kind of total equivalent of sex, her identity there; the need is precisely to come back on the production of sexuality, women and men (the reduction of sexuality to genitality in their representation), and to understand the history of the subject in difference from there, in the social relations of its symbolic order, in a possibility of transformation.

...

If a sexual reality is the condition of the symbolic, that through which the signifier comes into the world, then there is little to do, nature wins; if sexuality is always a symbolic production, then there is a place for a politics of the unconscious, for, that is, a grasp of the unconscious not as closed but as historically open, taken up in the historical process of its realisations, existing in transformation. The equation of woman and unconscious leads only to essence; the raising of questions as to the operation of an equation between the feminine and the unconscious as assignment of a place of woman and its complex effects with regard to resistance from that place within a history and economy of repression is a fully political task. It is the task engaged, for example, by the work of Irigaray ... its force the consideration of the links between current designations of the unconscious and the definition of the feminine, of the traces to be followed in those links of different logics, different economies ...

> Can I sketch out something of the content of what this other unconscious, woman's unconscious, would be?' No, of course not, since that supposes detaching the feminine from the present economy of the unconscious. It would be to anticipate a certain historical process and check its inter-pretation and movement by prescribing, as from now, themes and con-tents to the feminine unconscious. I could say, however, that there is something that has been singularly ignored, scarcely broached, in the theory of the unconscious: *the relation of the woman to the mother and the relation of women amongst themselves*. But would this, for all that, be a sketch of the 'content' of the 'feminine' unconscious? No. It is merely a question addressed to the way in which the functioning of the unconscious is interpreted. Why are psychoanalytic theory and practice so far so poor and reductive as regards those matters? Can the latter find a better interpretation in a patriarchal-type economy and logic? In the Oedipal systematic their formulation supposes? (Irigaray, 1977, 123–4)

A further issue arising is that of a determination by the problematic situation in the symbolic of a specific relation of woman and imaginary. Irigaray herself, often effectively thematically substantialising her question of the unconscious and the feminine and indeed running the feminine back into an anatomically mimetic expression of the body, stresses the 'rejection', the 'exclusion' of a feminine imaginary, a particular unfolding of woman's desire (Irigaray, 1977, 29). More generally, the idea of the woman's negative position in the symbolic order leads to emphasis on 'her privileged relation to the imaginary dyad, she is bound to the principle of reversibility which it contains' (Rose, 1976/7, 102), where the imaginary is a site of reference to the pre-Oedipal bond of daughter-mother (remember Lemoine-Luccioni's focus on the doubling of woman, mother and child): 'the imaginary also contains the realm of pre-Oedipality to which the sexuality of the woman is bound ... a repressed reference to the pre-Oedipal relation between the mother and the girl-child' (Rose, 1976/7, 102). In this form, the argument is in keeping with the view developed by Freud, the very term, 'pre-Oedipus phase' being introduced in the context of his late considerations of female sexuality and hinging on the surprise at the importance and intensity of the original attachment of girl to mother ('our insight into this early, pre-Oedipus, phase in girls comes to us as a surprise, like the discovery in another field of the Minoan-Mycenaean civilisation behind the civilisation of Greece': Freud, *SE*, 21: 226). The modern argument takes up the differentiation of men and women in terms of the significance of the pre-Oedipal ('the phase of exclusive attachment to the mother, which may be called the pre-Oedipus phase, possesses a far greater importance in women than it can have in men; many phenomena of female sexual life which were not properly understood before can be fully explained by reference to this phase': Freud, *SE*, 21: 230). and values the latter as difference, a specificity of the woman (no value is attributed by Freud to the strength of the pre-Oedipus phase; on the contrary, a major factor in the length and circuitousness of the path to the feminine form of the Oedipus complex which is all too often not surmounted at all, it marks the woman out as in some sense unfinished, apt for regression, slightly archaic). Montrelay offers a powerful development of this argument through her conception of a feminine primary imaginary, the woman confronted always on her own body with the original enjoyment of the mother, doubled in that: 'For the woman enjoys her body as she would the body of another. Every occurrence of a sexual kind (puberty, erotic experiences, maternity, etc) *happens to her* as if it came from a feminine other; every occurrence is the fascinating actualisation of *the* femininity of all women, but also and above all, of that of the mother. It is as if "to become a woman", "to be woman" gave access to a *jouissance* of the body as feminine *and/or* maternal. In the self-love she bears herself, the woman cannot differentiate her own body from that which was "the first object"' (Montrelay, 1977, 69; 1978, 91). What is then needed is the rediscovery, the revaluation of that body of the imaginary: 'Can we not ask ourselves whether the imaginary, by giving "consistency" (as Lacan puts it) to the symbolic which is a gap, is not just as operative, just as determining of the structure as are the real and the symbolic? Giving consistency, giving body to the symbolic dividing up: that operation preceeds any possible grasp of the subject in its image and that of the other. A primary imaginary exists which is not without its relation with feminine *jouissance*' (Montrelay, 1977, 155–6).

The movement that links feminine and imaginary and understands a specificity of and for women from there brings with it, again, problems of the foundation of difference. To define a difference on the basis of this imaginary, taken as specific value, with characteristic effects of stressed relations between woman and narcissism, regression, and so on, can seem very quickly to repeat a definition maintained in the existing order, whose own imaginary, and imagery, of the woman is heavily implicated in attributions of defining narcissism (woman and the mirror …) …

Perhaps it could be added here, a little aside, that the imaginary and the specular are not, as is too commonly thought, a simple equivalence; the latter – reflections, mirrorings, imagings – is part of the former but does not exhaust it. The analytic account of the construction of the subject is not one of a simple progression from imaginary to symbolic. True, Lacan sets the imaginary very precisely in the biographical moment of the mirror stage, but that is not to make it in any sense original, primary: symbolic, real are always there; the subject is a representation of the signifier held in a structuration which is the shifting imbrication – the knotting – of real, symbolic and imaginary, the latter modelling desire in the subject's image of itself from the structure, not some separate area prior to the subject that it is given in some way to possess. If imaginary and specular are taken as equivalent, the conception of the imaginary slides easily towards such a priority, the area to be repossessed, a separate enclosure; where the need is much rather to avoid limiting the imaginary to a biographical evolution of the individual, to grasp that it is a necessary and permanent function of the history of the subject, and, simultaneously, of the subject in history. It can then no longer be a question of 'rediscovering' (nor, conversely, of 'abandoning'), but one of displacing, transforming …

The preceding addition is finally not so intrusive since the one thing that has been constantly stressed here is that if there is a way of thinking that works in the specular-imaginary, it is well and truly that of difference – the establishment of the difference of one and the other sides from the fact of the biological division of the sexes, with its consequent motion of reversal of images, from side to side, the same images. Difference in these terms is always treacherous, reactionary; a tourniquet operates in which the real necessity to claim difference binds back, and precisely from the difference claimed, into the renewal of the same, a reflection of the place assigned, assigned as difference. Patriarchy, men in its order, has never said anything but that women are – the woman is –

different: they are *not men*, the difference maintained supports the status quo, the difference derived, derived ideologically, from nature, the appeal to the biological, 'undeniable'. The problem, for men as for women, is to pose specificity away from the specularity of difference; which means a critical attention to the certainties of difference, the certainty of the phallus, proposed in and from psychoanalysis itself.

. . .

VI

In discussions of a specifically feminine writing, emphasis is often put on the voice: 'all the feminine texts that I have read are very close to the *voice*, are very close to the flesh of the language, much more than in masculine texts' (Cixous, 1976, 14). A closeness to the voice as a trace of the intensity of the attachment to the mother: 'to write in the feminine is to put over what is cut off by the symbolic, the voice of the mother, it is to put over what is most archaic' (Cixous, 1976, 14); a closeness in the voice to words 'as in the first moments of life when they extended the body of the mother and simultaneously circumscribed the place of suspension of her desire' (Montrelay, 1977, 64; 1978, 87); a voice imagined in the field of the Other as invocation of the mother, movement through words to the invocatory 'grain of the voice' (Barthes, 1977, 182)

The emphasis is on the voice as against the look; in women's texts, writes Montrelay, 'no contour is traced on which the eye could rest' (Montrelay, 1977, 153). The look is a distance, an absence of grain[5] is 'theoretical' in Hegel's use of the term in the *Aesthetik* to privilege vision over the other senses: 'vision, on the contrary, finds itself in a purely theoretical relationship with objects, through the intermediary of light, that immaterial matter which truly leaves objects their freedom, lighting and illuminating without consuming them' (Hegel, 1927–8, 254).[6] Irigaray reverses the valuation in that description for women: 'Investment in the look is not privileged in women as in men. More than the other senses, the eye objectifies and masters. It sets at a distance, maintains the distance. In our culture, the predominance of the look over smell, taste, touch, hearing has brought an impoverishment of bodily relations. It has contributed to disembodying sexuality. The moment the look dominates, the body loses in materiality (Irigaray, 1978, 50). Cixous talks of 'looking with closed eyes' (1977, 487).

> She looked very lovely under her black hair hung loose over her neck and bosom, sparkling with drops to imitate dew, and it seemed a pity that only ladies were to look at her.
>
> Gustave was made to kneel down on the ground in front of the sofa, and support a round mirror, before which the wilful little lady had elected to try on the silken hose and dainty boots.

These brief passages are from a work of nineteenth-century pornography (an example of the common whipping literature of the period), the author and narrator of which is given as being a woman (Anson, 1857). This proposition of female author/narratorship is a convention that doubles over from and against itself in the spectacle of the book's discourse. The desire is the intimacy of the woman, the order of women, for the man, the intimacy existing only from the term of its intrusion, the male gaze; what is said is the intact beauty of the woman, all her flawless brilliance, and the absence of a look ('it seemed a pity ...') which is thus simultaneously present, in the enunciation, the very point of the passage and the point from which it is written, the spectacle constructed. The book's scenes are, without surprise, those of the whole panoply of the male, a mixture of voyeurism and fetishism: the young Gustave, man allowed into the fiction as child in order to preserve the intimacy and the fetishistic moment, at the woman's feet, holding the mirror, the spectator and the spectacularity of the woman, the objects of disavowal and its erotic – hose, boots. No doubt that the writing is a representation-representing in which subjects are joined in the perspective of 'the man' and 'the woman' from the site – and from the sight – of the man as model of the elaboration-translation of desire; the woman author/narrator is a fiction – and had a woman been the book's writer, she would have been that fiction of the man, a term of its repeated order. All this, it might be added, is not too far from Lacan's writing of St Teresa: there is an intimacy of the woman, a certain aura, call it *jouissance*, the truth of which it is ceaselessly necessary to surprise, to catch in the veil of its images with a look that masters, preserving the certainty, 'you only have to go and look ...'

... Freud poses from early on a libidinal investment in looking to see, in seeing: 'A desire to see the organs peculiar to each sex exposed is one of the original components of our libido ... The libido for looking ... is present in everyone in two forms, active and passive, male and female; and, according to the preponderance of the sexual character, one form or the other predominates' (Freud, SE, 8: 98). The pleasure in looking is in relation to knowledge which makes use of it, the looking to see, to know the other body. It was emphasised earlier how important to Freud is the appeal to the look to establish castration: boy and girl *see* the lack.

In this context, the following points may be noted:

(1) Seeing for Freud is 'an activity that ultimately is derived from touching' (Freud, SE, 7: 156) which it thus extends and displaces.

(2) The eye as organ is the locus of at least two functions: 'the eyes perceive not only alterations in the external world which are important for the pre-servation of life, but also characteristics of objects which lead to their being chosen as objects of love – their charms' (Freud, SE, 11: 216). There are more or less serious disturbances if the two functions are not held together in unity and the sexual aspect begins to dominate; Freud notes in this connection 'pathological consequences if the two fundamental instincts are disunited and if the ego maintains a repression of the sexual component instinct concerned ...

the sexual component instinct which makes use of looking – sexual pleasure in looking – has drawn upon itself defensive action by the ego instincts in consequence of its excessive demands …' (Freud, *SE*, 11: 216). The classic example of such psychogenic disturbance of vision is provided by the 'blindness' often found in hysterics but Freud is at pains to stress equally the common experience of this 'blindness of the seeing eye' (*SE*, 2: 117).

(3) The common experience is had by men and women. The fact of the importance of that experience, at its extreme, in hysteria, in the case of the women who alone furnish the material for the *Studies on Hysteria*, links it as much with the latter as with the former. Yet it is not by chance that Freud's major illustration for the disturbance caused by the conflict of sexual and ego in vision is the story of Peeping Tom, the active scopophilia (pleasure in seeing) of voyeurism: 'As regards the eye, we are in the habit of translating the obscure psychical processes concerned in the repression of sexual scopophilia and in the development of the psychogenic disturbance of vision as though a punishing voice was speaking from within the subject and saying: "Because you sought to misuse your organ of sight for evil sensual pleasures, it is fitting that you should not see anything at all any more", and as though it was in this way approving the outcome of the process. The idea of talion punishment is involved in this, and in fact our explanation of psychogenic disturbance of vision coincides with what is suggested by myths and legends. The beautiful legend of Lady Godiva tells how all the town's inhabitants hid behind their shuttered windows, so as to make easier the lady's task of riding naked through the streets in broad daylight, and how the only man who peeped through the shutters at her revealed loveliness was punished by going blind' (Freud, *SE*, 11: 217). Not by chance because Freud's constant emphasis elsewhere is on libidinal investment in the eye as phallus; which is what is at stake in the Lady Godiva/Peeping Tom legend: the scene of the woman, the violation, the blinding-castration. As Freud puts it in the essay on 'The uncanny', which is perhaps the most important reference for this emphasis, 'the substitutive relation between the eye and the male organ … is seen to exist in dreams and myths and phantasies' (*SE*, 17: 231). One might cite, as a kind of condensation here, the recorded case of a male patient who identified his eye with a speculum and was then racked with the fear of his look becoming 'stuck' on things and his losing his sight (Chazaud, 1973, 119).

(4) Lacan has it that the scopic drive is 'that which most completely eludes the term of castration', referring at the same time to Freud's paper on 'Instincts and their vicissitudes' (Lacan, 1973a, 74; 1978, 78). In that paper, written just after that introducing narcissism (*SE*, 14: 69–102, 111–40), Freud identifies an initial autoerotic element in scopophilia, not formulated in the description quoted earlier from 'Jokes and their relation to the unconscious', which distinguishes it from other drives: 'for the beginning of its activity the scopophilic instinct is auto-erotic: it has indeed an object, but that object is the subject's own body' (*SE*, 14: 130). This is the context of the imbrication of

specular and imaginary and of the importance of the mirror stage; the perceived image of the body gives the principle of unity, the one, identity – an identity that can never be other than that imaginary, in which, through the look, castration can be eluded, held off.

(5) The imaginary can then be taken as 'before' sexual difference ... Yet the symbolic, division, is always there, and, for example, in the mirror stage in the surrounds of the child who sees, the person who holds, encourages, confirms, but also accompanies from the place of the other. The scopic drive may elude the term of castration but the look returns the other, castration, the other – the evil – eye. Hence Lacan's long account of the dialectic of eye and look. The look presents itself to us in an uncanny contingence, symbolic of 'the lack that constitutes castration anxiety' (1973a, 70; 1978, 73): your look is never from where I see, my look is never what I want to see. In this dialectic, however, the look is constantly evanescent, elided in the self-turning power of the investment in the eye, in seeing, in the constitution of the imaginary, in 'that form of vision that is satisfied with itself in imagining itself as consciousness' (1973a, 71; 1978, 74), consciousness in its illusion 'of *seeing itself seeing itself*, in which the look is elided' (1973a, 79; 1978, 82). The world is given itself as spectacle by the subject, as vision, something like a pure consciousness, at rest, indifferent, all seeing (with the ambiguity there the catch of the subject in the imaginary): 'The world is omnivoyeur, not exhibitionistic – it does not provoke our look. When it does begin to provoke it, then begins too the feeling of strangeness' (1973a, 71–2; 1978, 75). Note that Lacan compares this all-seeingness to 'the satisfaction of a woman who knows that she is being looked at, on condition that she is not shown it' (1973a, 71; 1978, 194).

The comparison is significant. Throughout the discussion of the eye/look dialectic, Lacan indicates no sexual differentiation as between male and female or masculine and feminine, yet such a differentiation is not absent, the comparison is its trace.

The eye/look dialectic functions as division, symbolises lack, sets the subject in the field of the desire of the Other, with the imaginary of the eye, the evanescence of the look, then defined as the eluding of the term of castration. Which term is that of the articulation of symbolic and sexual difference. The imaginary is never 'before', it is always from, from the symbolic construction of the subject, is a join of the subject, its identifications of desire. The difficulty in the theory is that castration is the term both of the division of the subject in the movement of symbolic difference and of a sexual difference that differentiates individual subjects as between male and female; it crosses, in other words, from universal function to effective realisation without doubt, with the latter thus becoming the constant form of the former and, in fact, its nature – we are back with Freud's 'inadequate empirical and conventional equation', Lacan's 'through sexual reality that the signifier came into the world'.

The castration that is posed and eluded in the shifts of the eye/look dialectic is a relation of the symbolic in a specific production of sexual difference. The difference is specific in Lacan's account which pulls towards a voyeurism that is its underlying order: the dialectic is also, immediately, the look of the man, the image of the woman, the satisfaction of a woman who knows she is being looked at'. Everything turns on the castration complex and the central phallus, its visibility and the spectacle of lack; the subject, as Lacan puts it at one point, 'looks at itself in its sexual member' (1973a, 177; 1978, 194), and delights in being seen from that look. What the voyeur seeks, poses, is not the phallus on the body of the other but its absence as the definition of the mastering presence, the security, of his position, his seeing, his phallus (Peeping Tom behind the shutters, penetrating the space of the other, holding its image . . .); the desire is for the other to be spectacle not subject, or only the subject of that same desire, its exact echo – the echo that Lacan hears to *his* satisfaction when he talks of that 'satisfaction of a woman who knows she is being looked at'. Fetishism too, which often involves the scopophilic drive, has its scenario of the spectacle of castration; and where what is at stake is not to assert that the woman has the penis-phallus but to believe in the intact, to hold that the woman is not castrated, that nothing is lost, that his representation, and of him, works. Always, from voyeurism to fetishism, the erotisisation of castration.

'*The* woman' is the support of this erotisation, the whole scene of the phallus, *is* representation. There is a painting by Magritte that is clear in this respect (clear not from any certainty to be seen but from the elements it assembles as a statement on that very certainty). Entitled *Representation* (*La représentation*, 1937, Penrose Collection, London), it shows the frame of a mirror in the form of a keyhole, with, on the surface of the mirror, filling its frame, the keyhole, the torso of a nude woman, with the line of the thighs in a perfect discretion of any sex. The woman is to be seen, completely, she is all seeing, satisfied in that always there in the mirror, hidden and visible, behind the keyhole; which is to say that, omnivoyeur, spectacle of vision, she has no look, provokes only in image and not as subject in return; and, above all, no look of her sex. The discretion of the sex in the Magritte painting is an important element in its statement on representation. The history of the nude in western art from classical times is one of the omission of a sex for the woman (where the penis is figured readily on any statue of the nude man): what is thus presented in her representation is not any lack, not the lack, but nothing, the fully intact, the body smooth without break, the scopophilic defence of 'beauty' (Fliess, 1956, 171–2). For beauty is exactly *the* woman as all, undivided in herself, the perfect image. 'Like a god, just as empty, beauty can say only: *I am as I am*' (Barthes, 1970, 40; 1974, 33), and, within the *I am as I am*, the *I saw myself seeing myself* which Lacan regards as the 'theme' of 'femininity': the contained spectacle, for me, the man, and, as my desire, the support of my representation, for herself.

Here, a problem can be posed as follows:[7] agreed, the terms of representation classically are those of the production and representing of woman as all, beauty to see, the woman; it is nevertheless the case that the coming of the photograph changes something: something that can be grasped, for example, in developments in social pornography (pornography of wide and open distribution in society, e.g. *Penthouse*) where what are now given are directly vaginal images.[8] That there is change is certain; as to the transformation of the economy of representation, the question is more difficult.

By its weight of reality ('record', 'reproduction'), the photograph disturbs the established order of art and beauty; hence a kind of balance of tensions in its immediate practice and conception: the photograph is too real, obliterates beauty, is thus not fitted for the depiction of the body (Nadar, for instance, disapproves of the use of photography for the nude); the photograph because of that real is to be directly exploited as a commerce of the body seen, as the possession of its actuality in image ... Obviously, that commerce is not without its relations to the established representations of art: various sublimations of the photographic real of the body through strategies of focus, lighting, retouching, and so on; various 'reframings', realignments to the same attention, as with the massive speculation on the photograph of the nude girl child, the female-not-a-sexed-woman, before 'stream and river meet'.[9] It remains, however, that the photograph is not the painting; it points to a real as an immediate – as an immediately visible – source of its image, says somewhere an actuality of a body, a once-present here-now. In the painting or sculpture, the sex of the woman is not 'hidden', there is nothing 'not seen'; the photograph, posing the woman discretely, reproduces perhaps the same figure as of the nude in art but brings with it a certain effect of the withheld, the out-of-sight. The completely satisfiable curiosity of the real that is the photograph's view, its ideological currency, is inevitably the compulsion to 'show everything', to 'really present' the sex of the woman, women's sexual organs (it then being, in a mirror reversal from classic representation in the history of art, the depiction of the male sex that is problematic, that lags behind, only very recently a possibility for social pornography – as though the penis-phallus hold might be threatened).

And yet ... and yet the real of the photograph is a real that is always an image; the veil, the completion of representation, persists, a whole imaginary of the body's presence. The real of the body, the body now in its symbolic relation in the process of the individual as subject, is discordant, takes voice from the unconscious ('as though, precisely, it was not from the unconscious that the body had voice') (Lacan, 1973b, 20) not from the photograph, which is always in a sense concordant, making an image. The photograph can only show and can never show the woman's sex, 'her' sexuality retained as exhibition. Something changes but the economy remains more or less stable, still of the order of phallic castration. One, the man, perhaps the woman in place in his perspective, is assured of the sex of the woman, as of his own thereby (the look as phallus); assured again and again, since the unit here is not the possible knowledge of a single photograph but the continual confirmation of the series, the exhaustion of all women, the guarantee of *the* woman, in this image. Pornography plays exactly the series: the resumption from scene to scene, film to film, from one photograph to the next, one magazine issue to another; according to a kind of metonymisation of the imaginary, the finite number standing open for the total number of women which would make the final *one*. At any moment, moreover, the confirmation can never be sure, since its only basis is in the movement of the accountability for vision, an interminable summing; the photographer Henri Maccheroni takes 2,000 photographs of one woman's sex, envisages a further set ... [10] No truth is produced with the multiplication of such photographs other than that the woman is the difference of the man who is reassured in his place, compulsively reposing the fact of his certainty, his vision: sex and sexuality are brought back to the sex, woman is her sex, the phallic stakes are won over and over.

What then of the look for the woman, of woman subjects in seeing? The reply given by psychoanalysis is from the phallus. If the woman looks, the spectacle provokes, castration is in the air, the Medusa's head is not far off; thus, she must not look, is absorbed herself on the side of the seen, seeing herself seeing herself, Lacan's femininity. By virtue of the doubling unity of her specular relation to the mother, parent of the same sex, the woman is specified as being in a particular, different relation to the scopic function, to pleasure in seeing: 'For the girl, the setting at a distance is a difficult experience. She prefers to tip over into the image guaranteed for her (as she believes) by the quite as captive look of the mother and, later, by the all powerful look of the father. So she prefers to believe in that image. She believes she is herself. She thus equates herself with the full and flawless figure, no crack, which preserves and is preserved by the parental authority. In so doing, she substitutes for the person of the mother crucial in the *fort/da* game her own person figured by her body in the specular image; an image that the mother's look brings out, "causes". It is an inverted *fort/da*, and it is the whole body which becomes the stake of symbolisation, with the consequent risks of fragmentation and hysterical paralyses. But in thus offering herself to the look, in giving herself for sight, according to the sequence: see, see oneself, give oneself to be seen, be seen, the girl – unless she falls into the complete alienation of the hysteric – provokes the Other to an encounter and a reply which give her pleasure' (Lemoine-Luccioni, 1976, 85).

...

NOTES

1. [Where two dates are given, these indicate, in the first instance, the original publication in French of Lacan's *Écrits*; the English language edition contains only a selection of the essays, but where an essay is reproduced, Stephen Heath has also quoted from that, although in some cases he may have modified the translation. JW]
2. 'without symptoms, except from time to time mistakes in gender' ...

3. [The two dates refer to the French and English editions respectively; throughout Heath may have modified the translation. JW]

4. The dialectic of having and being is suggested in a late note by Freud: '"Having" and "being" in children. Children like expressing an object-relation by an identification: "I am the object". "Having" is the later of the two; after loss of the object it relapses into "being" ...' (SE 23: 299).

5. Unless, for instance, grain is to be sought somewhere with regard to colour – colour which finally disturbs perspective representation in the history of painting, colour which is a factor in 'the perversion of the sense of sight', in the 'blindness' often noted in hysteria, a shift in the balance of the intensities of the normal state of colour vision (cf. Charcot, 1886, 427–34).

6. Hegel also admits hearing as a theoretical sense but only in so far as he can separate it from any of that intimacy with the body stressed as the reality of the voice in feminine writing.

7. The problem is suggested by Griselda Pollock (1977, 25–34).

8. 'A directness that radically questions the psychoanalytically based analyses of images of women undertaken by Claire Johnston and Laura Mulvey and the notions of castration fears and the phallic woman' (Pollock, 1977, 30).

9. 'About nine out of ten, I think, of my child friendships get shipwrecked at the critical point "where the stream and river meet", and the child friends, once so affectionate, become uninteresting acquaintances whom I have no wish to set eyes on again.' C. L. Dodgson (ed. Gernsheim, 1969, 18).

10. A sample of Maccheroni's work can be found in 'Trente-deux photographies du sexe d'une femme' (1977, 313–28).

5.2

USING LACAN:
READING *TO THE LIGHTHOUSE*

James M. Mellard

...

THE IMAGINARY AND 'THE WINDOW'

In 'The Window', the longest of the three parts of *To the Lighthouse*, Virginia Woolf produces a virtual paradigm of the various features of the Lacanian Imaginary. Characters (that is, the subjects of unconscious desire) in this passage are almost totally caught up in the dualities brought on by the completion of the mirror phase. That means ... that subjects are involved in identificatory or aggressive contacts with others, whether these others (*les autres*) represent aspects of the intra- or the intersubjective configuration ... the Imaginary is both social and highly individual as it draws real images into the intrapsychic realm of symbols and symbolization ...

Oedipus and Jouissance

The very first section of 'The Window' establishes the divisions of the subject in a quite primal way – the conflict of son with father across the body of the mother. The section, moreover, establishes this conflict in Lacanian terms – the 'No' of the father (cum Father of the Symbolic) that defines difference versus the 'Yes' of the mother (the primal other) that defines the same, similarity, or nondifferentiation of one (I, me) from the other (only incipiently a *you*). Woolf's initial (and youngest) subject is James, the Ramsays' six-year-old son. At that

Extract from James M. Mellard, *Using Lacan, Reading Fiction* (University of Illinois Press), pp. 140–94.

age he still belongs, as Woolf writes, 'to that great clan which cannot keep this feeling [of extraordinary joy] separate from that [feeling], but must let future prospects, with their joys and sorrows, cloud what is actually at hand' (9). Woolf attributes the boy's propensity here to a personality type, to 'such people' in whom 'even in earliest childhood any turn in the wheel of sensation has the power to crystallise and transfix the moment upon which its gloom or radiance rests' (9). But the psychological fact is that the extreme pleasure the child attaches to the mother's positive words – her 'Yes, of course, if it's fine tomorrow' (9) – are much more likely to occur in the child of any 'sort' who has not yet really internalized the Symbolic word or Law of the Father, the child who in short has not yet accepted the lessons of the Oedipal condition. At the moment of his mother's 'Yes,' young James remains more firmly attached to the other who is also (m)Other than to the law of difference and negation to come. His powerful libidinal investment in Mrs Ramsay thus, as Woolf suggests, not only transfixes the moment, it also 'endows' other objects (in the type of metonymical transfer one would expect) with the same joy, even 'endowed the picture of a refrigerator, as his mother spoke, with heavenly bliss' (9).

Perhaps the most significant aspect of this moment in setting the tenor of the novel is its expression of *jouissance*. But more than that, this moment suggests how a literary text is created as a textual unconscious and mirrors the human unconsciousness, which for Lacan is an unconscious texture if not precisely a text. The active function inhabiting a text is *jouissance*. *Jouissance*, as Lacan defines it, is more than mere pleasure or enjoyment. 'There is no adequate translation in English of this word,' writes Alan Sheridan in his translator's note to *Écrits: A Selection;* '"Enjoyment" conveys the sense, contained in *jouissance*, of enjoyment of rights, of property, etc. Unfortunately, in modern English, the word has lost the sexual connotations it still retains in French. (*Jouir* is slang for 'to come.') "Pleasure", on the other hand, is pre-empted by "plaisir" – and Lacan uses the two terms quite differently' ... In James's extraordinary bliss there is clearly [a] sense of the sexual contained in his *jouissance*, as well as a sense of his transgression of law. The law is here especially Oedipal, for James, illustrating Lacan's dictum that 'Desire is a metonymy,' expressly transfers his desire for union with his mother to the objects around him. 'It', Woolf writes of this moment for James, 'was fringed with joy. The wheelbarrow, the lawnmower, the sound of poplar trees, leaves whitening before rain, rooks cawing, brooms knocking, dresses rustling – all these were so coloured and distinguished in his mind that he had already his private code, his secret language' (9–10). His 'language' is no more than the 'secret language' of desire and the unconscious. While it would not be proper to call this the birth of desire and the unconscious in James, it clearly mimes that birth in the advent of the Oedipal realization.

The birth of desire, the development of language (that is, of symbolization), and the Oedipal conflict are all conjoined in Lacan's conception of a *jouissance* discovered in the pre-mirror-stage objects that cause desire ... 'By placing the roots of the pleasure principle in the Imaginary union between infant and (m)Other,' says Ragland-Sullivan, 'Lacan redefined the pleasure principle as *jouissance* or a sense of Oneness, and reshaped the reality principle to refer to the separation evoked by language and Law (Castration), which ends the mirror stage' (1986, 139). The moment Woolf portrays here in James underscores the 'sense of Oneness' of the child with the mother, but already there exists the displacement of the child's feeling from her to the objects surrounding her. The moment suggests, in other words, that young James has indeed passed through his mirror phase ... and is already aware of his differentiation from his mother and of his necessary submission to the father's law. The at least symbolic castration effected by the Oedipal passage has thus occurred, a psychic fact suggested in further details Woolf gives of ... his mother's investment in him (contra the father) of something of the Law: '... his mother, watching him guide his scissors neatly round the refrigerator, imagined him all red and ermine on the Bench or directing a stern and momentous enterprise in some crisis of public affairs' (10).

Whereas Mrs Ramsay only imagines her son on the bench (as a symbol of the Law), the Law as it appears in the Imaginary father is in fact present in this moment. It is expressed in Mr Ramsay, the boy's father, who utters the fateful word of negating contrariety – '*But*'. '"But," said his father, stopping in front of the drawing-room window, "it won't be fine"' (10). This *but* represents the Symbolic No-of-the-father, the principle of contradiction and differentiation that counters the desire for union or oneness symbolized by the mother and expressed in *jouissance*. With the father's word comes the end of James's moment of bliss, but with it also come the hostilities of the Oedipal conflict. Woolf is explicit. The weapon (phallic) the boy wants (lacks) is represented in the father (phallic):

> Had there been an axe handy, or a poker, any weapon that would have gashed a hole in his father's breast and killed him, there and then, James would have seized it. Such were the extremes of emotion that Mr. Ramsay excited in his children's breasts by his mere presence; standing, as now, lean as a knife, narrow as the blade of one, grinning sarcastically, not only with the pleasure of disillusioning his son and casting ridicule upon his wife, who was ten thousand times better in every way than he was (James thought), but also with some secret conceit at his own accuracy of judgement. (10)

Each point of the Oedipal triangle is represented here in son, mother, father. And the imagery – of phallic weapons, of a phallic father, and of a universally valorized mother – is just right for the termination of the momentary transgression of the Law in James's *jouissance*. But Woolf herself does not permit her text to remain caught in James's or the mother's position, for she makes it plain that young James has indeed learned the Oedipal lesson, even if he has not yet fully internalized it ...

The miniature Oedipal drama Woolf represents in the opening paragraphs of 'The Window' establishes the section's modality of character relations and internal drives. The focus of this longest of the novel's sections is, simply, pleasure, *jouissance*, the fulfillment of the desire (in Lacan's terms) that translates physical (biological) needs into demands. The direction of intra- and intersubjective relations here is always against the current of the Oedipal Law ... pleasure 'proceeds paradoxically along the Desiring path of investing passion in simultaneous efforts to recreate the bonds of an impossible unity through substitutes and displacements and, thereby, to deny the reality principle of Castration' (1986, 139). But, as young James's experience in this inaugural moment portends, this paradoxical motivation (both to recreate an original plenitude and to substitute for it or to displace it in other directions) does not separate Desire and Law, but, rather, conjoins them in the very structuration of the subject ...

Desire and L'Objet Petit A

The remainder of part 1 of 'The Window' extrapolates the Oedipal drama seen in the child's relation to mother and father. It also suggests how desire and objects (or aims) of desire operate to create a textual unconscious, as James's portion had, but also how the vicissitudes of desire generate suspense or *narrative* drive in the unconscious of the text. Mr and Mrs Ramsay ... stand for the mother and the father in the text and in their relations to all other characters. 'The Window' in effect belongs to Mrs Ramsay, the figure of the mother. Thus the focus of events (which, in the novel, are essentially moments of consciousness rather than action) is this woman on whom the others project their desires. The mother is always the primal source of the subject's desire, although her role as source is repressed into the unconscious after the passage through the mirror stage and the Oedipal realization. In the beginning, the pre-mirror-stage subject is in a relation of being to the mother: that is, the child simply *is* that which the mother desires; after the mirror stage, the child is in a relation of having or wanting to have: that is, it desires to possess that which the mother desires, though the child does not (and can never) have it (the phallus) nor can the mother either, since the lesson of the Oedipal rule imposed by the father is that she too lacks (is lacking) it. What happens thereafter is that the subject finds substitutes or displacements for the missing thing, now repressed into (and thereby forming) the unconscious. Those substitutes or displacements thus fill the space of Desire, and will ever after represent an alienation of the subject from that which it desires, now symbolized in objects, Lacan's other 'little things' representing the *autre* – the *objet petit a*. This dialectical movement from recognition of lack to a desire to fill it is well illustrated in the Ramsays' relations with Charles Transley.

Like young James, Charles Tansley is still visibly struggling with his Oedipal relationships. Since Tansley obviously is beyond the mirror stage in his psychic development, his desire is represented in substitutions for his mother and father. Mr and Mrs Ramsay are those substitutes. The very evident substitution in his attempts to *be* Mr Ramsay means of course that he wants to be the *thing* desired by the mother. In his turn, Tansley also is the focus of substitutory displacement, for the Ramsays' children displace hostility toward their father onto Tansley. The language of their disapproval, however, suggests just how little Tansley possesses the thing he desires – the phallus: 'He was such a miserable specimen, the children said, all humps and hollows' (15) – that is, to them he represents more a feminine (in those humps and hollows) than the masculine image he longs to project. To have that masculine image he operates by way of imitation. He expropriates the dictum (the words of the Law) of the real father: '"There'll be no landing at the Lighthouse tomorrow," said Charles Tansley' (15). And he imitates Mr Ramsay in other ways, particularly in his peripatetic and intellectual habits. 'They knew what he liked best – to be for ever walking up and down, up and down, with Mr. Ramsay, and saying who had won this, who had won that, who was "brilliant but I think fundamentally unsound"' (15). Object of jealous projections, Tansley is ... roundly detested because he reminds others of their castrations, at the same time he competes with them for the object of their desires.

Against all odds, Tansley does have his moment of *jouissance* with Mrs Ramsay. It comes as a result of her recognition of him and is localized in the displacement/substitute of the *objet a*, Lacan's *objet petit a*. First comes the desire to be desired, recognized, by the Other here represented in Mrs Ramsay. That recognition occurs because Mrs Ramsay ... takes pity on Tansley and asks him to join her in an errand to town. Mrs Ramsay thus engages Tansley in a 'plot' of advance and retreat, small gains followed by immediate losses. We see in it the rhythm of desire. Talking with her, for example, makes Tansley 'better pleased with himself than he had done yet.' Then appears the *objet a* of displacement, for immediately he focuses his desire not on her person so much as, metonymically, on one of the objects – 'her little bag' (20) – associated with her. He asks to carry it for her, but even when she demurs, saying she always carries it herself, there comes a swell of emotion, the onset of a soon-to-be realized affect that links him to his forbidden *jouissance*. 'She did too. Yes, he felt that in her. He felt many things, something in particular that excited him and disturbed him for reasons which he could not give' (20). One of those unknown reasons, clearly, is represented in his fantasy of recognition by the (m)Other: 'He would like her to see him, gowned and hooded, walking in a procession' (20). Recognized by her, he feels for a moment the omnipotence of the infant at the bosom of the mother: 'A fellowship, a professorship, he felt capable of anything' (20).

But Tansley's joy is short-lived in this mini plot of small successes and minor retreats, for that moment is quashed when he notices she is not even watching him. She is watching someone else, and not just anyone else, but a man who has just one arm pasting a bill advertising a circus. Both the one-armed man and the circus poster evoke again Tansley's sense of lack, inadequacy. Yet once more Mrs Ramsay draws him out. Asking him if he had never been taken to circuses, Mrs Ramsay surmises that she had 'asked the very thing he wanted; had been longing all these days to say, how they did not go to circuses,' that, instead, he was from a large, but poor family, and had 'paid his own way since he was thirteen' (21). Thus she provides him a moment of recognition, a moment to explain himself, a moment to recover his self-confidence. He is on the verge once more of continuing his narcissistic ramblings when, inevitably, Mrs Ramsay interrupts him with an exclamation. She is captured by the beauty of the prospect of 'the hoary Lighthouse, distant, austere', 'in the midst' of a 'great plateful of blue water' before them. Once more, in the remark that the light-house, in effect, is the possession of Mr Ramsay, Mrs Ramsay reminds Tansley of his lack of that which he desires (23).

But his complete capture by *jouissance* in the company of Mrs Ramsay is merely interrupted, not forestalled entirely. He may still come in touch with it: 'Under the influence of that extraordinary emotion which had been growing all the walk, had begun in the garden when he had wanted to take her bag' (24), Tansley begins to 'see himself, and everything he had ever known gone crooked a little' (24). But, strange to him, he feels that somehow this woman can restore him to a lost vision of himself; as Lacan might say, she is the woman who is man's symptom. He even decides in what her power lies. Her power somehow resides in 'her little bag', and, 'determined to carry it', he simply takes it from her. Taking the *objet a* from her, he thus, symbolically, takes her as well; at the same time, the other's gaze, directed at her as the valued possession, takes him in, but also reifies his triumph: 'a man digging in a drain stopped digging and looked at her, let his arm fall down and looked at her; for the first time in his life Charles Tansley felt an extraordinary pride; felt the wind and the cyclamen and the violets for he was walking with a beautiful woman. He had hold of her bag' (25). Because of the obviousness of the connection, it is perhaps needless to point out the relation between Mrs Ramsay and her bag, on the one hand, and the (m)Other and the object associated with her (the breast), on the other. What might need pointing out is the way in which the successful achievement of Tansley's desire, however momentary, is a model of the way narrative texts operate in or upon readers. Tansley's story is an allegory of desire.

... The passages involving James and Tansley seem closer to the primally Oedipal situation than most of the other passages through *jouissance* in 'The Window'. For that reason, their passages represent most graphically the objects/objectives of the unconscious on a text and the text (especially the narrative text) as an unconscious ...

THE REAL AND 'TIME PASSES'

One of the most difficult concepts ... is Lacan's notion of 'the Real'. Similarly, one of the difficult passages ... is the middle section of Woolf's *To the Lighthouse* ... In Lacan's thought, the Real is not regarded as a register or an order quite on the same plane as either the Imaginary or the Symbolic, though inevitably it is inmixed with them ... The Real for Lacan is of course much involved with his conception of 'Reality', but since Reality, for Lacan, equals 'fantasy' and draws one into the domains of the Imaginary and the Symbolic, both of which are specifically human realms, the Real is not the same as Reality ... the Real involves the confrontation of the 'brute fact' of the phenomenological with the transformations of the Symbolic, whether regarded in Lacanian or Idealist terms.

The short middle section of *To the Lighthouse* may help us to understand what Lacan means by 'the Real', but at the same time the concept will help us understand the novel, as well as how difficult it is to interpolate the Real in a verbal medium. Though there is no subject consciousness dominating 'Time Passes' as there is in each of the other two sections, it is nonetheless accurate to say that what occurs in this section is both existential and phenomenological...

Time and Brute Fact

The Real seems to have been a necessary passage in the structure of *To the Lighthouse*. The dominance, in 'The Window', of Imaginary fusions with what Lacan calls *objets a* would seem to suggest that human *being* ... could somehow be complete without acknowledging the Real. Following the false or misleading plenitude of the novel's first section, what seems mandated is a passage through raw existence, a confrontation with 'the order of brute fact' and the domain of Symbolic and Imaginary time ... and the 'totally real' Heidegger calls death. While space and time are intertwined in the novel, we may begin with time. On the face of it, indeed, the aspect of time dominates 'Time Passes'. The first sentence of the section is 'Well, we must wait for the future to show' (189). But such a remark by an actual conscious subject (here Mr Bankes) is not characteristic of the section, for most of the temporal markers are located in the larger phenomenological framework of days and nights, weeks and months, and, especially, the rhythm of the seasons and the years. Woolf writes, for instance, 'But what after all is one night? A short space, especially when the darkness dims so soon, and so soon a bird sings, a cock crows, or a faint green quickens, like a turning leaf, in the hollow of the wave. Night, however, succeeds to night' (192). Beyond these markers are others tracing a longer rhythm. 'Nothing it seemed could break that image, corrupt that innocence, or disturb the swaying mantle of silence which, week after week, in the empty room, wove into itself the falling cries of birds, ships hooting, the drone and hum of the fields, a dog's bark, a man's shout, and folded them round the house in silence' (195).

Beyond the diurnal rhythm and the passage of weeks, of course, are the cycles of the seasons. These regularly mark off the passing years (ten in all) as the house stands vacant of human subjects ... while objects in space may represent the narrative's content, time is the most insistent medium in which this narrative moves, and one entire brief section (7) is devoted to its recording: 'Night after night, summer and winter, the torments of storms, the arrow-like stillness of fine weather, held their court without interference … [N]ight and day, month and year ran shapelessly together' (202–3).

Besides insisting through repetitions that time is a reality outside human control or being, Woolf equally insists on a spatial realm of 'brute fact' or materiality that acts as it will, apart from human intentions or meanings, regardless of any meaning to which one might subject it. In the world of physics, space is almost inextricably linked to light. One may say that space exists because it provides a container for, even if it does not create, light. As a measure of space, light thus becomes the virtual subject of space and time. Significantly, Woolf creates a metaphorical human world, a world containing – but outside – human consciousness, by use of a conventional metaphor of light. When there is no light, there is no subject or consciousness to fill Woolf's space. Thus darkness (and, as we shall see, death) subtends consciousness; it underlies so as to include the domain of subjectivity. 'So with the lamps all put out,' she says at the beginning of part 2 of 'Time Passes', with 'the moon sunk, and [with] a thin rain drumming on the roof, a downpouring of immense darkness began' (189). In this 'profusion of darkness,' human objects have lost their definition: 'Not only was furniture confounded,' she writes; 'there was scarcely anything left of *body* or *mind* by which one could say, "This is he" or "This is she"' (190; my emphasis). Eventually, light as it is perceived in nature does return to Woolf's Real domain here, but when it returns it does so without any metaphorical sense of its *being* consciousness. Instead, the lights represent objects searching *for* consciousness. 'And so, nosing, rubbing, they went to the window on the staircase, to the servants' bedrooms, to the boxes in the attics; descending, blanched the apples on the dining-room table, fumbled the petals of roses, tried the picture on the easel, brushed the mat and blew a little sand along the floor' (191). Because section 2 ends with a rare moment of conscious subjectivity, one is made more aware of its almost pervasive absence, for that moment occurs in one of those 'holes in the Real' rent by death that, as we shall see, Lacan associates with mourning and the reconstitution of the subject. It occurs in one of those bracketed moments of human consciousness Woolf occasionally gives readers. When Woolf tells us here that Augustus Carmichael reads Virgil, therefore, she presages, by the allusion, the deeper descent in 'Time Passes' into the netherworld of human subjectivity represented by Lacan's notion of the unspeakable, 'impossible' Real.

In a world without a subject, the forces of the Real, of brute fact and physical materiality, take over. For Woolf, this Real is something hidden behind a curtain, though no doubt Lacan would say it is only a curtain of language. Unfortunately, like any poet, the only way Woolf may represent the unrepresentable is in language. So whether behind language or some other veil, the Real is never available to us in any material way. Thus, while Woolf's aim within this passage seems evident enough, it is also true that even here the Real must truly remain hidden behind words, symbols, language. It neither speaks nor thinks itself before the advent of language and subjectivity in the human being …

The Disappearance of the Subject

... As space gives time substance, so human habitations offer consciousness a possible locale. One form of the human that *might* include consciousness is thus represented metonymically by the Ramsays' abandoned vacation house at Skye ... Woolf's main theme is *vacancy*; it is developed through a figure of 'airs', that which fills empty space; like lights, they seem to seek subjectivity, some human occupant. 'So with the house empty and the doors locked and the mattresses rolled round,' says Woolf, 'those stray airs, advance guards of great armies, blustered in, brushed bare boards, nibbled and fanned, met nothing in bedroom or drawing-room that wholly resisted them but only hangings that flapped, wood that creaked, the bare legs of tables, saucepans and china already furred, tarnished, cracked' (194).

As the house represents the body to be inhabited by mind, so human garments represent other metonymical forms of the body once inhabited by conscious subjects. Thus garments provide metonymical images of the diminished human, the human shape or form minus the awareness of the subject. These images, like the house, come under the sway of time and decay. 'What people had shed and left – a pair of shoes, a shooting cap, some faded skirts and coats in wardrobes,' writes Woolf, 'those alone kept the human shape and in the emptiness indicated how once they were filled and animated; how once hands were busy with hooks and buttons' (194). More than mere human presence, however, these images lead Woolf to another image that perfectly represents Lacan's own image of the moment of constitution of the subject. In her way, Woolf captures the mirror stage when she suggests that those garments express 'how once the looking-glass had held a face; had held a world hollowed out in which a figure turned, a hand flashed, the door opened, in came children rushing and tumbling; and went out again' (194). These are lovely images indeed, but what they represent is loss, absence, vacancy – what might have been or what might well come to be again, a nostalgia less for the past than for the future.

Even after the advent (in Mrs McNab) of an inchoate consciousness early on, the world vacated by the Ramsays remains dominated by a brute reality without consciousness. Much of that material Real manifests itself in what it does to the house. The house stands as Woolf's major representation of the body's potential for subjectivity. She catalogs in minute detail the displacements of a potentially mental space by the detritus of a brutish Real signifying death, death itself represented in the house-as-dead-body:

> The house was left; the house was deserted. It was left like a shell on a sandhill to fill with dry salt grains now that life had left it. The long night seemed to have set in; the trifling airs, nibbling, the clammy breaths, fumbling, seemed to have triumphed. The saucepan had rusted and the mat decayed. Toads had nosed their way in. Idly, aimlessly, the swaying shawl swung to and fro. A thistle thrust itself between the tiles in the

larder. The swallows nested in the drawing-room; the floor was strewn with straw; the plaster fell in shovelfuls; rafters were laid bare; rats carried off this and that to gnaw behind the wainscots. Tortoise-shell butterflies burst from the chrysalis and pattered their life out on the window-pane. Poppies sowed themselves among the dahlias; the lawn waved with long grass; giant artichokes towered among roses; a fringed carnation flowered among the cabbages; while the gentle tapping of a weed at the window had become, on winters' nights, a drumming from sturdy trees and thorned briars which made the whole room green in summer. (206–7)

Woolf suggests here that the incursions of natural fact, 'the sensibility of nature' (207), cannot be blocked by mere unconscious desire, by a dream such as Mrs McNab's 'dream of a lady, of a child, of a plate of milk soup' (207). There is no Symbolic here, no voice of the Father to set boundaries, to establish the law. There seems, Woolf says, nothing to say 'no to them' (208), not even the phallic lighthouse that once, when subjects were present, 'had laid itself with such authority ... in the darkness' (199–200).

Regarding human subjectivity, Lacan argues, the most insistent fact of the brute world outside of or beyond consciousness is death. Death is the great 'No' of life. As in Freud, in Lacan death has its place at the base of being and identity. For the subject to become a subject, Lacan insists, it must encounter death – the 'No' of the Father – in some form; whatever the specific form, it represents castration. In Woolf's novel it is clear that one drive is toward the negation of death. Perhaps the most troubling feature of 'Time Passes', indeed, is the death of consciousness represented in the disappearance of the subject and, worse, the subject's being relegated to a mere hole in the Real. Those half dozen bracketed passages in this section vividly express death and the loss of the subject, though at the same time they represent the gap within the Real through which subjectivity may reemerge. Since the very symbol of subjectivity in the novel's previous chapter, 'The Window', is Mrs Ramsay, her loss portends the greatest loss in the entire novel. But in the course of 'Time Passes' that loss is represented as a trivial moment, nothing more than a slight rent in the fabric of the Real – a mere punctuation mark in the discourse of time. The brackets signifying that hole, it is important to note, are Woolf's:

[Mr. Ramsay, stumbling along a passage one dark morning, stretched his arms out, but Mrs. Ramsay having died rather suddenly the night before, his arms, though stretched out, remained empty.] (194)

... Half the bracketed passages in 'Time Passes' rip ... immitigable holes in our experience of the novel. The other two deaths are Prue's and Andrew's.

[Prue Ramsay died that summer in some illness connected with child-birth, which was indeed a tragedy, people said, everything, they said, had promised so well.] (199)

[A shell exploded. Twenty or thirty young men were blown up in France, among them Andrew Ramsay, whose death, mercifully, was instantaneous.] (201)

In these passages bracketing death, Woolf shows that brute reality takes no notice of the human. In the large perspective of time and space, the human being is of no especial consequence. The pain of that recognition, however, will begin to regenerate a perspective, a subjectivity, that will again valorize life, mind, consciousness.

Death for the human being is not simply negation, for in Lacanian thought the fact of death permits, even insists on, the reemergence of the subject from the Real. In the perception of death, the nascent subject emerges through the formation of the register of the Symbolic. In 'Desire and the Interpretation of Desire in *Hamlet*', Lacan says the Symbolic fills those holes in the Real through the process of mourning Death, says Lacan, creates the hole in the Real that calls forth mourning in the subject, and mourning, with the aid of the primal signifier, begins to reestablish the subject against the screen of the Real ... What this process of mourning entails, Lacan says, is the reestablishment of the *logos*; the *logos* is that order founded on community and culture and identified by Lacan as the Symbolic. 'The work of mourning is first of all performed to satisfy the disorder that is produced by the inadequacy of signifying elements to cope with the hole that has been created in existence, for it is the system of signifiers in their totality which is impeached by the least instance of mourning' (38). But in the end, Lacan insists, the work of mourning is essentially to create – or, more properly, to recreate – the subject itself in what amounts to a repetition of the mirror stage.

From Death to Mourning

The narrative trajectory of 'Time Passes' thus represents the move from death to mourning to the reconstitution of the subject ... What the passage through mourning amounts to ... is a repetition of the mirror phase, the moment in the life of the subject when identity asserts itself through mirror reflections and creates the possibility of the Oedipal conflict and its attendant moment of castration. In the structure of *To the Lighthouse*, 'Time Passes' represents castration through the loss of subjectivity and the imposition of the fact of death, especially the loss through death of the primal object, the mother. But 'Time Passes' also represents the reemergence of subjectivity as well. It occurs through the mediation of none other than Mrs McNab. Woolf tells us, in indirect discourse attributed to the old woman: 'So she was dead; and Mr Andrew killed; and Miss Prue dead too, they said, with her first baby; but every one had lost some one these years' (205). Clearly, the mourning process has begun. Lacan says that 'ritual introduces some mediation of the gap [*béance*] opened up by mourning. More precisely, ritual operates in such a way as to make this gap coincide with that greater *béance*, the point x, the symbolic lack. The navel of the dream, to which Freud refers at one point, is perhaps nothing but the psychological counterpart of this lack' ('Desire in *Hamlet*' 40). In her recognition of the 'greater *béance*', Mrs McNab begins to mediate between brute insensibility and human subjectivity. By her process of mourning the lack of Mrs Ramsay, the Symbolic lack and the lack of the Symbolic, the old woman presides over the birth of human subjectivity in the Symbolic, in the ritual of things done (the house cleaning in preparation for the Ramsay's return), and the language of things said. Functioning as the Symbolic, these take care of the mourning and establish the power of the Symbolic over or in the face of the Real.

The human world is hollowed out of the Real by the Symbolic in the same way as the subject is formed in the mirror stage by a splitting of specular images. In 'Time Passes', that human, Symbolic world has been represented as departed or diminished or fragmented. Thus what has remained is a metonymical world of objects associated with the human that are now seeking a human subject. It is a world where shadows 'for a moment darkened the pool in which light reflected itself' (195), where there is nothing else but light to engage in the act of *reflection* – in any sense of the term ... Autistic, insensate, virtually without thought, such is the world, then, as Woolf represents it just before that inchoate consciousness in the form of Mrs McNab returns to the premises: 'Once only a board sprang on the landing; once in the middle of the night with a roar, with a rupture, as after centuries of quiescence, a rock rends itself from the mountain and hurtles crashing into the valley, one fold of [Mrs Ramsey's] shawl [covering the boar's skull] loosened and swung to and fro. Then again peace descended; and the shadow wavered; light bent to its own image in adoration on the bedroom wall, and Mrs. McNab, tearing the veil of silence with hands that had stood in the wash-tub, grinding it with boots that had crunched the shingle, came as directed to open all windows, and dust the bedrooms' (195–6).

But the threshold of consciousness represented by Mrs McNab for a long time hardly diminishes the grip of the brute Real on Woolf's landscape. Early on, this old woman seems barely more sensate as a subject than those abandoned clothes of the Ramsays. She would seem to be a negative counterpart to Mrs Ramsay ... Woolf's description of Mrs McNab makes the negative consciousness 'positive'. In the old woman, Woolf makes consciousness visible in the way of objects in a photographic negative: 'she lurched (for she rolled like a ship at sea) and leered (for her eyes fell on nothing directly, but with a sidelong glance that deprecated the scorn and anger of the world – she was witless, she knew it)' (196). As with those garments that once reminded one of subjects before the mirror, so Mrs McNab brings one back to it. The index of her nearly negative humanity is her inability to face it squarely. 'Rubbing the glass of the long looking-glass and leering side ways at her swinging figure a sound issued from her lips – something that ... was robbed of meaning, was like the voice of witlessness, humour, persistency itself' (196). But since darkness subtends being as the unconscious subtends consciousness,

Mrs McNab accomplishes a small, necessary step upward by her representing a break in the darkness: 'there must have been', Woolf writes, 'some cleavage of the dark ... , some channel in the depths of obscurity through which light enough issued to twist her face grinning in the glass' (197). Not much of a start, it is a start nonetheless.

Woolf's description offers a painful burlesque of Lacan's mirror stage, even to the questions asked. The old dance hall tune she mumbles might have given an answer to basic human questions – 'What am I', 'What is this?' (198) – but listeners would have had to be mystics or visionaries to understand that answer, and even so 'they could not say what it was' (198). Despite a social stratification here invidious to this old woman, it nevertheless seems that what Mrs McNab represents most of all is an absence, precisely the absence of Mrs Ramsay, who is Woolf's image of the positive, shaping, creating human consciousness. But as the absence of such consciousness, old Mrs McNab is no less than the human Real, the bare, witless rock on which a more symbolic 'Reality' eventually may be built. Though Woolf early on had implied that Mrs McNab's 'dream of a lady' – that is, of Mrs Ramsay – might not be a force sufficient to withstand the entropic slant of nature, she later suggests otherwise (207). 'But there was a force working; something not highly conscious; something that leered, some-thing that lurched; something not inspired to go about its work with dignified ritual or solemn chanting' (209). Consequently, asked to prepare the house, that empty metaphorical potential for consciousness, for their return by one of the daughters, Mrs McNab (and, now, her own mirror double, Mrs Bast) does indeed rescue the house 'from the pool of Time' (209). The whole process, Woolf suggests, is a sort of 'rusty laborious birth' (210), and what, ultimately, is borne out of it is subjectivity itself. Out of the loss of Mrs Ramsay, mediated by poor witless Mrs McNab, with her alter ego, Mrs Bast, comes once more Woolf's image of the new consciousness to replace the primal mother. It is not Mrs McNab who emerges to represent that new subjectivity; it is another for whom she has prepared the way. The other is the painter, Lily Briscoe. Within Lily Briscoe, who represents Woolf's figure of the artist, there once again sings 'the voice of the beauty of the world' (213). As we shall see in the novel's final chapter, 'The Lighthouse', the world whose beauty Lily commemorates is not that of the Real. Rather, it is that of the Imaginary 'reality' created in the signifiers of art and language – in, that is, the material of the Symbolic.

THE SYMBOLIC AND 'THE LIGHTHOUSE'

In the aesthetic arrangement of the three sections of To the Lighthouse it seems evident that, in the order of human existence, the second passage ('Time Passes') is somehow primal, quite fundamental in its representation of a subject's relation to the world external to consciousness. In Lacan's epistemol-ogy, that world – the Real – is 'full'; it is marked by a material plenitude, but it is also impossible, ineffable, unincorporable. Since it is outside or beyond language or symbolization, it thus can also, paradoxically, signify the lack that comes to mark the human subject once he or she (in, Lacan says, the mirror stage's recognition of – and relation to – an other not one's self) is separated from the (m)Other and cast into a universe alien to one's self. In this respect, the Real represented in 'Time Passes' is also associated with absence of being – with, therefore, death, both the ultimate Real and the incorrigibly alienated. As the generalized 'subject' of Woolf's novel moves, then, from the middle passage to the final one, 'The Lighthouse', it must reconcile to or internalize the fact of lack, loss, or absence of the object of desire through the work of mourning. Mourning itself is not adequately accomplished in 'Time Passes', though subjectivity is restored, nor do all subjects of 'The Lighthouse' respond to the object loss in the same ways when mourning is taken up. What we find is that Lily Briscoe quite overtly deals with the loss – that is, the loss of Mrs Ramsay as the (m)Other – and finds her own symbolic way to internalize it. But each of the Ramsays who stands in for the subject in this passage – Mr Ramsay, Cam, and James – finds other ways, other necessities for handling the *béance* in existence. For the children, the passage comes to represent castration and the internalization of the Oedipal complex; for the father it represents the final acceptance of the place of the Name-of-the-Father in whose name he speaks. In all instances (for Lily, Cam, James, and Mr Ramsay), the passage seems to represent a positive movement toward the Symbolic register in the domain of subjectivity. But the movement is only aesthetically fulfilling, for it is the case that the Symbolic does not represent a permanent plateau that, once attained, places the subject beyond the reach of the Imaginary. For 'normality', one has to achieve the Symbolic, but it is not a place one can move into and therein live happily ever after.

The Name-of-the-'F(Ather)'

Mrs Ramsay is the symbol for all characters of the object of desire; as her husband, Mr Ramsay is the first figure who must deal with the problem of mourning her loss. Woolf represents his accommodation within the first two sections of 'The Lighthouse'. As is his wont, Ramsay immediately attaches himself to the first woman available to him as a substitute object for his wife. Ramsay's drive is to satisfy a 'demand'; demand is a void that once may have been a physiological need ... but that is now a void hollowed out in the space of desire. Need becomes *démande* ... When Ramsay fastens his desire on Lily she is manifestly the object substituting for his lack, now more painful ... because it is permanent. That lack signifies his (and our) alienation in desire and in the world. Woolf makes all this clear (though she uses both *demand* and *need*) in the moment Lily perceives Ramsay's look: 'Suddenly Mr Ramsay raised his head as he passed and looked straight at her, with his distraught wild gaze which was yet so penetrating ... ; and she pretended to drink out of her empty coffee cup so as to escape him – to escape his demand on her, to put aside a moment longer that imperious need' (219).

Lacan recognizes that language may serve as well as real objects in satisfying demands of desire and mourning. In their effects, the words become real objects. Lily's first turn from Ramsay's demand on her is indeed toward language. As he strides by her, he mutters two words, 'Alone' and 'Perished'. These two words represent his isolation and loss, but around them might be woven what Lily thinks of as 'the truth of things' (219); for Lacan, too, they might *be* the truth of things since they signify alienation and death. 'Like everything else this strange morning,' Lily perceives, 'the words became symbols.' They 'wrote themselves all over the grey-green walls. If only she could put them together, she felt,' if only she could 'write them out in some sentence, then she would have got at the truth of things' (219). Desire, in fact, is a truth of things. It is a truth of objects, *objets a*, or, as Lacan says, a metonymy: 'Desire is a metonymy' (1977). It is caught up in a syntax of things. In the presence of Ramsay's need, Lily seems actually to recognize that fact, but she has trouble deciding what to do or what to say or on what objects to focus: 'she could say nothing; the whole horizon seemed swept bare of objects to talk about' (227). But Ramsay's demand is immense, having to do (Lacan would insist) with his very being since 'demand begins with the ideal ego's formation and answers finally to the superego, or the limits intrinsic to a specific *moi*' (Ragland-Sullivan, 1986, 86). Consequently, without her knowing what she does (as if, indeed, she were directed by an Other), Lily does alight upon the one object that will satisfy Ramsay's demand. She is directed to it/ them, no doubt by the Other in Ramsay, as he notices that his bootlaces are untied. 'Remarkable boots they were too,' Lily thought. They are 'sculptured; colossal; like everything that Mr. Ramsay wore,' Lily notes. 'She could see them walking to his room of their own accord, expressive in his absence of pathos, surliness, ill-temper, charm' (228–9). Though she thinks that to praise those boots is frivolous in the face of his demand, when she says, 'What beautiful boots!' Ramsay smiles and, remarkably, 'his infirmities fell from him' (229). Those boots are his *objet a*, and by her praise, Lily creates in him a moment of joy that can fill his sense of lack: 'They had reached', Lily thinks, ironically, 'a sunny island where peace dwelt, sanity reigned and the sun for ever shone.' It was, she thinks, 'the blessed island of good boots' (230).

One may feel that Ramsay's displacement of grief for the death of his wife is too easily accepted here. But, while it has indeed seemed facile, there is no reason to suspect that his pain is neither real nor substantial. He easily displaces the grief because (one must surmise) he has had to deal with it for quite some years, and, in a sense, long practice (of the unconscious, to be sure, not the conscious mind) has made it easier to master in each recurrence. The fact is, if he were not able to control the mourning rather easily by this time in his life we would have to regard him as somehow immature or undeveloped. He *is* an old man, over seventy now, and what has become absolutely incumbent upon him is to take his place in the normal structure of personality and family discourse. To remain caught up in mourning too long is to remain trapped in an unhealthy Imaginary relationship. One has to let go of the desired object, accept the loss or lack or absence of the beloved. One must accept, in short, castration in yet one more form, but that acceptance is part of an ongoing Symbolic process whether it occurs in the mourning of a Real loss as such or merely in the mourning of a lost object in which desire has been momentarily invested (as in Minta's brooch) ... early morning encounter with the psychic fact of mourning (brought on by demands dating back, one is sure, to infancy and to the real mother) is to pass once more through a displaced version of the mirror stage and the Oedipus encounter. Traversed successfully, this passage represents (once again) the passage from Imaginary to Symbolic.

Happily for Ramsay's children Cam and James, his passage is successful (as, again one is sure, it always has been for him), and Ramsay is enabled in the unconscious discourse he constructs with them to move into his proper place. He takes his place in relation to them (they are all, literally and figuratively, in the same boat) where the Name-of-the-Father resides in the Symbolic. He becomes Other to them, not merely antagonistic or narcissistic other in their Imaginary conflicts or projections. After praising those boots, Lily herself notes a change in Ramsay, though she may misunderstand its nature. But the shift in her attitude (from hostility to sympathy) and the appearance of Cam and James at this moment begin to suggest Ramsay's new role ... In this context, suddenly, the old man moves over to the place of the Other, of God-the-Father, a figure to be feared and worshipped. Thus Lily becomes angry at the boy and girl: 'But why was it like *that* that they came?' she wonders; 'they might have come more cheerfully; they might have given him what, now that they were off [to the light-house], she would not have the chance of giving him' (230-1). In short order, Ramsay has been transformed within Lily's mind (but, as we shall see, in the domain of the text as well) into the heroic Other. 'He had become a very distinguished, elderly man, who had no need of her whatsoever' (231). He becomes yet more heroic to her (though not yet to the children). 'He had all the appearance of a leader making ready for an expedition. Then, wheeling about, he led the way with his firm military tread, in those wonderful boots, carrying brown paper parcels, down the path, his children following him' (231). Lily's meditation on Ramsay ranges far in the next few moments, but the end result is precisely to acknowledge his representing Otherness, his withdrawal into 'that other final phase which was new to her and had, she owned, made herself ashamed of her own irritability, when it seemed as if he had shed worries and ambitions, and the hope of sympathy and the desire for praise, had entered some other region, was drawn on, as if by curiosity, in dumb colloquy, whether with himself or another, at the head of that little procession out of one's range' (233).

It is from within this 'other region' – the place of the Other – and 'in dumb colloquy' that Ramsay conducts his discourse with Cam and James hereafter. Representing this discourse, several sections are then devoted largely to the silent discourse of the children with the father. Essentially, their response is to the Law (which is silent) more than it is to the actual father, but, Oedipally, since they prefer to resist, they displace their resistance from the person toward a concept: 'they vowed, in silence,' we are told, 'to stand by each other and to carry out the great compact – to resist tyranny to the death' (243). Ramsay's power over them thus is more than biological or familial. 'Their grievance weighed them down,' we are told. 'They had been forced; they had been bidden. He had borne them down once more with his gloom and his authority, making them do his bidding, on this fine morning, [making them] come, because he wished it, carrying these parcels, to the Lighthouse; take part in these rites he went through for his own pleasure in memory of dead people' (246). In effect, Ramsay has now been identified with the silent dead, with Prue, Andrew and Mrs Ramsay, and progressively he moves more and more toward silence on the boat ride as he disappears into the pages of his (and Woolf's) book ... for Cam, James, and Lily Briscoe, Mr Ramsay has taken his proper place in the Symbolic. He takes his place in the Name-of-the-Father, but, portentously, the place he takes is the place of the dead as well.

Male Castration

Male and female castration are both manifested in the relations of Mr Ramsay with his children James and Cam. The theme is focused of course in the Oedipus complex. James's confrontation with the Oedipus, as we shall see, is less complicated than Cam's. The imagery in which it is represented is almost perfect. Since James and Cam are united in their pact to 'fight tyranny to the death', much of what we learn about the boy's response to his father comes through or in conjunction with his sister's. It is Cam, for example, who notes that Ramsay has thrust onto James the task of steering the boat to the lighthouse, a task that generates the antagonism and permits the reconciliation of the Oedipus conflict to occur. Cam notes, 'James would be forced to keep his eye all the time on the sail. For if he forgot, then the sail puckered and shivered, and the boat slackened, and Mr Ramsay would say sharply, "Look out! Look out!"' (244). The boy and girl are united in their vow to fight the tyrant, but since their father represents that dominating image of law to them, of him 'they were conscious all the time' (245). Steering the boat, however, James on occasion fantasizes escape rather than confrontation: he thinks that 'he might escape; he might be quit of it all. They might land somewhere; and be free then' (246–7). With his mother dead, James displaces his feelings regarding the mother toward his sister; thus he suffers moments of anger toward and alienation from Cam when he observes his father's entreaties for sympathy from the girl. His feelings at sixteen are little different from those seen at six. 'I shall be left to fight the tyrant alone. The compact would be left to him to carry out. Cam would never resist tyranny to the death, he thought grimly, watching her face, sad, sulky, yielding' (250). The threat of the girl's yielding to his father grows even more grim – incestuously so – when out of his unconscious emerges a very primal memory of the father's coming between the boy and his real mother. The memory comes, naturally enough, in that moment we shall call

Cam's secondary castration, in that moment when he identifies her with 'woman', with some primal otherness – some castrating 'they'. '*They* look down he thought, at their knitting or something. Then suddenly *they* look up' (251; my emphasis). What he is remembering here is that scene, when he was six, of Oedipal conflict represented in 'The Window' (9). 'It must have been his mother, he thought, sitting on a low chair, with his father standing over her' (251), he tall, erect, threatening, 'stopped dead, upright, over them' (252).

In this memory, James's consciousness reveals both how the unconscious works as a structure we may call a text and how the text contributes to the already formed unconscious for the reader. James plays upon this primal episode during the remainder of his journey to the lighthouse. It brings out all the latent violence in the boy's imagination. So when imagining the father's reprimands of him for the boat's slowing down, James explicitly recalls that other scene, that scene of the Oedipal other: 'once before he had brought his blade down among them on the terrace and she had gone stiff all over, and if there had been an axe handy, a knife, or anything with a sharp point he would have seized it and struck his father through the heart' (277). But in fact James's anger there is as much directed at the mother as at the father who intrudes, for he feels it is the mother who abandons him: 'She had gone stiff all over, and then, her arm slackening, so that he felt she listened to him no longer, she had risen somehow and gone away and left him there, impotent, ridiculous, sitting on the floor grasping a pair of scissors' (277–8). The ambivalence of James's anger accounts for the ambiguous role of the mother in castration in the Oedipal conflict ... in James's imagery, as in Lacanian theory, the figures associated with the intrusive 'father' may as easily be female as male. 'He had always kept this old symbol of taking a knife and striking his father to the heart. Only now, as he grew older, and sat staring at his father in an impotent rage, it was not him, that old man reading, whom he wanted to kill, but it was the thing that descended on him – without his knowing it perhaps: that fierce sudden black-winged harpy, with its talons and its beak all cold and hard, that struck and struck at you' (273).

In this ambivalence toward the androgynous 'black-winged harpy' (is it father? mother?) James actually is engaged in a necessary step toward gender maturation. One thing he needs to do to be gendered male is to identify his future as a male with his father; he needs to identify with the symbols and occupations of the father. He does that, strangely enough, even as he con-templates his Oedipal revenge: 'Whatever he did – (and he might do anything, he felt, looking at the Light-house and the distant shore) whether he was in a business, in a bank, a barrister, a man at the head of some enterprise, that he would fight, that he would track down and stamp out – tyranny, despotism, he called it – making people do what they did not want to do, *cutting off* their right to speak' (274; my emphasis). Thus, even while he cannot yet quite dissociate the *principle* of law or authority from his own father, James can recognize his identificatory link to him: 'he had come to feel, quite often lately, when his father said something or did something which surprised the others, [that] there were two pairs of footprints only; his own and his father's. They alone knew each other' (274–5). Feeling such an identification with his father, James thus begins to investigate the basis of the fear of and hostility toward 'this terror, this hatred' of the 'black-winged harpy'. He finds his explanation of the law of denial (castration) in a metaphor of cause and effect. He concludes that an instrument, say a wagon wheel crushing a foot, is not to be blamed for what it does; the fault lies somewhere else, in some causal agent. But who or what is that agent? James struggles toward an answer in the notion of Law, in abstract principle. It is Law, rather than the mere person who happens to be present, that is to be faulted. His imagery for that principle seems, finally, indeed to evoke castration, the fact of loss and alienation: 'It was in this world that the wheel went over the person's foot. Something, he remembered, stayed and darkened over him; would not move; something flourished up in the air, something arid and sharp descended even there, like a blade, a scimitar, smiting through the leaves and flowers even of that happy world and making it shrivel and fall' (276). If James exonerates his father-*as-father*, then he does so in the end at the expense of the mother, for while it must be she who resides behind the black wings of that harpy, the father it seems can withdraw behind the black robes of Law.

As part of James's identification with his father in the process of gender maturation, he begins consequently to mythologize the role of his mother in a different direction. She becomes lost to him as woman in the process, for in accordance with the Oedipus passage she must be desexualized. Thereafter, she reappears, precisely as Ragland-Sullivan suggests of woman in general, in the place of truth or knowledge. 'The absence of the signifier *woman*', moreover, 'also accounts for the illusion of the infinite,' Jacques-Alain Miller has said. 'The passion for things symbolic has no other source. Science exists because *woman* does not exist. Knowledge as such substitutes for knowing the other sex' (as quoted in Ragland-Sullivan, 1986, 297). Thus, James searches for both mother and woman and *knowledge* in the dominating presence of the phallic signifier represented by his father. The shift toward knowledge is evidenced in James's investigation of his haunting memory images. What he seems to want to do is to find out where his mother 'went' on that day when he was six and his father came between them. The imagery of that discovery is rather explicitly that of the primal scene. 'James stealthily, as if he were stealing downstairs on bare feet, afraid of waking a watchdog by a creaking board, went on thinking what was she like, where did she go that day?' (278). In his thoughts (as he steers the boat) James follows 'her from room to room' (278). But it is clear that like the father become the Law of the Father (the crushing wheel of what – of fate?), the mother has moved into the Symbolic as a form of the unknowable Other. She has moved into the same Symbolic realm. There, in the Symbolic, 'She alone spoke the truth; to her alone could he speak it. That was the source of her everlasting attraction for him, perhaps; she was a person to whom one could say what came into one's head' (278). But even there in the Symbolic the baleful, Oedipal presence of patriarchal authority tends to limit the search for or utterance of a truth displaced from the forbidden woman. 'But all the time he thought of her, he was conscious of his father following his thought, surveying it, making it shiver and falter. At last he ceased to think' (278).

The end of the Oedipal journey for James is the arrival at the lighthouse and the Symbolic. There, he comes to terms with his father and the symbol of his own masculinity. Section 12 of 'The Lighthouse' develops these themes overtly. First, James perceives his place in a paternal, identificatory lineage, for he sees that his father 'looked very old. He looked, James thought, getting his head now against the Lighthouse, now against the waste of waters running away into the open, like some old stone lying on the sand; he looked as if he had become physically ... that loneliness [the empty place vacated by woman] which was for both of them the truth about things' (301). Then he perceives and internalizes the symbolic power of the lighthouse: 'it was a stark tower on a bare rock. It satisfied him. It confirmed some obscure feeling of his about his own character' (301–2). In the starkness of the lighthouse, James sees the alienation of life and of his own identity. Finally, he internalizes the role of the father. He does that by imitation of the words of a father who shares the knowledge that life is bleak, hard: '"We are driving before a gale – we must sink," he began saying to himself, half aloud, exactly as his father said it' (302) ...

Female Castration

The psychic work that engages both Cam and James in 'The Lighthouse' is their internalization of the Law of the Father – their acceptance, that is, of the law of castration revealed in the passage through the Oedipus conflict ... The passage to the lighthouse is as much for Cam as for James the passage through the Oedipus complex. The two of them are as insistently oriented toward their father as the boat is oriented toward the lighthouse. For Cam the passage is slightly different from James's passage, because as a female she has a different relation to the phallus and its loss. While, like her brother, Cam has to realize that she cannot *be* the phallus for her mother, she never has to deal with having symbolically to lose the actual phallus possessed in the Real by the male child. Moreover, as a female, Cam seems in a favored relation to her father because she absorbs the values possessed by her mother-as-female. Thus Cam's relation to father and law may be symptomatic of the relatively less traumatic *primary* passage through Oedipus some Lacanians think the female may have. On the other hand, she also represents the greater difficulty the female experiences in what Ragland-Sullivan calls the *secondary* castration – the necessity of being identified *as* woman in a phallocentric, patriarchal Symbolic culture. Cam's image of the difference comes in relation to Macalister's story about the wintry shipwreck; Ramsay 'relished the thought of the storm and the dark night and the fishermen striving there. He liked that men should labour and sweat on the windy beach at night; pitting muscle and brain against the waves and the wind;

he liked men to work like that.' But what he likes of the woman is that she 'keep house, and sit beside sleeping children indoors, while men were drowned, out there in a storm' (245). Although the men are given the more dangerous options, at least they are given options outside home and hearth. 'Wild' Cam surely will recognize that difference – as it is clear Woolf herself did.

Cam's relation to Ramsay reveals the evolution of the female in the Oedipal passage. The dominant (castration) theme of that relation is difference, alienation, separation. The child is identified in its fusion with the mother's body, but it is further identified in the symbol of its differentiation through its relation to the father. In effect, in the face of the No-of-the-Father the child has also to enunciate its own 'No'. Cam does that in concert with James in their vow to resist 'tyranny', meaning of course the demands of the father that they do this or do that. But try as she might to 'resist tyranny to the death' (246), Cam cannot resist the place into which her father thrusts her in his own thoughts. That place insistently is not that of her as child; rather, it is of her as Woman, located in Ramsay's Imaginary, ambiguously, as fulfillment and obstacle to his demands. On the one hand Ramsay can rant inwardly because Cam does not know the points of the compass: 'women are always like that; the vagueness of their minds is hopeless' (249). On the other, he feels he must make up to her because he rather liked 'this vagueness in women. It was part of their extraordinary charm' (250). So he will try to make her smile by tempting her with an image of something a woman presumably cannot resist. He will tempt her by a 'little thing', just another *objet a* that may substitute for the missing phallus: 'There was a puppy. They had a puppy. Who was looking after the puppy today?' (250). The old man's surmise is plain: the way to a girl's – or woman's – heart is through the baby or the little object that may stand for one, the *objet* itself always standing in for the phallus.

The validity of Cam's acceptance of primary castration, her recognition of law, is illustrated in her confrontation with her father's Imaginary perception of her. Cam understands clearly that there is a higher authority than her father-as-father. In this scene she identifies that law, ironically, with the son, her brother James. All the while that Cam is trying to 'resist [Ramsay's] entreaty – forgive me, care for me' (251), James sits there representing 'the lawgiver, with the tablets of eternal wisdom laid open on his knee (his hand on the tiller had become symbolical to her),' he saying, 'Resist him. Fight him' (251). Even so, at this very moment James himself is casting Cam into the same realm of secondary castration as had her father. James, too, insists on her definition as woman, but as woman defined in the castrated mother's act of betrayal of the child: 'She'll give way, James thought, as he watched a look come upon her face, a look he remembered. They look down he thought, at their knitting or something. Then suddenly they look up. There was a flash of blue, he remembered, and then somebody sitting with him laughed, surrendered, and he was very angry. It must have been his mother' (251). What James is imposing upon Cam here, then, is ... 'double Castration' ...

Despite the Imaginary violence done to Cam's identity, however, the girl is able to deal with her father in a proper or normal way. She can resist his Imaginary importunities – she does not play his game of name-the-puppy, for example. But she can accept him – as well as the mother (seen in Cam's frequent references to images of the peaceful, protective island receding behind them) – for what the Symbolic makes of him. That is, he can be both a narcissistic and an anaclitic image for her. Narcissistically: 'For no one attracted her more; his hands were beautiful, and his feet, and his voice, and his words, and his haste, and his temper, and his oddity, and his passion, and his saying straight out before every one, we perish, each alone, and his remoteness' (253). Anacliti- cally, he is an image of the protector-father: 'for she was safe, while he sat there; safe, as she felt herself when she crept in from the garden, and took a book down, and the old gentleman, lowering the paper suddenly, said something very brief over the top of it' (283). Similarly, at the arrival at the lighthouse, Cam 'felt as she did in the study when the old men were reading *The Times*. Now I can go on thinking whatever I like, and I shan't fall over a precipice or be drowned, for there he is, keeping his eye on me' (304). Most of all she can internalize his image as the Other, that ultimate, arbitrary, silent interlocutor whose place is really in the unconscious: 'What was he thinking now? she wondered. What was it he sought, so fixedly, so intently, so silently?' (307) And it is his role as the Other, the one who is supposed to know, that permits him to pose for Cam the two dominant questions of one's being – death and plenitude, loss and fulfill- ment: 'He sat and looked at the island and he might be thinking, We perished, each alone, or he might be thinking, I have reached it. I have found it' (308). But as the silent Other, 'he said nothing' (308). Such has Ramsay's identity come to be for Cam (and James) at the moment he lightly springs 'on to the rock' of the lighthouse that possesses his Symbolic being. As a young woman, Cam, too, has arrived at her destination – or, more properly, her destiny within, we say redundantly, a patriarchal culture.

The Name-of-the-'M(Other)'

Aesthetically, the most significant of the passages into the Symbolic in 'The Lighthouse' is that accomplished by Lily Briscoe. Hers is so expansive in scope that it subsumes all others in its metapsychological sweep. Lily is the substitute in the last movement of the novel for Mrs Ramsay in that both represent (or come to represent) the novel's metaconsciousness, its over-soul of subjectivity. All the others – Ramsay, James, Cam – are subjects of course, but Lily enfigures the heightened, pervading subjectivity observed in Mrs Ramsay and character- ized by Woolf in the artist. As noted in the discussion of 'Time Passes', Lily represents the re-emergence of subjectivity following the loss of it in the dark, mournful passage through the order of the Real. Consequently, Woolf creates the sense that Lily is not entirely a whole consciousness at the start of 'The Lighthouse'. She has to move toward psychic reintegration. She begins in a state of denial, primarily denial of loss, *béance*, castration. The hole in the Real is still gaping in her consciousness. Woolf makes the point clearly: 'What does it mean?' Lily wonders; 'she could not, this first morning with the Ramsays, contract her feelings, could only make a phrase resound to cover the blankness of her mind until these vapours had shrunk. For really, what did she feel, come back after all these years and Mrs. Ramsay dead? Nothing, nothing – nothing that she could express at all' (217). Thus Woolf makes readers feel that Lily has not yet accomplished the work of mourning the loss of Mrs Ramsay and the others – 'Mrs. Ramsay dead; Andrew killed; Prue dead too – repeat it as she might, it roused no feeling in her' (219). What Lily does to reestablish 'the link that usually bound things together [and that] had been cut' (219) is to return to her painting, the picture she had abandoned ten years before.

Lily has an ambivalent relation to the painting, however. It obviously represents for her an *objet a*; it is a substitute for the thing desired (always, symbolically, the phallus), an object to fill the gap (always resulting, symbolically, from castration) that she suffers in being. But the painting is also a barrier she wishes to erect between her and the nearest representative of the phallus – Mr Ramsay. One sees that plainly in her almost frantic efforts to avoid his 'penetrating' gaze when he is searching for someone to fill his loss, while, that is, she is trying 'to escape his [sexual] demand on her' (219). The painting will fill the place of the phallus, for the construction represented in the work of art (as in the science of which Miller speaks) is a way to get 'at the truth of things' (219), though that 'truth' be nothing more than the denial of castration in its representation. That truth is also associated with a paternal metaphor, the lighthouse. But the lighthouse is as ambiguous to her as Ramsay's presence and demand. 'The extraordinary unreality was frightening; but it was also exciting. Going to the Lighthouse. But what does one send to the Lighthouse?' (220). Since she does not go with the others, what Lily sends there is consciousness, her heightened aesthetic perception. In Lily's mind the lighthouse becomes associated with her painting, for both are signifiers by which she will restore unity to a fragmented existence and fill 'the empty places' vacated by woman in the Oedipal passage (220). Seeing in Ramsay's demand a reminder of the loss, the castration, effected in Mrs Ramsay's death, Lily attempts to escape the work of mourning (and also of love) by plunging into her painting: 'It seemed as if the solution had come to her: she knew now what she wanted to do' (221).

But so long as the painting is merely a 'barrier, frail, but she hoped sufficiently substantial to ward off Mr. Ramsay' (223), Lily sees that she is only playing at painting, and that her playing is 'a kind of blasphemy' (224). Lily's sense of loss and frustration thus turns (in another example of woman's secondary castration) to anger at Mrs Ramsay: 'It was all Mrs. Ramsay's doing. She was dead. Here was Lily, at forty-four, wasting her time, unable to do a thing, standing there, playing at painting, playing at the one thing one did not play at, and it was all Mrs. Ramsay's fault. She was dead. The step where she used to sit was empty. She was dead' (223–4). The anger is the means by which Lily begins to perceive her loss, and the anger will eventually lead to the effective act of mourning. But at this point she merely questions the need to 'repeat this over and over again' (224), this effort 'to bring up some feeling she had not got' (224). But the one thing she can do, besides work at her painting, is to accept her role as a substitute for Mrs Ramsay in meeting Ramsay's need. She might at least accept her maternal role *vis-à-vis* the others, though she does not understand it yet. 'Surely, she could imitate from recollection the glow, the rhapsody, the self-surrender, she had seen on so many women's faces (on Mrs. Ramsay's, for instance) when on some occasion like this they blazed up – she could remember the look on Mrs. Ramsay's face – into a rapture of sympathy, of delight in the reward they had, which, though the reason of it escaped her, evidently conferred on them the most supreme bliss of which human nature was capable. Here he was, stopped by her side. She would give him what she could' (224–5). To give him what she could is to accept her role in the cultural Symbolic as 'a woman' instead of 'a peevish, ill-tempered, dried-up old maid' (226). Still, there is a hole where woman was, and Lily will try to fill it both with her painting and with her body.

If Lily's painting links to an *objet a*, the *objet a* emanates from the Other, the subject supposed to know. In this linkage, the painting or the act of painting for her thus represents what she feels about the maternal signifier, Mrs Ramsay. Consequently the dialogue between Lily and her painting modulates into a dialogue with Mrs Ramsay and therefore into a dialogue with the insufficiently mourned dead. Lily is like the child in the mirror stage, for she is now a split subject, divided between desire and loss. The split is represented in the relation between Mrs Ramsay and Ramsay, the one dead and gone, the other simply departed to the lighthouse. 'She felt curiously divided, as if one part of her were drawn out there' to the lighthouse, whereas 'the other had fixed itself doggedly, solidly, here on the lawn' with her canvas (233–4). At this moment Ramsay is merely Imaginary other; the canvas stands in the place of the Symbolic Other that interrogates her. For her the canvas is 'this formidable ancient enemy', 'this other thing, this truth, this reality, which suddenly laid hands on her, emerged stark at the back of appearances and commanded her attention' (236). What that Other creates in her is a resistance to the voice from the past of another of her Imaginary others, the one who – as he had to young James – says 'no' to her in imitation of the Name-of-the-Father: 'she heard some voice saying she couldn't paint, saying she couldn't create, as if she were caught up in one of those habitual currents in which after a certain time experience forms in the mind, so that one repeats words without being aware any longer who originally spoke them' (237). The voice from the past belongs to Charles Tansley, Lily's Imaginary other, her 'whipping boy' (293) from across the divide of all the years. What she needs to get on with her painting, the only form of reproduction she has chosen, is this almost sexual stimulation the memory of Tansley provides her. Woolf's language is explicit: it was 'as if some juice necessary for the lubrication of her faculties were spontaneously squirted' (237).

In her rememoration of Charles Tansley, Lily reenacts the mirror phase in which she becomes differentiated from the maternal figure at the same time she recognizes the place that that figure has filled in her life. As mirror image or alter ego for Lily, Tansley has the curious function of stimulating Lily to paint (which, judging from Woolf's language, is obviously an erotically charged activity for her), but he also enables her to recognize the loss she has experienced in Mrs Ramsay's death. Thinking of the time on the beach when she and Tansley were there together, Lily cannot avoid thinking of Mrs Ramsay, who was also there. 'When she thought of herself and Charles throwing ducks and drakes and of the whole scene on the beach, it seemed to depend somehow upon Mrs. Ramsay sitting upon the rock, with a pad on her knee, writing letters ... That woman sitting there writing under the rock resolved everything into simplicity; made these angers, irritations fall off like old rags' (239). What Lily sees in Mrs Ramsay is the principle of art, the ability to bring disparate things together and to preserve them. But that identification – of Mrs Ramsay and art – leads Lily to a recognition of loss. 'Mrs. Ramsay making of the moment something permanent (as in another sphere Lily herself tried to make of the moment something permanent) – this was of the nature of a revelation. In the midst of chaos there was shape; this eternal passing and flowing ... was struck into stability. Life stand still here, Mrs. Ramsay said. "Mrs. Ramsay!" she repeated. She owed it all to her' (241).

In this moment, as she begins to get control of her painting, Lily feels that she has been returned to the maternal space. Lily's painting, her link to her *objet a*, evokes in her the memory of another object, the boat or cork or cask she and Mrs Ramsay had seen on the ocean that long ago day ... More than that, Lily, as she works further into her painting, moves into a sort of womb: 'And Lily, painting steadily, felt as if a door had opened, and one went in and stood gazing silently about in a high cathedral-like place, very dark, very solemn' (255). What Lily feels she is enabled to capture at this moment is the fullness of being, that plenitude Lacan associates with the phallic signifier; in this moment she has become what Lacan would term the phallus. The setting, the painting, the memories welling up from her unconscious – all enable Lily to capture or to be the phallus, albeit for a moment only ...

Lily's moment of triumph over dead, dusty, out-of-date Mrs Ramsay is short-lived. Remembering Mrs Ramsay through the remembered tales told of her by William Bankes, Lily very shortly begins to feel other than triumphant. Using Augustus Carmichael now as if he were the silent Other in relation to her, Lily wants to ask him about everything that he, the subject who knows, 'like a creature gorged with existence' (265), might be able to tell her. But she realizes she will be unable to say to him what she feels, for what she feels is 'not one thing, but everything' (265). The talking cure will not be sufficient for her. 'Little words that broke up the thought and dismembered it said nothing. "About life, about death; about Mrs. Ramsay." ... Words fluttered sideways and struck the object inches too low ... For how could one express in words these emotions of the body? express that emptiness there?' (265). Lily, in this realization, is beginning to face the gap, loss, emptiness of being left by the death of the maternal figure. She is facing a repetition of the birth of desire in mourning, the emergence of desire out of a realization that one may not have what one misses. 'To want and not to have, sent all up her body a hardness, a hollowness, a strain. And then to want and not to have – to want and want – how that wrung the heart, and wrung it again and again! Oh, Mrs. Ramsay!' (266). Wanting to ask Carmichael what it all means and feeling that 'the whole world' has seemed to dissolve into 'a deep basin of reality' (266), Lily acknowledges, finally, the profound loss she has suffered in Mrs Ramsay's death. She recognizes, moreover, that while her painting might substitute in the Symbolic for Mrs Ramsay, it cannot ever bring her back.

Even so, by persisting in her feeling that Carmichael (as Other) has greater knowledge, that he is a being who sails 'serenely through a world which satisfied all his wants' (267), Lily manages to believe that the phallus might be restored. 'For one moment she felt that if they both got up, here, now on the lawn, and demanded an explanation, why was it so short, why was it so inexplicable, said it with violence, as two fully equipped human beings from whom nothing should be hid might speak, then, beauty would roll itself up; space would fill; those empty flourishes would form into shape; if they shouted loud enough Mrs. Ramsay would return. "Mrs. Ramsay!" she said aloud, "Mrs. Ramsay!" The tears ran down her face' (268). But Lily's moment here is counterpointed in what is perhaps the most blatantly literary symbolic event in the novel, the senseless mutilation of a fish by the Macalister boy on the boat heading to the lighthouse. That act, like the deaths of Mrs Ramsay, Prue and Andrew in 'Time Passes', is represented as a bracketed hole in the narration. But instead of forming a hole in the Real, the mutilation seems an intrusion here of the brute real into the Symbolic:

> [Macalister's boy took one of the fish and cut a square out of its side to bait his hook with. The mutilated body (it was alive still) was thrown back into the sea.] (268)

Beyond this Symbolic moment, as if from this crucifixion, which is outside her purview, though not that of the text or the textual unconscious, Lily suffers through her most intense pain of mourning, feeling an 'anguish [that] could reduce one to such a pitch of imbecility' as to cause her to 'step off her strip of board into the waters of annihilation' (269).

But beyond this moment, too, the anguish begins to subside; she has now felt the 'sorrow for Mrs. Ramsay' she thought she would never feel (269). Moreover, she takes a renewed interest in completing her painting, for again she feels that primary-process presence, a 'mysterious' 'sense of some one there, of Mrs. Ramsay, relieved for a moment of the weight that the world had put on her, staying lightly by her side and then ... raising to her forehead a wreath of white flowers with which she went' (269). In this image of the flower-wreathed Mrs Ramsay, Lily reenacts in memory the earlier scene of mourning that had accompanied the news of Mrs Ramsay's death. For Lily the scene has to be repeated constantly – it is a 'vision [that] must be perpetually remade' (270) – because she has not accepted the ultimacy of symbolic castration, the necessary shift from the fusional Imaginary to the distancing of the Symbolic. At the end of this scene of her imagining Mrs Ramsay's traversing the 'fields of death' (270), Lily finally seems prepared to shift her focus away from the maternal (m)Other to the paternal Other. That shift occurs as the result of another intrusive object, not remembered, but seen now on the ocean's surface; it is 'a brown spot in the middle of the bay' (270) that turns out to be Ramsay's boat heading toward the lighthouse. On that boat is the paternal signifier, and it is this signifier that Lily seems finally able to acknowledge and accept. 'Where was he, that very old man who had gone past her silently, holding a brown paper parcel under his arm?' (271). Now Lily is faced with achieving 'that razor edge of balance between two opposite forces: Mr. Ramsay and the picture' (287). Clearly, the balance of these two represents for Lily the balance between Mr and Mrs Ramsay, father and mother, male and female. When Lily, in her extensive rememoration of the past, imagines the marriage of these two, she is prepared to accept the place of the dominant signifier. Thus as Mrs Ramsay becomes for Lily a 'part of ordinary experience' (300), Lily becomes ready to yield to Mr Ramsay, the father in the Symbolic. 'Where was the boat now? And Mr. Ramsay? She wanted him' (300). As Lacan would say, it is he – and what he represents – that Lily 'wants', 'lacks', 'desires'.

When Lily surmises that Mr Ramsay 'must have reached' the lighthouse (308), the psychic fact is that she too has reached it, reached, that is, the phallic signifier, the domain of the Symbolic. The feeling Lily evinces in this moment is rather erotic, as well it might be … For her 'the effort of looking at it and the effort of thinking of him landing there, which both seemed to be one and the same effort, had stretched her body and mind to the utmost. Ah, but she was relieved. Whatever she had wanted to give him, when he left her that morning, she had given him at last' (308–9). At this ecstatic moment of submission to the phallic signifier, Lily turns to that other figure of the Other, Carmichael, now 'looking like an old pagan god' (309), like one who has the power to offer a benediction or 'sanctification' (Rosenthal, 1979, 127) to the passage Lily and the others have made to the lighthouse. 'Carmichael stood there as if he were spreading his hands over all the weakness and suffering of mankind; she thought he was surveying, tolerantly and compassionately, their final destiny. Now he has crowned the occasion, she thought, when his hand slowly fell, as if she had seen him let fall from his great height a wreath of violets and asphodels which, fluttering slowly, lay at length upon the earth' (309).

With this blessing from her more immediate Other from the domain of the Symbolic, Lily is enabled to complete her painting. The mark on the canvas that completes the painting is one that commemorates the lighthouse and the phallic signifier at the same time that it is a cut reifying the lesson of the Law (see Fleishman and Harrington for discussions of the 'central line'). In effect, Lily's brush becomes the blade in the air that Lily frequently imagines. 'With a sudden intensity, as if she saw it clear for a second, she drew a line there, in the centre. It was done; it was finished. Yes, she thought, laying down her brush in extreme fatigue, I have had my vision' (310). Her vision, Lacan might conclude, is precisely to picture the place of the Symbolic amidst the turmoil of the Imaginary in human life. As I have suggested before, the stay against confusion effected by Lily's painting and Woolf's novel is only momentary, as is the momentary triumph of the Symbolic over death and mourning. But it seems likely that Lacan and Woolf ... would agree that however momentary those Symbolic, aesthetic stays, they are the only ones we shall get. And they may also be all we shall need.

ANNOTATED BIBLIOGRAPHY

Freud, Sigmund. *The Standard Edition of the Complete Psychoanalytic Works of Sigmund Freud*, 24 vols, ed. and trans. James Strachey. London, 1953–74.

Often referred to as SE, this is the standard English translation of Freud's works. It contains his developing theories regarding infantile sexuality and the development of the Oedipus complex, his discovery of the unconscious mind, and his changing views of the drives towards both pleasure and death. He establishes the relationship, between linguistic ambiguity and the unconscious, especially with regard to jokes, parapraxes, Freudian slips and dreams. His discussions of case histories, such as 'The Wolf Man', 'Little Hans' and 'Dora' are essential reading, and scholarly debate especially among feminists about their conduct and status as evidence continues unabated.

Gallop, Jane. *The Daughter's Seduction: Feminism and Psychoanalysis*. Ithaca, NY, 1982.

Gallop spells out the fundamental feminist problems with psychoanalytic theory, particular with the move that traditional psychoanalytic theory sees in the female as committed to the course of maturation – from an attachment to the mother to an attachment to the father. Gallop works from within the concepts, of the discipline, and seeks, with Lacan, to redefine the phallus as a referent-free concept, or at least having a contingent and therefore shifting referent to do with those sources of power which institute the Symbolic order. When the phallus is freed from its association with the penis in this way, a criticism of essentialism in both psychoanalytic and feminist discourses becomes possible, without sacrificing the intellectually valuable linguistic and philosophical concepts of Freud, Lacan and other thinkers.

Lacan, Jacques. *Écrits: A Selection*, trans. Alan Sheridan. London, 1977.

This is a selection of the original French version of *Écrits* (ed. Jacques Alain Miller. Paris: Seuil, 1966). The short and comparatively readable essay on the Mirror Stage is widely misunderstood, and it is well worthwhile for students to form their own opinion of Lacan's views on this. Especially useful is the appended guide to Lacanian vocabulary and to reference points in the text where key terms are discussed and used.

Lacan, Jacques. *The Four Fundamental Concepts of Psychoanalysis*, trans. Alan Sheridan. London, 1977.

An extremely important and relatively readable set of articles edited from the lecture series and subsequent question-and-answer sessions. Lacan deals with the nature of psychoanalysis. In the first section he argues for the transformation of Freud's views of the unconscious mind into the Lacanian view of the unconscious as primarily linguistic. Section two on the gaze as *objet petit a* is of fundamental importance both to the visual arts and to the concept of the 'screen', discussed above. Finally, after a section on the transference as an exchange of psychic identifications between patient and analyst, Lacan moves to bring psychoanalytic practice and language theory into juxtaposition through the concepts of desire/lack.

Laplanche, J. and Pontalis, J. *The Language of Psychoanalysis*, intro. Daniel Lagache. London, 1973.

This encyclopaedic dictionary of psychoanalytic terminology is an extended reference work, containing substantial discussions of key terms from a variety of schools of psychoanalysis, including American and modern French. The invaluable bibliographical references give the locations in Freud's works and elsewhere where concepts originated, and thus form a guide to further reading. It is not designed for the literary critic, and some of the more arcane Lacanian formulations do not appear.

SUPPLEMENTARY BIBLIOGRAPHY

Adams, Parveen. *The Emptiness of the Image: Psychoanalysis and Sexual Differences.* London, 1996.

Barker, Jill. 'Does Edie Count? A Psychoanalytic Perspective on "Snowed Up"', in *Literary Theories: A Case Study in Critical Performance*, eds Julian Wolfreys and William Baker. London, 1996.

Bowie, Malcolm. *Freud, Proust and Lacan.* Cambridge, 1987.

———. *Lacan.* London, 1991.

———. *Psychoanalysis and the Future of Theory.* Oxford, 1991.

Brooks, Peter. 'The Idea of a Psychoanalytic Literary Criticism', in *Discourse in Psychoanalysis and Literature*, ed. Shlomith Rimmon-Kenan. London, 1987.

———. *Body Works: Objects of Desire in Modern Narrative.* Cambridge, MA, 1993.

Chase, Cynthia. 'Desire and Identification in Lacan and Kristeva', in *Feminism and Psychoanalysis*, eds Richard Feldstein and Judith Roof. Ithaca, NY, 1989.

Con Davis, Robert, ed. *The Fictional Father: Lacanian Readings of the Text.* Amherst, MA, 1981.

Ellmann, Maud, ed. *Psychoanalytic Literary Criticism.* London, 1994.

Felman, Shoshana. *Writing and Madness: Literature/Philosophy/Psychoanalysis.* Ithaca, NY, 1985.

———. *Jacques Lacan and the Adventure of Insight: Psychoanalysis in Contemporary Culture.* Cambridge, MA, 1987.

———, ed. *Literature and Psychoanalysis: The Question of Reading: Otherwise.* Baltimore, MD, 1982.

Ferrer, Daniel. 'To the Lighthouse', in *Psychoanalytic Literary Criticism*, ed. Maud Ellmann. London, 1994.

Gallop, Jane. *The Daughter's Seduction: Feminism and Psychoanalysis.* London, 1982.

Grosz, Elizabeth. *Jacques Lacan: A Feminist Introduction.* London, 1990.

Hartmann, Geoffrey. *Psychoanalysis and the Question of the Text.* Baltimore, MD, 1978.

Heath, Stephen. 'Difference', *Screen*, 19: 3, 1978.

Irigaray, Luce. *This Sex Which Is Not One*, Trans. Catherine Porter. Ithaca, NY, 1985.

————. *Speculum of the Other Woman*, trans. Catherine Gill. Ithaca, NY, 1985.

Kaplan, E. Ann. *Psychoanalysis and Cinema*. London, 1990.

Kerrigan, William, and Joseph H. Smith, eds. *Interpreting Lacan*. New Haven, CT, 1983.

Kristeva, Julia. *Desire in Language: A Semiotic Approach to Literature and Art*, trans. and ed. Leon S. Roudiez. New York, 1980.

————. *Powers of Horror: An Essay on Abjection*, trans. Leon S. Roudiez. New York, 1982.

————. *The Kristeva Reader*, ed. Toril Moi, trans. Sean Hand and Leon S. Roudiez. Oxford, 1986.

Lacan, Jacques. 'Desire and the Interpretation of Desire in *Hamlet*', *Yale French Studies*, 55–6, 1977.

————. *Écrits: A Selection*. Trans. Alan Sheridan. New York, 1977.

————. *The Four Fundamental Concepts of Psychoanalysis*, trans. Alan Sheridan. London, 1977.

————. *Speech and Language in Psychoanalysis: The Language of the Self*, trans., ed. and intro. Antony Wilden. Baltimore, MD, 1981.

MacCannell, Juliet Flower. *Figuring Lacan: Criticism and the Cultural Unconscious*. London, 1986.

Mellard, James M. *Using Lacan; Reading Fiction*. Urbana, IL, 1991.

Mitchell, Juliet and Jacqueline Rose, eds. *Feminine Sexuality: Jacques Lacan and the Ecole freudienne*. London, 1982.

Muller, John P. and William J. Richardson, eds. *The Purloined Poe: Lacan, Derrida and Psychoanalytic Reading*. Baltimore, MD, 1988.

Mulvey, Laura. 'Visual Pleasure and Narrative Cinema', in *Visual and Other Pleasures*. Basingstoke, 1989.

Rose, Jacqueline. *Sexuality in the Field of Vision*. London, 1986.

Vice, Sue, ed. *Psychoanalytic Criticism: A Reader*. Cambridge, 1996.

Wright, Elizabeth. *Psychoanalytic Criticism: Theory in Practice*. London, 1984.

Young, Robert, ed. *Untying the Text: A Post-Structuralist Reader*. London, 1981.

Žižek, Slavoj. *The Sublime Object of Ideology*. London, 1989.

————. *Enjoy Your Symptom! Jacques Lacan in Hollywood and Out*. London, 1992.

PART 6
DECONSTRUCTION

INTRODUCTION:
WHAT REMAINS UNREAD

Julian Wolfreys

PRELIMINARY STATEMENTS (REITERATING, IN OTHER WORDS)

Deconstruction is an old French word. *Déconstruire. Déconstruction. Se déconstruire.*

It's a very old word in the French language. (Derrida, 1996, 224)

It is also an English word, derived from French: *Deconstruction*. The same as the French. Almost. The same and not the same. *Deconstruction/Déconstruction*. What a difference an accent makes. The accent and its non-translation might be said to mark economically and in a violent fashion the fortunes of deconstruction.

The first known written appearance of the word in English is in 1882. As with its French predecessor, it has legal connotations: 'A reform the beginnings of which must be a work of deconstruction'.

Deconstruction presages reform.

Deconstruction is always immanent in the conceptual languages of Western metaphysics. Yet

> Operating necessarily from the inside, borrowing all the strategic and economic resources of subversion from the old structure, borrowing them structurally, that is to say without being able to isolate their elements and atoms, the enterprise of deconstruction always in a certain way falls prey to its own work. (Derrida, 1974, 24)

Deconstruction is associated with the texts of Jacques Derrida, especially his earlier publications from the 1960s, where he employs the term *deconstruction*.

The term is used on occasion as a possible translation for two German words, *Destruktion* and *abbau*, employed by Martin Heidegger.

Deconstruction is neither a concept nor a thing.

It does not name a methodology.

Deconstruction is one term among many used by Derrida in his writing. Among the other terms used are *hymen, écriture, différance, text, trace, arché-écriture*.

> Derrida had initially proposed [the word *deconstruction*] in a chain with other words – for example, difference, spacing, trace – none of which can command the series or function as a master word. (Kamuf, 1991, vii)

None of these words, *deconstruction* included, is privileged over any other. They are all used on different occasions, in different and differing contexts, without any term assuming an absolute value of use over any of the others. The use of the words is dictated by the object of analysis or text being analysed, and according to the range of contexts – historical, philosophical, conceptual, discursive – which determine the shape and structure of the object or text in question.

> We have taken a series of terms from Derrida, who took them from texts read not according to a program or a method ... but, at least in (irreducible) part, according to the flair and the chance of encounters with what is bequeathed or repressed by the tradition. We have said several times that these terms are singular in the sense that they remain more or less attached to the text from which they were taken, and never achieve the status of metalinguistic or metaconceptual operators. (Bennington, 1993, 267)

They, and others, constitute what Derrida calls non-synonymous substitutions. That is, they do not mean the same thing, nor do they serve the same purpose, yet they operate in the performance of Derrida's in a similar dislocating fashion to describe the unfolding of the functioning structure of a concept.

The purpose in exploring the structure of the structure – its structurality – is to show how all structures rely on a centring or grounding principle, idea, concept which, though never examined as such, guarantees the identity, meaning, value of the structure.

> ... the concept of structure and even the word 'structure' itself are as old as ... Western science and Western philosophy ... Structure – or rather the structurality of structure – although it has always been at work, has always been neutralized or reduced, and this by a process of giving it a center or of referring it to a point of presence, a fixed origin. The function of this center was not only to orient, balance, and organize the structure ... but above all to make sure that the organizing principle of the structure would limit what we might call the *play* of the structure. (Derrida, 1978, 278)

The text, a structure, an idea, an institution, a philosophy, all contain in themselves that which disturbs and is in excess of the serenity of the full, simple identity as such.

To show the structurality of structure is not to deconstruct a text.

You cannot deconstruct a text.

Derrida does not offer us a method of reading called 'deconstruction' which, once learned can be applied to anything we choose to read.

Deconstruction does not name an analysis which allows you to make the text mean anything you like, nor can you ignore either that which the text imposes on you or the structures which determine the singularity of the text.

Derrida provides us with exemplary discussions of text, of a word, a structure, a concept, the structuring principles of a concept. In these exemplary discussions, he has occasionally used the word 'deconstruction'.

Exemplary readings and discussions are faithful to the singularity of that which is being discussed.

Derrida's writing has on a number of occasions performed the exemplary tracing of the contours of whatever it takes to be its object of analysis. In this gesture of tracing, which doubles the writing being delineated in a transformative fashion, Derrida alights upon a single theme, term, word, concept. In so doing, he transforms the structure of the text – concept, institution, theme – through examining how that single figure operates in the structure as a whole, in excess of the structure. At the same time, Derrida does not only analyse this word or figure, standing back at a critical distance. He also puts it to work as a figure for determining the function of that which is being discussed.

The figure in question, far from calming down the production of a single meaning in the overall economy of the text, troubles that logic, making the univocal meaning undecidable. In unfolding the structurality of the structure, Derrida thus makes plain the *aporia* within the structural logic, on which the structure depends for its transmission, yet which it suppresses everywhere. In opening the structure's play to its own movement – already installed in the structure and not imposed from some supposed 'outside' – beyond the centre which the text is conventionally assumed to approve, or on which it is otherwise grounded, Derrida's discussion performs in other words the textual oscillation always already within the structure.

It is such oscillation which conventional and institutional acts of reading seek to damp down, often through institutionally approved methods and techniques of reading that aim to emphasize the harmony of identity, at the cost of difference and undecidability.

So, to reiterate: the exemplary reading cannot be rendered as a methodology, a technique, because, in being faithful to the contours of what is being analysed, the exemplary critique or analysis never applies a theory. On the other hand, the analysis is always already applied, in that it applies itself responsibly to its text. It offers the rigorous delineation of that which is in question, which, when performed, transforms the text, concept, institution, through the focus on that which moves the structure but which is not necessarily logical within the economy of the structure.

SUPPLEMENTARY STATEMENTS (DECONSTRUCTION, SPEAKING FOR ITSELVES)

You know the programme; [deconstruction] cannot be applied because deconstruction is not a doctrine; it's not a method, nor is it a set of rules or tools; it cannot be separated from performatives ... On the one hand, there is no 'applied deconstruction'. But on the other hand, there is nothing else, since deconstruction doesn't consist in a set of theorems, axioms, tools, rules, techniques, methods. If deconstruction, then, is nothing by itself, the only thing it can do is apply, to be applied, to something else, not only in more than one language, but also with something else. There is no deconstruction, deconstruction has no specific object ... Deconstruction cannot be applied and cannot *not* be applied. So we have to deal with this *aporia*, and this is what deconstruction is about. (Derrida, 1996, 217–18)

Deconstruction – which is never single or homogeneous, but which can here, at least provisionally, be identified with 'the work of Derrida' – is concerned with the lucid, patient attempt to trace what has not been read, what remains unread or unreadable within the elaboration of concepts and workings of institutions. (Royle, 1995, 160)

No doubt the success of deconstruction as a term can be explained in part by its resonance with *structure* which was then, in the 1960s, the reigning word of structuralism. Any history of how the word deconstruction entered a certain North American vocabulary, for instance, would have to underscore its critical use in the first text by Derrida to be translated in the United States, 'Structure, Sign, and Play in the Discourse of the Human Sciences.' [Derrida, 1978, 278–93] ... As used here 'de-construction' marks a distance (the space of a hyphen, later dropped [from the word 'de-construction']) from the structuring or construction of discourses ... that have uncritically taken over the legacy of Western metaphysics. If, however, it cannot be a matter of refusing this legacy ... then the distance or difference in question is in the manner of assuming responsibility for what cannot be avoided. Deconstruction is one name Derrida has given to this responsibility. It is not a refusal or a destruction of the terms of the legacy, but occurs through a re-marking and redeployment of these very terms, that is, the concepts of philosophy. (Kamuf, 1991, viii)

Deconstruction is not a theory or a project. It does not prescribe a practice more or less faithful to it, nor project an image of a desirable state to be brought about. (Bennington, 1988, 7)

Deconstruction is not a dismantling of the structure of the text but a demonstration that it has already dismantled itself. (Miller, 1991, 126)

Sentences of the form 'Deconstruction is so and so' are a contradiction in terms. Deconstruction cannot by definition be defined, since it presupposes the indefinability or, more properly, the 'undecidability' of all conceptual or generalizing terms. Deconstruction ... can only be exemplified, and the examples will all differ. (Miller, 1991, 126)

All of Derrida's texts are already applications, so there is no separate 'Derrida' in the form of theory who might *then* be applied to something else. Insofar as 'Deconstruction' tends to become a method or a school, we might say that it has forgotten this, and has begun at least to make Derrida into a theory which it wants to put into practice ... we cannot simply be content to claim that Derrida (sometimes) applies his own theory, or unites theory and practice, or performs theoretical practice ... (Bennington, 1996, 17)

I am not sure that deconstruction can function as a literary *method* as such. I am wary of the idea of methods of reading. The laws of reading are determined by that particular text that is being read. This does not mean that we should simply abandon ourselves to the text, or represent and repeat it in a purely passive manner. It means that we must remain faithful, even if it implies a certain violence, to the injunctions of the text. These injunctions will differ from one text to the next so that one cannot prescribe one general method of reading. In this sense deconstruction is not a method. (Derrida, 1983, 124)

The very idea of a nutshell is a mistake and a misunderstanding, an excess – or rather a defect – of journalistic haste and impatience, a ridiculous demand put by someone ... everything in deconstruction is turned toward opening, exposure, expansion, and complexification ... toward releasing unheard-of, undreamt-of possibilities *to come* ...

The very meaning and mission of deconstruction is to show that things – texts, institutions, traditions, societies, beliefs, and practices of whatever size and sort you need – do not have definable meanings and determinable missions, that they are always more than any mission would impose, that they exceed the boundaries they currently occupy ... A 'meaning' or a 'mission' is a way to contain and compact things, like a nutshell, gathering them into a unity, whereas deconstruction bends all its efforts to stretch beyond these boundaries ... Whenever deconstruction finds a nutshell – a secure axiom or a pithy maxim – the very idea is to crack it open and disturb this tranquillity ... cracking nutshells is what deconstruction *is*. In a nutshell. (Caputo, 1997, 31–2)

In short, deconstruction not only teaches us to read literature more thoroughly by attending to it *as language*, as the production of meaning through *différance* and dissemination, through a complex play of signifying traces; it also enables us to interrogate the covert philosophical and political presuppositions of institutionalized critical methods which generally govern our reading of a text ... It is not a question of calling for the destruction of such institutions, but rather of making us aware of what we are in fact doing when we are subscribing to this or that institutional way of reading. (Derrida, 1983, 125)

As a transformative strategy without finality, as the destabilizing differential effects always already at work everywhere, deconstruction is never single but necessarily multiple and incomplete. (Royle, 1995, 128)

I have often had occasion to define deconstruction as that which is – far from a theory, a school, a method, even a discourse, still less a technique that can be appropriated – at bottom *what happens or comes to pass* [ce qui arrive]. (Derrida, 1995, 17)

Concerning the institution that is the university put in question by the PC debate, the term 'deconstruction' is most often presumed to refer to a theory, a method, a school, perhaps even a doctrine, in any case, some identifiable or localizable 'thing' that can be positioned – posed and opposed – within that institution, but also that can be excluded from this defined enclosure. (Kamuf, 1997, 141)

[The premises of a discourse] ... are not absolute and ahistorical ... They depend upon socio-historical conditions, hence upon nonnatural relations of power that by essence are mobile and founded upon complex conventional structures that in principle may be analyzed ... and in fact, these structures are in the process of transforming themselves profoundly and, above all, very rapidly (this is the true source of anxiety in certain circles, which is merely revealed by 'deconstruction': for before becoming a discourse, an organized practice that *resembles* a philosophy, a theory, a method, which it is *not*, in regard to those unstable stabilities or this destabilization that it makes its principal theme, 'deconstruction' is firstly this destabilization on the move in, if one could speak thus, 'the things themselves'; but it is not negative. Destabilization is required for 'progress' as well. And the 'de-' of *de*construction signifies not the demolition of what is constructing itself, but rather what remains to be thought beyond the constructivist or destructionist scheme). What is at stake here is the entire debate, for instance, on the curriculum, literacy, etc. (Derrida, 1988, 147)

OBJECTIONS, HISTORIES, AND METHODS: SO-CALLED DECONSTRUCTION

Of course, I can hear the voices already. I've slanted the evidence in favour of the idea that deconstruction is neither an analysis, nor a critique, even less a method, a programme, a doctrine, a school of thought. Look at the names: Miller, Kamuf, Bennington, Royle, Caputo, Derrida himself, several times, on several occasions. Defending what he does by saying that he doesn't do it, and saying that he's never said this is what you do (even though he hasn't and he doesn't). As for the others, well, they're all deconstructionists (aren't they?), they all practice the methodology (more or less, now and then); they, and others like them ... well, that's deconstruction for you. It's all very slippery and its practitioners are among the slipperiest. Imagine: an introduction to 'deconstruction' in something called a 'reader and guide to literary theories', in a section, moreover, which gathers under the heading 'Deconstruction' three essays, by Jacques Derrida, J. Hillis Miller and Nicholas Royle, some of those very 'deconstructionists' who have already been quoted, which insists that there is no such thing as a deconstructive approach to literary studies, no such thing as a methodology or school of thought. Imagine. Why, *I* can imagine one of the voices saying, indignantly, I expect whoever's writing this, being a deconstructionist, has even written things like this before. (You're wrong, I'm not, for all the reasons above; but you're right, I have; 1996, 179–244; 1998a; 1998b, 1–49).

Deconstruction has to exist. It has to have an identity. It has to be identifiable, at least for some (see Kamuf, 1997, 141). And, usually, introductions, especially when they are introductions to what we call literary theory, are conventionally obliged to suppose that what is being introduced does, in fact, exist. Deconstruction is taught. It is taught, in universities, as a method of reading and analysis, even while it is given an institutional history. Usually these histories suggest that 'deconstruction' is a French mode of thought, originated by Jacques Derrida, then translated and imported, into the US and UK, into American-English and English-English, and established as a critical practice, especially in the US, in Departments of English (see Adamson, 1993, 25–31). Certainly, Derrida has commented on a number of occasions about the fortunes of deconstruction in North America in these terms, even though he dissociates himself to greater or lesser extents with those manifestations of 'deconstruction'.

Part of the history of 'deconstruction' is to suggest that it flourished as a critical methodology in the early 1970s, particularly at Yale University, where it was championed by four critics in particular, J. Hillis Miller, Geoffrey Hartman, Harold Bloom and Paul de Man (see Rorty, 1995, 178–9). This 'gang of four' were, along with Derrida, who was a visiting professor at Yale during these years, subsequently referred to, usually in the media, and elsewhere, among academics hostile to the idea of deconstruction (even though they never showed signs of really ever having understood it), as the Yale School. These critics practised deconstruction, it was claimed. They allegedly showed through readings of canonical and classical texts that there was no meaning in a work. You could talk about these texts endlessly because the texts could mean anything you chose. The critical discourse of these and other critics was assumed to rely on word play, on puns, on esoteric and obscurantist prose, on an inmixing of literary analysis, a neo- or quasi-Nietzschean renunciation of value and moral worth, and an importation of hard-to-read continental philosophers (especially Hegel and Heidegger!), which assaulted the value of literary masterpieces.

I may be accused of parodying here, but then it's hard to see how one can parody a range of misrepresentations which, themselves, not only verge on but often, and unintentionally, go right over the edge of parody. I have used the words 'claimed' and 'assumed' above to suggest that, in bad journalistic fashion – though a fashion not restricted to journalists alone, but adopted, often all too readily by certain academics – nothing much was *read*. Nothing is clearer, if you take the time to do the research, that, on these and other occasions (about which Nicholas Royle speaks in his essay below, in the section entitled 'Not reading Derrida'), many have not read either the texts of Derrida or those who are aligned with the word *deconstruction*. (The reader is also referred to Peggy Kamuf's discussion of a review from the *New York Review of Books*, and a letter which the review subsequently drew forth (1997, 141–5).) If there are similar concerns between the work of Jacques Derrida and that of, say Paul de Man, or Peggy Kamuf, Geoffrey Bennington, Hillis Miller or Philippe Lacoue-Labarthe, then there are also marked dissimilarities, which remain unread and which are equally as strong as the similarities, if not more so. However, the attempt to define deconstruction as a practice partakes of that tendency in the history of thought to assign resemblances between disparate things: conventionally, one erases the difference between thinkers, between texts, in the effort to domesticate the textual ground shared between them, producing a likeness into which all can be subsumed, at the cost of difference. Producing a theory is, therefore, producing what Derrida has described as a 'family atmosphere' (1989, 7), or tailoring a theoretical equivalent of the 'one-size-fits-all' garment.

However, there is neither the time nor the space, unfortunately, to do much more than to gesture, in a highly schematic manner, in the direction of the 'history of institutionalized deconstruction'. What the response to 'deconstruction' tells us is that 'deconstruction' whatever it may have or have not meant, had to be invented and given an institutional, unified identity, which, once defined and domesticated, could then be signalled, gestured towards, and often attacked, as merely one example of 'radical' thought 'infecting' 'our' – detractors and critics just love the bullying power which that plural pronoun affords them; they give themselves credit to speak for others, even though others haven't been consulted, and may even hold differing views – universities and colleges. I have yet to describe the conventional view of what deconstruction as a methodology might be, free from all critical attacks. Two brief examples will have to suffice.

The misreading or not-reading of Derrida emerges chiefly from responses to his *of Grammatology*, where, among other things, he examines and calls into question the operation of meaningful structures of binary opposition as these pertain throughout the history of western metaphysics. This assessment of what Derrida termed at the time 'logocentrism' – the conceptual movement of thought which calms movement in favour of locating centres, origins, essences – was part of the work of *Of Grammatology* to expose how any system, structure, form or concept, in orienting itself according to some centre or truth, necessarily suppresses that which remains undecidable according to the logical economy of the structure. Yet that which is undecidable, or that which contradicts the logic and identity of the subject, is also that which serves to articulate the structure. This 'movement' if you will, this trace of the undecidable, is not something foreign to the structure. It is always already of it and in it as a necessary feature of the structure or concept's identity, yet always in excess of that which is deemed proper to the identity in question.

Derrida's discussion was taken to be part of a general method, and this method was called by critics deconstruction. From such acts of translation, translating from the specific to the general, come the tendencies to theorise deconstruction and, in so doing, to give deconstruction the 'it-ness' of a discernible identity, to create for it the 'family resemblance', and to assign 'it' 'its' institutional home. We see gestures in this direction in discussions of deconstruction which attempt to come to terms with 'it' by Christopher Norris and Terry Eagleton. Norris suggests that:

> To deconstruct a text is to draw out conflicting logics of sense and implication, with the object of showing that the text never exactly means what it says or says what it means. (Norris, 1988, 7)

Clearly for Norris, deconstruction is an activity, available for the critical reader's mastery, and reliant upon that reader's active imposition of the method of analysis. Although the remark can be read as subject-sensitive (one could always draw out conflicting logics according to the peculiarities of the text), it is all too easy to see how such a remark, which is by no means untypical of definitions of deconstruction, can be amplified and otherwise worked up into a general programme for a critical purpose. Mistaking the drawing out of conflicting logics for what Derrida does or, worse, all that Derrida does, it is only another step to suggesting that this is what deconstruction does (as Norris in fact implies in the opening of the sentence). Eagleton offers a similar definition. Despite the fact that, in 1981, he had described deconstruction as a kind of 'left reformism' (1981, 133), giving it a provisional political identity, and subsequently made it plain that deconstruction was not 'of course, a system, or a theory, or even a method' (1981, 135), two years later here is Eagleton on the subject of deconstruction once more:

> 'deconstruction' is the name given to the *critical operation* by which . . . [binary] oppositions can be partly undermined, or by which they *can be shown* partly to undermine each other in the process of textual meaning . . . *The tactic of deconstructive criticism . . . is to show* how texts come to embarrass their own ruling systems of logic; and *deconstruction shows this* by fastening on the 'symptomatic' points, the *aporia* or impasses of meaning, where texts get into trouble, come unstuck, offer to contradict themselves. (Eagleton, 1983, 132, 133–4; emphases added)

Eagleton's view is similar to Norris's; phrases such as 'critical operation' and 'the tactic of deconstructive criticism' invent the possibility that one can deconstruct. The phrases I've highlighted all nod in the direction of a weary pedagogy, a quasi-scientifism of teaching by example. The implication, obviously, is that the reader can study Derrida's texts with the purpose of extracting a critical practice and then, having gained control over the niceties of this form of criticism, rendering it, that is, as a theory or method, can go away and apply the extracted model to whichever text he or she wishes.

This is not the case, however. If you spend some time with the texts of Jacques Derrida, or with the three texts published here, by Derrida, Miller and Royle; if you spend time, moreover with other texts in this reader, where Derrida is invoked or otherwise has left a ghostly trace (see Sedgwick, Butler, Dollimore, Bhabha, Lydon, just for starters), you will find that there is no method, no reproducible structure of critique, except the act of responsible attentiveness.

EXEMPLARY ESSAYS: TRANSLATION, TRANSFERENCE, TRANSPORT

Each of the essays presented here deals in some sense with the movement between languages, between texts, even within the same language. Such movement is necessary and inevitable as that which makes meaning possible, even though the attempt to read after meaning is one which aims to still the movement. The three essayists do not work with a common theory of language and its effects. Derrida employs the occasion of the possible translation of *deconstruction* into Japanese to translate *deconstruction* from its translated, transformed institutional reception in the university. Miller reads a poem by Thomas Hardy to consider issues of communication and transference, where the transmission determines the identity of the addressee ahead of its arrival. Royle considers the tripartite relationship between the trope of not reading in Derrida, the not-reading of Derrida within the academy, and Derrida's professed inability to read Samuel Beckett. Each essay differs from every other essay, except in the respect paid to the singularity of that which is being read. There is no method here, no applied theory as such. Yet Royle, Miller and Derrida each share a similar attentiveness and patience to that which interests them.

As just mentioned, the occasion of Derrida's letter is the discussion of the possibilities of translating 'deconstruction' (see Bennington, 1993, 166–79). Immediately, Derrida turns the discussion of translation to the desire to avoid negative connotations for 'deconstruction', initiating a clearing of the ground by indicating that the significance of 'deconstruction' is best approached by considering what it ought not to be. At the same time, Derrida stresses that one cannot simply say what deconstruction is or is not because no univocal or unequivocal meaning pertains to the word, even if one stays in the same language, French. The sense of the word is always multiple within itself, and it cannot be traced to a single sense or source. Also, the word changes its meaning according to use. Thus, there is already a translation effect at work within one language and within one word. Moreover, Derrida points out, the meanings of 'deconstruction' have been translated or transferred according to the contexts of use. Here, Derrida is speaking of that translation which 'deconstruction' undergoes in the conceptual, technical and institutional (as, for example, in the transformation of 'deconstruction' into a technical name for a critical operation practised in an institutional guise).

For Derrida the question of deconstruction is always one of translation within the history of Western thought. Deconstruction *qua* translation is the movement which inhabits and informs the 'conceptual corpus' of western thought. The question is one of how we effect the movement in thought between conceptual structures, other than by translation. Moreover, what is taken with us, what is transformed, and what remains untranslatable? To put this final question another way, what are the remains of deconstruction? What remains to be read in 'deconstruction' which the Anglo-American translation of 'deconstruction' has left unread? Derrida continues, explaining how the word imposed itself upon him in his search for the adequate translation, from German to French, of those terms used by Heidegger already mentioned, that avoided negative connotations. Derrida's opening advice in his correspondence is recalled, transferred, as he returns to an anterior moment of confrontation over the issue of translation. Explaining his choices, enumerating the linguistic, semantic and technical possibilities of 'deconstruction', Derrida re-presents the variety of meanings available in the family of words which, while offering 'models', do not represent 'the totality of what deconstruction aspires to at its most ambitious'. Furthermore, each 'model' cannot merely be accepted; its conceptual structure must first be questioned.

Remaining 'deconstruction', deconstruction nonetheless becomes translated. Derrida points to certain translations of 'deconstruction' which have occurred as a result of more obvious lexical meanings. From this he proceeds to elaborate the sense of 'deconstruction', not in some general, abstract or conceptual fashion (for that is impossible). Instead, he insists on discussing the possibility of the word's possible significations only within certain contexts. It should be clear from this that deconstruction is not to be thought of as a conceptual term which arrives 'ready-made' to determine the meaning of a situation (such as the terms True/False might conventionally be said to do). Derrida grounds his use of the word by sketching a brief history of the emergence of 'deconstruction' as, initially, a 'structuralist' gesture, but also as a response to structuralism. Importantly here, 'deconstruction' is signalled as naming in part the comprehension and reconstruction or reformation of the structural 'ensemble' of, say, a concept. As Derrida puts it, deconstruction names a 'genealogical restoration'.

Deconstruction cannot therefore be 'reduced to some methodological instrumentality or to a set of rules and transposable procedures', because that which is read as deconstructive, what remains elsewhere unread and yet translated into the language of the system, is intrinsic to the structurality of the structure. As Derrida says in this piece, deconstruction is neither 'an *analysis* nor a *critique*'. Furthermore, it is not a method, even if it appears to have suffered a history of translation aiming at the wilful reinvention of the term as a 'technical and methodological' metaphor for a process or procedure.

Derrida continues, pointing out that we should also avoid thinking of deconstruction as an act awaiting application to a text, object or theme (see Norris and Eagleton, above). If deconstruction *is* anything, it is an 'event'. It takes place, as the French reflexive verb suggests, everywhere, *in* every structure, theme, concept, conceptual organisation, ahead of any consciousness. Its event is not the same every time but is a condition of or (we might say) translated by the structure in which it insists. Reading the taking place of deconstruction gives us to understand the operation of the structure, allowing the possibility of comprehension and reform. In effect, this comprehension and reformation (both terms requiring a patient analysis of their conceptual constitution) is what Derrida imagines as he sketches the possibility of translating deconstruction. His own text gestures towards the performance, if we can put it this way, of the deconstruction of deconstruction. This is not because Derrida's letter is a deconstructive reading, but because he analyses, within the limits of a specific use and reception, a specific history, the 'incapacity of the word to be equal to a "thought"'. Thus, this letter addresses itself, in anticipating its addressee and the future transmission of deconstruction, to deconstruction's previous communications.

J. Hillis Miller's essay also concerns the possible effects of transmission and communication. In presenting a reading of Thomas Hardy's poem 'The Torn Letter', Miller situates his discussion, providing a 'line of communication', via Franz Kafka and Jacques Derrida, in order to consider the performative effects of a letter on the addressee as this is given exemplary expression through Hardy's text. Writing, Miller points out, citing Kafka, dislocates. It spaces addresser and addressee, not only from one another, but also from themselves, within themselves. The self is translated in the event of writing into 'multiple simultaneous selves'. Writing thus marks a differentiation, a spacing, as well as always having the power to transform 'you' into the 'you' which it addresses. This is not Miller's theory, and neither is it Derrida's, even though both men have, on numerous occasions, discussed the temporal and spatial dislocations, deferrals and differentiations traced in writing. It is precisely not a theory, as Miller's essay economically demonstrates, because this understanding of writing is effectively performed by both Kafka and Hardy, ahead of and in anticipation of any so-called 'theory of deconstruction'. For Miller, writing, even as it seeks to communicate and to connect, only serves in its very movement to displace by the very rhythm and spacing of its transport and transference. Indeed, displacement, dislocation, are always already the movement *of* and *in* writing, ahead of any transference or communication.

In situating his discussion of the performative effects of writing, particularly the act of writing a letter, Miller has recourse to Derrida's 'Télépathie'. In this essay, Derrida, Miller asserts and shows, discusses the possible performative effects of the letter on its recipient. As Miller puts it, the letter is capable, unintentionally, of creating the identity of the addressee. The performative power of the letter is in its ability to 'produce its recipient', as Derrida suggests.

The letter, before the event of its transference, carries in it the anticipated translation of the self, 'just as poor Boldwood, in Thomas Hardy's novel *Far from the Madding Crowd*, becomes the bold lover Bathsheba's valentine seems to tell him he is'. In drawing out the logic of Derrida's commentary on the performative capability of epistolary acts, Miller effectively shows how Hardy's poem, quite unintentionally, anticipates Derrida's argument. Derrida, writes Miller, 'has been programmed by the poem to write an interpretation of it before, beside, or after the letter, so to speak, in displacement from any conscious encounter with it.' Derrida's essay does not therefore invent a theory of epistolary transmission; he merely responds to that which the epistolary performs, 'translating' what is already there in writing, without ever having read Hardy's poem. Hardy's poem for Miller makes the same claims concerning transmission and performativity as Derrida's essay, albeit in a highly different, singular manner. Opening the lines of communication, Miller shows how, in a certain way, writing operates upon the reading self, who becomes not the 'I' who speaks, who thinks, who writes this poem letter, a letter in fragments, in ruins, but the self who becomes instead that 'you' to whom the poem addresses itself. Taking this to be the case, we should return to 'Letter to a Japanese Friend' in order to comprehend how the letter assumes the identity of a 'you' who we become if we receive its address carefully, no longer seeking to think of 'deconstruction' as a theory or method, but instead as that which traces all articulation of identities.

If there is a question here of reception and the construction of identity, then it must also be acknowledged, as does Nicholas Royle, that 'a writer's work can be received without being read: texts can have effects without being read'. Once more, though in a manner significantly different from either Miller or Derrida, the emphasis here is on communication, transmission, translation. Indeed, Royle, in beginning his essay, stresses a certain translation of Derrida's work as an effect of having not read Derrida. Royle's interest in having not read Derrida, Derrida not reading, and not reading in Derrida's work all concern Royle's principal interest in the 'spectral character of writing'. Miller speaks of the ghostly as an effect of writing, of writing's ability to produce ghosts. This interest is pursued as Royle traces the relationship between Derrida's 'professed inability to write about' Samuel Beckett and the ways in which Beckett's work might be read so as to illuminate the questions of reading and writing after Derrida.

Thus the critic employs a reading of Beckett, much as Miller had provided a reading of Hardy, to address issues raised by these writers, but which they share with Derrida, albeit articulated in a manner very different from Derrida's own explorations. (Once more, the point here, in passing, is that Derrida's concerns do not originate with him, nor do they amount to a theory. They are, often, the concerns of literature but, within the conventional and even, in some cases, current horizon of expectations of literary analysis, remain unread.) Royle's concern in so doing is to move from conventional wisdom on Derrida –

that his work is either 'philosophical' or 'literary' – in order to suggest that in part, because of the constant enunciation of authority vested in the articulation of 'I', Derrida is not sufficiently literary enough.

Royle draws on Derrida's work on citationality and iterability as a condition of writing, the possibility that for writing to be readable, it can be transferred, transmitted, translated, outside its context or initial inscription (see Derrida, 1982, 309–30; 1991, 11–48). Take briefly the form of the proper name. Although the proper name is supposedly unique, in order that it be meaningful or readable, it must operate as does language in general: it must be capable of retransmission outside of its supposedly original occasion, unique status or authoritative inscription (see Bennington, 1993, 104–14, 148–66; also, see Bennington on the title, 241–58). In being iterable, the proper name is not proper, but is wholly typical of writing's movements and translations. This quality of iterability pertains to all language, determining the fact of its readability. For Royle, that writing is iterable suggests that, far from having been read, definitively, it remains as a possible future iteration, still to be read, not yet having been read. The iterable movement of writing dissolves all authority, and specifically that, in this essay, of 'I'. 'I', that which 'I' write as a sign of my authority and control, also as an iterable re-mark, bears in it, in the possibility of its function and comprehension, the iteration beyond me, beyond my death (Bennington, 1993, 110). Thus, *in* the articulation of what Royle calls 'identity-as-authority' is traced the displacement of authority, not read, not yet read, awaiting reading.

Taking Derrida's professed feeling of proximity to Beckett as the instance of not reading in Derrida, Royle turns to Beckett's text. Beckett's writing enacts for Royle this displacement of authority, where 'I' is not attributable to any source, but is, instead, the articulation of the spectral as the space of what is called the literary. The critic traces the instances of pronominal markers across the text of Beckett as the dislocation of authority through the written trace, which remains (as) unattributable. In this reading, the 'space of literature ... disables and dissolves the very possibility of "one's own position"'. Derrida's writing, on the other hand, is, unlike Beckett's, marked by numerous signs of 'identity-as-authority', especially, as Royle shows, in their opening gambits of numerous essays where 'I' appears everywhere, centre-stage, apparently seeking to control the scene.

For this reason, Derrida's writing may be tentatively understood, the critic warily proposes, as not literary enough. From the perspective of the reading of Beckett, and juxtaposing Beckett with Derrida, the latter's writings are seen to 'deploy and rely on authority effects', which subsequently are 'dissolved and dispossessed' in the space of literature and by the effect of writing. Thus writing deconstructs the sovereign 'I'. 'I', in being written, deconstructs the assumption of it-self as a univocal location. *Se déconstruire*: it (itself) deconstructs (itself). In this understanding, if the literary is that which dispossesses one of all authority, Derrida's writing, which is taken as performing the deconstruction of the subject, in assuming the subject position only to displace that, does not go far enough, and needs 'to be further radicalised'. Realising the 'folly' of such a proposal, Nicholas Royle concludes by imagining a future moment of not reading Derrida, where Derrida is no longer cited, but is, in Royle's term *ex-cited*; quoted nowhere, but having passed spectrally into the language.

To the extent that deconstruction is still termed a method or a school of thought, the communication has not yet reached its destination. Having gone awry through the passages of translation, deconstruction remains unread in its guise as that which names an identity. The conventional narratives of so-called deconstruction leave deconstruction unread in their constructivist or determinist efforts to introduce 'deconstruction', to produce for 'it' a stable identity, to offer it up as one more, somewhat idiosyncratic yet nonetheless typical conceptual structure in the family atmosphere of western metaphysics. What can be said in conclusion is that, if, as a provisional definition after Royle, deconstruction is that multiplicity of traces which remain unread in the structurality of any text, structure, institution or concept, then deconstruction, we might say, is also that, precisely, which remains unread, in the texts of Jacques Derrida. Hence the need and the inescapable double-bind (not) to (not) read this signature, Jacques Derrida, as the authorising source of deconstruction.

6.1

LETTER TO A JAPANESE FRIEND

Jacques Derrida

10 July 1983

Dear Professor Izutsu,[1]

At our last meeting I promised you some schematic and preliminary reflections on the word 'deconstruction'. What we discussed were prolegomena to a possible translation of this word into Japanese, one which would at least try to avoid, if *possible*, a negative determination of its significations or connotations. The question would be therefore what deconstruction is not, or rather *ought* not to be. I underline these words 'possible' and 'ought'. For if the difficulties of translation can be anticipated (and the question of deconstruction is also through and through *the* question of translation, and of the language of concepts, of the conceptual corpus of so-called Western metaphysics), one should not begin by naively believing that the word 'deconstruction' corresponds in French to some clear and univocal signification. There is already in 'my' language a serious [*sombre*] problem of translation between what here or there can be envisaged for the word and the usage itself, the reserves of the word. And it is already clear that even in French, things change from one context to another. More so in the German, English, and especially American contexts, where the *same* word is already attached to very different connotations, inflections, and emotional or affective values. Their analysis would be interesting and warrants a study of its own.

When I choose this word, or when it imposed itself upon me – I think it was

Extract from Jacques Derrida, *A Derrida Reader: Between the Blinds*, ed. Peggy Kamuf (Columbia University Press, 1991), pp. 270–6.

in *Of Grammatology* – I little thought it would be credited with such a central role in the discourse that interested me at the time. Among other things I wished to translate and adapt to my own ends the Heideggerian word *Destruktion* or *Abbau*. Each signified in this context an operation bearing on the structure or traditional architecture of the fundamental concepts of ontology or of Western metaphysics. But in French 'destruction' too obviously implied an annihilation or a negative reduction much closer perhaps to Nietzschean 'demolition' than to the Heideggerian interpretation or to the type of reading that I proposed. So I ruled that out. I remember having looked to see if the word 'deconstruction' (which came to me it seemed quite spontaneously) was good French. I found it in the *Littré*: The grammatical, linguistic, or rhetorical senses [*portées*] were found bound up with a 'mechanical' sense [*portée 'machinique'*]. This association appeared very fortunate and fortunately adapted to what I wanted at least to suggest. Perhaps I could cite some of the entries from the *Littré*. '*Déconstruction*: action of deconstructing. Grammatical term. Disarranging the construction of words in a sentence. 'Of deconstruction, common way of saying construction,' Lemare, *De la manière d'apprendre les langues*, chap. 17, in *Cours de langue Latine. Déconstruire*. I. To disassemble the parts of a whole. To deconstruct a machine to transport it elsewhere. 2. Grammatical term ... To deconstruct verse, rendering it, by the suppression of meter, similar to prose. Absolutely. ('In the system of prenotional sentences, one also starts with translation and one of its advantages is never needing to deconstruct,' Lemare, ibid., 3. *Se déconstruire* [to deconstruct itself] ... to lose its construction. 'Modern scholarship has shown us that in a region of the timeless East, a language reaching its own state of perfection is deconstructed [*s'est déconstruire*] and altered from within itself according to the single law of change, natural to the human mind,' Villemain, *Préface du Dictionnaire de l'Académie.*'

Naturally it will be necessary to translate all of this into Japanese but that only postpones the problem. It goes without saying that if all the significations enumerated by the *Littré* interested me because of their affinity with what I 'meant' ['*voulais-dire*'], they concerned, metaphorically, so to say, only models or regions of meaning and not the totality of what deconstruction aspires to at its most ambitious. This is not limited to a linguistico-grammatical model, nor even a semantic model, let alone a mechanical model. These models themselves ought to be submitted to a deconstructive questioning. It is true then that these 'models' have been behind a number of misunderstandings about the concept and word of 'deconstruction' because of the temptation to reduce it to these models.

It must also be said that the word was rarely used and was largely unknown in France. It had to be reconstructed in some way, and its use value had been determined by the discourse that was then being attempted around and on the basis of *Of Grammatology*. It is to this use value that I am now going to try to give some precision and not some primitive meaning or etymology sheltered from or outside of any contextual strategy.

A few more words on the subject of 'the context'. At that time structuralism was dominant. 'Deconstruction' seemed to be going in the same direction since the word signified a certain attention to structures (which themselves were neither simply ideas, nor forms, nor syntheses, nor systems). To deconstruct was also a structuralist gesture or in any case a gesture that assumed a certain need for the structuralist problematic. But it was also an antistructuralist gesture, and its fortune rests in part on this ambiguity. Structures were to be undone, decomposed, desedimented (all types of structures, linguistic, 'logocentric', 'phonocentric' – structuralism being especially at that time dominated by linguistic models and by a so-called structural linguistics that was also called Saussurian – socio-institutional, political, cultural, and above all and from the start philosophical). This is why, especially in the United States, the motif of deconstruction has been associated with 'poststructuralism' (a word unknown in France until its 'return' from the United States). But the undoing, decomposing, and desedimenting of structures, in a certain sense more historical than the structuralist movement it called into question, was not a negative operation. Rather than destroying, it was also necessary to understand how an 'ensemble' was constituted and to reconstruct it to this end. However, the negative appearance was and remains much more difficult to efface than is suggested by the grammar of the word (de-), even though it can designate a genealogical restoration [remonter] rather than a demolition. That is why this word, at least on its own, has never appeared satisfactory to me (but what word is), and must always be girded by an entire discourse. It is difficult to effect it afterward because, in the work of deconstruction, I have had to, as I have to here, multiply the cautionary indicators and put aside all the traditional philosophical concepts, while reaffirming the necessity of returning to them, at least under erasure. Hence, this has been called, precipitously, a type of negative theology (this was neither true nor false but I shall not enter into the debate here).[2]

All the same, and in spite of appearances, deconstruction is neither an *analysis* nor a *critique* and its translation would have to take that into consideration. It is not an analysis in particular because the dismantling of a structure is not a regression toward a *simple element*, toward an *indissoluble origin*. These values, like that of analysis, are themselves philosophemes subject to deconstruction. No more is it a critique, in a general sense or in a Kantian sense. The instance of *krinein* or of *krisis* (decision, choice, judgment, discernment) is itself, as is all the apparatus of transcendental critique, one of the essential 'themes' or 'objects' of deconstruction.

I would say the same about *method*. Deconstruction is not a method and cannot be transformed into one. Especially if the technical and procedural significations of the words are stressed. It is true that in certain circles (university or cultural, especially in the United States) the technical and methodological 'metaphor' that seems necessarily attached to the very word 'deconstruction' has been able to seduce or lead astray. Hence the debate that has developed in these circles: Can deconstruction become a methodology for reading and for interpretation? Can it thus let itself be reappropriated and domesticated by academic institutions?

It is not enough to say that deconstruction could not be reduced to some methodological instrumentality or to a set of rules and transposable procedures. Nor will it do to claim that each deconstructive 'event' remains singular or, in any case, as close as possible to something like an idiom or a signature. It must also be made clear that deconstruction is not even an *act* or an *operation*. Not only because there would be something 'patient' or 'passive' about it (as Blanchot says, more passive than passivity, than the passivity that is opposed to activity). Not only because it does not return to an individual or collective *subject* who would take the initiative and apply it to an object, a text, a theme, etc. Deconstruction takes place, it is an event that does not await the deliberation, consciousness, or organization of a subject, or even of modernity. *It deconstructs it-self. It can be deconstructed. [Ça se déconstruit.]* The 'it' *[ça]* is not here an impersonal thing that is opposed to some egological subjectivity. *It is in deconstruction* (the *Littré* says, 'to deconstruct it-self *[se déconstruire]* . . . to lose its construction'). And the 'se' of 'se déconstruire', which is not the reflexivity of an ego or of a consciousness, bears the whole enigma. I recognize, my dear friend, that in trying to make a word clearer so as to assist its translation, I am only thereby increasing the difficulties: 'the impossible task of the translator' (Benjamin). This too is what is meant by 'deconstructs'.

If deconstruction takes place everywhere it *[ça]* takes place, where there is something (and is not therefore limited to meaning or to the text in the current and bookish sense of the word), we still have to think through what is happening in our world, in modernity, at the time when deconstruction is becoming a motif, with its word, its privileged themes, its mobile strategy, etc. I have no simple and formalizable response to this question. All my essays are attempts to have it out with this formidable question. They are modest symptoms of it, quite as much as tentative interpretations. I would not even dare to say, following a Heideggerian schema, that we are in an 'epoch' of being-in-deconstruction, of a being-in-deconstruction that would manifest or dissimulate itself at one and the same time in other 'epochs'. This thought of 'epochs' and especially that of a gathering of the destiny of being and of the unity of its destination or its dispersions *(Schicken, Geschick)* will never be very convincing.

To be very schematic I would say that the difficulty of *defining* and therefore also of *translating* the word 'deconstruction' stems from the fact that all the predicates, all the defining concepts, all the lexical significations, and even the syntactic articulations, which seem at one moment to lend themselves to this definition or to that translation, are also deconstructed or deconstructible, directly or otherwise, etc. And that goes for the *word*, the very unity of the *word* deconstruction, as for every *word*. *Of Grammatology* questioned the unity 'word' and all the privileges with which it was credited, especially in its *nominal* form. It is therefore only a discourse or rather a writing that can make up for the incapacity of the word to be equal to a 'thought'. All sentences of the type 'deconstruction is X' or 'deconstruction is not X' *a priori* miss the point, which is to say that they are at least false. As you know, one of the principal things at stake in what is called in my texts 'deconstruction' is precisely the delimiting of ontology and above all of the third person present indicative: S *is* P.

The word 'deconstruction', like all other words, acquires its value only from its inscription in a chain of possible substitutions, in what is too blithely called a 'context'. For me, for what I have tried and still try to write, the word has interest only within a certain context, where it replaces and lets itself be determined by such other words as 'écriture', 'trace', 'differance', 'supplement', 'hymen', 'pharmakon', 'marge', 'entame', 'parergon', etc.[3] By definition, the list can never be closed, and I have cited only names, which is inadequate and done only for reasons of economy. In fact, I should have cited the sentences and the interlinking of sentences which in their turn determine these names in some of my texts.

What deconstruction is not? everything of course!

What is deconstruction? nothing of course!

I do not think, for all these reasons, that it is a *good word [un bon mot]*. It is certainly not elegant *[beau]*. It has definitely been of service in a highly determined situation. In order to know what has been imposed upon it in a chain of possible substitutions, despite its essential imperfection, this 'highly determined situation' will need to be analyzed and deconstructed. This is difficult and I am not going to do it here.

One final word to conclude this letter, which is already too long. I do not believe that translation is a secondary and derived event in relation to an original language or text. And as 'deconstruction' is a word, as I have just said, that is essentially replaceable in a chain of substitution, then that can also be done from one language to another. The chance, first of all the chance of (the) 'deconstruction', would be that another word (the same word and an other) can be found in Japanese to say the same thing (the same and an other), to speak of deconstruction, and to lead elsewhere to its being written and transcribed, in a word which will also be more beautiful.

When I speak of this writing of the other which will be more beautiful, I clearly understand translation as involving the same risk and chance as the poem. How to translate

'poem'? a 'poem'? ...

With my best wishes,
Jacques Derrida

Translated by David Wood and Andrew Benjamin

NOTES

1. Toshiko Izutsu is a well-known Japanese Islamologist. – Ed.
2. Derrida enters into this question at length in 'How to Avoid Speaking' [1987].
3. Derrida has often exploited the contradictory semantic possibilities of all these

terms: 'entame', for example, comes from a verb that means to incise, to cut or bite into, and thus also to begin something; 'parergon' is that which is neither simply inside nor outside the work or 'ergon', like the frame of a painting. Derrida takes the term as the title of his essay on Kant's *Third Critique* in his *The Truth in Painting* [1978]. – Ed.

THOMAS HARDY, JACQUES DERRIDA AND THE 'DISLOCATION OF SOULS'

J. Hillis Miller

My focus is a poem by Thomas Hardy, 'The Torn Letter'. As a way into this admirable poem, a passage from Kafka's *Letters to Milena* and a recent essay by Jacques Derrida will provide a line of communication. First Kafka:

> The easy possibility of letter-writing must – seen merely theoretically – have brought into the world a terrible dislocation [*Zerrüttung*] of souls. It is, in fact, an intercourse with ghosts, and not only with the ghost of the recipient but also with one's own ghost which develops between the lines of the letter one is writing and even more so in a series of letters where one letter corroborates the other and can refer to it as a witness. How on earth did anyone get the idea that people can communicate with one another by letter! Of a distant person one can think, and of a person who is near one can catch hold – all else goes beyond human strength. Writing letters, however, means to denude oneself before the ghosts, something for which they greedily wait. Written kisses don't reach their destination, rather they are drunk on the way by the ghosts. It is on this ample nourishment that they multiply so enormously ... The ghosts won't starve, but we will perish. (Kafka, 1954, 229)[1]

Thinking and holding are here opposed to writing. The former belongs to 'the real world' of persons, bodies, and minds, of distance and proximity. If a person is near, one can touch him, hold him, kiss him (or her). If a person is

Extract from J. Hillis Miller, *Tropes, Parables, Performatives* (Duke University Press, 1991), pp. 171–80.

distant one can think of that person. Such thinking relates one real 'soul' to another. It is as genuine a 'means of communication' as touch. The souls or selves pre-exist the thinking that joins them, as much as two bodies pre-exist their kiss. Writing is another matter. Nothing is easier than writing – a letter, for example. The writing of a poem, a story, a novel, is no more than an extension of the terrible power of dislocation involved in the simplest 'gesture' of writing a note to a friend. The dislocation is precisely a 'dislocation of souls'. Writing is a dislocation in the sense that it moves the soul itself of the writer, as well as of the recipient, beyond or outside of itself, over there, somewhere else. Far from being a form of communication, the writing of a letter dispossesses both the writer and the receiver of themselves. Writing creates a new phantom written self and a phantom receiver of that writing. There is correspondence all right, but it is between two entirely phantasmagorial or fantastic persons, ghosts raised by the hand that writes. Writing calls phantoms into being, just as the ghosts of the dead appear to Odysseus, to Aeneas, or to Hardy in his poem 'In Front of the Landscape'. In this case, however, the ghosts are also of the witnesses of those ghosts. The writer raises his own phantom and that of his correspondent. Kafka's ghosts, in his 'commerce with phantoms', drink not blood but written kisses. They flourish and multiply on such food, while the one who writes the kisses and the correspondent they do not reach die of hunger, eaten up by the very act through which they attempt to nourish one another at a distance.

Now Derrida: Some remarkable paragraphs in 'Télépathie'[2] (Derrida, 1981, 5–41) seem almost to have been written with 'second sight', that is, with prophetic foreknowledge that I would need to cite them here to support my reading of Hardy. In this essay Derrida speculates on the performative power a letter (in the epistolary sense) may have in order to bring into existence an appropriate recipient. If a letter happens to fall into my hands I may become the person that letter needs as its receiver, even though that new self is discontinuous with the self I have been up till now. Derrida's argument is peripherally attached as an appendage to his polemic, in 'Le facteur de la vérité' (Derrida, 1980), against Jacques Lacan's idea that a letter always reaches its destination. For Derrida, in 'Télépathie', a letter reaches its destination all right, but not because the proper recipient, the self to which the letter corresponds, is waiting there for it, already in full-formed existence as a self. No, the letter creates the self appropriate to itself. It creates it by performing (in the strict Austinian sense of performative (Austin, 1967), though with a twist) the utmost violence on the already existing self of the hapless person who accidentally reads the letter. The 'twist' lies in the fact that the performative power of the letter is not foreseen or intended. This is contrary to the strict concept of a performative utterance as defined by Austin, but it may be that Austin, here as in other aspects of his theory, was unsuccessfully attempting to limit the terrible and always to some degree unpredictable power of a performative utterance:

> Why, [asks Derrida] do the theoreticians of the performative or of the pragmatic interest themselves so little, to my knowledge, in the effects of written things, notably in letters? What do they fear? If there is something performative in the letter, how is it that a letter can produce all sorts of these ends, foreseeable and unforeseeable, and in fact even produce its recipient? All of this, to be sure, according to a properly performative causality, if there is such a thing, and which is purely performative, not at all according to another sequence extrinsic to the act of writing. I admit that I do not fully know what I want to say by that; the unforeseen should not be able to be part of the performative structure in the strict sense, and yet ... ('Télépathie', 9; my translation)

As an example of this strange coercive and yet unpredictable power of the written word, Derrida has suggested on the previous page that someone might determine his whole life according to the 'program' of a letter or of a postcard that he accidentally intercepts, a missive not even intended for him. The recipient becomes the self the letter invites him to be (but there is no 'him' before he receives the letter), just as poor Boldwood, in Thomas Hardy's novel *Far from the Madding Crowd*, becomes the bold lover Bathsheba's valentine seems to tell him he is:

> I do not [says Derrida] make the hypothesis of a letter which would be the external occasion, in some way, of an encounter between two identifiable subjects – and which would be already determined. No, rather of a letter which after the fact seems to have been projected toward some unknown recipient at the moment it was written, predestined receiver unknown to himself or to herself, if that can be said, and who determines himself or herself, as you know so well how to do, on receipt of the letter; this is therefore an entirely different thing from the transfer of a message. Its content and its end no longer precede it. Here it is then: you identify yourself and you engage your life according to the program of the letter, or perhaps better still of a postcard, a letter open, divisible, at once trans-parent and encrypted ... Then you say: it is I, uniquely I who can receive this letter, not that it is meant especially for me, on the contrary, but I receive as a present the happenstance to which this card exposes itself. It chooses me. And I choose that it should choose me by chance, I wish to cross its trajectory, I wish to encounter myself there, I am able to do it and I wish to do it – its transit or its transfer. In short, by a gentle and yet terrifying choice you say: 'It was I.' ... Others would conclude: a letter thus *finds* its recipient, he or she. No, one cannot say of the recipient that he exists before the letter. ('Télépathie', 7–8; my translation)

It almost seems, as I have said, that these sentences were written with a kind of retrospective prevision of their appropriateness as a commentary on Hardy's 'The Torn Letter', or as if 'The Torn Letter' had been written with foresight of

Jacques Derrida's meditations on July 9, 1979, though so far as I know Derrida had not then and has not yet read Hardy's poem. Even so, Hardy's poem, which is a 'letter' in the first person written to an unnamed 'you', has found its proper recipient at last in the unwitting Derrida. Derrida has become its reader without even knowing it. He has been programmed by the poem to write an interpretation of it before, beside, or after the letter, so to speak, in displacement from any conscious encounter with it. He has become the person the poem-letter invites him to be, in a confirmation of his theories of which he is unaware.

Here is Hardy's poem:

> The Torn Letter
>
> I
>
> I tore your letter into strips
>   No bigger than the airy feathers
>   That ducks preen out in changing weathers
> Upon the shifting ripple-tips.
>
> II
>
> In darkness on my bed alone
>   I seemed to see you in a vision,
>   And hear you say: 'Why this derision
> Of one drawn to you, though unknown?'
>
> III
>
> Yes, eve's quick need had run its course,
>   The night had cooled my hasty madness;
>   I suffered a regretful sadness
> Which deepened into real remorse.
>
> IV
>
> I thought what pensive patient days
>   A soul must know of grain so tender,
>   How much of good must grace the sender
> Of such sweet words in such bright phrase.
>
> V
>
> Uprising then, as things unpriced
>   I sought each fragment, patched and mended;
>   The midnight whitened ere I had ended
> And gathered words I had sacrificed.
>
> VI
>
> But some, alas, of those I threw
>   Were past my search, destroyed for ever:
>   They were your name and place; and never
> Did I regain those clues to you.
>
> VII
>
> I learnt I had missed, by rash unheed,
>   My track; that, so the Will decided,

In life, death, we should be divided,
And at the sense I ached indeed.
VIII
That ache for you, born long ago,
Throbs on: I never could outgrow it.
What a revenge, did you but know it!
But that, thank God, you do not know.
(Hardy, 1976, 307)

'The Torn Letter' contains several characteristic Hardyan ironic turns away from the straightforward notion that a letter may have a performative power to determine the self of its recipient. Derrida has the general idea of the letter-poem from Thomas Hardy right, but the message seems to have got garbled or overlaid with static and interference on the way. Some parts are twisted a bit or missing entirely, perhaps because somewhere along the line they have been switched or translated from Hardy's pungent and acerb English into Derrida's idiomatic French. In the latter, for example, the recipient of a letter is called its *destinataire*, with suggestions that the receiver is predestined, a latent fatality or doomed end point of the message. These overtones are missing in the equivalent English words, such as those I have used in my translation of 'Derrida's' ideas back into English.

'The Torn Letter' is spoken or written by someone who has received a letter from an unknown admirer, apparently a woman. Before concluding that the speaker-writer is 'Hardy' it must be remembered that Hardy claims most of his poems are 'personative', spoken or written by imaginary personages. The poem is addressed to the sender of the letter, but, paradoxically, the poem is posited on the assumption that she will never receive his message and therefore cannot learn how much her letter had made him suffer: 'But that, thank God, you do not know.' If the poem is thought of as spoken or perhaps as silently thought, then the woman will indeed never know. In fact it is written down (or how else could we be reading it?). The poem itself, in its physical existence, contradicts its own affirmation. It is always possible, perhaps even inevitable, that the poem will fall into the woman's hands and tell her what he says he thanks God she cannot know. If her 'revenge' on him for destroying the letter is the permanent ache of a remorse for not having kept it and answered it, his revenge on her is to let her know this in the act of saying she does not and cannot know. The poem is a version of that sort of mind-twisting locution, discussed elsewhere by Derrida,[3] which imposes disobedience to its own command: 'Do not read this,' or 'Burn this without reading it.'

Ashamed or embarrassed at receiving such a letter from a stranger (though the reader is never told just what she said), the speaker-writer of the poem has turned her letter into strips, tiny unreadable fragments 'No bigger than the airy feathers / That ducks preen out in changing weathers / Upon the shifting ripple-tips.' The 'I' has divided and subdivided the letter until its bits are mere useless objects like molted feathers. The scraps are no longer able to carry legible words or to communicate any message. The letter has been reduced to detached letters or fragments of words. The fragments are no longer able to form part of a whole and to 'fly', so to speak, in the sense of rising above the matter on which the message is written into the airy freedom of meaning. Unlike Farmer Boldwood, the 'I' here has such a violent resistance to receiving the letter, responding to it, becoming subject to its performative power, turning into the person it would by perlocution make him be, that he tries to destroy the letter and all its latent power. He wants to turn it back into senseless matter. This is a striking example of part at least of what Derrida may mean by the 'divisibility' of the letter. Derrida has in mind a letter's detachment from any single conscious emitting mind or self. He means also a letter's readiness to divide itself indiscriminately at the receiving end and to branch out to exert its power over any number of recipients, *destinataires*. For Derrida, and for Hardy too, a letter or a poem is divisible, and divided, at its origin, in itself, and at its end. In 'The Torn Letter' the initial emphasis is on its physical divisibility. The letter by no means has the 'organic unity' that used to be attributed to the single text. It can be turned into a thousand tiny pieces.

It will surprise no reader of Hardy to discover that neither this theoretical divisibility, nor the fact that the 'I' turns theory into practice and fragments the letter, inhibits one bit its implacable performative power. To the contrary. The message is somehow distributed throughout the whole 'signifying chain', like the proper name repeated beneath the text in one of Saussure's 'hypograms' (Starobinski, 1971). The message can operate through any fragment of it, as a single cell contains the DNA message for reconstructing the whole organism of which it is a minute part, or as, in one of the more grotesque experiments of modern biology, one worm may learn behavior from another worm that has been pulverized and fed to the first worm. The genetic code or imprint passes by ingestion.

The 'I' regrets his rash act. His 'regretful sadness' at his 'derision' 'of one drawn to him though unknown' deepens 'into real remorse' as the night wears on. He seems to see the writer of the letter 'in a vision', reproaching him. The letter has invoked this vision. It has raised the ghost or hallucination of the lady. It has operated as a prosopopoeia, a speech to the absent or dead. Or perhaps it would be better to say that the act of tearing the letter to pieces, reducing the letter to dead letters, so to speak, has made it act as a magic invocation, as a man might be haunted by the ghost of the woman he had killed, or as 'Hardy', in another poem, 'In Front of the Landscape', haunted by the phantoms of those he has betrayed. The poet rises up, collects the fragments of the letter, and pieces them together again.

The 'Hardyan twist' is that the speaker cannot find all the pieces of the torn letter. Those lost are the ones with the lady's name and address. The speaker's act, with a reversal of the sexes, is like that of Isis gathering up the fragments of the body of the Osiris she has murdered. In both cases something is missing, the phallus of Osiris in one case, the lady's identification in the other, head source of meaning in both cases. Once again, as in that strange myth, the story Hardy tells is of the dispersal, fragmentation, defacing, depersonification, or even unmanning of the self, since in the end the reader of the poem, as I shall argue, becomes not the speaker, receiver of the letter, but the unattainable woman to whom the poem is spoken. The speaker cannot, after all, write back to the lady. He cannot initiate a correspondence and a relationship in which he would, in spite of his initial resistance to doing so, become the self the letter invited him to be:

> I learnt I had missed, by rash unheed,
>> My track; that, so the Will decided,
>> In life, death, we should be divided,
> And at the sense I ached indeed.

The Will here is of course the Immanent Will, that unconscious energy within what is, which, in Hardy's phrase, 'stirs and urges everything' (1976, 307). The Will is Hardy's name for the fact that things happen as they do happen. This volition is will as force, not will as conscious intent. Its 'decisions' are the decisions of fortuity, the fact, for example, that the poet could not find the scraps with the woman's name and address. This means that the track he should have followed, the destiny that waited for him, remains untrodden. The divisibility of the letter means that he must remain divided from the correspondent, by a 'decision' that is another form of division, separating this possibility from that one, this track from that.

'I had missed, by rash unheed, / My track' – the phrasing is odd. On the one hand, the track was truly his. It was fated for him by the Will. The track pre-exists his taking it, and with the track the self appropriate to it also exists. This track is his destiny. How can a man avoid his destiny, even by the 'rash unheed' of not responding to the woman's call? On the other hand, 'the Will decided' that he should not, as punishment for his rash unheed, take the track that was nevertheless destined for him. It is as if he were two separate persons, or two superposed persons, the one who took the track and the one who did not take it, as in Borges' 'The Garden of the Forking Paths'.

Though the divisibility of the letter did not mean that its power could be destroyed, that power was partially inhibited, and so another form of division takes place, the poet's permanent division from the lady. On the other hand, the paradox of the poem, another wry ironic turn, is that by missing his track he only follows it more surely and securely. He becomes more deeply and more permanently marked by the letter just because he has lost the name and address of its sender and so cannot answer it back, follow out the track it lays out. The letter is detached from the real name and self of its sender and liberated to have an anonymous or universal power to make new selves and join them. Again, as in Saussure's hypograms, what is 'proper' to the letter is not a proper name and place attached to it on the outside but a power distributed throughout its minutest parts, its letters, a power to bring into existence the phantom selves of both sender and destined receiver. The fact that the letter lacks the proper name and address is just what gives it its power of the dislocation of souls. This might be defined by saying that although the torn and then reconstructed letter operates as an apostrophe or prosopopoeia, the ghost that is invoked is that dislocated new self of the reader of the letter, the self the letter personified into existence, if such a transitive use of the word may be made. It is as though the letter were being written on my mind, inscribed there, thus giving that blank page a personality it did not have.

Had the speaker answered the letter the episode would have run its course, as always happens in Hardy. Warmth, intimacy, love perhaps, would have been followed by coolness, betrayal, the wrenching apart of a final division. For Hardy it is always the case that 'Love lives on propinquity, but dies of contact') (F. E. Hardy, 1965, 220). If he had followed the track he would ultimately have gone off the track and ceased forever to be the self the letter commands him to be. As it is the ache remains: 'That ache for you, born long ago, / Throbs on: I never could outgrow it.' For Hardy, the only relation to another person that can last is one that is in some way inhibited, prevented from moving on from propinquity to contact. In this case, the ache remains, like an unhealed and unhealable wound. One part of the 'I' does become and remain the self the letter 'performs' into existence. I say 'one part' because, as Derrida affirms, 'all is not recipient [*destinataire*] in a recipient, a part only which accommodates itself to the rest' ('Télépathie', 9–10; my translation). For Hardy, as for Derrida, or as for Nietzsche in paragraph 490 of *The Will to Power* (1968, 279–81),[4] the divisibility of the self is not only along the diachronic track, but synchronically, in the moment. At any given time the 'self' is a commonwealth of many citizens. The self is the locus of many different selves dwelling uneasily with one another. Each struggles to dominate the others and to become the sole ruler, the single self within the domain of the self. For the speaker-writer in 'The Torn Letter', one of those selves will remain the self who would have answered the unknown woman's letter.

One more thing must be said of the significance of the missing name and address in 'The Torn Letter'. The fact that he cannot attach the letter to a proper name and to a specific place puts the 'I' of the poem in the same situation as the reader of this or of many other poems by Hardy. The reader is told precious little of the stories at which Hardy's poems hint. He is given a fragment only, usually lacking names, dates and places. The poem is cut off from what came before and from what came after. It is the bare sketch of an episode. Vital facts are missing that would allow the reader to attach the poem with certainty to Hardy's biography or to actual places on a map of Dorset. Far from reducing the poems' power to haunt their readers, to stick in the mind and lodge there permanently, as an ache or throb the reader can never outgrow, the absence of these specifications multiplies the poems' powers over the reader a hundredfold. The poems produce something like that tantalizing sense that there is a proper name one cannot quite remember. This incompletion gives the poems their power to dwell within the reader, like a ghost, or like an unrealized self, or like a parasite within its host. Each of Hardy's poems is an unsolved and unsolvable mystery. It is a track the reader cannot take or reach the end of, and so he remains fascinated by it. One part of the reader, too, becomes, by the law of multiple simultaneous selves, permanently the self the poem performatively creates.

As Derrida observes, it is not necessary for a letter that brings a new self into existence in me to contain detailed instructions about what that self should be. Far from it. The performative power of the letter works best if it remains a sketch, like Hardy's poems. If, as Derrida says, 'you identify yourself and engage your life according to the program of the letter,' it is also the case that

> the program says nothing, it announces or enunciates nothing at all, not the least content, it does not even present itself as a program. One cannot even say that it 'works' as a program, in the sense of appearing like one, but without looking like one, it *works*, it programs. ('Télépathie', 8; my translation)

'The Torn Letter' is a striking confirmation of this. Just because the poem is so bereft of details, like the torn letter itself, it is able to perform its magic on any reader who happens to read it. It is as if he had accidentally come upon a letter intended for someone else. Reading the poem, I, you, or anyone becomes its addressee, since it has no name or specified destination. Hardy is forced to communicate with his lost correspondent by sending out a general letter to the world and publishing it in a book of poems, just as radio telescopists send out messages beamed into outer space in hopes they may be intercepted by some intelligent beings, somewhere: 'Is anybody there?'

The reader of 'The Torn Letter' becomes not so much, through a familiar kind of negative capability, the self of the speaker-writer of the poem, the 'I' who has received the letter and is haunted by it, as, by a far stranger form of metamorphosis, the 'you' to whom the poem is spoken or written. The reader becomes the woman who has caused the 'I' so much ache. The poem becomes a letter in its turn, a letter missing the name and address of its destined receiver, and so anyone who happens to read it is put in the place of that unnamed receiver and programmed ever after to be, a part of him or her at least, the self that letter-poem calls into being. If letters or postcards perform that fearful dislocation of souls of which Kafka speaks, putting a man beside himself, as it were, drinking his life in the creation of a phantom self and a phantom correspondent for that self, a phantom who intercepts the most passionate of written kisses so that they never reach their destination, works of literature can enact a similar dispossession. A poem, too, may dislocate its reader. It may make her someone else somewhere else, perhaps without power ever to go back to herself.

NOTES

1. Translation slightly altered: for the German, see Kafka (1952, 259–60).

2. See, for example, 'Envois' (7–273; 3–256). [The page numbers refer to the French and English language editions respectively. JW]
3. For example, in 'Envois', *La carte postale*.
4. For the German see *Werke*, vol. 3 (1966, 473–4).

6.3

ON NOT READING: DERRIDA AND BECKETT

Nicholas Royle

One night as he sat trembling head in hands from head to foot a man appeared to him and said, I have been sent by – and here he named the dear name – to comfort you. Then drawing a worn volume from the pocket of his long black coat he sat and read till dawn. Then disappeared without a word.

Samuel Beckett, 1986, 447

Be alert to these invisible quotation marks, even within a word ...

LO, 76

It may be said that, to date, there have been two broad characterisations of the work of Jacques Derrida. On the one hand it has been seen as primarily 'philosophical' and subsequently as seriously disruptive in relation to distinctions between the philosophical and the literary. The 'literary', that is to say, is here being thought from the side of or starting from the 'philosophical'. This characterisation is faithful to statements made by Derrida himself, for example when he speaks of the primary importance of being 'true to philosophy' (OCP, 218) or when he says that he always places himself 'in relation to philosophy' (IJD, 136).[1] On the other hand, there is the (mostly ill-informed) view of Derrida's work as basically 'literary' or 'non-philosophical' and subsequently as not seriously disruptive of anything much at all. In this chapter I wish to question both of these 'mainstream' perspectives, in particular by exploring the

---

Extract from Nicholas Royle, *After Derrida* (Manchester University Press, 1995), pp. 159–74.

(perhaps differently disruptive) idea that Derrida's work might be considered from the perspective of being, in some curious way, not 'literary' *enough*. I acknowledge in advance the manifest folly of such an exploration. I feel it coming all the same. I will circle around three concerns: not reading Derrida, not reading in Derrida's work, and Derrida not reading. In doing so I shall attempt to focus on the relationship between the writings of Derrida and Beckett and to consider (1) what might be involved in Derrida's professed inability to write about Beckett's work and (2), conversely, what light Beckett's work might cast on the question of reading and writing *after Derrida*.

NOT READING DERRIDA

The recent and somewhat unusual Cambridge farce – about whether or not Jacques Derrida should be given an honorary degree by that university – highlighted once again, in English culture but no doubt also beyond it, the extraordinary importance of not reading. For it was clear that many of those opposing his nomination to this honorary degree – opposing him on the grounds that his work is 'nihilistic', 'unintelligible', 'meaningless' and so on – had not read Derrida's texts.[2] What is involved here? Even (or perhaps especially) if the writings of Derrida themselves remain unread, they have indelibly marked contemporary culture. A writer's work can be received without being read: texts have effects without being read.[3] Evoked here, then, is a sort of culture of hallucination, a culture of telepathy in which people's thoughts and values, their ideas and beliefs, are variously determined and dictated, transmitted and inscribed, by thinkers whose work has not been read.

NOT READING IN DERRIDA'S WORK

Of course, there is not reading and there is not reading. Indeed it is in the reading and untangling of various figurations of 'not reading' that we might want to situate the importance of deconstruction. Deconstruction – which is never single or homogeneous, but which can here, at least provisionally, be identified with 'the work of Derrida' – is concerned with the lucid, patient attempt to trace what has not been read, what remains unread or unreadable within the elaboration of concepts and the workings of institutions. Frequently this concern has been construed by critics as the negative, irresponsible or unethical character of deconstruction: deconstruction is concerned with nihilistically giving priority to the unreadable.[5] In this respect, the unreadable corresponds to the notion of the indeterminate. By way of trying to clarify a fundamental misunderstanding of Derrida's work – characteristic, as we have seen, of criticism such as Geoffrey Hartman's, but also pervasive in the Cambridge affair – let us merely propose that deconstructive thought is concerned not with indeterminacy but rather with undecidability.

To classify a text, or a moment in a text, as indeterminate is to put an end to the question of judging: it is, in a sense, the opposite of undecidability. To talk about undecidability is not to suggest that making decisions or judgements is impossible but rather that any and every judgement is haunted by an *experience* of the undecidable, the effects of which remain to be read. To refer to the meaning of a text, or a moment in a text, as indeterminate is in fact to determine a reading, to stop the process of reading. As Derrida summarily observes in 'Living On', 'unreadability does not arrest reading' (LO, 116). To encounter the unreadable is not to bring reading to an end, but rather to acknowledge the demand that reading cannot stop, that reading begin again, that reading always and necessarily belongs to another time. Such an acknowledgement is suggested by the aphorism from Pascal about which Derrida speaks in *Mémoires*: 'When one reads too swiftly or too slowly one understands nothing' (M, 88, n.3).[5] This aphorism constitutes a kind of 'authoritative ellipsis' (M, 88, n.3) and evokes what is perhaps the most succinct definition of deconstruction, that is to say 'the *experience of the impossible*' (Aft, 200). 'When one reads too swiftly or too slowly one understands nothing': to read this is at once straightforward and impossible. The sentence must and cannot be read at the right speed, according to a proper sense of time. Aphorism in ruin, once again.

The unreadable is fixed only to the extent that it is apprehended as that which remains to be read, even if that reading is theorised (as it is in Derrida's work) as belonging as much to an immemorial past as to the future. An example of this would be the piece of graffiti quoted by Derrida in 'Border Lines': '"do not read me"' (BL, 145). This injunction must and cannot be read. It is, as he points out, 'the sort of order that can be obeyed only by transgressing it beforehand' (BL, 145). This piece of graffiti concisely illustrates the double-bind of deconstruction, in other words the necessity and impossibility of deconstructive reading. It demands and dissolves the strange time, which is never proper, never *on* time, of reading. The reading of this injunction not to read can never catch up with itself, can never coincide with itself, not least because it can never have adequate authority to authorise its own reading (its 'authoritative ellipsis' is, again, also an ellipsis of authority) and because its very readability cannot be derived: what is readable is indissociable from what is iterable. The readable has no origin, it is immemorial, it precedes us and our reading.[6] By the same token the readable would be necessarily still to come.[7] It is still to come not as an act or event that might one day become present, but rather in the structural sense of a promise, a promise which is – in its affirmation and nonfulfilment – a double-bind.[8] In this sense, Derrida's work will never be readable. The reading of Derrida's texts is always still to come. If the readings advanced in the present study come after Derrida, they are by the same token still *after* Derrida in the sense of seeking after: reading 'after Derrida' can never arrive at itself.

DERRIDA NOT READING

Derrida has given seminars, in a 'stammering' fashion, on Beckett's work (see TSICL, 61). In the interview with Richard Kearney, published in 1984, he refers to Beckett in the context of the notion of literature, saying:

> when I speak of literature it is not with a capital L; it is rather an allusion to certain movements which have worked around the limits of our logical concepts, certain texts which make the limits of our language tremble, exposing them as divisible and questionable. This is what the works of Blanchot, Bataille or Beckett are particularly sensitive to. (DO, 112)

But Derrida has not (as yet) published work on Beckett and indeed has expressed an unwillingness, inability or avoidance in the face of such a prospect. We might wonder what is implied here. Is there some sense in which this professed inability might be seen as figuring a kind of fissure, or twilight zone, in Derrida's oeuvre?

Derrida's comments on his relation to the work of Beckett, in particular in the 1989 interview with Derek Attridge published in *Acts of Literature*, are somewhat enigmatic. Attridge asks Derrida why he has never written on Beckett. He responds:

> This is an author to whom I feel very close, or to whom I would like to feel myself very close; but also too close. Precisely because of this proximity, it is too hard for me, too easy and too hard. I have perhaps avoided him a bit because of this identification ... How could I write in French in the wake of or 'with' someone who does operations on this language which seem to me so strong and so necessary, but which must remain idiomatic? How could I write, sign, countersign performatively texts which 'respond' to Beckett? How could I avoid the platitude of a supposed academic metalanguage? (TSICL, 60)

No doubt the very form of an interview (so valuably and necessarily questioned around twenty years earlier, in *Positions*) tends to promote the kinds of 'platitude' to which Derrida refers, but the terms in which his relation to Beckett's work are being presented here are nevertheless provocative.

First, Derrida's remarks are strikingly author-centred. Beckett is 'an author' to whom he feels very close; Beckett is 'someone' who 'does operations' on the French language. However doomed to failure, my attempt to think about the writings of Beckett and Derrida in non-author-centred terms can perhaps be reinforced here by the fact that Beckett is no longer alive: his death, a few months after the Attridge–Derrida interview, casts an appropriate spectrality and passivity on the 'operations' to which Derrida refers. For it is, among other things, with precisely this spectral character of writing that the present study is preoccupied. Whether it is a question of Beckett or Derrida, Shakespeare or Toni Morrison, the focus here is on the ghostly, on the author as always already dead – that is to say, 'dead insofar as his text has a structure of survival even if he is living' (DTB, 183).

Second, and beyond the paradoxical claim of what is, in Derrida's 'proximity' to 'Beckett', at once 'too easy' and 'too hard' (an ease or easiness which can in effect be neither proven nor refuted), there is this enigmatic appearance of the word 'but': 'How could I write in French in the wake of or "with" someone who does operations on this language which seem to me so strong and so necessary, but which must remain idiomatic?' How should we read (or perhaps, rather, *not* read) this 'but'? The strangeness of this 'but' (and the proviso of the 'idiomatic' which ensues) seems perhaps only to be increased when, a little later in the interview, and still on the question of 'Beckett', Derrida refers to the idiomatic dimension of his own writing. He is not concerned with reading, he says, even in the case of the works of Joyce, Celan or Blanchot: 'I will never claim to have "read" or proposed a general reading of these works. I wrote a text, which in the face of the event of another's text, as it comes to me at a particular, quite singular, moment, tries to "respond" or to "countersign", in an idiom which turns out to be mine' (62).

Derrida claims not to be able to 'respond' to Beckett's texts because they do not permit him what he calls 'writing transactions'. Consequently he concludes by saying: 'That wasn't possible for me with Beckett, whom I will thus have "avoided" as though I had always already read him and understood him too well' (61). What is going on in this, perhaps deceptively gentle and loving, appropriation?[9] What could it mean to have 'understood' Beckett 'too well'? What transformational forces of reading (or *not reading*) might be inscribed in this authoritative ellipsis, this peculiar abdication from reading what is nevertheless alleged to have been 'as though ... always already read'?

NOT READING WHAT NOT

Is it possible to read Beckett, even one or two words? Is it possible to read the word 'I', for example, or 'me', or not? Or what? What 'what'? And if not, what 'not'?

> Mr. Knott was a good master, in a way.
> Watt had no direct dealings with Mr. Knott, at this period. Not that Watt was ever to have any direct dealings with Mr. Knott, for he was not.
> (Beckett, 1976, 64)

Mastery and authority, including what Leo Bersani has called 'identity *as* authority' (1990, 3), is constitutively disabled, dislocated, dispossessed in the fiction of Beckett. Engaged in a reading of *The Unnamable*, for example, who are 'we'? The disturbance of identity is not only a matter of acknowledging, for example, that our names carry death (in that they structurally outlive their bearers) or that any 'operations' which we – as readers or as writers – may carry out *in our names* are likewise always already touched by the hand of death. For the 'unnamable' referred to in the title of that text concerns an unnamability affecting entitlement itself, the very entitlement of and to identity.[10] This logic pertains not only to the 'I' *in* the text but also to 'we', 'you', and 'they'. The notion of identity is food, it could be said, not for thought but 'for delirium' (Beckett, 1966, 337).[11] We/they are this text's constitutively multiple, irreducibly heterogeneous, anonymous, impossible readers:

> Do they believe I believe it is I who am speaking? That's theirs too. To
> make me believe I have an ego all my own, and can speak of it, as they of
> theirs. Another trap to snap me up among the living. It's how to fall into
> it they can't have explained to me sufficiently. (*U*, 348)

'I', 'they', 'we', and 'you' in turn are all ghosts within this scene of reading.[12]
There is no I to whom the speaking, writing or reading of *The Unnamable* can
be attributed. *The Unnamable*, more spectrally perhaps than any other work of
twentieth-century literature *or* philosophy, calls for a reading that would itself
be unnamable, resistant to authority and identity in general, contumacious (to
evoke a 'nice image' (*U*, 383)) in advance of every identification.

There would seem to be in Derrida's texts, on the other hand, the recurrent
deployment of a kind of implicit or working assumption of the equation of
identity-as-authority. The deployment of the 'I' in Derrida's work, in this
respect, would appear to be radically different from that in Beckett's. A brief
consideration of some of the opening statements of Derrida's texts may provide
some indication of the regularity with which they seem to start out with such a
deployment, even if they just as regularly proceed to a deconstruction or
deconstitution of the identity of that 'I': 'I will speak, therefore, of a letter'
(Diff, 3); 'Francis Ponge – from here I call him, for greeting and praise, for
renown, I should say, or renaming' (*S*, 2); 'Genres are not to be mixed. I will
not mix genres' (LG, 223); 'You might read these *envois* as the preface to a book
that I have not written' (E, 3); 'What else am I going to be able to invent?' (PIO,
25); 'I have never known how to tell a story' (*M*, 3); 'I shall speak of ghost
[*revenant*], of flame, and of ashes' (OS, 1); 'C'est ici un devoir, je dois
m'adresser à vous en anglais. This is an obligation, I must *address* myself to
you in English' (FL, 921). The narrator of *Murphy* famously observes: 'In the
beginning was the pun' (1973, 41).[13] Even the phrase 'the fiction of Beckett'
could be said to constitute a pun. The fictionality of authority – including or
especially that of authorial identity, the writerly 'I' – would appear to set 'the
fiction of Beckett' at odds with 'the work of Derrida'. Against the reading (or
misreading) of Derrida as a 'punning', 'playful' (i.e. 'literary') writer, it might
then seem possible to suggest that his texts are marked by a kind of literary
'insufficiency', a limiting of the 'literary' that renders itself readable through
juxtaposition with the writings of Beckett.

To set out to suggest that Derrida's texts are not sufficiently 'literary' may
seem like taking on the mantle of a somnambulist in a minefield. Quite apart
from anything else, there is the danger of appearing to offer a 'strong reading',
in the sense of that phrase glossed by David Wood: 'The paradox of *strong
reading* is that it is strong precisely to the extent that it is not a reading, but the
use of a sacrificial victim to exhibit one's own position' (1992, 2). Wood's
point makes sense so long as it is assumed that there is or can be such a thing as
'one's own position'. My concern here, however, has to do with the paradoxical, eerie but perhaps also laughable acknowledgement of a concern that

can never be appropriated, never seriously be proposed as 'mine'. In this respect one must listen out for the pause that follows the somnambulist murmuring, 'Minefield? What minefield? There is no mine ...' It is as the ghost of a somnambulist, then, that I reflect here on the concern with an 'unnamable', deconstructive reading of identity-as-authority, a reading that would identify (with) the space of literature as that which disables and dissolves the very possibility of 'one's own position'. This deconstructive reading is indeed, I would like to suggest, 'not a reading', but a kind of *not* reading at variance with what 'not' might be understood to mean in the context of Wood's formulation. It is with an elucidation of this rather different sense of 'not reading' that this essay will attempt to conclude.

A reading of the fiction of Beckett would appear to foreground the extent to which Derrida's writings deploy and rely on authority-effects (above all that of the identity-as-authority of an authorial 'I') which are dissolved and dispossessed, obliterated in the space of literature. Inevitably evoked here is the strange space of Maurice Blanchot's *The Space of Literature*, in which for instance we may read: 'The writer belongs to a language which no one speaks, which is addressed to no one, which has no centre, and which reveals nothing. He may believe that he affirms himself in this language, but what he affirms is altogether deprived of self' (1982, 26). Such an account may be distinguished from the kind of 'space of literature' evoked by Derrida in 'This Strange Institution Called Literature', where literature is described as 'the institution which allows one to *say everything*' (36). Following Blanchot and Beckett, the space of literature might be characterised rather as that in which one loses the authoritative capacity to say 'one' at all. 'Where now? Who now? When now? Unquestioning. I, say I. Unbelieving' (*U*, 293): it may be said that these, the opening words of *The Unnamable*, 'must remain idiomatic', in other words resistant both to a 'strong reading' and even to the most gentle and loving appropriation, precisely to the extent that already, before starting, they will have dramatised the (fiction of the) unnamable, putting the 'I' into play as always already dispossessed, the authority of identity always already cast into question, dislocated, beyond belief.

Reading Beckett alongside or 'with' Derrida, then, tends to draw attention to the various ways in which Derrida's work seems to presuppose and impose the figure of a self-identical author or writer, valorising (even if it goes on to deconstitute) the inaugurating presence of the producer of 'writing transactions', the writerly 'I'. Such would appear to be the 'I', for example, which inaugurates the essay 'Force of Law: The "Mystical Foundation of Authority"' and which can later declare: 'I authorise myself – but by what right? – to multiply protocols and detours' (FL, 945). If, as has been suggested elsewhere, the subject of deconstruction is the deconstruction of the subject, (e.g. Readings, 1989, 241, n. 24), it may be recalled too that this deconstruction is a strategy without finality, a disseminatory strategy or series of strategies still being (and always still to be) elaborated and unfolded. It is a fundamental, if in some quarters still prevalent, misreading of Derrida's work to suppose that deconstruction is concerned with getting rid of the human subject. As he stresses, for example, in the interview with Richard Kearney, when he says: 'I have never said that the subject should be dispensed with. Only that it should be deconstructed ... My work does not, therefore, destroy the subject; it simply tries to resituate it' (DO, 125).[14] In the twilight zone of the Beckettian reading that has been tentatively advanced here, however, it might be suggested that Derrida's work *does not go far enough* with its deconstruction of the subject, and that a deconstructive resituating of the subject calls to be further radicalised.

AFTER DERRIDA: EXCITATION

Complete madness. The madness of the day. A light unlike any other. I posthume as I breathe. Folly. Sheer kink. Nothing more or less than a folly to suggest that it could be appropriate to characterise Derrida's work in terms of a maintenance of identity as authority, of a legitimation of the violence of self-authorisation, of a persistence in valorising the writing 'I'. What is the word? Folly. In ruins. Beckett and Derrida, these two ghosts – each of them, like every ghost, double and more than double – are up to the same thing, in their different ways. If Beckett's work shows how – in Bersani's words – 'the strategies for continuing talk survive the absence of psychological subjects' (1990, 169), Derrida's work is likewise concerned with working through the deconstitution of psychological subjects, but *from the perspective of their presence*, from the experience of self-presence and, indeed, of *narcissism*. Derrida says as much, for example in that ghostly polyphonic text, 'Right of Inspection', which calls for 'a new understanding of narcissism, a new "patience", a new passion for narcissism'. The ghostly voice goes on: 'The right to narcissism must be rehabilitated, it needs the time and the means. More narcissism or else none at all [*Plus de narcissisme*]' (RI, 80).[15]

Beckett and Derrida: their laughter is almost indistinguishable. They repeat and repeat themselves, never the same. They give and efface themselves, these ghosts, with a humility, passion and patience that is at once inimitable ('like nobody else') and 'like nobody'.

It is time we disappeared. We, ghosts from another future.

We would like, finally, to disappear without a word, or at least with a word which, like the 'unnamable' or like 'deconstruction', may not be one. One way of trying to conceive of a practice of writing and reading after Beckett and after Derrida might be in terms of a theory of *excitation*. This term, in so far as it could be described as such (it would be no more a *term* than 'the unnamable' or 'deconstruction'), is pronounced so as to conceal as best it can the heterophonic pun it nevertheless harbours, like a foreign body. Excitation, that is to say, cannot be read without a logic of ex-citation, of that which dispossesses, ex-propriates or para-cites every citation. Excitation would have to do, among other things, with an absence of quotation marks. Be alert to these invisible quotation marks, even within a word: excitation. This would be the site, and sighting, of another apparent distinction between the ghostly I's, between

Derrida and Beckett: Derrida's texts evince an almost constant pleasure in quotation and in the employment of quotation marks; Beckett's tend to avoid quotation marks altogether.[16] In Derrida's bizarre 'autobiothanatoheterographical' text entitled 'Circumfession', for example, we can read:

> and then I remember having gone to bed very late after a moment of anger or irony against a sentence of Proust's, praised in a book in this collection 'Les Contemporains', which says: 'A work in which there are theories is like an object on which one has left the price tag', and I find nothing more vulgar than this Franco-Britannic decorum, European in truth, I associate it with Joyce, Heidegger, Wittgenstein, and a few others, the salon literature of that republic of letters, the grimace of a good taste naive enough to believe that one can efface the labor of theory, as if there wasn't any in Pr., and mediocre theory at that. (*JD ii*, 62–3)

This passage not only presents a good example of Derrida's liking for quotations (including, here, the citing of authorial proper names) but also indicates the relentlessness with which his own writing is concerned with 'theory' and with making 'the labor of theory' explicit.

Of course to characterise Derrida's texts in terms of a love for citation and quotation marks can only be done on condition of acknowledging that these texts are at the same time constantly, implacably engaged with showing how distinctions between quotation and non-quotation, use and mention, etc., are subject to a logic of contamination, of repetition and difference, in other words subject to that which always already destabilises citation, linking it to iterability.[17] A practice of writing after Derrida, that is to say a theory of excitation, might be figured in terms of a notion of passing into the language. Recalling the question of reading and not reading Derrida's work in relation to the idea of a culture of telepathy, we might conclude by trying to take account of his suggestion, made in *Mémoires*, that the 'ideal signature' is 'the one which *knows how to efface itself*' (*M*, 26). The best signature would be that which dissolves, no longer lets itself be read or lets itself be read only as a kind of ghost. No longer the (de)construction site of citation, but rather a space of excitation. Geoffrey Bennington's recent study of Derrida, 'Derridabase', which claims not to quote a single sentence of Derrida, signals the way towards such a writing and such a theory. It would no longer be necessary to cite Derrida: the most effective kind of writing after Derrida would be that in which Derrida, the proper name, and everything ostensibly belonging to it, or presumed to enable a reader to read and identify the singularity of a corpus (even that of a sentence) signed 'Derrida', had disappeared, passed into the language.[18] We would return then, with an uncanny difference, to a notion of 'not reading Derrida'. This would be to envisage a kind of fictional, theoretical writing, in other words, in which 'theory' has passed into the language.

Which is not to suppose that one could 'efface the labor of theory', as if there weren't any in Beckett (or Proust) – but rather to speculate on a theoretically vigilant, rigorous and inventive writing which would be radically excitational. Such a writing might seem, in some ways, closer to the work of Beckett than to that of Derrida, and yet it would be inconceivable without Derrida, without the telepathic hymen, the delirious excitation of both.

NOTES

[The abbreviations throughout this essay refer to the following works of Jacques Derrida, full details of which are to be found in the 'Works Cited' list. JW]

Aft	'Afterw.rds: or, at least, less than a letter about a letter less'
ATED	'Afterword: Toward an Ethic of Discussion'
BL	'Border Lines'
DA	'Deconstruction in America: An Interview with Jacques Derrida'
Diff	'Différance'
DO	'Deconstruction and the Other'
DTB	'Des Tours de Babel'
E	'Envois'
FL	'Force of Law: The Mystical "Foundation of Authority"'
IJD	'An "Interview" with Jacques Derrida'
JD i	Geoffrey Bennington, 'Derridabase', from Bennington and Derrida (1993)
JD ii	Jacques Derrida, 'Circumfession', from Bennington and Derrida (1993)
LG	'The Law of Genre'
LI	'Limited Inc a, b, c …'
LO	'Living On'
M	*Mémoires: for Paul de Man.*
OCP	'On Colleges and Philosophy: Jacques Derrida and Geoff Bennington'
OS	*Of Spirit: Heidegger and the Question*
P	*Positions*
PIO	'Psyche: Inventions of the Other'
POO	'Passions: "An Oblique Offering"'
RI	'Right of Inspection'
S	*Signéponge/Signsponge*
TSICL	'This Strange Institution Called Literature'

1. See too Derrida's illuminating comments on this topic in the interview with Derek Attridge entitled 'This Strange Institution Called Literature', where he compares literature and philosophy and mediates on the reasons for having been drawn personally and professionally to the latter. He reminisces on his unease about the 'innocence', 'irresponsibility' and 'impotence' of literature and his associating literature with 'the experience of a dissatisfaction or a lack, an impatience' (TSICL, 39). Philosophy, on the other hand, he says, 'also seemed more political, let's say more capable of posing politically the question of literature with the political seriousness and consequentiality it requires' (39). It should perhaps be added that, in what follows, I do not want to ignore or deny the extent to which Derrida's work is engaged, for example, with a mutual contamination of the philosophical and the literary, but rather I wish to continue an elaboration, initiated in *Telepathy and Literature: Essays on the Reading Mind* (1991), of what happens if one tries (however perversely) to be 'true to literature', to place oneself primarily 'in relation to literature', and thus stage differently a certain priority of what might be called *not I*.

2. See, for example, Derrida's own remarks in this context, in 'An "interview" with Jacques Derrida (IJD), 131–9. Here he talks about the various 'distorting and malicious representations of his work and of those opponents to his degree nomination, 'whose every sentence proves clearly that they either haven't read or haven't understood one line of the texts they wish to denounce' (132).

3. In this context we might recall (though, for obvious reasons by now perhaps

sufficiently evident, without feeling obliged to endorse the rhetoric of mastery and discipleship marking it) a suggestion made by Paul de Man in 'Sign and Symbol in Hegel's *Aesthetics*': 'whether we know it, or like it, or not, most of us are Hegelians and quite orthodox ones at that ... Few thinkers have so many disciples who have never read a word of their master's writings' (1982, 763).

4. For some particularly clear and stimulating refutations of such characterisations, see Derrida's 'Afterword: Toward an Ethic of Discussion' (ATED).

5. This aphorism is also of course the epigraph to Paul de Man's *Allegories of Reading: Figural Language in Rousseau, Nietzsche, Rilke, and Proust* (1979).

6. See Derrida's remarks in 'How to Avoid Speaking' (1989, 3–70). These remarks are perhaps also pertinent to any theory of reading, of not reading, or of how to avoid reading: 'Thus, at the moment when the question "How to avoid speaking?" arises, it is already too late. There was no longer any question of not speaking. Language has started without us, in us and before us. This is what theology calls God, and it is necessary, it will have been necessary, to speak. This "it is necessary" [*il faut*] is *both* the trace of undeniable necessity – which is another way of saying that one cannot avoid denying it, one can only deny it – *and* of a past injunction. Always already past, hence without a past present' (29).

7. See Samuel Weber, 'Reading and Writing *chez* Derrida', in his *Institution and Interpretation* (1987, 85–101). Weber notes that 'every text ... is both structurally unreadable and yet destined to be read. It is structurally unreadable inasmuch as it can never be definitively delimited or situated (*casé*); it *is* only *as* the repetition of other readings, which in turn are the reinscription of other writings; and hence, the desire to repeat it for once and for all, to read it properly, is inevitably frustrated. And yet, at the same time, this desire is also unavoidable' (97–8).

8. This might be compared with Derrida's remarks in 'This Strange Institution Called Literature' on a concept of democracy as 'linked to the to-come' [*à-venir*, cf. *avenir*, future], to the experience of a promise engaged, that is always an endless promise' (TSICL, 38). Cf. too Geoffrey Bennington's characterisation of politics as being '*now*, not projected into a utopian future, but in the even of the tension which is not to be *resolved*' (JD i, 257).

9. That reading and writing necessarily entail a double movement, a movement that is violent as well as loving, faithful and identificatory, is a consistent emphasis in Derrida's work. On the notion of practising a 'double writing' that is 'simultaneously faithful and violent', for example, see *Positions* (P, 6). It is in the interviews in *Positions* also, we may recall, that Derrida emphasises what he calls 'The effective violence of disseminating writing' (85). The linking of violence and fidelity might further be compared with his comments on 'loving and violating' (TSICL, 61) language in the context of Beckett (and Artaud). Will the reading of Derrida offered here itself be construed as 'violating' as well as loving? Perhaps such an impression is unavoidable. But at the same time, and beyond this, I would also dare to hope that the present reading might be viewed as taking a little further, or approaching from another direction, Derrida's hypothesis in 'Afterword: Toward an Ethic of Discussion', that 'if ... violence remains in fact (almost) ineradicable, its analysis and the most refined, ingenious account of its conditions will be the least violent gestures, perhaps even nonviolent, and in any case those which contribute most to transforming the legal-ethical-political rules: *in* the university and *outside* the university' (ATED, 112).

10. This also applies to the notion of the identity of a national language: for a good account of some of the complexities of trying to think about Beckett's work in terms of 'operations' on a language, at once French and/or English but also irreducible to either, see Leslie Hill, *Beckett's Fictions: In Different Words* (1990, esp. 40–58).

11. Hereafter cited in text as U.

12. See Leo Bersani and Ulysse Dutoit's recent reading of *Company* (1992, 1–19), in which they suggest that 'you' is also unnamable' (13) in this late text.

13. Cited by Jonathan Culler in his Introduction to *On Puns: The Foundation of Letters* (1988, 16).
14. Cf. too 'Deconstruction in America: An Interview with Jacques Derrida', in which he observes: 'the notion of *"writer"* and the notion of the subject, *is* a logocentric product ... The subject is a logocentric concept. That doesn't mean that we can get rid of it just like that. It's not a question of getting rid of it, moreover' (DA, 16).
15. For the paradox of this '*Plus de narcissisme*', cf. Derrida's remark, in 'Passions: "an Oblique Offering"', that it is 'impossible to construct a non-contradictory or coherent concept of narcissism' (POO, 12).
16. Beckett's first novel *Murphy* (1938) would be the obvious exception to this rule. Interestingly, this pattern follows the work of Joyce: quotation marks are deployed in *Dubliners*, but not in *A Portrait, Ulysses* or *Finnegans Wake*.
17. See, in particular, 'Limited Inc' (LI) and 'Living On: Border Lines' (LO/BL).
18. Cf. Bennington's speculation at the end of 'Derridabase', regarding the absorption of Derrida 'into a textuality in which he may well have quite simply disappeared' (JD i, 316).

ANNOTATED BIBLIOGRAPHY

de Man, Paul. *Allegories of Reading: Figural Language in Rousseau, Nietzsche, Rilke, and Proust*. New Haven, CT, 1979.

The essays collected here demonstrate the author's fascination with European Romanticism and its legacy, the rhetoric of identity and the relationship between figural language and reality. Paul de Man takes language as a form of reflection, which, for him is a fraught and problematic process. The author works through a series of close readings, demonstrating how the relationship between word and thing is conventional, not phenomenal. See the references to this text in Reader-Response Theory above and Poststructuralism below.

Derrida, Jacques, and John D. Caputo. *Deconstruction a Nutshell: A Conversation with Jacques Derrida*. New York, 1997.

The first part of this book is a roundtable discussion with Derrida, in which he responds to questions concerning deconstruction, improvising and elaborating points concerning philosophy, justice, responsibility, the gift, the idea of messianism, community and his writings on James Joyce. From the roundtable discussion, Caputo elaborates on issues raised in the roundtable in seven chapters, which do double service as a commentary on the discussion and a lucid introduction to certain major topics in the text of Jacques Derrida, without reducing Derrida's text to a systematic or formulaic methodology.

Derrida, Jacques. *Of Grammatology*, trans. Gayatri Chakravorty Spivak. Baltimore, MD, 1975.

Divided in two sections, the first considers the nature of writing in relation to the concept of Being. It proposes through its own practice or performance a critical or 'grammatological' reading which examines the aporetic in metaphysical thought. Derrida posits the idea that metaphysics relies on the suspension of logical movement and the hierarchical manipulation of binary oppositions which support such thinking. Derrida examines the oppositions 'voice/writing' and 'presence/absence' to examine how in the history of western metaphysical thought the former term is always privileged over the latter. The idea of writing is examined for the lack of attention paid to its operations in philosophy and for the way it is distrusted as a form of communication.

Derrida works with a number of terms which have subsequently been considered by those who insist on the idea of deconstruction as a critical methodology as essential to the lexicon of deconstruction: trace, inscription, logocentrism, reserve, gramme, *différ-ance*, supplement, logocentrism.

Derrida, Jacques. *Aporias*, trans. Thomas Dutoit. Stanford, CA, 1993.

Two essays, 'Finis' and 'Awaiting (at) the Arrival', comprise this publication, which Derrida considers the aporia between singularity and the general, while also addressing various modes of specificity of experience. The aporetic obligation involved in playing host to the foreign while respecting its foreignness is considered. Derrida's interests are articulated around a critique of various cultural histories and theorizations of death.

Kamuf, Peggy. *The Division of Literature or the University in Deconstruction.* Chicago, 1997.

Kamuf offers a sustained historicization of the development of literary studies in the university, while looking also at the political aspect of debates concerning the perception of 'deconstruction' and its assumed relationship to the question of 'political correctness' among academics and within institutions. Kamuf pursues this discussion also through a consideration of the figure of 'credit' in, among others, Herman Melville and G. W. F. Hegel.

Lacoue-Labarthe, Philippe. *Typography: Mimesis, Philosophy, Politics*, intro. Jacques Derrida, trans. Christopher Fynsk et al. Cambridge, MA, 1989; rpt. Stanford University Press, 1998.

A selection of essays from the French edition; the English-language edition is introduced by Derrida, whose discussion of Lacoue-Labarthe's work focuses on the latter's analysis of mimesis. Concentrating on both philosophy and poetics, particularly in the texts of Hölderin, the essays offer radical reappraisals of questions of subjectivity, paradox and mimesis, politics, mimesis and supplementarity, and the logic of identity, demonstrating the indirect yet powerful influence of Derrida on certain aspects of philosophical thought in France today.

SUPPLEMENTARY BIBLIOGRAPHY

Beardsworth, Richard. *Derrida and the Political.* London, 1996.

Bennington, Geoffrey. *Legislations: The Politics of Deconstruction.* London, 1994.

————and Jacques Derrida. *Jacques Derrida,* trans. Geoffrey Bennington. Chicago, 1993.

Brandt, Joan. *Geopoetics: The Politics of Mimesis in Poststructuralist French Poetry and Theory.* Stanford, CA, 1997.

Brannigan, John, Ruth Robbins and Julian Wolfreys, eds. *Applying: to Derrida.* Basingstoke, 1996.

Caputo, John D. *The Prayers and Tears of Jacques Derrida: Religion without Religion.* Bloomington, IN, 1997.

Caruth, Cathy. *Unreclaimed Experience: Trauma, Narrative, and History.* Baltimore, MD, 1996.

Clark, Timothy. *Derrida, Heidegger, Blanchot: Sources of Derrida's Notion and Practice of Literature.* Cambridge, 1992.

Critchley, Simon. *The Ethics of Deconstruction: Derrida and Levinas.* Oxford, 1992.

Derrida, Jacques. *Dissemination,* trans. and intro. Barbara Johnson. Chicago, 1981.

————. *Glas,* trans. John P. Leavey, Jr and Richard Rand. Lincoln, NE, 1986.

————. *The Post Card: From Socrates to Freud and Beyond,* trans. Alan Bass. Chicago, 1987.

————. *The Truth in Painting,* trans. Geoff Bennington and Ian McLeod. Chicago, 1987.

————. *Of Spirit: Heidegger and the Question,* trans. Geoffrey Bennington and Rachel Bowlby. Chicago, 1989.

————. *Given Time: I. Counterfeit Money,* trans. Peggy Kamuf. Chicago, 1992.

————. *The Other Heading: Reflections on Today's Europe,* trans. Pascale-Anne Brault and Michael B. Naas, intro. Michael B. Naas. Bloomington, IN, 1992.

————. *Aporias,* trans. Thomas Dutoit. Stanford, CA, 1993.

————. *Specters of Marx: The State of the Debt, the Work of Mourning, and the New International,* trans. Peggy Kamuf, intro. Bernd Magnus and Stephen Cullenberg. New York, 1994.

—————. *Archive Fever: A Freudian Impression*, trans. Eric Prenowitz. Chicago, 1995.

—————. *The Gift of Death*, trans. David Wills. Chicago, 1995.

—————. *On the Name*, ed. Thomas Dutoit, trans. David Wood, John P. Leavey, Jr and Ian McLeod. Stanford, CA, 1995.

—————. *Points . . . : Interviews, 1974–1994*, ed. Elizabeth Weber, trans. Peggy Kamuf et al. Stanford, CA, 1995.

—————. *The Politics of Friendship*, trans. George Collins. London, 1997.

—————. *Resistances of Psychoanalysis*, trans. Peggy Kamuf, Pascale-Anne Brault and Michael Naas. Stanford, CA, 1998.

Hart, Kevin. *The Trespass of the Sign: Deconstruction, Theology and Philosophy*. Cambridge, 1989.

Johnson, Barbara. *The Critical Difference: Essays in the Contemporary Rhetoric of Reading*. Baltimore, MD, 1980.

Johnson, Christopher. *System and Writing in the Philosophy of Jacques Derrida*. Cambridge, 1993.

Lacoue-Labarthe, Philippe. *Typography: Mimesis, Philosophy, Politics*, ed. Christopher Fynsk with Linda M. Brooks, intro. Jacques Derrida. Cambridge, MA, 1989; rpt. Stanford, CA, 1998.

Miller, J. Hillis. *Topographies*. Stanford, CA 1995.

Nancy, Jean-Luc. *The Birth to Presence*, trans. Brian Holmes et al. Stanford, CA, 1993.

Plotnitsky, Arkady. *Complementarity: Anti-Epistemology after Bohr and Derrida*. Durham, NC, 1994.

Ronell, Avital. *The Telephone Book: Technology, Schizophrenia, Electric Speech*. Lincoln, NE, 1989.

Sartilliot, Claudette. *Citation and Modernity: Derrida, Joyce, and Brecht*. Norman, OK, 1993.

Smith, Robert. *Derrida and Autobiography*. Cambridge, 1995.

Steigler, Bernard. *Technics and Time, 1: The Fault of Epimetheus*, trans. Richard Beardsworth and George Collins. Stanford, CA, 1998.

Wolfreys, Julian, John Brannigan and Ruth Robbins, eds. *The French Connections of Jacques Derrida*. Albany, NY, 1999.

Wood, David, ed. *Derrida: A Critical Reader*. Oxford, 1993.

PART 7
POSTSTRUCTURALISM

INTRODUCTION:
CRITICISM AND CONCEIT

Mark Currie

The most controversial moment in Paul de Man's essay 'Semiology and Rhetoric' is an aside in his final sentence which claims that the difference between literature and criticism is delusive. I want to use this as a point of entry to poststructuralist literary theory. In different ways it is a proposition which takes its place in the work of many of poststructuralism's key thinkers from Barthes's formula that there are no more critics, only writers, to the inventive critical styles of Derrida and other deconstructors. Its explanation opens up other questions, such as the genealogy of poststructuralism, the issue of reference in language, the possibility of scientific objectivity, and the knowability of the past. It also helps to define the legacy of poststructuralism, particularly in terms of the destruction of literary theory as we knew it, and the rise of storytelling as a critical activity, both in the novel and in the new historicisms.

There is nevertheless something quite obnoxious about a critic demolishing the boundary between literary and critical writing. It seems to involve an unjustified self-elevation on the critic's part, from the secondary and derivative role of a commentator to that of a primary creative producer, and in the same stroke it drags literature down by implying that its importance lies in the critical knowledge that it yields about itself and literature at large. Both of these tendencies are evident in poststructuralist approaches. There is an attitude of apparent self-importance, a feeling that the reading is more important than the thing read, and a recurring claim that valued literary texts speak only of themselves, no matter how strong the illusion that they are capable of reference to something else. Given these apparent aspirations to literariness, it is ironic that the language of poststructuralist discourse sets new standards of ugly complexity, pretentious neologism and puerile over-abstraction. Perhaps the real delusion lies in this chippy re-arrangement of an established hierarchy.

But de Man was not blowing his own trumpet in this way, nor expecting *Allegories of Reading* to displace Proust in the canon. He was responding to a kind of reciprocity between literature and criticism in the twentieth century that seemed to set them on a convergent course. A useful rubric under which to describe this convergence is the notion of the decline of realism, a process which can be traced in parallel through literary modernism and formalist criticism. There is a clear sense in which the modernist novel draws much of its experimental energy from the rejection of realistic conventions established in the eighteenth and nineteenth centuries. On one hand there is the ironisation of those conventions, a kind of illusion-breaking candour about fictional techniques, a baring of devices, which foregrounds the illusory and constructed nature of the realistic effect. This species of illusion-breaking irony includes techniques such as dramatising the process of fictional production, parodying past styles, the use of surrogate authors and readers, the poeticisation of prose style and narrative self-commentary. It is a kind of literary self-referentiality which seems to incorporate critical distance in a novel, and gives it a critical function in relation to its own history of rules and procedures. On the other hand there is the assertion of a different kind of reality: a more subjective, interior and contingent reality than the stable social, physical and external world of the conventional novel. To this tendency we could attribute technical innovations such as multiple narrators, sustained focalisation, stream of consciousness, an increasingly suggestive symbolism and the use of outside worlds as metaphors for inner landscapes. In short, the modernist novel contributes to a growing doubt over the viability of realism as a concept by highlighting its artificiality and its fluidity.

There are two points to be made here about the decline of realism and the ascent of reading. The first is that novels like this tend to generate more ambiguous and multiple meanings than those rooted in the faithful representation of a pre-existing reality, placing a greater burden on reading as a process of rendering the text intelligible. The second is that if reality is seen as contingent and constructed, there is a sense in which realism itself is a reading, one possible reading among others, or a collective agreement over what constitutes reality. To view realistic literature as a kind of reading is to emphasise that reality is not prior to language and interpretation but a product of it, as well as to extend massively the scope of the term *reading*. There is a feeling that realism is a kind of sham: a discourse that effaces its own techniques, language and role in projecting structure onto experience which has no shape *per se*. And this feeling is in evidence in much of the literary criticism of the first half of the twentieth century, which seemed to accept the critical insights of the modernist novel and incorporate them into their own critical readings. So, for example, in Russian formalism and early structuralism, one of the main concerns is to expose the sham of realism, by baring its devices and revealing its role in projecting shape and form onto the world.

If the critique of realism was underway within the novel itself in the modernist period, it was only a part of more widespread awareness of the role of language and convention in structuring reality. At around same time, Saussure was making a similar claim not only for realistic fiction, but for the conditions of linguistic reference in general: that words are capable of reference only because they project their system of differences onto the non-linguistic world. Like literary realism, then, the language system at large generates an illusion that words can refer directly and objectively to reality, but their ability to do so depends on the hidden conditions – conventions, codes and differences – which make reference possible. In the light of this proposition, the role of the critic shifts from being a commentator on the illusion generated by language (say the fictional world) to that of someone who unveils these hidden conditions, revealing the underlying structural relationships that enable meaning.

There is clearly a common philosophical denominator between these approaches to realism and reference, and therefore a reciprocity between them. But the contemporaneity of Saussure's *Course* and the modernist critique of fictional realism can be slightly misleading. There may well have been unseen historical forces contributing to this climate of scepticism, relativism and anti-realism, forces also at work in the emergence of scientific relativity, existential philosophy or psychoanalysis. But the actual reciprocity between fictional and structuralist critiques of realism was not apparent, especially in the Anglo-American tradition, until much later in the twentieth century, when Saussure's work was taken up in the humanities and the anti-realist tendencies in criticism found their theoretical underpinnings. But if Saussure's account of the sign acts as a kind of linguistic premise for structuralist thought the same cannot really be said of poststructuralism. If we take Derrida's dealings with Saussure as an example, we do not find him paying homage to structural linguistics as an origin of anti-realist thinking. His reading of Saussure's account of the sign in *Of Grammatology* is as a symptom of something much larger, namely the tendency in anti-realist thinking to remain implicated with realism no matter how hard it may strive to escape. In his early work, Derrida calls this inescapable condition the 'metaphysics of presence', which he describes as an ineluctable desire to ground general explanations and theories in some form of presence. To the extent that this desire is at work in Saussure, it is worth pointing out that for Derrida, Saussure is just one example of the anti-realist tendency with a much longer history, not its origin, and that it is considerably easier to find proclamations in Derrida's work of the foundational influence of modernist writers on his thinking than of *The Course in General Linguistics*. I say this partly to support the idea of the convergence of literature and criticism that de Man advances, but also to correct a wide misconception often spread by critical commentators that structuralism was based on some radical new premise about language, and that poststructuralism found a way of making it more radical still. As Derrida is always reminding us, questions about realism, or the ability of language to refer to an extra-linguistic reality, have been with us at least since Plato, and can be traced throughout the history of western metaphysics, including literature.

Returning for a moment to Derrida's relation to Saussure, we find him talking of the sign not as some radical new hypothesis but as a concept inherited from the old dualist tradition of metaphysical thinking, the key characteristic of which was to separate the form and the content of language. But the radical impact of Saussure's thesis lay in the proposition that in language 'there are only differences without positive terms', a proposition taken by most structuralists to mean that the content of a word was a kind of illusion, a referential illusion, and that its real content was in fact the hidden system of differences which enabled that illusion to occur. Derrida's claim is that this proposition is undermined by the fact that Saussure still understands the sign as a two-sided entity, a *signifier* and a *signified*. If Saussure was attempting to articulate a monistic theory of the form and content of language and argue for their inseparability, the distinction of signifier and signified is unnecessary. It is nothing more than a residue of dualistic metaphysics which subverts the monism which the *Course* proposes. Worse than that, it installs an ambiguity in the premise of structuralist thought which can be traced through literary structuralism as a kind of slippage between two markedly different attitudes to linguistic analysis. Does a structuralist critic deny the presence of content in language or merely ignore it? Many commentators give the impression that the radical reputation of structuralist criticism was founded on the outright denial of referential content in language, and that structural linguistics provided the hypothesis that, however powerful the referential illusion, language could only ever refer to itself. But this kind of hypothesis is not easily found in the work of structural linguists.

If we take Roman Jakobson, whose work on the question of reference and self-reference was enormously influential on this kind of commentary, we find no such denial of referential content. In 'Closing Statement' in 1960, he argued that any utterance or act of communication had several distinguishable aspects or functions occurring simultaneously in different degrees. For example it is possible for an utterance to convey meaning about the outside world, the language system, and the message itself at the same time, or in his own terminology, to be at once referential, metalingual and poetic. Some discourses, he argues, seem more orientated towards one of these functions than others. Poetry, for example, foregrounds the poetic function of language by drawing attention to the way in which things are said, to the point where reference seems like a lesser consideration; prose, on the other hand, seems to use language in a more transparent way and so foregrounds the referential function. But if the poetic function seems to dominate in poetry, this does not mean that the referential function is negated or absent, nor that the poetic function of prose is absent. A linguistic analysis can focus on any aspect of the communication that it pleases – the poetic function of prose for example – so that the analyst has some input into which aspect of the communication to foreground. In other words, foregrounding is not something determined only by the nature of the language under analysis: it is also an active process on the part of the analysis, the critic or the reader. Put simply this means that if you ask a question about the metalingual aspect of an utterance, you get a metalingual answer, but this doesn't mean that the referential aspect dissolves, or that the outside world ceases to exist. Sometimes it seems that the radical reputation of structuralism is based on a mistake or an exaggeration, and the occasional commentator dares to say so. 'The student who says in a university seminar that Lawrence is splendidly true to life will be answered with smiles of conscious superiority as if he had committed some mild betise,' notes A.D. Nuttall in his discussion of Jakobson's similarly uncontroversial argument in 'Realism in Art'. The mistaken assumption according to Nuttall is 'that modern literary theory has exploded the idea that literature is in any way authentically true to life' (Nuttall, 1983, 54). If this is a mistake, and the radical reputation of literary structuralism rests on nothing more than a claim that realism has a conventional element, the ambiguity in structuralist approaches to reference has a lot to answer for.

The ambiguity between bracketing off and denying the referential dimension of language is the starting point for de Man's essay below: 'By an awareness of the arbitrariness of the sign (Saussure) and of literature as an autotelic statement "focused on the way it is expressed" (Jakobson), the entire question of meaning can be bracketed, thus freeing the critical discourse from the debilitating burden of paraphrase' (de Man, 1979, 5). For de Man, then, the epistemological issue of meaning is merely sidestepped by semiology, whereas any radical critique of reference will focus on referential meaning in conjunction with its formal and figural aspects. Later in *Allegories of Reading*, to which this essay serves as an introduction, he finds this critique in Rousseau, whose 'radical critique of referential meaning never implied that the referential function of language could in any way be avoided, bracketed, or reduced to being just one contingent linguistic property among others, as it is postulated, for example, in contemporary semiology' (de Man, 1979, 204). In other words, semiology implicitly denies reference by ignoring it and transforming form into the primary content of a discourse, but de Man is looking for a less ambiguous position capable of bringing referential meaning into confrontation with other aspects of language in a way which will more explicitly purge language of its referential content. It is clear in the discussion below of Yeats that de Man rejects any Jakobsonian sense of an easy co-presence of different aspects of language or of any decision to give priority to one aspect over another. There is also an unmistakable revulsion to the idea of reference which is imaged variously as a trickster, a disease or the victim of some horrible collision.

The argument against reference in *Allegories of Reading* can be summarised like this. If Jakobson sees the total meaning of a discourse as the sum of the six functions he identifies, the bracketing-off of reference in the name of *poetics* produces a partial reading of that discourse. No matter how much scientific attention is poured onto the formal and self-referential aspects of that discourse, the referential aspect is still there, lurking but ignored, in happy coexistence with the other functions. De Man argues instead that reading should sustain the contradiction between different aspects of language. If semiology gives the impression that form *is* the *total* meaning of a discourse, it does so by ignoring its other aspects and allowing a partial reading to present itself as a total reading. This is *totalisation* – the great enemy of deconstruction – or *synecdoche*, whereby a part stands for the whole. This is a useful preliminary way of understanding the impact of deconstruction in literary theory: a deconstruction reads a narrative for contradictions, aims to sustain them, and not reduce the text to a stable, single structure or meaning.

One of the interesting aspects of de Man's attitude to reference is that he cannot express it theoretically: it is 'a difficulty which puts its precise theoretical exposition beyond my powers' (1979, 9). It is only by reading texts that a critique of referential meaning emerges, so that the linguistic theory is always embedded in the reading of a particular text and remains unextractable from that context. In his two examples here, of ambiguous rhetorical questions, and in the more extended analyses later in *Allegories of Reading*, there is a clear sense that ambiguity is a much more catastrophic condition than we would normally assume, that literary language exists in this condition more than most, and that the *victim of the catastrophe is referential meaning*. Characteristically, de Man tends to move from readings which emphasise the collision of different aspects of linguistic meaning into general claims about the nature of language, its self-referentiality, its inability to refer to the outside or the impossibility of separating the literal from the metaphorical. Simple as the strategy may seem, it represents a profound shift for literary theory. For Jakobson, the linguistic model is a foundation or a premise for the analysis of a literary text. For de Man, the text is the premise which yields linguistic knowledge. In other words the direction of the relationship between linguistics and literature has been reversed. The linguistic model in structuralism tended to reduce the rich diversity of literary texts to some bland common denominator, as instances of grammatical rules, or as abstract structures illustrating the enabling conventions of meaning. Poststructuralist readings tend to use the complexity of individual texts to demolish the neat categories and methods which the linguistic model brings to texts. Or to use Barthes's language, the relation of the linguistic model to literature has shifted from one of *deduction* to one of *induction*, no longer moving from general rules about language to the analysis of particular texts, but from the analysis of texts towards a negative knowledge of those general rules.

If my account a moment ago of the impact of poststructuralism in criticism was that it refused the view of a text as a stable structure, there is now an important qualification. The text is not only something that can't be pinned down by scientific (semiological) analysis. By being unpindownable, it destabilises the model of analysis and in this sense yields its own linguistic knowledge.

For de Man, one model of analysis at stake is what he calls the inside/outside model in literary studies. The main characteristic of the inside/outside model is that nobody knows which is which. The opposition of form and content implies that form is external, yet in another sense the form of a work is within it while its content is often something which is pointed to outside the work. For this reason the opposition of intrinsic and extrinsic criticism has never been clear. Intrinsic criticism in the hands of New Criticism was formalist while extrinsic brought external information such as historical, biographical or referential perspectives to bear. Many critics after the New Criticism began to express the relationship between the outside of literature and formalism the other way around. Here is A. D. Nuttall again: 'There are two languages of criticism, the first "opaque", external, formalist, operating outside the mechanisms of art and taking those mechanisms as its object, the second "transparent", internal, realist, operating within the world presented in the work' (1983, 80). This confusion is really a facet of the ambiguity surrounding structuralist attitudes to reference, as well as being de Man's version of Derrida's engagement with Saussure: 'The recurrent debate opposing intrinsic to extrinsic criticism stands under the aegis of an inside/outside metaphor that is never being seriously questioned' (1979, 5). The problem with literary semiology, for de Man, is that even if it seems to understand reference, on Saussurean lines, as a purely internal effect of language, it still imports the inside/outside model by distinguishing between, for example, the referential and the autotelic. If Derrida saw the distinction of signifier and signified as a residual dualist presupposition, this is exactly the problem for de Man with the inside/outside model. Speaking of Saussure's justification to base his study of language on speech – the pure inside of language – as opposed to writing which is merely an external representation of speech, Derrida characterises the new relationship between the poles: 'the outside bears with the inside a relationship which is, as usual, anything but simple exteriority. The meaning of the outside was always present within the inside, imprisoned outside the outside, and vice versa' (1976, 100).

Derrida's engagements with linguistic theory are often humorously complex: they illustrate that language itself does not cooperate with any model which seeks to stabilise it, reduce it, or close down its infinite complexity. Linguistic terminology in Derrida's work tends to take on ironic force, no longer naming some feature of language, but naming some problem in a prior theory or tradition. *Differance* is a good example of a term which does its utmost not to designate anything except the unstoppable motion of language in the face of attempts to keep it still for a moment; or, to put it another way, if it designates anything it is the inadequacy of the Saussurean term difference. Simple terms such as writing, metaphor and signifier are used by Derrida in ironic ways to upturn and collapse the oppositions to which they belong in linguistic theory at large, designating the presuppositions of former accounts of meaning without asserting anything about the nature of language: language will always undermine the categories and distinctions by which linguists attempt to define and totalise it.

Perhaps the most famous misrepresentation of Derrida's engagement with language theory is the way that critics and philosophers have interpreted the slogan *Il n'y a pas de hors-texte*. If I am right in the paragraph above that Derrida never attempts to say anything of his own about language, but only to show that it disrupts, exceeds and resists its own analysis, the slogan does not mean there is nothing outside of the text as most commentators have taken it. It is closer to there is no outside-text. Derrida does not mean that reality does not exist except as an illusion foisted on us by language, but that it is not possible to distinguish categorically between what is within and what is outside. So, for example, the idea often associated with Derrida that all language is metaphorical is a problem in the definition of literal meaning, not an ontological claim. Those who claim that poststructuralism rests on a theory of language which denies reference to the outside world are mistaken on two grounds. First, they assume that the linguistic model comes first, like a premise which is then applied to instances – the realistic novel for example – of language. As I have said, theoretical knowledge, however negative, comes if anything from reading narratives against the grain of any linguistic model for analysis. Second, they assume that poststructuralism is a knowledge of language when it would be safer to see it as an argument against the knowability of language which shifts attention away from knowledge of language towards the language of knowledge.

This shift points to the real cataclysm of poststructuralist thought, which emerges from a glaring contradiction in structuralist thought. I began this discussion with the argument that the impetus behind structuralism derived from a view that language constructed rather than reflected the world, created rather than revealed the structures that we think of as reality. And yet the structuralist seems to assume, on the whole, that a metalanguage such as linguistics is capable of describing language from a stance of scientific objectivity. If language creates, rather than reveals, the world surely metalanguage also creates, rather than reveals, the structures of language. Reference to language is after all no different from reference to the so-called outside world. There can surely be no position outside of language from which language can be viewed objectively. Derrida calls this a repetition and a redoubling of structuralism's basic insight.

If structuralist thought is to remain true to its own basic insight, the idea of metalingual distance on which most literary criticism is dependant is no longer viable. How can criticism deny the transparency of language in general only to assume the transparency of its own descriptions? This conundrum takes us back into the conflation of literature and criticism from which we started, since the boundary between literary and critical writing disappears as a consequence of the impossibility of metalingual distance. Much of the notorious difficulty of poststructuralist writing derives from this collapse of metalingual distance. Criticism moves into a phase in which it can no longer posit the objectivity of its insights and abounds instead with new creative practices. De Man's formula for an allegory of reading is typical of the way that such practices ambiguously divide responsibility for an insight between the critic and the text itself: is he speaking of an allegory about reading within the text, or is the allegory a property of the reading? There is one line of argument in de Man that indicates that allegory is not an intentional structure but a kind of translation performed by the critic according to his own interests; and yet there is another which claims that the deconstruction 'is not something we have added to the text, but it constituted the text in the first place' (1979, 17). Either way, the consequence is that poststructuralist critics characteristically translate some of our best-loved literary works into unrecognisable metalingual tracts: for example Proust's *A la Recherche du temps perdu* becomes, in the hands of Gilles Deleuze, a metalanguage better capable of exploring the semiotics of narrative than any critical language, or in Paul de Man's, a deconstruction of the distinction between metaphor and metonomy.

An equally apparent consequence of the collapse of metalingual distance is the increasing opacity of poststructuralist critical writing, that jargonesque and neologistic tendency about which I was so rude at the start of this piece. It is possible to defend this kind of opacity and difficulty as a kind of self-conscious awareness of the role of critical language in projecting structure onto the language under analysis. This is certainly true of a neologism such as Derrida's *differance*, a term which precludes any easy transparency to its analytical objects and foregrounds its graphic materiality by transposing Saussure's 'e' to an 'a'. This may sound like the death of critical reason, and many have argued that it was. It certainly compels a different definition of literary theory and criticism. Writing four years after his attempts to evangelise his readers on behalf of the objectivity of the linguistic model, Barthes provides a useful alternative when he proposes that 'theoretical does not of course mean abstract. From my point of view it means *reflexive*, something which turns back on itself' (1973, 44). If a theoretical discourse is one which turns back on itself, reflects upon itself, the canon of literary theoretical texts is suddenly opened up to hundreds of literary texts, especially modernist and postmodernist novels, but equally the Canterbury Tales, Shakespeare plays, Romantic and modernist lyrics, not to mention television advertisements, sitcoms, cartoons and films. Contemporary criticism is awash with such claims, that theory is no longer a discourse about critical discourse, no longer a set of propositions about propositions, but a kind of knowledge yielded by discourses everywhere. Or to use the most influential terminology, theory and criticism are no longer constative (truth-telling) discourses, but performatives, or discourses which enact and perform their views rather than state them. Theory as reflexivity, then, is a way of avoiding what Derrida calls the 'platitude of a supposed academic metalanguage' (Derrida, 1992, 60), or what Barthes sees as the 'hypocritical distance of a fallacious metalanguage' (1973, 44), and ensure that criticism begins, in de Man's words, to practise what it preaches, namely writing.

There are many places where this new performative criticism has led since its inception in the 1970s, and not all of them in my view are positive. If I had to point to negative outcomes, I would gesture in the direction of New Historicist anecdote, which often strikes me as a retreat from theory into a metaphorical discourse bristling with theoretical suggestivity, but without the faintest idea of what it is suggesting. On the other side of the traditional borderline, I think there are negative outcomes for literature. The ascendance of metafictional self-contemplation, for example, into the orthodoxy of historiographic metafiction – fiction which endlessly highlights the artificiality of its own retrospect – seems to me a kind of dumbing down of poststructuralist approaches to historical reference. But I don't have the space to argue these cases at length here.

At any rate, the theorisation of fiction and the aestheticisation of theory both seem to stand or fall on a principle more akin to the traditional vagaries of aesthetic value than the rules of critical reason. But on a more positive note, I agree with de Man below when he asserts that 'metaphors are much more tenacious than facts', and that the 'apparent glorification of the critic-philosopher in the name of truth is in fact a glorification of the poet as the primary source of this truth' (1979, 17). If we look at Derrida's output since the mid-1980s, there is a clear acknowledgement of the power of metaphor to outstrip that of conventional reason, and his work presents a litany of theoretical metaphors such as postcards, gifts, various forms of technology and ghosts which scrupulously avoid the platitude of a metalanguage.

In this tradition I would also locate Avital Ronell's reading of *Madame Bovary*, which is extracted from her book *Crack Wars* (1992). Elsewhere in the study, Ronell poses the problem that we have been charting of 'the exhaustion of language': 'Where might one go today, to what sources can one turn, in order to activate a just constativity?' Explicitly repudiating the traditional, constative values of literary criticism, she resorts instead to a very literary kind of criticism under the following justification: 'Why should I begin my study of *Madame Bovary* in the mode of fiction? To fill a prescription; namely that the provisions of the simulacrum be doubled' (1992, 64). If the 'simulacrum' refers to a postmodern logic in which real things and simulated representations cannot be distinguished, this doubling recalls the fusion of subject and object which presided over Derrida's redoubling of structuralism's basic insight. Similarly, Ronell invokes Deleuze in *Difference and Repetition* when he claims that philosophy 'ought to be a very particular kind of crime story' and that it should 'resemble science fiction'. Clearly then we are in a tradition which cannot separate the activities of creative writing and criticism.

I claimed above that an ambiguity operates in de Man's work between insights that belong to an object text and those that belong to the critic, and the same confusion reigns here in the relation between Ronell and Flaubert. This is partly a source of comedy produced by the tension between a novel published in 1857 and a descriptive vocabulary located firmly in contemporary drug culture. There are certainly strong elements of parody implicit in this technique, surfacing in bad jokes and painful puns, and becoming explicit in the concluding section of the work which casts Derrida, Heidegger, Freud, Benjamin, Emma Bovary and others in comic stage dialogue. There are also performative gestures of a Derridean nature, graphic jokes which signal the materiality of writing on the page as if invoking poststructuralist thematics, yet deployed in such purposeless ways that their intent can only be sardonic. I hope I am not wrong. But the serious project of the reading is to construct a chain of connotative links between the novel's own motifs and broader themes of intoxication and dependency. Chief among these links is the analogy, established with the help of Derrida between fiction and drug addiction, the pleasure taken in an experience without truth, in exile from reality. Responsibility for this overriding analogy lies partly with Flaubert, the plotting of Emma's alienation and will to escape, and the text's tropological connections to other libidinal pleasures through images of ingestion such as love and feeding, vampirism and parasitism. But if these are aspects of the novel, they are also links actively forged by the critical reading, in metaphoric and metonymic ways rather than by reasoned analogy to the point where they are capable of entering into substitution with each other, in phrases such as 'hallucinating literature', the 'books she's consumed', 'seduced by a hallucination', 'her dosage of fantasy', 'incorporations of a foreign body' or her many puns on words such as *purity, substance* and *prescription.*

This is one sense in which metaphors are more tenacious than facts: they exist in this middle ground between the subject and the object, between the discovery of the novel's own metaphoric system and the invention of that system by the creative imagery of the critical language. Perhaps this is also the trace of a set of psychoanalytic assumptions which allow this slippage between discovery and invention. Attempting to understand eating as a metonymy of introjection, for example, Ronell clearly locates her chain of connotative links in a textual unconscious: 'It is important to figure this out, for devouring, reading, swallowing, and suicide are linked as one great train rushing through the novel's underground.' Here is a metaphor (and a pun) describing a chain of metaphoric links in the novel's unconscious while at the same time foregrounding the invention of those links, the performativity of critical language itself, in a way that characterises the poststructuralist legacy. Contemporary criticism abounds with this kind of highlighted metaphor, with this spirit of tropological creativity derived from linguistic and psychoanalytic poststructuralism no more than from literature itself. It represents the insertion of the critic into what de Man calls, in his closing sentence, the most rigorous and the most unreliable language in terms of which she names and transforms herself, and helps to plot the connection between criticism and conceit.

7.1

SEMIOLOGY AND RHETORIC

Paul de Man

To judge from various recent publications, the spirit of the times is not blowing in the direction of formalist and intrinsic criticism. We may no longer be hearing too much about relevance but we keep hearing a great deal about reference, about the nonverbal 'outside' to which language refers, by which it is conditioned and upon which it acts. The stress falls not so much on the fictional status of literature – a property now perhaps somewhat too easily taken for granted – but on the interplay between these fictions and categories that are said to partake of reality, such as the self, man, society, 'the artist, his culture and the human community', as one critic puts it. Hence the emphasis on hybrid texts considered to be partly literary and partly referential, on popular fictions deliberately aimed towards social and psychological gratification, on literary autobiography as a key to the understanding of the self, and so on. We speak as if, with the problems of literary form resolved once and forever, and with the techniques of structural analysis refined to near-perfection, we could now move 'beyond formalism' towards the questions that really interest us and reap, at last, the fruits of the ascetic concentration on techniques that prepared us for this decisive step. With the internal law and order of literature well policed, we can now confidently devote ourselves to the foreign affairs, the external politics of literature. Not only do we feel able to do so, but we owe it to ourselves to take this step: our moral conscience would not allow us to do otherwise. Behind the assurance that valid interpretation is possible, behind the recent interest in writing and reading

Extract from *Diacritics*, 3:3 (Fall 1973), pp. 27–33.

as potentially effective public speech acts, stands a highly respectable moral imperative that strives to reconcile the internal, formal, private structures of literary language with their external, referential, and public effects.

I want, for the moment, to consider briefly this tendency in itself, as an undeniable and recurrent historical fact, without regard for its truth or falseness or for its value as desirable or pernicious. It is a fact that this sort of thing happens, again and again, in literary studies. On the one hand, literature cannot merely be received as a definite unit of referential meaning that can be decoded without leaving a residue. The code is unusually conspicuous, complex, and enigmatic; it attracts an inordinate amount of attention to itself, and this attention has to acquire the rigor of a method. The structural moment of concentration on the code for its own sake cannot be avoided, and literature necessarily breeds its own formalism. Technical innovations in the methodical study of literature only occur when this kind of attention predominates. It can legitimately be said, for example, that, from a technical point of view, very little has happened in American criticism since the innovative works of New Criticism. There certainly have been numerous excellent books of criticism since, but in none of them have the techniques of description and interpretation evolved beyond the techniques of close reading established in the thirties and the forties. Formalism, it seems, is an all-absorbing and tyrannical muse; the hope that one can be at the same time technically original and discursively eloquent is not borne out by the history of literary criticism.

On the other hand – and this is the real mystery – no literary formalism, no matter how accurate and enriching in its analytic powers, is ever allowed to come into being without seeming reductive. When form is considered to be the external trappings of literary meaning or content, it seems superficial and expendable. The development of intrinsic, formalist criticism in the twentieth century has changed this model: form is now a solipsistic category of self-reflection, and the referential meaning is said to be extrinsic. The polarities of inside and outside have been reversed, but they are still the same polarities that are at play: internal meaning has become outside reference, and the outer form has become the intrinsic structure. A new version of reductiveness at once follows this reversal: formalism nowadays is mostly described in an imagery of imprisonment and claustrophobia: the 'prison house of language', 'the impasse of formalist criticism', etc. Like the grandmother in Proust's novel ceaselessly driving the young Marcel out into the garden, away from the unhealthy inwardness of his closeted reading, critics cry out for the fresh air of referential meaning. Thus, with the structure of the code so opaque, but the meaning so anxious to blot out the obstacle of form, no wonder that the reconciliation of form and meaning would be so attractive. The attraction of reconciliation is the elective breeding-ground of false models and metaphors; it accounts for the metaphorical model of literature as a kind of box that separates an inside from an outside, and the reader or critic as the person who opens the lid in order to release in the open what was secreted but inaccessible inside. It matters little whether we call the inside of the box the content or the form, the outside the meaning or the appearance. The recurrent debate opposing intrinsic to extrinsic criticism stands under the aegis of an inside/outside metaphor that is never being seriously questioned.

Metaphors are much more tenacious than facts, and I certainly don't expect to dislodge this age-old model in one short try. I merely wish to speculate on a different set of terms, perhaps less simple in their differential relationships than the strictly polar, binary opposition between inside and outside and therefore less likely to enter into the easy play of chiasmic reversals. I derive these terms (which are as old as the hills) pragmatically from the observation of developments and debates in recent critical methodology.

One of the most controversial among these developments coincides with a new approach to poetics or, as it is called in Germany, poetology, as a branch of general semiotics. In France, a semiology of literature comes about as the outcome of the long-deferred but all the more explosive encounter of the nimble French literary mind with the category of form. Semiology, as opposed to semantics, is the science or study of signs as signifiers; it does not ask what words mean but how they mean. Unlike American New Criticism, which derived the internalization of form from the practice of highly self-conscious modern writers, French semiology turned to linguistics for its model and adopted Saussure and Jakobson rather than Valéry or Proust for its masters. By an awareness of the arbitrariness of the sign (Saussure) and of literature as an autotelic statement 'focused on the way it is expressed' (Jakobson) the entire question of meaning can be bracketed, thus freeing the critical discourse from the debilitating burden of paraphrase. The demystifying power of semiology, within the context of French historical and thematic criticism, has been considerable. It demonstrated that the perception of the literary dimensions of language is largely obscured if one submits uncritically to the authority of reference. It also revealed how tenaciously this authority continues to assert itself in a variety of disguises, ranging from the crudest ideology to the most refined forms of aesthetic and ethical judgment. It especially explodes the myth of semantic correspondence between sign and referent, the wishful hope of having it both ways, of being, to paraphrase Marx in the German Ideology, a formalist critic in the morning and a communal moralist in the afternoon, of serving both the technique of form and the substance of meaning. The results, in the practice of French criticism, have been as fruitful as they are irreversible. Perhaps for the first time since the late eighteenth century, French critics can come at least somewhat closer to the kind of linguistic awareness that never ceased to be operative in its poets and novelists and that forced all of them, including Sainte Beuve, to write their main works 'contre Sainte Beuve'. The distance was never so considerable in England and the United States, which does not mean, however, that we may be able, in this country, to dispense altogether with some preventative semiological hygiene.

One of the most striking characteristics of literary semiology as it is practiced today, in France and elsewhere, is the use of grammatical (especially syntactical) structures conjointly with rhetorical structures, without apparent awareness of a possible discrepancy between them. In their literary analyses, Barthes, Genette, Todorov, Greimas, and their disciples all simplify and regress from Jakobson in letting grammar and rhetoric function in perfect continuity, and in passing from grammatical to rhetorical structures without difficulty or interruption. Indeed, as the study of grammatical structures is refined in contemporary theories of generative, transformational, and distributive grammar, the study of tropes and of figures (which is how the term *rhetoric* is used here, and not in the derived sense of comment or of eloquence or persuasion) becomes a mere extension of grammatical models, a particular subset of syntactical relations. In the recent *Dictionnaire encyclopédique des sciences du langage*, Ducrot and Todorov write that rhetoric has always been satisfied with a paradigmatic view over words (words substituting for each other), without questioning their syntagmatic relationship (the contiguity of words to each other). There ought to be another perspective, complementary to the first, in which metaphor, for example, would not be defined as a substitution but as a particular type of combination. Research inspired by linguistics or, more narrowly, by syntactical studies, has begun to reveal this possibility – but it remains to be explored. Todorov, who calls one of his books a *Grammar of the Decameron*, rightly thinks of his own work and that of his associates as first explorations in the elaboration of a systematic grammar of literary modes, genres, and also of literary figures. Perhaps the most perceptive work to come out of this school, Genette's studies of figural modes, can be shown to be assimilations of rhetorical transformations or combinations to syntactical, grammatical patterns. Thus a recent study, now printed in *Figures III* and entitled *Metaphor and Metonymy in Proust*, shows the combined presence, in a wide and astute selection of passages, of paradigmatic, metaphorical figures with syntagmatic, metonymic structures. The combination of both is treated descriptively and nondialectically without considering the possibility of logical tensions.

One can ask whether this reduction of figure to grammar is legitimate. The existence of grammatical structures, within and beyond the unit of the sentence, in literary texts is undeniable, and their description and classification are indispensable. The question remains if and how figures of rhetoric can be included in such a taxonomy. This question is at the core of the debate going on, in a wide variety of apparently unrelated forms, in contemporary poetics. But the historical picture of contemporary criticism is too confused to make the mapping out of such a topography a useful exercise. Not only are these questions mixed in and mixed up within particular groups or local trends, but they are often co-present, without apparent contradiction, within the work of a single author.

Neither is the theory of the question suitable for quick expository treatment. To distinguish the epistemology of grammar from the epistemology of rhetoric is a redoubtable task. On an entirely naïve level, we tend to conceive of grammatical systems as tending towards universality and as simply generative, i.e. as capable of deriving an infinity of versions from a single model (that may govern transformations as well as derivations) without the intervention of another model that would upset the first. We therefore think of the relationship between grammar and logic, the passage from grammar to propositions, as being relatively unproblematic: no true propositions are conceivable in the absence of grammatical consistency or of controlled deviation from a system of consistency no matter how complex. Grammar and logic stand to each other in a dyadic relationship of unsubverted support. In a logic of acts rather than of statements, as in Austin's theory of speech acts, that has had such a strong influence on recent American work in literary semiology, it is also possible to move between speech acts and grammar without difficulty. The performance of what is called illocutionary acts such as ordering, questioning, denying, assuming, etc., within the language is congruent with the grammatical structures of syntax in the corresponding imperative, interrogative, negative, optative sentences. 'The rules for illocutionary acts', writes Richard Ohman in a recent paper, 'determine whether performance of a given act is well-executed, in just the same way as *grammatical* rules determine whether the product of a locutionary act – a sentence – is well formed ... But whereas the rules of grammar concern the relationships among sound, syntax, and meaning, the rules of illocutionary acts concern relationships among people' (1972, 50). And since rhetoric is then conceived exclusively as persuasion, as actual action upon others (and not as an intralinguistic figure or trope), the continuity between the illocutionary realm of grammar and the perlocutionary realm of rhetoric is self-evident. It becomes the basis for a new rhetoric that, exactly as is the case for Todorov and Genette, would also be a new grammar.

Without engaging the substance of the question, it can be pointed out, without having to go beyond recent and American examples, and without calling upon the strength of an age-old tradition, that the continuity here assumed between grammar and rhetoric is not borne out by theoretical and philosophical speculation. Kenneth Burke mentions *deflection* (which he compares structurally to Freudian displacement), defined as 'any slight bias or even unintended error', as the rhetorical basis of language, and deflection is then conceived as a dialectical subversion of the consistent link between sign and meaning that operates within grammatical patterns; hence Burke's well-known insistence on the distinction between grammar and rhetoric. Charles Sanders Peirce, who, with Nietzsche and Saussure, laid the philosophical foundation for modern semiology, stressed the distinction between grammar and rhetoric in his celebrated and so suggestively unfathomable definition of the sign. He insists, as is well known, on the necessary presence of a third element, called the interpretant, within any relationship that the sign entertains with its object. The sign is to be interpreted if we are to understand the idea it is to convey, and this is so because the sign is not the thing but a meaning derived from the thing by a process here called representation that is not simply generative, i.e. dependent on a univocal origin. The interpretation of the sign is not, for Peirce, a meaning but another sign; it is a reading, not a decodage, and this reading has, in its turn, to be interpreted into another sign, and so on *ad infinitum*. Peirce calls this process by means of which 'one sign gives birth to another' pure rhetoric, as distinguished from pure grammar, which postulates the possibility of unproblematic, dyadic meaning, and pure logic, which postulates the possibility of the universal truth of meanings. Only if the sign engendered meaning in the same way that the object engenders the sign, that is, by representation, would there be no need to distinguish between grammar and rhetoric.

These remarks should indicate at least the existence and the difficulty of the question, a difficulty which puts its concise theoretical exposition beyond my powers. I must retreat therefore into a pragmatic discourse and try to illustrate the tension between grammar and rhetoric in a few specific textual examples. Let me begin by considering what is perhaps the most commonly known instance of an apparent symbiosis between a grammatical and a rhetorical structure, the so-called rhetorical question, in which the figure is conveyed directly by means of a syntactical device. I take the first example from the sub-literature of the mass media: asked by his wife whether he wants to have his bowling shoes laced over or laced under, Archie Bunker answers with a question: 'What's the difference?' Being a reader of sublime simplicity, his wife replies by patiently explaining the difference between lacing over and lacing under, whatever this may be, but provokes only ire. 'What's the difference' did not ask for difference but means instead 'I don't give a damn what the difference is.' The same grammatical pattern engenders two meanings that are mutually exclusive: the literal meaning asks for the concept (difference) whose existence is denied by the figurative meaning. As long as we are talking about bowling shoes, the consequences are relatively trivial; Archie Bunker, who is a great believer in the authority of origins (as long, of course, as they are the right origins) muddles along in a world where literal and figurative meanings get in each other's way, though not without discomforts. But suppose that it is a *de*-bunker rather than a 'Bunker', and a de-bunker of the arche (or origin), an archie De-bunker such as Nietzsche or Jacques Derrida for instance, who asks the question 'What is the Difference' – and we cannot even tell from his grammar whether he 'really' wants to know 'what' difference is or is just telling us that we shouldn't even try to find out. Confronted with the question of the difference between grammar and rhetoric, grammar allows us to ask the question, but the sentence by means of which we ask it may deny the very possibility of asking. For what is the use of asking, I ask, when we cannot even authoritatively decide whether a question asks or doesn't ask?

The point is as follows. A perfectly clear syntactical paradigm (the question) engenders a sentence that has at least two meanings, of which the one asserts and the other denies its own illocutionary mode. It is not so that there are simply two meanings, one literal and the other figural, and that we have to decide which one of these meanings is the right one in this particular situation. The confusion can only be cleared up by the intervention of an extra-textual intention, such as Archie Bunker putting his wife straight; but the very anger he displays is indicative of more than impatience; it reveals his despair when confronted with a structure of linguistic meaning that he cannot control and that holds the discouraging prospect of an infinity of similar future confusions, all of them potentially catastrophic in their consequences. Nor is this intervention really a part of the mini-text constituted by the figure which holds our attention only as long as it remains suspended and unresolved. I follow the usage of common speech in calling this semiological enigma 'rhetorical'. The grammatical model of the question becomes rhetorical not when we have, on the one hand, a literal meaning and on the other hand a figural meaning, but when it is impossible to decide by grammatical or other linguistic devices which of the two meanings (that can be entirely incompatible) prevails. Rhetoric radically suspends logic and opens up vertiginous possibilities of referential aberration. And although it would perhaps be somewhat more remote from common usage, I would not hesitate to equate the rhetorical, figural potentiality of language with literature itself. I could point to a great number of antecedents to this equation of literature with figure; the most recent reference would be to Monroe Beardsley's insistence in his contribution to the *Essays* to honor William Wimsatt, that literary language is characterized by being 'distinctly above the norm in ratio of implicit [or, I would say rhetorical] to explicit meaning' (1973, 37).

Let me pursue the matter of the rhetorical question through one more example. Yeats's poem 'Among School Children' ends with the famous line: 'How can we know the dancer from the dance?' Although there are some revealing inconsistencies within the commentaries, the line is usually interpreted as stating, with the increased emphasis of a rhetorical device, the potential unity between form and experience, between creator and creation. It could be said that it denies the discrepancy between the sign and the referent from which we started out. Many elements in the imagery and the dramatic development of the poem strengthen this traditional reading; without having to look any further than the immediately preceding lines, one finds powerful and consecrated images of the continuity from part to whole that makes synecdoche into the most seductive of metaphors: the organic beauty of the tree, stated in the parallel syntax of a similar rhetorical question, or the convergence, in the dance, of erotic desire with musical form:

> O chestnut-tree, great-rooted blossomer,
> Are you the leaf, the blossom or the bole?
> O body swayed to music, O brightening glance,
> How can we know the dancer from the dance?

A more extended reading, always assuming that the final line is to be read as a rhetorical question, reveals that the thematic and rhetorical grammar of the poem yields a consistent reading that extends from the first line to the last and that can account for all the details in the text. It is equally possible, however, to read the last line literally rather than figuratively, as asking with some urgency the question we asked earlier within the context of contemporary criticism: *not* that sign and referent are so exquisitely fitted to each other that all difference between them is at times blotted out but, rather, since the two essentially different elements, sign and meaning, are so intricately intertwined in the imagined 'presence' that the poem addresses, how can we possibly make the distinctions that would shelter us from the error of identifying what cannot be identified? The clumsiness of the paraphrase reveals that it is not necessarily the literal reading which is simpler than the figurative one, as was the case in our first example; here, the figural reading, which assumes the question to be rhetorical, is perhaps naïve, whereas the literal reading leads to greater complication of theme and statement. For it turns out that the entire scheme set up by the first reading can be undermined, or deconstructed, in the terms of the second, in which the final line is read literally as meaning that, since the dancer and the dance are not the same, it might be useful, perhaps even desperately necessary – for the question can be given a ring of urgency, 'Please tell me, how *can* I know the dancer from the dance' – to tell them apart. But this will replace the reading of each symbolic detail by a divergent interpretation. The oneness of trunk, leaf, and blossom, for example, that would have appealed to Goethe, would find itself replaced by the much less reassuring Tree of Life from the Mabinogion that appears in the poem 'Vacillation', in which the fiery blossom and the earthly leaf are held together, as well as apart, by the crucified and castrated God Attis, of whose body it can hardly be said that it is 'not bruised to pleasure soul'. This hint should suffice to suggest that two entirely coherent but entirely incompatible readings can be made to hinge on one line, whose grammatical structure is devoid of ambiguity, but whose rhetorical mode turns the mood as well as the mode of the entire poem upside down. Neither can we say, as was already the case in the first example, that the poem simply has two meanings that exist side by side. The two readings have to engage each other in direct confrontation, for the one reading is precisely the error denounced by the other and has to be undone by it. Nor can we in any way make a valid decision as to which of the readings can be given priority over the other; none can exist in the other's absence. There can be no dance without a dancer, no sign without a referent. On the other hand, the authority of the meaning engendered by the grammatical structure is fully obscured by the duplicity of a figure that cries out for the differentiation that it conceals.

Yeats's poem is not explicitly 'about' rhetorical questions but about images or metaphors, and about the possibility of convergence between experiences of consciousness such as memory or emotions – what the poem calls passion, piety, and affection – and entities accessible to the senses such as bodies, persons, or icons. We return to the inside/outside model from which we started out and which the poem puts into question by means of a syntactical device (the question) made to operate on a grammatical as well as on a rhetorical level. The couple grammar/rhetoric, certainly not a binary opposition since they in no way exclude each other, disrupts and confuses the neat antithesis of the inside/outside pattern. We can transfer this scheme to the act of reading and interpretation. By reading we get, as we say, *inside* a text that was first something alien to us and which we now make our own by an act of understanding. But this understanding becomes at once the representation of an extra-textual meaning; in Austin's terms, the illocutionary speech act becomes a perlocutionary actual act – in Frege's terms, *Bedeutung* becomes *Sinn*. Our recurrent question is whether this transformation is semantically controlled along grammatical or along rhetorical lines. Does the metaphor of reading really unite outer meaning with inner understanding, action with reflection, into one single totality? The assertion is powerfully and suggestively made in a passage from Proust that describes the experience of reading as such a union. It describes the young Marcel, near the beginning of Combray, hiding in the closed space of his room in order to read. The example differs from the earlier ones in that we are not dealing with a grammatical structure that also functions rhetorically but have instead the representation, the dramatization, in terms of the experience of a subject, of a rhetorical structure – just as, in many other passages, Proust dramatizes tropes by means of landscapes or descriptions of objects. The figure here dramatized is that of metaphor, an inside/outside correspondence as represented by the act of reading. The reading scene is the culmination of a series of actions taking place in enclosed spaces and leading up to the 'dark coolness' of Marcel's room.

> I had stretched out on my bed, with a book, in my room which sheltered, tremblingly, its transparent and fragile coolness from the afternoon sun, behind the almost closed blinds through which a glimmer of daylight had nevertheless managed to push its yellow wings, remaining motionless between the wood and the glass, in a corner, poised like a butterfly. It was hardly light enough to read, and the sensation of the light's splendor was given me only by the noise of Camus ... hammering dusty crates; resounding in the sonorous atmosphere that is peculiar to hot weather, they seemed to spark off scarlet stars; and also by the flies executing their little concert, the chamber music of summer: evocative not in the manner of a human tune that, heard perchance during the summer, afterwards reminds you of it but connected to summer by a more necessary link: born from beautiful days, resurrecting only when they return, containing some of their essence, it does not only awaken their image in our memory; it guarantees their return, their actual, persistent, unmediated presence.
>
> The dark coolness of my room related to the full sunlight of the street as the shadow relates to the ray of light, that is to say it was just as luminous and it gave my imagination the total spectacle of the summer, whereas my senses, if I had been on a walk, could only have enjoyed it by fragments; it matched my repose which (thanks to the adventures told by my book and stirring my tranquility) supported, like the quiet of a motionless hand in the middle of a running brook the shock and the motion of a torrent of activity. (1985, 83)

For our present purpose, the most striking aspect of this passage is the juxtaposition of figural and metafigural language. It contains seductive metaphors that bring into play a variety of irresistible objects: chamber music, butterflies, stars, books, running brooks, etc., and it inscribes these objects within dazzling fire- and water-works of figuration. But the passage also comments normatively on the best way to achieve such effects; in this sense, it is metafigural: it writes figuratively about figures. It contrasts two ways of evoking the natural experience of summer and unambiguously states its preference for one of these ways over the other: the 'necessary link' that unites the buzzing of the flies to the summer makes it a much more effective symbol than the tune heard 'perchance' during the summer. The preference is expressed by means of a distinction that corresponds to the difference between metaphor and metonymy, necessity and chance being a legitimate way to distinguish between analogy and contiguity. The inference of identity and totality that is constitutive of metaphor is lacking in the purely relational metonymic contact: an element of truth is involved in taking Achilles for a lion but none in taking Mr Ford for a motor car. The passage is *about* the aesthetic superiority of metaphor over metonymy, but this aesthetic claim is made by means of categories that are the ontological ground of the metaphysical system that allows for the aesthetic to come into being as a category. The metaphor for summer (in this case, the synesthesia set off by the 'chamber music' of the flies) guarantees a presence which, far from being contingent, is said to be essential, permanently recurrent and unmediated by linguistic representations or figurations. Finally, in the second part of the passage, the metaphor of presence not only appears as the ground of cognition but as the performance of an action, thus promising the reconciliation of the most disruptive of contradictions. By then, the investment in the power of metaphor is such that it may seem sacrilegious to put it in question.

Yet, it takes little perspicacity to show that the text does not practice what it preaches. A rhetorical reading of the passage reveals that the figural praxis and the metafigural theory do not converge and that the assertion of the mastery of metaphor over metonymy owes its persuasive power to the use of metonymic structures. I have carried out such an analysis in a somewhat more extended context;[1] at this point, we are more concerned with the results than with the procedure. For the metaphysical categories of presence, essence, action, truth, and beauty do not remain unaffected by such a reading. This would become clear from an inclusive reading of Proust's novel or would become even more explicit in a language-conscious philosopher such as Nietzsche who, as a philosopher, has to be concerned with the epistemological consequences of the kind of rhetorical seductions exemplified by the Proust passage. It can be shown that the systematic critique of the main categories of metaphysics undertaken by Nietzsche in his late work, the critique of the concepts of causality, of the subject, of identity, of referential and revealed truth, etc., occurs along the same pattern of deconstruction that was operative in Proust's text; and it can also be shown that this pattern exactly corresponds to Nietzsche's description, in texts that precede *The Will to Power* by more than fifteen years, of the structure of the main rhetorical tropes. The key to this critique of metaphysics, which is itself a recurrent gesture throughout the history of thought, is the rhetorical model of the trope or, if one prefers to call it that, literature. It turns out that in these innocent-looking didactic exercises we are in fact playing for very sizeable stakes.

It is therefore all the more necessary to know what is linguistically involved in a rhetorically conscious reading of the type here undertaken on a brief fragment from a novel and extended by Nietzsche to the entire text of post-Hellenic thought. Our first examples dealing with the rhetorical questions were rhetorizations of grammar, figures generated by syntactical paradigms, whereas the Proust example could be better described as a grammatization of rhetoric. By passing from a paradigmatic structure based on substitution, such as metaphor, to a syntagmatic structure based on contingent association such as metonymy, the mechanical, repetitive aspect of grammatical forms is shown to be operative in a passage that seemed at first sight to celebrate the self-willed and autonomous inventiveness of a subject. Figures are assumed to be inventions, the products of a highly particularized individual talent, whereas no one can claim credit for the programmed pattern of grammar. Yet, our reading of the Proust passage shows that precisely when the highest claims are being made for the unifying power of metaphor, these very images rely in fact on the deceptive use of semi-automatic grammatical patterns. The deconstruction of metaphor and of all rhetorical patterns such as mimesis, paronomasia, or personification that use resemblance as a way to disguise differences, takes us back to the impersonal precision of grammar and of a semiology derived from grammatical patterns. Such a reading puts into question a whole series of concepts that underlie the value judgments of our critical discourse: the metaphors of primacy, of genetic history, and, most notably, of the autonomous power to will of the self.

There seems to be a difference, then, between what I called the rhetorization of grammar (as in the rhetorical question) and the grammatization of rhetoric, as in the readings of the type sketched out in the passage from Proust. The former end up in indetermination, in a suspended uncertainty that was unable to choose between two modes of reading, whereas the latter seems to reach a truth, albeit by the negative road of exposing an error, a false pretense. After the rhetorical reading of the Proust passage, we can no longer believe the assertion made in this passage about the intrinsic, metaphysical superiority of metaphor over metonymy. We seem to end up in a mood of negative assurance that is highly productive of critical discourse. The further text of Proust's novel, for example, responds perfectly to an extended application of this pattern: not only can similar gestures be repeated throughout the novel, at all the crucial articulations or all passages where large aesthetic and metaphysical claims are being made – the scenes of involuntary memory, the workshop of Elstir, the septette of Vinteuil, the convergence of author and narrator at the end of the novel – but a vast thematic and semiotic network is revealed that structures the entire narrative and that remained invisible to a reader caught in naïve metaphorical mystification. The whole of literature would respond in similar fashion, although the techniques and the patterns would have to vary considerably, of course, from author to author. But there is absolutely no reason why analyses of the kind here suggested for Proust would not be applicable, with proper modifications of technique, to Milton or to Dante or to Hölderlin. This will in fact be the task of literary criticism in the coming years.

It would seem that we are saying that criticism is the deconstruction of literature, the reduction to the rigors of grammar of rhetorical mystifications. And if we hold up Nietzsche as the philosopher of such a critical deconstruction, then the literary critic would become the philosopher's ally in his struggle with the poets. Criticism and literature would separate around the epistemological axis that distinguishes grammar from rhetoric. It is easy enough to see that this apparent glorification of the critic-philosopher in the name of truth is in fact a glorification of the poet as the primary source of this truth; if truth is the recognition of the systematic character of a certain kind of error, then it would be fully dependent on the prior existence of this error. Philosophers of science like Bachelard or Wittgenstein are notoriously dependent on the aberrations of the poets. We are back at our unanswered question: does the grammatization of rhetoric end up in negative certainty or does it, like the rhetorization of grammar, remain suspended in the ignorance of its own truth or falsehood?

Two concluding remarks should suffice to answer the question. First of all, it is not true that Proust's text can simply be reduced to the mystified assertion (the superiority of metaphor over metonymy) that our reading deconstructs. The reading is not 'our' reading, since it uses only the linguistic elements provided by the text itself; the distinction between author and reader is one of the false distinctions that the reading makes evident. The deconstruction is not something we have added to the text but it constituted the text in the first place. A literary text simultaneously asserts and denies the authority of its own rhetorical mode, and by reading the text as we did we were only trying to come closer to being as rigorous a reader as the author had to be in order to write the sentence in the first place. Poetic writing is the most advanced and refined mode of deconstruction; it may differ from critical or discursive writing in the economy of its articulation, but not in kind.

But if we recognize the existence of such a moment as constitutive of all literary language, we have surreptitiously reintroduced the categories that this deconstruction was supposed to eliminate and that have merely been displaced. We have, for example, displaced the question of the self from the referent into the figure of the narrator, who then becomes the *signifié* of the passage. It becomes again possible to ask such naïve questions as what Proust's, or Marcel's, motives may have been in thus manipulating language: was he fooling himself, or was he represented as fooling himself and fooling us into believing that fiction and action are as easy to unite, by reading, as the passage asserts?

The pathos of the entire section, which would have been more noticeable if the quotation had been a little more extended, the constant vacillation of the narrator between guilt and well-being, invites such questions. They are absurd questions, of course, since the reconciliation of fact and fiction occurs itself as a mere assertion made in a text, and is thus productive of more text at the moment when it asserts its decision to escape from textual confinement. But even if we free ourselves of all false questions of intent and rightfully reduce the narrator to the status of a mere grammatical pronoun, without which the narrative could not come into being, this subject remains endowed with a function that is not grammatical but rhetorical, in that it gives voice, so to speak, to a grammatical syntagm. The term *voice*, even when used in a grammatical terminology as when we speak of the passive or interrogative voice, is, of course, a metaphor inferring by analogy the intent of the subject from the structure of the predicate. In the case of the deconstructive discourse that we call literary, or rhetorical, or poetic, this creates a distinctive complication illustrated by the Proust passage. The reading revealed a first paradox: the passage valorizes metaphor as being the 'right' literary figure, but then proceeds to constitute itself by means of the epistemologically incompatible figure of metonymy. The critical discourse reveals the presence of this delusion and affirms it as the irreversible mode of its truth. It cannot pause there however. For if we then ask the obvious and simple next question, whether the rhetorical mode of the text in question is that of metaphor or metonymy, it is impossible to give an answer. Individual metaphors, such as the chiaroscuro effect or the butterfly, are shown to be subordinate figures in a general clause whose syntax is metonymic; from this point of view, it seems that the rhetoric is superseded by a grammar that deconstructs it. But this metonymic clause has as its subject a voice whose relationship to this clause is again metaphorical. The narrator who tells us about the impossibility of metaphor is himself, or itself, a metaphor, the metaphor of a grammatical syntagm whose meaning is the denial of metaphor stated, by antiphrasis, as its priority. And this subject-metaphor is, in its turn, open to the kind of deconstruction to the second degree, the rhetorical deconstruction of psycholinguistics, in which the more advanced investigations of literature are presently engaged, against considerable resistance.

We end up therefore, in the case of the rhetorical grammatization of semiology, just as in the grammatical rhetorization of illocutionary phrases, in the same state of suspended ignorance. Any question about the rhetorical mode of a literary text is always a rhetorical question which does not even know whether it is really questioning. The resulting pathos is an anxiety (or bliss, depending on one's momentary mood or individual temperament) of ignorance, not an anxiety of reference – as becomes thematically clear in Proust's novel when reading is dramatized, in the relationship between Marcel and Albertine, not as an emotive reaction to what language does, but as an emotive reaction to the impossibility of knowing what it might be up to. Literature as well as criticism – the difference between them being delusive – is condemned (or privileged) to be forever the most rigorous and, consequently, the most unreliable language in terms of which man names and transforms himself.

NOTE

1. [de Man is referring here to part of Chapter Three, 'Reading (Proust)' of *Allegories of Reading: Figural Language in Rousseau, Nietzsche, Rilke, and Proust* (1979, 57–78), particularly 59–67. JW]

7.2

SCORING LITERATURE

Avital Ronell

. . .

III

Flaubertian leaks

The writing of secretion

In many ways, *Madame Bovary* is a novel about suicidal anguish, about exploring the limits of interiorizing violence. The motivation to suicide never simply involves the extinction of one person, but tends to arrive from another agency. It hits you with the violence of a non-address. Innocent bystander at the event of your suicide, you sometimes miss, that is, you have made an attempt. But this time you did not miss the Other. This means: at the extreme limits of experience, the gesture offers a lever for killing something or someone, the Persecutor. The death rush disposes – sometimes – of the harassing other, eliminating him. You succeed in secreting the other. At the place where existence and finitude touch, the harassed one threatens to take someone down with him, producing an ultimatum, and sometimes you win.

Madame Bovary committed total suicide; her nullity affirms itself and it is not immediately clear who or what she took with her. Her death establishes no discernible order of being for or beyond herself. On the contrary, a certain narcosis spreads its effects through the body of the text, numbing its articulations ... a certain economy has been exhausted ... she goes broke. She has passed at the level of low energy rather than from a revealed side of destructive *jouissance*. The after-effects of her suicide are no less dim. Her husband locks himself into mourning and breaks with a more original Madame

Extract from Avital Ronell, *Crack Wars: Literature, Addiction, Mania* (University of Nebraska Press, 1992), pp. 93–135, 172–5.

Bovary, his mother. (In fact, there were two Madame Bovarys prior to Emma, who starts on the edge of degenerescence.) Her brutalized child, Berthe, suffers a fading, sacrificed by Flaubert at the novel's end to a series of humiliations. (He leaves little doubt about it, Emma Bovary was a child abuser.) Her father, devastated, leaves; her lovers endure remote and pitiless lives. The poison-giver, Justin, experiences hysterical grief. And so, Emma's has passed out of circulation, vacating the premises.

In short, it seems that nothing much happens that would surrender a sign or a revealing from Emma Bovary's death. No one figure turns up to explain the cause for her murderous rage ... She does not manage to eliminate any particular force or figure, though it is said that ink flows from her mouth. In this nothingness that menaces death with a loss of symbology, two discrete events take place, however. Flaubert has attacks of nausea and throws up while committing Emma Bovary to suicide. And, in the novel, the apothecary, Homais, survives to receive a national prize. This survival signals the commencement of the pharmaceutical wars.

IV

If the novel goes on after the death of Madame Bovary, drawn out by Homais, it is in order to territorialize another kind of drug story. The same store from which Emma drew the suicidal poison returns to occupy the scene at the end of the novel. In the wake of a great nothingness, the pharmacy is figured to exceed the commerce of hell: 'il fait une clientèle d'enfer' (366) ('Mr. Homais now has more patients than the devil himself could handle' [302]). The erection of this institution (over Emma's dead body) calls attention to itself, and not only because it is shown to be the institution of institutions, the storehouse of prescriptive language and pseudoscientific writing. It acquires legal sanctity from a structure at once fragile and constant, a mix of fable and belief. Thus, of its guardian, the *homme* and homeopath, we learn: 'l'autorité le ménage et l'opinion publique le protège' (366) ('the authorities treat him with deference and public opinion supports him' [303]). Following the uncontrolled patterns of ingestion which had organized Emma Bovary's losing economy, a condensation and restoration occur: every medical dispensary holds in reserve a store of poison. In a sense, Flaubert's novel breaks the ground for a modern drug store chain. Beyond evil, the drug store is a signifying chain that leaves even the devil in the dust ...

Despite the grim irony with which Flaubert sets up Homais for life, something very serious occurs by means of an underground thematics that has led to the consolidation of a drug store monopoly. For the drug store in *Madame Bovary* guarantees the preservation of a cadaverous presence while marking the place of its otherness to itself. The drug store figures a legalized reproach to uncontrolled or street drugs but at the same time argues for the necessity of a certain drug culture. Indeed, the critical question that Flaubert poses through the novel concerns the possibility of culture divested of hallucinogens. There is no culture without a drug culture, even if this is to be sublimated to pharmaceuticals.

V

At a time when the concept itself of politics is dissolving into a unanimous war against drugs, Flaubert urges upon us a reading of the untimely, that is, of the phantasms and phantoms that invest the institution of a drug store.

VI

The narrative allegorizes the split over drug control and a condemnation of street drugs at a number of corners that organize the textual cartography: '"Drunkenness ought to be dealt with more severely!" said the apothecary' (132). The injunction comes around the bend, crashing through the text, driven as it is by an unruly coachman. The scene of the uncontrolled coach, a sort of public *bateau ivre*, presents the complementary 'other' to the drive of amorous pursuit ...

... [T]he apothecary['s] ... faculty for judgment was aroused by the disjunctive movements of a carriage: 'The coachman, who was drunk, suddenly dozed off, and in the distance the mass of his body could be seen above the hood, between the two lanterns, swaying back and forth with the pitching of the thorough braces' (132).

The apothecary, whose calling depends almost entirely upon a stock market of public opinion, would like to see a bulletin board put up on the door of the town hall 'for the special purpose of posting a list of the names of everyone who's been intoxicated by alcohol during the week. It would be useful from a statistical point of view, too, because it would constitute a public record that could' – we in fact never learn what this record could do, for its promise dissolves into ellipses. Still, this may constitute the first declaration of war on unregulated drugs, passing from an apothecary's mouth to a public denunciation of guilty parties. The public record would keep tabs on the deconstituting body.

The drunk, like the adulterous Emma, liberates uncontrolled signs into a public sphere. Their display irradiates a mimetic poisoning which, once absorbed, would set off an entire population of innocent bystanders in the same movement of dissolution. Like the work which contains them, they become killer texts, triggering a chain reaction of uncontained mimetic caliber ...

They – the adulterers of morals – stage for the socius an irremediable destructive satisfaction; in other words, they stage the literality of the satisfaction derived from auto-destruction. The automobility of this small cartel is what interests us here.

If the scenes of drunkenness and adulterous trespass are constantly put into communication with one another, this is in the first place because Flaubert seems to register gradations of the word 'adultery' according to the distillation of its etymology. Adultery means that which alters the mind, falsifying and modifying its natural inflection. In its concept adultery is indissociable from what today we call mind-altering drugs: 'Adultery comes from a Latin verb that signifies *alter*, and nothing in fact more alters things and feelings' (Lucas 1840, 3: 265). The mind-altering project casts about for a premise of which it can presume an original purity of mind, a non-contaminated naturalness that would be in harmony with convention and lawful conduct. ... That which has avoided the zone of experience marked by *adultery* fits simultaneously in the groove of the natural as it inscribes the institution. Out of this tension of doubling and loosening the stakes of adultery, Flaubert concocts an entire ethos of drug culture avant la lettre. A seamless collapse of drugs into crime, of *adultery* into outlaw, is something that his probing sensibility would not hazard. Still, he was always up against the law.

VII

It is still necessary to demonstrate the structure of addiction that governs Emma's conduct in the novel, the drug wars which she originates and which range from her dependence on chemical prostheses, as in the case of make-up, to the intoxication which she imperiously seeks. The 'objects' of her intoxication consist of non-containable substances whose traces we still have to analyze. While the drug store, as social investment, is on the side of truth (science, remedy, statistics), Emma is a subject of the simulacrum ...

...

IX

The structure of addiction, and even of drug addiction in particular, is anterior to any empirical availability of crack, ice or street stuff. This structure and necessity are what Flaubert discovers and exposes. A quiver in the history of madness (to which no prescription of reason can be simply and rigorously opposed), the chemical prosthesis, the mushroom or plant, respond to a fundamental structure, and not the other way around. Of course, one can be hooked following initiation and exposure but even this supposes a prior disposition to admitting the injectable phallus ...

Any way you look at it, Emma Bovary carries the marks of her many incorporations of a foreign body. We have yet to grasp the male sex she carries with her, for Emma is not a simply gendered woman. Her prime injections of a foreign body follow the multiple lines of an interiorizing violence.

'a pince-nez which she carried, like a man, tucked in between two buttons of her bodice'

X

In the first place, Emma's moments of libidinal encounter are frequently described as experiences of intoxication. The second place, however, may be of more interest. In the second place, then, we discover that drugs, when submitted to Flaubert's precision of irony, are after all not viewed as a conduit of escape but as present at the base of life:

What do we hold against the drug addict?

> He seemed to her contemptible, weak and insignificant. How could she get rid of him? What an endless evening! She felt numb, as though she had been overcome by opium fumes. (217)

An evening with her husband, Charles Bovary. How could she get rid of him?

Emma judges Charles to be a weak man. The judgment is sounded from a position of feminine virility. His nullity, overwhelming, turns her into a hit man (how to get rid of him?). From the sense of the deadening infinitude of this confrontation, the threatening limitlessness of what is mediocre, Emma reconstitutes existence as an effect of an overdrawn downer. Not only does this passage argue for the refinement of difference – this opiate acts differently from other insinuations of her substance/husband abuse – it also shows the opium base to be at the bottom of life. Life in its essential normalcy (they are at the dinner table when she ODs) yields to death because it is on the side of an endlessness that numbs. And so Emma Bovary's body gets rigid with the presentiment of nothingness ... She suffers endlessly from her finitude, sitting there face to face with her husband. 'She felt numb,' which is to say, she felt **Life's vacant** non-feeling. Life assigns itself to her with a drained sensation of its own **terror** nothingness. If Emma is going to take drugs seriously, it will be only in order to diminish the power, to decrease the dosage that numbs. She needs a counter-drug, something to repel the ruthless continuity of the opiate, 'life' ... Going nowhere fast ... Madame Bovary ... signs up for the drug program to the extent that she resumes the violence of non-address.

> She had bought herself a blotter [*un buvard*], writing-case, pen-holder, and envelopes although *she had no one to write to* ... (52) (italics added)[1]

With nowhere to go and little to do, these missives, along with the equipment that maintains them, can only be routed inwardly. But it is an inwardness of diminished interiority, a kind of dead letter box – an impasse in destination. Still, writing for no one to no address counts for something; it is the writer's common lot. For Flaubert, this movement of the simulacrum without address (or in another idiom: without purpose, point) is associated with the toxic pleasure of a certain narcissism:

> I have condemned myself to write for myself alone, for my own personal amusement, the way one smokes or rides. (Steegmuller, 1977, 108)

It is important to weigh this violence of non-address because it designates a **Flaubert** most vulnerable type of writing that is, like smoking, susceptible to acts of **E** nihilism, burning out. Unaddressed or unchanneled pleasure, condemnation to **M** solitary confinement, with or without a community of smokers, belongs to the **M** registers of a 'feminine' writing in the sense that it is neither phallically aimed **A** nor referentially anchored, but scattered like cinders. At no point a prescriptive **N** language or pharmacological ordinance, it is rather a writing on the loose, **I** running around without a proper route, even dispensing with the formalities of **N** signing. The impropriety of such writing – which returns only to haunt itself, **E** refusing to bond with community or affirm its health and value – consistently **W** reflects a situation of depropriation, a loss of the proper. Thus the heroine **R** (who is also, sometimes, Flaubert: 'Madame Bovary, c'est moi!') not only has **I** no one to write to, but also lacks a proper name ('"Madame Bovary! Everyone **T** **I** **N** **G** calls you that! And it's not even your name – it's someone else's ... someone else's!" He buried his face in his hands' [134].) Still, this is the name that entitles the book, and cosigns its cover. But the countersignatory functions like a bad check, destined to collapse upon itself and bounce ...

XI

... On the narrative level of textual experience, the eruption of paranoia is felt at those times when Emma Bovary gets a hit. When signs are everywhere readable, signification becomes persecutory. Take one morning when 'she glanced around uneasily, looking intently at every figure moving on the horizon, at every dormer window in the village from which she might be seen. She listened for the sound of footsteps, voices and plows, and whenever she heard something she would stop in her tracks, paler and more trembling than the leaves of the poplars swaying above her head.

> One morning as she was coming back she suddenly thought she saw a long rifle being aimed at her. (142–3)

Such passages of sensitive terror dominate the residue of intoxication. And so the narrative, as codependent and accomplice, shows Emma adopting strategies to help her avoid coming down from what it calls 'love'. 'Love had intoxicated (*enivrée*) her at first, and she had thought of nothing beyond it. But now that it had become an essential part of her life she was afraid she might lose part of it, or even that something might arise to interfere with it' (142). On the loose and on the run, she dives into a paranoid crash position which organizes her 'downfall' in the novel.

'and her soul, sinking into that intoxication'

XII

What goes hand in hand with her decline is a kind of crash economy, an exorbitant expenditure with no reserve: we call this 'narcodollars'. Quite understandably, little has been said about Emma Bovary's radically losing economy, save to mention perhaps her creditor, a certain Mr High and Happy – Monsieur Lheureux. No doubt this topos fails to gain easy currency within readings that limit themselves to variants of housewifely neurosis, unmastered love-sickness, 'Bovarysme', or even frustrated writing habits. Yet all these conditions are linked to expenditure. To support her habit – while to a certain degree objectless, it is still maintained as a substance in the novel – Emma Bovary invests a field of liquidity that involves incredible manipulation of interest rates, capital gains, mortgaging and even, indeed, laundered money. She keeps a whole village economy vibrating, cutting deals like a shrewd cartel. She is dealing however for her own consumption and not trading properly. She borrows too much (in the way she borrows – cites, lives off – literature). At any rate, Lheureux pulls a fast one and the narcodollars overwhelm her. In the end, she's liquidated.

GOING DOWN

liquidare (med.)

The momentum of a savage cash flow cannot be contained by a reading of *Madame Bovary* that restricts itself merely to following her down the adulterous path, however … charming this might seem. There's the question of a libidinal economy, of course, and of the spermatic economy in which she spends herself. Her lovers, fairly well endowed with capital flow, do not leave clues as to why she should be running such a relentlessly losing economy. Her uncontrollable expenditure at once points to a complete divestiture of property (she secretly sells the inheritance and property of her husband) and to the flow that is being drawn from her. She quite literally is being drained of resources: something is vampirizing Emma Bovary. Now this drainage which in itself produces nothing – there is no transfer of energy or funds – will terminate only when the cash flow gushes out of her mouth at the scene of her suicide. This is when the concept itself of currency becomes assimilated to her circulatory systems. Within the larger economy of the novel, these speculations are nothing new, for the narrative has dropped hints along the way.

liquidare (med.)

When we first came upon her, Emma Bovary, displaying symptoms of auto-vampirism, was running an internally regulated circulation, a currency whose losses she could initially absorb:

> as she sewed, she kept pricking her fingers and raising them to her lips to suck them. (12)

Suturing and opening, stitching and wounding – she at once textures and bleeds. Into her mouth. The marks of a vampire should in any case come as no surprise to anyone familiar with Charles's taste in women, for his first wife – the second Madame Bovary – 'was skinny; she had long teeth' (16). When, on the other hand, Emma's vampiric traits arise, they are accompanied by another trademark of a foreign body invasion, which is to say, she begins to exhibit virile features, she enters a semiosis of masculine properties: 'She had a shell-rimmed pince-nez which she carried, like a man, tucked in between two buttons of her bodice' (13). Or, again:

> Finally even those who still had doubts lost them when she was seen stepping out of the Hirondelle one day wearing a tight, mannish-looking vest … (165)

Periodically growing signs of an indwelling alterity, Emma Bovary appears to suffer incorporation. There is something other gnawing at her, a beloved, but at the same time a Persecutor whom she has to feed and nourish. This may in part furnish an explanation for her inability to

nurture
her
child.

XIII

Crack Baby Of the scandals that the novel provoked, one concerned precised her brutal-ization of Baby. The budget cuts that she initiates belong elsewhere; money is associated with futurity in general but with her daughter's *Bildung* in particular. This is no sentimental education. Refusing to save money, Emma ruins the future and equally refuses to save her daughter, Berthe. There will be no growth, no development. Absolute bankruptcy. At the end, diminished and irrecuperably down on her luck, Berthe, ruined by her mother, more or less indentures herself to a distant relative, encountering the virtual dead end of a humiliated afterlife. ('An aunt took charge of the child's upbringing. She is poor and has put her to work in a cotton mill to earn her living' [302].)

But Emma was from the first a child-abuser, and this leads us to wonder what's eating her. Manifestly developing a structure of dependency, she cannot herself sustain a dependent. It is rather clearly stated that she cannot admit another woman into her life. Seeing her child for the first time, she faints, abandons it to a wet nurse and finally, supported by her suitor, Léon, visits it and quickly becomes disgusted. The child throws up on the mother who will keep it down until the end.

The scene of this disgust, shared by mother and daughter, has skirted a cemetery.

> The nausea of motherhood.

> To reach the wet-nurse's house they had to run left at the end of the street, as though going to the cemetery. (79)

One could see, runs the description, 'a pig on a manure pile, or cows wearing breast harnesses ... while in front of them a swarm of flies buzzed in the warm air' (79). These passages, setting up the maternal demand, constitute the place to which we shall have to return. Incessantly. The house in which she had stowed away her child, marking an utter inversion of the Mosaic myth, is set where

> A stream of dirty water was trickling over the grass, and all around were a number of nondescript rags, knitted stockings, a short red calico wrapper and a large, thick sheet spread out on the hedge. At the sound of the gate the wet-nurse appeared, carrying with one arm a child that was sucking her breast. With her other hand she was pulling a poor sickly little boy whose face was covered with scrofula sores. He was the son of a Rouen knit-goods dealer; too busy with their shop to take care of him, his parents had boarded him out in the country ... a Mathieu Laensberg almanac lay on the dusty mantelpiece among gun flints, candle ends and pieces of tinder. The clutter in the room was completed by a picture of Fame blowing her trumpet; it had no doubt been cut out of some perfume advertisement and was now fastened to the wall with six shoe nails ... standing in the midst of such squalor ... Madame Bovary blushed; turned away, fearing there might have been a certain impertinence in his eyes. Then she put the baby back in its cradle: it had just thrown up on her collar. The wet-nurse quickly wiped it off, assuring her it wouldn't show. (80)

> It had just thrown up on her collar.

> But Madame Bovary was not too busy to take care of her child.

Destructed landscape. Libidinal rescue attempts. Blush. Disgust. Madame Bovary is freaked. We – we have to stick to this scene, if only because it returns. The communication of nausea from mother to daughter is unremitting. Where does the circuit commence? ... Grazing the cemetery, Flaubert unfolds a scene of natural bodies, all somehow ironized and polluted by the dirty stream – the nurturing cow, harnessed, the mother body of the wet-nurse. In this landscape of dreary but resolute naturalness, Emma stands out like an artifice, an obstinate resistance to the organic. And this is something to keep in mind: her refusal of the organic body, her startling capacity for disgust and toxicity, gradually grow into the figuration par excellence of the addicted subject. What do we hold against the addict?

> In the name of this organic and originary naturalness of the body we declare and wage war on drugs. (Derrida, ed. Herviev, 1989, 205)

In the work containing Madame Bovary, the only originary naturalness is drawn from the body of a cow. But in order to evoke naturality, it bears the marks of equipment and artifice; the moment the animal body enters literature, it, too, belongs to technicity and artifice. Natural bodies are those of the cows, and horses, that travel the text. The nature of the human is shown to be on the edge of decay and dilapidation, whereas everything that is staked on beauty is on the side of artifice or the somehow foreign (this can be Paris). The tensions rumbling through the novel derive from a secret war against artificial, pathogenetic and foreign invasions. And thus Emma Bovary invades the space of the infant as a missile of toxicity, an emetic mother, artificial and dangerous. Invading and polluting what is naturally polluted ('dirty water'), she inspires toxic desire in others. As she is about to leave, the wet-nurse thus asks Emma Bovary for coffee and alcohol.

> 'If you'd just let me have' – she gave her a supplicating look – 'a little jug of brandy,' she said at last. (81)

She is dealing, even over the body of her child.

Tenderness   'I'll rub your little girl's feet with it; they're as tender as your tongue.' (81)

Emma, in any case, cannot feed her child, she cannot bend her body to postures of maternal abundance or 'natural' forms of vampirism. She will not let her child eat her, but something is eating her and she herself cannot stop consuming. We still have to deal with the cemetery ...

XIV

... The cemetery is linked to a manifest thematics of eating and vampirism through the agency of M. Lestiboudois, who exploits the land of the dead in order to grow potatoes. Potatoes – this dead vegetable, a somewhat inorganic organic fruit, dotted with eyes, blind like the seer of Emma's end – bloat the novel like the gastronomic fillers that they are: morbid accompaniment to meat, they organize a kind of *objet petit a* on the plate of desire. The novel tells us that the experience of eating is implanted in the experience of mourning.

This goes for the potato as well as the cold turkey and apricots, Emma's blood stains, his coffee. Who runs this farm of the undead?

If the novel has a plot, it is located in the cemetery. Entering this space – it is public, democratic, you all have access to it – we will discover that there are in effect two bodies lying in wait there, one on which Emma continues symbolically to feed, and another that remote controls her. In fact, they are both parasitically bound to her, but the first body is symbolically rooted in what we might call the *toxic maternal*. We shall examine this body closely, not only because Flaubert delights in fixing the gaze of autopsy but also because this body continues to transmit through Emma the persecutory rules that govern her habits, and hence rule her out. The *toxic maternal* means that while mother's milk is poison, it still supplies the crucial nourishment that the subject seeks. It suggests, moreover, that the maternal is too close, invading the orifices and skin with no screen protection, as it were, no intervening law to sever the ever-pumping umbilicus. This is what it means to find the men surrounding Emma 'weak': they are too weak to sever or divert the toxic maternal. It taps back into her own daughter. It recommences. Emma is absorbing medicine that nourishes by poisoning. And this poison still circulates through the textual body, haunting its every move, hunting down the heroine whose phobic maternal fits we have already noted.

'You're feeding on the dead, Lestiboudois!'

XV

When Emma Rouault, bored by the nothingness enveloping her, first met Charles Bovary, she thought she liked him. She was not simply listless, but bored to death. One day the seduction began, and here is what she told her suitor:

On being bored to death.

> She talked to him about her mother and the cemetary, and even showed him the flower bed in the garden from which, on the first Friday of every month, she picked flowers to place on her grave ... And, according to what she was saying, her voice was either clear or shrill; or, suddenly becoming languorous, it would trail off into inflections that ended almost in a murmur, as though she were talking to herself. Sometimes her eyes would open wide in guileless joy, then her eyelids would droop while her face took on an expression of profound boredom and her thoughts seemed to wander aimlessly. (19)

Tightly regimented, the sequencing of a language of seduction centers itself on 'her mother and the cemetery', moving toward a kind of murmur of non-address that leaves off on profound boredom. She is bored stiff. In the meantime, the lover's discourse has been held over the abyss of a graveyard, with everything, including eyelids, being pulled by a downward tug in the narrative.

As symptom, boredom is co-originary with melancholia. It pervades everything, and cannot be said simply to erupt. Nor does it desist of its own. It is prior to signification, yet it appears to be a commentary on life; it is, at least for

Emma, the place of deepest struggle. It also makes her American: when dialectically tilted, she can be viewed as fun-loving (Flaubert was fascinated with America, and particularly with California). Boredom, with its temporal slowdown and edge of anguish, is also an authentic mode of being-in-the-world. Boredom inflects a sonic quality, it attunes a murmur or an attitude of voice. Infusing the whole text with its ground level of non-sense, Emma's boredom appears to exhaust a certain reserve before it has been tapped. It is companion to loss, but raised on tranquilizers. In *Madame Bovary*, boredom opens a listening to disappearance, fabricating a society's holding pattern over the death that traverses us. It fills the extreme side of passive receptivity, threading through a nothingness which reminds us that Flaubert has wanted nothing more:

> What I would like to write is a book about nothing at all – almost no subject. (Steegmuller, 1977, 247)

This forms the threshold through which the existence of Emma Bovary is made to pass, a zone of experience that conspires with 'nothing at all', the extenuation of the subject. Something like an ontology of boredom announces its necessity here ...

And even when the life of Emma Bovary erupts periodically into an experience without precedent, it is reappropriated only by means of absorption and inhalation. Thus the appointed metonymy of the magnificent ball, a cigar box, needs to be taken repeatedly, as an imperious compulsion: 'She would look at it, open it and sniff its lining, which was impregnated with an odor of verbena and tobacco' (49).

Living boredom on the outer fringes of hysteria, Emma Bovary accedes to a domestic drug administration:

> She grew pale and had palpilations of the heart. Charles gave her valerian and camphor baths. Everything he tried seemed to make her more overwrought than ever.
>
> There were days when she chattered feverishly for hours on end; and this overexcitement would be abruptly followed by a period of torpor during which she neither spoke nor moved. She would then revive herself by pouring a bottle of eau de Cologne over her arms. (58)

. . .

XIX

'"Of course," continued Homais, "there's bad literature, just as there's bad pharmacy."' Bad pharmacy well exposes the allegory of dissolution to which Emma Bovary's relationship with Léon succumbs. Their encounter begins and ends with mediated pharmacy. Habitually, she would go to see him on Thursdays. In Rouen.

One day the pharmacist calamitously invades their Thursday with the

Timed release

352

expectation that Léon might divert him. Emma in the hotel room, expecting Léon to divert her: 'Léon hesitated, as though struggling against the pharmacist's spell' (243). Homais puts him in a trance, immobilizes him where Emma stimulates, exhausts him. He cannot cut it, 'Léon hesitated.'

Emma had begun to poison his life; the pharmacist casts a spell. Caught between the charm and the poison, Léon yields to the spell of the pharmacy. The blow is struck, and each member of the couple chooses a drug. Emma, for her part, will try to recuperate the couple's losses by dispensing letters whose effects are intended to pump up the fiction of desire. As if to underscore her experience of craving for external supplements, the narrative alerts us to the 'naive expedients of a weakened passion trying to stimulate itself by external means' (244). These refer to the letters she henceforth sends to him, or rather the letters that send her, for they arouse the hope that 'her next trip would bring her profound bliss' (244). The addicted body slips something between them:

> And yet, in that forehead covered with beads of cold sweat, in those stammering lips, those wild eyes and those clutching arms, Léon felt the presence of something mad, shadowy and ominous, something that seemed to be subtly slipping between them, as though to separate them. (244)

If Léon's thoughts appear to be capable of exceptional lucidity, this is not because they are inspired by a mood of sobriety. He, for his part, gets caught in the negativity of failing abstinence:

> He even tried to force himself to stop loving her, but as soon as he heard her footsteps he would feel helplessly weak, like a drunkard at the sight of liquor. (244)

Poison and alcohol. Emma kicks in, like a drug circulating alongside the prescriptive precincts of pharmacy. Léon loses his grip, his job is coming apart, time and money condense. Ever since their carriage ride he can't stay on the wagon. The encapsulated vehicle soon yielded to hard liquor. He can't let go. When compared with Emma, the pharmacist possesses a certain charm.

Destroyed by the one, Léon is held spellbound by the other. Marked as illicit and harmful, Emma Bovary belongs to the domain of books. While Léon grows increasingly more desperate and weak, Emma takes recourse in those 'naive expedients', external supplements. He disintegrates. Meanwhile, her rapport to him benefits from the coherency of delirium. She is the hallucinator. Emma, she had longed for the 'ineffable sentiments of love which she had tried to imagine from her books!' (245).

> The first months of her marriage, her rides in the forest, her waltzes with the viscount, Lagardy singing – everything passed before her eyes ... (245)

But her hallucinations are gapped. They are connected to longing and to a certain knowledge of what is not there. The delirium stops short, breaking open the distance. Unable to coincide with the books she's consumed, he will never answer to the hysteric's demand for eternity. It cracks: 'And Léon suddenly appeared to her as remote as the others' (245).

Distance has asserted itself not as an enabling condition for love or thought, but as punishment. He joins the procession of the phantomal others. She cannot go into withdrawal. She will increase the dosages, accelerate the need, in order to gather up what

can

not

be

had.

'Why was life so unsatisfying? Why did everything she leaned on instantly crumble into dust?' (245). And here we find the suturing lament, the dispersal of support into dust, the crumbling other that she was to consume incessantly, as dust, in part because something – she calls it life – was relentlessly insistent upon withholding what might have satisfied her. Here we might suggest that the distinction, so rigorously maintained in the Hegelian Lacan, between need and desire, may be the luxury of the sober.

NOTE

1. I should like to point out that 'a blotter' and '*un buvard*' recuperate the link between writing and drinking in the novel, but also refer us to the proper name of its title: buvard, bovary. Cf. 'to be blotto', to be smashed, drunk.

ANNOTATED BIBLIOGRAPHY

Culler, Jonathan. *Literary Theory: A Very Short Introduction*. Oxford, 1997.
  Probably the best short introduction to contemporary theory, and particularly useful on the critical trend towards performativity.

de Man, Paul. *Allegories of Reading: Figural Language in Rousseau, Nietzsche, Rilke, and Proust*. New Haven, CT, 1979.
  Somewhat bossy, complex and logically slippery, a fascinating account of 'figural' language in literature and the way it often yields knowledge of what de Man describes as the 'impossibility' of pinning language down with linguistic terminology. A stunning display of deconstruction as allegorical interpretation. See the entry for this book in Deconstruction and Reader-Response Theory, above.

Derrida, Jacques. *Acts of Literature*, ed. Derek Attridge. New York, 1992.
  An anthology of Derrida's writings on literature, useful for the illustration of performative readings after the collapse of metalingual distance in criticism, particularly in 'Ulysses Gramophone'. The collection contains an introductory interview concerned with the relation of literature and criticism.

Nuttall, A. D. *A New Mimesis: Shakespeare and the Representation of Reality*. London, 1983.
  A lucid counter-argument to poststructuralist critiques of realism, sometimes wrong-headed, but touching usefully on Jakobson and other structuralist approaches to realism.

Young, Robert, ed. *Untying the Text: a Post-Structuralist Reader*. London, 1981.
  A stimulating collection including Barthes's 'Theory of the Text' containing his critique of criticism as a metalanguage, and a useful introduction on the same subject.

SUPPLEMENTARY BIBLIOGRAPHY

Barthes, Roland. 'Introduction to the Structural Analysis of Narratives', in *Image-Music-Text*, trans. and ed. Stephen Heath. London, 1977.

Deleuze, Gilles. *The Logic of Sense*, trans. Mark Lester with Charles Stivale, ed. Constantin V. Boundas. New York, 1990.

de Man, Paul. 'The Epistemology of Metaphor', *Critical Inquiry*, 5: 1, Autumn 1978.

————. *Allegories of Reading: Figural Language in Rousseau, Nietzsche, Rilke, and Proust*. New Haven, CT, 1979.

————. *Blindness and Insight: Essays in the Rhetoric of Contemporary Criticism*, 2nd edn. London: Methuen, 1983.

————. *The Resistance to Theory*. Manchester, 1986.

Derrida, Jacques. *Of Grammatology*, trans. and intro. Gayatri Chakravorty Spivak. Baltimore, MD, 1976.

————. *Writing and Difference*, trans. Alan Bass. Chicago, 1978.

————. 'White Mythology: Metaphor in the Text of Philosophy', trans. F. C. T. Moore, *New Literary History*, 6: 1, Autumn 1974; rpt. Derrida, *Margins of Philosophy*, trans. Alan Bass. Chicago, 1982.

Gasché, Rodolphe. *The Tain of the Mirror: Derrida and the Philosophy of Reflection*. Cambridge, MA, 1986.

Hutcheon, Linda. *A Poetics of Postmodernism: History, Theory, Fiction*. New York, 1988.

Jakobson, Roman. 'Closing Statement: Linguistics and poetics', in *Style in Language*, ed. Thomas A. Sebeok. Cambridge, MA, 1960.

————. 'On Realism in Art'. *Readings in Russian Poetics*, eds L. Matedjka et al. Ann Arbor, MT, 1978.

MacCabe, Colin. *James Joyce and the Revolution of the Word*. London, 1978.

Melville, Stephen. *Philosophy Beside Itself: On Deconstruction and Modernism*. Minneapolis, MN, 1986.

Riffaterre, Michael. *Fictional Truth*. Baltimore, MD, 1990.

Ronell, Avital. *Crack Wars: Literature, Addiction, Mania*. Lincoln, NE, 1992.

Saussure, Ferdinand de. *Course in General Linguistics*, trans. Roy Harris. London, 1972.

PART 8
POSTMODERNISM

INTRODUCTION: POSTMODERNISM? NOT REPRESENTING POSTMODERNISM

Leah Wain

> With postmodernism it is as if we pass through the looking-glass of western reason. As we do so, apparently reliable conceptual distinctions are inverted or abolished altogether ... Postmodernism attempts a radical break with all of the major strands of post-Enlightenment thought. (West, 1996, 189)

WHAT ABOUT POSTMODERNISM?

Although the earliest use of the term *postmodernism* dates back to the 1930s by Federico de Onis as a definition of a 'conservative reflux within modernism itself', as Perry Anderson has recently pointed out in his *The Origins of Postmodernity* (1998, 3), one of the first uses of the term in the English-speaking world was in the late 1940s, as a definition for a style of architecture. It was first used among literary critics (Leslie Fielder, Frank Kermode) as a definition for experimental fictional writing which came after modernism, but it did not become appropriated as the name for theoretical approaches or schools of thought until the 1970s and 1980s. Even today, postmodernism signals unsteadily not a consensus of opinion with a discernible object of study, but, instead, a range of debates that are far from in agreement with one another. The composite word, composed of *post* and *modern*, gives the impression that it was the movement to take over from modernism. Indeed, the last fifty years have been known as the postmodern period and the artistic developments which have taken place during this time are often, though sometimes vaguely, referred to as postmodernism, where the term is somewhat synonymous with a knowing self-referentiality in a work of art. However, postmodernism, the theory which evolves as a result of these developments, resists such simple definition. As David West says, '"postmodernity" and "postmodernism" are not always straightforwardly cognate terms' (1996, 189).

Historically, western philosophy has operated on a system of replacement theories. New ways of thinking have superseded older systems of thought, making way for 'better' ways of processing our understanding of society. However, postmodernism suspends ideas of right and wrong, completion and truth. It has been argued that postmodernism breaks with modernism in so far as modernism advocates ideas of unity and representation, albeit in an indirect manner. Yet, postmodernist ethics prevent it from rejecting and opposing these or any ideas, and thus protect it from the 'spiraling negativity' alluded to by Baudrillard below; postmodernism suspends answers and defers completion, though it does not ignore the possibility. Therefore, postmodernism can be seen rather as a continuation in a certain manner of the project of modernism. For example, where modernism argues for fragmentation of narratives, postmodernism performs their dissemination. Postmodernism also elides any attempts to locate it historically. This is because postmodernism resists historicism and performs ahistorically. A postmodern response to history is that it is a form of fiction or, at the very least, a narrative which has neither more nor less a claim to authoritative status than any other competing narrative. Thus any historical anchorage, authority or legitimacy which may be claimed by a theoretical school, class or institution dissolves. The only point of reference for postmodernism, in the absence of anything else, is itself, as self-reference.

Having questioned the fixing of postmodernism historically through brief attention to its own claims, it may seem contradictory to now suggest it has a cultural context. Yet some critics of postmodernism agree that postmodernism is part of the condition of late capitalist society. The symbiotic relationship between postmodernism and capitalism generates debate within the theory, not least in postmodern-Marxist and postmodern-feminist narratives. Adjunct of a free-market economy, postmodernism concerns itself with mass-production and image. In this environment previously perceived realistic representations of products, which the consumer desires and believes to be obtainable, become derealised. Somewhere along the chain of successful advertising and mass consumerism the image has become its own referent. As Baudrillard demonstrates, the simulacrum gives itself value and need not equate with any real thing. The copy no longer refers to a reality. What we call the 'real' thing is, and must be in order to sell, a copy of the copy on the billboard or TV screen. Cola is not the 'real thing' in a Baudrillardian world, but Coke – the logo – is. The image is as far removed from the product as it is removed from the mode of production. This is the capitalist state of postmodernism in which we live.

POSTMODERNISM IN PERFORMANCE

Unlike other theoretical schools which approach texts with prepared hypotheses, postmodernism's only agenda is that it (claims it) does not have one. It seeks to uncover no particular hidden meaning. Indeed, it suspends the idea that a text hides 'truth' or reality, but resists taking the opposite stance that all is fiction, which only reinforces the idea of reality. This is what Baudrillard refers to when he writes of the 'ideological blanket' enacted by theme parks such as Disneyland, which cover over a 'third-order simulation'. By producing texts that can be termed fictional, the implication is always there that anything which is not contained within that fiction-margin is 'reality'. This works on a system of binary oppositions which has been used as a power tool to justify exclusion and oppression throughout western history. The fiction-margin, writes Baudrillard 'is a deterrence machine set up in order to rejuvenate in reverse the fiction of the real'. It thus reinforces the binary oppositions of true and false. Moreover it perpetuates the myth that the first term ('truth') holds a higher value. The true/false antitheses could be replaced by another oppositional pair in which the first term is privileged, like man/woman. The ideological blanket performs a similar function. Baudrillard avoids the fiction/reality dichotomy in textual practice by introducing into the discourse of the postmodern the notion of the 'hyperreal', a third term the operation of which suspends the binary dialectic. Hyperreality is a simulacrum and not a referent. Once we learn to view the world as such, suggests Baudrillard, (who has been prematurely accused of being extremist and glib for such a suggestion), we undermine those institutions which rely on such power structures. A postmodern text, then, is merely a 'referent', if it can be put this way, only to the non-referentiality of the text. It is self-referential. Referring to itself, and to its non-referential status, the self-referring postmodern text undoes the power of reference on which realist narrative constructs rely.

Words often associated with the notion of postmodernism are allegory and parody. Yet, if the postmodern text, or a postmodern reading of a text, does not refer to or represent any external thing, then perhaps pastiche would be a more appropriate term. To break this down a little: if, as Baudrillard claims, everything is simulation or composed of simulacra, then no text is original. If something is not original it surely refers to something preceding it. Yet, in order to avoid perpetuating a negative power struggle, it must not be a referent. Postmodern pastiche has many textual referents, each of equal and no value. As a text, therefore, it has no one point of reference. Postmodern pastiche destabilises the genres from which it borrows its composite parts. It disseminates texts so that no central or original point of reference can be located and scatters the fragments randomly to form an eclectic work.

Dissemination and eclectic postmodernism seem perfect textual performances for a theory which defers value-judgements. Yet, Lyotard warns, eclectic art is vulnerable, on the one hand, to the machinations and, on the other, the critique of a capitalist order. Under the protective guise of 'aestheticism' institutions 'impose a priori criteria of the "beautiful"' and begin to categorise and marginalise. Postmodern art can be turned against itself. Lyotard explains.

> It is easy to find a public for eclectic works. When art makes itself kitsch, it panders to the disorder that reigns in the 'taste' of the patron. Together, artist, gallery owner, critic and public indulge one another in the Anything Goes.

Self-referentiality, which can result in beautiful eclecticism, is easily abused and attacked by both neo-conservative versions of postmodernism and neo-conservative anti-postmodernist narratives. Lyotard continues, 'this realism of Anything Goes is the realism of money: in the absence of aesthetic criteria it is still possible and useful to measure the value of works of art by the profits they realize'. Works become commodities which both feed and produce a desire for the easily accessible and elide any responsibility because they are 'aesthetic'.

In definitions of postmodernist theory, it often seems easier to articulate that which postmodernism does not do to, or expect from, a text. This in itself is a postmodern performance. For the postmodern text represents the unrepresentable, not by seeking to represent it, but by attesting to unrepresentability. Postmodernism *is not*. What *is* postmodernism *not*? There is no succinct answer to this question because, to refer to Lyotard's essay, one possible 'Answer to the question: What is the postmodern?' *is* 'What is the postmodern?' However, one thing that the postmodern is not is unitary. The text is not a complete unit and no one reading is beyond question. That does not mean to say that a postmodern reading is non-unitary. For that would be to presume that theories of non-unitarity or in-completion are themselves beyond question. Thus postmodernism would have written itself into its own paradigm. It escapes this double-bind, however, by writing that it has written itself into a paradigm and thereby writing itself out of it again. This is how self-referentiality can work. Postmodernism does not prohibit the text from writing an answer to the questions it asks. It answers questions with questions and defers any final answer, implying that all answers are relative and provisional.

This discussion on postmodernism has continued as if that which we term the postmodern were self-conscious and could actually define itself in much the same way as articles such as this claim to be able to contain it with definitives. This is because western metaphysical thought has conventionally based itself on myths of presence and self-presence. This inevitably affects our construction of any discourse of the real. The history of western thought can be provisionally constructed from certain perspectives as a narrative, a growing self-consciousness. Paradoxically, because postmodernism has abandoned the myth of self-presence – as in the examples of hyperreality and the simulacrum – we can now be more self-conscious than ever, even though Jürgen Habermas has 'attacked postmodernism as a new form of conservatism, which has prematurely abandoned the uncompleted project of the Enlightenment' (West, 1996, 200), a project which aims at human emancipation 'through the application of reason' (1996, 200). However, to highlight an overlap with poststructuralism, assumptions of presence, reason or rationality have been questioned in that transcendental values, just as theories of 'progression', have been used to justify many kinds of oppression. The alternative *a*rational, rather than irrational (that which Habermas sees as the project of postmodernism, and which is merely oppositional), suggests the relativity of 'reason', whether that be religious or scientific, and suspends the opposition between rationality and irrationality. The self-conscious postmodern 'play' that ensues in this space of undecidability often provokes critics of postmodernism to make accusations that the postmodern is either nihilistic or adopts a cavalier, glib attitude towards the grim disintegration of society (see Habermas, 1990, 86–94, 136–40). Yet, the critical distance which arationality produces allows us to be self-conscious in a dissident and ironic fashion about the society in which we live. Far from championing nihilism, the radical scepticism and arationality of postmodernist discourse (Lyotard's version, at least) requires an ever more constant vigilance in the name of justice (Lyotard, 1979, 66). As Jameson points out, the defamiliarisation we sense as we look at ourselves in retrospect is the closest we can get to objectivity.

Postmodernist discourse reads inclusively and non-categorically. In theory, this makes it a potentially attractive theory for many politically marginalised groups (although this is not in itself unproblematic, as Teresa Ebert has demonstrated in her feminist critique of postmodernist discourse, particularly that model put forward by Fredric Jameson (Ebert, 1996, 129–80). Indeed, like the word itself, postmodernism as a discourse and concept is composite and heterogeneous by nature, as well as embodying an ethics of non-progress and arational thought. Postmodernism replaces grand narratives with little narratives (see Currie, 1998, 106–13). Yet this in itself excludes, or rather cannot include, the political discourse of some of its members. Many feminisms, not least essentialist feminism, are based on gender-exclusive concepts and once a postmodern suggestion concerning the myth of gender is made, the foundations of that school of thought are shaken. This is simplifying the argument greatly but suffices to show the complex relationship postmodernism has with other political theories and why it can experience a hostile reception.

The compromise many postmodern Marxists, such as Fredric Jameson, face is not only that of being part of that capitalist cultural condition called postmodernism while remaining committed to Marxist socialism, but also believing (to greater or lesser extents) in the grand narrative of Marxism, while working with a postmodern theory which continually defers the model of progress inherent in grand narratives, distrusting that particular metanarrative. Jameson comments on the postmodern text: 'viewers and protagonists still have to feel that they are on their way somewhere', but 'there is no longer anything to discover at the end of the line'. Jameson reads this lack of progress as 'aimlessness', concluding that the postmodern pastiche, as well as disrupting other genres, constitutes its own 'lack of identity'. In so defining postmodern pastiche, Jameson argues that

> ... in the process of trying to identify its own present at the same time that [it] illuminate[s] the failure of this attempt ... [it] seems to reduce itself to the recombination of various stereotypes of the past.

In a postmodernist age, Marxists like Jameson do not risk delusions of nostalgia for the past, but neither can they be comforted by a vision of progress toward a future.

SOME READINGS OF POSTMODERN READINGS

Having discussed postmodernism in a fairly abstract manner, which is perhaps the only way to attempt a definition of a self-conflicting discourse which advocates acknowledging the unrepresentational, the remainder of this essay will highlight certain aspects of the essays, by Lyotard, Baudrillard and Jameson, reprinted here. These writers demonstrate postmodernist criticism in performance, which should clarify and contextualise the concepts of post-modernism introduced in the previous sections. There are many commentaries possible, following their readings, and this example is by no means definitive. It will examine the questions of non-representation, undecidability, fragmenta-tion and dissemination, which are suspended by the discussions of Lyotard, Baudrillard and Jameson.

In 'Nostalgia for the Present' Jameson comments on, while trying not to represent, the textual practice and cinematography of three 'postmodern' films which can be read as avoiding forms of representation. One way in which these texts enable the reader to conceive of that which they cannot represent is through the use of allegory. Of *Blue Velvet* Jameson comments,

> The later insistence on robins with worms twisting desperately in their beaks also reinforces this cosmic *sense* of the dizzying and nauseating violence of all nature – *as though* ... (emphasis added)

The point that director, David Lynch, is trying to make for the critic is that he wants to make a point *about* something, something Jameson calls 'cosmic', but which cannot be directly represented. The image, therefore, invites the viewer to glean a *sense* of that which the director feels. This process relies on the active participation of the viewer, in this case Jameson. He must respond to the image. Jameson continues this allegorical process when he writes (to us) *as though*. This adds to the non-referential referential chain which leads only to itself, which, according to postmodernists, is the most ethical mode of rep-resentation: non-representation.

Postmodern non-representation, Jameson points out, is the effort to avoid representation which perpetuates the myth of presence. Postmodernists are interested in the mechanisms of textual non-representation; they are interested in saying that nothing can be said directly by saying something about the un(re)presentable through indirection. Ironically, this provides 'greater cogni-tive as well as existential contact with the thing itself'. Non-representation is, in this sense, the most rhetorically convincing form of representation. Noticing that both the historical novel and the science-fiction narrative defamiliarise the reader from a text which, presented under another realist genre, would reproduce the myth of presence, Jameson suggests that what is important here is the process of locating the text in a historical other. He explains:

> what is at stake is essentially a process of reification whereby we draw back from our immersion in the here and now (not yet identified as a

'present') and grasp it as a kind of thing – not merely a 'present' but a present that can be dated and called the eighties or the fifties.

This is reading the present (text) as not present. It does not represent presence or the present, but represents presence or the present as un(re)presentable. The paradox is that, in the process of not representing presence or the present, the text achieves just that. Jameson uses the example of film actors to illustrate this point. The actor 'playing' Ray in *Something Wild* is 'the representation of someone playing at being evil', 'Nothing about Ray, indeed, is particularly authentic'. We cease to be drawn in by the character of 'evil' Ray, as though he were in some manner merely a representation of a real person. We are forced to step back and read the postmodern allegory in performance. Jameson argues that we thus become aware of an image of collective otherness being constructed through the representation of presence as unrepresentable. This reading of *Something Wild* enables Jameson to maintain a postmodernist perspective without compromising his Marxist need 'to identify the deeper ideological purpose[s]' of the infrastructure. However, Jameson's Marxist grand narrative sits somewhat uneasily with the postmodernist destabilising repetition of self-reference.

The destabilisation of historical narratives in order to replace them with other totalising narratives is what persuades Lyotard to question these terms and to follow an alternative narrative which involves desire and the Sublime. Lyotard's postmodern belief in the Sublime can be explained in that non-representation signals absence and, whereas Jameson wishes to fill that space with a Marxist narrative, this non-event perpetuates the desire (itself an event) for something, that other thing, which is yet unrepresented. Lyotard offers the following, 'Thou shalt not make unto Thee any graven image' (Exodus 20: 4), as an example of 'the most sublime moment in the Bible, in that it forbids any presentation [representation] of the absolute'. Lyotard uses the biblical text, widely accepted as the representation of the Sublime in that it names it as 'God', to demonstrate it as a text which is most sublime when it is actively trying not to be. Postmodernism does not dispute that 'We can conceive of the absolutely great', but does demonstrate that when we try and reproduce it as a perceivable shape it 'appears sadly lacking to us'. It 'appears' 'lacking'. It is present only in its absence, knowable only through its un-representability. We would do better, according to Lyotard, to perform 'negative presentation' (Kantian formlessness) and invite the postmodern reader to 'see only by prohibiting [them] from seeing'. Postmodern non-representation, for Lyotard, is the most ethical and divine blank text and should not be written over.

Baudrillard also values the postmodern principle of non-representation, but differs from both Jameson and Lyotard in his performance. His simulations and simulacra cover over that abyss which Lyotard calls the Sublime. Moreover, Baudrillard refers to the 'precession of simulacra'. In much the same way that postmodernism cannot be located historically, Baudrillard posits the copy, the map, the simulacra both before and after *'the desert of the real itself'*. The simulacra is ahistorical and, therefore, extends the question of whether the absent sublime or the simulacra came first. The answer to that question is not important yet. Postmodernism is more concerned with the posing of the question. For Baudrillard this does not threaten the idea *of* the sublime, despite Lyotard's insistence on formlessness. It does, however, disrupt 'the Platonic idea of God', that named and fixed image of the Sublime. Baudrillard expands this critique of western philosophy,

> But what if God himself can be simulated, that is to say, reduced to signs which attest to his existence? Then the whole system becomes weightless; it is no longer anything but a gigantic simulacrum; not unreal, but a simulacrum, never again exchanging for what is real, but exchanging in itself, in an uninterrupted circuit without reference or circumference.

Baudrillard is not insisting that the absolutely Sublime which we name 'God' is a simulacrum. He is merely extending the question to the dogmatic answer that religious icons (simulations) are wrong as graven images of (representations of) the sublime. As representations, they expose God as merely a copy of a copy. If, as Lyotard suggests, the Sublime (God) cannot be represented, then simulacra merely reinforce this suggestion and signify only themselves. They perform the absence, which Lyotard claims can also be performed through avant-garde formlessness, and do not represent the sublime at all. The non-representation (self-representation) performed through simulation gestures towards the thing, the other, without seeking to represent it at all. Postmodern simulation does claim equivalence.

Postmodernism is then fragmentary and made of disparate elements, of little narratives that resist globalisation through relative particularity (see Currie, 1998, 111–12). These three readings of non-representation are taken from essays which all attempt to be faithful to the (undefinable) idea of the postmodern. Yet they demonstrate irreducible and unresolvable difference. They are what Lyotard calls *differends*, described by Mark Currie as 'incommensurable disputes between little narratives where there are no external criteria for litigation or judgement' (1998, 111). This in itself begs the question, once more, 'What is postmodernism?' for the discursiveness and dissemination produced so far by this reading of postmodern readings defers any possible claims we may wish to make about the 'truth' of postmodernism.

We cannot begin to make claims about postmodern truths because the notion of 'Truth' is held in suspension in postmodernist discourse. Not only do postmodernist thinkers resist claiming truths, they question the reality of predetermined truths. Reality is not part of the postmodern discourse because it belongs to the discourse of mastery and oppression. Postmodernism responds to reality, not unlike its treatment of history, as a myth which is perpetuated in order to sustain political hierarchies. Baudrillard exposes the scandal of the Watergate scandal. The scandal, for the postmodernist, is that this was exposed as a scandal. Not unlike Disneyland's marginalisation of fiction in order to prove reality, the politicians behind the Watergate scandal marginalise so-called immorality in order to prove the existence of (and need for) morality in that space which is not the designated area of 'scandal'. This inadvertently creates a need for the law to instigate and uphold 'morality'. However, Baudrillard does not simply accuse the Watergate politicians of reinforcing the status quo. Postmodern texts rely on the response of the reader and this fabrication depended on the outrage of the public. As Baudrillard points out, 'denunciation of scandal always pays homage to the law' and the law upholds the political order. The scandal refers to a law, which must draw an arbitrary line between moral and immoral. As soon as someone reacts to the supposed scandal as a scandal that demarcation line between right and wrong becomes absolute. Postmodernism does not accept absolute claims and, therefore, Baudrillard does not respond to 'Watergate' as a reality. He is careful, however, not to declare Watergate a fiction either (as many have similarly misinterpreted his suggestions concerning the 'reality' of the Gulf War and its status as 'hyperreal media event'; see Currie, 1998, 90), for that would be to accept that there is another referent for reality. Alternatively, for Baudrillard, a text without a referent belongs to 'hyperreality'. In the world of the hyperreal, events and language lose fixed meanings and we can no longer say with confidence what they mean because the meanings are generated as competing truth claims which, political in themselves, allow no access to the real.

Baudrillard explains how hyperreality can become part of the critical discourse of postmodernism. To borrow from Structuralism's semiological understanding, the ideological concept of reality depends upon the acceptance that language operates as a range of fixed referents and not as a structure of difference. For example, the myth that 'Watergate' means one thing (immorality) and not another (morality) depends on the static relationship between the image (visual or acoustic) 'Watergate' and a concept of that 'event'. In this scheme, Watergate is a metaphor for immorality. Postmodernist critics such as Baudrillard process the image 'Watergate' syntagmatically along a chain of meanings which continually recede, never concluding on an ultimate truth. This postmodern process is concerned with the very process of processing the image, not with an ultimate static reality. Baudrillard comments on this hyperreality.

A hyperreal henceforth sheltered from the imaginary, and from any distinction between the real and the imaginary, leaving room only for the orbital recurrence of models and the simulated generation of difference.

Meaning is lost along an endless chain of referents. Dissemination produces hyperreality. The narratives of the Watergate scandal, threats of nuclear war or terrorist attacks now refer to no *one* thing, but circulate within a general substitution of images serving various ideological purposes. According to Baudrillard, all is postmodern and part of hyperreality. This 'claim', if it can be called such – for surely it is a deferral of claims – has received much criticism. Lyotard's notion of reality is not dissimilar and offers a sense of why Baudrillard actively doesn't make the claims that others passively do.

Lyotard begins his article by citing a number of proto-modernist statements concerning unity, which he then undercuts. He exposes them as frightened reactions to simulated reality. Indeed, he allows the arguments themselves to argue his point for him:

> I have read a talented theatrologist who says that the tricks and caprices of postmodernism count for little next to authority, especially when a mood of anxiety encourages that authority to adopt a politics of totalitarian vigilance in the face of the threat of nuclear war.

What soon becomes apparent, however, is that threats such as nuclear war are part and parcel of narrative 'tricks and caprices' of an authority which needs to justify its position of power, which it is the purpose of postmodern scepticism to display. Lyotard notes that this produces a public desire, in the face of a 'real' threat, for a 'real' solution. Postmodernists such as Lyotard are repelled by realism because, in his words, 'Realism . . . can be defined only by its intention of avoiding the question of reality implied in the question of art'. Postmodernism questions and suggests possibilities. It does not, Lyotard argues, deny possibilities. This would be to enter into that totalitarian discourse he decries. At the same time, Lyotard's essay is a wonderful example of how postmodernism is not simply a cynical or negative discourse. As he explains, the postmodern age of technology and science need not be at odds with postmodernist resistances to the idea of 'progress'. The continuation of science (rather than 'progress' of science) relies on the possibility, the question, of nonprogress. 'There would be no physics had doubt not been cast on the Aristotolian theory of movement', suggests Lyotard, 'discovery of the *lack of reality* . . . is linked to the invention of other realities'. Postmodernism continually questions, opening up and encouraging discursiveness.

Suspending the question of reality, Lyotard suggests the possibility of multiple realities. He is constantly aware that desire is manipulated by authority in the form of capital and treated as a commodity. The simulation of a 'dangerous' threat creates a desire for a solution. Mass consumerism, working on the principal of supply and demand as Baudrillard explains, is 'the hysteria of production and reproduction [simulation] of the real'. Jameson similarly reads the 'reality myth' as a capitalist construction and more explicitly describes it as bourgeois self-justification. He highlights the political sales pitch of high art which perpetuates consumerist desire with images of 'false' happiness, the gratifications of the new car, the TV dinner and your favorite program on the sofa – which are now themselves secretly a misery, an unhappiness that doesn't know its name, that has no way of telling itself apart from genuine satisfaction and fulfillment since it has presumably never encountered this last.

The simulated reality creates a desire for that simulation which, when obtained, produces simulated contentment. This, notes Jameson, is realism, that which the high culture decides represents reality and which self-image is reinvented by subsequent generations. All of these images are simulated for political gain. In much the same way, the historical novel was a mode by which the middle classes (to the exclusion of other classes) could write their own history and safely anchor themselves. This genre is now outdated, according to Jameson, in an age of postmodernity. The postmodern text seeks 'to stress the conditions of possibility' and not the 'existential experience' of history. Yet, perhaps not unlike Lyotard, Jameson is sensitive to our desire to historicize. He posits science fiction as postmodernism's historical novel. For, 'Historicity is . . . neither a representation of the past nor a representation of the future' but 'a perception of the present as history'. The reality referent of 'history' is now suspended by postmodernism. Texts which question the possibilities of futur-ology not only defamiliarize us from the 'present' text, but also serve the dual purpose of familiarising us with future threats, as discussed by Lyotard and Baudrillard, desensitising us to them. Future otherness has already been anticipated in the present and is no longer completely other. However, despite the victory over 'the shock of otherness' there is still a terror in Jameson's article. This is fear of not fearing for a future under capitalism. He therefore asks the question whether postmodernism brings about 'an ultimate historicist breakdown in which we can no longer imagine the future at all, under any form – Utopian or catastrophic'. Jameson, then, questions the possibilities of the possibilities which postmodernism questions in his own search and desire for Socialist Utopia. The postmodern performance, for Jameson, is not political enough. Postmodernist questions are their own answers. 'Unlike politics, alas,' writes Jameson, 'the "search" automatically becomes the thing itself: to set it up is by definition to realize it'. The postmodern suspension of reality, and of desire, *is* postmodern desire and hyperreality.

Postmodernism, for Jameson, is useful because it unsettles the realist histori-cism that has been used as a power-tool by ruling orders for centuries. Ahistor-ical narratives empower us by providing us with an unfamiliar look at the present, exposing history as myth (much like reality) and sheltering us from, and familiarising us with, the possibilities of the near-future. Yet, many who desire and seek 'real' political change see postmodernism as deferring just that. Jameson's questioning of the postmodern, however, is an effective theoretical strategy. For in the mode of questioning, the critic acknowledges his belonging to an age of postmodernity, like it or not, and the game-play has altered.

These three postmodern articles, which differ and yet work together against a system of realist totalitarian unity, are, in a sense, differends, competing little narratives concerned with dismantling the metanarratives of authority, of capital and politics. Lyotard calls us to fight with 'active differends'. This does not mean breaking down differences into sameness. Baudrillard does not suggest that we fragment systems in order to build a complete model of the lack of meaning. Under postmodernism, language and meaning have no one meeting point, but many. In the words of David West:

> Postmodernism can be understood as a new way of conceiving the relationship between intellectual disciplines, challenging conventional academic boundaries ... Postmodernism has also become a topic of discussion within a number of different disciplines: in art, art theory and criticism, cultural studies, communication theory, philosophy, history, sociology, anthropology and geography among others. (West, 1996, 217)

This suggests that multiple meanings are possible and any single meaning is suspended. It would be impossible and unethical to pretend to draw the articles in this anthology (or others) together and present one single definition of postmodernism. They have been fragmented. They meet and disagree at different points. There is no single point of reference to this article other than that there is no single point of reference. All three articles succeed in not representing postmodernism. They are, then, accurate 'representations' of those theories, schools of thought, concepts or things we call postmodernism.

8.1

ANSWER TO THE QUESTION, WHAT IS THE POSTMODERN?

Jean-François Lyotard

To Thomas E. Carroll

Milan, May 15, 1982

A DEMAND

We are in a moment of relaxation – I am speaking of the tenor of the times. Everywhere we are being urged to give up experimentation, in the arts and elsewhere. I have read an art historian who preaches realism and agitates for the advent of a new subjectivity. I have read an art critic who broadcasts and sells 'transavantgardism' in the market-place of art. I have read that in the name of postmodernism architects are ridding themselves of the Bauhaus project, throwing out the baby – which is still experimentation – with the bathwater of functionalism. I have read that a new philosopher has invented something he quaintly calls Judeo-Christianism, with which he intends to put an end to the current impiety for which we are supposedly responsible. I have read in a French weekly that people are unhappy with *A Thousand Plateaus* [by Deleuze and Guattari] because, especially in a book of philosophy, they expect to be rewarded with a bit of sense. I have read from the pen of an eminent historian that avant-garde writers and thinkers of the 1960s and 1970s introduced a reign of terror into the use of language, and that the imposition of a common mode of speech on intellectuals (that of historians) is necessary to reestablish the conditions for fruitful debate. I have read a young Belgian philosopher of

Extract from Jean-François Lyotard, *The Postmodern Explained* (University of Minnesota Press, 1982), pp. 1–16, and Jean-François Lyotard, *The Postmodern Explained to Children* (© The Power Institute, 1992), pp. 1–16.

language complaining that Continental thought, when faced with the challenge of talking machines, left them to look after reality; that it replaced the paradigm of referentiality with one of adlinguisticity (speaking about speech, writing about writing, intertextuality). He thinks it is time language recovered a firm anchoring in the referent. I have read a talented theatrologist who says the tricks and caprices of postmodernism count for little next to authority, especially when a mood of anxiety encourages that authority to adopt a politics of totalitarian vigilance in the face of the threat of nuclear war.

I have read a reputable thinker who defends modernity against those he calls neoconservatives. Under the banner of postmodernism they would like, he believes, to extricate themselves from the still-incomplete project of modernity, the project of Enlightenment. By his account, even the last partisans of the *Aufklärung* (the Enlightenment), for example, Popper and Adorno, were able to defend that project only in particular spheres of life – politics for the author of *The Open Society*, art for the author of *Aesthetic Theory*. Jürgen Habermas (you will have recognized him) thinks that if modernity has foundered, it is because the totality of life has been left to fragment into independent specialties given over to the narrow competence of experts, while concrete individual experiences 'desublimated meaning' and 'destructured form', not as a libera-tion, but in the manner of that immense ennui Baudelaire described over a century ago.

Following Albrecht Wellmer's lead, the philosopher believes the remedy for this parceling of culture and its separation from life will only come from a 'change in the status of aesthetic experience when it is no longer primarily expressed in judgments of taste', when instead 'it is used to illuminate a life-historical situation' – that is to say, when 'it is related to the problems of existence.' For this experience 'then enters into a language game which is no longer just that of the aesthetic critic'; it intervenes 'in cognitive procedures and normative expectations'; it 'changes the way these different moments *refer* to one another.' In short, Habermas demands of the arts and the experience they provide that they form a bridge over the gap separating the discourses of knowledge, ethics, and politics, thus opening the way for a unity of experience.

My problem is to be positive about what sort of unity Habermas has in mind. What is the end envisaged by the project of modernity? Is it the constitution of a sociocultural unity at the heart of which all elements of daily life and thought would have a place, as though within an organic whole? Or is the path to be cut between heterogeneous language games – knowledge, ethics, and politics – of a different order to them? And if so, how would it be capable of realizing their effective synthesis?

The first hypothesis, Hegelian in inspiration, does not call into question the notion of a dialectically totalizing *experience*. The second is closer in spirit to the *Critique of Judgment*, but like the *Critique* it must be submitted to the severe reexamination postmodernity addresses to the thought of the Enlightenment, to the idea of a uniform end of history and the idea of the subject. This critique was started not only by Wittgenstein and Adorno, but also by other thinkers, French or otherwise, who have not had the honor of being read by Professor Habermas. At least this spares them getting bad marks for neoconservatism.

REALISM

The demands I cited to you at the beginning are not all equivalent. They may even be contradictory. Some are made in the name of postmodernism, some in opposition to it. It is not necessarily the same thing to demand the provision of a referent (and objective reality), or a meaning (and credible transcendence), or an addressee (and a public), or an addressor (and expressive subjectivity), or a communicative consensus (and a general code of exchange, the genre of historical discourse, for example). But in these various invitations to suspend artistic experimentation, there is the same call to order, a desire for unity, identity, security, and popularity (in the sense of *Öffentlichkeit*, 'finding a public'). Artists and writers must be made to return to the fold of the community; or at least, if the community is deemed to be ailing, they must be given the responsibility of healing it.

There exists an irrefutable sign of this common disposition: for all these authors, nothing is as urgent as liquidating the legacy of the avant-gardes. The impatience of so-called transavantgardism is a case in point. The replies an Italian critic recently gave to French critics leave no doubt on the matter. The procedure of mixing avant-gardes together means that artists and critics can feel more confident of suppressing them than if they attacked them head-on. They can then pass off the most cynical eclecticism as an advance on the no doubt partial nature of earlier explorations. If they turned their backs on such explorations overtly, they would expose themselves to ridicule for neoacademicism. At the time the bourgeoisie was establishing itself in history, the salons and academies assumed a purgative function, awarding prizes for good conduct in the plastic and literary arts under the guise of realism. But capitalism in itself has such a capacity to derealize familiar objects, social roles, and institutions that so-called realist representations can no longer evoke reality except through nostalgia or derision – as an occasion for suffering rather than satisfaction. Classicism seems out of the question in a world where reality is so destabilized that it has no material to offer to experience, but only to analysis and experimentation.

This theme is familiar to readers of Walter Benjamin. Still, its precise implications need to be grasped. Photography did not pose an external challenge to painting any more than did industrial cinema to narrative literature. The former refined certain aspects of the program of ordering the visible elaborated by the Quattrocento, and the latter was able to perfect the containment of diachronies within organic totalities – the ideal of exemplary educative novels since the eighteenth century. The substitution of mechanical and industrial production for manual and craft production was not a catastrophe in itself, unless the essence of art is thought to be the expression of individual genius aided by the skills of an artisanal elite.

The greatest challenge lay in the fact that photographic and cinematic processes could accomplish better and faster – and with a diffusion a hundred thousand times greater than was possible for pictorial and narrative realism – the task that academicism had assigned to realism: protecting consciousness from doubt. Industrial photography and cinema always have the edge over painting and the novel when it is a matter of stabilizing the referent, of ordering it from a point of view that would give it recognizable meaning, of repeating a syntax and lexicon that would allow addressees to decode images and sequences rapidly, and make it easy for them to become conscious both of their own identities and of the approval they thereby receive from others – since the structures in these images and sequences form a code of communication among them all. So effects of reality – or the phantasms of realism, if you prefer – are multiplied.

If the painter and novelist do not want to be, in their turn, apologists for what exists (and minor ones at that), they must renounce such therapeutic occupations. They must question the rules of the art of painting and narration as learned and received from their predecessors. They soon find that such rules are so many methods of deception, seduction, and reassurance that make it impossible to be 'truthful'. An unprecedented split occurs in both painting and literature. Those who refuse to reexamine the rules of art will make careers in mass conformism, using 'correct rules' to bring the endemic desire for reality into communication with objects and situations capable of satisfying it. Pornography is the use of photographs and film to this end. It becomes a general model for those pictorial and narrative arts that have not risen to the challenge of the mass media.

As for artists and writers who agree to question the rules of the plastic and narrative arts and perhaps share their suspicions by distributing their work – they are destined to lack credibility in the eyes of the devoted adherents of reality and identity, to find themselves without a guaranteed audience. In this sense, we can impute the dialectic of the avant-gardes to the challenge posed by the realisms of industry and the mass media to the arts of painting and literature. The Duchampian readymade does no more than signify, actively and parodically, this continual process of the dispossession of the painter's craft, and even the artist's. As Thierry de Duve astutely observes, the question of modern aesthetics is not 'What is beautiful?' but 'What is art to be (and what is literature to be)?'

Realism – which can be defined only by its intention of avoiding the question of reality implied in the question of art – always finds itself somewhere between academicism and kitsch. When authority takes the name of the party, realism and its complement, neoclassicism, triumph over the experimental avant-garde by slandering and censoring it. Even then, 'correct' images, 'correct' narratives – the correct forms that the party solicits, selects, and distributes – must procure a public that will desire them as the appropriate medicine for the depression and anxiety it feels. The demand for reality (that is, for unity, simplicity, communicability, etc.) did not have the same intensity or continuity for the German public between the wars as it had for the Russian public after the revolution: here one can draw a distinction between Nazi and Stalinist realism.

All the same, any attack on artistic experimentation mounted by political authority is inherently reactionary: aesthetic judgment would only have to reach a verdict on whether a particular work conforms to the established rules of the beautiful. Instead of the work's having to bother with what makes it an art object and whether it will find an appreciative audience, political academicism understands and imposes a priori criteria of the 'beautiful', criteria that can, in one move and once and for all, select works and their public. So the use of categories in an aesthetic judgment would be similar to their use in a cognitive judgment. In Kant's terms, both would be determinant judgments: an expression is first 'well formed' in the understanding; then, only those 'cases' that can be subsumed within this expression are retained in experience.

When authority does not take the name of the party but that of capital, the 'transavantgardist' solution (postmodernist in [Christopher] Jencks's sense) turns out to be more appropriate than the antimodern one. Eclecticism is the degree zero of contemporary general culture: you listen to reggae; you watch a western; you eat McDonald's at midday and local cuisine at night; you wear Paris perfume in Tokyo and dress retro in Hong Kong; knowledge is the stuff of TV game shows. It is easy to find a public for eclectic works. When art makes itself kitsch, it panders to the disorder that reigns in the 'taste' of the patron. Together, artist, gallery owner, critic, and public indulge one another in the Anything Goes – it's time to relax. But this realism of Anything Goes is the realism of money: in the absence of aesthetic criteria it is still possible and useful to measure the value of works of art by the profits they realize. This realism accommodates every tendency just as capitalism accommodates every 'need' – so long as these tendencies and needs have buying power. As for taste, there is no need to be choosy when you are speculating or amusing yourself. Artistic and literary investigation is doubly threatened: by 'cultural politics' on one side, by the art and book market on the other. The advice it receives, from one or another of these channels, is to provide works of art that, first, relate to subjects already existing in the eyes of the public to whom they are addressed and, second, are made ('well formed') in such a way that this public will recognize what they are about, understand what they mean, and then be able to grant or withhold its approval with confidence, possibly even drawing some solace from those it accepts.

THE SUBLIME AND THE AVANT-GARDE

This interpretation of the contact of the mechanical and industrial arts with the fine arts and literature is acceptable as an outline, but you would have to agree it is narrowly sociologistic and historicizing – in other words, one-sided. Notwithstanding the reservations of Benjamin and Adorno, it should be remembered that science and industry are just as open to suspicion with regard to reality as art and writing. To think otherwise would be to subscribe to an excessively humanist idea of the Mephistophelian functionalism of science and technology. One cannot deny the predominance of technoscience as it exists today, that is, the massive subordination of cognitive statements to the finality of the best possible performance – which is a technical criterion. Yet the mechanical and the industrial, particularly when they enter fields traditionally reserved for the artist, are bearers of something more than the effects of power. The objects and thoughts issuing from scientific knowledge and the capitalist economy bring with them one of the rules underwriting their possibility: the rule that there is no reality unless it is confirmed by a consensus between partners on questions of knowledge and commitment.

This rule is of no small consequence. It is the stamp left on the politics of both the scientist and the manager of capital by a sort of escape of reality from the metaphysical, religious, and political assurances the mind once believed it possessed. This retreat is indispensable to the birth of science and capitalism. There would be no physics had doubt not been cast on the Aristotelian theory of movement; no industry without the refutation of corporatism, mercantilism, and physiocracy. Modernity, whenever it appears, does not occur without a shattering of belief, without a discovery of the *lack of reality* in reality – a discovery linked to the invention of other realities.

What would this 'lack of reality' mean if we were to free it from a purely historicizing interpretation? The phrase is clearly related to what Nietzsche calls nihilism. Yet I see a modulation of it well before Nietzschean perspectivism, in the Kantian theme of the sublime. In particular, I think the aesthetic of the sublime is where modern art (including literature) finds its impetus, and where the logic of the avant-garde finds its axioms.

The sublime feeling, which is also the feeling of the sublime, is, according to Kant, a powerful and equivocal emotion: it brings both pleasure and pain. Or rather, in it pleasure proceeds from pain. In the tradition of the philosophy of the subject coming from Augustine and Descartes – which Kant does not radically question – this contradiction (which others might call neurosis or masochism) develops as a conflict between all of the faculties of the subject, between the faculty to conceive of something and the faculty to 'present' something. There is knowledge, first, if a statement is intelligible and, second, if 'cases' that 'correspond' to it can be drawn from experience. There is beauty if a particular 'case' (a work of art), given first by the sensibility and with no conceptual determination, arouses a feeling of pleasure that is independent of any interest and appeals to a principle of universal consensus (which may never be realized).

Taste in this way demonstrates that an accord between the capacity to conceive and the capacity to present an object corresponding to the concept – an accord that is undetermined and without rule, giving rise to what Kant calls a reflective judgment – may be felt in the form of pleasure. The sublime is a different feeling. It occurs when the imagination in fact fails to present any object that could accord with a concept, even if only in principle. We have the Idea of the world (the totality of what is), but not the capacity to show an example of it. We have the Idea of the simple (the nondecomposable), but we cannot illustrate it by a sensible object that would be a case of it. We can conceive of the absolutely great, the absolutely powerful, but any presentation of an object – which would be intended to 'display' that absolute greatness or absolute power – appears sadly lacking to us. These Ideas, for which there is no possible presentation and which therefore provide no knowledge of reality (experience), also prohibit the free accord of the faculties that produces the feeling of the beautiful. They obstruct the formation and stabilization of taste. One could call them unpresentable.

I shall call modern the art that devotes its 'trivial technique', as Diderot called it, to presenting the existence of something unpresentable. Showing that there is something we can conceive of which we can neither see nor show – this is the stake of modern painting. But how do we show something that cannot be seen? Kant himself suggests the direction to follow when he calls *formlessness*, the *absence of form*, a possible index to the unpresentable. And, speaking of the empty *abstraction* felt by the imagination as it searches for a presentation of the infinite (another unpresentable), he says that it is itself like a presentation of the infinite, its *negative presentation*. He cites the passage 'Thou shalt not make unto Thee any graven image . . .' (Exodus 20:4) as the most sublime in the Bible, in that it forbids any presentation of the absolute. For an outline of an aesthetic of sublime painting, there is little we need to add to these remarks: as painting, it will evidently 'present' something, but negatively. It will therefore avoid figuration or representation; it will be 'blank' [*blanche*] like one of Malevich's squares; it will make one see only by prohibiting one from seeing; it will give pleasure only by giving pain. In these formulations we can recognize the axioms of the avant-gardes in painting, to the extent that they dedicate themselves to allusions to the unpresentable through visible presentations. The systems of reasoning in whose name or with which this task could support and justify itself warrant a good deal of attention; but such systems cannot take shape except by setting out from the vocation of the sublime, with the aim of legitimating this vocation – in other words, of disguising it. They remain inexplicable without the incommensurability between reality and concept implied by the Kantian philosophy of the sublime.

I do not intend to analyze in detail here the way the various avant-gardes have, as it were, humiliated and disqualified reality by their scrutiny of the pictorial techniques used to instill a belief in it. Local tone, drawing, the blending of colors, linear perspective, the nature of the support and of tools, 'execution', the hanging of the work, the museum: the avant-gardes continually expose the artifices of presentation that allow thought to be enslaved by the gaze and diverted from the unpresentable. If Habermas, like Marcuse, takes this work of derealization as an aspect of the (repressive) 'desublimation' characterizing the avant-garde, it is because he confuses the Kantian sublime with Freudian sublimation, and because for him aesthetics is still an aesthetics of the beautiful.

THE POSTMODERN

What then is the postmodern? What place, if any, does it occupy in that vertiginous work of questioning the rules that govern images and narratives? It is undoubtedly part of the modern. Everything that is received must be suspected, even if it is only a day old ('Modo, modo,' wrote Petronius). What space does Cézanne challenge? The Impressionists'. What object do Picasso and Braque challenge? Cézanne's. What presupposition does Duchamp break with in 1912? The idea that one has to make a painting – even a cubist painting. And [Daniel] Buren examines another presupposition that he believes emerged intact from Duchamp's work: the place of the work's presentation. The 'generations' flash by at an astonishing rate. A work can become modern only if it is first postmodern. Thus understood, postmodernism is not modernism at its end, but in a nascent state, and this state is recurrent.

I would not wish, however, to be held to this somewhat mechanistic use of the word. If it is true that modernity unfolds in the retreat of the real and according to the sublime relationship of the presentable with the conceivable, we can (to use a musical idiom) distinguish two essential modes in this relationship. The accent can fall on the inadequacy of the faculty of presentation, on the nostalgia for presence, experienced by the human subject and the obscure and futile will that animates it in spite of everything. Or else the accent can fall on the power of the faculty to conceive, on what one might call its 'inhumanity' (a quality Apollinaire insists on in modern artists), since it is of no concern to the understanding whether or not the human sensibility or imagination accords with what it conceives – and on the extension of being and jubilation that come from inventing new rules of the game, whether pictorial, artistic, or something else. A caricatured arrangement of several names on the chessboard of avant-gardist history will show you what I mean: on the side of *melancholy*, the German Expressionists, on the side of *novatio*, Braque and Picasso; on the one hand, Malevich, on the other, El Lissitsky; on one side, De Chirico, on the other, Duchamp. What distinguishes these two modes may only be the merest nuance: they often coexist almost indiscernibly in the same piece, and yet they attest to a *différend* [a difference of opinion] within which the fate of thought has, for a long time, been played out, and will continue to be played out – a differend between regret and experimentation.

The works of Proust and Joyce both allude to something that does not let itself be made present. Allusion (to which Paolo Fabbri has recently drawn my attention) is perhaps an indispensable mode of expression for works that belong to the aesthetic of the sublime. In Proust the thing that is eluded as the price of this allusion is the identity of consciousness, falling prey to an excess of time. But in Joyce it is the identity of writing that falls prey to an excess of the book, or literature. Proust invokes the unpresentable by means of a language that keeps its syntax and lexicon intact, and a writing that, in terms of most of its operators, is still part of the genre of the narrative novel. The literary institution as Proust inherits it from Balzac or Flaubert is undoubtedly subverted, since the hero is not a character but the inner consciousness of time, and also because the diachrony of the diegesis, already shaken by Flaubert, is further challenged by the choice of narrative voice. But the unity of the book as the odyssey of this consciousness is not disturbed, even if it is put off from chapter to chapter: the identity of the writing with itself within the labyrinth of its interminable narration is enough to connote this unity, which some have compared to that of *The Phenomenology of Spirit*. Joyce makes us discern the unpresentable in the writing itself, in the signifier. A whole range of accepted narrative and even stylistic operators is brought into play with no concern for the unity of the whole, and experiments are conducted with new operators. The grammar and vocabulary of literary language are no longer taken for granted; instead they appear as academicisms, rituals born of a piety (as Nietzsche might call it) that does not alter the invocation of the unpresentable.

So this is the differend: the modern aesthetic is an aesthetic of the sublime. But it is nostalgic; it allows the unpresentable to be invoked only as absent content, while form, thanks to its recognizable consistency, continues to offer the reader or spectator material for consolation and pleasure. But such feelings do not amount to the true sublime feeling, which is intrinsically a combination of pleasure and pain: pleasure in reason exceeding all presentation, pain in the imagination or sensibility proving inadequate to the concept.

The postmodern would be that which in the modern invokes the unpresentable in presentation itself, that which refuses the consolation of correct forms, refuses the consensus of taste permitting a common experience of nostalgia for the impossible, and inquires into new presentations – not to take pleasure in them, but to better produce the feeling that there is something unpresentable. The postmodern artist or writer is in the position of a philosopher: the text he writes or the work he creates is not in principle governed by preestablished rules and cannot be judged according to a determinant judgment, by the application of given categories to this text or work. Such rules and categories are what the work or text is investigating. The artist and the writer therefore work without rules and in order to establish the rules for what *will have been made*. This is why the work and the text can take on the properties of an event; it is also why they would arrive too late for their author, or, in what amounts to the same thing, why the work of making them would always begin too soon. *Postmodern* would be understanding according to the paradox of the future (*post*) anterior (*modo*).

It seems to me that the essay (Montaigne) is postmodern, and the fragment (the *Athenaeum*) is modern.

Finally, it should be made clear that it is not up to us to *provide reality*, but to invent allusions to what is conceivable but not presentable. And this task should not lead us to expect the slightest reconciliation between 'language games'. Kant, in naming them the faculties, knew that they are separated by an abyss and that only a transcendental illusion (Hegel's) can hope to totalize them into a real unity. But he also knew that the price of this illusion is terror. The nineteenth and twentieth centuries have given us our fill of terror. We have paid dearly for our nostalgia for the all and the one, for a reconciliation of the concept and the sensible, for a transparent and communicable experience. Beneath the general demand for relaxation and appeasement, we hear murmurings of the desire to reinstitute terror and fulfill the phantasm of taking possession of reality. *The* answer is this: war on totality. Let us attest to the unpresentable; let us activate the differends and save the honor of the name.

8.2

SIMULACRA AND SIMULATIONS

Jean Baudrillard

The simulacrum is never that which conceals the truth – it is the truth which
conceals that there is none.
The simulacrum is true.

Ecclesiastes

If we were able to take as the finest allegory of simulation the Borges tale where
the cartographers of the Empire draw up a map so detailed that it ends up
exactly covering the territory (but where, with the decline of the Empire this
map becomes frayed and finally ruined, a few shreds still discernible in the
deserts – the metaphysical beauty of this ruined abstraction, bearing witness to
an imperial pride and rotting like a carcass, returning to the substance of the
soil, rather as an aging double ends up being confused with the real thing), this
fable would then have come full circle for us, and now has nothing but the
discrete charm of second-order simulacra.

Abstraction today is no longer that of the map, the double, the mirror or the
concept. Simulation is no longer that of a territory, a referential being or a
substance. It is the generation by models of a real without origin or reality: a
hyperreal. The territory no longer precedes the map, nor survives it. Henceforth, it is the map that precedes the territory – *precession of simulacra* – it is
the map that engenders the territory and if we were to revive the fable today, it
would be the territory whose shreds are slowly rotting across the map. It is the
real, and not the map, whose vestiges subsist here and there, in the deserts

Extract from Jean Baudrillard, *Simulacra and Simulations*, trans. Paul Foss, Paul Patton and Philip
Beitchman (Autonomedia/Sémiotext(e), 1983), pp. 1–13, 23–49, and *Jean Baudrillard: Selected
Writings*, ed. Mark Porter (Stanford University Press, 1988), pp. 166–83.

which are no longer those of the Empire, but our own. *The desert of the real itself.*

In fact, even inverted, the fable is useless. Perhaps only the allegory of the Empire remains. For it is with the same imperialism that present-day simulators try to make the real, all the real, coincide with their simulation models. But it is no longer a question of either maps or territory. Something has disappeared: the sovereign difference between them that was the abstraction's charm. For it is the difference which forms the poetry of the map and the charm of the territory, the magic of the concept and the charm of the real. This representational imaginary, which both culminates in and is engulfed by the cartographer's mad project of an ideal coextensivity between the map and the territory, disappears with simulation, whose operation is nuclear and genetic, and no longer specular and discursive. With it goes all of metaphysics. No more mirror of being and appearances, of the real and its concept; no more imaginary coextensivity: rather, genetic miniaturization is the dimension of simulation. The real is produced from miniaturized units, from matrices, memory banks and command models – and with these it can be reproduced an indefinite number of times. It no longer has to be rational, since it is no longer measured against some ideal or negative instance. It is nothing more than operational. In fact, since it is no longer enveloped by an imaginary, it is no longer real at all. It is a hyperreal: the product of an irradiating synthesis of combinatory models in a hyperspace without atmosphere.

In this passage to a space whose curvature is no longer that of the real, nor of truth, the age of simulation thus begins with a liquidation of all referentials – worse: by their artificial resurrection in systems of signs, which are a more ductile material than meaning, in that they lend themselves to all systems of equivalence, all binary oppositions and all combinatory algebra. It is no longer a question of imitation, nor of reduplication, nor even of parody. It is rather a question of substituting signs of the real for the real itself; that is, an operation to deter every real process by its operational double, a metastable, programmatic, perfect descriptive machine which provides all the signs of the real and short-circuits all its vicissitudes. Never again will the real have to be produced: this is the vital function of the model in a system of death, or rather of anticipated resurrection which no longer leaves any chance even in the event of death. A hyperreal henceforth sheltered from the imaginary, and from any distinction between the real and the imaginary, leaving room only for the orbital recurrence of models and the simulated generation of difference.

THE DIVINE IRREFERENCE OF IMAGES

To dissimulate is to feign not to have what one has. To simulate is to feign to have what one hasn't. One implies a presence, the other an absence. But the matter is more complicated, since to simulate is not simply to feign: 'Someone who feigns an illness can simply go to bed and pretend he is ill. Someone who simulates an illness produces in himself some of the symptoms' (Littre). Thus, feigning or dissimulating leaves the reality principle intact: the difference is always clear, it is only masked; whereas simulation threatens the difference between 'true' and 'false', between 'real' and 'imaginary'. Since the simulator produces 'true' symptoms, is he or she ill or not? The simulator cannot be treated objectively either as ill, or as not ill. Psychology and medicine stop at this point, before a thereafter undiscoverable truth of the illness. For if any symptom can be 'produced', and can no longer be accepted as a fact of nature, then every illness may be considered as simulatable and simulated, and medicine loses its meaning since it only knows how to treat 'true' illnesses by their objective causes. Psychosomatics evolves in a dubious way on the edge of the illness principle. As for psychoanalysis, it transfers the symptom from the organic to the unconscious order: once again, the latter is held to be real, more real than the former; but why should simulation stop at the portals of the unconscious? Why couldn't the 'work' of the unconscious be 'produced' in the same way as any other symptom in classical medicine? Dreams already are.

The alienist, of course, claims that 'for each form of the mental alienation there is a particular order in the succession of symptoms, of which the simulator is unaware and in the absence of which the alienist is unlikely to be deceived.' This (which dates from 1865) in order to save at all cost the truth principle, and to escape the specter raised by simulation: namely that truth, reference and objective caues have ceased to exist. What can medicine do with something which floats on either side of illness, on either side of health, or with the reduplication of illness in a discourse that is no longer true or false? What can psychoanalysis do with the reduplication of the discourse of the unconscious in a discourse of simulation that can never be unmasked, since it isn't false either?

What can the army do with simulators? Traditionally, following a direct principle of identification, it unmasks and punishes them. Today, it can reform an excellent simulator as though he were equivalent to a 'real' homosexual, heart-case or lunatic. Even military psychology retreats from the Cartesian clarities and hesitates to draw the distinction between true and false, between the 'produced' symptom and the authentic symptom. 'If he acts crazy so well, then he must be mad.' Nor is it mistaken: in the sense that all lunatics are simulators, and this lack of distinction is the worst form of subversion. Against it, classical reason armed itself with all its categories. But it is this today which again outflanks them, submerging the truth principle.

Outside of medicine and the army, favored terrains of simulation, the affair goes back to religion and the simulacrum of divinity: 'I forbade any simulacrum in the temples because the divinity that breathes life into nature cannot be represented.' Indeed it can. But what becomes of the divinity when it reveals itself in icons, when it is multiplied in simulacra? Does it remain the supreme authority, simply incarnated in images as a visible theology? Or is it volatilized into simulacra which alone deploy their pomp and power of fascination – the visible machinery of icons being substituted for the pure and intelligible Idea of God? This is precisely what was feared by the Iconoclasts, whose millennial quarrel is still with us today. Their rage to destroy images rose precisely because they sensed this omnipotence of simulacra, this facility they have of erasing God from the consciousnesses of people, and the overwhelming, destructive truth which they suggest: that ultimately there has never been any God; that only simulacra exist; indeed that God himself has only ever been his own simulacrum. Had they been able to believe that images only occulted or masked the Platonic idea of God, there would have been no reason to destroy them. One can live with the idea of a distorted truth. But their metaphysical despair came from the idea that the images concealed nothing at all, and that in fact they were not images, such as the original model would have made them, but actually perfect simulacra forever radiant with their own fascination. But this death of the divine referential has to be exorcised at all cost.

It can be seen that the iconoclasts, who are often accused of despising and denying images, were in fact the ones who accorded them their actual worth, unlike the iconolaters, who saw in them only reflections and were content to venerate God at one remove. But the converse can also be said, namely that the iconolaters possessed the most modern and adventurous minds, since, underneath the idea of the apparition of God in the mirror of images, they already enacted his death and his disappearance in the epiphany of his representations (which they perhaps knew no longer represented anything, and that they were purely a game, but that this was precisely the greatest game – knowing also that it is dangerous to unmask images, since they dissimulate the fact that there is nothing behind them).

This was the approach of the Jesuits, who based their politics on the virtual disappearance of God and on the worldly and spectacular manipulation of consciences – the evanescence of God in the epiphany of power – the end of transcendence, which no longer serves as alibi for a strategy completely free of influences and signs. Behind the baroque of images hides the grey eminence of politics.

Thus perhaps at stake has always been the murderous capacity of images: murderers of the real; murderers of their own model as the Byzantine icons could murder the divine identity. To this murderous capacity is opposed the dialectical capacity of representations as a visible and intelligible mediation of the real. All of Western faith and good faith was engaged in this wager on representation: that a sign could refer to the depth of meaning, that a sign could *exchange* for meaning and that something could guarantee this exchange – God, of course. But what if God himself can be simulated, that is to say, reduced to the signs which attest his existence? Then the whole system becomes weightless; it is no longer anything but a gigantic simulacrum: not unreal, but a simulacrum, never again exchanging for what is real, but exchanging in itself, in an uninterrupted circuit without reference or circumference.

So it is with simulation, insofar as it is opposed to representation. Representation starts from the principle that the sign and the real are equivalent (even if this equivalence is Utopian, it is a fundamental axiom). Conversely, simulation starts from the Utopia of this principle of equivalence, *from the radical negation of the sign as value*, from the sign as reversion and death sentence of every reference. Whereas representation tries to absorb simulation by interpreting it as false representation, simulation envelops the whole edifice of representation as itself a simulacrum.

These would be the successive phases of the image:

1 It is the reflection of a basic reality.
2 It masks and perverts a basic reality.
3 It masks the *absence* of a basic reality.
4 It bears no relation to any reality whatever: it is its own pure simulacrum.

In the first case, the image is a *good* appearance: the representation is of the order of sacrament. In the second, it is an *evil* appearance: of the order of malefice. In the third, it *plays at being* an appearance: it is of the order of sorcery. In the fourth, it is no longer in the order of appearance at all, but of simulation.

The transition from signs which dissimulate something to signs which dissimulate that there is nothing, marks the decisive turning point. The first implies a theology of truth and secrecy (to which the notion of ideology still belongs). The second inaugurates an age of simulacra and simulation, in which there is no longer any God to recognize his own, nor any last judgement to separate truth from false, the real from its artificial resurrection, since everything is already dead and risen in advance.

When the real is no longer what it used to be, nostalgia assumes its full meaning. There is a proliferation of myths of origin and signs of reality; of second-hand truth, objectivity and authenticity. There is an escalation of the true, of the lived experience; a resurrection of the figurative where the object and substance have disappeared. And there is a panic-stricken production of the real and the referential, above and parallel to the panic of material production. This is how simulation appears in the phase that concerns us: a strategy of the real, neo-real and hyperreal, whose universal double is a strategy of deterrence.

HYPERREAL AND IMAGINARY

Disneyland is a perfect model of all the entangled orders of simulation. To begin with it is a play of illusions and phantasms: pirates, the frontier, future world, etc. This imaginary world is supposed to be what makes the operation successful. But, what draws the crowds is undoubtedly much more the social microcosm, the miniaturized and *religious* revelling in real America, in its delights and drawbacks. You park outside, queue up inside, and are totally abandoned at the exit. In this imaginary world the only phantasmagoria is in the inherent warmth and affection of the crowd, and in that sufficiently excessive number of gadgets used there to specifically maintain the multitudinous affect. The contrast with the absolute solitude of the parking lot – a veritable concentration camp – is total. Or rather: inside, a whole range of gadgets magnetize the crowd into direct flows; outside, solitude is directed onto a single gadget: the automobile. By an extraordinary coincidence (one that undoubtedly belongs to the peculiar enchantment of this universe), this deep-frozen infantile world happens to have been conceived and realized by a man who is himself now cryogenized; Walt Disney, who awaits his resurrection at minus 180 degrees centigrade.

The objective profile of the United States, then, may be traced throughout Disneyland, even down to the morphology of individuals and the crowd. All its values are exalted here, in miniature and comic-strip form. Embalmed and pacified. Whence the possibility of an ideological analysis of Disneyland ... : digest of the American way of life, panegyric to American values, idealized transposition of a contradictory reality. To be sure. But this conceals something else, and that 'ideological' blanket exactly serves to cover over a *third-order simulation*: Disneyland is there to conceal the fact that it is the 'real' country, all of 'real' America, which *is* Disneyland (just as prisons are there to conceal the fact that it is the social in its entirety, in its banal omnipresence, which is carceral). Disneyland is presented as imaginary in order to make us believe that the rest is real, when in fact all of Los Angeles and the America surrounding it are no longer real, but of the order of the hyperreal and of simulation. It is no longer a question of a false representation of reality (ideology), but of concealing the fact that the real is no longer real, and thus of saving the reality principle.

The Disneyland imaginary is neither true nor false: it is a deterrence machine set up in order to rejuvenate in reverse the fiction of the real. Whence the debility, the infantile degeneration of this imaginary. It is meant to be an infantile world, in order to make us believe that the adults are elsewhere, in the 'real' world, and to conceal the fact that real childishness is everywhere, particularly among those adults who go there to act the child in order to foster illusions of their real childishness.

Moreover, Disneyland is not the only one. Enchanted Village, Magic Mountain, Marine World: Los Angeles is encircled by these 'imaginary stations' which feed reality, reality-energy, to a town whose mystery is precisely that it is nothing more than a network of endless, unreal circulation: a town of fabulous proportions, but without space or dimensions. As much as electrical and nuclear power stations, as much as film studios, this town, which is nothing more than an immense script and a perpetual motion picture, needs this old imaginary made up of childhood signals and faked phantasms for its sympathetic nervous system.

POLITICAL INCANTATION

Watergate. Same scenario as Disneyland (an imaginary effect concealing that reality no more exists outside than inside the bounds of the artificial perimeter): though here it is a scandal-effect concealing that there is no difference between the facts and their denunciation (identical methods are employed by the CIA and the *Washington Post* journalists). Same operation, though this time tending towards scandal as a means to regenerate a moral and political principle, towards the imaginary as a means to regenerate a reality principle in distress.

The denunciation of scandal always pays homage to the law. And Watergate above all succeeded in imposing the idea that Watergate *was* a scandal – in this sense it was an extraordinary operation of intoxication: the reinjection of a large dose of political morality on a global scale. It could be said along with Bourdieu that: 'The specific character of every relation of force is to dissimulate itself as such, and to acquire all its force only because it is so dissimulated'; understood as follows: capital, which is immoral and unscrupulous, can only function behind a moral superstructure, and whoever regenerates this public morality (by indignation, denunciation, etc.) spontaneously furthers the order of capital, as did the *Washington Post* journalists.

But this is still only the formula of ideology, and when Bourdieu enunciates it, he takes 'relation of force' to mean the *truth* of capitalist domination, and he *denounces* this relation of force as itself a *scandal*: he therefore occupies the same deterministic and moralistic position as the *Washington Post* journalists. He does the same job of purging and reviving moral order, an order of truth wherein the genuine symbolic violence of the social order is engendered, well beyond all relations of force, which are only elements of its indifferent and shifting configuration in the moral and political consciousnesses of people.

All that capital asks of us is to receive it as rational or to combat it in the name of rationality, to receive it as moral or to combat it in the name of morality. For they are *identical*, meaning *they can be read another way*: before, the task was to dissimulate scandal; today, the task is to conceal the fact that there is none.

Watergate is not a scandal: this is what must be said at all cost, for this is what everyone is concerned to conceal, this dissimulation masking a strengthening of morality, a moral panic as we approach the primal (mise-en-)scene of capital: its instantaneous cruelty; its incomprehensible ferocity; its fundamental immorality – these are what are scandalous, unaccountable for in that system of moral and economic equivalence which remains the axiom of leftist thought, from Enlightenment theory to communism. Capital doesn't give a damn about the idea of the contract which is imputed to it: it is a monstrous unprincipled undertaking, nothing more. Rather, it is 'enlightened' thought which seeks to control capital by imposing rules on it. And all that recrimination which replaced revolutionary thought today comes down to reproaching capital for not following the rules of the game. 'Power is unjust; its justice is a class justice; capital exploits us; etc.' – as if capital were linked by a contract to the society it rules. It is the left which holds out the mirror of equivalence, hoping that capital will fall for this phantasmagoria of the social contract and fulfill its obligation towards the whole of society (at the same time, no need for revolution: it is enough that capital accept the rational formula of exchange).

Capital in fact has never been linked by a contract to the society it dominates. It is a sorcery of the social relation, it is a *challenge to society* and should be responded to as such. It is not a scandal to be denounced according to moral and economic rationality, but a challenge to take up according to symbolic law.

MOEBIUS: SPIRALLING NEGATIVITY

Hence Watergate was only a trap set by the system to catch its adversaries – a simulation of scandal to regenerative ends. This is embodied by the character called 'Deep Throat', who was said to be a Republican grey eminence manipulating the leftist journalists in order to get rid of Nixon – and why not? All hypotheses are possible, although this one is superfluous: the work of the Right is done very well, and spontaneously, by the Left on its own. Besides, it would be naive, to see an embittered good conscience at work here. For the Right itself also spontaneously does the work of the Left. All the hypotheses of manipulation are reversible in an endless whirligig. For manipulation is a floating causality where positivity and negativity engender and overlap with one another; where there is no longer any active or passive. It is by putting an *arbitrary* stop to this revolving causality that a principle of political reality can be saved. It is by the *simulation* of a conventional, restricted perspective field, where the premises and consequences of any act or event are calculable, that a political credibility can be maintained (including, of course, 'objective' analysis, struggle, etc.) But if the entire cycle of any act or event is envisaged in a system where linear continuity and dialectical polarity no longer exist, in a field *unhinged by simulation*, then all determination evaporates, every act terminates at the end of the cycle having benefited everyone and been scattered in all directions.

Is any given bombing in Italy the work of leftist extremists; or of extreme right-wing provocation; or staged by centrists to bring every terrorist extreme into disrepute and to shore up its own failing power; or again, is it a police-inspired scenario in order to appeal to calls for public security? All this is equally true, and the search for proof – indeed the objectivity of the fact – does not check this vertigo of interpretation. We are in a logic of simulation which has nothing to do with a logic of facts and an order of reasons. Simulation is characterized by a *precession of the model*, of all models around the merest fact – the models come first, and their orbital (like the bomb) circulation constitutes the genuine magnetic field of events. Facts no longer have any trajectory of their own, they arise at the intersection of the models; a single fact may even be engendered by all the models at once. This anticipation, this precession, this short-circuit, this confusion of the fact with its model (no more divergence of meaning, no more dialectical polarity, no more negative electricity or implosion of poles) is what each time allows, for all the possible interpretations, even the most contradictory – all are true, in the sense that their truth is exchangeable, in the image of the models from which they proceed, in a generalized cycle.

The communists attack the socialist party as though they wanted to shatter the union of the Left. They sanction the idea that their reticence stems from a more radical political exigency. In fact, it is because they don't want power.

But do they not want it at this conjuncture because it is unfavorable for the Left in general, or because it is unfavorable for them within the union of the Left – or do they not want it by definition? When Berlinguer declares, 'We mustn't be frightened of seeing the communists seize power in Italy,' this means simultaneously:

1 That there is nothing to fear, since the communists, if they come to power, will change nothing in its fundamental capitalist mechanism.
2 That there isn't any risk of their ever coming to power (for the reason that they don't want to); and even if they do take it up, they will only ever wield it by proxy.
3 That in fact power, genuine power, no longer exists, and hence there is no risk of anybody seizing it or taking it over.
4 But more: I, Berlinguer, am not frightened of seeing the communists seize power in Italy – which might appear evident, but not so evident, since:
5 It can also mean the contrary (no need for psychoanalysis here): *I am frightened* of seeing the communists seize power (and with good reason, even for a communist).

All the above is simultaneously true. This is the secret of a discourse that is no longer only ambiguous, as political discourses can be, but that conveys the impossibility of a determinate position of power, the impossibility of a determinate position of discourse. And this logic belongs to neither party. It traverses all discourses without their wanting it.

Who will unravel this imbroglio? The Gordian knot can at least be cut. As for the Moebius strip, if it is split in two, it results in an additional spiral without there being any possibility of resolving its surfaces (here the reversible continuity of hypotheses). Hades of simulation, which is no longer one of torture, but of the subtle, maleficent, elusive twisting of meaning – where even those condemned at Burgos are still a gift from Franco to Western democracy, which finds in them the occasion to regenerate its own flagging humanism, and whose indignant protestation consolidates in return Franco's regime by uniting the Spanish masses against foreign intervention? Where is the truth in all that, when such collusions admirably knit together without their authors even knowing it?

The conjunction of the system and its extreme alternative like two ends of a curved mirror, the 'vicious' curvature of a political space henceforth magnetized, circularized, reversibilized from right to left, a torsion that is like the evil demon of commutation, the whole system, the infinity of capital folded back over its own surface: transfinite? And isn't it the same with desire and libidinal space? The conjunction of desire and value, of desire and capital. The conjunction of desire and the law; the ultimate joy and metamorphosis of the law (which is why it is so well received at the moment): only capital takes pleasure, Lyotard said, before coming to think that *we* take pleasure in capital. Overwhelming versatility of desire in Deleuze: an enigmatic reversal which brings this desire that is 'revolutionary by itself, and as if involuntarily, in wanting what it wants,' to want its own repression and to invest paranoid and fascist systems? A malign torsion which reduces this revolution of desire to the same fundamental ambiguity as the other, historical revolution.

All the referentials intermingle their discourses in a circular, Moebian compulsion. Not so long ago sex and work were savagely opposed terms: today both are dissolved into the same type of demand. Formerly the discourse on history took its force from opposing itself to the one on nature, the discourse on desire to the one on power: today they exchange their signifiers and their scenarios.

It would take too long to run through the whole range of operational negativity, of all those scenarios of deterrence which, like Watergate, try to revive a moribund principle by simulated scandal, phantasm, murder – a sort of hormonal treatment by negativity and crisis. It is always a question of proving the real by the imaginary; proving truth by scandal; proving the law by transgression; proving work by the strike; proving the system by crisis and capital by revolution; and for that matter proving ethnology by the dispossession of its object (the Tasaday). Without counting: proving theater by anti-theater; proving art by anti-art; proving pedagogy by anti-pedagogy; proving psychiatry by anti-psychiatry, etc., etc.

Everything is metamorphosed into its inverse in order to be perpetuated in its purged form. Every form of power, every situation speaks of itself by denial, in order to attempt to escape, by simulation of death, its real agony. Power can stage its own murder to rediscover a glimmer of existence and legitimacy. Thus with the American presidents: the Kennedys are murdered because they still have a political dimension. Others – Johnson, Nixon, Ford – only had a right to puppet attempts, to simulated murders. But they nevertheless needed that aura of an artificial menace to conceal that they were nothing other than mannequins of power. In olden days the king (also the god) had to die – that was his strength. Today he does his miserable utmost to pretend to die, so as to preserve the *blessing* of power. But even this is gone.

To seek new blood in its own death, to renew the cycle by the mirror of crisis, negativity and anti-power: this is the only alibi of every power, of every institution attempting to break the vicious circle of its irresponsibility and its fundamental nonexistence, of its déjà-vu and its déjà-mort.

STRATEGY OF THE REAL

Of the same order as the impossibility of rediscovering an absolute level of the real, is the impossibility of staging an illusion. Illusion is no longer possible, because the real is no longer possible. It is the whole *political* problem of the parody, of hypersimulation or offensive simulation, which is posed here.

For example: it would be interesting to see whether the repressive apparatus would not react more violently to a simulated hold up than to a real one? For a real hold up only upsets the order of things, the right of property, whereas a simulated hold up interferes with the very principle of reality. Transgression and violence are less serious, for they only contest the *distribution* of the real. Simulation is infinitely more dangerous since it always suggests, over and above its object, that *law and order themselves might really be nothing more than a simulation.*

But the difficulty is in proportion to the peril. How to feign a violation and put it to the test? Go and simulate a theft in a large department store: how do you convince the security guards that it is a simulated theft? There is no 'objective' difference: the same gestures and the same signs exist as for a real theft; in fact the signs incline neither to one side nor the other. As far as the established order is concerned, they are always of the order of the real.

Go and organize a fake hold up. Be sure to check that your weapons are harmless, and take the most trustworthy hostage, so that no life is in danger (otherwise you risk committing an offence). Demand ransom, and arrange it so that the operation creates the greatest commotion possible. In brief, stay close to the 'truth', so as to test the reaction of the apparatus to a perfect simulation. But you won't succeed: the web of artificial signs will be inextricably mixed up with real elements (a police officer will really shoot on sight; a bank customer will faint and die of a heart attack; they will really turn the phoney ransom over to you). In brief, you will unwittingly find yourself immediately in the real, one of whose functions is precisely to devour every attempt at simulation, to reduce everything to some reality: that's exactly how the established order is, well before institutions and justice come into play.

In this impossibility of isolating the process of simulation must be seen the whole thrust of an order that can only see and understand in terms of some reality, because it can function nowhere else. The simulation of an offence, if it is patent, will either be punished more lightly (because it has no 'consequences') or be punished as an offence to public office (for example, if one triggered off a police operation 'for nothing') – but *never as simulation*, since it is precisely as such that no equivalence with the real is possible, and hence no repression either. The challenge of simulation is irreceivable by power. How can you punish the simulation of virtue? Yet as such it is as serious as the simulation of crime. Parody makes obedience and transgression equivalent, and that is the most serious crime, since it *cancels out the difference upon which the law is based.* The established order can do nothing against it, for the law is a second-order simulacrum whereas simulation is a third-order simulacrum, beyond true and false, beyond equivalences, beyond the rational distinctions upon which function all power and the entire social stratum. Hence, *failing the real*, it is here that we must aim at order.

This is why order always opts for the real. In a state of uncertainty, it always prefers this assumption (thus in the army they would rather take the simulator as a true madman). But this becomes more and more difficult, for it is practically impossible to isolate the process of simulation; through the force of inertia of the real which surrounds us, the inverse is also true (and this very reversibility forms part of the apparatus of simulation and of power's impotency): namely, *it is now impossible to isolate the process of the real*, or to prove the real.

Thus all hold ups, hijacks and the like are now as it were simulation hold ups, in the sense that they are inscribed in advance in the decoding and orchestration rituals of the media, anticipated in their mode of presentation and possible consequences. In brief, where they function as a set of signs dedicated exclusively to their recurrence as signs, and no longer to their 'real' goal at all. But this does not make them inoffensive. On the contrary, it is as hyperreal events, no longer having any particular contents or aims, but indefinitely refracted by each other (for that matter like so-called historical events: strikes, demonstrations, crises, etc.), that they are precisely unverifiable by an order which can only exert itself on the real and the rational, on ends and means: a referential order which can only dominate referentials, a determinate power which can only dominate a determined world, but which can do nothing about that indefinite recurrence of simulation, about that weightless nebula no longer obeying the law of gravitation of the real – power itself eventually breaking apart in this space and becoming a simulation of power (disconnected from its aims and objectives, and dedicated to *power effects* and mass simulation).

The only weapon of power, its only strategy against this defection, is to reinject realness and referentiality everywhere, in order to convince us of the reality of the social, of the gravity of the economy and the finalities of production. For that purpose it prefers the discourse of crisis, but also – why not? – the discourse of desire. 'Take your desires for reality!' can be understood as the ultimate slogan of power, for in a nonreferential world even the confusion of the reality principle with the desire principle is less dangerous than contagious hyperreality. One remains among principles, and there power is always right.

Hyperreality and simulation are deterrents of every principle and of every objective; they turn against power this deterrence which is so well utilized for a long time itself. For, finally, it was capital which was the first to feed throughout its history on the destruction of every referential, of every human goal, which shattered every ideal distinction between true and false, good and evil, in order to establish a radical law of equivalence and exchange, the iron law of its power. It was the first to practice deterrence, abstraction, disconnection, deterritorialization, etc.; and if it was capital which fostered reality, the reality principle, it was also the first to liquidate it in the extermination of every use value, of every real equivalence, of production and wealth, in the very sensation we have of the unreality of the stakes and the omnipotence of manipulation. Now, it is this very logic which is today hardened even more *against* it. And when it wants to fight this catastrophic spiral by secreting one last glimmer of reality, on which to found one last glimmer of power, it only multiplies the *signs* and accelerates the play of simulation.

As long as it was historically threatened by the real, power risked deterrence and simulation, disintegrating every contradiction by means of the production of equivalent signs. When it is threatened today by simulation (the threat of vanishing in the play of signs), power risks the real, risks crisis, it gambles on remanufacturing artificial, social, economic, political stakes. This is a question of life or death for it. But it is too late.

Whence the characteristic hysteria of our time: the hysteria of production and reproduction of the real. The other production, that of goods and commodities, that of *la belle epoque* of political economy, no longer makes any sense of its own, and has not for some time. What society seeks through production, and overproduction, is the restoration of the real which escapes it. That is why *contemporary 'material' production is itself hyperreal*. It retains all the features, the whole discourse of traditional production, but it is nothing more than its scaled-down refraction (thus the hyperrealists fasten in a striking resemblance a real from which has fled all meaning and charm, all the profundity and energy of representation). Thus the hyperrealism of simulation is expressed everywhere by the real's striking resemblance to itself.

Power, too, for some time now produces nothing but signs of its resemblance. And at the same time, another figure of power comes into play: that of a collective demand for *signs* of power – a holy union which forms around the disappearance of power. Everybody belongs to it more or less in fear of the collapse of the political. And in the end the game of power comes down to nothing more than the *critical* obsession with power: an obsession with its death; an obsession with its survival which becomes greater the more it disappears. When it has totally disappeared, logically we will be under the total spell of power – a haunting memory already foreshadowed everywhere, manifesting at one and the same time the satisfaction of having got rid of it (nobody wants it any more, everybody unloads it on others) and grieving its loss. Melancholy for societies without power: this has already given rise to fascism, that overdose of a powerful referential in a society which cannot terminate its mourning.

But we are still in the same boat: none of our societies know how to manage their mourning for the real, for power, for the *social itself*, which is implicated in this same breakdown. And it is by an artificial revitalization of all this that we try to escape it. *Undoubtedly this will even end up in socialism.* By an unforeseen twist of events and an irony which no longer belongs to history, it is through the death of the social that socialism will emerge – as it is through the death of God that religions emerge. A twisted coming, a perverse event, an unintelligible reversion to the logic of reason. As is the fact that power is no longer present except to conceal that there is none. A simulation which can go on indefinitely, since – unlike 'true' power which is, or was, a structure, a strategy, a relation of force, a stake – this is nothing but the object of a social *demand*, and hence subject to the law of supply and demand, rather than to violence and death. Completely expunged from the *political* dimension, it is dependent, like any other commodity, on production and mass consumption. Its spark has disappeared; only the fiction of a political universe is saved.

Likewise with work. The spark of production, the violence of its stake no longer exists. Everybody still produces, and more and more, but work has subtly become something else: a need (as Marx ideally envisaged it, but not at all in the same sense), the object of a social 'demand', like leisure, to which it is equivalent in the general run of life's options. A demand exactly proportional to the loss of stake in the work process. The same change in fortune as for power: the *scenario* of work is there to conceal the fact that the work-real, the production-real, has disappeared. And for that matter so has the strike-real too, which is no longer a stoppage of work, but its alternative pole in the ritual scansion of the social calendar. It is as if everyone has 'occupied' their work place or work post, after declaring the strike, and resumed production, as is the custom in a 'self-managed' job, in exactly the same terms as before, by declaring themselves (and virtually being) in a state of permanent strike.

This isn't a science-fiction dream: everywhere it is a question of a doubling of the work process. And of a double or locum for the strike process – strikes which are incorporated like obsolescence in objects, like crises in production. Then there are no longer any strikes or work, but both simultaneously, that is to say something else entirely: a wizardry of work, a trompe l'oeil, a sceno-drama (not to say melodrama) of production, collective dramaturgy upon the empty stage of the social.

It is no longer a question of the *ideology* of work – of the traditional ethic that obscures the 'real' labour process and the 'objective' process of exploitation – but of the scenario of work. Likewise, it is no longer a question of the ideology of power, but of the *scenario* of power. Ideology only corresponds to a betrayal of reality by signs; simulation corresponds to a short-circuit of reality and to its reduplication by signs. It is always the aim of ideological analysis to restore the objective process; it is always a false problem to want to restore the truth beneath the simulacrum.

This is ultimately why power is so in accord with ideological discourses and discourses on ideology, for these are all discourses of *truth* – always good, even and especially if they are revolutionary, to counter the mortal blows of simulation.

8.3

NOSTALGIA FOR THE PRESENT

Fredric Jameson

There is a novel by Philip K. Dick, which, published in 1959, evokes the fifties:
President Eisenhower's stroke; Main Street, USA; Marilyn Monroe; a world of
neighbors and PTAs; small retail chain stores (the produce trucked in from the
outside); favorite television programs; mild flirtations with the housewife next
door; game shows and contests; sputniks distantly revolving overhead, mere
blinking lights in the firmament, hard to distinguish from airliners or flying
saucers. If you were interested in constructing a time capsule or an 'only
yesterday' compendium or documentary-nostalgia video film of the 1950s, this
might serve as a beginning: to which you could add short haircuts, early rock
and roll, longer skirts, and so on. The list is not a list of facts or historical
realities (although its items are not invented and are in some sense 'authentic'),
but rather a list of stereotypes, of ideas of facts and historical realities. It
suggests several fundamental questions.

First of all, did the 'period' see itself this way? Did the literature of the period
deal with this kind of small-town American life as its central preoccupation;
and if not, why not? What other kinds of preoccupations seemed more
important? To be sure, in retrospect, the fifties have been summed up culturally
as so many forms of protest against the fifties 'themselves'; against the
Eisenhower era and its complacency, against the sealed self-content of the
American small (white, middle-class) town, against the conformist and the
family-centered ethnocentrism of a prosperous United States learning to

Extract from Frederic Jameson, *Postmodernism, or, The Cultural Logic of Late Capitalism* (Duke
University Press, 1991), pp. 279–96.

consume in the first big boom after the shortages and privations of the war, whose immediacy has by now largely lost its edge. The first Beat poets; and occasional 'antihero' with 'existentionalist' overtones; a few daring Hollywood impulses; nascent rock and roll itself; the compensatory importation of European books, movements, and art films; a lonely and premature political rebel or theorist like C. Wright Mills: such, in retrospect, seems to be the balance sheet of fifties culture. All the rest is Peyton Place, best-sellers, and TV series. And it is indeed just those series – living-room comedies, single-family homes menaced by *Twilight Zone*, on the one hand, and gangsters and escaped convicts from the outside world, on the other – that give us the content of our positive image of the fifties in the first place. If there is 'realism' in the 1950s, in other words, it is presumably to be found there, in mass cultural representation, the only kind of art willing (and able) to deal with the stifling Eisenhower realities of the happy family in the small town, of normalcy and nondeviant everyday life. High art apparently cannot deal with this kind of subject matter except by way of the oppositional: the satire of Lewis, the pathos and solitude of Hopper or Sherwood Anderson. Of naturalism, long after the fact, the Germans used to say that it 'stank of cabbage'; that is, it exuded the misery and boredom of its subject matter, poverty itself. Here too the content seems somehow to contaminate the form, only the misery here is the misery of happiness, or at least contentment (which is in reality complacency), of Marcuse's 'false' happiness, the gratifications of the new car, the TV dinner and your favorite program on the sofa – which are now themselves secretly a misery, an unhappiness that doesn't know its name, that has no way of telling itself apart from genuine satisfaction and fulfillment since it has presumably never encountered this last.

When the notion of the oppositional is contested, however, in the mid eighties, we will know a fifties revival in which much of this 'degraded mass culture' returns for possible reevaluation. In the fifties, however, it is high culture that is still authorized to pass judgment on reality, to say what real life is and what is, on the other hand, mere appearance; and it is by leaving out, by ignoring, by passing over in silence and with the repugnance one may feel for the dreary stereotypes of television series, that high art palpably issues its judgments. Faulkner and Hemingway, the southerners and the New Yorkers, pass this small-town US raw material by in a detour considerably greater than the proverbial ten-foot pole; indeed, of the great writers of the period, only Dick himself comes to mind as the virtual poet laureate of this material: of squabbling couples and marital dramas, of petit bourgeois shopkeepers, neighborhoods, and afternoons in front of television, and all the rest. But, of course, he does something to it, and it was already California anyway.

This small-town content was not, in the postwar period, really 'provincial' any longer (as in Lewis or John O'Hara, let alone Dreiser): you might want to leave, you might still long for the big city, but something had happened – perhaps something as simple as television and the other media – to remove the pain and sting of absence from the center, from the metropolis. On the other hand, today, none of it exists any longer, even though we still have small towns (whose downtowns are now in decay – but so are the big cities). What has happened is that the autonomy of the small town (in the provincial period a source of claustrophobia and anxiety; in the fifties the ground for a certain comfort and even a certain reassurance) has vanished. What was once a separate point on the map has become an imperceptible thickening in a continuum of identical products and standardized spaces from coast to coast. One has the feeling, however, that the autonomy of the small town, its complacent independence, also functioned as an allegorical expression for the situation of Eisenhower America in the outside world as a whole – contented with itself, secure in the sense of its radical difference from other populations and cultures, insulated from their vicissitudes and from the flaws in human nature so palpably acted out in their violent and alien histories.

This is clearly, however, to shift from the realities of the 1950s to the representation of that rather different thing, the 'fifties', a shift which obligates us in addition to underscore the cultural sources of all the attributes with which we have endowed the period, many of which seem very precisely to derive from its own television programs; in other words, its own representation of itself. However, although one does not confuse a person with what he or she thinks of himself/herself, such self-images are surely very relevant indeed and constitute an essential part of the more objective description or definition. Nonetheless, it seems possible that the deeper realities of the period – read, for example, against the very different scale of, say, diachronic and secular economic rhythms, or of synchronic and systemic global interrelationships, have little to do with either our cultural stereotypes of years thus labeled and defined in terms of generational decades. The concept of 'classicism', for example, has a precise and functional meaning in German cultural and literary history which disappears when we move to a European perspective in which those few key years vanish without a trace into some vaster opposition between Enlightenment and Romanticism. But this is a speculation which presupposes the possibility that at an outer limit, the sense people have of themselves and their own moment of history may ultimately have nothing whatsoever to do with its reality: that the existential may be absolutely distinct, as some ultimate 'false consciousness', from the structural and social significance of a collective phenomenon, surely a possibility rendered more plausible by the fact of global imperialism, in terms of which the meaning of a given nation-state – for everyone else on the globe – may be wildly at odds from their own inner experiences and their own interior daily life. Eisenhower wore a well-known smile for us but an equally well-known scowl for foreigners beyond our borders, as the state portraits in any US consulate during those years dramatically attested.

There is, however, an even more radical possibility; namely, that period concepts finally correspond to no realities whatsoever, and that whether they are formulated in terms of generational logic, or by the names of reigning

monarchs, or according to some other category or typological and classificatory system, the collective reality of the multitudinous lives encompassed by
such terms is nonthinkable (or nontotalizable, to use a current expression) and
can never be described, characterized, labeled, or conceptualized. This is, I
suppose, what one could call the Nietzschean position, for which there are no
such things as 'periods', nor have there ever been. In that case, of course, there
is no such thing as 'history' either, which was probably the basic philosophical
point such arguments sought to make in the first place.

This is the moment, however, to return to Dick's novel and record the twist
that turns it into science fiction: for it transpires, from an increasing accumulation of tiny but aberrant details, that the environment of the novel, in which we
watch the characters act and move, is not really the fifties after all ... It is a
Potemkin village of a historical kind: a reproduction of the 1950s – including
induced and introjected memories and character structures in its human
population – constructed (for reasons that need not detain us here) in 1997,
in the midst of an interstellar atomic civil war. I will only note that a twofold
determination plays across the main character, who must thus be read according to a negative and a positive hermeneutic simultaneously. The village has
been constructed in order to trick him, against his will, into performing an
essential wartime task for the government. In that sense, he is the victim of this
manipulation, which awakens all our fantasies of mind control and unconscious exploitation, of anti-Cartesian predestination and determinism. On this
reading, then, Dick's novel is a nightmare and the expression of deep, unconscious, collective fears about our social life and its tendencies.

Yet Dick also takes pains to make clear that the 1950s village is also very
specifically the result of infantile regression on the part of the protagonist, who
has also, in a sense, unconsciously chosen his own delusion and has fled the
anxieties of the civil war for the domestic and reassuring comforts of his own
childhood during the period in question. From this perspective, then, the novel
is a collective wish-fulfillment, and the expression of a deep, unconscious
yearning for a simpler and more human social system and a small-town Utopia
very much in the North American frontier tradition.

We should also note that the very structure of the novel articulates the
position of Eisenhower America in the world itself and is thereby to be read as
a kind of distorted form of cognitive mapping, an unconscious and figurative
projection of some more 'realistic' account of our situation, as it has been
described earlier: the hometown reality of the United States surrounded by the
implacable menace of world communism (and, in this period to a much lesser
degree, of Third World poverty). This is also, of course, the period of the classic
science fiction films, with their more overtly ideological representations of
external threats and impending alien invasions (also generally set in small
towns). Dick's novel can be read in that way – the grimmer 'reality' disclosed
behind the benign and deceptive appearance – or it can be taken as a certain
approach to self-consciousness about the representations themselves.

What is more significant from the present perspective, however, is the paradigmatic value of Dick's novel for questions of history and historicity in general. One of the ways of thinking about the subgenre to which this novel belongs – that 'category' called science fiction, which can be either expanded and dignified by the addition of all the classical satiric and Utopian literature from Lucian on or restricted and degraded to the pulp-and-adventure tradition – is as a historically new and original form which offers analogies with the emergence of the historical novel in the early nineteenth century. Lukács has interpreted this last as a formal innovation (by Sir Walter Scott) which provided figuration for the new and equally emergent sense of history of the triumphant middle classes (or bourgeoisie), as that class sought to project its own vision of its past and its future and to articulate its social and collective project in a temporal narrative distinct in form from those of earlier 'subjects of history' such as the feudal nobility. In that form, the historical novel – and its related emanations, such as the costume film – has fallen into disrepute and infrequency, not merely because, in the postmodern age, we no longer tell ourselves our history in that fashion, but also because we no longer experience it that way, and, indeed, perhaps no longer experience it at all.

One would want, in short, to stress the conditions of possibility of such a form – and of its emergence and eclipse – less in the existential experience of history of people at this or that historical moment than rather in the very structure of their socioeconomic system, in its relative opacity or transparency, and the access its mechanisms provide to some greater cognitive as well as existential contact with the thing itself. This is the context in which it seems interesting to explore the hypothesis that science fiction as a genre entertains a dialectical and structural relationship with the historical novel – a relationship of kinship and inversion all at once, of opposition and homology ... But time itself plays a crucial role in this generic opposition, which is also something of an evolutionary compensation. For if the historical novel 'corresponded' to the emergence of historicity, of a sense of history in its strong modern post-eighteenth-century sense, science fiction equally corresponds to the waning or the blockage of that historicity, and, particularly in our own time (in the postmodern era), to its crisis and paralysis, its enfeeblement and repression. Only by means of a violent formal and narrative dislocation could a narrative apparatus come into being capable of restoring life and feeling to this only intermittently functioning organ that is our capacity to organize and live time historically. Nor should it be thought overhastily that the two forms are symmetrical on the grounds that the historical novel stages the past and science fiction the future.

Historicity is, in fact, neither a representation of the past nor a representation of the future (although its various forms use such representations): it can first and foremost be defined as a perception of the present as history; that is, as a relationship to the present which somehow defamiliarizes it and allows us that distance from immediacy which is at length characterized as a historical perspective. It is appropriate, in other words, also to insist on the historicality of the operation itself, which is our way of conceiving of historicity in this particular society and mode of production; appropriate also to observe that what is at stake is essentially a process of reification whereby we draw back from our immersion in the here and now (not yet identified as a 'present') and grasp it as a kind of thing – not merely a 'present' but a present that can be dated and called the eighties or the fifties ...

Time Out of Joint ... offers ... what one might in the strong sense call a trope of the future anterior – the estrangement and renewal as history of our own reading present, the fifties, by way of the apprehension of that present as the past of a specific future. The future itself – Dick's 1997 – is not, however, centrally significant as a representation or an anticipation; it is the narrative means to a very different end, namely the brutal transformation of a realistic representation of the present, of Eisenhower America and the 1950s small town, into a memory and a reconstruction. Reification is here indeed built into the novel itself and, as it were, defused and recuperated as a form of praxis: the fifties is a thing, but a thing that we can build, just as the science fiction writer builds his own small-scale model. At that point, then, reification ceases to be a baleful and alienating process, a noxious side-effect of our mode of production, if not, indeed, its fundamental dynamic, and is rather transferred to the side of human energies and human possibilities. (The reappropriation has, of course, a good deal to do with the specificity of Dick's own themes and ideology – in particular, the nostalgia about the past and the 'petit bourgeois' valorization of small craftsmanship, as well as small business and collecting.)

This novel has necessarily become for us a historical one: for its present – the 1950s – has become our past in a rather different sense than that proposed by the text itself. The latter still 'works': we can still feel and appreciate the transformation and reification of its readers' present into a historical period; we can even, by analogy, extrapolate something similar for our own moment in time. Whether such a process today can be realized concretely, in a cultural artifact, is, however, a rather different question. The accumulation of books like *Future Shock*, the incorporation of habits of 'futurology' into our everyday life, the modification of our perception of things to include their 'tendency' and of our reading of time to approximate a scanning of complex probabilities – this new relationship to our own present both includes elements formerly incorporated in the experience of the 'future' and blocks or forestalls any global vision of the latter as a radically transformed and different system. If catastrophic 'near-future' visions of, say, overpopulation, famine, and anarchic violence are no longer as effective as they were a few years ago, the weakening of those effects and of the narrative forms that were designed to produce them is not necessarily due only to overfamiliarity and overexposure; or rather, this last is perhaps also to be seen as a modification in our relationship to those imaginary near futures, which no longer strike us with the horror of otherness and radical difference. Here a certain Nietzscheanism operates to defuse anxiety and even fear: the conviction, however gradually learned and acquired, that there is only the present and that it is always 'ours', is a kind of wisdom that cuts both ways. For it was always clear that the terror of such near futures – like the analogous terror of an older naturalism – was class based and deeply rooted in class comfort and privilege. The older naturalism let us briefly experience the life and the life world of the various underclasses, only to return with relief to our own living rooms and armchairs: the good resolutions it may also have encouraged were always, then, a form of philanthropy. In the same way, yesterday's terror of the overcrowded conurbations of the immediate future could just as easily be read as a pretext for complacency with our own historical present, in which we do not yet have to live like that. In both cases, at any rate, the fear is that of proletarianization, of slipping down the ladder, of losing a comfort and a set of privileges which we tend increasingly to think of in spatial terms: privacy, empty rooms, silence, walling other people out, protection against crowds and other bodies. Nietzschean wisdom, then, tells us to let go of that kind of fear and reminds us that whatever social and spatial form our future misery may take, it will not be alien because it will by definition be ours. *Dasein ist je mein eigenes* – defamiliarization, the shock of otherness, is a mere aesthetic effect and a lie.

Perhaps, however, what is implied is simply an ultimate historicist breakdown in which we can no longer imagine the future at all, under any form – Utopian or catastrophic. Under those circumstances, where a formerly futurological science fiction (such as so-called cyberpunk today) turns into mere 'realism' and an outright representation of the present, the possibility Dick offered us – an experience of our present as past and as history – is slowly excluded. Yet everything in our culture suggests that we have not, for all that, ceased to be preoccupied by history; indeed, at the very moment in which we complain, as here, of the eclipse of historicity, we also universally diagnose contemporary culture as irredeemably historicist, in the bad sense of an omnipresent and indiscriminate appetite for dead styles and fashions; indeed, for all the styles and fashions of a dead past. Meanwhile, a certain caricature of historical thinking – which we may not even call *generational* any longer, so rapid has its momentum become – has also become universal and includes at least the will and intent to return upon our present circumstances in order to think of them – as the nineties, say – and to draw the appropriate marketing and forecasting conclusions. Why is this not historicity with a vengeance? and what is the difference between this now generalized approach to the present and Dick's rather cumbersome and primitive laboratory approach to a 'concept' of his own fifties?

In my opinion, it is the structure of the two operations which is instructively different: the one mobilizing a vision of the future in order to determine its return to a now historical present; the other mobilizing, but in some new allegorical way, a vision of the past, or of a certain moment of the past. Several recent films (I will here mention *Something Wild* and *Blue Velvet*) encourage us to see the newer process in terms of an allegorical encounter; yet even this formal possibility will not be properly grasped unless we set in place its preconditions in the development of nostalgia film generally. For it is by way of so-called nostalgia films that some properly allegorical processing of the past becomes possible: it is because the formal apparatus of nostalgia films has trained us to consume the past in the form of glossy images that new and more complex 'postnostalgia' statements and forms become possible. I have elsewhere tried to identify the privileged raw material or historical content of this particular operation of reification and of the transformation into the image in the crucial antithesis between the twenties and the thirties, and in the historicist revival of the very stylistic expression of that antithesis in art deco. The symbolic working out of that tension – as it were, between Aristocracy and Worker – evidently involves something like the symbolic reinvention or production of a new Bourgeoisie, a new form of identity. Yet like photorealism, the products themselves are bland in their very visual elegance, while the plot structures of such films suffer from a schematization (or typification) which seems to be inherent in the project. While we may anticipate more of these, therefore, and while the taste for them corresponds to more durable features and needs in our present economicopsychic constitution (image fixation *cum* historicist cravings), it was perhaps only to be expected that some new and more complicated and interesting formal sequel would rapidly develop.

What was more unexpected – but very 'dialectical' indeed, in a virtually textbook way – was the emergence of this new form from a kind of cross, if not synthesis, between the two filmic modes we had until now been imagining as antithetical: namely, the high elegance of nostalgia films, on the one hand, and the grade-B simulations of iconoclastic punk film, on the other. We failed to see that both were significantly mortgaged to music, because the musical signifiers were rather different in the two cases – the sequences of high-class dance music, on the one hand, the contemporary proliferation of rock groups, on the other. Meanwhile, any 'dialectical' textbook of the type already referred to might have alerted us to the probability that an ideologeme of 'elegance' depends in some measure on an opposite of some kind, an opposite and a negation which seems in our time to have shed its class content (still feebly alive when the 'beats' were felt to entertain a twin opposition to bourgeois respectability and high modernist aestheticism), and to have gradually migrated into that new complex of meanings that bears the name *punk*.

The new films, therefore, will first and foremost be allegories of that, of their own coming into being as a synthesis of nostalgia-deco and punk: they will in one way or another tell their own stories as the need and search for this 'marriage' (the wonderful thing about aesthetics – unlike politics, alas – being that the 'search' automatically becomes the thing itself: to set it up is by definition to realize it). Yet this resolution of an aesthetic contradiction is not gratuitous, because the formal contradiction itself has a socially and historically symbolic significance of its own.

But now the stories of these two films need to be briefly outlined. In *Something Wild* a young 'organization man' is abducted by a crazy girl, who initiates him into cutting corners and cheating on credit cards, until her husband, an ex-convict, shows up and, bent on vengeance, pursues the couple. In *Blue Velvet*, on the other hand, a young high-school graduate discovers a severed ear, which puts him on the trail of a torch singer mysteriously victimized by a local drug dealer, from whom he is able to save her.

Such films indeed invite us to return somehow to history: the central scene of *Something Wild* ... is a class reunion, the kind of event which specifically demands historical judgments of its participants: narratives of historical trajectories, as well as evaluations of moments of the past nostalgically reevoked but necessarily rejected or reaffirmed. This is the wedge, or opening, through which a hitherto aimless but lively filmic narrative suddenly falls into the deeper past (or that deeper past into it); for the ten-year reunion in reality takes us back twenty more, to a time when the 'villain' unexpectedly emerges, over your shoulder, marked as 'familiar' in all his unfamiliarity to the spectator (he is the heroine's husband, Ray, and worse). 'Ray' is, of course, in one way yet another reworking of that boring and exhausted paradigm, the gothic, where – on the individualized level – a sheltered woman of some kind is terrorized and victimized by an 'evil' male. I think it would be a great mistake to read such literature as a kind of protofeminist denunciation of patriarchy and, in particular, a protopolitical protest against rape. Certainly the gothic mobilizes anxieties about rape, but its structure gives us the clue to a more central feature of its content which I have tried to underscore by means of the word *sheltered*.

Gothics are indeed ultimately a class fantasy (or nightmare) in which the dialectic of privilege and shelter is exercised: your privileges seal you off from other people, but by the same token they constitute a protective wall through which you cannot see, and behind which therefore all kinds of envious forces may be imagined in the process of assembling, plotting, preparing to give assault ... That its classical form turns on the privileged content of the situation of middle-class women – the isolation, but also the domestic idleness, imposed on them by newer forms of middle-class marriage – adds such texts, as symptoms, to the history of women's situations but does not lend them any particular political significance (unless that significance consists merely in a coming to self-consciousness of the disadvantages of privilege in the first place). But the form can also, under certain circumstances, be reorganized around young men, to whom some similarly protective distance is imputed: intellectuals, for example, or 'sheltered' young briefcase-carrying bureaucrats, as in *Something Wild* itself. (That this gender substitution risks awakening all kinds of supplementary sexual overtones is here self-consciously dramatized in the extraordinary tableau moment in which the stabbing, seen from behind – and from the woman's visual perspective – looks like a passionate embrace between the two men.) The more formal leap, however, will come when for the individual 'victim' – male or female – is substituted the collectivity itself, the US public, which now lives out the anxieties of its economic privileges and its sheltered 'exceptionalism' in a pseudo-political version of the gothic – under the threats of stereotypical madmen and 'terrorists' (mostly Arabs or Iranians for some reason). These collective fantasies are less to be explained by some increasing 'feminization' of the American public self than by its guilt and the dynamics of comfort already referred to. And like the private version of the traditional gothic romance, they depend for their effects on the revitalization of ethics as a set of mental categories, and on the reinflation and artificial reinvigoration of that tired and antiquated binary opposition between virtue and vice, which the eighteenth century cleansed of its theological remnants and thoroughly sexualized before passing it on down to us.

The modern gothic, in other words – whether in its rape-victim or its political-paranoid forms – depends absolutely in its central operation on the construction of *evil* (forms of the good are notoriously more difficult to construct, and generally draw their light from the darker concept, as though the sun drew its reflected radiance from the moon). Evil is here, however, the emptiest form of sheer Otherness (into which any type of social content can be poured at will). I have so often been taken to task for my arguments against ethics (in politics as well as in aesthetics) that it seems worth observing in passing that Otherness is a very dangerous category, one we are well off without; but fortunately, in literature and culture, it has also become a very tedious one. Ridley Scott's *Alien* may still get away with it (but then, for science fiction, all of Lem's work – in particular the recent *Fiasco* – can be read as an argument against the use of such a category even there); but surely Ray of *Something Wild* and Frank Booth of *Blue Velvet* don't scare anybody any longer; nor ought we really to require our flesh to creep before reaching a sober and political decision as to the people and forces who are collectively 'evil' in our contemporary world.

On the other hand, it is only fair to say that Ray is not staged demonically, as a representation of evil as such, but rather as the representation of someone *playing at being evil*, which is a rather different matter. Nothing about Ray, indeed, is particularly authentic; his malevolence is as false as his smile; but his clothes and hairstyle give a further clue and point us in a different direction from the ethical one. For not only does Ray offer a simulation of evil, he also offers a simulation of the *fifties*, and that seems to me a far more significant matter. I speak of the oppositional fifties, to be sure: the fifties of Elvis rather than the fifties of Ike, but I'm not sure we can really tell the difference any more, as we peer across our historical gap and try to focus the landscape of the past through nostalgia-tinted spectacles.

At this point, however, the gothic trappings of *Something Wild* fall away and it becomes clear that we have to do here with an essentially allegorical narrative in which the 1980s meet the 1950s. What kind of accounts actuality has to settle with this particular historicist ghost (and whether it manages to do so) is for the moment less crucial than how the encounter was arranged in the first place: by the intermediary and the good offices of the 1960s, of course – inadvertent good offices to be sure, since Audrey/Lulu has very little reason to desire the connection, or even to be reminded of her own past, or Ray's (he has just come out of prison).

Everything turns, therefore, or so one would think, on this distinction between the sixties and the fifties: the first desirable (like a fascinating woman), the second fearful and ominous, untrustworthy (like the leader of a motorcycle gang). As the title suggests, it is the nature of 'something wild' which is at stake, the inquiry into it focused by Audrey's first glimpse of Charley's nonconformist character (he skips out on his lunch bill). Indeed, the nonpaying of bills seems to function as the principal index for Charley's 'hipness' or 'squareness' – it being understood that neither of these categories (nor those of conformity/ nonconformity used above) corresponds to the logic of this film, which can be seen as an attempt very precisely to construct new categories with which to replace those older, historically dated and period-bound (uncontemporary, unpostmodern) ones. We may describe this particular 'test' as involving white-collar crime, as opposed to the 'real', or lower-class, crime – grand theft and mayhem – practiced by Ray himself. Only it is a petit-bourgeois white-collar crime (even Charley's illicit use of company credit cards is scarcely commensurable with the genuine criminality his corporation can be expected, virtually by definition, to imply). Nor are such class markers present in the film itself, which can in another sense be seen very precisely as an effort to repress the language and categories of class and class differentiation and to substitute for them other kinds of semic oppositions still to be invented.

Those necessarily emerge in the framework of the Lulu character, within the sixties allegory (which is something like the 'black box' of this particular semic transformation). The fifties stands for genuine rebellion, with genuine violence and genuine consequences, but also for the *romantic representations* of such rebellion, in the films of Brando and James Dean. Ray thus functions both as a kind of gothic villain, within this particular narrative, and also, on the allegorical level, as the sheer *idea* of the romantic hero – the tragic protagonist of another kind of film, that can no longer be made. Lulu is not herself an alternate possibility, unlike the heroine of *Desperately Seeking Susan*. The framework here remains exclusively male, as the lamentable ending – her chastening, or taming – testifies, along with the significance of clothing, which we will look at in a moment. Everything depends, therefore, on the new kind of *hero* Lulu somehow allows or enables. Charley to become, by virtue of her own semic composition (since she is a good deal more than a mere woman's body or fetish).

What is interesting about that composition is that it first of all gives us the sixties seen, as it were, through the fifties (or the eighties?): alcohol rather than drugs. The schizophrenic, drug-cultural side of the sixties is here systematically excluded along with its politics. What is dangerous, in other words, is not Lulu at her most frenzied but rather Ray; not the sixties and its countercultures and 'life-styles' but the fifties and its revolts. Yet the continuity between the fifties and the sixties lay in what was being revolted *against*, in what life-style the 'new' life-styles were alternatives *to*. It is, however, difficult to find any content in Lulu's stimulating behavior, which seems organized around sheer caprice; that is to say, around the supreme value of remaining unpredictable and immune to reification and categorization … The costume changes lend this otherwise purely formal unpredictability a certain visual content; they translate it into the language of image culture and afford a purely specular pleasure in Lulu's metamorphoses (which are not really psychic).

Yet viewers and protagonist still have to feel that they are on their way somewhere (at least until the appearance of Ray gives the film a different kind of direction): as thrilling and improvised as it seems, therefore, Lulu's abduction of Charley from New York has at least an empty form that will be instructive, for it is the archetypal descent into Middle America, into the 'real' United States, either of lynching and bigotry or of true, wholesome family life and American ideals; one doesn't quite know which. Nonetheless, like those Russian populist intellectuals in the nineteenth century setting forth on foot to discover 'the people', something like this journey is or was the *scène à faire* for any American allegory worthy of its vocation: what this one reveals, however, is that there is no longer anything to discover at the end of the line. For Lulu/Audrey's family – reduced in this case to a mother – is no longer the bourgeoisie of sinister memory: neither the sexual repression and respectability of the fifties nor the Johnsonian authoritarianism of the sixties. This mother plays the harpsichord, 'understands' her daughter, and is fully as much an oddball as everybody else. No Oedipal revolts are possible any longer in this American small town, and with them all the tension goes out of the social and cultural dynamics of the period. Yet if there are no longer any 'middle classes' to be found in the heartland, there is something else that may serve as something for a substitute for them, at least in the dynamic of narrative structure itself: for what we find at Lulu's class reunion (besides Ray and her own past) is Charley's business colleague, that is to say, a yuppie bureaucrat, along with his pregnant wife. These are unquestionably the baleful parents we sought, but of some distant and not quite imaginable future, not of the older, traditional American past: they occupy the semic slot of the 'squares', but without any social basis or content any longer (they can scarcely be read as embodiments of the Protestant ethic, for example, or of puritanism or white racism or patriarchy). But they at least help us to identify the deeper ideological purpose of this film, which is to differentiate Charley from his fellow yuppies by making him over into a hero or protagonist of a different generic type than Ray. Unpredictability, as we have shown, is a matter of *fashion* (clothing, hairstyle, and general body language): Charley himself must therefore pass through this particular matrix, and his metamorphosis is concretely realized, appropriately enough, when he sheds his suit for a more relaxed and tourist-type disguise (T-shirt, shorts, dark glasses, etc.). At the end of the film, of course, he also sheds his corporate job; but it would probably be asking too much to wonder what he does or can become in its stead, except in the 'relationship' itself, where he becomes the master and the senior partner ...

... *Blue Velvet* ... tries to place sadomasochism squarely on the mass-cultural map with an earnestness altogether lacking in the Demme movie (whose handcuff love scene is as sexy as it is 'frivolous'). S&M thus becomes the latest and the last in the long line of those taboo forms of content which, beginning with Nabokov's nymphets in the 1950s, rise one after the other to the surface of public art in that successive and even progressive widening of transgressions which we once called the counterculture, or the sixties. In *Blue Velvet*, however, it is explicitly related to drugs, and therefore to crime – although not exactly organized crime, rather to a collectivity of misfits and oddballs – the transgressive nature of this complex of things being tediously reinforced by repetitive obscenity (on the part of the Dennis Hopper character).

Yet if history is discreetly evoked and invoked in *Something Wild*, it is rather its opposite – Nature – which is given us as the overall frame and inhuman, transhuman perspective in which to contemplate the events of *Blue Velvet*. The father's stroke, which opens the film like an incomprehensible catastrophe ... is itself positioned by David Lynch (director of *Eraserhead* and *Dune*) within the more science fictional horizon of the Darwinian violence of all nature. From the shot of the father lying paralyzed, the camera withdraws into the bushes surrounding the house, enlarging its microscopic focus as it does so, until we confront a horrible churning which we take first and generically, in good horror-film format, to be the hidden presence of the maniac, until it proves to be the mandibles of an insatiable insect. The later insistence on robins with worms twisting desperately in their beaks also reinforces this cosmic sense of the dizzying and nauseating violence of all nature – as though within this ferocity without boundaries, this ceaseless bloodshed of the universe as far as the eye can see or thought can reach, a single peaceful oasis had been conquered by the progress of humanity and whatever divine providence guided it; namely – unique in the animal kingdom as well as in the horrors of human history as well – the North American small town. Into this precious and fragile conquest of civilized decorum wrenched from a menacing outside world, then, comes violence – in the form of a severed ear; in the form of an underground drug culture and of a sadomasochism about which it is finally not yet really clear whether it is a pleasure or a duty, a matter of sexual gratification or just another way of expressing yourself.

History therefore enters *Blue Velvet* in the form of ideology, if not of myth: the Garden and the Fall, American exceptionalism, a small town far more lovingly preserved in its details like a simulacrum or Disneyland under glass somewhere than anything the protagonists of *Something Wild* were able to locate on their travels, complete with high-school leads on the order of the most authentic fifties movies. Even a fifties-style pop psychoanalysis can be invoked around this fairy tale, since besides a mythic and sociobiological perspective of the violence of nature, the film's events are also framed by the crisis in the paternal function – the stroke that suspends paternal power and authority in the opening sequence, the recovery of the father and his return from the hospital in the idyllic final scene. That the other father is a police detective lends a certain plausibility to this kind of interpretation, which is also strengthened by the abduction and torture of the third, absent, father, of whom we only see the ear. Nonetheless the message is not particularly patriarchal-authoritarian, particularly since the young hero manages to assume the paternal function very handily: rather, this particular call for a return to the fifties coats the pill by insistence on the unobtrusive benevolence of all these fathers – and, contrariwise, on the unalloyed nastiness of their opposite number.

For this gothic subverts itself fully as much as *Something Wild*, but in a rather different way. There, it was the simulated nature of Ray's evil that was underscored for us even while he remained a real threat: revolt, statutory illegality, physical violence, and ex-convicts are all genuine and serious matters. What *Blue Velvet* gives us to understand about the sixties, in contrast, is that despite the grotesque and horrendous tableaux of maimed bodies, this kind of evil is more distasteful than it is fearful, more disgusting than threatening: here evil has finally become an image, and the simulated replay of the fifties has generalized itself into a whole simulacrum in its own right. Now the boy without fear of the fairy tale can set out to undo this world of baleful enchantment, free its princess (while marrying another), and kill the magician. The lesson implied by all this – which is rather different from the lesson it transmits – is that it is better to fight drugs by portraying them as vicious and silly, than by awakening the full tonal range of ethical judgments and indignations and thereby endowing them with the otherwise glamorous prestige of genuine Evil, of the Transgressive in its most august religious majesty. Indeed, this particular parable of the end of the sixties is also, on another metacritical level, a parable of the end of theories of transgression as well, which so fascinated that whole period and its intellectuals. The S&M materials, then – even though contemporary with a whole new postmodern punk scene – are finally called on to undo themselves and to abolish the very logic on which their attraction/repulsion was based in the first place.

Thus these films can be read as dual symptoms: they show a collective unconscious in the process of trying to identify its own present at the same time that they illuminate the failure of this attempt, which seems to reduce itself to the recombination of various stereotypes of the past. Perhaps, indeed, what follows upon a strongly generational self-consciousness, such as what the 'people of the sixties' felt, is often a peculiar aimlessness. What if the crucial identifying feature of the next 'decade' is, for example, a lack of just such strong self-consciousness, which is to say a constitutive lack of identity in the first place? This is what many of us felt about the seventies, whose specificity seemed most of the time to consist in having no specificity, particularly after the uniqueness of the preceding period. Things began to pick up again in the eighties, and in a variety of ways. But the identity process is not a cyclical one, and this is essentially the dilemma. Of the eighties, as against the seventies, one could say that there were new political straws in the wind, that things were moving again, that some impossible 'return of the sixties' seemed to be in the air and in the ground. But the eighties, politically and otherwise, have not really resembled the sixties, especially, particularly if one tried to define them as a return or a reversion. Even that enabling costume-party self-deception of which Marx spoke – the wearing of the costumes of the great moments of the past – is no longer on the cards in an ahistorical period of history. The generational *combinatoire* thus seems to have broken down at the moment it confronted serious historicity, and the rather different self-concept of 'postmodernism' has taken its place.

Dick used science fiction to see his present as (past) history; the classical nostalgia film, while evading its present altogether, registered its historicist deficiency by losing itself in mesmerized fascination in lavish images of specific generational pasts. The two 1986 movies, while scarcely pioneering a wholly new form (or mode of historicity), nonetheless seem, in their allegorical complexity, to mark the end of that and the now open space for something else.

ANNOTATED BIBLIOGRAPHY

Amiram, Eyal, and John Unsworth, eds. *Essays in Postmodern Culture*. New York, 1993.
Interdisciplinary in nature and drawing on a range of theoretical models, the essays in this collection are drawn from the journal *Postmodern Culture*, which first existed as an on-line journal, one of the first of its kind. The essays address the politics of post-modernism through various manifestations of postmodern culture in art, disease, literature, cyborgs, hypertexts, cities and the body, while also discussing issues of representation and history in postmodern culture.

Appignanesi, Lisa, ed. *Postmodernism: ICA Documents*. London, 1989.
A collection of essays, documents and interviews drawn from events held at the Institute of Contemporary Arts, London. The various documents discuss the postmo-dern relation to epistemology, the arts and architecture, television, the sublime and popular culture. Contributors to this highly useful collection include Jean-François Lyotard, Philippe Lacoue-Labarthe and Jacques Derrida.

Baudrillard, Jean. *Jean Baudrillard: Selected Writings*, ed. Mark Poster. Stanford, CA, 1988.
A thought-provoking collection of essays drawn from the range of Baudrillard's publications. Essay topics include advertising and commodity culture, as well as simulation and desire. Baudrillard's writing presents a sustained critique of cultural production in western society through an understanding of the ways in which human subjectivity has come to be defined by the flow of commodified images as part of a larger 'hyperreality'.

Jameson, Fredric. *Postmodernism, or the Cultural Logic of Late Capitalism*. London, 1991.
From the Hegelian high-ground of his politicised discourse, Jameson pursues the concept of the postmodern and its various definitions through a variety of discourses and disciplines, such as architecture, film studies, literature, literary theory, cultural studies and economics. His discussions include considerations of video as the 'dominant form' of postmodern art, the disappearance of the subject, space and nostalgia, as these inform and are transformed by the narratives of the postmodern. The volume turns, as

Jameson puts it, on four themes: interpretation, Utopia, survivals of the modern, and 'returns of the repressed' of historicity.

Lyotard, Jean-François. *The Postmodern Condition: A Report on Knowledge*, trans. Geoff Bennington and Brian Massumi. Foreword Fredric Jameson. Minneapolis, MN, 1984.

Lyotard defines the object of his study as 'the condition of knowledge in the most highly developed societies', and gives the name *postmodern* to that condition. He examines how the grand narratives of modernism have collapsed and given way to flows of information and knowledge controlled by science and technology, and by their self-legitimating discourses in the contemporary moment of advanced industrial societies. Lyotard proposes a 'technocracy', which determines the social form of knowledge, and questions this through the consideration of narrative and scientific knowledge, the nature of research and education, and issues of legitimation and delegitimation.

SUPPLEMENTARY BIBLIOGRAPHY

Amiram, Eyal and John Unsworth, eds. *Essays in Postmodern Culture*. Oxford, 1993.
Appiah, Kwame Anthony. 'Is the Post- in Postmodernism the Post- in Post-Colonial?', *Critical Inquiry*, 17, Winter 1991.
Appignanesi, Lisa, ed. *Postmodernism: ICA Documents*. London, 1989.
Baudrillard, Jean. *The Mirror of Production*, trans. Mark Poster. New York. 1975.
————. *Simulations*, trans. Paul Foss, Paul Patton and Philip Beitchman. New York, 1983.
————. *America*, trans. Chris Turner. London, 1988.
————. *Cool Memories*, trans. Chris Turner. London, 1990.
————. *The Perfect Crime*, trans. Chris Turner. London, 1996.
Bauman, Zygmunt. *Postmodern Ethics*. Oxford, 1993.
Bewes, Timothy. *Cynicism and Postmodernity*. London, 1997.
Connor, Steven. *Postmodern Culture: An Introduction to the Theories of the Contemporary*. Oxford, 1989.
Currie, Mark. *Postmodern Narrative Theory*. Basingstoke, 1998.
Debord, Guy. *The Society of the Spectacle*. Detroit, MI, 1967.
Dellamora, Richard, ed. *Postmodern Apocalypse: Theory and Cultural Practice at the End*. Philadelphia, 1996.
Durham, Scott. *Phantom Communities: The Simulacrum and the Limits of Postmodernism*. Stanford, CA, 1998.
Eagleton, Terry. 'Capitalism, Modernism and Postmodernism', *New Left Review*, 152, July/August 1985.
Ebert, Teresa L. *Ludic Feminism and After: Postmodernism, Desire, and Labor in Late Capitalism*. Ann Arbor, MI, 1996.
Elam, Diane. *Romancing the Postmodern*. New York, 1992.
Elliott, Anthony. *Subject to Ourselves: Social Theory, Psychoanalysis and Postmodernity*. Cambridge, 1996.
Foster, Hal, ed. *Postmodern Culture*. London, 1985.
Gregson, Ian. *Contemporary Poetry and Postmodernism: Dialogue and Estrangement*. Basingstoke, 1996.

Halberstam, Judith and Ira Livingston, eds. *Posthuman Bodies*. Bloomington, IN, 1995.

Harvey, David. *The Condition of Postmodernity*. Oxford, 1989.

Hutcheon, Linda. *A Poetics of Postmodernism: History, Theory, Fiction*. New York, 1988.

——. *The Politics of Postmodernism*. London, 1993.

Jameson, Fredric. *Postmodernism or, The Cultural Logic of Late Capitalism*. London, 1991.

Kellner, Douglas. *Jean Baudrillard: From Marxism to Postmodernism and Beyond*. Stanford, CA, 1989.

Lyotard, Jean-François. *The Postmodern Condition: A Report on Knowledge*, trans. Geoff Bennington and Brian Massumi, foreword Fredric Jameson. Minneapolis, MN 1979.

——. *The Postmodern Explained*, trans. Don Barry et al., eds Julian Pefanis and Morgan Thomas, afterword Wlad Godzich. Minneapolis, MN, 1992.

McHale, Brian. *Postmodernist Fiction*. New York, 1987.

Moi, Toril. 'Feminism, Postmodernism, and Style: Recent Feminist Criticism in the United States', *Cultural Critique*, 9, Spring 1988.

Norris, Christopher. *What's Wrong with Postmodernism: Critical Theory and the Ends of Philosophy*. Baltimore, MD, 1990.

——. *The Truth About Postmodernism*. Oxford, 1993.

Smith, Bruce Gregory. *Nietzsche, Heidegger, and the Transition to Postmodernity*. Chicago, 1996.

Soja, Edward. *Postmodern Geographies*. London, 1989.

PART 9
NEW HISTORICISM

INTRODUCTION:
HISTORY, POWER AND POLITICS
IN THE LITERARY ARTIFACT

John Brannigan

THE HISTORY AND THEORY OF THE NEW HISTORICISM

In the late 1970s and early 1980s literary critics seemed to become more interested in the relationship between literature and history. In Britain and the USA the contents of literary journals, the subject of critical books, university courses and the titles of academic conferences were reflecting a growing interest in examining how literature reflected, shaped and represented history. Although feminist, Marxist and postcolonial critics were at the forefront of this development in literary criticism, it was a group of American critics known as the new historicists who were responsible chiefly for the prominence of historicist approaches to literature in the 1980s and 1990s. Where many previous critical approaches to literary texts assumed that texts had some universal significance and essential ahistorical truth to impart, new historicist critics tended to read literary texts as material products of specific historical conditions. New historicism approached the relationship between text and context with an urgent attention to the political ramifications of literary interpretation. In the eyes of new historicist critics, texts of all kinds are the vehicles of politics insofar as texts mediate the fabric of social, political and cultural formations. This view is evident in the work of new historicist critics who read historical context through legal, medical and penal documents, anecdotes, travel writings, ethnological and anthropological narratives and, of course, literary texts.

An important realisation of the new historicism is that literature and history are inseparable. History is not a coherent body of objective knowledge which can simply be applied to a literary text in order to discover what the text does or does not reflect. Literature is a vehicle for the representation of history, and it does contain insights into the formation of historical moments. It reveals the processes and tensions by which historical change comes about. But it does not behave passively towards history; it does not, in other words, reflect history as a mirror. Literature shapes and constitutes historical change. Literary texts can have effects on the course of history, on the social and political ideas and beliefs of their time. For new historicism the object of study is not the text and its context, not literature and its history, but rather literature *in* history. This is to see literature as a constitutive and inseparable part of history in the making, and therefore rife with the creative forces, disruptions and contradictions, of history.

The issues with which new historicist critics are most concerned are the role of historical context in interpreting literary texts and the role of literary rhetoric in mediating history. Louis Montrose argued that the key concern of new historicist critics was 'the historicity of texts and the textuality of history'. He explained that by 'the historicity of texts' he meant that all texts were embedded in specific social and cultural contexts, and by 'the textuality of history' he meant that all of our knowledge and understanding of the past could only exist through the 'surviving textual traces of the society in question', the very survival of which suggested that they were subject to 'complex and subtle social processes of preservation and effacement' (Montrose, in Veeser, 1989, 20). Literature and history, in Montrose's view, were fully interdependent, and no knowledge existed outside of the realms of narrative, writing or discourse.

The work of these critics follows from, and develops further, the interests and beliefs of previous generations of Marxist and historicist critics who re-evaluated the stories that past societies had told of themselves. Historicist critics introduced a degree of scepticism concerning the construction of historical narratives, and the place of the critic or historian within those narratives. Historicism understands the stories of the past as society's way of constructing a narrative which unconsciously fits its own interests. Marxist critics, borrowing from the lessons of historicism, see history as the procession of stories favourable to the victor, the ruling class, with literary texts as much as historical texts taking part in that procession. On a simple level Marxism fractures the idea that history is singular and universal by positing that all history is rife with class struggle, in which the interests of the dominant economic group are represented as the interests of society in general while the interests of the proletariat, those who sell their labour for wages, are not represented, or are represented as those of a particular minority. One direct consequence of this view is evident in the work of Marxist historians who have revisited conventional accounts of the past with a view to telling stories of how the working or labouring classes lived. New historicists have followed a somewhat similar path in revisiting the literature of the past in order to tell stories about women, the colonised, the insane, the heretics and the persecuted. There is a significant difference between the work of Marxists and new historicists, however. Marxists tend to think of their critical practice as, in some ways, emancipatory, of liberating the story of the oppressed from being lost to history. New historicists return to stories of the oppressed only in order to discover how these stories mark the effectiveness of the apparatus of oppression.

Gallagher's essay on the relationship between Marxism and new historicism traces the history of left-wing criticism in the US, and in particular the debt of new historicist critics to the radical campaigns of the new left in the 1960s and early 1970s. She situates the new historicism within left-wing criticism, despite the problems which Marxists have with the political quietism of new historicist practice. Gallagher explains the evolution of the central concerns and characteristics of new historicism from the influences of Marxism, feminism and deconstruction on literary studies, and defends the reasons why new historicists found themselves in the position whereby 'we could neither renew our faith in Marxism nor convert to deconstruction'. The questions with which she follows this defence indicate the differences between new historicism and the political agendas of other literary theories:

> Was it possible, we asked, that certain forms of subjectivity that felt oppositional were really a means by which power relations were maintained? Was a politics organized by the discourse of liberation inevitably caught inside modern America's terms of power? Was it theoretically possible even to differentiate the individual subject from a system of power relationships?

In part, new historicism is an analysis of the failure of the left-wing politics of student radicalism in the 1960s and 1970s to instigate social and political change, hence the questions which Gallagher asks all suggest the bewilderment of someone disillusioned by the rhetoric of oppositionality, liberation and individual subjectivity. The answers to these questions are all gloomy, from the point of view of an emancipatory practice: certain forms of 'oppositional' subjectivity do help to sustain power relations, discourses of liberation were indeed informed by and trapped within America's 'terms of power', and no, it was not possible to distinguish the individual subject from power relationships.

Gallagher suggests some ways in which new historicism is a direct challenge to some comfortable illusions of contemporary literary studies – various notions of the political and ideological imports of literature – and she defends new historicism against its detractors. She attempts to rescue it from the charge of being complicit in the power relationships it describes by arguing that it is instrumental in introducing to the classroom a whole range of non-canonical texts and compelling political issues. She fails to address the most serious concern of left-wing opponents of the new historicism, however, which is the political import of what it teaches students. In ranging through the history of western imperialism and the ideological discourses of gender oppression, new historicism teaches students that resistance plays clumsily and helplessly into the hands of existing power relationships, that struggle is merely the most visible sign of co-option, and that power seeps into every facet of routine, daily life. Moreover, by refusing to define the location or specific, localisable nature of power relationships, and by insisting 'that power cannot be equated with economic or state power', new historicists might also be accused of going beyond deflating the utopian project of Marxism to embracing the politics of conservatism.

For new historicists, literary texts have specific functions within a network of power relations in society. Literature can serve to persuade us of the justice of particular causes, or can police the dominant ideas of a particular time by representing alternatives or deviations as threatening. In Shakespeare's time, for example, the idea prevailed that the ruling order was sanctioned by religious providentialism, and it was maintained by a wide range of representations which formed a consensual discourse, of which literary texts were a part. In our own time, the idea that individuals should be free to choose between competing products and services is widely accepted as of universal benefit, and this is maintained by representations as diverse as television advertisements, legal documents, literary texts and company reports. These representations serve to ratify the existing social order, by participating in a consensus which marginalises or alienates any form of dissent from the social order.

New historicists were influenced by Claude Lévi-Strauss's recognition that culture is a self-regulating system, just like language, and that a culture polices its own customs and practices in subtle and ideological ways, as they were influenced also by the anthropological studies of cultural systems by Clifford Geertz and Abner Cohen. For new historicists this recognition has been extended to the 'self', particularly in Stephen Greenblatt's early and seminal study, *Renaissance Self-Fashioning*. What makes the operations of power particularly complex is the fact that the self polices and regulates its own desires and repressions. This removes the need for power to be repressive. No physical or military force need be deployed or exercised for power to have operated effectively in the interests of dominant ideological systems when the self, ideologically and linguistically constructed, will reproduce hegemonic operations. In this respect, representations and discourses are involved more heavily in policing and bolstering the authority of the social order than the physical or military apparatus of the state.

This kind of approach to literature did mark a significant turn away from the humanist idea that literature could teach human beings valuable lessons in moral and civil behaviour. New historicists replaced this notion of literature as the benevolent, kindly teacher with the view that literature was rather a loyal watchdog, patrolling the fences of a conservative social order. Shakespeare was not the teacher of morals, but the guardian of the state. To show this is the case, new historicist critics have examined the ways in which Shakespeare's plays performed vital roles in support of state and church ideologies. The Renaissance period, and Shakespeare in particular, has been an important object of study for new historicists, partly because it marks the beginnings of the modern era of history, but partly also because of the canonical status of Shakespeare and some of his contemporaries in twentieth-century literary studies. New historicists have sought to politicise Shakespeare, not least because this would reveal that even the most revered literature is implicated in the grubby business of power relations and state ideology.

THE CRITICAL PRACTICE OF NEW HISTORICISM

New historicism emerged as a recognisable practice in 1980, when Greenblatt published *Renaissance Self-Fashioning* and Montrose published his essay, 'Eliza, Queene of Shepheardes', on state ideologies in Elizabethan pastoral forms, both of which are seminal works in the formation of a distinct critical practice. Greenblatt gave this critical practice the name of 'new historicism' in 1982, although he later claimed that he was amazed at how the name acquired currency. There are significant differences between the various new historicist critics in how they read literature in relation to history, and in how they see literature behaving towards and within the social order. Stephen Greenblatt, Louis Montrose, Catherine Gallagher, D. A. Miller, Joel Fineman and Walter Benn Michaels have all pursued very different critical approaches and focused on different themes and interests. But they do share common practices and assumptions, particularly concerning methodological issues and the nature of power relations. They had succeeded in drawing attention to a turn towards history in literary studies, and, although many of them were not always comfortable with the label 'new historicism', they shared some common theoretical assumptions which made them identifiable loosely as a group. In his anthology of essays on the new historicism in 1989, H. Aram Veeser summarised these common assumptions as follows:

1. that every expressive act is embedded in a network of material practices;
2. that every act of unmasking, critique, and opposition uses the tools it condemns and risks falling prey to the practice it exposes;
3. that literary and non-literary 'texts' circulate inseparably;
4. that no discourse, imaginative or archival, gives access to unchanging truths nor expresses inalterable human nature;
5. finally ... that a critical method and a language adequate to describe culture under capitalism participate in the economy they describe.

(Veeser, 1989, xi)

Veeser's list of common theoretical assumptions is general enough, which is to say non-specific enough, to allow for the wide range of differences in new historicist ideas, practices and applications. These are the assumptions which underpin the thought and practice of new historicism, but they also share common strategies of reading and analysing texts. There are, in general, four characteristics which I want to suggest are common to new historicist critics. Firstly, new historicists tend to examine widely different texts in order to show that those texts play a key role in mediating power relations within the state. Secondly, they treat literary texts as inseparable from other texts and forms, and inseparable from the social and political contexts in which they are embedded. Thirdly, they share the view that literature, like other written sources, raises the possibility of subversion against the state only to contain, and make safe, that subversion. Fourthly, it is common to all new historicist analyses to study a range of texts in the same epoch, and to assume, or argue, that each epoch has its own mode of power.

We can examine how these reading strategies and theoretical assumptions work in the essay by Montrose extracted below. Louis Montrose's essay, '"Shaping Fantasies"', appeared in the second issue of *Representations*, the flagship journal of the new historicism which was launched in 1983. The subject of Montrose's essay is the construction of a powerful mythical identity for Elizabeth I through narratives and dramas which played out the 'shaping fantasies' of Elizabethan culture. Shakespeare's *A Midsummer Night's Dream* is the principal subject of Montrose's essay, but he also examines a dream recounted in the autobiography of Simon Forman, a popular Elizabethan medical guide, a colonial travel narrative by Sir Walter Raleigh and other travel tales of the Amazon. Montrose shows how these texts share common images, themes and metaphors which have a direct bearing on the representation of power in Elizabethan society. Although he devotes much of his discussion to Shakespeare's play, he does not privilege the play with greater insight or understanding of its time than the other texts. Nor is it any less implicated in political representations. Montrose examines Shakespeare's play in relation to these medical, colonial and travel narratives in order to explain how the persona of Elizabeth I was invented and disseminated. In this essay, then, literary texts and other texts are interdependent, and they are not only produced by social and political discourse, but are also in fact the makers of this discourse, as Montrose sees *A Midsummer Night's Dream* playing a vital role in shaping the cult of Elizabeth.

Shakespeare's play does so not at the behest, or under the express authority, of the Queen, for as Montrose argues 'the Queen was as much the creature of her image as she was its creator ... her power to fashion her own strategies was itself fashioned by her culture and constrained within its mental horizon'. Subjectivity is shaped by power relations as much as it has any effect on their outcome. Montrose's conception of the relationship between power and subversion is slightly more complex than that of Stephen Greenblatt. For Greenblatt, texts of all kinds offer us glimpses of subversion, but only in order to contain subversive elements effectively. Power requires the representation of subversion at some level in order to justify its own practices, and so subversion is always exposed only to be made safe. For Montrose, however, representations of Elizabethan forms of power are less effective in containing subversive possibilities than Greenblatt allows. Montrose shows that Elizabeth was precariously placed as a woman at the head of a strongly patriarchal society, and her power was then a series of contradictions and complications which had to be manipulated and managed, both on a bureaucratic and a symbolical level, in order to secure her interests as a flawless head of state. Shakespeare's play threatens to subvert the powerful image of the Queen as mother of the state by instating male prerogatives, and marks a point of transition in which the iconography of a virgin Queen as head of a patriarchal state begins to become precarious. Montrose entertains a more complex and inherently unstable notion of power than does Greenblatt or, indeed, D. A. Miller. On our final criterion, that each epoch is characterised by its own mode of power, this is true of Montrose's argument too. The subject of his analysis is the specific modes and media of power which shape the reign of Elizabeth I, and the texts which he analyses in relation to each other are all from that same epoch. This suggests that these texts, in circulation with each other at a particular time, come together to form a common discourse of power relations in that time. In suggesting that Shakespeare's play joined with others in the later decades of the sixteenth century to mark the growing instability of representations of the virgin Queen, Montrose is also indicating that there is soon to be a change of epoch, and with it new set of relations and modes of power.

We can compare the work of Montrose with D. A. Miller to see what new historicists share in common.[1] D. A. Miller's essay, 'Discipline in Different Voices', takes up Foucault's (and, less directly, Baudrillard's) interest in the carceral and looks at the way in which Dickens's *Bleak House* represents and makes visible the carceral in mid-nineteenth-century England. Miller's emphasis in this essay is on one novel, and therefore is not interested in tracing the shift in power relations or in the mode of representation of power through widely different texts and contexts, as is the common practice of Greenblatt and Montrose. The essay focuses almost exclusively on Dickens's novel alone, and therefore doesn't deal with a discursive formation constituted by several texts of various genres, as is evident in Montrose's essay. Miller's essay is then more of an application of a Foucauldian idea to a literary text than a genealogy of power.

Miller resembles Montrose in the sense that he treats literary texts as inseparable from their contexts and indeed the very idea that *Bleak House* acts as a vehicle for the carceral in Victorian Britain demonstrates his belief that literary texts are embedded in social and political discourses. According to Miller the novel has a precise function within these discourses, to comfort readers with the illusion of a difference between the penal or institutional space in which power acts repressively against individuals and the liberal society 'outside' which is free, private and safe, and is usually regarded as the home of the happy family. Although Miller makes no explicit comment on the possibilities of subversion in this society, it is implicit in his argument that power works through the medium of cultural forms like Dickens's novel in order to secure its own interests against subversion. *Bleak House*, he argues, serves to remind its readers and their families that outside the comfort and security of home awaits the violence of the prison, the workhouse and the mental hospital, and therefore warns against any disruption of the cosy economy and values of the home and the family. In a simplification of Foucauldian notions of the social function of the text, Miller argues that the novel bears a message for society to reform its institutions and for the family to avoid disruption and conflict. It is also clear in the essay that the relationship between the novel and the carceral is a product of the particular forms which both took in the Victorian period, and that this Victorian period therefore has its own particular mode of power. With the exception of the first of our criteria, Miller's essay broadly shares the characteristics of new historicist critical practice as defined above, and perhaps the most important similarity is that all regard literary texts, and texts of all kinds, as vehicles of power.

CRITICISMS AND PROBLEMS

If new historicism emerged in opposition to types of literary criticism and of historical investigation which failed to theorise cultural and historical differences in their own work, and failed to recognise the temporal and generic specificity of texts and events, new historicism was also subject to the same criticisms by the mid-1980s. From that time onwards, the criticisms of new historicism have proliferated and become stronger. In particular, these criticisms have focused on the new historicist tendency to reduce all representations of history to the same basic model of power relations, and the tendency to subject texts to a superficial and generalised reading, locating the ostensible positions of texts in the grid of discursive formations without interrogating the interpretability of those texts.

To take the first criticism, Carolyn Porter has articulated this particularly well in her article from 1988, 'Are we being historical yet?':

> New historicism projects a vision of history as an endless skein of cloth smocked in a complex, overall pattern by the needle and thread of Power. You need only pull the thread at one place to find it connected to another. (Porter, 1988, 765)

Porter argues that new historicism has succeeded in displacing the grand narrative of progress which dominated the old historicism, and indeed which shaped the development of empirical history, only to replace it with another grand narrative, that of power. Moreover, she suggests that the effect of this model of power relations in new historicism is to consider all historical events the subject of an elusive but generalised and universal condition of power. To Porter it seems ironic that a practice which claims to be historicising texts and events ends up making them the product of an ahistorical, universal and apparently omnipotent force. Frank Lentricchia attributes the centrality of this ill-defined and seemingly rampant and universal 'power' in new historicist analyses to the influence of Foucault, whose 'depressing message' of a power 'saturating all social relations to the point that all conflicts and "jostlings" among social groups become a mere show of political dissension' is repeated uncritically by the new historicists (Lentricchia, in Veeser, 1989, 235).

It is certainly the case that, whether examining pastoral poems in the Elizabethan period, confessions of an Italian heretic in the sixteenth century, the realist novel in Victorian England or the encounters between colonisers and natives in the New World, new historicists seem to find the same model, whereby power produces its own subversion in order to contain and control subversion more effectively. Power is everywhere, in every facet of western society and culture, but nowhere is it clear what power is, how it is made, where it fails or ends, what is outside of power, or even how power emerges. The new historicist conception of power is borrowed from Foucault's *History of Sexuality*, Volume One. Lentricchia's claim that it is accepted uncritically by the new historicists is shared by Lee Patterson, who sees the new historicist interest in circularity demonstrated in their critical practice when he writes: 'There is no space outside power because power is the only term in the analyst's arsenal' (Patterson, in Ryan, 1996, 96). Power is everywhere, because it is sought for everywhere, and at the same time it erases the specificity of the historical moment. Effectively, new historicism silences dissent and subversion, and eradicates difference, by looking only for power.

The second major criticism of new historicism is that it tends to subject texts to the most superficial and generalised readings as a result of an interest in the function rather than the interpretability of texts. If Louis Montrose can make texts of various genres, from medical to travel narratives, from a Shakespeare play to an essay justifying colonial expansion, perform the very same function in a general discourse, and make them repeat the same formulation, it is easy to see why new historicism has been criticised for a lack of sensitivity to the complexity of literary texts. When this criticism has been expressed by formalist critics we might choose to regard it as the result of an opposition to historical criticism. But when the deconstructionist critic J. Hillis Miller rebuked new historicism as 'an exhilarating experience of liberation from the obligation to read' (Miller, 1991, 313), as a flight of fancy away from an ethical obligation to the other, even to the otherness of the past, we may expect his opposition to be based on more than a desire to return to an ahistorical practical criticism. And when the historicist critic Kiernan Ryan argues that new historicism 'is undoubtedly the poorer for its reluctance to meet the complex demands of a text's diction and formal requirements' (Ryan, 1996, xviii), he does so from the desire to see a radical historical criticism which engages with the detail of the text in order to show even more clearly the historical and political implications and locations of the text.

We can trace the new historicist focus on the function of a text rather than its interpretability to Foucault. Foucault focuses on the position of texts and statements within discursive formations. Texts are, in Foucault's conception, pawns in the game of discursive transformations, and are therefore subject to an interrogation of what position they occupy, but not of what they mean. Foucault's archaeological analysis seeks to uncover the participation of texts and statements in discourse, not to scrutinise the varieties of meaning which may be produced from texts and statements. Reading the text is not, it seems, a necessary part of this process, and is certainly not as necessary as a knowledge of how texts connect with other texts, how the textuality of history forms a kind of discursive fabric. If new historicism fails to read literary texts, and seems to be completely insensitive to the differences between texts, between genres and indeed between textual and historical events, it is a product of following, perhaps too rigidly, the Foucauldian model of discursive analysis.

THE USES OF NEW HISTORICISM

Primarily through the work of new historicists, Foucault brought to the discipline of literary studies an emphasis on the function and condition of texts within a network of power relations, on the positions of subjectivity within those texts, and on the contests for meaning and control of meaning displayed in the reception and criticism of texts. New historicists have contributed to literary studies a close attention to the effects and functions of literature in history, and to how literature plays a part in constructing a society's sense of itself. As a critical practice, it is useful principally in showing how literary texts circulate with other texts in a particular period to construct and shape the power relations of that society. By adopting new historicist strategies, and abiding by its theoretical assumptions, we can explore the relationship between literature and colonialism, gender oppression, slavery, criminality or insanity. We can examine the degrees to which literature participates in forming the dominant ideological assumptions of a particular time.

Of course, new historicists differ on how we might do this. Miller adopts Foucault's writings on incarceration and discipline to reveal the part that Dickens's *Bleak House* plays in policing and disciplining mid-Victorian society. Montrose reconstructs a network of myths and writings of the Elizabethan period to show how these various texts circulated with each other to produce a discourse of Elizabethan power. In each case, the focus is the same – the relationship between literature and the power relations of the past. Miller's essay is simpler than Montrose's in that it tends towards a method of applying Foucault's ideas on the carceral and on discipline to a literary text in an attempt to show how penal discourses are refracted through the text. Montrose's method, on the other hand, juggles with a variety of literary genres to fashion a discourse of power, which itself is complex and fraught with contradictions and conflicts. Montrose shows how one text jars against another, producing the possibility of incoherence or instability, and explores the extents to which discourses of power are always shifting, insecure and rife with tensions.

These new historicist essays enable us to see how literary texts which may be read as entertainments, as character studies, or as complex, formal and linguistic structures, can also be read for their comprehension of cultural manifestations and mediations of power and political control. They are useful not in helping us to locate the the specific political position of a text, but in formulating the ways and means by which literature is complicit in the operations of power. New historicism is the most important indication of a turn to history in literary studies, and although it may be criticised for exercising a kind of violence to the specificity of historical events in constructing what appear to be seamless narratives of power through long periods of time, it is also responsible for revealing the capacity of literary texts as political acts or historical events. New historicist strategies of reading enable us to construct alternative political and historical stories out of the relationship between literature and other forms of representation, to fashion alternative histories of oppression and power through the surviving textual traces of the past.

NOTE

1. The editor of this volume and the compiler of this part had planned to include an extract from D. A. Miller's essay 'Discipline in Different Voices'. However, Professor Miller declined permission to reprint the extract unless the essay could be reproduced in full. In view of constraints on the size of this volume the essay is too long to be reproduced in full and unfortunately has had to be deleted.

9.1

MARXISM AND THE
NEW HISTORICISM

Catherine Gallagher

Critics of the 'new historicism' have given wildly different accounts of its political implications, but they generally agree that its politics are obnoxious. Charged on the one hand with being a crude version of Marxism and on the other with being a formalist equivalent of colonialism,[1] the new historicism attracts an unusual amount of specifically political criticism for a criticism whose politics are so difficult to specify. One could, of course, simply stand back, amused, and let the countervailing charges collide and explode each other, but one might also be curious about why a phenomenon of such apparent political indeterminacy should seem such a general political irritant.

There is no mystery about why the new historicism's politics should attract speculation. Although there has been a certain amount of controversy over just what the new historicism is, what constitutes its essence and what its accidents, most of its adherents and opponents would probably agree that it entails reading literary and nonliterary texts as constituents of historical discourses that are both inside and outside of texts and that its practitioners generally posit no fixed hierarchy of cause and effect as they trace the connections among texts, discourses, power, and the constitution of subjectivity. Since these are the issues new historicists study, it's hardly surprising that they have kindled speculation about their own discursive contexts, commitments to and negotiations of power, or the constitution of their historical subjectivity. Such speculation is obviously very much in the spirit of their own inquiries and can hardly be called impertinent or irrelevant.

Extract from *The New Historicism*, ed. H. Aram Veeser (Routledge, 1989), pp. 37–48.

However, the insistence on finding a *single*, unequivocal political meaning for this critical practice, indeed in some cases on reducing it to a politics or a relation to power, is puzzling and certainly runs counter to what seem to me to be new historicism's most valuable insights: that no cultural or critical practice is simply a politics in disguise, that such practices are seldom *intrinsically* either liberatory or oppressive, that they seldom contain their politics as an essence but rather occupy particular historical situations from which they enter into various exchanges, or negotiations, with practices designated 'political'. The search for the new historicism's political essence can be seen as a rejection of these insights. Critics on both the right and left seem offended by this refusal to grant that literature and, by extension, criticism either ideally transcend politics or simply are politics when properly decoded.

To ask what is the intrinsic political meaning or content of the new historicism, then, is to pose the question in terms that wipe out the assumptions on which many critics who are routinely called new historicists might base a reply. Consequently, the following remarks proceed from a different question: what are the historical situations of the new historicism and how have these defined the nature of its exchanges with explicitly political discourses?

Having formulated this more congenial question, I must at once admit my inability to answer it adequately. I have neither the space nor the knowledge to identify the situations and sources of such a vast and various phenomenon; I can only write from what may seem a highly unusual perspective, that of critics who have arrived at new historicist postions via continental Marxist theory and 1960s radical politics. Marxist critics[2] have themselves called attention to this filiation by accusing new historicists of 'left disillusionment'. Whereas I acknowledge the 'left' inspiration in the work of many new historicists, I disagree that 'disillusionment' intervened between our current work and our more 'optimistic' youth. I'll be arguing, on the contrary, that American radicalism of the sixties and early seventies bred just those preoccupations that have tended to separate new historicist from Marxist critics in the eighties and that the former preserve and continue, rather than react against, many of the characteristic tendencies of New Left thought. I'll be concentrating especially on new historicism's residual formalism, its problematization of representation, and its dual critique and historicization of the subject.

We should bear in mind that American left-wing literary critics had developed a strong, optimistic and politically problematic brand of formalism a generation before the New Left. In its most independent and intelligent sectors, the American left offered its children in the post-war years a politics that had already begun to transfer its hopes from the traditional agent of revolutionary change, the proletariat, to a variety of 'subversive' cultural practices, the most prominent of which was aesthetic modernism. The transferral had started in the earlier belief that modernism was a support for revolutionary social change of an anti-Stalinist kind; writers such as Philip Rahv, William Phillips, Dwight Macdonald, Harold Rosenberg, and Mary McCarthy, were reacting in the

1930s against the popular front for its Stalinism, its uncritical embrace of Democratic Party politics and its sentimental, traditional cultural nationalism. The very difficulty of modernist forms, they believed, cut against the grain of American conservatism. Hence we find Harold Rosenberg, for example, trying even in the 1940s to yoke the modern working class, modernist culture, traditionless America, and his own immigrant experience into one complex of radical forces. But the joining soon became a substitution of elements whereby cultural modernism and the rootless intellectual were increasingly valued as the privileged representations of latent and repressed social contradictions.

The generation of cultural critics that came of age in the 1960s, therefore, might have inherited a belief in the political efficacy of certain aesthetic forms, for left formalism had reached a high level of sophistication before the war. If these aspiring critics had then merely read the available continental Marxist aesthetic theory in the sixties and early seventies, they might have stayed very much within this legacy. The Marxist criticism that circulated most widely in those years tended to be the work of Western Marxists, especially Lukács and members of the Frankfurt School. From these sources one might have picked up a number of different critical orientations toward the dominant culture. For example, one would probably have learned that culture as a realm differentiated itself from the social whole during the period of bourgeois ascendancy for the purpose of creating false resolutions for social contradictions. Its function, according to this account, was to create a consciousness capable of at once acknowledging these contradictions and justifying them by ascribing them to any number of supra-social causes. The Marxist literary critic committed to this model of bourgeois culture saw her job as the undoing of the false resolution, the detection in the text of the original contradiction and the formal signs of its irresolvability. She believed that identifying such signs exposed the false ideological solution, that turning the text back on its moments of instability confronted the culture with things it could not stand to acknowledge.

Alternatively, to take another influential Western Marxist commonplace from that period, she might have viewed the bourgeois work of art's imperfect attempts at harmonious resolution as expressions of utopian hopes and hence as potential incitements to subversive realizations. To be sure, the job of the critic was still the exposure of the gap between conflict and resolution, for the reader must be made to understand that only action in the social world could resolve the conflict. Nevertheless, the imperfect formal reconciliation itself became in this view more than a functional component of bourgeois ideology; it became a disfunctional moment as well, a vision of fulfillment not yet achieved and hence a disturbance of the status quo.

A third strand of continental Marxist aesthetics, that of the Brecht revival of the late sixties, probably also had an effect on this generation of critics. Brechtian aesthetics emphasized, like the other available Marxisms, the role of culture and cultural analysis in exposing ideological contradictions. Among Brechtians, moreover, a critic with close ties to American Left formalism might have felt very much at home, since, despite serious political differences, both tendencies believed in the almost magical subversive power of modernist forms. But whether pro- or anti-modernist, whether cognitive or affective in its orientation, whether concentrating on critical or creative practice, the continental Marxist aesthetics that was being circulated in this country in the late sixties and early seventies tended to confirm the left formalist's belief in a privileged realm of representation and her optimism about the efficacy of exposing ideological contradictions.

Such confirmation, however, might easily have collided with the implied cultural and aesthetic assumptions of the life one was actually living in the late sixties. For this generation of critics was not just reading Marxist aesthetic theory produced decades earlier; many of its members were also living, reading, writing and acting the political culture of the New Left. And it is to that culture, inchoate as it was, that we should look for several important departures from what had been the influential Marxist models.

First, for a variety of reasons, the New Left dispensed with what we might call a politics of substitution that relied on a hierarchy of causation to determine just what the crucial contradictions were. Most obviously, the intellectual activist herself did not claim to stand or speak for some other oppressed group. New Left activists notoriously invoked the principle of individual and group liberation in justifying rebellion instead of invoking their connection to the objective interests of a universal class. In the 1940s, Harold Rosenberg had taken pains to show that the ideological crisis informing his own immigrant experience could be traced back, not just to other conflicts, but to the one conflict that counted: class conflict. In contrast, New Left intellectuals generally, avoided the implicit causal hierarchy of such analyses and their logic of substitution.

For example, in New Left rhetoric particular struggles were often joined to the general interest through a logic of decentered distribution, in which each group, in speaking for itself, spoke against a 'system' that was oppressing all. This was the case at the outset of the 'movement,' when middle-class, white, civil rights activists learned that they could not think of themselves as representing or even as altruistically aiding black people, for altruism implied condescension. Indeed, the roots of the movement in black civil rights struggles was no doubt a strong factor obviating the rhetoric of representation for white radicals,[3] who claimed instead to be freeing themselves from racism. And the avoidance of substitutional politics only increased as group after group claimed the legitimacy of action on its own behalf.

This is not to deny the importance of such slogans as 'serve the people' or the vehemence of New Left anti-middle-class sentiments. But the slogan, after all, only proves my general point: 'the people' was a category designed to include oneself and anyone else content to join a decentered coalition of disaffected groups. Certainly, solidarity was as important to the radicals of the sixties as it had been to those of the thirties, but the grounds of solidarity had shifted from an identification with a designated specific class to a recognition of shared oppressions that cut across class divisions. Moreover, 'serving the people' was often imagined to be a means of self-transformation, even the realization and liberation of self stifled by middle-class conventionality.

Thus, because of its sociological base in groups outside the organized traditional proletariat – its reliance on upwardly mobile sectors of racial minorities, women of all races, and college students in general – important segments of the New Left devised a profoundly anti-representational form of political activism. One no longer needed to justify her own cause by claiming that it ultimately substituted for the crucial cause, the cause of the universal class. Instead, one could believe that a number of local contests, a number of micro-contradictions, would condense into a systemic crisis, a revolutionary conjunction.

All of this has been said before, but its consequences for the budding cultural critic have generally not been remarked. First, it led to an emphasis, still very influential in 'oppositional' American criticism, on indeterminant negativity. It was no longer necessary, indeed it was impossible, to specify the inverse positive valence on every group's oppositional stance toward the 'system.' Indeed, in certain quarters, indeterminant negativity came to be seen as superior to positive programs because less liable to cooptation. Negativity and marginality became values in themselves.

Second, but perhaps more important for the future of literary studies in general, was simply the collapse of the logic of representation itself. There was no longer a privileged realm of representation any more than there was a privileged referent. Cultural activity itself in this context began discarding its claim to separate status; lived and symbolic experience were consciously merged in guerilla theater, in happenings, in attempts to live a radical culture. Everything was equally symbolic and immanent, readable and opaque, and something (unspecified) in excess of itself.

This, rather than continental Marxist theory, was the intellectual and political experience that prepared the way for the American reception of French post-structuralist thought in left-wing circles, where it was often filtered through an increasingly attenuated Althusserianism. For some, Althusserianism became a step toward re-Marxification, for others it was a step toward the deconstructive critique of representation. In either case it reformulated the problem of the constitution of the subject, giving it a new, linguistic emphasis. When this was then supplemented by Jacques Derrida's work, a method of analysis resulted that accorded with some aspects of New Left political thought and contravened others. Specifically, although Derridean critiques also decentered a 'system', collapsed the distinction between things and signs, and concentrated on the fungibility of a series of diacritical moments, they often defined the system as nothing but its diacritical moments and implied that those moments displace one another in an endless chain of signification instead of condensing in a revolutionary conjunction. What came to be called 'deconstruction', then, could be used both to confirm important New Left tenets and, at the very time when the movement was losing momentum, to provide an explanation for that loss.

Many of us, however, found that we could neither renew our faith in Marxism nor convert to deconstruction, for neither seemed sufficient to explain the permutations of our own historical subjectivities and our relationship to a system of power, which we still imagined as decentered, but which we no longer viewed as easily vulnerable to its own contradictions. At this juncture, the process that had begun when the hierarchy of contradictions was abandoned, the process of rethinking the relationship between power and apparently oppositional subjectivity, became exigent. This was not so much a process of disillusionment as it was an extension of our belief in the efficacy of combining personal and political self-reflection. Was it possible, we asked, that certain forms of subjectivity that felt oppositional were really a means by which power relations were maintained? Was a politics organized by the discourse of liberation inevitably caught inside modern America's terms of power? Was it theoretically possible even to differentiate the individual subject from a system of power relationships?

This sort of self-questioning had extensive left-wing credentials, not only in the works of Louis Althusser, but also in Herbert Marcuse's highly influential repressive desublimation thesis. Such self-questioning became all the more urgent as feminist self-consciousness spread among activists. Indeed, the women's liberation movement taught us several things that are apposite here. First, it forced us to see that the more 'personal' and 'mundane' the issues, the more resistance to change we encountered. We could achieve what at the time seemed virtual generational consensus for abolishing the draft, winning a strike, reorganizing a university, ending the war, and passing affirmative action laws. But there was no such consensus about sharing the housework, reorganizing childcare, exposing family violence, or ending exploitative sexual relations. In the early years of the women's liberation movement, we were repeatedly told that we were siphoning off energy from significant political activities and wasting it in trivial, personal confrontations. Of course, we took such resistance, including the very rhetoric of triviality, as a token of the radical significance of our movement. Finally, we thought, we had penetrated the deepest, least questioned and most inaccessible region of social formation: the formation of ourselves as gendered subjects.

Thus we went beyond dismantling the old hierarchy of significance and began erecting a new one in which those aspects of life whose continuity was assured by their classification under the category of the trivial came to seem the most important. But this lesson had a second implication as well; by focusing attention on our gendered individuation as the deepest moment of social oppression, some of us called into question the political reliability of our own subjectivity. We effectively collapsed the self/society division and began regarding our 'normal' consciousness and 'natural' inclinations as profoundly untrustworthy. We, along with our erstwhile political optimism, became for ourselves the objects of a hermenuetics of suspicion. We wondered at our pre-feminist radical consciousness, which had imagined social arrangements to be relatively fragile. Could the illusion of fragility maintained by a belief that the system could not bear an exposure of its contradictions be a functioning part of its endurance? This was not the end of politics for many of us, but it was the end of a naive faith in the transparency of our own political consciousness.

The women's liberation movement had a third relevant consequence. We became fascinated with the history of gender, of how things have changed and how they don't change. The work of the Annales school and other anthropologically inspired historians gave some methodological direction in the mid-seventies, and in those years Michel Foucault's work appeared, addressing exactly the issues that preoccupied us.

These were the seed years for the new historicist work that has been appearing in the eighties. In many ways this work has maintained New Left assumption about the sources, nature, and sites of social conflict and about the issue of representation. Instead of resubscribing, as some Marxist critics have, to a historical meta-narrative of class conflict, we have tended to insist that power cannot be equated with economic or state power, that its sites of activity, and hence of resistance, are also in the micro-politics of daily life. The traditionally important economic and political agents and events have been displaced or supplemented by people and phenomena that once seemed wholly insignificant, indeed outside of history: women, criminals, the insane, sexual practices and discourses, fairs, festivals, plays of all kinds. Just as in the sixties, the effort in the eighties has been to question and destabilize the distinctions between sign systems and things, the representation and the represented, history and text.

In all of these ways, much new historicist work can be said to possess a remarkable continuity with certain cultural assumptions of the New Left. But the work has also exposed and taken off from a number of contested moments within those assumptions, especially those regarding form and ideological contradiction. Despite the critique of substitutionalist politics and the supposed de-privileging of a realm of representation during the sixties and seventies, left formalism managed to thrive. In its Althusserian form, it tended, ironically, to reestablish many former Hegelian notions about the special status of art as a displayer of ideological contradictions. The art *form*, according to Althusser and Pierre Macherery, created internal distantiations which allow us to 'see' the gaps and fissures, the points of stress and incoherence, inside the dominant ideology. 'Seeing' was not to be confused with 'knowing'; nevertheless, Althusserian literary criticism in practice made very little of this distinction and proceeded as if form were in itself revelatory.[4] This did not entail the privileging of any particular form, but of all forms. It was against such claims for the automatic subversiveness of art, as well as parallel deconstructive claims for literature's self-referential and therefore anti-ideological rhetoricity, that many new historicists directed their critiques. Their effort was, and still is, to show that under certain historical circumstances, the display of ideological contradictions is completely consonant with the maintenance of oppressive social relations. New historicists were often bent on proving that the relationship between form and ideology was neither one of simple affirmation, in which form papers over ideological gaps, nor one of subversive negation, in which form exposes ideology and thereby helps render it powerless. The contribution of the new historicism has been to identify a third alternative in which the very antagonism between literature and ideology becomes, in specific historical environments, a powerful and socially functional mode of constructing subjectivity.

This could be seen as the final de-privileging of the realm of representation, the final blow to left formalism, and hence a further extension of a New Left tendency. But it is precisely this mode of construing the relationship between literature and ideology that other left-wing critics have found not only quietistic in its implications but also formalist[5] in its assumptions. I will treat the second of these charges first, since it seems to me undeniable. The actual procedures of many new historicist analyses are often not very different from those of left formalists. We too often take the text as a constant, the very instability of which is stable across time, so that its historical impact can be determined from an analysis of its structures and the logic of their disintegration when set against other discourses. Historical reception studies are sometimes suggested as an antidote to such formalism,[6] and, despite the fact that these often import their own epistemological naivete, they certainly deserve much more of our attention than they currently receive. However, there is no simple solution to the problem of formalism – one variant of the problem of textuality – in historical studies; we can only hope to maintain a productive tension between the textualist and historicist dimensions of our work.

The charge of quietism in response to attacks on left formalism returns us to the issue with which we began, the issue of the relationship between politics and criticism. To argue that it is inherently quietistic to deny literature an inherent politics is, first of all, to reason tautologically. Such reasoning begins with the assumption that everything has *a* politics; a denial of this assumption must also have *a* politics, no doubt reactionary. Such reasoning is impervious to evidence; the accusers need not do the difficult work of examining how critical orientations interact with specific political initiatives, even in the most immediate arena of academic politics. They need not ask, for example, what impact the new historicism has had on curricula in literature departments, whether or not it has had a role in introducing non-canonical texts into the classroom, or in making students of literature more aware of the history and significance of such phenomena as imperialism, slavery, and gender differentiation in western culture. It is my guess, although the evidence is yet to be gathered, that new historicists have been, along with Marxists and feminists, fairly active in achieving these goals, which are generally considered to be on the 'left' of the academic political spectrum.

All this is oddly irrelevant to critics of the new historicism on the left, while it forms the basis of political complaints coming from the right.[7] Left-wing critics would concede that new historicists often read the right texts and ask the right questions, but they complain that such readings yield the wrong answers. Specifically, they tend to complain that new historicists fail to emphasize that the text is a site of subversive potential and that the critic's job is to activate it.[8] They imply that the new historicist, in describing how texts may create modern subjectivity by playing the literary against the ideological, somehow becomes complicit in the process described.[9] There are many versions of this argument, some more persuasive than others, but they share a dismay at the new historicist's tendency to identify precisely the things in texts that had been named subversive, destabilizing, and self-distantiating, as inscriptions of the formative moments, not the disruptions, of the liberal subject. The negativity of literary culture is not denied but is rather re-presented as a potential basis of its positivity. Such a representation seems in itself quietistic to some critics because it apparently presents culture as achieving, through its very fracturing, an inescapable totalizing control. It could thus, the argument runs, convince people of the uselessness of opposition. And it certainly discredits the left-formalist assumptions that have underwritten much of this generation's emotional investment in the study of literature.

There is no doubt, then, that those new historicists who emphasize that modern subjectivity is subtended by what we might call a sub-tension pose a challenge to the usual methods of left-wing criticism. But it does not follow that this is a reactionary or quietistic challenge to the left. Indeed, one can find no more generally agreed-upon proposition in all sectors of literary criticism than the proposition that literature shakes us up and disturbs our moral equilibrium (liberal humanism), destabilizes the subject (deconstruction), and self-distantiates ideological formations (Marxism). New historicists find the terms of this consensus fascinating, and far from imagining that it has a politics, simply point to the ways in which it can take the place of many politics. As D. A. Miller has succinctly expressed it, 'even if it were true that literature exercises a destabilizing function in our culture, the current consensus that it does so does not' (1987, xi). By posing challenges to the left-wing version of this consensus, indeed by simply pointing out that there is such a consensus, new historicists on the left ask more traditional leftists to see how the 'subversion hypothesis', to use Miller's words again, 'tends to function within the overbearing cultural "mythologies" that will already have appropriated it.' This is not an attempt to demoralize the left, but it can be seen as an attempt to de-moralize our relationship to literature, to interrupt the moral narrative of literature's benign disruptions with which we soothe ourselves.

What is the political import of this interruption? It doesn't have *one*. Even if its political origins were wholly comprised in the history I have sketched – of course, they are not – its tendencies and potential affiliations are never fully determined. We can reasonably predict, however, that new historicism's most active interlocutors will continue to be Marxists and other 'oppositional' critics, and that the effects of their debate might be to alter long-standing critical procedures. For new historicism and Marxism are nudging one another toward previously undeveloped evidentiary bases for their conclusions and away from a belief in the self-consistency or constant 'difference' of the text over time that warrants deriving historical effect from formal features or 'rigorous' readings.

But we probably cannot predict a happy collaboration in the future, because some new historicists will continue to resist the goal of synthesizing their historical, literary critical, and political consciousnesses into one coherent entity. The new historicist, unlike the Marxist, is under no nominal compulsion to achieve consistency. She may even insist that historical curiosity can develop independently of political concerns; there may be no political impulse whatsoever behind her desire to historicize literature. This is not to claim that the desire for historical knowledge is itself historically unplaced or 'objective'; it is, rather, to insist that the impulses, norms, and standards of a discipline called history, which has achieved a high level of autonomy in the late twentieth century, are a profound part of the subjectivity of some scholars and do not in all cases require political ignition.

Moreover, even for those of us whose political and historical concerns quite clearly overlap, a perfect confluence between the two might arouse more suspicion than satisfaction, for what would such a confluence be based on but the myth of a self-consistent subject impervious to divisions of disciplinary boundaries and outside the constraints of disciplinary standards? The demands that one so often hears on the left for self-placement, for exposing the political bases of one's intellectual endeavors, for coming clean about one's political agenda, for reading and interpreting everything as a feminist or a Marxist or an anti-imperialist, for getting to and shoring up a solid political foundation for all of one's endeavors, demands often made in the name of historical self-consciousness, resound only in a historical vacuum, so deeply do they mistake the constitution of modern subjectivity.

One could retort, using the analyses of some new historicists, that this modern subject, whose supposed nonidentity often facilitates the circulation of disciplinary power, is precisely what needs to be overcome. Such a retort would temporarily reverse the positions of the interlocutors, for the people who call for a single political-historical-critical enterprise often celebrate the subversive potential of the nonidentical subject, while the new historicist finds herself insisting on the very nonidentity she has so often shown to be part of disciplinary processes. In doing so, however, new historicists have not claimed that the historical experience of nonidentity is merely chimerical and can be overcome by simply dismissing it as a literary effect underneath which some essential consistency can be unearthed. In fact, it does not follow from new historicist arguments either that the subject can or should be reconstituted on an identitarian model. Rather, the effort of this criticism has been to trace the creation of modern subjectivity in the necessary failures of the effort to produce a stable subject. It is difficult to see how attempts at producing stable critical subjects on a political model will escape repeating this circuit, will not result once again in an experience of decentered helplessness.

Of course, many of the points I'm making here come from inside the Marxist tradition; Lukács, Adorno, Althusser, indeed, Marx himself all warned against subordinating theory, critique, or historical scholarship to practical political goals. New historicism confronts Marxism now partly as an amplified record of Marxism's own edgiest, uneasiest voices. Those Marxists who listen carefully may hear many of their own unanswered doubts and questions. To dismiss such challenges as the mere echoes of a reactionary defeatism would be a serious mistake.

NOTES

1. For the former charge, see Edward Pechter (1987, 292–303); for the latter see Carolyn Porter, 'Are we Being Historical Yet?' ... (1990, 27–62). An argument similar to but less substantial and sophisticated than Porter's is made by Marguerite Waller (1987, 2–20). It must be noted that all of the above and most of the critics yet to be cited here focus their attacks on the work of Stephen Greenblatt. I've attempted in this article to discuss only those charges that seem to me applicable to other critics, outside the field of Renaissance literature, who are routinely called new historicists.
2. Carolyn Porter uses this term, quoting Walter Cohen (1987).
3. I am grateful to Houston Baker for this suggestion.
4. Michael Sprinker has recently explicated this distinction (1987, esp. 101–4 and 267–95).
5. On the issue of formalism, see Cohen (1987).
6. Both Porter and Cohen have made this suggestion.
7. According to David Brooks of *The Wall Street Journal*, the new historicism is a left-wing plot to destroy the canon and substitute a political agenda for a loving exploration of 'literary excellence': 'Annabel Patterson of Duke is typical. She uses Shakespeare, she says as a vehicle to illuminate the way 17th-century society mistreated women, the working class and minorities. This emphasis is called the New Historicism' (1988, 24, cols 3–5). And according to *Newsweek*, new historicism is one among many schools prescribing the study of books not because of their moral or esthetic value but because they permit the professor to advance a political, often Marxist agenda' (Lehman, 1988, 62). Frederick Crews, to whom these sentiments are attributed in the article, has energetically repudiated them in a letter to the editor, insisting that they are Lehman's own construction. There may be a certain amount of confusion evident in these mass-media attacks, but they are, in their own way, arguably accurate about the new historicism's usual affiliations in the overall politics of the discipline.
8. See both Cohen and Waller.
9. For the argument that new historicists themselves repeat the marginalization and/or containment of disruptive elements accomplished by the discursive practices they analyze, see Porter (1990), and Lynda Boose, 'The Family in Shakespeare Studies; or – Studies in the Family of Shakespeareans; or – The Politics of Politics', forthcoming in *Renaissance Quarterly*.

9.2

'SHAPING FANTASIES': FIGURATIONS OF GENDER AND POWER IN ELIZABETHAN CULTURE

Louis Adrian Montrose

I

... My intertextual study of Shakespeare's *Midsummer Night's Dream*[1] ... construes the play as calling attention to itself, not only as an end but also as a source of cultural production ... in writing of 'shaping fantasies', I mean to suggest the dialectical character of cultural representations: the fantasies by which the text of *A Midsummer Night's Dream* has been shaped are also those to which it gives shape. I explore this dialectic within a specifically Elizabethan context of cultural production: the interplay between representations of gender and power in a stratified society in which authority is everywhere invested in men – everywhere, that is, except at the top.

...

III

The beginning of *A Midsummer Night's Dream* coincides with the end of a struggle in which Theseus has been victorious over the Amazon warrior:

> Hippolyta, I woo'd thee with my sword,
> And won thy love doing thee injuries;
> But I will wed thee in another key,
> With pomp, with triumph, and with revelling.
>
> (1.1.16–19)

Extract from *Representations*, 2 (Spring 1983), pp. 61–94.

Descriptions of the Amazons are ubiquitous in Elizabethan texts ... The Amazons' penchant for male infanticide is complemented by their obvious delight in subjecting powerful heroes to their will ...

Sixteenth-century travel narratives often recreate the ancient Amazons of Scythia in South America or in Africa. Invariably, the Amazons are relocated just beyond the receding boundary of *terra incognita* ... [European] cultural fantasy assimilates Amazonian myth, witchcraft, and cannibalism into an anti-culture which precisely inverts European norms of political authority, sexual license, marriage practices, and inheritance rules. The attitude toward the Amazons expressed in such Renaissance texts is a mixture of fascination and horror. Amazonian mythology seems symbolically to embody and to control a collective anxiety about the power of the female not only to dominate or reject the male but to create and destroy him. It is an ironic acknowledgment by an androcentric culture of the degree to which men are in fact dependent upon women: upon mothers and nurses, for their birth and nurture; upon mistresses and wives, for the validation of their manhood.

Shakespeare engages his wedding play in a dialectic with this mythological formation. The Amazons have been defeated before the play begins; and nuptial rites are to be celebrated when it ends. *A Midsummer Night's Dream* focuses upon different crucial transitions in the male and female life cycles: the fairy plot, upon taking 'a little changeling boy' from childhood into youth, from the world of the mother into the world of the father; the Athenian plot, upon taking a maiden from youth into maturity, from the world of the father into the world of the husband. The pairing of the four Athenian lovers is made possible by the magical powers of Oberon and made lawful by the political authority of Theseus. Each of these rulers is preoccupied with the fulfillment of his own desires in the possession or repossession of a wife. Only after Hippolyta has been mastered by Theseus may marriage seal them 'in ever-lasting bond of fellowship' (1.1.85). And only after 'proud Titania' has been degraded by 'jealous Oberon' (2.1.60, 61), has 'in mild terms begg'd' (4.1.57) his patience, and has readily yielded the changeling boy to him, may they be 'new in amity' (4.1.86).

The diachronic structure of *A Midsummer Night's Dream* eventually re-stores the inverted Amazonian system of gender and nurture to a patriarchal norm. But the initial plans for Theseus' triumph are immediately interrupted by news of yet another unruly female. Egeus wishes to confront his daughter Hermia with two alternatives: absolute obedience to the paternal will, or death. Theseus intervenes with a third alternative: if she refuses to marry whom her father chooses, Hermia must submit

> Either to die the death or to abjure
> Forever the society of men.
> ...
> For aye to be in shady cloister mew'd,

Chanting faint hymns to the cold, fruitless moon.
Thrice blessed they that master so their blood
To undergo such maiden pilgrimage;
But earthlier happy is the rose distill'd
Than that which, withering on the virgin thorn,
Grows, lives, and dies, in single blessedness.

                                    (1.1.65–6, 71–8)

Theseus has characteristically Protestant notions about the virtue of virginity: maidenhood is a phase in the life-cycle of a woman who is destined for married chastity and motherhood. As a permanent state, 'single blessedness' is mere sterility. Theseus expands Hermia's options only in order to clarify her constraints. In the process of tempering the father's domestic tyranny, the Duke affirms his own interests and authority. He represents the life of a vestal as a *punishment*, and it is one that fits the nature of Hermia's crime. The maiden is surrounded by men, each of whom – as father, lover, or lord – claims a kind of property in her. Yet Hermia dares to suggest that she has a claim to property in herself: she refuses to 'yield [her] virgin patent up / Unto his lordship whose unwished yoke / [Her] soul consents not to give sovereignty' (1.1.80–2). Like Rosalind, in *As You Like It*, Hermia wishes the limited privilege of giving herself. Theseus appropriates the source of Hermia's fragile power: her ability to deny men access to her body. He usurps the power of virginity by imposing upon Hermia his own power to deny her the use of her body. If she will not submit to its use by her father and by Demetrius, she must 'abjure forever the society of men', and 'live a barren sister all [her] life' (1.1.65–6, 72). Her own words suggest that the female body is a supreme form of property and a locus for the contestation of authority. The self-possession of single blessedness is a form of power against which are opposed the marriage doctrines of Shakespeare's culture and the very form of his comedy.

In devising Hermia's punishment, Theseus appropriates and parodies the very condition which the Amazons sought to enjoy. They rejected marriages with men and alliances with patriarchal societies ... The separatism of the Amazons is a repudiation of men's claims to have property in women. But if Amazonian myth figures the inversionary claims of matriarchy, sisterhood, and the autonomy of women, it also figures the *repudiation* of those claims in the act of Amazonomachy ...

Shakespeare's play naturalizes Amazonomachy in the vicissitudes of courtship. Heterosexual desire disrupts the innocent pleasures of Hermia's girlhood: 'What graces in my love do dwell, / That he hath turn'd a heaven unto a hell!' (1.1.206–7). Hermia's farewell to Helena is also a farewell to their girlhood friendship, a delicate repudiation of youthful homophilia:

And in the wood, where often you and I
Upon faint primrose beds were wont to lie,
Emptying our bosoms of their counsel sweet,

> There my Lysander and myself shall meet;
> And thence from Athens turn away our eyes,
> To seek new friends, and stranger companies.
>
> (1.1.214–19)

Before dawn comes to the forest, the 'counsel' shared by Hermia and Helena, their 'sisters' vows ... school-days' friendship, childhood innocence' (3.2.198, 199, 202), have all been torn asunder, to be replaced at the end of the play by the primary demands and loyalties of wedlock. On the other hand, by dawn the hostilities between the two male youths have dissolved into 'gentle concord' (4.1.142). From the beginning of the play, the relationship between Lysander and Demetrius has been based upon aggressive rivalry for the same object of desire: first for Hermia, and then for Helena. Each youth must despise his previous mistress in order to adore the next; and a change in one's affections provokes a change in the other's ... the maidens remain constant to their men at the cost of inconstancy to each other. If Lysander and Demetrius are flagrantly inconstant to Hermia and Helena, the pattern of their inconstancies nevertheless keeps them constant to each other. The romantic resolution transforms this constancy from one of rivalry to one of friendship by making each male to accept his own female. In Puck's charmingly crude formulation:

> And the country proverb known,
> That every man should take his own,
> In your waking shall be shown:
> Jack shall have Jill,
> Nought shall go ill:
> The man shall have his mare again, and all shall be well.
>
> (3.2.458–63)

At the end of *A Midsummer Night's Dream*, as at the end of *As You Like It*, the marital couplings dissolve the bonds of sisterhood at the same time that they forge the bonds of brotherhood.[2] ... In *A Midsummer Night's Dream*, as in other Shakespearean comedies, the 'drive toward a festive conclusion' is, specifically, a drive toward a wedding. And in its validation of marriage, the play is less concerned to sacrimentalize libido than to socialize it.

In the opening scene, Egeus claims that he may do with Hermia as he chooses because she is his property: 'As she is mine, I may dispose of her' (1.1.142). This claim is based upon a stunningly simple thesis: she is his because he has *made* her. Charging that Lysander has 'stol'n the impression' (1.1.32) of Hermia's fantasy, Egeus effectively absolves his daughter from responsibility for her affections because he cannot acknowledge her capacity for volition. If she does not – cannot – obey him, then she should be destroyed. Borrowing Egeus' own imprinting metaphor, Theseus explains to Hermia the ontogenetic principle underlying her father's vehemence:

> To you your father should be as a god:
> One that compos'd your beauties, yea, and one
> To whom you are but as a form in wax
> By him imprinted, and within his power
> To leave the figure or disfigure it.
>
> (1.1.47–51)

Theseus represents paternity as a cultural act, an art: the father is a demiurge or *homo faber*, who composes, in-forms, imprints himself upon, what is merely inchoate matter. Conspicuously excluded from Shakespeare's play is the relationship between mother and daughter – the kinship bond through which Amazonian society reproduces itself. The mother's part is wholly excluded from this account of the making of a daughter. Hermia and Helena have no mothers; they have only fathers. The central female characters of Shakespeare's comedies are not mothers but mothers-to-be, maidens who are passing from fathers to husbands in a world made and governed by men.

In effect, Theseus' lecture on the shaping of a *daughter* is a fantasy of male parthenogenesis. Titania's votaress is the only biological mother in *A Midsummer Night's Dream*. But she is an absent presence who must be evoked from Titania's memory because she has died in giving birth to a *son*. Assuming that they do not maim their sons, the Amazons are only too glad to give them away to their fathers. In Shakespeare's play, however, Oberon's paternal power must be directed against Titania's maternal possessiveness:

> For Oberon is passing fell and wrath,
> Because that she as her attendant hath
> A lovely boy, stol'n from an Indian king –
> She never had so sweet a changeling;
> And jealous Oberon would have the child
> Knight of his train to trace the forest wild;
> But she perforce withholds the loved boy,
> Crowns him with flowers, and makes him all her joy.
>
> (2.1.20–7)

A boy's transition from the female-centered world of his early childhood to the male-centered world of his youth is given a kind of phylogenetic sanction by myths recounting a cultural transition from matriarchy to patriarchy. Such a myth is represented at the very threshhold of *A Midsummer Night's Dream*: Theseus' defeat of the Amazonian matriarchate sanctions Oberon's attempt to take the boy from an infantilizing mother and to make a man of him. Yet 'jealous' Oberon is not only Titania's rival for the child but also the child's rival for Titania: making the boy 'all her joy', 'proud' Titania withholds herself from her husband; she has 'forsworn his bed and company' (2.1.62–3). Oberon's preoccupation is to gain possession, not only of the boy but of the woman's desire and obedience; he must master his own dependency upon his wife.

Titania has her own explanation for her fixation upon the changeling:

> His mother was a votress of my order
> And in the spiced Indian air, by night,
> Full often hath she gossip'd by my side;
> And sat with me on Neptune's yellow sands,
> Marking th'embarked traders on the flood:
> When we have laugh'd to see the sails conceive
> And grow big-bellied with the wanton wind;
> Which she, with pretty and with swimming gait
> Following (her womb then rich with my young squire),
> Would imitate, and sail upon the land
> To fetch me trifles, and return again
> As from a voyage rich with merchandise.
> But she, being mortal, of that boy did die;
> And for her sake do I rear up her boy;
> And for her sake I will not part with him.
>
> (2.1.123–37)

Titania's attachment to the changeling boy embodies her attachment to the memory of his mother. What Oberon accomplishes by substituting Bottom for the boy is to break Titania's solemn vow. As in the case of the Amazons, or of Hermia and Helena, the play again enacts a male disruption of an intimate bond between women: first by the boy, and then by the man. It is as if, in order to be freed and enfranchised from the prison of the womb, the male child must *kill* his mother: 'She, being mortal, of that boy did die.' Titania's words suggest that mother and son are potentially mortal to each other: the matricidal infant complements the infanticidal Amazon. As is later the case with Bottom, Titania both dotes upon and dominates the child, attenuating his imprisonment to the womb: 'And for her sake I will not part with him.' Thus, within the changeling plot are embedded transformations of the male fantasies of motherhood which are figured in Amazonian myth.

Titania represents her bond to her votaress as one that is rooted in an experience of female fecundity, an experience for which men must seek merely mercantile compensations. The women 'have laugh'd to see the sails conceive / And grow big-bellied with the wanton wind'; and the votaress has parodied such false pregnancies by sailing to fetch trifles while she herself bears riches within her very womb. The notion of maternity implied in Titania's speech counterpoints the notion of paternity formulated by Theseus in the opening scene. In Theseus' description, neither biological nor social mother – neither *genetrix* nor *mater* – plays a role in the making of a daughter; in Titania's description, neither *genitor* nor *pater* plays a role in the making of a son. The father's daughter is shaped from without; the mother's son comes from within her body: Titania dwells upon the physical bond between mother and child, as manifested in pregnancy and parturition. Like an infant of the Elizabethan upper classes, however, the changeling is nurtured not by his natural mother but by a surrogate. By emphasizing her own role as a foster mother to her gossip's offspring, Titania links the biological and social aspects of parenthood together within a wholly maternal world, a world in which the relationship between women has displaced the relationship between wife and husband. Nevertheless, despite the exclusion of a paternal role from Titania's speech, Shakespeare's embryological notions remain distinctly Aristotelian, distinctly phallocentric: the mother is represented as a *vessel*, as a container for her son; she is not his *maker*. In contrast, the implication of Theseus' description of paternity is that the male is the only begetter; a daughter is merely a token of her father's potency. Thus these two speeches may be said to formulate in poetic discourse, a proposition about the genesis of gender and power: men make women, and make themselves through the medium of women. Such a proposition reverses the Amazonian practice, in which women use men merely for their own reproduction. But much more than this, it seems an overcompensation for the *natural* fact that men do indeed come from women; an overcompensation for the *cultural* facts that consanguineal and affinal ties *between* men are established through mothers, wives, and daughters. *A Midsummer Night's Dream* dramatizes a set of claims which are repeated throughout Shakespeare's canon: claims for a spiritual kinship among men that is unmediated by women; for the procreative powers of men; and for the autogeny of men.

[I]n Shakespeare's age … although biological maternity was readily apparent, biological paternity was a cultural construct for which ocular proof was unattainable. More specifically, the evidence for *unique* biological paternity, for the physical link between a particular man and child, has always been exiguous. And, in Shakespearean drama, this link is frequently a focus of anxious concern, whether the concern is to validate paternity or to call it in question. Thus, Lear tells Regan that if she were *not* glad to see him, 'I would divorce me from thy mother's tomb, / Sepulchring an adult'ress' (*King Lear*, 2.4.131–2). And Leontes exclaims, upon first meeting Florizel, 'Your mother was most true to wedlock, Prince, / For she did print your royal father off, / Conceiving you' (*The Winter's Tale*, 5.1.124–6). In the former speech, a vulnerable father invokes his previously unacknowledged wife precisely when he wishes to repudiate his child; while in the latter, a vulnerable husband celebrates female virtue as the instrument of male self-reproduction.

The role of genetrix is self-evident but the role of genitor is not. As Launcelot Gobbo puts it, in *The Merchant of Venice*, 'it is a wise father that knows his own child' (MV, 2.2.76–7). This consequence of biological asymmetry calls forth an explanatory – and compensatory – asymmetry in many traditional embryological theories: paternity is procreative, the formal and/or efficient cause of generation; maternity is nurturant, the material cause of generation. For example, according to *The Problemes of Aristotle*, a popular Elizabethan medical guide that continued to be revised and reissued well into the nineteenth century,

> The seede [i.e. of the male] is the efficient beginning of the childe, as the builder is the efficient cause of the house, and therefore is not the materiall cause of the childe ... The seedes [i.e. both male and female] are shut and kept in the wombe: but the seede of the man doth dispose and prepare the seed of the woman to receive the forme, perfection, or soule, the which being done, it is converted into humiditie, and is fumed and breathed out by the pores of the matrix, which is manifest, bicause onely the flowers [i.e. the menses] of the woman are the materiall cause of the yoong one. (Anon. 1597, sigs. E3^r–E4^r)

Conflating Aristotelian and Galenic notions, the text registers some confusion about the nature of the inseminating power and about its attribution to the woman as well as to the man. Although the contributions of both man and woman are necessary, the female seed is nevertheless materially inferior to that of the male. The notion of woman as an unperfected, an inadequate, imitation of man extends to the analogy of semen and menses: 'The seede ... is white in man by reason of his greate heate, and because it is digested better ... The seede of a woman is red ... because the flowers is corrupt, undigested blood' (Anon., 1597). Whether in folk medicine or in philosophy, notions of maternity have a persistent natural or physical bias, while notions of paternity have a persistent social or spiritual bias. And such notions are articulated within a belief-system in which nature is subordinated to society, and matter is subordinated to spirit. The act of generation brings man and woman into a relationship that is both complementary and hierarchical. Thus, there exists a homology between the cultural construction of sexual generation and the social institution of marriage: genitor is to genetrix as husband is to wife.

While Shakespeare's plays reproduce these legitimating structures, they also reproduce challenges to their legitimacy. For, like the ubiquitous jokes and fears about cuckoldry to which they are usually linked, the frequent allusions within Shakespeare's texts to the incertitude of paternity point to a source of tension, to a potential contradiction, within the ostensibly patriarchal sex/gender system of Elizabethan culture. Oberon's epithalamium represents procreation as the union of man and woman, and marriage as a relationship of mutual affection:

> To the best bride-bed will we,
> Which by us shall blessed be;
> And the issue there create
> Ever shall be fortunate.
> So shall all the couples three
> Ever true in loving be.
> (5.1.389–94)

This benign vision is predicated upon the play's reaffirmation of the father's role in generation and the husband's authority over the wife. But at the same time that the play reaffirms essential elements of a patriarchal ideology, it also calls that reaffirmation in question; irrespective of authorial intention, the text intermittently undermines its own comic propositions. Oberon assures himself that, by the end of the play, 'all things shall be peace' (3.2.377). But the continuance of the newlyweds' loves and the good fortune of their issue are by no means assured. Indeed, as soon as the lovers have gone off to bed, Puck begins to evoke an uncomic world of labor, fear, pain, and death (5.1.357–76). This invocation gives some urgency to Oberon's subsequent ritual blessing: the dangers are imminent and the peace is most fragile. *A Midsummer Night's Dream* ends, not only with the creation of new children but with the creation of new mothers and new fathers; it ends upon the threshhold of another generational cycle, which contains *in potentia* a renewal of the strife with which the play began. The status of 'jealous' Oberon and 'proud' Titania as personifications of forces in Nature at once sanctions and subverts the doctrine of domestic hierarchy. For, as personified in Shakespeare's fairies, the divinely ordained imperatives of Nature call attention to themselves as the humanly constructed imperatives of Culture: Shakespeare's naturalization and legitimation of the domestic economy deconstructs itself. The all-too-human struggle between the play's already married couple provides an ironic prognosis for the new marriages.

The promised end of romantic comedy is not only undermined by dramatic ironies but also contaminated by a kind of inter-textual irony. The mythology of Theseus is filled with instances of terror, lust, and jealousy which are prominently recounted and censured by Plutarch in his *Life of Theseus* and in his subsequent comparison of Theseus with Romulus. Shakespeare uses Plutarch as his major source of Theseus-lore but does so highly selectively, excluding those events 'not sorting with a nuptial ceremony' (5.1.55) nor with a comedy ... [T]he text of Shakespeare's play is permeated by echoes not only of Plutarch's parallel lives of Theseus and Romulus but also of Seneca's *Hippolitus* and his *Medea* ... Thus, sedimented within the verbal texture of *A Midsummer Night's Dream* are traces of those forms of sexual and familial violence which the play would suppress: acts of bestiality and incest, of parricide, uxoricide, filicide, and suicide; sexual fears and urges erupting in cycles of violent desire – from Pasiphae and the Minotaur to Phaedra and Hippolitus. The seductive and destructive powers of women figure centrally in Theseus' career; and his habitual victimization of women, the chronicle of his rapes and disastrous marriages, is a discourse of anxious misogyny which persists as an echo within Shakespeare's text, no matter how much it has been muted or transformed.

The play actually calls attention to the mechanism of mythological suppression by an ironically meta-dramatic gesture: Theseus demands 'some delight' with which to 'beguile / The lazy time' (5.1.40–1) before the bedding of the brides. The list of available entertainments includes 'The battle with the Centaurs, to be sung / By an Athenian eunuch to the harp,' as well as 'The riot of the tipsy Bacchanals, / Tearing the Thracian singer in their rage'

(5.1.44–5, 48–9). Theseus rejects both – because they are already too familiar. These brief scenarios encompass the extremes of reciprocal violence between the sexes. The first performance narrates a wedding that degenerates into rape and warfare; the singer and his subject – Athenian eunuch and phallic Centaur – are two antithetical kinds of male-monster. In the second performance, what was often seen as the natural inclination of women toward irrational behavior is manifested in the Maenads' terrible rage against Orpheus. The tearing and decapitation of the misogynistic Ur-Poet at once displaces and vivifies the Athenian singer's castration; and it also evokes the fate of Hippolytus, the misogynistic offspring of Theseus and Hippolyta. It is in its intermittent ironies, dissonances, and contradictions that the text of *A Midsummer Night's Dream* discloses – perhaps, in a sense, despite itself – that patriarchal norms are compensatory for the vulnerability of men to the powers of women.

IV

Such moments of textual disclosure also illuminate the interplay between sexual politics in the Elizabethan family and sexual politics in the Elizabethan monarchy: for the woman to whom *all* Elizabethan men were vulnerable was Queen Elizabeth herself. Within legal and fiscal limits, she held the power of life and death over every Englishman; the power to advance or frustrate the worldly desires of all her subjects. Her personality and personal symbolism helped to mold English culture and the consciousness of Englishmen for several generations.

Although the Amazonian metaphor might seem suited to strategies for praising a woman ruler, it was never popular among Elizabethan encomiasts (see Schleiner, 1978, 162–80). Its associations must have been too sinister to suit the personal tastes and political interests of the Queen. However, Sir Walter Ralegh did boldly compare Elizabeth to the Amazons in his *Discoverie of Guiana*.[3] In his digression on the Amazons, who are reported to dwell 'not far from Guiana', Ralegh repeats the familiar details of their sexual and parental practices, and notes that they 'are said to be very cruel and blood-thirsty, especially to such as offer to invade their territories' (28). At the end of his narrative, Ralegh exhorts Elizabeth to undertake a

> Her Majesty heereby shall confirme and strengthen the opinions of al nations, as touching her great and princely actions. And where the south border of *Guiana* reacheth to the Dominion and Empire of the *Amazones*, those women shall heereby heare the name of a virgin, which is not onely able to defend her owne territories and her neighbors, but also to invade and conquere so great Empyres and so farre removed (120).

Ralegh's strategy for convincing the Queen to advance his colonial enterprise is to insinuate that she is both like and unlike an Amazon; that Elizabethan imperialism threatens not only the Empire of the Guiana but the Empire of the Amazons; and that Elizabeth can definitively cleanse herself from contamination by the Amazons if she sanctions their subjugation. The Amazonomachy which Ralegh projects into the imaginative space of the New World is analogous to that narrated by Spenser within the imaginative space of Faeryland. Radigund, the Amazon Queen, can only be defeated by Britomart, the martial maiden who is Artegall's betrothed and the fictional ancestress of Elizabeth. Radigund is Britomart's double, split off from her as an allegorical personification of everything in Artegall's beloved which threatens him. Having destroyed Radigund and liberated Artegall from his effeminate 'thraldome', Britomart reforms what is left of Amazon society: she

> The liberty of women did repeale,
> Which they had long usurpt; and them restoring
> To mens subjection, did true Justice deale:
> That all they as a Goddesse her adoring,
> Her wisedome did admire, and hearkned to her loring.
>
> (FQ, 5.7.42)

... For Ralegh's Elizabeth, as for Spenser's Britomart, the woman who has the prerogative of a goddess, who is authorized to be out of place, can best justify her authority by putting other women in their places.

...

The Queen herself was too politic, and too ladylike, to wish to pursue the Amazonian image very far. Instead, she transformed it to suit her purposes, representing herself as an androgynous martial maiden, like Spenser's Britomart. Such was her appearance at Tilbury in 1588, where she had come to review her troops in expectation of a Spanish invasion. On that momentous occasion, she rode a white horse and dressed in white velvet; she wore a silver cuirass on her breast and carried a silver truncheon in her hand. The theme of her speech was by then already familiar to her listeners: she dwelt upon the womanly frailty of her body natural and the masculine strength of her body politic – a strength deriving from the love of her people, the virtue of her lineage, and the will of her God: 'I have always so behaved myself that, under God, I have placed my chiefest strength and safeguard in the loyal hearts and good will of my subjects ... I know I have the body of a weak and feeble woman, but I have the heart and stomach of a king, and of a king of England too.'[4] As the female ruler of what was, at least in theory, a patriarchal society, Elizabeth incarnated a contradiction at the very center of the Elizabethan sex/gender system ...

... Queen Elizabeth was a cultural anomaly; and this anomalousness – at once divine and monstrous – made her powerful, and dangerous. By the skillful deployment of images that were at once awesome and familiar, this perplexing creature tried to mollify her male subjects while enhancing her authority over them.

At the beginning of her reign, Elizabeth formulated the strategy by which she turned the political liability of her gender to advantage for the next half century. She told her first parliaments that she was content to have as her epitaph 'that a Queen, having reigned such a time, lived and died a virgin'; that her coronation ring betokened her marriage to her subjects; and that, although after her death her people might have many stepdames, yet they should never have 'a more natural mother than [she] meant to be unto [them], all' (See Neale, 1958, 49, 109). One way in which she actualized her maternal policy was to sponsor more than a hundred godchildren, the offspring of nobility and commoners alike (Williams, 1967, 218) ...

In a royal household comprising some fifteen hundred courtiers and retainers, the Queen's female entourage consisted of merely a dozen ladies of high rank – married or widowed – and half a dozen maids of honor from distinguished families, whose conduct was of almost obsessive interest to their mistress. Sir John Harington, the Queen's godson and an acute observer of her ways, wrote in a letter that 'she did oft aske the ladies around hir chamber, If they lovede to thinke of marriage? And the wise ones did conceal well their liking hereto; as knowing the Queene's judgment in this matter.' He goes on to relate an incident in which one of the maids of honor, 'not knowing so deeply as hir fellowes, was asked one day hereof, and simply said – "she had thought muche about marriage, if her father did consent to the man she lovede."' Thereupon, the Queen obtained the father's consent that she should deal as she saw fit with her maid's desires. 'The ladie was called in, and the Queene tould her father had given his free consente. "Then," replied the ladie, "I shall be happie and please your Grace." – "So thou shalte; but not to be a foole and marrye. I have his consente given to me, and I vow thou shalte never get it into thy possession ... I see thou art a bolde one, to owne thy foolishnesse so readilye"' (Harington, 1930, 124). The virgin Queen threatened her vestal with the prospect of living a barren sister all her life. Directly, in cases such as this, and indirectly through the operation of the Court of Wards, the Queen reserved to herself the traditional paternal power to give or withhold daughters. Among the aristocracy, marriage was not merely a legal and affective union between private persons but also a political and economic alliance between powerful families; it was an institution over which a careful and insecure monarch might well wish to exercise an absolute control. Behavior which, in the context of Elizabeth's body natural, may have been merely peevish or jealous was, in the context of her body politic, politic indeed.

Elizabeth's self-mastery and mastery of others were enhanced by an elaboration of her maidenhood into a cult of virginity which 'allows of amorous admiration but prohibits desire' (Bacon, 1860, 11: 460); the displacement of her wifely duties from a household to a nation; and the sublimation of her temporal and ecclesiastical authority into a nurturing maternity. She appropriated not only the suppressed cult of the Blessed Virgin but also the Tudor conception of the Ages of Woman. By fashioning herself into a singular combination of Maiden, Matron, and Mother, the Queen transformed the normal domestic life-cycle of an Elizabethan female into what was at once a social paradox and a religious mystery ... Because she was always uniquely herself, Elizabeth's rule was not intended to undermine the male hegemony of her culture. Indeed, the emphasis upon her *difference* from other women may have helped to reinforce it. As she herself wrote in response to Parliament in 1563, 'though I can think [marriage] best for a private woman, yet I do strive with myself to think it not meet for a prince' (Neale, 1958, 127). The royal exception could prove the patriarchal rule in society at large.

Nevertheless, from the very beginning of her reign, Elizabeth's parliaments and counselors urged her to marry and produce an heir. There was a deeply felt and loudly voiced need to insure a legitimate succession, upon which the welfare of the whole people depended. But there must also have been another, more obscure motivation behind these requests: the political nation, which was wholly a nation of men, seems at times to have found it frustrating or degrading to serve a female prince – a woman who was herself unsubjected to any man ... In the 1560s and 1570s, Elizabeth witnessed allegorical entertainments boldly criticizing her attachment to a life of 'single blessedness'. For example, in the famous Kenilworth entertainments sponsored by the Earl of Leicester in 1575, Diana praised the state of fancy-free maiden meditation and condemned the 'wedded state, which is to thraldome bent.' But Juno had the last word in the pageant: 'O Queene, O worthy queene,/ Yet never wight felt perfect blis / But such as wedded beene.'[5] By the 1580s, the Queen was past childbearing; Diana and her virginal nymph, Eliza, now carried the day in such courtly entertainments as Peele's *Araygnment of Paris*. Although 'as fayre and lovely as the queene of Love', Peele's Elizabeth was also 'as chast as Dian in her chast desires' (ed. Benbow, 1970, ii. 1172–3).[6] By the early 1590s, the cult of the unaging royal virgin had entered its last and most extravagant phase. In the 1590 Accession Day pageant, there appeared 'a Pavilion ... like unto the sacred Temple of the Virgins Vestal.'[7] Upon the altar there were presents for the Queen – offerings from her votaries. At Elvetham, during the royal progress of 1591, none other than 'the Fairy Queene' gave to Elizabeth a chaplet that she herself had received from 'Auberon, the Fairy King' (Nichols, 1966, 3:118–19). From early in the reign, Elizabeth had been directly engaged by such performances: debates were referred to her arbitration; the magic of her presence civilized savage men, restored the blind to sight, released errant knights from enchantment, and rescued virgins from defilement. These social dramas of celebration and coercion played out the delicately balanced relationship between the monarch and her greatest subjects. And because texts and descriptions of most of them were in print within a year of their performance, they may have had a cultural impact far greater than their occasional and ephemeral character might at first suggest.

A Midsummer Night's Dream is permeated by images and devices that suggest these characteristic forms of Elizabethan court culture. However, whether or not its provenance was in an aristocratic wedding entertainment, Shakespeare's play is neither focused upon the Queen nor structurally dependent upon her presence or her intervention in the action. On the contrary, it might be said to depend upon her absence, her exclusion. In the third scene of the play, after Titania has remembered her Indian votaress, Oberon remembers his 'imperial votaress'. He has once beheld

> Flying between the cold moon and the earth,
> Cupid all arm'd; a certain aim he took
> At a fair vestal, throned by the West,
> And loos'd his love-shaft smartly from his bow
> As it should pierce a hundred thousand hearts.
> But I might see young Cupid's fiery shaft
> Quench'd in the chaste beams of the watery moon;
> And the imperial votress passed on,
> In maiden meditation, fancy-free.
> Yet mark'd I where the bolt of Cupid fell:
> It fell upon a little western flower,
> Before milk-white, now purple with love's wound:
> And maidens call it 'love-in-idleness'.
> . . .
> The juice of it, on sleeping eyelids laid,
> Will make or man or woman madly dote
> Upon the next live creature that it sees.
> (2.1.156–68, 170–2)

The evocative monologues of Titania and Oberon are carefully matched and contrasted: the fairy queen speaks of a mortal mother from the east; the fairy king speaks of an invulnerable virgin from the west. Their memories express two myths of origin: Titania's provides a genealogy for the changeling and an explanation of why she will not part with him; Oberon's provides an aetiology of the metamorphosed flower which he will use to make her part with him. The floral symbolism of female sexuality begun in this passage is completed when Oberon names 'Dian's bud' (4.1.72) as the antidote to 'love-in-idleness'. With Cupid's flower, Oberon can make the Fairy Queen 'full of hateful fantasies' (2.1.258); and with Dian's bud, he can win her back to his will. The vestal's invulnerability to fancy is doubly instrumental to Oberon in his reaffirmation of romantic, marital, and parental norms that have been inverted during the course of the play. Thus, Shakespeare's royal compliment re-mythologizes the cult of the Virgin Queen in such a way as to sanction a relationship of gender and power that is personally and politically inimical to Elizabeth.

Unlike the fair vestal, Shakespeare's comic heroines are in a transition between the states of maidenhood and wifehood, daughterhood and mother-hood. These transitions are mediated by the wedding rite and the act of defloration, which are brought together at the end of *A Midsummer Night's Dream*: when the newlyweds have retired for the night, Oberon and Titania enter the court in order to bless the 'bride-bed' where the marriages are about to be consummated. By the act of defloration, the husband takes physical and symbolic possession of his bride. The sexual act in which the man draws blood from the woman is already implicit, at the beginning of the play, in Theseus' vaunt: 'Hippolyta, I woo'd thee with my sword, / And won thy love doing thee injuries.' The impending injury is evoked – and dismissed with laughter – in the play-within-the-play which wears away the hours 'between our after-supper and bedtime' (5.1.34): Pyramus finds Thisbe's mantle 'stain'd with blood', and concludes that 'lion vile hath here deflower'd [his] dear' (5.1.272, 281). The image in which Oberon describes the flower's metamorphosis suggests the immanence of defloration in the very origin of desire: 'the bolt of Cupid fell / ... Upon a little western flower, / Before milk-white, now purple with love's wound.' Cupid's shaft violates the flower when it has been deflected from the vestal: Oberon's purple passion flower is procreated in a displaced and literalized defloration. Unlike the female *dramatis personae*, Oberon's vestal virgin is *not* subject to Cupid's shaft, to the frailties of the flesh and the fancy. Nor is she subject to the mastery of men. Isolated from the experiences of desire, marriage and maternity, she is immune to the pains and pleasure of human mutability. But it is precisely her bodily and mental impermeability which make possible Oberon's pharmacopoeia. Thus, ironically, the vestal's very freedom from fancy guarantees the subjection of others. She is necessarily excluded from the erotic world of which her own chastity is the efficient cause.

Within *A Midsummer Night's Dream*, the public and domestic domains of Elizabethan culture intersect in the figure of the imperial votaress. When a female ruler is ostensibly the virgin mother of her subjects, then the themes of male procreative power, autogeny, and mastery of women acquire a seditious resonance. In royal pageantry, the Queen is always the cynosure; her virginity is the source of magical potency. In *A Midsummer Night's Dream*, however, magical power is invested in the King. Immediately after invoking the royal vestal and vowing to torment the Fairy Queen, Oberon encounters Helena in pursuit of Demetrius. In Shakespeare's metamorphosis of Ovid, 'the story shall be chang'd / Apollo flies, and Daphne holds the chase' (2.1.230–1). Oberon's response is neither to extinguish desire nor to make it mutual but to restore the normal pattern of pursuit: 'Fare thee well, nymph; ere he do leave this grove / Thou shalt fly him and he shall seek thy love' (2.1.245–6) ... Unlike Elizabeth, Oberon uses his mastery over Nature to subdue others to their passions. The festive conclusion of *A Midsummer Night's Dream* depends upon the success of a process by which the female pride and power manifested in misanthropic warriors, possessive mothers, unruly wives, and willful daughters are brought under the control of lords and husbands. When the contentious young lovers have been sorted out into pairs by Oberon, then Theseus can invite them to share his own wedding day. If the Duke finally overbears Egeus' will (4.1.178), it is because the father's obstinate claim to 'the ancient privilege of Athens' (1.1.41) threatens to obstruct the very process by which Athenian privilege and Athens itself are reproduced. Hermia and Helena are granted their desires – but those desires have themselves been shaped by a social imperative. Thus, neither for Oberon nor for Theseus does a contradiction exist between mastering the desires of a wife and patronizing the desires of a maiden. In the assertion of an equivalence between the patriarchal family and the patriarchal state, the anomalous Elizabethan relationship between gender and power is suppressed.

In his letters, Sir John Harington wrote of Elizabeth as 'oure deare Queene, my royale godmother, and this state's natural mother'; as 'one whom I both lovede and fearede too.' After her death, he reflected slyly on how she had manipulated the filial feelings of her subjects: 'Few knew how to aim their shaft against her cunninge. We did all love hir, for she saide she loved us, and muche wysdome she shewed in thys matter.'[8] So much for Elizabeth's maternal strategies. As for her erotic strategies, Bacon provides perhaps the most astute contemporary analysis:

> As for those lighter points of character, – as that she allowed herself to be wooed and courted, and even to have love made to her; and liked it; and continued it beyond the natural age for such vanities; – if any of the sadder sort of persons be disposed to make a great matter of this, it may be observed that there is something to admire in these very things, which ever way you take them. For if viewed indulgently, they are much like the accounts we find in romances, of the Queen in the blessed islands, and her court and institutions, who allows of amorous admiration but prohibits desire. But if you take them seriously, they challenge admiration of another kind and of a very high order; for certain it is that these dalliances detracted but little from her fame and nothing from her majesty, and neither weakened her power nor sensibly hindered her business. (1860, 11: 460)

Bacon appreciates that the Queen's personal vanity and political craft are mutually reinforcing. He is alert to the generic affinities of the royal cult, its appropriation and enactment of the conventions of romance. And he also recognizes that, like contemporaneous romantic fictions, the Queen's romance could function as a political allegory. However, symbolic forms may do more than *represent* power: they may actually help to *generate* the power that they represent. Thus – although Bacon does not quite manage to say so – the Queen's dalliances did not weaken her power but strengthened it; did not hinder her business but furthered it.

By the same token, the Queen's subjects might put the discourse of royal power to their own uses. Consider the extravagant royal entertainment of 1581, in which Philip Sidney and Fulke Greville performed as 'Foster Children of Desire' (Nichols, 1996, 2: 312–19). 'Nourished up with [the] infective milke' (313) of Desire – 'though full oft that dry nurse Dispaier indevered to wainne them from it' (314) – the Foster Children boldly claimed and sought to possess The Fortress of Perfect Beauty, an allegorical structure from within which Elizabeth actually beheld the 'desirous assault' (317) mounted against her. The besieged Queen was urged that she 'no longer exclude vertuous Desire from perfect Beautie' (314). During two days of florid speeches, spectacular self-displays, and mock combats, these young, ambitious, and thwarted courtiers acted out a fantasy of political demand, rebellion, and submission in metaphors of resentment and aggression that were alternately filial and erotic. They seized upon the forms in which their culture had articulated the relationship between sovereign and subjects: they demanded sustenance from their royal mother, favors from their royal mistress. The nobility, gentlemen, and hangers-on of the court generated a variety of pressures that constantly threatened the fragile stability of the Elizabethan regime. At home, personal rivalries and political dissent might be sublimated into the agonistic play-forms of courtly culture; abroad, they might be expressed in warfare and colonial enterprise – displaced into the conquest of lands that had yet their maidenheads.

The Queen dallied, not only with the hearts of courtiers but with the hearts of commoners, too. For example, in 1600, a deranged sailor named Abraham Edwardes sent 'a passionate ... letter unto her Majesty', who was then sixty-eight years old. Edwardes was later committed to prison 'for drawing his dagger in the [royal] presence chamber'. The Clerk of the Privy Council wrote to Cecil that 'the fellow is greatly distracted, and seems rather to be transported with a humour of love, than any purpose to attempt anything against her Majesty.' He recommended that this poor lunatic and lover 'be removed to Bedlam' (Waad, 1600, 10: 172–3). By her own practice of sexual politics, the Queen may very well have encouraged the sailor's passion – in the same sense that her cult helped to fashion the courtly performances and colonial enter-prises of courtiers like Sidney or Ralegh, the dream-life of Doctor Forman, the dream-play of Master Shakespeare. This being said, it must be added that the Queen was as much the creature of her image as she was its creator, that her power to fashion her own strategies was itself fashioned by her culture and constrained within its mental horizon. Indeed, in *A Midsummer Night's Dream*, as in *The Faerie Queene*, the ostensible project of elaborating Queen Elizabeth's personal mythology inexorably subverts itself – generates ironies, contradictions, resistances which undo the royal magic. Such processes of disenchantment are increasingly evident in Elizabethan cultural productions of the 1580s and 1590s. The texts of Spenser and other Elizabethan courtly writers often fragment the royal image, reflecting aspects of the Queen 'in mirrours more then one' (FQ, 3.Proem.5). In a similar way, Shakespeare's text splits the triune Elizabethan cult image between the fair vestal, an unattainable *virgin*; and the Fairy Queen, an intractable *wife* and a dominating *mother*. Oberon uses one against the other in order to reassert male prerogatives. Thus, the structure of Shakespeare's comedy symbolically neutralizes the forms of royal power to which it ostensibly pays homage. It would be an over-simplification and a distortion to characterize such cultural processes merely as an allegorical encoding of political conflict. The spiritual, maternal, and erotic transformations of Elizabethan power are not reduceable to instances of

Machiavellian policy, to intentional mystifications. Relationships of power and dependency, desire and fear, are inherent in both the public and domestic domains. Sexual and family experience were invariably politicized; economic and political experience were invariably eroticized: the social and psychological force of Elizabethan symbolic forms depended upon a thorough conflation of these domains. ...

NOTES

1. All quotations of MND will follow *The Arden Shakespeare* edition, ed. Harold F. Brooks (1979) and will be cited in the text by act, scene and line. Quotations from other Shakespearean plays follow the texts in *The Riverside Shakespeare* ... (1974).
2. For detailed analysis, see Montrose (1981, 28–54).
3. References will be to this edition.
4. Quoted in Paul Johnson (1974, 320). Contemporary representations of the event are quoted and discussed in Schleiner (1978).
5. I quote the printed text of the Kenilworth entertainment (1576) from *The Complete Works of George Gascoigne* (1910, 2: 107, 120).
6. See Montrose (1980, 433–61).
7. Described in Sir William Segar (1966, 3: 41–50); quotation from Nichols (3: 46). One of the most popular iconographic attributes of Queen Elizabeth is the sieve, which identifies her with the vestal virgin Tuccia.
8. Letters to Lady Mary Harington (1602) and Robert Markham (1606) (1930, 96, 123–5).

ANNOTATED BIBLIOGRAPHY

Greenblatt. Stephen. *Renaissance Self-Fashioning: From More to Shakespeare*. Chicago, 1980.

Although this was not Greenblatt's first book, it was the first in which he employed the concepts of power, discourse and subjectivity to analyse literary texts, a practice which became known subsequently as new historicism. Greenblatt argues in this book that in the Renaissance period there was a transformation in the social and cultural structures which changed the character of subjectivity. He analyses the ways in which writers and individuals like Thomas More, William Tyndale, Thomas Wyatt, Edmund Spenser and Christopher Marlowe fashioned their self-identities through a network of social, psychological, political and intellectual discourses.

Greenblatt. Stephen. 'Invisible Bullets: Renaissance Authority and its Subversion'. *Glyph*, 8, 1981: 40–61.

One of the most influential new historicist essays, by which I mean that it has been widely discussed and widely anthologised. Greenblatt begins with an anecdote about an Italian heretic, Menocchio, whose radical subversiveness got him burned at the stake on the authority of the Inquisition. Greenblatt uses this anecdote to explain his argument that subversiveness is necessary in order for power to become visible and fearsome, and to extend his argument to suggest that seemingly orthodox texts generate subversive insights which are an integral part of a society's policing apparatus. He then proceeds to examine this argument in relation to Thomas Harriot, the author of a report on England's first colony America, and to Shakespeare's *I Henry IV*. He finds in each case that power produces the appearance of subversion in order to contain and police subversion more effectively.

Miller. D. A. *The Novel and the Police*. Berkeley, CA, 1988.

Miller differs from the new historicists in Renaissance studies, like Greenblatt and Montrose, in that he applies Foucault's concepts directly and explicitly to literary texts, rather than owing some of his implicit assumptions to Foucault. Miller takes Foucault's work on discipline, punishment, policing and incarceration and explores what kind of readings emerge from the application of those concepts to Victorian novels. Miller focuses on Charles Dickens, Anthony Trollope and Wilkie Collins in his study.

Veeser. H. Aram, ed. *The New Historicism*. London, 1989.

The first of Veeser's collections of essays on the new historicism, in this volume Veeser gathered together essays on the emergence, reception and criticism of new historicism, which include contributions from prominent practitioners like Louis Montrose, Joel Fineman, Catherine Gallagher and Stephen Greenblatt to critics like Brook Thomas, Frank Lentricchia, Vincent Pecora and Hayden White. Veeser's introduction attempts to define the characteristics of the new historicism, and in general this anthology is useful for reading debates on what the new historicism represents in literary studies, including its shortcomings and weaknesses.

Veeser. H. Aram, ed. *The New Historicism Reader*. London, 1994.

Whereas the first of Veeser's collections published essays about the new historicism, the second anthology published examples of the critical practice of new historicism. It included classic new historicist essays by Stephen Orgel, Stephen Greenblatt, Louis Montrose, Joel Fineman, Walter Benn Michaels, Catherine Gallagher and many others. Some of the essays included, such as the essays by Brook Thomas and Eve Kosofsky Sedgwick, do not follow the classic new historicist formula, which Veeser usefully describes as the process of 'converting details into knowledge' by five measured operations: 'anecdote, outrage, resistance, containment, and the critic's autobiography – all in a tight twenty-five pages' (5).

SUPPLEMENTARY BIBLIOGRAPHY

Armstrong, Nancy. *Desire and Domestic Fiction: A Political History of the Novel.* Oxford, 1987.

———— and Leonard Tennenhouse, eds. *The Violence of Representation: Literature and the History of Violence.* London, 1989.

Brannigan, John. *New Historicism and Cultural Materialism.* Basingstoke, 1998.

Boyarin, Daniel. '"Language Inscribed by History on the Bodies of Living Beings": Midrash and Martyrdom', *Representations*, 25, Winter 1989.

Brown, Marshall, ed. *The Uses of Literary History.* Durham, NC, 1995.

Bruster, Douglas. 'New Light on the Old Historicism: Shakespeare and the Forms of Historicist Criticism', *Literature and History*, 5: 1, Spring 1996.

Cox, Jeffrey N. and Larry J. Reynolds, eds. *New Historical Literary Studies: Essays on Reproducing Texts, Representing History.* Princeton, NJ, 1993.

Dimock, Wai-Chee. 'Feminism, New Historicism and the Reader', *American Literature*, 63: 4, 1991.

During, Simon. 'New Historicism', *Text and Performance Quarterly*, 11: 3, July 1991.

Foucault, Michel. *The Archaeology of Knowledge*, trans. A. M. Sheridan Smith. London, 1972.

————. *Discipline and Punish: The Birth of the Prison*, trans. Alan Sheridan. London, 1979.

————. *The History of Sexuality, Volume 1: An Introduction*, trans. Robert Hurley. London, 1981.

Gallagher, Catherine. *The Industrial Reformation of English Fiction: Social Discourse and Narrative Form 1832–1867.* Chicago, 1985.

Geertz, Clifford. *The Interpretation of Cultures.* London, 1993.

Goldberg, Jonathan. *James I and the Politics of Literature: Johnson, Shakespeare, Donne and their Contemporaries.* Baltimore, MD, 1983.

————, ed. *Queering the Renaissance.* Durham, NC, 1994.

Greenblatt, Stephen. *Learning to Curse: Essays in Early Modern Culture.* New York, 1990.

————. *Marvelous Possessions: The Wonder of the New World.* Oxford, 1991.

Hamilton, Paul. *Historicism.* London, 1996.

Hawthorn, Jeremy. *Cunning Passages: New Historicism, Cultural Materialism and Marxism in the Contemporary Literary Debate*. London, 1996.

Howard, Jean. 'The New Historicism in Renaissance Studies', *English Literary Renaissance*, 16, 1986.

Michaels, Walter Benn. *The Gold Standard and the Logic of Naturalism: American Literature at the Turn of the Century*. Berkeley, CA, 1987.

Miller, D. A. 'Discipline in Different Voices: Bureaucracy, Police, Family and *Bleak House*', *Representations*, 1: 1, 1983; rpt. in *The Novel and the Police*. Berkeley, CA, 1988.

Miller, J. Hillis. 'Presidential Address 1986: the Triumph of Theory, the Resistance to Reading, and the Question of the Material Base', *Theory Now and Then*. Hemel Hempstead, 1991.

Montrose, Louis Adrian. '"Shaping Fantasies": Figurations of Gender and Power in Elizabethan Culture'. *Representations*, 1: 2, Spring 1983.

————. 'Renaissance Literary Studies and the Subject of History', *English Literary Renaissance*, 16, 1986.

————. '"Eliza, Queene of Shepheardes", and the Pastoral of Power', *The New Historicism Reader*, ed. H. Aram Veeser. London, 1994.

Newton, Judith. 'History as Usual? Feminism and the "New Historicism"', *Cultural Critique*, 9, Spring 1988.

Porter, Carolyn. 'Are We Being Historical Yet?', *The South Atlantic Quarterly*, 87: 4, Fall 1988.

————. 'History and Literature: "After the New Historicism"', *New Literary History*, 21, 1990.

Ryan, Kiernan, ed. *New Historicism and Cultural Materialism: A Reader*. London, 1996.

Tennenhouse. Leonard. *Power on Display: The Politics of Shakespeare's Genres*. London, 1986.

Thomas, Brook. *The New Historicism and Other Old-Fashioned Topics*. Princeton, NJ, 1991.

————. 'Walter Benn Michaels and the New Historicism: Where's the Difference?' *Boundary 2: An International Journal of Literature and Culture*, 18: 1, Spring 1991.

Wilson, Richard, and Richard Dutton, eds. *New Historicism and Renaissance Drama*. Harlow, 1992.

PART 10
POSTCOLONIAL THEORY

INTRODUCTION:
THE DIFFICULTY OF DIFFERENCE

Gail Ching-Liang Low

One significant aspect of the modern world has been the impact and legacy of imperialism, colonial territorial acquisition and control – particularly of European imperialism. From the nineteenth century, European powers started a major scramble for territory so much so that by 1914, more than three-quarters of the world was controlled by Europeans. The processes associated with European modernity emerged on the back of imperialism and, in many ways, represents its darker underside. Postcolonial theory has emerged from an interdisciplinary area of study which is concerned with the historical, political, philosophical, social, cultural and aesthetic structures of colonial domination and resistance; it refers to a way of reading, theorising, interpreting and investigating colonial oppression and its legacy that is informed by an oppositional ethical agenda. In relation to colonial history, some of the basic questions that preoccupied critics include: Are there common structures to colonial domination across different geographies and different histories? What is the relation between material and hegemonic forms of oppression, between power and representation in specific situations? Is power total? What kinds of challenges are possible and what forms do they take? If official history is the history of the powerful, how do we recover these anti-colonial oppositions? How, and in what way, have some of the founding assumptions of the Enlightenment such as rationality, progress, beauty and taste been produced by colonial history? Questions relating to political independence – to the *post*-colonial – are equally important: What is at stake in the articulation of cultural or national identity? Can one hope to recover or create identities, artistic and representational forms and culture which is not overdetermined by that imperial legacy? Is writing in a colonial language and tradition a form of 're-' rather than 'de-'colonisation? Who is postcolonial when global capitalism contributes to a neocolonial world? Finally, because of its commitment to interrogate structures of domination, postcolonial theory has of necessity had to address institutions, intellectuals and the role they play in the network of power and knowledge. Accordingly, especially recently, postcolonial theory has been more critical and self-reflexive of its own theoretical presumptions and its institutional location in perpetuating an unequal global exchange.

The publication of Edward Said's *Orientalism* (1978) emerges as a key moment in the development of postcolonial theory within the academy. Drawing on Foucault and Gramsci, Said's monograph is a polemical and critical study of the ways in which the Occident has sought to objectify the Orient through the discourses of the arts and the human and social sciences. His definition of Orientalism as a 'discourse' was distinctly enabling for the emerging field of postcolonial theory because it enabled critics to see how different sorts of cultural and representational texts contributed to the formation of structures of power. Said sees an intimate connection between systems of knowledge and strategies of domination and control; hence his critique is an interdisciplinary interrogation of western intellectual, aesthetic scholarly and cultural traditions.

The Essex Sociology of Literature conference for 1984, which Edward Said attended, was entitled 'Europe and its Others' and provided a forum for an international collection of scholars to address colonial issues. The Essex conference also provided the venue for introducing two other leading figures, Homi Bhabha and Gayatri Spivak, who together with Said have been hailed somewhat cheekily by Robert Young as the 'holy trinity' of postcolonial theory. (Bhabha offered a paper on Said and colonial discourse at the earlier 'The Politics of Theory' conference in 1982.) Bhabha's work, informed by psychoanalysis, enunciation theory and deconstruction, and latterly by postmodern theory, emerged from the space of *Orientalism* but was also framed as a distinct challenge to its representation of colonial hegemony as omnipotent and uniform. Bhabha's essays, 'The Other Question' (1983) interrogates racism and racial stereotyping through a theory of racial fetishism (further developed in Bhabha's 1986 critical introduction to Fanon's *Black Skins/White Masks*); in 'Of Mimicry and Man' (1984) he develops the idea of ambivalence; 'Signs Taken for Wonders' (1985) elaborates ambivalence and mimicry through a new term, 'hybridity', while 'DissemiNation' (1990) develops their implicit conceptual critique of origins in the direction of national identities and narratives of the nation. Later essays will explore the difficulty of (theorising) agency, given Bhabha's post-structuralist approach. Bhabha's account of the conflictual economy of colonial discourse has been enormously productive for the field of colonial literary criticism, of which Gail Ching-Liang Low's book is but one example.

Gayatri Spivak's work is immensely influential in the field of colonial historiography, feminist studies, cultural studies and postcolonial studies and her writing has always sought to bring together the insights of poststructuralism, deconstruction, Marxism, psychoanalysis and feminism in active collision. Sceptical of grand, ambitious and overreaching explanatory frameworks, she points out the usefulness of these theories and critiques their limitations. Spivak is concerned with what she calls the 'epistemic violence' of imperialism; she is also noted for her relentless questioning of institutions, institutional power and the role of intellectuals in institutions (*Outside in the Teaching Machine*, 1993). Her critique of the Subaltern Studies project of recovering peasant – as opposed to elite – history is emblematic of the necessity and the impossibility of speaking for/or on behalf of oppressed groups ('Subaltern Studies: Deconstructing Historiography', 1985). Critical of western feminism's humanist assumptions, she also poses the question of what it means to address woman (femininity, sexual difference) as a unifying universal analytic category, especially when different cultures, histories and political-legal contexts have produced very different notions of the 'sexed' subject ('French Feminism in an International Frame', 1981; 'Three Women's Texts and a Critique of Imperialism', 1985; 'The Political Economy of Women as seen by a Literary Critic', 1989). 'Can the Subaltern Speak?' (1988), Spivak's most influential and controversial early essay, suggests that one particular 'regulative psycho-biography' for women is *sati* or sanctioned suicide, a site of contradictory subject positions assigned to women in India by both indigenous patriarchal and British colonial regimes.

The Essex conference also provided the impetus for the emergence of the Group for the Critical Study of Colonial Discourse and its occasional bulletin, *Inscriptions*, based at the University of California, Santa Cruz. The group's aim was to foster contact between scholars and researchers on representation and colonialism; some of the figures who participated in the group and contributed papers, such as James Clifford, Caren Kaplan, Lata Mani, David Lloyd, Peter Hulme, Mary Louise Pratt and Trinh Minh-ha, from adjacent disciplinary backgrounds, were later to become established critics in postcolonial studies. Special numbers and guest editors in prestigious academic journals in this period of the 1980s consolidated the influence of colonial discourse and postcolonial theory, and also its crossovers into other aspects of literary theory; Henry Louis Gates' guest editorship of *Critical Inquiry* in 1985, entitled 'Race, Writing and Difference', contains influential figures like Jacques Derrida on apartheid, Edward Said on the reassessment of Orientalism, Abdul JanMohamed on Manichean aesthetics, Mary Louis Pratt on travel narratives, Patrick Brantlinger on empire and fiction, Homi Bhabha on ambivalence in colonial discourse and Gayatri Spivak on imperialism and feminism. The American special number is joined, on the British side of the Atlantic, by the 1988 *Oxford Literary Review* special number on colonialism and postcolonialism. OLR includes Gauri Viswanathan's well-known work on English education in India and Benita Parry's influential critique of Bhabha, Spivak and JanMohamed. Parry's turn to the revolutionary Fanon, as opposed to Bhabha's earlier psychoanalytic Fanon, signals the inclusion of theories of colonialism from a different time and history to its fold, and the intense contestation over the work of the revolutionary theorist, activist and psychoanalyst. Parry's recuperation of nationalism, 'Resistance Theory/Theorising Resistance or Two Cheers for Nativism', is supported by Neil Lazarus' positive but critical review of the place of intellectuals in 'National Consciousness and the Specificity of (Post)-colonial intellectualism'. Both essays are collected in *Colonial Discourse/Postcolonial theory* (1994) and present an important alternative strand to what is sometimes seen as a celebratory 'hybridity' and anti-essentialism in some significant domains of postcolonial theory; the volume also contains Anne McClintock's much cited critique of the term 'postcolonialism'.

Another genealogy of postcolonial theory is possible if one also incorporates the work done in postcolonial criticism and Commonwealth writing. This position is argued by critics associated with the development of 'Commonwealth literature' or 'new literatures in English' in Britain and the Commonwealth. Alan Lawson, Leigh Dale, Helen Tiffin, Shane Rowlands, Stephen Slemon and Bart Moore-Gilbert all contend that the work done by creative writers like Raja Rao, Wilson Harris and Wole Soyinka foreshadow colonial discourse theory. The Leeds' conference of 1964 is marked as a key moment in the establishment of Commonwealth teaching, with writers such as Chinua Achebe and R. K. Narayan contributing lectures; some of its themes and issues such as identity, nationality, landscape, pedagogy and language would be taken up over the next decade. In their recent collective introduction to a comparative survey of postcolonial literatures and theories in English, Lawson, Dale, Tiffin and Rowlands argue for overlaps between what is sometimes taken to be two separate genealogies. 'Commonwealth post-colonialism', a term they coin, initially focused more on creative efforts and channelled energies, especially in the 1970s, into anti-colonial criticism and the writing and teaching of national or regional literatures. The African presence is particularly strong in this period of the 1970s with Chinua Achebe's *Morning Yet on Creation Day* (1975), Wole Soyinka's *Myth, Literature and the African World* (1976) and Ngugi Wa Thiongo's *Homecoming: Essays on African and Caribbean Literature* (1972) following the setting up of Heinemann's African Writers Series. (This period also witnessed the creation of Dangaroo Press based in Denmark publishing critical, theoretical and literary work from the Commonwealth.) Slemon and Moore-Gilbert contend that concepts like creolization and hybridization in Carribean writers and theorists such as Edward Brathwaite and Wilson Harris resemble the ambivalence that will surface with Bhabha's work in the 1980s. Bill Ashcroft, Gareth Griffiths and Helen Tiffin's *The Empire Writes Back* (1989) would provide a landmark teaching text where postcolonial Commonwealth literary criticism takes on board more self-consciously postcolonial theory. The publication of anthologies of postcolonial theory and criticism, notably Laura Chrisman and Patrick Williams's *Colonial Discourse and Post-Colonial Theory* (1993). Bill Ashcroft, Gareth Griffiths and Helen

Tiffin's *The Postcolonial Studies Reader* (1995) and the more US-oriented *Contemporary Postcolonial Theory: A Reader* (1996) by Padmini Mongia, also marks the canonisation and commodification of the field in academic studies.

The recent critical and sometimes hostile reassessment of postcolonial theory and its impact marks a phase in which the theory has come of age; Vijay Mishra and Bob Hodge's 'What is Post(-)colonialism?' (1991) points out the limitations of the all-embracing nature of *The Empire Strikes Back*, while Ella Shohat's 'Notes on the Post-Colonial' (1992) attempts a reflexive archaeology of the term post-colonial. Aijaz Ahmad's *In Theory* (1992) attempts to rejuvenate the Marxist connections and, like Arif Dirlik's *The Postcolonial Aura* (1997), warns against a lack of historical specificity and objects to the radical chic of metropolitan theorising, a caution already sounded in Spivak's early work. Dirlik's academic connections are to China Studies as is Rey Chow's work; this is just a small indication of how widespread the current disciplinary affiliations and geographical concerns are in the area of postcolonial theory, and how much these disparate bases have added to, problematised and reshaped what has previously taken to be the central ground. Crossovers with the field of cultural studies and cultural theory have also been particularly productive with Stuart Hall and Paul Gilroy's interrogation of racism and representation, ethnic absolutism and nationalism. Gilroy's recent monumental study of the African Diaspora, *The Black Atlantic* (1993), argues for an ethnohistorical approach to modernity. His charting of transnational and intercultural flow of ideas about ethnicity and identity in black vernacular culture and nationalist thought develops one of the central tropes of postcolonial migration. Rey Chow's study of Chinese cinema, *Primitive Passions* (1995), Ella Shohat and Robert Stam's *Unthinking Eurocentrism: Multiculturalism and the Media* (1994), which explores the central role of the media and popular culture in shaping both Eurocentric thinking and an oppositional aesthetics of resistance, are good examples of the current willingness to apply theory to more popular forms to see how they revise and revitalise terms and concepts.

The articles by Bhabha, Low and Chow reproduced here represent, in my mixed metaphor, moments in the vast terrain and hybrid concerns of postcolonial theory and its applications. Bhabha's 'Of Mimicry and Man' belongs to the early phase of Bhabha's work which is concerned with how stereotyping, imitation and mimicry all reflect an ambivalence and hybridity in colonial discourse that troubles its smooth delivery. Bhabha argues that Orientalism is as much about the colonial production of knowledges as it is about projection of fears and desires; Said acknowledges this split in his appropriation of the Freudian terms of dream analyses, manifest and latent, but understandably focuses exclusively on *Orientalism*'s disciplinary power and effectivity. In an effort to avoid the reification of colonial power, history and subjectivity, Bhabha's arguments will question precisely the effectivity of colonial authority at the level of discourse. Consequently, his reading will emphasise the vacillation between Orientalism as the authoritative discourse of knowledge, learning and information and Orientalism as fantasy; such a vacillation renders a much more fractured and ambivalent discourse than *Orientalism* puts forward.

One significant pole of Bhabha's arguments then relies on psychoanalytic theories of identity formation, and the adoption of the mirror as the figure for discussing how vision and difference contributes to self-image. Accordingly, the colonial situation provides the opportunity for narcissistic identification in the image of the colonised as 'a reformed, recognisable Other'; such figures can be found in the image of the anglicised native, which in Thomas Macaulay's words, form the 'class of persons Indian in blood and colour, but English in tastes, in opinions, in morals and in intellect'. But this reformed image of the other is also a product of the colonial gaze which must insist on difference – not quite/not white, not English but anglicised – in order to justify continued colonial rule. The discriminatory discourse must also produce the other as poor imitations of the self because these 'mimic men' cannot ever arrive at the threshold of humanity that is identified with the coloniser; hence, the ambivalence, indeterminacy and self-contradictory nature of colonial discourse which 'must continually produce its slippage, its excess, its difference' in order to be effective. Here Bhabha also draws on the psychoanalytic theory of fetishism as avowal and disavowal of castration. (Bhabha makes no apologies or concessions for invoking the gendered bias in the equation of castration with lack and femininity). Racial fetishism is argued to possess a similar dynamic of avowal and disavowal in its primal encounter with the difference of skin colour; racial stereotyping is an 'arrested, fixated form of representation' based on the subject's denial of difference and desire that 'all men have the same skin/ colour/race'.

The reformed other has the potential to unsettle and threaten the self precisely because it resembles the image of the self. Like Freud's uncanny, which catches the ease by which the self can be alienated (literally estranged or made strange) through the double, colonial mimicry is at once resemblance and menace. Colonial mimicry produces another knowledge of the self by producing a vision of the self from (an)other place; for example, in Charles Grant's treatise on the morality and necessity of Christian education and reform, the civilising mission is mirrored as an immoral form of social control. Mimicry need not be restricted to colonial history but can be also found in postcolonial literatures. For example, in *The Enigma of Arrival*, V. S. Naipaul's ambivalent mediations on Englishness, it is the narrator's loving (mis)identification with the English and veneration of things English that also enable him to see it as an invention of tradition – the handiwork of impresarios. The investment in origins is precisely what enables an intimate knowledge of its production.

The disruption of colonial discourse can also be traced, deconstructively, on a more historical front. An understanding of the discursive economy of fetishism as posed between the twin poles of metonymy and metaphor provides the link. Bhabha uses the term 'metonymy of presence' to signal the distance between the metropolitan point of articulation and origination, and the colonial periphery that colonial discourse has to travel to. In this theory, metaphor, which presumes an identity of meaning across boundaries, is supplemented by metonymy, which registers different social, cultural and political displacements. Discourse as it is translated into a colonial context brings about hybridisation and ambivalence, and points to the lie of universalism that underwrites colonial authority. The insertion into colonial discourse of beliefs, assumptions and languages that are deemed foreign to it enables a resistance or blockage; it is also employed as a strategy by postcolonial writers who work within a metropolitan literary tradition, but who want also to insist on their difference, and their resistance to a master(ing) discourse.

Bhabha's insights into the conflictual nature of colonial subjectivities is helpful for its refusal of the easy binary polarities of coloniser/colonised and colonialist/nationalist, and claims to a stable, whole and unitary identity on both sides of the divide. The ambivalence of colonial discourse opens up a space to think about how power and paranoia are linked, and paves the way for a less reductive reading of colonial texts. But Bhabha does not differentiate between the different positions the critic, the text and the context occupies in the production of ambivalence; his vacillation between all three fields makes it difficult to assess what kinds of resistance are possible to colonial authority and the status of such resistance. Also, Bhabha's psychoanalytic and deconstructive approach enables the more troubled and conflictual reading but, as Robert Young in *White Mythologies* has pointed out, it is by no means certain if this is the distinct mark of the colonial situation, or is, following deconstruction and psychoanalysis, a characteristic of all texts and all psyches.

Gail Low attempts a more nuanced reading and assessment of two key figures in imperial myth-making of the late nineteenth century; her work is enabled by the spaces opened up by Bhabha's exploration of ambivalence of colonial texts, and by the literary theoretical turn to psychoanalysis to explore questions of power, desire, pleasure, displeasure, mastery and defence in the representation of colonial relations. Contrary to the conventional dismissal of Kipling's writing as simple imperial proselytising, she asks the question: 'What kind of jingoism and what kind of effectivity?' She discovers in Kipling's early writing a fascination with figures who cross cultural and social boundaries, especially white men 'gone native', whose transgressive status is sometimes recuperated for the colonial state, and sometimes shunned as 'beyond the pale'. Unlike the 'mimic men' of Bhabha's piece, who are figures of comedy and estrangement, the white man who can pass for native is invested with extraordinary energy within the stories. To use the psychoanalytic term, they are 'subjects who presume to know'; their distinctive status resides in their being subjects outside the circuit of desire. Hence, their fascination and power as imperial symbols lies not in the figures themselves but transferential dynamics. Here Low follows the line of Peter Brooks in arguing for the similarity between the psychoanalytic and narrative structures; the transferential dynamics of the analytic situation are similar to the transferential dynamics of storytelling and its seduction.

In the chapter that is reproduced, Low is concerned with the 'Loafer' or vagrant in what is sometimes taken to be the quintessential parable of empire, 'The Man Who Would Be King'. Positive responses to the loafers have often taken the line that the tale's moral lies in its expression of 'universal desire for power and domination'; these readings have remarked on the loafer's breathless daring and impudence. But Low argues that such readings of what is a much more open tale is only possible after transference has taken place; the 'truth' or moral of the tale in this way is understood to be more a retroactive product of desire than internal to the text. Focusing not on the central characters of the tale, but their relationship to each other and critics' relationship to them, Low reads in Kipling's elaborate use of various frame-narrators and focalisation his sense of his own role as writer, his awareness of contemporary culture and a canny understanding of how narration is built on voyeurism, novelty and seduction. For Low, the strengths of the tale lies not in its audacious representation of conquest but in its understanding of the impudent processes of imperial mythologising. The artist as loafer represents the flip side to the traditional portrait of Kipling as imperial bard, 'responsible for some of the founding legends of Empire'; Low's Kipling emerges as an opportunistic 'flaneur-tramp, [with an] inquisitive and often deliberately voyeuristic gaze', a figure who fantasises about crossing cultural boundaries, and a writer who turns others into narrative and commercial profit.

Low's reading of 'The Man Who Would Be King' is useful for calling attention to Kipling's complex handling of narrative. But her piece suffers from some of the same flaws exhibited by Bhabha's text; her desire to read historically and to read psychoanalytically elides what is distinctly attributable to the colonial situation and what to more ahistorical structures of narrative or the psyche. In addition, the relationship between commerce, novelty, journalism and Empire, while suggestive, is not fully developed nor worked into the story's structure.

The difficulty of cultural crossings in a postcolonial world that bears the legacy of imperialism is at the heart of Rey Chow's work on the (re)presentation of Chinese cinema both within and without its national boundaries. The questions she asks are very much central to postcolonial theory: How do postcolonial cultural and artistic endeavours in the cinema engage with the epistemic violence of colonialism, and what do they have to offer us on different sides of the cultural divide? How should a western(ised) critic discourse on non-western expressive cultures? How should a non-western critic discourse on cultural forms that are enabled by 'western' technologies? What kinds of institutional politics are involved in such cross-cultural problems and how do we circumvent their more oppressive and repressive effects? How do non-westerners deal with the postmodern extension of an Orientalist legacy?

Chow's book is a calculated intervention for cross-cultural exchanges against the mutual hostilities of cultural essentialism and the guilt-ridden anxieties of the liberal western intellectual in an age of postcolonialism. To this effect, she employs the term ethnography for her model of cultural exchange. Here, ethnography is divested of its disciplinary claims to truth and knowledge, and read as 'autoethnography', which is fully cognisant of its subjective origins. Chow follows Mary Louise Pratt's definition of these forms of self-representation by colonised others which appropriate and engage with the traditions of their colonisers, but her interrogation of subject/object split in the Orientalist gaze leads her to focus on visuality both literally and metaphorically. Revising Laura Mulvey's theorisation of the male gaze, Chow argues, in autoethnography 'the experience of being looked at' and the 'memory of past objecthood' is 'the primary event in cross-cultural representation'. Hence, the anthropological impasse of a world divided between subject and object, seer and seen, active and passive, us and them is no longer tenable: '"viewed object" is now looking at "viewing subject" looking'. In a memorable scene in Zhang YiMou's *JuDou*, the heroine deliberately disrobes and displays her bruised body before her peeping-tom nephew, the voyeurism and eroticism of the spectacle of the female body rapidly fades into a self-conscious realisation of the violence of the structures which enable such an scene. Likewise, Chow's autoethnographic exchanges are forms of cross-cultural narrative by which the 'less powerful (cultures) negotiate the [violence of the] imposition of the agenda of the powerful'. Reading Gianni Vattimo alongside Walter Benjamin, Chow argues that they are contradictory fabular forms by which the previously ethnographized survive in the media marketplace by engaging with, amplifying ironizing and displaying the terms of their subjection, calling attention to the interplay of power, myth and image. In doing so, their subversive gaze points towards 'the weakened foundations of Western metaphysics as well as the disintegrated bases of Eastern traditions'.

In reading New Chinese Cinema (associated with the Fifth Generation film directors) as autoenthographic and a fabular form of ethnography, she disrupts the disciplinary professionalism which claims a truth or documentary function for the genre, and aligns herself with the postmodernist scepticism of 'metaphysical truth claims and metaphysical systems of logic' (Vattimo, 1988, xiii). But, more importantly, reading narrative cinema as (auto)ethnographic allows her to read the concept of national cinema differently: as inscriptive cultural record of images, sounds and stories, as a translation between cultures and, with postmodern hindsight, as the transformation of culture through the media. Autoethnographic forms of representation address questions of identity, ethnicity, sexuality, gender, authenticity, elite and popular by situating the national within a transnational global traffic of mixed media and commodity capitalism. This form of culture writing engages with the hybridity, mediation, 'contamination' and 'corruption' of postcolonial forms of expression. In their content and narrative structure, distribution and reception, they enable an interrogation of the myth of authentic native and the exotic primitive within nationalistic and Euro-modernist discourses by showing them to be the structural product of displacement and identification. Correspondingly, and here Chow's text shows the influence of deconstruction, the critic's task is not to reinstate the deep-seated prejudice and privilege of depth, originality and fidelity which governs critical conventions; 'we [have to] take seriously the deconstructionist insistence that the "first" and "original" as such is always already difference – always already translated'. The desire to return to one's origin is shown to be a paradoxical desire to remove it from the very structuration that renders it 'original' in the first place. Chow argues that the 'dismantling' of the notion of origin and alterity both within and without the western world allows one to open one's eyes to – and take responsibility for – the 'coevalness of cultures' in the contemporary world:

> This notion of the other – not as idealised lost origin to be rediscovered or resurrected but as our contemporary – allows for a context of cultural translation in which these 'other' cultures are equally engaged in the contradictions of modernity, such as the primitivization of the under-privileged, the quest for new foundations and new monuments, as so forth ... The coevalness of cultures, is not simply the peaceful co-existence among plural societies but the co-temporality of power structures ... that mutually support and reinforce the exploitation of underprivileged social groups, nonhuman life forms, and ecological resources throughout the world.

The focus on film in postcolonial discourse analysis is particularly welcomed, for the terrain of postcolonial critiques has tended to focus more on the literary than on popular media forms; yet, in an transnational world, it is the latter which increasingly and more complexly impact on our feelings of belonging and exclusions. In this, we see also see the merits and the limitations of her study. Film textual analysis offers the joys of 'close reading' and allows discussion of the spectacle of postmodern consumer culture; but the claims for a quintessential postcolonial subversiveness for the Fifth Generation is perhaps weakened by the relative exclusion of even more popular media forms and by the absence of what Ella Shohat and Robert Stam have called the different and multiple registers of spectatorship.

Nevertheless, Chow's criticism, which is a good example of the domain of postcolonial discourse analysis, intersects productively with the preoccupations and insights of deconstruction, poststructuralism, postmodernism, psychoanalysis and feminism, and is careful to take note of the relentless migrations of her subject between cultures, histories and media. Her reading of the work of the Fifth Generation of Chinese film directors shows the enormous difficulties and rewards of the postcolonial critic who takes seriously the task of cross-cultural exchange. For her critiques interrogate not only the construction of images and narratives, their attendant aesthetic and political histories, but are also aware of the processes of identification and displacement that signal a critic's location and investment in the subject matter. The difficulty and rewards of postcolonial theory and criticism is, to use Said's phrase in *Culture and Imperialism* (1993), nothing less than an attempt to come to terms with 'overlapping territories and intertwined histories'.

10.1

OF MIMICRY AND MAN: THE AMBIVALENCE OF COLONIAL DISCOURSE

Homi K. Bhabha

Mimicry reveals something in so far as it is distinct from what might be called an itself that is behind. The effect of mimicry is camouflage . . . It is not a question of harmonizing with the background, but against a mottled background, of becoming mottled – exactly like the technique of camouflage practised in human warfare.

Jacques Lacan (1977, 99)

It is out of season to question at this time of day, the original policy of a conferring on every colony of the British Empire a mimic representation of the British Constitution. But if the creature so endowed has sometimes forgotten its real significance and under the fancied importance of speakers and maces, and all the paraphernalia and ceremonies of the imperial legislature, has dared to defy the mother country, she has to thank herself for the folly of conferring such privileges on a condition of society that has no earthly claim to so exalted a position. A fundamental principle appears to have been forgotten or overlooked in our system of colonial policy – that of colonial dependence. To give to a colony the forms of independence is a mockery; she would not be a colony for a single hour if she could maintain an independent station.

Sir Edward Cust, 'Reflections on West African affairs . . . addressed to the Colonial Office', Hatchard, London 1839

The discourse of post-Enlightenment English colonialism often speaks in a tongue that is forked, not false. If colonialism takes power in the name of history, it repeatedly exercises its authority through the figures of farce. For the epic intention of the civilizing mission, 'human and not wholly human' in the famous words of Lord Rosebery, 'writ by the finger of the Divine' (cit. Stokes,

Extract from Homi K. Bhabha, *The Location of Culture* (Routledge, 1994), pp. 85–92.

1960, 17–18) often produces a text rich in the traditions of *trompe-l'œil*, irony, mimicry and repetition. In this comic turn from the high ideals of the colonial imagination to its low mimetic literary effects mimicry emerges as one of the most elusive and effective strategies of colonial power and knowledge.

Within that conflictual economy of colonial discourse which Edward Said (1978, 240) describes as the tension between the synchronic panoptical vision of domination – the demand for identity, stasis – and the counter-pressure of the diachrony of history – change, difference – mimicry represents an *ironic* compromise. If I may adapt Samuel Weber's formulation of the marginalizing vision of castration (1973, 112), then colonial mimicry is the desire for a reformed, recognizable Other, *as a subject of a difference that is almost the same, but not quite*. Which is to say, that the discourse of mimicry is constructed around an *ambivalence*; in order to be effective, mimicry must continually produce its slippage, its excess, its difference. The authority of that mode of colonial discourse that I have called mimicry is therefore stricken by an indeterminacy: mimicry emerges as the representation of a difference that is itself a process of disavowal. Mimicry is, thus, the sign of a double articulation; a complex strategy of reform, regulation and discipline, which 'appropriates' the Other as it visualizes power. Mimicry is also the sign of the inappropriate, however, a difference or recalcitrance which coheres the dominant strategic function of colonial power, intensifies surveillance, and poses an immanent threat to both 'normalized' knowledges and disciplinary powers.

The effect of mimicry on the authority of colonial discourse is profound and disturbing. For in 'normalizing' the colonial state or subject, the dream of post-Enlightenment civility alienates its own language of liberty and produces another knowledge of its norms. The ambivalence which thus informs this strategy is discernible, for example, in Locke's Second Treatise which *splits* to reveal the limitations of liberty in his double use of the word 'slave': first simply, descriptively as the locus of a legitimate form of ownership, then as the trope for an intolerable, illegitimate exercise of power. What is articulated in that distance between the two uses is the absolute, imagined difference between the 'Colonial' State of Carolina and the Original State of Nature.

It is from this area between mimicry and mockery, where the reforming, civilizing mission is threatened by the displacing gaze of its disciplinary double, that my instances of colonial imitation come. What they all share is a discursive process by which the excess or slippage produced by the *ambivalence* of mimicry (almost the same, *but not quite*) does not merely 'rupture' the discourse, but becomes transformed into an uncertainty which fixes the colonial subject as a 'partial' presence. By 'partial' I mean both 'incomplete' and 'virtual'. It is as if the very emergence of the 'colonial' is dependent for its representation upon some strategic limitation or prohibition *within* the author-itative discourse itself. The success of colonial appropriation depends on a proliferation of inappropriate objects that ensure its strategic failure, so that mimicry is at once resemblance and menace.

A classic text of such partiality is Charles Grant's 'Observations on the state of society among the Asiatic subjects of Great Britain' (1792; 1812–13, 10: 282) which was only superseded by James Mills's *History of India* as the most influential early nineteenth-century account of Indian manners and morals. Grant's dream of an evangelical system of mission education conducted un-compromisingly in the English language, was partly a belief in political reform along Christian lines and partly an awareness that the expansion of company rule in India required a system of subject formation – a reform of manners, as Grant put it – that would provide the colonial with 'a sense of personal identity as we know it'. Caught between the desire for religious reform and the fear that the Indians might become turbulent for liberty, Grant paradoxically implies that it is the 'partial' diffusion of Christianity, and the 'partial' influence of moral improvements which will construct a particularly appropriate form of colonial subjectivity. What is suggested is a process of reform through which Christian doctrines might collude with divisive caste practices to prevent dangerous political alliances. Inadvertently, Grant produces a knowledge of Christianity as a form of social control which conflicts with the enunciatory assumptions that authorize his discourse. In suggesting, finally, that 'partial reform' will produce an empty form of 'the *imitation* [my emphasis] of English manners which will induce them [the colonial subjects] to remain under our protection' (Ch. 4, 104). Grant mocks his moral project and violates the Evidence of Christianity – a central missionary tenet – which forbade any tolerance of heathen faiths.

The absurd extravagance of Macaulay's 'Minute' (1835) – deeply influenced by Charles Grant's 'Observations' – makes a mockery of Oriental learning until faced with the challenge of conceiving of a 'reformed' colonial subject. Then, the great tradition of European humanism seems capable only of ironizing itself. At the intersection of European learning and colonial power, Macaulay can conceive of nothing other than 'a class of interpreters between us and the millions whom we govern – a class of persons Indian in blood and colour, but English in tastes, in opinions, in morals and in intellect' (1958, 49) – in other words a mimic man raised 'through our English School', as a missionary educationist wrote in 1819, 'to form a corps of translators and be employed in different departments of Labour' (Thomason, 1821, 54–5). The line of descent of the mimic man can be traced through the works of Kipling, Forster, Orwell, Naipaul, and to his emergence, most recently, in Benedict Anderson's excellent work on nationalism, as the anomalous Bipin Chandra Pal (1983, 88). He is the effect of a flawed colonial mimesis, in which to be Anglicized is *emphatically* not to be English.

The figure of mimicry is locatable within what Anderson describes as 'the inner compatibility of empire and nation' (1983, 88–9). It problematizes the signs of racial and cultural priority, so that the 'national' is no longer naturalizable. What emerges between mimesis and mimicry is a *writing*, a mode of representation, that marginalizes the monumentality of history, quite simply mocks its power to be a model, that power which supposedly makes it imitable. Mimicry *repeats* rather than *re-presents* and in that diminishing perspective emerges Decoud's displaced European vision of Sulaco in Conrad's *Nostromo* as:

> the endlessness of civil strife where folly seemed even harder to bear than its ignominy ... the lawlessness of a populace of all colours and races, barbarism, irremediable tyranny ... America is ungovernable. (Conrad, 1979, 161)

Or Ralph Singh's apostasy in Naipaul's *The Mimic Men*:

> We pretended to be real, to be learning, to be preparing ourselves for life, we mimic men of the New World, one unknown corner of it, with all its reminders of the corruption that came so quickly to the new. (1967, 146)

Both Decoud and Singh, and in their different ways Grant and Macaulay, are the parodists of history. Despite their intentions and invocations they inscribe the colonial text erratically, eccentrically across a body politic that refuses to be representative, in a narrative that refuses to be representational. The desire to emerge as 'authentic' through mimicry – through a process of writing and repetition – is the final irony of partial representation.

What I have called mimicry is not the familiar exercise of *dependent* colonial relations through narcissistic identification so that, as Fanon has observed (1970, 109) the black man stops being an actional person for only the white man can represent his self-esteem. Mimicry conceals no presence or identity behind its mask: it is not what Césaire describes as 'colonization-thingification' (1972, 21) behind which there stands the essence of the *présence Africaine*. The *menace* of mimicry is its *double* vision which in disclosing the ambivalence of colonial discourse also disrupts its authority. And it is a double vision that is a result of what I've described as the partial representation/recognition of the colonial object. Grant's colonial as partial imitator, Macaulay's translator, Naipaul's colonial politician as play-actor, Decoud as the scene setter of the *opéra bouffe* of the New World, these are the appropriate objects of a colonialist chain of command, authorized versions of otherness. But they are also, as I have shown, the figures of a doubling, the part-objects of a metonymy of colonial desire which alienates the modality and normality of those dominant discourses in which they emerge as 'inappropriate' colonial subjects. A desire that, through the repetition of *partial presence*, which is the basis of mimicry, articulates those disturbances of cultural, racial and historical difference that menace the narcissistic demand of colonial authority. It is a desire that reverses 'in part' the colonial appropriation by now producing a partial vision of the colonizer's presence; a gaze of otherness, that shares the acuity of the genealogical gaze which, as Foucault describes it, liberates marginal elements and shatters the unity of man's being through which he extends his sovereignty (1977, 153).

I want to turn to this process by which the look of surveillance returns as the displacing gaze of the disciplined, where the observer becomes the observed and 'partial' representation rearticulates the whole notion of *identity* and alienates it from essence. But not before observing that even an exemplary history like Eric Stokes' *The English Utilitarians and India* acknowledges the anomalous gaze of otherness but finally disavows it in a contradictory utterance:

> Certainly India played *no* central part in fashioning the distinctive qualities of English civilisation. In many ways it acted as a disturbing force, a magnetic power placed at the periphery tending to distort the natural development of Britain's character (1959, xi, my emphasis)

What is the nature of the hidden threat of the partial gaze? How does mimicry emerge as the subject of the scopic drive and the object of colonial surveillance? How is desire disciplined, authority displaced?

If we turn to a Freudian figure to address these issues of colonial textuality, that form of difference that is mimicry – *almost the same but not quite* – will become clear. Writing of the partial nature of fantasy, caught *inappropriately*, between the unconscious and the preconscious, making problematic, like mimicry, the very notion of 'origins', Freud has this to say:

> Their mixed and split origin is what decides their fate. We may compare them with individuals of mixed race who taken all round resemble white men but who betray their coloured descent by some striking feature or other and on that account are excluded from society and enjoy none of the privileges. (1915, 14: 190–1)

Almost the same but not white: the visibility of mimicry is always produced at the site of interdiction. It is a form of colonial discourse that is uttered *inter dicta*: a discourse at the crossroads of what is known and permissible and that which though known must be kept concealed; a discourse uttered between the lines and as such both against the rules and within them. The question of the representation of difference is therefore always also a problem of authority. The 'desire' of mimicry, which is Freud's 'striking feature' that reveals so little but makes such a big difference, is not merely that impossibility of the Other which repeatedly resists signification. The desire of colonial mimicry – an interdictory desire – may not have an object, but it has strategic objectives which I shall call the *metonymy of presence*.

Those inappropriate signifiers of colonial discourse – the difference between being English and being Anglicized; the identity between stereotypes which, through repetition, also become different; the discriminatory identities constructed across traditional cultural norms and classifications, the Simian Black, the Lying Asiatic – all these are *metonymies* of presence. They are strategies of desire in discourse that make the anomalous representation of the colonized something other than a process of 'the return of the repressed', what Fanon unsatisfactorily characterized as collective catharsis (1970, 103). These instances of metonymy are the non-repressive productions of contradictory and multiple belief. They cross the boundaries of the culture of enunciation through a strategic confusion of the metaphoric and metonymic axes of the cultural production of meaning.

In mimicry, the representation of identity and meaning is rearticulated along the axis of metonymy. As Lacan reminds us, mimicry is like camouflage, not a harmonization of repression of difference, but a form of resemblance, that differs from or defends presence by displaying it in part, metonymically. Its threat, I would add, comes from the prodigious and strategic production of conflictual, fantastic, discriminatory 'identity effects' in the play of a power that is elusive because it hides no essence, no 'itself'. And that form of *resemblance* is the most terrifying thing to behold, as Edward Long testifies in his *History of Jamaica* (1774). At the end of a tortured, negrophobic passage, that shifts anxiously between piety, prevarication and perversion, the text finally confronts its fear; nothing other than the repetition of its resemblance 'in part': '[Negroes] are represented by all authors as the vilest of human kind, to which they have little more pretension of resemblance *than what arises from their exterior forms*' (1774, 2: 353, my emphasis).

From such a colonial encounter between the white presence and its black semblance, there emerges the question of the ambivalence of mimicry as a problematic of colonial subjection. For if Sade's scandalous theatricalization of language repeatedly reminds us that discourse can claim 'no priority', then the work of Edward Said will not let us forget that the 'ethnocentric and erratic will to power from which texts can spring' (1979, 184) is itself a theatre of war. Mimicry, as the metonymy of presence, is, indeed, such an erratic, eccentric strategy of authority in colonial discourse. Mimicry does not merely destroy narcissistic authority through the repetitious slippage of difference and desire. It is the process of the *fixation* of the colonial as a form of cross-classificatory, discriminatory knowledge within an interdictory discourse, and therefore necessarily raises the question of the *authorization* of colonial representations; a question of authority that goes beyond the subject's lack of priority (castration) to a historical crisis in the conceptuality of colonial man as an *object* of regulatory power, as the subject of racial, cultural, national representation.

'This culture ... fixed in its colonial status', Fanon suggests, '[is] both present and mummified, it testified against its members. It defines them in fact without appeal' (1967, 44). The ambivalence of mimicry – almost but not quite – suggests that the fetishized colonial culture is potentially and strategically an insurgent counter-appeal. What I have called its 'identity-effects' are always crucially *split*. Under cover of camouflage, mimicry, like the fetish, is a part-object that radically revalues the normative knowledges of the priority of race, writing, history. For the fetish mimes the forms of authority at the point at which it deauthorizes them. Similarly, mimicry rearticulates presence in terms of its 'otherness', that which it disavows. There is a crucial difference between this *colonial* articulation of man and his doubles and that which Foucault describes as 'thinking the unthought' (1971, Ch. 9) which, for nineteenth-century Europe, is the ending of man's alienation by reconciling him with his essence. The colonial discourse that articulates an *interdictory* otherness is precisely the 'other scene' of this nineteenth-century European desire for an authentic historical consciousness.

The 'unthought' across which colonial man is articulated is that process of classificatory confusion that I have described as the metonymy of the substitutive chain of ethical and cultural discourse. This results in the *splitting* of colonial discourse so that two attitudes towards external reality persist; one takes reality into consideration while the other disavows it and replaces it by a product of desire that repeats, rearticulates 'reality' as mimicry.

So Edward Long can say with authority, quoting variously Hume, Eastwick and Bishop Warburton in his support, that: 'Ludicrous as the opinion may seem I do not think that an orangutang husband would be any dishonour to a Hottentot female' (1774, 2: 364).

Such contradictory articulations of reality and desire – seen in racist stereotypes, statements, jokes, myths – are not caught in the doubtful circle of the return of the repressed. They are the effects of a disavowal that denies the differences of the other but produces in its stead forms of authority and multiple belief that alienate the assumptions of 'civil' discourse. If, for a while, the ruse of desire is calculable for the uses of discipline soon the repetition of guilt, justification, pseudo-scientific theories, superstition, spurious authorities, and classifications can be seen as the desperate effort to 'normalize' *formally* the disturbance of a discourse of splitting that violates the rational enlightened claims of its enunciatory modality. The ambivalence of colonial authority repeatedly turns from *mimicry* – a difference that is almost nothing but not quite – to *menace* – a difference that is almost total but not quite. And in that other scene of colonial power, where history turns to farce and presence to 'a part', can be seen the twin figures of narcissism and paranoia that repeat furiously, uncontrollably.

In the ambivalent world of the 'not quite/not white', on the margins of metropolitan desire, the *founding objects* of the Western world become the erratic, eccentric, accidental *objets trouvés* of the colonial discourse – the part-objects of presence. It is then that the body and the book lose their part-objects of presence. It is then that the body and the book lose their representational authority. Black skin splits under the racist gaze, displaced into signs of bestiality, genitalia, grotesquerie, which reveal the phobic myth of the undifferentiated whole white body. And the holiest of books – the Bible – bearing both the standard of the cross and the standard of empire finds itself strangely dismembered. In May 1817 a missionary wrote from Bengal:

> Still everyone would gladly receive a Bible. And why? – that he may lay it up as a curiosity for a few pice; or use it for waste paper. Such it is well known has been the common fate of these copies of the Bible ... Some have been bartered in the markets, others have been thrown in snuff shops and used as wrapping paper. (Anon., 1817, 186)

LOAFERS AND STORY-TELLERS

Gail Ching-Liang Low

... The loafer presents a perennial source of fascination in Kipling's early stories; on the one hand, the loafer represents the complete opposite of sanctioned figures of authority such as colonial policemen or district officers, and on the other, he represents the logical extension of the very modes of cultural transgression that give figures like Strickland and Kim their special status. The loafer is ... characterised as cynical and machiavellian ... his energies are not harnessed by the state for law-enforcement. He is a character who appears repeatedly in Kipling's narratives as one who rejects fair play and advocates colonial exploitation. In contrast to the district officers who uphold selflessly the ideals of the imperial cause, loafers are vagrants and confidence tricksters who live by their wits and their ability to exploit the situations and the people they come across. They have an uncanny knowledge of Indian life and custom and may, when inclined to do so, pass as native. Their presence in Kipling's texts is yet another indication of ambivalence and contradiction. Loafers voice populist irritation with the rhetorical trappings of Anglo-Indian statecraft and its civilising mission; they preach a simple politics of opportunism, and promote a brutalised version of native society. If their marginality and distance from the centres of imperial power permits the articulation of such desires, those very qualities are recuperated for the centres of imperial power.

... What I want to make clear ... is that the 'subject who is presumed to know' – 'the very place where meaning, and *knowledge* of meaning, reside' (Brooks, 1994, 58) – is produced through narrative. In particular, my analysis

Extract from Gail Ching-Liang Low, *White Skins, Black Masks* (Routledge, 1996), pp. 238–76.

of 'The Man Who Would Be King' aims to explore the transferential mechanics of story-telling. Kipling's short story has a number of different story-tellers and different listeners; each story told to each listener catches him/her in a position of transference. The dynamics of the transferential experience activated by the frame narrator of the tale are similar to the dynamics of seduction in story-telling. The framed narrator's fascination with the two loafers secures our interest; his interest becomes an expression of our desire to know more about their transgressive life-stories. The framed story of the loafers' rise and subsequent fall in 'The Man Who Would Be King' provides readers with a clear-sighted exploration of a colonial grammar and syntax of desire; but it also presents the colonial text as a hoax – a 'scam' – pulled off by enterprising vagabond story-tellers. In this respect, Kipling's fascination with the figure of the loafer represents the shadowy side to his persona as imperial story-teller; loaferdom presents an alternative portrait of the artist as journalist always in search of a good story and the artist as petty thief and trader of lies and lives. It is perhaps not the conventional portrait of Kipling but one necessary to do justice to the complexity of his writing ...

THE POLITICS OF LOAFERDOM

'The Man Who Would Be King', like many of Kipling's other short stories, seems to be a parable but one whose moral instructions are either ironised or rendered ambivalent. It invites conflicting interpretations; it tells the tale of two enterprising drifters, Peachey Carnehan and Daniel Dravot, who manage to stage the biggest confidence trick of all time by convincing the inhabitants of some far-flung territory of their divine right to rule. The story presents fraud and cynical opportunism as the founding legend of Empire. Carnehan and Dravot run out of places and people to dupe in British India; bemoaning the lack of entrepreneurial initiative in governmental circles, Carnehan tells the narrator,

> you can't lift a spade, nor chip a rock, nor look for oil, nor anything like that without all the Government saying – 'Leave it alone and let us govern'. Therefore [we will] ... go away to some other place where a man isn't crowded and can come into his own. (Kipling, 1914, 212)

Disguised first as a native priest and his servant and later as 'heathens' armed with rifles and ammunition, they journey to Kafiristan to create nothing less than an alternative Pax Britannica. Their kingdom is established through superior firepower and through a cynical manipulation of Freemason symbolism, after a chance discovery uncovers Kafiristan's similar religious and ritual ancestry. Their downfall is caused by Dravot, who commits the fatal error of believing his own propaganda and desires a queen to rule by his side. When his bride-to-be unmasks his humanity, the natives of Kafiristan shout, 'neither God nor Devil but a man!' Dravot is killed on a bridge of his own construction, and Carnehan is crucified. Much later, Carnehan returns in a state of delirium and madness to tell his story to his friend, the journalist. It is Carnehan's tale, and the story of their meeting, that the journalist frame-narrator imparts to us.

Carnehan and Dravot are first and foremost 'loafers'. A definition of the term would perhaps be useful. The etymology of the word in the *Oxford English Dictionary* begins with its American meaning, 'to loaf', 'to thieve'. In its later usages, the word is also taken to refer to someone who spends his life in idleness – as contrasted with those who do purposeful work . . .

David Arnold's study of European orphans and vagrants in nineteenth-century India is . . . useful for the specific context which we have to deal with; Arnold's work is a reminder of the harsh attitudes towards loafers prevalent among Anglo-Indians who were concerned with racial respectability. Loafers' vices such as drunkenness, debt, liaisons with native and Eurasian women were listed as factors bringing the white race into disrepute. The Commissioner of Patna writing to the Judicial Secretary of Bengal in 1867 asserted that 'the sight of Europeans in the lowest depths of degradation brought on by drinking and profligacy must . . . degrade [the white] race in the eyes of all who see them'. Fellow Anglo-Indians noted the wearing of Indianised costume with displeasure and were quick to condemn costume which made these European vagrants seem 'more like a Native than a European'. Lord Canning declared that a 'floating population of Indianised English loosely brought up, and exhibiting the worse qualities of both races' was a 'glaring reproach' (Arnold, 1979, 114, 110).

The perception of loafing as a disreputable activity, linked with thieving and vagrancy, is preserved in Kipling's characterisation of loafers. Yet his fascination with these drifters also endows them with a certain transgressive desirability. In 'Letters of Marque', he highlights their potential for embarrassment; but it is an embarrassment that is expressive of a populist dislike of bureaucracy and anger at the concessions made to Indian society. Loafers in 'Letters' are the *Doppelgänger* of the 'hat-marked castes' – the district officers and 'bridge builders' – whose duty and servitude is at the heart of official imperial mythology. Loafers animate the other side of the colonial identity by voicing an aggressive megalomania; in contrast with what they see as a policy of 'extreme scrupulousness' in handling native affairs, they would advocate a policy that 'made [people] . . . sit up' (Kipling, 1919, 181, 198). The 'politics of loaferdom' is a candid brutality which 'sees things from the underside where the lath and plaster is not smoothed off' (Kipling, 1914, 201). If loafers are a lost generation, whose decadence, hedonism, and lack of principles make them morally reprehensible, their politics of unrestrained self-gratification points to a different brand of government. To be a loafer is to have no illusions about the 'civilising mission' or the white man's burden. Carnehan has no qualms about blackmailing the nobility of the Central Indian States for 'hush' money; he bemoans the Residents' interference in his attempt to extort money in the Princely States: 'the Residents finds you out, and then you get escorted to the Border *before you've time to get your knife into them*' (Kipling, 1914, 202 [my emphasis]) . . .

Typically, Carnehan and Dravot's vision of Empire-building reflects a loafer's view of Empire as the acquisition of territory through sheer will and military hardware. Boasting that they can build an alternative 'Sar-a-whack' in Kafiristan, they load camel bags with rifles and travel to the north disguised in native costume. Native disguise in Kipling's stories ... functions as an indicator of transgressive knowledge or empowerment; 'The Man Who Would Be King' is no exception to the rule. Here native costume signifies the loafers' lack of inhibition in crossing moral and social boundaries for their own ends; for Dravot in particular, it also denotes an intimate knowledge of native affairs – a knowledge that is put to devastating effect in his quest to be king. Knowledge and power are twinned in a revealing sequence where Dravot, proud of his ability to be 'complete to the native mind', breaks his disguise. Dravot momentarily drops the guise of the mad priest to direct the frame-narrator's hands to rifle butts under his camel bags, 'twenty of 'em ... and ammunition to correspond, under the whirligigs and the mud dolls'. On arrival in Kafiristan, they easily overwhelm the native population, '[picking] them off with rifles before they knew where they was' (Kipling, 1914, 225). The loafers' audacity culminates in Dravot's installation as tribal God and King.

AN ALLEGORY OF EMPIRE?

The very title of Kipling's short story, 'The Man Who Would Be King', leads readers to expect a parable with an easy moral. It begins with the frame-narrator's elucidation of a moral precept that prefaces the narrative of king-ship, 'Brother to a Prince and fellow to a beggar if he be found worthy'. Addressing readers directly as if to reply to the question of merit, he offers to tell the story of his strange association with loafers and their tale of sover-eignty: 'I once came near to kinship with what might have been a veritable King and was promised the reversion of a Kingdom – army, law-courts, revenue and policy all complete'. Subsequent anecdotal references to historical kings con-firm that the issue of real or worthy sovereigns remains the fable's central concern.

But the main protagonists of the tale do not, in any ordinary sense, represent the conventional material of worthy monarchs. At best, Carnehan and Dravot seem to be audacious but likeable 'overreachers' in their quest for personal and political power. Yet the question of how seriously one is to treat the story of these men who would be kings is a question that all critical interpretations of the story have to address. Louis Cornell encourages us to see the story of the two loafers as a straightforward parable of Empire ...

> Dravot and Carnehan recapitulate the British conquest. Like Clive and the great generals who follow him, they prove that a disciplined native army, provided with effective weapons, is a match for a much larger force of untrained tribesmen. Like great Anglo-Indian administrators, they find the land divided by petty rulers: they put an end to internecine war,

establish the Pax Britannica, and win the support of the tribesmen who prefer subjection to anarchy. (Cornell, 1966, 163)

... Cornell's argument solves none of the problems of interpretation ... The story's narrative frame courts alternative interpretations – is the story true, an instance of the frame-narrator's proximity to veritable kings, or is the story false, and the product of the fevered imagination of loafer or frame-narrator.

One of the obvious difficulties for an interpretation which has this story as an unproblematic allegory of Empire-building lies in the status of Kafiristan and its inhabitants. The people of Kafiristan are introduced early as sharing the same racial group as the natives of England. Carnehan and Dravot's attempts at finding more information about the country which they seek to conquer unearth some surprising facts. Carnehan's researches result in a surprising find, 'Blow Bellew! ... this book here says they think they're related to us English' (Kipling, 1914, 214). Later, his description of the tribes in question builds on this connection: 'They were fair men – fairer than you, or me – with yellow hair and remarkable well built' (Kipling, 1914, 225). This link between the natives of Kafiristan and Englishmen is kept up throughout Carnehan's story of their rise and fall. Dravot's inaugural speech as Grand-Master and king repeats the impression of racial commonality: 'I know you won't cheat me because you're white people – sons of Alexander – and not common, black Mohammedans' (Kipling, 1914, 234). Furthermore, when planning the expansion of his empire, Dravot refers to his subjects as English. The full irony of this parable of Empire is apparent in his ravings:

> 'I won't make a Nation,' says he. 'I'll make an Empire! These men aren't niggers; they're English. Look at their eyes – look at their mouths. Look at the way they stand up. They sit on chairs in their own houses ... Two million people – two hundred and fifty thousand fighting men – and all English! They only want the rifles and a little drilling.' (Kipling, 1914, 236)

Carnehan's story is the tale of two vagrants who attempt to build an Empire through discipline; their version of discipline and character-building turns on educating the white natives of Kafiristan on how to drill in formation. Is 'The Man Who Would Be King' a parody of Empire? ... The irreverent image of Empire-building as consisting primarily of rifles and stiff parades reads more like a practical joke than a founding legend ... James Harrison and Tim Bascom ... ask whether these two men representing the 'scum of Anglo-Indian society' (who yet seek to civilise the sons of Alexander) are Kipling's idea of a joke (Bascom, 1987, 170, 173). As Harrison puts it, 'Can Kipling be scurrilously parodying the British acquisition of India?' One could ... read the story as a narrative which stages the imperial scenario with breathless impudence, but also takes the edge off its boldness through a pleasurable and comic characterisation of the two loafers' antics. Cornell's reading would more or less fall into this category. Yet, I would suggest, a more literal and less pleasurable reading may also be found if one reads Kipling's tale as a parody of imperial mythologising ...

TRANSFERENCE: PARABLE OR PARODY?

The frame-narrator is crucial to the manner in which a narrative trap is set for the reader. The frame-narrator's role within the narrative structure of the story encompasses two very distinct spheres of reference: the prosaic world of nineteenth-century reality and the epic and fabular world of the two loafer-kings' adventures. The frame-narrator occupies both the position of story-teller and listener; he is the figure to whom Carnehan directs his story and the figure that mediates Carnehan's story. For some readers, his location within the historical reality of nineteenth-century British India facilitates a better acceptance of what would otherwise be the incredible achievements of two loafers. For others, his specific contribution lies in the complex framing of the story, enabling an allegorical reading. As Tim Bascom argues, the improbability of the story is softened by the narrative frame which lets us commit ourselves to the telling of the tale, if not its actual content. Yet it is the narrator's presence in the historical world of Pax Britannica that makes the Kafiristan empire seem less real, 'prompting us to view it parabolically' (Bascom, 1987, 162) ...

The frame-narrator is positioned in relation to the two loafers as an intra-textual listener of their story; his reading position – one of attentive fascination – is a position that the extra-textual reader is encouraged to replicate. The frame-narrator listens to Carnehan's story just as we read his account of it. But Carnehan also catches the frame-narrator in a transferential relationship, because he embodies for the frame-narrator the subject who is presumed to know (the realpolitik behind Empire), the subject that 'knows' the frame-narrator's desires. The frame-narrator attracts our identification because he initiates and expresses our desire for more knowledge about the loafers, who are presented as the object of fascination.

The relationship between the loafers and the frame-narrator cannot be characterised as disinterested. Concerned about the fate of the two loafers at the hands of Native Princes, he informs the authorities of their presence in Rajasthan. He does not turn them away when they appear in his office but allows them access to his library. More importantly, the narrator, Carnehan and Dravot are all brothers in the Mother Lodge; masonic allegiances bind the narrator firmly to the loafers' narrative and their brand of myth-making. The frame-narrator's first meeting with Carnehan marks his fascination quite clearly; Carnehan's presence in the 'intermediate' train carriage, which holds only travellers 'most properly looked down on', catches his eye. The frame-narrator finds himself in instant rapport with Carnehan; we are told that 'he was a wanderer like [himself]' with stories to tell of amazing things seen and done in 'out-of-the-way corners of Empire' (Kipling, 1914, 201). The loafer's politics of opportunism are shared by the frame-narrator: '"if India was filled with men like you and me ... it isn't seventy millions of revenue the land would be paying – it's seven hundred millions … " I looked at his mouth and chin [and] … was disposed to agree with him' (Kipling, 1914, 201). Later, the frame-narrator's initial response to Dravot partakes of the same veneration that Carnehan has for his companion. If Dravot's face, described as 'great and shining' identifies him as a special figure, it is also the first in a series of messianic references that accrue to the visionary figure of the red-bearded loafer (even though it is Carnehan, not Dravot, who is crucified).

The main meeting between Carnehan and the frame-narrator shows that the latter is caught in transferential identification. His absorbed silence on hearing Carnehan's strange tale of his efforts in Kafiristan reflects his affective involvement. He readily agrees with Carnehan's request for an audience; he steadies the loafer's straying mind with references to their past associations in order to overcome Carnehan's narrative blockages. Story-teller and listener are intimately bound. Carnehan's entreaty – 'Keep looking at me, or maybe my words will go all to pieces. Keep looking at me in my eyes and don't say anything' – is met with the frame-narrator's response: 'I leaned forward and looked into his face as steadily as I could. He dropped one hand upon the table and I grasped it by the wrist' (Kipling, 1914, 222). In the exchange of looks the frame-narrator, mesmerised by Carnehan's narration, prompts him for more information:

> The punkah-coolies had gone to sleep. Two kerosene lamps were blazing in the office, and the perspiration poured down my face and splashed on the blotter as I leaned forward. Carnehan was shivering, and I feared that his mind might go. I wiped my face, took a fresh grip of the piteously mangled hands, and said: – 'What happened after that?' (Kipling, 1914, 247)

By positioning Carnehan as the subject who possesses knowledge or a secret worth unveiling, the frame-narrator imbues the loafer with narrative authority in a chain of displaced desire. Bascom remarks that by identifying with the loafers, we let Carnehan (and by implication Dravot) act as our character surrogates, and they become figures that express our covert desires. But Bascom's reading begs the question why Carnehan/Dravot should be privileged figures that command attention; the question of how their alleged knowledge is linked with desire is ignored. Carnehan's knowledge is not separate from the frame-narrator's desire but, in Bascom's reading, neither is the frame-narrator's knowledge separate from the critic's desire. As Peter Brooks points out, story-telling relies on the transferential relation between speaker and listener and this relies on desire as much as 'truth'. In a particularly revealing passage, Brooks links meaning and knowledge to desire through narrative:

> Narrative truth, then, seems to be a matter of conviction, derived from the plausibility and well-formedness of the narrative discourse, and also what we might call its force, its power to create further patterns of connectedness … Calling Lacan as a gloss to Freud, one could say that

narrative truth depends as much on the discourse of desire as on the claims of past event. The narrative discourse – like the discourse of analysis – must restage the past history of desire as it exercises its pressure toward meaning in the present. The past never will be recollected at all except insofar as it insists on continuing to mean, to repeat its charge of affect in the present. (Brooks, 1994, 59)

The transferential relationship is first and foremost founded on the axis of desire. But the subject does not really possess knowledge; he is perceived to have knowledge simply by virtue of being a subject of desire, or where desire is focused. Slavoj Žižek's work on the temporal loop of narrative analysis foregrounds the retroactive nature of transference. Žižek argues that 'truth' (that the subject is presumed to know) is an illusion; 'it does not really exist in the other, the other does not really possess it, it is constituted afterwards, through our – the subject's – signifier's working'. Yet it is a 'necessary illusion', a misrecognition, for 'we may paradoxically elaborate this knowledge only by means of the illusion that the other already possesses it and that we are only discovering it' (Žižek, 1989a, 56–7). Žižek puts a different twist on Brooks's more optimistic understanding of dialogue between narrator and narratee in the transferential dynamics of story-telling by introducing ideology into the equation. In Žižek's re-reading of Althusser through Lacan, the dynamics of transference are linked to ideological interpellation; in his estimation, transference marks the point of 'attachment' that produces ideological knowledge inscribed retroactively; it is 'the point of attachment that links his very desire to the resolution of that which is to be revealed [that is to say the "truth" of ideology]'.

    ... The frame-narrator ... requires the listener's transferential identification in order to activate meaning – as opposed to a competing reading which might see in Carnehan's tale a literal parody of Empire, or the comic hallucinations of an insane man. In order to read the tale of loafers as the parable of men who would be kings, that is to say, in order to activate the allegorical or parabolic meaning of Kipling's tale, one must have already given in to the colonial fantasy of power and domination ... Surely the moral of the tale is not that the silent participation of the narrator and sympathetic reader is a *universal* desire for power and domination but that such a dream (or nightmare) is peculiar to colonialism – and one which is to haunt the very image of the colonial civil state. To help us locate one final set of transferential relations that repeat colonial desire across listeners and tellers, we must make a distinction between Carnehan and Dravot, and scrutinise closely the manner of Carnehan's narration.

THE GREAT GAME

Dravot and Carnehan's characters are more sympathetic and likeable when compared with their earlier prototype in 'Letters of Marque'. The loafer in Kipling's travels in Rajasthan appears to be unnaturally obsessed with the alleged wealth and deviousness of the Princely States. In contrast to the normal practices of colonial governors and British Residents, the Rajasthan loafer would be ruthless with his collection of revenue: 'I'm a pauper, an' you're a pauper – we 'aven't got anything hid in the ground – an' so's every white man in this forsaken country. But the Injian he's a rich man ... if you send half a dozen swords at him and shift the thatch off his roof, he'll pay' (Kipling, 1898: 182–3). Philip Mallet is correct to observe that the softening of the loafer's portrait in 'The Man Who would Be King' is achieved by excluding much of Carnehan's and Dravot's past and by excluding much of the paranoiac and exploitative characterisation of the Rajasthan loafer.

Dravot and Carnehan make attractive characters because they insist on taking an anarchic, impudent and cynical view of the colonial status quo. Their actions are predicated primarily on the thrill of a prank and the audacity with which they perform their various hoaxes for personal profit. As long as they remain in a position of relative powerlessness, their madcap schemes for exploiting situations and peoples can be viewed with indulgence. It is when Dravot and Carnehan are able to amass a store of rifles and ammunition that the context and reception of their gaming should change. But the text, in fact, records no such change.

Dravot's intervention in the Kafiristan tribal wars is told in more or less the same language and manner of his previous madcap schemes. His decision to aid the aggressors rather than the victimised is purely arbitrary; no reason is supplied by Carnehan who is simply recorded as saying, 'Says Dravot, un-packing the guns – "This is the beginning of the business. We'll fight for the ten men"'. Whilst in their relatively impecunious state, these men's scrapes amount to nothing more than minor irritations for all concerned; but on acquiring the fire-power needed to subdue hostile territory, their actions have devastating consequences. Yet Carnehan's third-person narration betrays little change:

> he fires two rifles at the twenty men, and drops one of them at two hundred yards ... The other men began to run, but Carnehan and Dravot sits on the boxes picking them off at all ranges, up and down the valley. Then we goes up to the ten men that had run across the snow too, and they fires a footy little arrow at us. Dravot he shoots above their heads and they all falls down flat. Then he walks over them and kicks them, and then he lifts them up and shakes hands all round to make them friendly like. He calls them and gives them boxes to carry, and waves his hand for all the world to see as though he was King already. (Kipling, 1914, 225)

Carnehan's narration registers no visible difference between the severity of the present situation and the previous schemes the loafers engage in. His language is kept at a purely descriptive level and proceeds by substituting one action for another in an accumulative series of deeds that is devoid of any emotional or moral response. Words such as 'drop' and 'picking them off' function as euphemisms for killing and are in keeping with the deliberately anti-climactic and prosaic account of events. Carnehan's distanced account of their participation in the war reads more like stage farce than historic imperial battle; the description of event is aligned more with music hall or vaudeville than with historic battles staged to conquer real kingdoms. Carnehan's dead-pan narration gives the story of loafer-kings its curious sense of absurdity and fabular timelessness. It also imparts to the story a relentless logic and reality. J. H. Millar records his impressions in a review of 1898, 'the reader, falling more and more under the master's spell, is whirled along triumphantly to the close. No time to take breath or to reflect, so impetuous and irresistible is the torrent' (Green, 1971, 208).

Mallett's observations on Carnehan's narrative viewpoint are pertinent. Carnehan tells his story with little or no interjections from the frame-narrator; Carnehan's tale is also told without any moralising comment. Framing Carnehan's story in this manner means that readers have access to Dravot only through Carnehan's perspectival limits of 'scams' and tricks: 'Dravot is seen only ... in terms of his personality, and the only [intra-textual] moral relation in which he stands is his relation to Carnehan, his friend and his fellow in their enterprise' (Mallet, 1989, 104). Hence, Carnehan's limits are the parameters of the story's transferential frame; identification is effected only through Carnehan's viewpoint as loafer. Because Carnehan provides the story's only moral perspective on Dravot, the latter is presented as morally reprehensible only within Carnehan's own frame of reference (Mallet, 1989, 104).

If Dravot's actions are reprehensible, they are also recuperable, for the text's use of Carnehan as focaliser means that any crime Dravot commits can be redeemed; in his friend's eyes, 'he [Dravot] can atone for his flaws by admitting them and magnanimously offering to die alone' (Mallett, 1989, 104). Such an atonement within the story's narrative structure helps elevate Dravot's stature from that of a misguided fool to that of a tragic hero. By the close of the tale, Dravot has acquired the virtues of self-knowledge and dignity. Because the narrative excludes the experiences of the natives of Kafiristan, their interpellation of Dravot as God and King is read not as (Carnehan's and) Dravot's desire inscribed retroactively (the product of transference) but as a fulfilment of prophecy/fate. Furthermore, the natives of Kafiristan function as the object lesson for Dravot's overreaching ambition. They remind him of his humanity, and enable him to die with dignity. 'The Man Who Would Be King' may be read as a parable of Empire with a moral difference: Empire becomes the means by which men may discover themselves. Mallett remarks, 'on these terms, what counts is not what the white man offers the subject peoples, but [that they] are the occasion for him to learn self-mastery and loyalty and what are sometimes embarrassingly called the masculine virtues' (Mallett, 1989, 106). What Kipling's 'The Man Who Would Be King' contains is a parable within a parable. If the inner parable offers a moral lesson in 'masculine virtues' or a moral truism in vicarious excitement, such readings are predicated on the act of transmission, where the reader enters into the transferential space; if the story 'has "taken hold", the act of transmission resembles psychoanalytic transference' (Brooks,

1994, 51). But the story in question is one told by a loafer noted for his confidence tricks and imaginative presentations of himself 'for a few day's food' (Kipling, 1914, 201). There is perhaps a more substantial link between loafer and journalist-narrator than simply that of Freemasonry. To adopt Conrad's metaphor, the meaning of the story lies not inside, like a kernel, but outside. Carnehan's story proves to be a powerful one in terms of the effects it produces on the frame-narrator, but perhaps Carnehan's story (and its effects) also provide an analogy for Kipling's story (and its effects). In this reading, not only is the frame-(journalist-)narrator's position identical to Carnehan's, but Kipling's own position as writer is identical to Carnehan's; both Kipling and Carnehan are ever in search of a new situation or new trick to play on their listeners. For part of the frame-narrator's avowed function as a journalist in the text is to record curious and unexpected incidents of Anglo-Indian life; the frame-narrator spends his time in search of a good story to report to his readers. He finds such a story in Carnehan's fantasmatic account of his adventures in Kafiristan. What 'The Man Who Would Be King' offers is a parable of story-telling: the colonial text as a hoax – a 'scam' – pulled off by enterprising vagabond story-tellers. Kipling's fascination with the figure of the loafer represents the artist as petty thief who steals and trades in stories of other people's lives. The interface between story-teller and journalist is clearly worth scrutiny.

THE IMPERIAL STORY-TELLER

The preface to *Life's Handicap* records a conversation between a native story-teller, Gobind, and the author–narrator of the series of short stories that follows. Gobind, whose tales were 'true but could not be printed in an English book', is firmly located within the oral traditions of story-telling as opposed to the narrator's avowed role as *kerani* or writer. He is likened to the native bazaar craftsman 'speak[ing] straight to men and women' and performs his stories within the locale of communal and stable agrarian societies. Gobind advises Kipling the narrator–writer:

> Tell them first of the things thou hast seen and they have seen together. Thus their knowledge will piece out thy imperfections. Tell them of what thou alone hast seen, then what thou hast heard, and since they be children, tell them of battles and kings, horses, devils, elephants and angels, but omit not to tell them of love and such like. (Kipling, 1897, ix)

Robert Kellogg argues that story-tellers thrive on the creation of an alternative heroic world to the ordinary real world of their listeners. Odysseus or Boccaccio's narrators 'keep alive heroic desires when they cannot be acted out in actual circumstances'. Kellogg suggests that the framed narrative is one method of keeping alive story-telling's archaic and magical functions: 'we readers know that there are not more heroes, demons, saints, magicians, or gods left in the world; but it comforts us mightily to know they exist in stories' (Bascom, 1987, 163). Benjamin's alternative homage to the archaic and magical properties of story-telling is captured in the figure of the travelling journeymen: 'in it was combined the lore of faraway places, such as a much-travelled man brings home, with the lore of the past, as it best reveals itself to natives of the place' (Benjamin, 1973, 85). Benjamin contrasts the communal aspects of story-telling with the solitary sensation of the novelistic experience driven by print technology – 'the story-teller takes what he tells from experience ... his own or that reported by others. And he in turn makes it the experience of those who are listening to his tale' (Benjamin, 1969, 87).

Sir Walter Besant, a contemporary critic and novelist, perceived Kipling as essentially a story-teller; he emphasised the marvellous and magical which the traveller as story-teller is privileged to convey, and the communal and experiential knowledge that is passed on from story-teller to audience. Kipling, the narrator of colonial desire, acts as the privileged point of transference:

> Kipling ... knows the world – especially the Anglo-Saxon world – the world of our empire and the world of the American republic. He is one of those thrice blessed who have not only received the gifts of observation and of sympathy – the gift of story-telling with the dramatic instinct and the power of selection and grouping – but he has obtained the gift of opportunity; he has lived in the lands where there are still adventures and the adventurous ... where there are still unknown mysteries of hills and forests; he has found mines of material diverse and new and marvellous, and he has worked these mines as they have never been worked before (Green, 1971, 254)

Besant even describes a performance in which Kipling, as frame-narrator–journalist, told the story of 'The Man Who Would Be King'. I have no evidence that such a performance happened but Besant's description confirms my version of the powerful transferential relation between story-teller and listener that is inscribed within some of these tales:

> While that story was told, there was not heard in the whole of the vast audience a sound, a whisper, a breath. In the dead silence it was received; in the dead silence it concluded – in a dead silence save for the sigh which spoke of a tension almost too great to be borne. Perhaps that sigh might be taken for applause. Perhaps the story-teller himself took it for pleasure. (Green, 1971, 255)

Kipling was on occasion not adverse to promoting this version of his writing self. Late in life, he presented himself as the imperial legend-founder, the man 'afflicted with the magic of the necessary word' whose task it is to write the record of his tribe:

> all it suggests is that the man with the Words shall wait upon the man with achievement, and step by step with him try to tell the story of the Tribe ... When it is done this is the literature of which it will be said, in due time, that it fitly represents its age. (Kipling, 1928, 6–7)

Kipling's *Recessional*, written in 1897, is a hymnic call to the nation not to forget the duties of British 'dominion over palm and pine' (Kipling, 1969, 328). Benita Parry calls Kipling 'an exemplary artist of imperialism' whose 'homilies on the development of character in the metropolitan population, hymned in one of the verses as adherence to a code of Law, Order, Duty and Restraint, Obedience, Discipline', and whose 'projection of the white race as the natural rulers of a global space' worked towards the 'fabrications of England's mysterious imperialist identity and destiny' (Parry, 1988, 61–2). His *Puck* stories may be seen as attempts to create a mythic-text of the British Empire, which produces the figure of the child at the centre of its narrative enchantment. After all, Kipling's children are no ordinary children, they are the heroes and heroines who will inherit the duties, power and responsibilities of the whole of the British Empire.

Or the Artist as Loafer?

We are used to describing Kipling as the imperial story-teller or the preeminent bard of Empire, but I also hope to show an alternative portrait of Kipling, and one indebted more to journalism and its quest for novelty. For what is equally apparent in his early texts is a journalistic flair for the dramatic potential of a good story. The Anglo-India stories, many later collected in anthologies such as *Plain Tales* and *Life's Handicap*, were published as newspaper fiction (literal 'turnovers') and included impressionistic and fragmented, specular bit-part sketches of native life. His narratives often employ the persona of journalist–narrator as the narrative correspondent: the man-on-the-spot who relays information for a reading audience. While his narrative persona is not always objective or distanced from the events that unfold, his function within the narrative is akin to journalistic mediation and interpretation of news. In 'The Return of Imray' and 'The Mark of the Beast' his presence serves to verify the authenticity of strange affairs and to mediate their experience for readers. In 'The Strange Ride' and 'The Man Who Would Be King' he comes across unusual incidents, which he (re)stages for readers' benefit. In 'The City of Dreadful Night' and 'To be Filed For Reference' his nightly exploration of parts of the native city yield tableaus of native and colonial lives. In this respect, his narrator is often a petty pilferer or loafer, either stealing bits of other people's lives or stories of their lives to fashion a novel story.

Kipling's narrator is usually a journalist who has an affinity for the underside of official life. In 'The Man Who Would Be King', his narrator classifies himself as a 'wanderer and vagabond' whose occupation sanctions his experience of things in 'out-of-the-way-corners of Empire'. The epigram which prefaces the tale – brother to a beggar and to a prince – indicates not only 'the right sort of king' but his worth as a writer. While it is dangerous to equate the frame-narrator with Kipling, there are passages in 'The Man Who Would Be King' which are lifted directly from Kipling's record of his own travel experiences in the Princely States. On assignment for the *Pioneer* in Rajasthan (which resulted in 'Letters of Marque'), he describes himself in a letter to his cousin Margaret Burne-Jones in similar terms as his frame-narrator. He describes himself as having 'railed and rode and drove and tramped' and 'slept in King's palaces or under the stars' with natives in 'desolate wayside stations'.[1] Diverse experiences contribute to the narrator's authority; 'wonderful and awful things' experienced during the journey become fodder for his writing. Kipling's early years as a journalist in India show a marked fascination with peripheral figures and experiences outside the pale. To return to the Burne-Jones letter quoted earlier:

> Underneath our excellent administrative system; under the piles of reports and statistics; the thousands of troops: the doctors: and the civilian runs wholly untouched and unaffected the life of the peoples of the land ... immediately outside of our own English life, is the dark and crooked and fantastic; and wicked: and awe-inspiring life of the 'native' ... I have done my best to penetrate into it and have put the little I have learnt into the pages of 'Mother Maturin' – Heaven send that she may grow into a full blown novel before I die. My experiences of course are only a queer jumble of opium dens, night houses, night strolls with natives; evenings spent in their company in their own homes (in the men's quarter of course) and the long yarns my native friends spin me, and one or two queer things I've come across in my own office experience.[2]

This passage contributes to the myth of Kipling as a great mediator of native culture. His knowledge is imaged as comprehensive and covers not only the everyday official life of the administrator but also its hidden native counterpart. The contact is illicit and vaguely sexual; but the underworld with its 'dark, crooked and fantastic' forms and stories provide the source and inspiration of his tales. The most compelling image that emerges from this description of his nightwalks is an image of the artist as loafer or flaneur. The artist walks through Indian streets in the same manner as the Baudelairean flaneur strolls along the pedestrian mall of the Parisian city, taking in the sights, or as a Dickensian nightwalker on his slumming expeditions in London. India yields a similar magic-lantern of familiar and phantasmagoric images.

There is a touch of the romantic and the bohemian in Kipling's (descriptions of his) expedition. Kipling speaks of how 'little an Englishman can hope to understand [these natives]': 'I would that you see some of the chapters in Mother Maturin and you will follow more closely what I mean'. Here, then, is the contradictory movement in Kipling's project. His task is both to mystify and to reveal native life for all to see. Mother Maturin is Kipling's unfinished (lost) novel about the 'unutterable horrors of lower class Eurasian and native life'; it is said to have been gleaned from his own 'experiences' in India. The Orientalist influence of the French Symbolists, the romantic heritage of decadent artists and the literary influence of Dickens may have contributed to the novel but, as a result of family disapproval, the novel was never published. But there is more than a glimpse of this aspect of Kipling's persona in his relation to the underworld of Lahore City away from departmental life. In a letter to his ex-editor Kay Robinson, Kipling writes:

> I hunt and rummage among 'em; knowing Lahore City – that wonderful, dirty, mysterious ant hill – blindfold and wandering through it like Haroun-al-Raschid in search of strange things ... the bulk of my notes and references goes to enrich a bruised tin tea-box where lies – 350 fcp. pages thick – my Mother Maturin. The novel that is always being written and yet gets no furrader ... heat and smells of oil and spices, and puffs of temple incense, and sweat, and darkness, and dirt and lust and cruelty, and above all, things wonderful and fascinating innumerable. Give me time Kay – give me seven years and three added to them and abide the publishment of 'Mother Maturin'. Then you shall sit down in your gas-lit, hot water pipe warmed office, at midnight, and shall indite a review saying that the book ought never to have been written.[3]

The letter is built on a series of contrasts: dirty/clean, magical (strange)/rational, sensual/sensible (ordinary, safe), dangerous/'gas-lit, hot water pipe warmed office' which depict experiences outside the English official world. 'The House of Suddhoo', 'The Gate of Hundred Sorrows', 'The City of Dreadful Night' (two versions) and 'To Be Filed For Reference' are all obsessed with journeys into the native quarter and with meeting figures who know it well. I will comment here only on the short story 'To Be Filed For Reference', because it deals directly with the aesthetics of loaferism that we have been discussing.

'To Be Filed' is the very last tale to be included in the first book-form collection of his short stories, *Plain Tales From The Hills*. The narrative recounts a meeting with a loafer who has gone native. Formerly an Oxford man, McIntosh Jellalludin is now a dissolute drunk, who is married to a native woman 'not pretty to look at'. As a literary aesthete turned 'Mussulman', he is also, the narrator records, 'the most interesting loafer that I had had the pleasure of knowing for a long time' (Kipling, 1898, 302). The narrator's nocturnal visits to his loafer friend are a form of education. McIntosh Jellaludin's mind was a 'perfect rag-bag of useless things', a hybrid list of classical quotations, literary knowledge, native customs and languages. But it is precisely this hybrid world which attracts the narrator's attention and it is McIntosh Jellaludin's knowledge of native customs that the frame-narrator covets for his own artistic ends: '[that] he had his hand on the pulse of native life ... was a fact ... As Mohammedan *faquir* – as McIntosh Jellaludin – he was all that I wanted for my own ends. He smoked several pounds of my tobacco, and taught me several ounces of things worth knowing' (Kipling, 1898, 303).

McIntosh Jellaludin's claim on posterity lies in a big bundle of papers, 'all numbered and covered with fine cramped writing', which he calls, in the manner of the Bible, 'the Book of McIntosh Jellaludin'. The bundle of papers is an account of the loafer's knowledge and experience of India: 'showing what he saw and how he lived, and what befell him and others ...'; this text, like all romantic visionary texts, is described as being 'paid for ... in seven years' damnation'. A literary child of two or more cultures, the book (described by the loafer as 'my only child') will be the lost gospel of British India. Strickland's legendary knowledge of things native will pale in comparison. McIntosh dies exhorting the narrator to publish it: 'do not let my book die in its present form ... Listen Now! I am neither mad nor drunk! That book will make you famous' (Kipling, 1898, 309).

Is it stillborn or still to be born? McIntosh's book is also the book of Mother Maturin, 'being also the account of the life and sins and death of Mother Maturin'. The narrative of 'To Be Filed For Reference' ends on a note of ambiguity. It is stillborn because the child who is a product of two cultures must be a sterile hybrid and because Strickland, the wise policeman and expert on native life and custom 'thought the writer an extreme liar'. But McIntosh Jellaludin's book is still-to-be-born because by the close of the story, 'Mother Maturin' has yet to be published. The references to McIntosh Jellaludin's 'Mother Maturin' matches what we know of Kipling's own unpublished novel; his own descriptions of the content of his '350 fcp. pages' of writing kept in a tea tin matches the narrator's descriptions of the loafer McIntosh's book.

Kipling's book contains 'all things wonderful and fascinating innumerable' and was to show his 'hand on the pulse of native life'. Kipling's 'Mother Maturin' by all accounts seems to have been as contentious and provocative a piece of work as McIntosh Jellaludin's book. In a letter to his Aunt Edith Mcdonald on July 30 1885, Kipling describes the early drafts:

> Further I have really embarked to the tune of 237 foolscap pages on my novel – Mother Maturin – an Anglo Indian episode. Like Topsy it 'growed' while I wrote and I find myself now committed to a two volume business at least. Its not one bit nice or proper but it carries a grim sort of a moral with it and tries to deal with the unutterable horrors of lower class Eurasian and native life as they exist outside reports and reports and reports. I haven't got Pater's verdict on what I've done. He comes up in a couple of days and will then sit in judgement. Trixie says its awfully horrid: Mother says its nasty but powerful and I know it to be in a large measure true.[4]

At this time, the manuscript exerted a powerful hold over Kipling, who describes it as an 'unfailing delight', and his own writing at a 'stage where characters are living with me always'. Mrs Hill, a close friend of Kipling in India, read parts of the earlier work and describes the story as that 'of an old Irishwoman who kept an opium den in Lahore. She married a civilian and came to live in Lahore – hence a story how government secrets came to be known in the Bazaar and vice versa' (Carrington, 1970, 423). The seedier side of Indian and Anglo-Indian urban life in all its 'unutterable horrors' is part and parcel of Kipling's poetics of decadence; the book is 'nasty but powerful'. When Kipling returned to London in the nineties, the novel was still unfinished. Kipling's letter to his former editor Kay Robinson, written in a bout of depression, speaks of his frustration at London's literary scene and his desire to return to India as an Anglo-Indian writer. 'Mother Maturin' is again invoked as a book that would launch his literary career.[5]

'To Be Filed For Reference' does not belong to the original 'Plain Tales' series of stories in the *Civil and Military Gazette*; it is also placed at the end of the anthology. Hence, 'To Be Filed' gestures towards the significant new novel that Kipling hoped to publish in the near future. Yet 'To Be Filed' contains a coda disclaiming authorship. The disclaimer is strategic, given the negative reception of his unfinished novel. In this light, one may be forgiven for taking McIntosh Jellaludin to be a *Doppelgänger* of the respectable journalist of the text. McIntosh Jellaludin, the loafer gone 'fantee' must be disavowed in order to preserve the integrity of the narrator's colonial identity. But Kipling's disavowal coexists with his avowal; it is present, for example, in the transferential relation between journalist and loafer.

In one of his last essays, Freud discusses fetishism's dual and contradictory attitudes towards external reality, and its effects on subjectivity (Freud, 23: 1964, 23). He argues that the contrary dynamics of avowal and disavowal produces a 'splitting of the ego': 'everything has to be paid for in one way or another, and this success is achieved at the price of a rift in the ego which never heals but which increases as time goes on' (Freud, 23: 1964: 275–6). I would argue that in this context, Kipling's contradictory attitudes towards 'Mother Maturin' result in a splitting which is *repeated* in the conflict between the respectable journalist and the disreputable loafer. It is the unstable doubling of the loafer/journalist–author that results in the joke which closes 'To Be Filed': 'If the thing is ever published, some one may perhaps remember this story, now printed as a safeguard to prove that McIntosh Jellaludin and not myself wrote the Book of Mother Maturin. I don't want the *Giant's Robe* to come true in my case' (Kipling, 1897, 310).

The case of McIntosh Jellaludin is interesting because it reminds us that there is a side to Kipling's story-telling other than that of imperial bard and visionary, who was responsible for some of the 'founding legends' of Empire. In this final tale of *Plain Tales*, and in my reading of some of the early short stories, Kipling also emerges as flaneur–tramp, whose inquisitive and often deliberately voyeuristic gaze uses others for his own ends. Kipling's early collections consist of a rag-bag of different stories. The two sides are part of one whole. The narrator's occupation enables him to take up a privileged position as collector of experiences; it allows him to function as a sympathetic ear for local gossip and to traverse racial and class boundaries in search of a good story. As both listener and teller of the tale, he is free from the network of social taboos which keep him within the strict boundaries of Anglo-Indian society. His voyeurism is parasitic on the society he moves in and out of and his position as writer and journalist sanctions such voyeurism.

Kipling as imperial story-teller offers both the magic and enchantment of the Indian story and its voyeurism; Edmund Gosse's reference to Kipling as 'the master of a new kind of terrible and enchanting peepshow' with readers that 'crowd around him begging for "just one more look"' (Green, 1971, 108) captures the spirit of his early work. Gosse's comment also hints at the spirit of commerce which informs the trade in stories and lives. Kipling's acknowledgement of his occupation as journalist–writer is an acknowledgement of the market forces and commodity relations which characterise the literary scene in the late nineteenth century. The journalist–writer's response to Gobind's advice in the preface to *Life's Handicap* underscores a commercial awareness:

> in regard to our people they desire new tales, and when all is written they rise up and declare that the tale were told better in such and such a manner ... Nay, but with our people, money having passed, it is their right; as we should turn against a shoeseller in regard to shoes if these wore out. If then I make a book you shall see and judge. (Kipling, 1897, x)

John Rignall asserts a close relation between the flaneur and the commodity culture of the nineteenth century by highlighting the 'significant affinity' between spectator and reader (Rignall, 1992). Not only are both spectator and the realist novel products of the commercial culture of the nineteenth century, but 'the novel, itself a commodity, presents in the figure of this observer an image of the very consumer on whom it depends' (Rignall, 1992, 4). Sara Suleri's is perhaps the most perceptive comment: writing about *Kim* she observes that Kipling's genius lies in his 'apprehension of the applicability of journalism to imperial narration'. For journalism revels in novelty and the text's youthful celebration of novelty and its successive 'montage of autonomous moment' is a major part of its picaresque attraction (Suleri, 1992, 111, 112). The same might be said for Kipling's short fiction; in displacing the figure of the traditional story-teller for that of the *kerani, Life's Handicap* and *Plain Tales'* juxtaposition of short stories – 'collected from all places, and all sorts of people' – produces an entertaining timeless montage of other worlds. Chronology, Suleri argues, is always a thorny issue for the 'story of empire' and imperial narratives display both coyness and discomfort when dealing with 'their situatedness' within history. 'To name the present tense of history is of course to turn to journalism ... in the story of journalism, history is perpetually novel and necessarily occurs in the absence of precedent.' In Kipling, we have a 'brilliant literalization of the colonial moment' where 'empire confronts the necessary perpetuation of its adolescence in relation to its history' (Suleri, 1992, 111).

NOTES

1. Letter to Margaret Burne-Jones dated January 25, 1888. Kipling's letters to his cousin are found in *The Kipling Papers*, University of Sussex Manuscripts, Box 11, File 6–7.
2. Letter to Margaret Burne-Jones dated November 28, 1885, ibid.
3. Letter to Kay Robinson April 30, 1886, ibid., Box 17, File 25.
4. Letter to Edith Mcdonald, ibid., Box 11, File 10.
5. Letter to Kay Robinson April 30, 1886, ibid., Box 17, File 25.

10.3

FILM AS ETHNOGRAPHY; OR, TRANSLATION BETWEEN CULTURES IN THE POSTCOLONIAL WORLD

Rey Chow

> For if the sentence is the wall before the language of the original, literalness is the arcade. (Denn der Satz ist die Mauer vor der Sprache des Originals, Wörtlichkeit die Arkade.)
> — Walter Benjamin, 'The Task of the Translator'

...

I will in the following pages argue for a redefinition of ethnography by explicitly linking ethnography with translation. Before doing that, I will explain how a focus on visuality as such is really the first step toward a dismantling of the classic epistemological foundations of anthropology and ethnography.

THE PRIMACY OF TO-BE-LOOKED-AT-NESS

In an essay on representation and anthropological knowledge, Kirsten Hastrup writes: 'For the non-anthropologist, all films dealing with exotic cultures may look equally anthropological, while to professional anthropologists it is much more a question of method and theory than of subject-matter' (1992, 17).

Contrary to Hastrup's suggestion, the increasingly blurred distinction between 'theory and method' on the one hand and 'subject matter' on the other is, I think, precisely the new object of ethnographic work in the postcolonial world. Rethought rigorously, ethnography can no longer be the 'science' that its practitioners once imagined it to be, nor is it simply a 'documentation' of 'other' ways of life. Despite its traditional claims to objectivity, ethnography is a kind

Extract from Rey Chow, *Primitive Passions: Visuality, Sexuality, Ethnography, and Chinese Cinema* (Columbia University Press, 1995), pp. 176–202, 238–43.

of representation with subjective origins. But how do we come to terms with such subjective origins? *Whose* subjective origins should concern us? Instead of simply arguing for the necessity of discursive self-reflexivity on the part of *Western* practitioners, with the politically correct admonition that we must watch what we say more carefully, I think it is by focusing on visuality that we can come to terms with the subjective origins of ethnography most productively. In other words, I do not think that an ethnography alternative to the one we have been criticizing can materialize simply through a call for 'self-consciousness' – 'let's look at ourselves, our language, and our assumptions more carefully' – since such a call only confirms, once again, what was long ago established by Hegel as the distinguishing trait of Western Man, his capacity for being aware of himself. Rather, I believe that *a new ethnography is possible only when we turn our attention to the subjective origins of ethnography as it is practiced by those who were previously ethnographized and who have, in the postcolonial age, taken up the active task of ethnographizing their own cultures.*

This, however, does not mean exploring subjectivity in the verbal realm only. How are the 'subjective origins' of the previously ethnographized communicated in *visual* terms? They are, I think, communicated not so much through the act of looking as through what may be called 'to-be-looked-at–ness' – the visuality that once defined the 'object' status of the ethnographized culture and that now becomes a predominant aspect of that culture's self-representation. We remember that in her famous article 'Visual Pleasure and Narrative Cinema', Laura Mulvey alerts us to 'to-be-looked-at–ness' as what constitutes not only the spectacle but the very way vision is organized; the state of being looked at, she argues, is built into the way we look. Because in our culture, looking and being looked at are commonly assigned respectively to men and women, vision bears the origins of gender inequality (Mulvey, 1985, 2: 303: 15). Supplementing Mulvey's argument with the anthropological situation, we may argue, in parallel, that vision bears the origins of ethnographic inequality. But we must go one step further: the state of being looked at not only is built into the way non-Western cultures are viewed by Western ones; more significantly it is part of the *active* manner in which such cultures represent – ethnographize – themselves.

What this means is that in the vision of the formerly ethnographized, the subjective origins of ethnography are displayed in amplified form but at the same time significantly redefined: what are 'subjective' origins now include a memory of past *objecthood* – the experience of being looked at – which lives on in the subjective act of ethnographizing like an other, an optical unconscious.[1] If ethnography is indeed autoethnography – ethnography of the self and the subject – then the perspective of the formerly ethnographized supplements it irrevocably with the understanding that being-looked-at–ness, rather than the act of looking, constitutes the primary event in cross-cultural representation.

With visuality as its focus, this reformulation of ethnography destroys the operational premises – of a world divided in the form of us and them, of viewing subject and viewed object – of classical anthropology. 'Us' and 'them' are no longer safely distinguishable; 'viewed object' is now looking at 'viewing subject' looking. Moreover, through the reading of films that are not documentary and hence not ethnographic in the conventional sense, this reformulated ethnography challenges as well the factualism that typifies anthropology's hold on representation. These lines from Dai Vaughan on the documentary may be used as a critique of such factualism – if we substitute the words *ethnographers* and *ethnography* for *documentarists* and *documentary*: 'Documentarists ... like to believe that documentary is the "natural" form of cinema. But fiction film, like painting and literature, rests no special claims upon the provenance of its linguistic elements. It must surely be clear that it is documentary which is the paradoxical, even aberrant form' (1992, 102). In studying contemporary Chinese films as ethnography and autoethnography, I am thus advocating nothing less than a radical deprofessionalization of anthropology and ethnography as 'intellectual disciplines'. Once these disciplines are deprofessionalized – their boundaries between 'us' and 'them' destabilized; their claims to documentary objectivity deconstructed – how do we begin to reconceive the massive cultural information that has for so long been collected under their rubric? It is at this juncture that I think our discussion about ethnography must be supplemented by a theory of translation.

A similar observation is made by Thomas Elsaesser in his study of the New German cinema of the 1970s. Concluding that German cinema was the consequence of 'a vast transcription process', Elsaesser introduces the notion of translation as a way to understand it:

> [The New German cinema] was an attempt to gather, record and report the images, sounds and stories – including those that the cinema itself produced – which make up the memory of a generation, a nation and a culture, and *to translate them, from their many perishable supports in people's minds to the one medium that, after all, promises paradoxically to be the most permanent: the cinema.* Literature, popular culture, architecture, fashion, memorabilia and the contents of junk shops have all been enlisted in a vast effort to preserve the traces of lives lived for oblivion. This hastily accumulated visual wealth has not yet been tapped or even properly inspected for its meanings or uses. As *a source of understanding the changes from a culture living mainly by the written text to one dominated by the image,* the New German Cinema still awaits to be discovered. (1989, 322–3, my emphases)

... Elsaesser's rich passage suggests, crucially, that there are at least two types of translation at work in cinema. First, translation as inscription: a generation, a nation, and a culture are being translated or permuted into the medium of film; and second, translation as transformation of tradition and change between media: a culture oriented around the written text is in the process of transition and of being translated into one dominated by the image.

Elsaesser's words are equally applicable to other 'national' cinemas such as the Chinese, because these 'national' cinemas are, in themselves, at the crossroads of different types and stages of cultural translation. The bulk of [*Primitive Passions*], then, has in effect been dealing with the filmic transcriptions of Chinese modernity as processes of cultural translation ...

TRANSLATION AND THE PROBLEM OF ORIGINS

Etymologically, the word *translation* is linked, among other things, to 'tradition' on the one hand and to 'betrayal' on the other.[2] The Italian expression *Traduttore, traditore* – 'Translator, traitor' – allows us to grasp the pejorative implication of infidelity that is often associated with the task of translating. Because faithfulness is such a crucial issue here, the analogy between translation and a human convention such as matrimony is, as Barbara Johnson writes, far-reaching: 'It might seem ... that the translator ought, despite or perhaps because of his or her oath of fidelity, to be considered not as a duteous spouse but as a faithful bigamist, with loyalties split between a native language and a foreign tongue' (1985, 143). To complicate things further, the matrimony that is translation is seldom established on the basis of the equality of the partners. In the classical thinking about translation, Johnson goes on, it is the signified, not the signifier, that is given priority: 'Faithfulness to the text has meant faithfulness to the semantic tenor with as little interference as possible from the constraints of the vehicle. Translation, in other words, has always been the translation of *meaning*' (1985, 145).

Given these deeply entrenched assumptions about translation, it is hardly surprising that the rendering of 'China' into film, even at a time when the literary bases of Chinese society are increasingly being transformed by the new media culture, is bedeviled by suspicion and replete with accusations of betrayal. While these suspicions and accusations may express themselves in myriad forms, they are always implicitly inscribed within the ideology of fidelity. For instance ... is not the distrust of 'surfaces' – the criticism of Zhang Yimou's lack of depth – a way of saying that surfaces are 'traitors' to the historical depth that is 'traditional China'? And yet the word *tradition* itself, linked in its roots to translation and betrayal, has to do with handing over. Tradition itself is nothing if it is not a transmission. How is tradition to be transmitted, to be passed on, if not through translation?

The common assumption about translation is that it is a rendering of one language into another language. Even though what is involved is actually the traffic between two languages, we tend to suppress our awareness of this by prioritizing one language over the other, by pretending that the traffic goes in one direction only. How does this happen? Consider the terminology we use, which reveals the epistemological uncertainties involved and hence the ideological need to prioritize: we call one language the 'original' and the other the 'translation' (meaning 'unoriginal' and 'derivative'). This terminology suppresses the fact that the 'unoriginal' language may well be the 'native tongue' –

that is, the original language – of the translator, whose translating may involve turning the 'original' which is actually *not* her native/original language into her 'native'/'original' language ...

Precisely because translation is an activity that immediately problematizes the ontological hierarchy of languages – 'which is primary and which is secondary?' – it is also the place where the oldest prejudices about origins and derivations come into play most forcefully. For instance, what does it mean to make a translation sound 'natural'? Must the translation sound more like the 'original', which is not the language into which it is translated – meaning that it is by resemblance to the 'original' that it becomes 'natural'? Or, must it sound more like the language into which it is translated, in which case sounding 'natural' would mean forgetting the 'origin'? When we say, derogatorily, 'This reads like a translation,' what we mean is that even though we understand what the 'original' meaning might be, we cannot but notice its translatedness – and yet is that not precisely what a translation is supposed to be – *translated* rather than 'original'? As in all bifurcated processes of signification, translation is a process in which the notion of the 'original', the relationship between the 'original' and its 'derivations', and the demand for what is 'natural' must be thoroughly reexamined.

Using contemporary Chinese cinema as a case in point, I think the criticism (by some Chinese audiences) that Zhang and his contemporaries 'pander to the tastes of the foreign devil' can itself be recast by way of our conventional assumptions about translation. The 'original' here is not a language in the strict linguistic sense but rather 'China' – 'China' as the sum total of the history and culture of a people; 'China' as a content, a core meaning that exists 'prior to' film. When critics say that Zhang's films lack depth, what they mean is that the language/vehicle in which he renders 'China' is a poor translation, a translation that does not give the truth about 'China'. For such critics, the film medium, precisely because it is so 'superficial' – that is, organized around surfaces – mystifies and thus distorts China's authenticity. What is implicitly assumed in their judgment is not simply the untranslatability of the 'original' but that translation is a unidirectional, one-way process. It is assumed that translation means a movement from the 'original' to the language of 'translation' but not vice versa; it is assumed that the value of translation is derived solely from the 'original', which is the authenticator of itself and of its subsequent versions. Of the 'translation', a tyrannical demand is made: the translation must perform its task of conveying the 'original' without leaving its own traces; the 'originality of translation' must lie 'in self-effacement, a vanishing act'.[3]

Our discussion here can be facilitated by turning to the work of Walter Benjamin, not least because Benjamin himself was writing at the crossroads of cultural transformation. Though Benjamin's essay 'The Work of Art in the Age of Mechanical Reproduction' may seem most immediately relevant to our topic in that it deals with the transformation of traditional art (which possesses 'aura') to mass-produced images such as those of photography and film (1969,

217–51), I find his essay 'The Task of the Translator' to be more useful in helping me think through the problem of translation between cultures (1969, 68–82). In this latter essay, Benjamin offers a theory of translation that is distinctively different from most theories.

It is often assumed, writes Benjamin, that the point of translation is to impart information or convey the meaning of the original; this is, however, not so. Instead, what needs to be translated is an 'intention' ('intentio') in the 'original' that Benjamin calls 'the great longing for linguistic complementation' (79). His mystical language notwithstanding, Benjamin is arguing for a materialist though elusive fact about translation – that translation is primarily a process of *putting together*. This process demonstrates that the 'original', too, is something that has been put together. But this 'putting together' is not, as I will go on to argue, simply a deconstructive production of differences. It is *also* a process of 'literalness' that *displays* the way the 'original' itself was put together – that is, in its violence.

Before elaborating this last point, we need to examine closely the way Benjamin discusses the 'putting together' that is linguistic translation. What needs to be translated from the original, he writes, is not a kind of truth or meaning but the way in which 'the original' is put together *in the basic elements of human language* – words. Hence it is words – in their wordness, their literality – rather than sentences, that matter the most in translation. A real translation, Benjamin writes, 'may be achieved, above all, by a literal rendering of the syntax which proves words rather than sentences to be the primary element of the translator. For if the sentence is the wall before the language of the original, literalness is the arcade' (79).

The German 'original' of this passage indicates that where Benjamin's English translator, Harry Zohn, uses the words *literal* and *literalness*, Benjamin has used the word *Wörtlichkeit*. But even though the English translation does not exactly reproduce Benjamin's word, a verbatim translation of which would be something like 'word-by-word–ness', it nonetheless supplements Benjamin's text in an unexpected, perhaps fateful, manner. To be 'literal' in the English language is to be 'verbatim', to follow the word strictly. At the same time, 'literal' can also connote a certain *lack* – in the sense of that which is matter-of-fact, without imagination, without metaphor, without depth; that which is superficial, crude, or naive. It is this second notion of literalness – this supplement that exists in the translation but not in the original – that brings out, I think, the precise sense of Benjamin's *Wörtlichkeit*: a real translation is not only that which translates word by word but also that which translates literally, depthlessly, naively.

It is obvious that here I depart significantly from the view of literalness held by deconstructionist critics. For Jacques Derrida and Paul de Man, for instance, *literal* is a problematic word that designates 'proper', in a way that is opposed to (their preferred) 'metaphoric' or 'figural'. De Man's reading of Rousseau, for instance, is that Rousseau's language tells the story of 'the necessary degradation ... of metaphor into literal meaning', and that a 'literal world' is one 'in which appearance and nature coincide' whereas a 'figural world' is one 'in which this correspondence is no longer a priori posited' (de Man, 1983, 136; 1979, 151).[4] For me, however, literalness is not simply 'proper', but it is not simply 'figural'/'metaphorical', either. Rather, I use the term to refer to a third area that is defined by neither of the two categories – the area we may loosely describe as the obvious, the superficial, and what immediately presents itself in signification. This 'literal' area is what lacks and/or exceeds the clear boundary implied by Derrida and de Man between the categories of the 'proper' and the 'figural'/'metaphorical'.

Zohn's translation-cum-supplement, then, makes explicit something that was merely lurking in the original in the form of what Benjamin himself calls the original's 'intention'. Remarkably, the 'original' intention is what can only be grasped as a supplement, as what is added (because translated): 'In all language and linguistic creations there remains *in addition to* what can be conveyed something that cannot be communicated; depending on the context in which it appears, it is something that symbolizes or something symbolized' (79, my emphasis). For Benjamin, the task of the translator consists in communicating this additional something that nonetheless could come across as a lack and a deprivation. (I will return to this point once again toward the end.)

The elusiveness of his approach to the 'original' makes it seem that Benjamin is saying with 'translation' what deconstructionists are saying with 'language', namely, that the original is self-différance. Examples of the deconstructionist definition of language include statements such as these: 'Language ... can only exist in the space of its own foreignness to itself,' 'the original text is always already an impossible translation that renders translation impossible' (Johnson, 1985, 146), and so forth. However, even though a deconstructionist reading of Benjamin is useful and necessary, it is inadequate. In the preceding passage by Benjamin, if we take the word *symbol* to mean not a full and complete representation of something but a sign that stands for something else, then what Benjamin is saying would suggest that the 'original' intention is not only a *self-*différance, but also a process of standing-for-something-*else*, something other than the 'self'. For Benjamin, the act of translation is less a confirmation of language's 'own' impossibility than it is a *liberation*, in a second language, of the 'intention' of standing-for-something-else that is already put together but imprisoned – 'symbolized' – in the original; hence 'it is the task of the translator to release in his own language that pure language which is under the spell of another, to liberate the language imprisoned in a work in his re-creation of that work' (80).

Because Benjamin's notion of the 'original' intention comprises *both* self-différance and the act of symbolizing (standing for an other), it is important to emphasize that his theory is not simply that translation is the original's deconstruction, which is the reading proposed, for instance, by de Man. De Man's reading is a persuasive one, but it does not do justice to Benjamin's theory. In his typical manner, de Man zeroes in on the inherent *negativity* of writing: hence he elaborates on the notion of 'failure' inscribed in the German title of Benjamin's piece, proving thus that translation is ultimately a failure – a failure, moreover, that is already present in the 'original'. Comparing the activity of translation to those of critical philosophy, literary theory, and history, de Man writes that all such *intralingual* activities have in common a disarticulation of the original: 'They reveal that their failure, which seems to be due to the fact that they are secondary in relation to the original, reveals an *essential* failure, an *essential* disarticulation which was already there in the original' (1986, 84, my emphases).

Because its rigor is a negative one, de Man's deconstructive reading is eminently useful in desacralizing and decanonizing the original. But deconstruction as such nonetheless does *not* depart from the view that there *is* some original – even if that should prove to be an illusion – to begin with. By concentrating its effects on the disarticulated and unstable 'essence' of the 'original', the deconstructive reading in fact makes it unnecessary for one to move outside or down from the realm of the original. Translation would thus remain one-way in the sense that it is intralingual, with all the differences/misreadings it produces moving back to (deconstruct the self that is) the original. This is demonstrated, best of all, by de Man's own reading, in which he repeatedly shows Benjamin's translators up for missing Benjamin's points. In spite of his sacrilegious intentions, therefore, de Man returns a kind of sacredness – now defined as intralingual instability – to the original that is Benjamin's text. De Man's deconstructive reading does not in the end deviate significantly from the conventional, dogmatic belief in the purity or untranslatability of any original. Were a 'translation' of culture to be based on de Man's reading, it would be, as he says, a failure: such a translation would be little more than the vicious circle of a search for a complete freedom from the 'origin' that is the past, which nonetheless would keep haunting us like the indelible memory of a nightmare.

For Benjamin, on the other hand, translation is not simply deconstructive but, even more important, a 'liberation' that is mutual and reciprocal *between* the 'original' and the 'translation'. In Benjamin's text, the nihilistic rigor of deconstruction is combined with a messianic utopianism, a sense of openness that is absent in de Man. For Benjamin, both 'original' and 'translation', as languages rendering each other, share the 'longing for linguistic complementarity' and gesture together toward something larger: 'A translation, instead of resembling the meaning of the original, must lovingly and in detail incorporate the original's mode of signification, thus making both the original and the translation recognizable as fragments of a greater language, just as fragments are part of a vessel' (78).[5] ...

... Benjamin's argument ... [is that] most work of translation is done in the wish to make the 'foreign' sound more like the 'native', with the assumption that the 'native' is the 'original' point of reference; whereas translation is a process in which the 'native' should let the foreign affect, or infect, itself, and vice versa. This radical notion of translation is what leads Jean Laplanche to

describe Benjamin's theory as an 'anti-ethnocentric' one: 'Benjamin participates in the great "anti-ethnocentric" movement ... or what I call the "anti-
auto- or self-centred" movement of translation (*le mouvement anti-autocen-
trique de la traduction*): a movement that doesn't want translation to be self-
enclosed and reduce the other to the terms of that self, but rather a movement
out towards the other' (1992, 201). The question then is, How is this 'movement out towards the other' to be conceived and theorized?

TRANSLATION AS 'CULTURAL RESISTANCE'

In a recent work, *Siting Translation*, Tejaswini Niranjana takes up the formidable task of rethinking translation in the context of postcolonial postmodernity.
Basing her arguments on poststructuralist theories of language, signification,
and representation, Niranjana deconstructs the humanistic, binary oppositional assumptions underlying traditional notions of translation. Moreover,
she proposes that both the theory and the practice of translation must be seen in
the context of Western imperialism and colonialism, in which the European/
Europeanist notions of knowledge reproduce themselves in Europe's encounter
with and 'translation' of its 'others' (1992)[6] ... If my critique of her book below
is a strong one, it is also offered in full appreciation of the significance of her
intervention in a context where 'cultural translation' is still by and large
dominated by Western discourse. This critique will, I hope, be read as an
interaction in alliance with that intervention rather than as its opposition.

If, in the hands of deconstructionists such as de Man, translation is that
originary intralingual self-différance, in Niranjana's analysis, translation is an
interlingual practice – the exchange of ideas, beliefs, and information between
different languages (and thus cultures). Because Niranjana's goal is to rescue the
term *translation* for 'cultural resistance' even while she criticizes its use by the
culturally dominant, the status of 'translation' in her analysis is an ambivalent,
empty, and ultimately idealist one: translation is fundamentally a 'philosopheme' (2, 31). The idealist status of the term is what allows Niranjana implicitly
to think of translation by differentiating between the good and the bad.

The bad: this is the European translation of its 'others' that is otherwise
known as 'orientalism'. Situating translation in the postcolonial context,
Niranjana criticizes such orientalist texts for being imperialist and ethnocentric, for simply reinscribing in the 'others' the orientalists' own preferences
and prejudices. *The good*: on the other hand, Niranjana also wants to turn
translation into something that Europe's colonized peoples can use. Translation is here given many analogies, chief of which is that it is an 'act of
resistance' when practiced by 'natives' doing their own ethnography (84–5).
Translation is, alternately, a 'problematic' and a 'field' (8), a 'transactional
reading' (42), a 'hybrid' act (46), a kind of citation and rewriting (172). Finally,
translation is what must be 'put under erasure' (48, n. 4).

These multiple analogies demonstrate the moves typical of a certain kind of
poststructuralist discourse, which may be paraphrased as follows: deconstruct

the danger and pitfalls of a term in its conventional usage; rescue that term for its inherent 'heterogeneity' and 'difference'; affirm this 'heterogeneity' and 'difference' *when it is used by certain groups of people*. By implicitly distinguishing between an incorrect and a correct practice of translation, what this type of poststructuralist rendering accomplishes is a *rationalist* understanding of 'translation.' This rendering returns 'translation' to an *idea* (hence translation is first and foremost a 'philosopheme'), debunks the dirty practice of the West, and reinstates the cleaner practice of the West's 'others' as the alternative. Apart from idealism, this poststructuralist discourse also tends to invest heavily in the form of attentiveness that is a vigilance to words. Reading the *verbal text* meticulously becomes the fundamental way to 'resist' the pitfalls of corrupt translation. In this regard, Niranjana's argument about translation does not add anything to the complex, nuanced arguments of writing, supplementarity, and différance that we already find in Derrida's work. 'History' is here rewritten as a careful reading, with the verbal text as its primary and predominant frame of reference.

The idealism and verbalism of her parameters mean that Niranjana must leave unasked the entire question of translation from verbal language into other sign systems and, more important, of *the translation of ethnic cultures from their previous literary and philosophical bases into the forms of contemporary mass culture*, a translation that is, arguably, European colonialism's foremost legacy in the non-European world. The privileging of verbal texts prevents the poststructuralist critic from coming to terms with significations whose value does not necessarily reside in their linguistic profundity and complexity – that is, their hermeneutic depth. Since 'to make complicated' remains poststructuralist textualism's primary strategy of resisting domination, surfaces, simplicities, and transparencies can only be distrusted as false. If Niranjana's point is that we need to bring 'history' into 'legibility', it is a legibility in the sense of a dense text. The decoding of this dense text, however, could mean exactly a perpetuation of the existing institutional practice of scholarly close reading.

On the other hand, does cross-cultural 'translation' not challenge precisely the scholarly mode of privileging the verbal text? If translation is 'transactional reading', must the emphasis fall on 'reading'? What if the emphasis is to fall on 'transaction', and what if the transaction is one between the verbal text and the visual image? It would seem that no consideration of cultural translation can afford to ignore these questions, simply because the translation between cultures is never West translating East or East translating West in terms of verbal languages alone but rather a process that encompasses an entire range of activities, including the change from tradition to modernity, from literature to visuality, from elite scholastic culture to mass culture, from the native to the foreign and back, and so forth.

If de Man's notion of translation ultimately revalorizes the 'original' that is the untranslatability of the (original) text, there is a way in which contemporary cultural studies, in the attempt to vindicate the cultures of the West's 'others', end up revalorizing the 'original' that is the authentic history, culture, and language of such 'others'. In spite of its politically astute intentions, what a work such as Niranjana's accomplishes in reversing are the asymmetrical, hierarchical power relations between West and East but *not* the asymmetrical, hierarchical power relations between 'original' and 'translation'. In an attempt to do justice to the East, Niranjana, like many antiorientalist critics, deconstruct/destabilize the West by turning the West into an *unfaithful translator/ translation* that has, as it were, betrayed, corrupted, and contaminated the 'original' that is the East. When this revalorization of the 'original' is done through a concentration on the depths and nuances of verbal texts, what continues to be obliterated is the fact that such texts are traditionally the loci of literate and literary culture, the culture through which *class hierarchy is established not only in Western but also in Eastern societies.*

THE 'THIRD TERM'

My concerns about cultural translation up to this point can be summarized as follows: First, can we theorize translation between cultures without somehow valorizing some 'original'? And second, can we theorize translation between cultures in a manner that does not implicitly turn translation into an *interpretation* toward depth, toward 'profound meaning'?

To answer such questions, we would need to move beyond the intralingual and interlingual dimensions of translation that we have seen in de Man and Niranjana, and include within 'translation' the notion of intersemiotic practices, of translating from one sign system to another.[7] Specifically, translation would need to encompass the translation, as Elsaesser suggests, of a 'culture' into a medium such as film. Such translation, however, is not to be confused with 'expression', 'articulation', or even 'representation', simply because these terms would too easily mislead us back into the comfortable notion that some pure 'original' was there to be expressed, articulated, or represented. Instead, the notion of translation highlights the fact that it is an activity, a transportation between two 'media', two kinds of already-mediated data, and that the 'translation' is often what we must work with because, for one reason or another, the 'original' as such is unavailable – lost, cryptic, already heavily mediated, already heavily translated. On the other hand, as I clarify in my discussion of de Man, I do not think that intersemiotic translation is simply 'deconstruction', either, because the negative momentum of deconstruction, while effectively demystifying the spontaneism and mimeticism of terms such as expression, articulation, and representation, remains incapable of conveying a sense of the new medium into which the 'original' is being transported.

What is useful from deconstruction, as is always the case, is the lesson about the 'original' – a lesson I am pushing to the extreme here by asking that even in translation, where it usually goes without saying (even for deconstructionists) that the 'original' is valued over the translated, we take absolutely seriously the deconstructionist insistence that the 'first' and 'original' as such is always already différance – always already translated. There are two possible paths from this lesson: one leads, as in the case of de Man, back to the painstaking study of the 'original' as an original failure; the other leads to the work of translations and the values arising from them without privileging the 'original' simply because it was there first. The choice of either path constitutes a major political decision.

And it is here, rather than in the opposition between 'language' and 'history' as Niranjana argues, that Benjamin's essay on translation, together with Benjamin's interest in mass culture, is most useful for a theory of cultural translation.[8]

There are multiple reasons why a consideration of mass culture is crucial to cultural translation, but the predominant one, for me, is precisely that asymmetry of power relations between the 'first' and the 'third' worlds. Precisely because of the deadlock of the more or less complete Europeanization of the world, which has led not only to the technocratic homogenization of world cultures but also to an organization of these cultures by way of European languages, philosophies, and sciences, the recourse to the archaic, authentic *past* of other cultures, in the assumption that somehow such past is closer to the original essence of humanity than Western culture, is a futile one. Critiquing the great disparity between Europe and the rest of the world means not simply a deconstruction of Europe as origin or simply a restitution of the origin that is Europe's others but a thorough dismantling of *both* the notion of origin and the notion of alterity as we know them today. This dismantling would be possible only if we acknowledge what Johannes Fabian speaks of as the *coevalness* of cultures (1983) and consider the intersemiotic transformations that have happened as much to non-Western societies as to Western ones. The mass culture of our media, into which even the most 'primitive' societies have been thrown, makes this coevalness ineluctable. The 'primitive' is not 'of another time' but is our contemporary …

WEAKNESS, FLUIDITY, AND THE FABLING OF THE WORLD

To elaborate my argument further, I will turn briefly to the work of Gianni Vattimo (1988, 1992). Basing his philosophy primarily on readings of Nietzsche and Heidegger, Vattimo's concern is that of figuring out possibilities of survival that are *practically* available in the deadlock of the European domination, homogenization, and standardization of the world. Among the most compelling ideas in Vattimo's writings is that of a weakening Western metaphysics, which he theorizes by drawing upon Nietzsche's idea of the death of God and Heidegger's notions of *Andenken* (recollection) and *Verwindung* (the overcoming that is not a transcendence but an acceptance and that carries with it the meaning of a cure, a convalescence).[9] For Vattimo, weakening – in the sense of a gradual decline, an ability to die – signals not a new, radical beginning but rather a turning and twisting of tradition away from its metaphysical foundations, a movement that makes way for the hybrid cultures of contemporary society.

Reading specifically for a tactics of translation between cultures, I find Vattimo's writings useful in several ways. First, he takes as his point of departure, realistically, the deadlock of the anthropological situation that has resulted from Western hegemony and that has led to the disappearance of alterity. Second, he refuses to think through this deadlock by constructing a brand-new beginning that is typical of the heroic radicalism of modernist narratives. Third, he attempts an alternative way of conceiving of the coeval-ness of cultures that is neither cynical and negative (in its criticism of the West) nor idealist and idealistic (by valorizing the East). Most important, Vattimo urges that we need to recognize the fact that these 'other' cultures, rather than being lost or disappearing, are themselves transforming and translating into the present. He cites from Remo Guidieri:

> Those who have lamented the deaths of cultures have neither known how to see, nor wanted to see, that these same cultures – which are as obsessed as we are with the myth of abundance – have nevertheless produced their own specific way of entering into the Western universe. Although they may be paradoxical, irrational, or even caricatural, these modalities are just as authentic as the ancient ways, tributary as they are to the cultural forms from which they derive their condition of possibility. The non-Western contemporary world is an immense construction site of traces and residues, in conditions which have still to be analysed. (1980, 60, cit. Vattimo, 1988, 158)

This notion of the other – not as the idealized lost origin to be rediscovered or resurrected but as our contemporary – allows for a context of cultural transla-tion in which these 'other' cultures are equally engaged in the contradictions of modernity, such as the primitivization of the underprivileged, the quest for new foundations and new monuments, and so forth, that have been blatantly exhibited by Western nations. The coevalness of cultures, in other words, is not simply a peaceful co-existence among plural societies but the co-temporal-ity of power structures ... that mutually support and reinforce the exploita-tion of underprivileged social groups, nonhuman life forms, and ecological resources *throughout the world*.

Once the coevalness of cultures is acknowledged in this manner, cultural translation can no longer be thought of simply in linguistic terms, as the translation between Western and Eastern verbal languages alone. Instead, cultural translation needs to be rethought as the co-temporal exchange and contention between different social groups deploying different sign systems that may not be synthesizable to one particular model of language or repre-sentation. Considerations of the translation of or between cultures would thus have to move beyond verbal and literary languages to include events of the media such as radio, film, television, video, pop music, and so forth, without writing such events off as mere examples of mass indoctrination. Conversely, the media, as the loci of cultural translation, can now be seen as what helps to weaken the (literary, philosophical, and epistemological) foundations of Western domination and what makes the encounter between cultures a fluid and open-ended experience:

> Contrary to what critical sociology has long believed (with good reason, unfortunately), standardization, uniformity, the manipulation of consensus and the errors of totalitarianism *are not* the only possible outcome of the advent of generalized communication, the mass media and reproduction. Alongside these possibilities – which are objects of political choice – there opens an alternative possible outcome. The advent of the media enhances the inconstancy and superficiality of experience. In so doing, it runs counter to the generalization of domination, insofar as it allows a kind of 'weakening' of the very notion of reality, and thus a weakening of its persuasive force. The society of the spectacle spoken of by the situationists is not simply a society of appearance manipulated by power: it is also the society in which reality presents itself as softer and more fluid, and in which experience can again acquire the characteristics of oscillation, disorientation and play. (Vattimo, 1992, 59)

What the fluidity of the co-presence of cultures signifies is not the harmony but – to use a word from Vattimo – the thorough 'contamination' of the world, so thorough that it has made the world become 'soft' and tender. If the Western domination of the world has been the result of rationalistic progress, a progress that moves the world toward the general transparency that is evidenced by our media, this transparency is also a recovery, a convalescence from rationalistic progress in that it shows the world to be, finally, a fable:

> Instead of moving toward self-transparency, the society of the human sciences and generalized communication has moved towards what could, in general, be called the 'fabling of the world.' The images of the world we receive from the media and the human sciences, albeit on different levels, are not simply different interpretations of a 'reality' that is 'given' regardless, but rather constitute the very objectivity of the world. 'There are no facts, only interpretations,' in the words of Nietzsche, who also wrote that 'the true world has in the end become a fable.' (Vattimo, 1992, 24–5)[10]

In the transcultural world market, contemporary Chinese films can be understood by way of this transparency becoming fable. In order to see this, we need to return once again to the problem of translation and to Walter Benjamin's essay.

THE LIGHT OF THE ARCADE

We come to what is perhaps the most difficult point in Benjamin's discussion: besides the 'longing for linguistic complementarity', what exactly is that 'active force in life' (79) that Benjamin describes as being imprisoned in the original and that the translation should liberate? How is this 'active force' related to the 'longing for linguistic complementarity'? Much as Benjamin's phrase carries with it a kind of organicist baggage, I propose that we think of it in terms other than organicism. By way of contemporary Chinese film, I would suggest that, *first*, the 'active force of life' refers to the cultural violence that is made evident or apparent by the act of translation. In its rendering of the prohibitions, the oppressive customs, and the dehumanizing rituals of feudal China, for instance, the translation that is film enables us to see how a culture is 'originally' put together, in all its *cruelty*. This putting together constitutes the violent active force to which the culture's members continue to be subjugated. For anyone whose identity is sutured with this culture, filmic representation thus makes it possible to see (with discomfort) one's 'native origins' as foreign bodies.

Second, the 'active force of life' refers also to the act of transmission. While the callousness and viciousness of 'tradition' is clearly visible on the screen, what makes it possible for Chinese audiences to become not simply inheritors of but also foreigners to their 'tradition' is the act of transmission – the fact that whatever they experience, they experience as a passing-on. Writing in another context, Benjamin has defined transmission as what distinguishes Franz Kafka's work from that of his contemporaries. A work's transmissibility, Benjamin writes, is in opposition to its 'truth':

> The things that want to be caught as they rush by are not meant for anyone's ears. This implies a state of affairs which negatively charac-terizes Kafka's works with great precision ... Kafka's work presents a *sickness of tradition* ... [The haggadic] consistency of truth ... has been lost. Kafka was far from being the first to face this situation. Many had accommodated themselves to it, clinging to truth or whatever they happened to regard as truth and, with a more or less heavy heart, [forsaking] its transmissibility. Kafka's real genius was that he tried something entirely new: he sacrificed truth for the sake of *clinging to its transmissibility*, its haggadic element (1969, 143–4, my emphases)

Following Benjamin, we may argue that transmissibility is what *intensifies* in direct proportion to the sickness, the weakening of tradition. Ironically, then, it is indeed 'tradition' that is the condition of possibility for transmission, but it is tradition in a debilitated and exhausted state.

Furthermore, in the age of multimedia communication, transmissibility is that aspect of a work which, unlike the weight of philosophical depth and interiority, is literal, transparent, and thus capable of offering itself to a popular or naive *handling*. What is transmissible is that which, *in addition to* having meaning or 'sense', is accessible. This last point, incidentally, is quite the opposite of the manner in which we usually think of accessibility, which is typically regarded as a *deprivation*, a *lack* of depth and meaning. For Benja-min, however, transmissibility and accessibility are not pejorative or negligible qualities; instead they are what enable movement – that is, translation – from language to language, from medium to medium. Transmissibility and accessibility are what give a work its afterlife.

Once we see these implications of transmission, the 'literalness' or *Wörtlichkeit* in Benjamin's essay that I have already discussed can be further defined as a transmissibility oriented toward a here and now – that is, a simultaneity rather than an alterity in place and time. Rather than a properly anchored 'truth', 'literalness' signifies mobility, proximity, approximation. Thus 'literalness' is, as Benjamin writes, an arcade, a passageway.

Juxtaposing 'The Task of the Translator' with Benjamin's interest in mass culture, we can now say that the 'literalness' of popular and mass culture is not 'simplistic' or 'lacking' as is commonly thought. Rather, in its naive, crude, and literal modes, popular and mass culture is a supplement to truth, a tactic of passing something on. In the language of visuality, what is 'literal' is what acquires a light *in addition to* the original that is its content; it is this light, this transparency, that allows the original/content to be transmitted and translated: 'A real translation is transparent; it does not cover the original, does not block its light, but allows the pure language, as though reinforced by its own medium, to shine upon the original all the more fully' (79).

For most interpreters, Benjamin's notion of 'light' and 'transparency' in this passage corroborates that of 'literalness' and 'arcade' in the sense of 'letting light through'. Derrida, for instance, writes that 'whereas the wall braces while concealing (it is *in front of* the original), the arcade supports while letting light pass and the original show' (1985, 187–8)[11] ...

By putting the emphasis on the arcade as a letting-light-through, critics such as Derrida ... alert us correctly to the 'passageway' that is the *conventional* meaning of the arcade. Insofar as it understands the relationship between 'original' and 'translation' in terms of clarity and obscurity, this is a familiar move, which Derrida himself has described and critiqued in the following terms: 'The appeal to the criteria of clarity and obscurity would suffice to confirm ... [that the] entire philosophical delimitation of metaphor already lends itself to being constructed and worked by "metaphors." How could a piece of knowledge or a language be properly clear or obscure?' (1992, 252).

We may borrow Derrida's passage to critique the way *translation* is often evaluated (even by himself) in terms of clarity and obscurity, light and blockage. 'Light' in this common philosophical tradition is assumed to be transparent in the sense of a *nonexisting* medium – and the arcade, which is equated with light, implicitly becomes a *mere* passageway. Since the 'arcade' also corresponds in this context to translation, we are back once again in the classical situation in which 'translation' is a mere vehicle, disposable once it completes its task.

And yet, does light not have another kind of transparency, the transparency of our media and consumer society? Such transparency moves us, it seems to me, not back to the 'original' but rather to the *fabulous constructedness* of the world as spoken of by Nietzsche and Vattimo. Rather than some original text, it is the brilliance of this 'fabling of the world' to which Benjamin's 'arcade' leads us.

What is forgotten, when critics think of translation only in terms of literary and philosophical texts, is that the arcade, especially in the work of Benjamin, is never simply a linguistic passageway; it is also a commercial passageway, a passageway with shop fronts for the display of merchandise.[12] I would therefore emphasize this *mass culture aspect of the arcade* in order to show that the light and transparency allowed by 'translation' is also the light and transparency of commodification. This is a profane, rather than pure and sacred, light, to which non-Western cultures are subjected if they want a place in the contemporary world. In 'literal', 'superficial' ways, this arcade is furnished with exhibits of modernity's 'primitives' such as the women in contemporary Chinese film, who stand like mannequins in the passageways between cultures. The fabulous, brilliant forms of these primitives are what we must go through in order to arrive – not at the new destination of the truth of an 'other' culture but at the weakened foundations of Western metaphysics as well as the disintegrated bases of Eastern traditions. In the display windows of the world market, such 'primitives' are the toys, the fabricated play forms with which the less powerful (cultures) negotiate the imposition of the agenda of the powerful.[13] They are the 'fables' that cast light on the 'original' that is our world's violence, and they mark the passages that head not toward the 'original' that is the West or the East but toward survival in the postcolonial world.[14]

Contemporary Chinese films are cultural 'translations' in these multiple senses of the term. By consciously exoticizing China and revealing China's 'dirty secrets' to the outside world, contemporary Chinese directors are translators of the violence with which the Chinese culture is 'originally' put together. In the dazzling colors of their screen, the primitive that is woman, who at once unveils the corrupt Chinese tradition and parodies the orientalism of the West, stands as the naive symbol, the brilliant arcade, through which 'China' travels across cultures to unfamiliar audiences. Meanwhile, the 'original' that is film, the canonically Western medium, becomes destabilized and permanently infected with the unforgettable 'ethnic' (*and* foreign) images imprinted on it by the Chinese translators ...

Like Benjamin's collector, the Chinese filmmakers' relation to 'China' is that of the heirs to a great collection of treasures, the most distinguished trait of which, writes Benjamin, 'will always be its transmissibility' (1969, 66). If translation is a form of betrayal, then the translators pay their debt by bringing fame to the ethnic culture, a fame that is evident in recent years from the major awards won by Chinese films at international film festivals in Manila, Tokyo, Nantes, Locarno, London, Honolulu, Montréal, Berlin, Venice, and Cannes.[15] Another name for fame is afterlife. It is in translation's faithlessness that 'China' survives and thrives. A faithlessness that gives the beloved life – is that not ... faithfulness itself?

NOTES

1. Walter Benjamin first used the term *optical unconscious* in the essay 'A Small History of Photography' (1931), in *One-Way Street* (1979, 240–57); he again refers to 'unconscious optics' in 'The Work of Art in the Age of Mechanical Reproduction', in *Illuminations* (1969, 217–51).
2. See the comments under the root *do* in Joseph T. Shipley (Shipley, 1984, 73); also the comments under the root *do* in the 'Indo-European Roots Appendix' in *The American Heritage Dictionary of the English Language*, 3rd edn (1992, 2101).
3. See the pertinent discussion by Laurence Venuti (1992, 4).
4. For Derrida's discussion, see, e.g., Jacques Derrida, 'White Mythology: Metaphor in the Text of Philosophy' (1992, 207–71).
5. De Man would argue, instead, that 'the translation is the fragment of a fragment ... There was no vessel in the first place' (1986, 91). He relies for his argument on a firm notion of one correct translation – his own – of Benjamin's text.
6. See in particular Ch. 2 for an erudite account of the traditions and theories of translation.
7. Roman Jakobson calls intersemiotic translation *transmutation*, which he differentiates from both intralingual translation (which he terms *rewording*) and interlingual translation (which he terms *translation proper*) (1959, 233).
8. The sidestepping of mass culture in Niranjana's reconsideration of translation can be glimpsed in the way she rewrites Benjamin's word *image*. Where Benjamin intends by *image* a concrete means – a constellation – for understanding the activity called reading, Niranjana elides such implications and rewrites *image* purely as *reading* in the deconstructive sense. In other words, where Benjamin's emphasis is on *image*, Niranjana's is on *reading* (171–2).
9. See Snyder's lucid and helpful introduction in *The End of Modernity* (Vattimo, 1988).
10. 'How the "Real World" at Last Became a Myth [Fable]' is a chapter in Nietzsche's *Twilight of the Idols* (1889). See Friedrich Nietzsche (1968, 40–1).
11. Derrida's discussions of Benjamin's essay on translation, which are centered largely on verbal language, can also be found in *The Ear of the Other: Otobiography Transference Translation* (1988, 93–161).
12. I can merely refer to Benjamin's arcade's project here. For an authoritative study in English, see Susan Buck-Morss (1989).
13. I borrow this observation from Jeffrey Mehlman (1993). Commenting on one of Benjamin's writings on toys, Mehlman writes: 'The toy is thus above all that wherein the child negotiates the imposition of an adult agenda. A precarious coming to terms that is marked by a tearing apart (*Auseinandersetzung*), it is shot through with the unmastered "traces" of the other' (4).
14. In the 1990s, even the communist state has to adopt market strategies to promote its ideas. For an informed discussion, see Geremie Barmé (1992, sec. 13, 1–52).
15. These include Chinese films from Taiwan and Hong Kong as well. In 1992 and 1993 alone, major awards were won by Stanley Kwan's *Ruan Lingyu (Center Stage)*, Xie Fei's *Xianghun nü (Oilmakers' Family)*, and Ang Lee's *Xiyan (The Wedding Banquet)* at the Berlin Film Festival; Zhang Yimou's *The Story of Qiuju* at the Venice Film Festival; and Chen Kaige's *Bawang bie ji (Farewell to My Concubine)* at the Cannes Film Festival. Films by Ang Lee, Zhang Yimou, and Chen Kaige have also been nominated for the award for 'Best Foreign Language Film' in various years at the Oscars.

ANNOTATED BIBLIOGRAPHY

Ashcroft, Bill, Gareth Griffiths and Helen Tiffin, eds. *The Post-Colonial Studies Reader*. London, 1995.
Commendable attempt to come to terms with the diversity and heterogeneity of postcolonial theory and criticism. This reader sacrifices some detail and depth for a comprehensive sweep; it is also perhaps more deliberately focused on the literary and literary teaching than other social and political issues. Yet its sampling of work from influential metropolitan theorists from the past and the present, and its willingness to include major non Euro-American writers and thinkers offers much by way of an introduction to both the student and teacher. The reader is organised into different sections with helpful introduction to the range of critical positions and debate. There is also a very helpful bibliography at the end of the volume which enables further research.
Bhabha, Homi K. *The Location of Culture*. London, 1994.
Collected essays which enable one to chart Bhabha's work on colonial subjectivity, narratives of origin, ambivalence and authority, and his postcolonial interrogation of Western modernity over a ten year period. It contains most of the famous pieces. In grappling with the problem of cultural and racial difference, Bhabha consistently attempts to think beyond the binary boundaries and homogenous categories of race, nation and class to consider the interstitial and the interlocutional. His term, the 'third space', the space of cultural translation where subject-positions are continually shifting and mutating, is just such an outcome.
Said, Edward. *Orientalism*. London, 1978.
Ambitious and seminal work on race, empire and representation which has influenced postcolonial literary theory and criticism significantly over the last twenty years. Said argues that the invention of the Orient as the object of study and representation goes hand in hand with imperial domination and control. He looks at major European traditions on Africa, Asia and the Middle East but the focus of the discussion is on the Middle East and Islamic cultures. Said's discussion of individuals does not always fit easily into the introductory monolithic model of Orientalism and there are tensions and contradictions in its attempt to marry a humanist vision with an anti-humanist critique, but the basic argument holds true.

Shohat, Ella and Robert Stam. *Unthinking Ethnocentrism: Multiculturalism and the Media*. London, 1994.

Ambitious interrogation of Eurocentrism as formed and challenged by popular media and film that is concerned to explore the connections between history, literature, film and theory. The sampling of films is remarkably wide – generically, commercially and culturally; Shohat and Stam's essays range from classical Hollywood films to some of the influential Third (World) cinema of resistance and their discussions encompass film as documentary and as entertainment. In arguing for a 'polycentric' multiculturalism and an ethnography of spectatorship, Shohat and Stam attempt to come to terms with contemporary transnational global capitalism in terms of its impact and its resistance.

Spivak, Gayatri Chakravorty. *Outside in the Teaching Machine*. London, 1993.

Challenging collection from Spivak which follows on from her earlier influential volume of essays, *Other Worlds*. In her forward, Spivak describes the shift in her work from 'strategic essentialism' and anti-essentialism, to a preoccupation with agency and rethinking marginality in relation to the 'teaching machine'. She advocates breaking down the barriers of discipline, languages and canons in the academic agenda in order to deal seriously with the complexity of the transnational study of culture. Essays also interrogate the role of intellectuals (academic and artistic) and the relation between migrancy and postcoloniality; with the lessons of Marxism, deconstruction and feminism in mind, she repeatedly warns us of the historical problems inherent in (re)presenting the oppressed which does (yet again) not render them silent.

SUPPLEMENTARY BIBLIOGRAPHY

Achebe, Chinua. *Morning Yet on Creation Day*. London, 1975.
————. *Hopes and Impediments: Selected Essays 1965–1987*. London, 1988.
Adam, Ian and Helen Tiffin, eds. *Past the Post: Theorizing Post-Colonialism and Post-Modernism*. Hemel Hempstead, 1991.
Ahmad, A. *Theory: Classes, Nations and Literatures*. London, 1992.
Anderson, Benedict. *Imagined Communities*. London, 1983.
Appiah, Kwame Anthony. *My Father's House: Africa in the Philosophy of Culture*. London, 1992.
Ashcroft, Bill, Gareth Griffiths and Helen Tiffin, eds. *The Empire Writes Back: Theory and Practice in Post-Colonial Literatures*. London, 1989.
————, Gareth Griffiths and Helen Tiffin, eds. *The Post-Colonial Studies Reader*. London, 1995.
Azin, Firdous. *The Colonial Rise of the Novel*. London, 1993.
Barker, Francis, Peter Hulme, Margaret Iversen and Diana Loxley, eds. *Europe and its Others*, 2 vols. Colchester, 1985.
————, Peter Hulme and Margaret Iversen, eds. *Colonial Discourse/Postcolonial Theory*. Manchester, 1994.
Bhabha, Homi K., ed. *Nation and Narration*. London, 1990.
————. *The Location of Culture*, London, 1994.
Brantlinger, Patrick. *Rule of Darkness: British Literature and Imperialism 1830–1914*. Ithaca, NY, 1988.
Brathwaite, Edward. *The Development of Creole Society in Jamaica 1770–1820*. Oxford, 1971.
————. *History of the Voice: The Development of Nation Languages in Anglophone Caribbean Poetry*. London, 1984.
Brooks, Peter. *Psychoanalysis and Storytelling*. Oxford, 1994.
Césaire, Aimé. *Discourse on Colonialism*. New York, 1972.
Chow, Rey. *Writing Diaspora: Tactics of Intervention in Contemporary Cultural Studies*. Bloomington, IN, 1993.
————. *Primitive Passions: Visuality, Sexuality, Ethnography and Contemporary Chinese Cinema*. New York, 1995.

Clifford, James. *The Predicament of Culture*. Cambridge, MA, 1988.

Coetzee, J. M. *White Writing: On the Cultures of Letters in South Africa*. New Haven, CT, 1988.

Dirlik, Arif. *The Postcolonial Aura: Third World Criticism in the Age of Global Capitalism*. Boulder, CO, 1997.

Fabian, Johannes. *Time and the Other: How Anthropology Makes its Object*. New York, 1983.

Fanon, Frantz. *The Wretched of the Earth*. Harmondsworth, 1983.

————. *Black Skins, White Masks*. London, 1986.

Frankenberg, Ruth and Mani, Lata. 'Crosscurrents, Crosstalk: Race, "Postcoloniality" and the Politics of Location', *Cultural Studies*, 7: 2, 1993.

Fuss, Diana. 'Interior Colonies: Frantz Fanon and the Politics of Identification', *Diacritics*, 23: 2/3, 1994.

Gates, Henry L., ed. *'Race', Writing and Difference*, special issue of *Critical Inquiry*, 12: 1, 1985.

Gilroy, Paul. *There Ain't No Black the Union Jack*. London, 1987.

————. *The Black Atlantic: Modernity and Double Consciousness*. London, 1993.

Guha, Ranajit and Gayatri Spivak, eds. *Selected Subaltern Studies*. New Delhi, 1988.

Hall, Stuart. 'Cultural Identity and Diaspora'. *Identities*, ed. Jonathan Rutherford. London, 1990.

————. 'When was the Post-Colonial?', in *The Post-Colonial Question*, eds Iain Chambers and Lidia Curti. London, 1996.

Harris, Wilson. *Tradition, the Writer and Society*. London, 1973.

————. *The Womb of Space*. Westport, CT, 1983.

Hulme, Peter. *Colonial Encounters: Europe and the Native Caribbean 1492–1797*. London, 1992.

JanMohamed, Abul. *Manichean Aesthetics: The Politics of Literature in Colonial Africa*. Amherst, MA, 1983.

Joshi, Svati. *Rethinking English: Essays in Literature, Language, History*. New Delhi, 1991.

Lamming, George. *The Pleasures of Exile*. London, 1960.

Landry, Donna and Gerald MacLean, eds. *The Spivak Reader*. London, 1996.

Loomba, Ania. *Gender, Race, Renaissance Drama*. Manchester, 1989.

————. 'Dead Women Tell No Tales: Issues of Female Subjectivity, Subaltern Agency and Tradition in Colonial and Post-Colonial Writings on Widow Immolation in India', *History Workshop Journal*, 36, 1993.

Low, Gail Ching-Liang. *White Skins/Black Masks: Representation and Colonialism*. London, 1996.

Lazarus, Neil. *Resistance in Postcolonial African Fiction*. New Haven, CT, 1990.

————. 'National Consciousness and Intellectualism'. In *Colonial Discourse/Post-colonial Theory*, eds F. Barker, P. Hulme and M. Iverson. Manchester, 1994.

Lawson, Alan, Leigh Dale, Helen Tiffin and Shane Rowlands, eds. *Post-Colonial Literatures in English: General, Theoretical and Comparative 1970–1993*. New York, 1997.

Kaplan, Caren. *Questions of Travel: Postmodern Discourses of Displacement*. Durham, NC 1996.

McClintock, Anne. 'The Angel of Progress: Pitfalls of the term "Post-Colonialism"', *Social Text*, 31/32, 1992.

————. *Imperial Leather*. London, 1995.

Mani, Lata. 'Contentious Traditions: The Debate on Sati in Colonial India', in *Recasting Women*, eds K.K. Sangari and S. Vaid. New Delhi, 1989.

————. 'Cultural Theory, Colonial texts: Reading Eyewitness Accounts of Widow Burning', in *Cultural Studies*, eds L. Grossberg, C. Nelson and P. Treichler. New York, 1992.

Mohanty, Chandra Talpade. 'Under Western Eyes', *Feminist Review*, 3, 1988.

Moore-Gilbert, Bart. *Postcolonial Theory: Contexts, Practices, Politics*. London, 1997.

Parry, Benita. 'Problems in Current Theories of Colonial Discourse', *Oxford Literary Review*, 9: 1–2, 1987.

Nandy, Ashish. *The Intimate Enemy: Loss and Recovery of Self under Colonialism*. New Delhi, 1983.

Ngugi Wa Thiongo. *Homecoming*. London, 1972.

———. *Decolonising the Mind: The Politics of Language in African Literature*. London, 1986.

Pratt, Mary. *Imperial Eyes*. New York, 1992.

Said, Edward. *Culture and Imperialism*. New York, 1994.

Sharpe, Jenny. *Allegories of Empire: The Figure of Woman in the Colonial Text*. London, 1993.

Shohat, Ella. 'Notes on the Post-Colonial', *Social Text*, 31/32, 1992.

Slemon, Stephen. 'Post-Colonial Allegory and the Transformation of History', *Journal of Commonwealth Literature*, 23: 1, 1988.

———. 'Reading for Resistance in Post-Colonial Literatures', in *A Shaping of Connections: Commonwealth Literature Studies – Then and Now: Essays in Honour of A. N. Jeffares*, eds Hena Maes-Jelinek, Kirsten Holst Petersen and Anna Rutherford. Mundelstrup, 1989.

———. 'The Scramble for Post-Colonialism', *De-Scribing Empire: Post-Colonialism and Textuality.*, eds Chris Tiffin and Alan Lawson. London, 1994.

Spivak, Gayatri Chakravorty. *In Other Worlds*. London, 1988.

———. *The Post-Colonial Critic: Interviews, Strategies, Dialogues*. London, 1990.

Suleri, Sara. *The Rhetoric of English India*. Chicago, 1992.

Taussig, Michael. *Shamanism, Colonialism and the Wild Man*. Chicago, 1987.

Tiffin, Helen. 'Lie Back and Think of England: Post-Colonial Literatures and the Academy', in *A Shaping of Connections: Commonwealth Literature Studies – Then and Now: Essays in Honour of A. N. Jeffares*, eds Hena Maes-Jelinek, Kirsten Holst Petersen and Anna Rutherford. Mundelstrup, 1989.

Viswanthan, Gauri. *Masks of Conquest*. London, 1990.

Young, Robert. *White Mythologies: Writing, History and the West*. London, 1990.

———. *Colonial Desire: Hybridity in Theory, Culture and Race*. London, 1995.

PART II
GAY STUDIES/QUEER THEORY

INTRODUCTION: WORKS ON THE WILD(E) SIDE – PERFORMING, TRANSGRESSING, QUEERING

Jane Goldman

The manifold formulations of 'gay studies' and 'queer theory' owe much to the work of Eve Kosofsky Sedgwick, Jonathan Dollimore (although he is the only one in the following selection not to make use of the term 'queer') and Judith Butler. It is difficult to find a writer in this field who does not invoke and engage with one, if not all three, of these theorists. The field, however, would not be as it is without the achievements of two others: Oscar Wilde and Michel Foucault. Wilde's writings, his life and his iconic 'queer' status, and Foucault's founding work on sexuality, are touchstones in the work of Sedgwick, Dollimore and Butler and many other gay and queer theorists. In his *History of Sexuality*, Foucault demonstrates, among other things, the nineteenth-century cultural emergence and construction of 'the homosexual' as 'a species' (1970, 43); Oscar Wilde, in the twentieth century, has come to personify for many a transhistorical and transcultural model of homosexual or queer identity, at once both enabling and limiting. Gay studies and queer theory address the political ramifications, the advantages and dangers, of culturally 'fixed' categories of sexual identities and the ways in which they may, in the terms given such potent currency by Sedgwick, Dollimore and Butler, be performed, transgressed and queered.

Before considering the work of Sedgwick, Dollimore and Butler it is worth considering some of the broader claims and definitions, positionings and criticisms, of gay studies and queer theory. Both of these interrelated theoretical spheres are enmeshed in the material politics of their time – from Stonewall to ACT UP and Queer Nation – and caught up in the politics of identity where declaration (or confession) of one's own positionality is almost *de rigeur* for any author contributing to its debates. (Call me old-fashioned, but I'm not about to oblige here.) The slash in 'gay studies/queer theory' communicates both the progressive consolidation of these categories – queer theory, a dominant force in the 1990s, may be understood as a legacy of earlier (1970s on) gay studies (itself in complex alliance with feminist and gender studies) – and the tensions between them – there is a sense in which queer theory undoes (queers) the orthodoxies, however recently established, of gay studies. 'Gay studies' may be taken to both embrace and elide 'lesbian' studies, just as 'queer theory', in turn, has simultaneously subsumed, expanded and undone gay studies, not least by marking 'a disturbing *mobility* or non-fixity between diverse sexualities' (Luckhurst, 1995, 333). If even the *naming* of this field, or fields, of study seems excruciatingly and preciously provisional (suggested also in the tendency to resort to scare quotes for whatever our chosen terms), it is because the fraught politics of naming and categorisation are so much its very business.

'Queer theory' has been claimed and refuted as the field in which we might most productively explore what is at stake for politics and people identified in terms of a range of sexualities, troubling not only the oppositional categories of heterosexuality/homosexuality, but also those of the apparently stable 'same-sex' labels of gay and lesbian too. 'Queer theory' has been claimed as giving voice to those elided or marginalised by 'gay' and 'lesbian' studies – bisexuals, transsexuals, sado-masochists, for example – and yet also refuted for silencing such voices. Queer theory is alive to its own paradoxes, playing on the tensions between its emergence as a naming, and therefore fixing category, and the possibilities opened up by its own catachrestic – *mis*naming – semantics. 'The minute you say "queer"', it has been remarked, 'you are necessarily calling into question exactly what you mean when you say it ... Queer includes within it a necessarily expansive impulse that allows us to think about potential differences within that rubric' (Harper, White and Cerullo, 1993, 30). With such positions and contradictions in mind, queer theory intervenes in – *queers* – already familiar debates: particularly the projects preoccupying feminist and gender studies to separate gender and sexuality, and involving the delicate and vexing issues of the politics of subjectivity (essentialist/constructionist), of identity/difference, of modernism/postmodernism, of sexuality and textuality, of margins and centre, of race, class, representation and so on.

Indeed, it was as a possible way out of a theoretical *impasse* located in many of these issues that one of the earliest formulations of queer theory made its mark. Teresa de Lauretis, in 'Queer Theory: Lesbian and Gay Sexualities', a special issue of the journal *differences* (1991), considers how queer theory might negotiate and transcend the racism and sexism evident in gay and lesbian communities of the previous two decades. She proposes that:

> rather than marking the limits of the social space by designating a place at the edge of culture, gay sexuality in its specific female and male cultural (or subcultural) forms acts as an agency of social process whose mode of

functioning is both interactive and yet resistant, both participatory and yet distinct, claiming at once equality and difference, demanding political representation while insisting on its material and historical specificity. (1991, iii)

De Lauretis's use of a colon, in her title, to separate 'queer' from 'lesbian and gay', marks for Sally O'Driscoll 'an ambiguity in the multiple meanings of *queer* as it is currently used', and played out in the tension between its semantic poles of identity and anti-identity:

> The existence of queer theory would be unimaginable without the pre-ceding decades of work in lesbian and gay studies and politics; yet the goal of queer theory as defined by many critics is precisely to interrogate the identity positions from which that work is produced. Using the same word to refer to both fields has produced confusion and even some bitterness on the part of those who fear that queer theory's critique of the subject undermines their visibility and political ground. (1996, 30)

It seems from O'Driscoll's summation that we might easily read 'queer theory' as 'postmodernism', for they seem to share the same good intentions and pitfalls. Queer, 'irreducible, undefinable, enigmatic, winking at us as it flouts convention', has become, according to Suzanne Walters, 'the perfect postmo-dern trope, a term for the times, the epitome of knowing ambiguity. Good-bye simulacra, adios panopticon, arrivederci lack, adieu jouissance: hello *queer*!' (1996, 837).

Whether or not queer theory is a resolution to, or merely a restatement of, familiar difficulties remains to be seen. De Lauretis's definition, according to Brett Beemyn and Mickey Eliason, 'is built on the very dualisms that much of queer theory purports to disrupt or dismantle (female and male, equality and difference), and De Lauretis never provides evidence to prove that queer theory actually does transcend lines of difference. For instance, how does queer theory address issues of racial and gender oppression?' (1996, 164). Beemyn and Eliason are themselves somewhat nebulous in introducing their (1996) collec-tion, *Queer Studies: A Lesbian, Gay, Bisexual, and Transgender Anthology*, with the promise that queer theory 'allows us to view the world from perspectives other than those which are generally validated by the dominant society; we can put a queer slant, for example, on literature, movies, television news reports, and current events. Such queer(ed) positions can challenge the dominance of heterosexist discourses.' Their collection sets out to fulfil queer theory's '*potential* to be inclusive of race, gender, sexuality, and other areas of identity by calling attention to the distinctions between identities, commu-nities, and cultures' (1996, 165). They point up the conscious exclusion of the category of, and essays on, bisexuality from an earlier conference anthology (Dorenkamp and Henke's *Negotiating Lesbian and Gay Subjects*, 1995, 1), and suggest that queer theory can redress such omissions and others: 'by including the voices of people whose lived experiences involve non-normative race, gender, and sexual identities/practices, queer theory can stretch the limits of current thought and possibly revolutionize it' (1995, 166). Yet this is possibly to stretch the limits of queer theory to the point of rendering it an ineffectual catch-all, cure-all, universalising term. Michael Warner in his introduction to *Fear of a Queer Planet*, as Beemyn and Eliason recognise, also comes close to this point in defining queer theory, by virtue of its very performativity, as 'elaborating, in ways that cannot be predicted in advance, this question: What do queers want?' (1993, vii). Beemyn and Eliason worry that 'from this definition ... queer theory is almost anything and everything that the author wants it to be' (1996, 163).

Using queer theory to examine heterosexuality, Lynne Segal, in *Straight Sex: The Politics of Pleasure* (1994), seems to want it to be merely a denotation of dissident catachresis (Luckhurst, 1995, 335). 'Straight feminists', she concludes, 'like gay men and lesbians, have everything to gain from asserting our noncoercive desire to fuck if, when, how and as we choose' (1994, 318). The inclusivity of such broad definitions of queer and queer theory has not pleased other feminists (Sheila Jeffreys, Biddy Martin and Suzanne Walters, for example) since it so often, paradoxically, elides lesbian experiences, work and theories in favour of those of male gays. Terry Castle regards both 'queer' and '*gay*' as 'pseudo-umbrella terms' to be avoided when 'speaking of lesbianism'. She understands the popularity of the term queer to be in part 'precisely because it makes it easy to enfold female homosexuality back "into" male homosexuality and disembody the lesbian once again' (1993, 12). Adrienne Rich's (much earlier) definition of 'the lesbian continuum' (a concept indebted to the work of Carroll Smith-Rosenberg) has attracted similar criticism for building too broad a kirk. Just as 'the lesbian continuum' risks subsuming and homogenising lesbian and 'straight' women's experience, so the queer continuum, we might say, risks subsuming and homogenising, even as it boasts of celebrating and foregrounding, a broad range of same-sex and dissident sexual identities. Walters is concerned about 'the implications involved in claiming "queerness" when one is not gay or lesbian' (1987, 841), and while half-jokingly observing that in academe 'you don't have to be gay to do [queer theory], in fact it is much better if you're not', points up a sinister

> kind of reigning dogma in progressive and postmodern academic circles these days that constructs an 'old-time' feminism in order to point out how the sex debates, postmodernism, and queer theory have nicely superseded this outmoded, reformist, prudish, banal feminism of old. Is it possible that queer theory's Other is feminism, or even lesbianism, or lesbian-feminism? (Rich, 1987, 842)

Much has been made of authorial positionality in these contexts. There is, for example, 'a rumorology [a Sedgwick coinage] that surrounds' Butler and Sedgwick, as Roger Luckhurst observes: 'Butler, the lesbian, does her theory "straight", with demanding and rigorous close readings; Sedgwick, the "straight" who cross-identifies with gay men, does her theory in a highly camp and digressive style' (1995, 334). Walters satirises the extremes to which identification and confession of positionality have been taken in academic discourse where for some (she exempts Sedgwick and Butler) 'we are what we do in bed' (1996, 863), and points up the potential for 'relentless narcissism and individualism' in 'narratives of queer theory'. She continues:

> 'I pack a dildo, therefore I am.' It is sort of like, let us make a theory of our own sexual practices (e.g., 'I'm a cross-dressing femme who likes to use a dildo while watching gay male porn videos with my fuck buddy who sometimes like to do it with gay men. Hmm, what kind of a theory can I make of that?') (Walters, 1996, 857)

Yet queer (theory) has its uses even for some of its sceptics (including Walters); but perhaps, like postmodernism, one of its few defining qualities *is* scepticism. Alan Sinfield confesses to using the term in his book title, *Cultural Politics – Queer Reading* (1994, a chapter of which is presented in the section on cultural studies in this anthology), 'only after considerable hesitation'. Although 'male gayness' dominates his discussion – 'because it is part of [his] argument that intellectuals should work in their own subcultural constituencies' – he invokes lesbian texts and theories, writing 'inclusively of lesbians and gay men wherever that has seemed plausible – but this signals a proposed political alignment, not an assertion that "we" are "the same" (indeed, not all gay men are the same).' He succumbs, then, to the collective term 'queer' in his title, aware both that 'it may be too limiting – yielding up too easily the aspiration to hold a politics of class, race, and ethnicity alongside a politics of gender and sexuality', and that 'it may be over-ambitious' since 'many people outside activist circles still find "queer" too distressing for reappropriation; and there is still the danger that inclusion will lead to effacement' (Sinfield, 1994, x). On the other hand, Sinfield's usage of 'queer' and 'gay' in another book of the same year, *The Wilde Century: Effeminacy, Oscar Wilde and the Queer Moment* (1994), depends on a historicised account of the terms: 'for the sake of clarity' he writes 'queer' for that historical phase when, after Wilde, 'that stereotype ... prevailed in the twentieth century ... not contradicting, thereby, its recent revival among activists'; and he writes "gay" for post-Stonewall kinds of consciousness' (Sinfield, 1994, 3). 'Gay', he points out, 'was established as a way of moving on from' the earlier 'Wildean model' of 'queer', before being superseded by the newly reappropriated 'queer' in the 1990s. The selection of such terms is strategic:

> The aggression and ambition in the readoption of 'queer' are directly proportionate to the degree to which its use proposes to overturn the historic, hostile meaning. It plays for much higher stakes than if we tried to reinstate, say, 'the third sex' ... 'Queer' says, defiantly, that we don't

care what they call us. Also it keeps faith with generations of people, before us, who lived their oppression and resistance in its initial terms. (Sinfield, 1994, 204)

This book has on its cover a picture of Oscar Wilde collagistically sporting a 'Queer as Fuck' T-shirt, an emblem of 1990s queer politics. The political ramifications of this anachronism inform Sinfield's 'constructionist' argument 'about the emergence of a queer identity around Wilde' which 'holds that sexualities ... are not essential, but constructed within an array of prevailing social possibilities.' He takes up Diana Fuss's observations, in *Essentially Speaking: Feminism, Nature and Difference*, that 'homosexuality is not a transhistorical, transcultural, eternal category but a socially contingent and variant construction' (1989, 107–8), to chart its construction in the nineteenth century. 'It is not that our idea of "the homosexual" was hiding beneath other phases,' Sinfield concludes, 'or lurking unspecified in the silence, like a statue under a sheet, fully formed but waiting to be unveiled; it was in the process of becoming constituted. The concept was *emerging* around and through instances like ... Wilde' (Sinfield, 1994, 8). It is not necessarily helpful, therefore, to read Wilde or Shakespeare, for example, or figures in their work, transhistorically as 'homosexual' or 'gay' or 'lesbian' or 'queer', but it is certainly productive to consider how these writers, and readings of their lives and works, contribute to the cultural constitution of such terms and identities.

Sedgwick, in 'Tales of the Avunculate: Queer Tutelage in *The Importance of Being Earnest*', which follows 'Queer and Now' in her collection of essays, *Tendencies*, moves beyond the raft of deconstructive readings of Wilde's play which celebrate Wilde 'for being Derrida or Lacan *avant la lettre*' (1993, 55) and which are (understandably) preoccupied with 'the Name of the Father' in its denouement, to consider how that term has been 'superseded, in a process accelerating over the last century and a half, very specifically by what might be termed the Name of the Family' (1993, 72). Typical of her general *modus operandi*, which Dollimore in *Sexual Dissidence* calls 'a unique integration of insightful literary analysis and persuasive cultural critique' (1993, 29), Sedgwick's reading of *The Importance of Being Earnest* opens out into explorations of contemporary lesbian and gay concerns with legal, social and political definitions of 'the family'. Also typical of her work, particularly in *Tendencies*, are 'the performance strategies of autobiographical "personal criticism"' (Luckhurst, 1995, 334). Sedgwick's activism in queer politics and AIDS campaigns, her bereavements to AIDS, her chemotherapy for breast cancer, her vilifying treatment by the right-wing press – for the notorious essay, 'Jane Austen and the Masturbating Girl' (also in *Tendencies*), for example – all inform her writing. Her first book, *Between Men: English Literature and Male Homosocial Desire*, is credited with breaking new ground for gay studies in introducing readings of nineteenth-century literature with an analysis of homosexuality, homosociality and homophobia in terms of 'erotic triangles'. She examines here the 'special relationship between male homosocial (*including* homosexual) desire and structures for maintaining and transmitting patriarchal power' (1985, 25). Sedgwick's 'arrangement of social and sexual relations', as Joseph Bristow observes in his helpful book, *Sexuality*, 'has one profound point to make: it remains difficult indeed to keep this particular cultural order intact. For the privilege granted to male–male relations stands in dangerous proximity to the very homosexuality that patriarchal fellowship is obliged to condemn' (1997, 205).

Sedgwick's second book, *Epistemology of the Closet* (1990), remains a landmark for queer theory. Here she argues 'that an understanding of virtually any aspect of modern Western culture must be, not merely incomplete, but damaged in its central substance to the degree that it does not incorporate a critical analysis of modern homo/heterosexual definition; and ... assume[s] that the appropriate place for that critical analysis to begin is from the relatively decentred perspective of modern gay and antihomophobic theory.' Following Foucault's 'axiomatic' findings on the privileged relation of sexuality 'to our most prized constructs of individual identity, truth, and knowledge', Sedgwick suggests that 'the language of sexuality not only intersects with but transforms the other languages and relations by which we know', and draws attention to

> performative aspects of texts, and to what are often blandly called their 'reader relations,' as sites of definitional creation, violence, and rupture in relation to particular readers, particular institutional circumstances ... The relations of the closet – the relations of the known and the unknown, the explicit and the inexplicit around homo/heterosexual definition – have the potential for being peculiarly revealing, in fact, about speech acts more generally.

Epistemology of the Closet, as she explains in her foreword to *Tendencies*, explores minoritising/universalising views of homo/heterosexuality and hypothesises 'that modern homo/heterosexual definition has become so exacerbated a cultural site because of an enduring incoherence about whether it is to be thought of as an issue only for a minority of (distinctly lesbian or gay) individuals, or instead as an issue that cuts across every locus of agency and subjectivity in the culture' (1990, xii). *Epistemology of the Closet* has met with both acclaim and consternation. Sedgwick's 'redefinition of the closet as an epistemological predicament rather than a logistical strategy', as Eric Savoy remarks, 'has galvinized subsequent queer theory, and disturbed activists, through the deployment of two axiomatic constructions: her emphasis on closetedness as performative, and her suggestion that it can never be finally disrupted' (1994, 138). The academic critic's and reader's delight in Sedgwick's virtuoso queer deconstructive readings of literary texts is here set against the often very different aspirations and experiences of those engaged in queer politics on the street.

Tendencies makes for Sedgwick 'a counterclaim' against the 'obsolescence' of queer: 'a claim that something about *queer* is inextinguishable.' Somewhat mystically she elaborates by drawing on the term's etymology:

> Queer is a continuing moment, movement, motive – recurrent, eddying, *troublant*. The word 'queer' itself means *across* – it comes from the Indo-European root *-twerkw*, which also yields the German *quer* (transverse), Latin *torquere* (to twist), English *athwart* ... The *queer* of these essays is transitive – multiply transitive. The immemorial current that *queer* represents is antiseparatist as it is antiassimilationist. Keenly, it is relational, and strange' (1993, xii)

Certainly 'Queer and Now' performs queerly in its traversing of several different spheres of personal and political experience, individual and collective, from the troubling statistics on adolescent gay and lesbian suicides, and thoughts on sexual identity and familial formations, to the status of academic and intellectual work of queer theorists. Sedgwick takes stock of her achievements and sets out prospectuses for new work – on transgendered desire and identifications, on 'Queer Performativity', and on the 'politics explicitly oriented around grave illness'. Perhaps the most significant passage in the essay is where Sedgwick, overlapping with Butler's work in some ways, proposes that part of the 'experimental force [of "queer"] as a speech act is the way in which it dramatizes locutionary position itself. Anyone's use of "queer" about themselves means differently from their use of it about someone else'. In this account, to declare oneself 'queer' is almost like bearing witness in a charismatic faith:

> A hypothesis worth making explicit: that there are important senses in which 'queer' can signify only *when attached to the first person*. One possible corollary: that what it takes – all it takes – to make the description 'queer' a true one is the impulse *to* use it in the first person.

As Luckhurst explains:

> Queer is a performative signifier, in that it does not identify and represent a group 'prior' to its naming, but *enacts* a sodality through its very enunciation, in that sense the dissonance of the groups it nominates is productive in the unforseeability of the political 'bodies' it produces. (1995, 333–4)

Sedgwick's point is that its force derives from its performance in the first person (whether singular or plural she does not specify here). O'Driscoll argues that Sedgwick's hypothesis

> elides a real difference between the chosen and the imposed. In practical terms, *queer* has the *same* sense when used in the first and second person, when it refers to lesbians and gay men; the difference between choosing to call oneself queer and being attacked on the street by people who call one queer is evident. This indicates the difference between a category that constitutes identity and one that does not.

'Queer', she continues, 'as used by theorists is not an identity category' like 'woman', 'black', 'white', 'male', in that it is not 'contingent on cultural recognition (1996, 34). Sedgwick's project, however, recognises the strategic, and contestive, political force of constructing and performing a new category of identity that itself transgresses and overturns identity categorisation.

In his outline to *Sexual Dissidence: Augustine to Wilde, Freud to Foucault*, in which his essay, 'Post/modern: On the Gay Sensibility, or the Pervert's Revenge on Authenticity – Wilde, Genet, Orton and Others', appears, Dollimore, citing *Between Men* and the pilot essay, 'Epistemology of the Closet' (1988), pays tribute to Sedgwick whose 'ongoing project' he 'share[s] and strongly endorse[s]' (1991, 29). He coins the term 'sexual dissidence' to describe

> one kind of resistance, operating in terms of gender, [that] repeatedly unsettles the very opposition between the dominant and the subordinate ... The literature, histories, and subcultures of sexual dissidence, though largely absent from current debates (literary, psychoanalytic, and cultural), prove remarkably illuminating for them. (1991, 21)

Much of the material considered above, of course, is testimony to the many critical correctives to such an absence emerging in the period since this observation was made.

Dollimore recognises

> that dissidence may not only be repressed by the dominant (coercively and ideologically), but in a sense actually produced by it, hence consolidating the powers which it ostensibly challenges. This gives rise to the subversion/containment debate, one of the most important areas of dispute in contemporary cultural theory. (1991, 26–7)

Subsequently, his discussion of homosexuality explores

> why in our own time the negation of homosexuality has been in direct proportion to its symbolic centrality; its cultural marginality in direct proportion to its cultural significance; why, also, homosexuality is so strangely integral to the selfsame heterosexual cultures which obsessively denounce it, and why history – history rather than human nature – has produced this paradoxical position. (1991, 28)

Anticipating the self-consciousness of queer theorists to come, Dollimore explains his use of 'homosexual' as 'always provisional and context dependent'. Instead of scare quotes he 'resort[s] again to the occasional use of a typographically pretentious "/" as a reminder that the construction of homo/sexuality emerges from a larger discriminatory formation of hetero/sexuality which it continues to be influenced by, but cannot be reduced to' (1991, 32).

The figure of Wilde is dominant in Dollimore's work. The first part of *Sexual Dissidence* considers an 'encounter' between Wilde and André Gide in Algiers in 1895 (and the book returns to a similar scenario at its close). Dollimore's reading of this event and of various writings by both authors, leads him to contrast Gide's essentialism with Wilde's anti-essentialism, 'a contrast which epitomizes one of the most important differences within the modern history of transgression' (1991, 11). It follows that Gide's (essentialist) transgressive aesthetic is 'obviously indebted to, yet also formed in reaction against, Wilde's own' (1991, 17). Citations from Wilde and Gide also inform 'Post/modern: On the Gay Sensibility, or the Pervert's Revenge on Authenticity – Wilde, Genet, Orton and Others', which appears in a section of the book entitled 'Transgressive Reinscriptions, Early Modern and Post-modern', as the postmodern counterpart to the preceding essay, 'Early Modern: Cross-Dressing in Early Modern England'. This section explores these two different instances of 'transgressive reinscription' which Dollimore defines in terms of 'the perverse dynamic', signifying 'that fearful interconnectedness whereby the antithetical inheres within, and is partly produced by, what it opposes' (1991, 33). In keeping with the 'dangerous proximity', identified by Bristow in Sedgwick's account, of patriarchy's privileged 'male–male' relations to the homosexuality it is obliged to condemn, Dollimore shows that 'the significance of the *proximate* in "metaphysical constructions of the Other", is that 'the proximate is often constructed as the other, and in a process which facilitates displacement. But the proximate is also what enables a tracking-back of the "other" in the "same".' This is Dollimore's 'transgressive reinscription, which, also provisionally may be regarded as the return of the repressed and/or the suppressed and/or the displaced via the proximate' (1991, 33). The 'Early Modern' essay is concerned with how the female transvestite of that period 'appropriated, inverted, and substituted for, masculinity – in a word, perverted it. This was primarily a question of style rather than sexual orientation.' Similarly the 'Post/modern' essay below considers how

> the elusive, probably non-existent, gay sensibility perverts the categories of the aesthetic and the subjective, restoring both to the cultural and social domains which, in the modern period, they have been assumed to transcend, but which in the early modern period they were always known to be a part of. (1991, 34)

The 'Post/modern' essay begins with a critique of Susan Sontag's and George Steiner's work on homosexual sensibility which Dollimore counters with the view that 'the very notion ... is a contradiction in terms', but that there is possibly an aspect of it which may be understood 'in terms *of* that contradiction – a parodic critique of the essence of sensibility as conventionally understood'. He reads Wilde, Genet and Orton through this model while identifying similarities with and departures from postmodernist and poststructuralist models of pastiche and parody. Not surprisingly, Dollimore draws on Butler's ground-breaking work on gender as performance in *Gender Trouble: Feminism and the Subversion of Identity* (1990), which makes much of parody, cross-dressing and repetition in its exploration of deconstructive models of subjectivity. As Dollimore summarises, Butler 'sees deviant sexualities ... as parodic subversive repetitions which displace rather than consolidate heterosexual norms', and cites her much quoted dictum 'gay is to straight *not* as copy is to original, but, rather as copy is to copy'. Attending to Butler's emphasis on the 'importance of *repetition* in the process of resistance and transformation', Dollimore underlines how gay subcultures are both a crucial enabling condition of, and constituting force for, the transgressive reinscription of gender.

Dollimore, in a more recent essay, 'Bisexuality, Heterosexuality, and Wishful Theory' (1996), critiques some of Butler's assertions on homo/hetero/sexuality in an essay published after *Gender Trouble* (in Fuss's collection), where she posits heterosexuality's 'profound dependency upon the homosexuality that it seeks fully to eradicate' (1991, 23). Dollimore underlines this as 'something generally missed by those who have mis/appropriated her work for a facile politics of subversion':

> In Butler's account gay desire usually figures *in an intense relationship to* heterosexuality – so much so that it might be said to have an antagonistic desire *for* it; reading Butler one occasionally gets the impression that gay desire is not complete unless somehow it is installed inside heterosexuality. [This] generalized description of how homosexuality and heterosexuality relate [is to Dollimore] obviously and verifiably wrong. (1996, 535)

In *Bodies that Matter: On the Discursive Limits of 'Sex'*, the last chapter of which is 'Critically Queer', Butler clarifies, defends and elaborates on her propositions in *Gender Trouble*, particularly with regard to criticisms of her notion of gender performativity and cross-dressing which was mistakenly understood to suggest the existence, prior to performance, of 'a willful and instrumental subject ... who decides *on* its gender ... and fails to realize that its existence is already decided *by* gender' (1993, x), and of a perceived lack of attention in her thesis to 'the materiality of the body' (1993, ix). She sets out to find 'a way to link the question of the materiality of the body to the performativity of gender' while taking into account 'the category of "sex" ... within such a relationship' (1993, 1), and, drawing on Derrida's work on the repetitional qualities of 'performative utterance' as 'citation', puts forward a model of performativity as citationality. Butler asks:

> To what extent does discourse gain the authority to bring about what it names through citing the conventions of authority? And does a subject appear as author of its discursive effects to the extent that the citational practice by which he/she is conditioned and mobilized remains unmarked? Indeed, could it be that the production of the subject as originator of his/her effects is precisely a consequence of this dissimulated citationality?

She considers the ramifications of this model for 'subjection to the norms of sex': 'the norm of sex takes hold to the extent that it is "cited" as such a norm, but it also derives its power through the citations that it compels' (1993, 13). In 'Critically Queer' Butler suggests that 'the contentious practices of "queerness" might be understood not only as an example of citational politics, but as a specific reworking of abjection into political agency that might explain why "citationality" has contemporary political promise' (1993, 21).

Of related significance in the essay is Butler's exploration of drag as an allegory of '*heterosexual melancholy*, the melancholy by which a masculine gender is formed from the refusal to grieve the masculine as a possibility of love; a feminine gender ... through the incorporative fantasy by which the feminine is excluded as a possible object of love'. Butler offers the somewhat startling observation that 'the "truest" lesbian melancholic is the strictly straight woman, and the "truest" gay male melancholic is the strictly straight man'. She describes the resultant 'culture of heterosexual melancholy' which 'can be read in the hyperbolic identifications by which mundane heterosexual masculinity and femininity confirm themselves'. Dollimore, in 'Bisexuality, Heterosexuality, and Wishful Theory', remarks that this is 'such a theoretically exquisite irony that it seems churlish to wonder whether it is true', or whether Butler is not herself partaking of that hyperbole she has just discerned in that 'mundane heterosexual masculinity and femininity' (1996, 537). Savoy's concerns over the work of both Butler and Sedgwick are echoed here: 'the rich ironies that accrue at the site of such deconstructive operations permit fine analysis of representation, but they infuriate activists ... who see theory as having an increasingly attenuated relationship to the risks and exigencies experienced by actual lesbians and gay men' (1994, 139).

Butler is tentative about the longevity of the term 'queer'. As a

> site of collective contestation ... it will have to remain that which is ... never fully owned, but always and only redeployed, twisted, queered from a prior usage and in the direction of urgent and expanding political purposes. This also means that it will doubtless have to be yielded in favor of terms that do that political work more effectively.

But a term so unruly and so alive to its own provisionality and mortality is perhaps paradoxically better equipped to survive than most. For, as Butler says elsewhere, 'normalizing the queer would be, after all, its sad finish' (1994, 21).

11.1

QUEER AND NOW

Eve Kosofsky Sedgwick

A MOTIVE

I think everyone who does gay and lesbian studies is haunted by the suicides of adolescents. To us, the hard statistics come easily: that queer teenagers are two to three times likelier to attempt suicide, and to accomplish it, than others; that up to 30 percent of teen suicides are likely to be gay or lesbian; that a third of lesbian and gay teenagers say they have attempted suicide; that minority queer adolescents are at even more extreme risk (Gibson, 1989, 3: 110–42).

The knowledge is indelible, but not astonishing, to anyone with a reason to be attuned to the profligate way this culture has of denying and despoiling queer energies and lives. I look at my adult friends and colleagues doing lesbian and gay work, and I feel that the survival of each one is a miracle. Everyone who survived has stories about how it was done

> – an outgrown anguish
> Remembered, as the Mile
> Our panting Ankle barely passed –
> When Night devoured the Road –
> But we – stood whispering in the House –
> And all we said – was 'Saved'!

(as Dickinson has it) (1960, poem 325, 154). How to tell kids who are supposed never to learn this, that, farther along, the road widens and the air

---

Extract from Eve Kosofsky Sedgwick, *Tendencies* (Duke University Press, 1993), pp. 1–20.

brightens; that in the big world there are worlds where it's plausible, our demand to *get used to it*.

EPISTEMOLOGIES

I've heard of many people who claim they'd as soon their children were dead as gay. What it took me a long time to believe is that these people are saying no more than the truth. They even speak for others too delicate to use the cruel words. For there is all the evidence. The preponderance of school systems, public and parochial, where teachers are fired, routinely, for so much as intimating the right to existence of queer people, desires, activities, children. The routine denial to sexually active adolescents, straight *and* gay, of the things they need – intelligible information, support and respect, condoms – to protect themselves from HIV transmission. (As a policy aimed at punishing young gay people with death, this one is working: in San Francisco for instance, as many as 34 percent of the gay men under twenty-five being tested – and 54 percent of the young black gay men – are now HIV infected (1991, 2: 298)). The systematic separation of children from queer adults; their systematic sequestration from the truth about the lives, culture, and sustaining relations of adults they know who may be queer. The complicity of parents, of teachers, of clergy, even of the mental health professions in invalidating and hounding kids who show gender-dissonant tastes, behavior, body language. In one survey 26 percent of young gay men had been forced to leave home because of conflicts with parents over their sexual identity (Remafedi, cit. Gibson); another report concludes that young gays and lesbians, many of them throwaways, comprise as many as a quarter of all homeless youth in the United States (Gibson, 1989, 3: 113–15).

And adults' systematic denial of these truths to ourselves. The statistics on the triple incidence of suicide among lesbian and gay adolescents come from a report prepared for the U.S. Department of Health and Human Services in 1989; under congressional pressure, recommendations based on this section of the report were never released. Under congressional pressure, in 1991 a survey of adolescent sexual behavior is defunded. Under the threat of congressional pressure, support for all research on sexuality suddenly (in the fall of 1991) dries up. Seemingly, this society wants its children to know nothing; wants its queer children to conform or (and this is not a figure of speech) die; and wants not to know that it is getting what it wants.

PROMISING, SMUGGLING, READING, OVERREADING

This history makes its mark on what, individually, we are and do. One set of effects turns up in the irreducible multilayeredness and multiphasedness of what queer survival means – since being a survivor on this scene is a matter of surviving *into* threat, stigma, the spiraling violence of gay- and lesbian-bashing, and (in the AIDS emergency) the omnipresence of somatic fear and wrenching loss. It is also to have survived into a moment of unprecedented cultural richness, cohesion, and assertiveness for many lesbian and gay adults.

Survivors' guilt, survivors' glee, even survivors' responsibility: powerfully as these are experienced, they are also more than complicated by how permeable the identity 'survivor' must be to the undiminishing currents of risk, illness, mourning, and defiance.

Thus I'm uncomfortable generalizing about people who do queer writing and teaching, even within literature; but some effects do seem widespread. I think many adults (and I am among them) are trying, in our work, to keep faith with vividly remembered promises made to ourselves in childhood: promises to make invisible possibilities and desires visible; to make the tacit things explicit; to smuggle queer representation in where it must be smuggled and, with the relative freedom of adulthood, to challenge queer-eradicating impulses frontally where they are to be so challenged.

I think that for many of us in childhood the ability to attach intently to a few cultural objects, objects of high or popular culture or both, objects whose meaning seemed mysterious, excessive, or oblique in relation to the codes most readily available to us, became a prime resource for survival. We needed for there to be sites where the meanings didn't line up tidily with each other, and we learned to invest those sites with fascination and love. This can't help coloring the adult relation to cultural texts and objects; in fact, it's almost hard for me to imagine another way of coming to care enough about literature to give a lifetime to it. The demands on both the text and the reader from so intent an attachment can be multiple, even paradoxical. For me, a kind of formalism, a visceral near-identification with the writing I cared for, at the level of sentence structure, metrical pattern, rhyme, was one way of trying to appropriate what seemed the numinous and resistant power of the chosen objects. Education made it easy to accumulate tools for this particular formalist project, because the texts that magnetized me happened to be novels and poems; it's impressed me deeply the way others of my generation and since seem to have invented for themselves, in the spontaneity of great need, the tools for a formalist apprehension of other less prestigious, more ubiquitous kinds of text: genre movies, advertising, comic strips.

For me, this strong formalist investment didn't imply (as formalism is generally taken to imply) an evacuation of interest from the passional, the imagistic, the ethical dimensions of the texts, but quite the contrary: the need I brought to books and poems was hardly to be circumscribed, and I felt I knew I would have to struggle to wrest from them sustaining news of the world, ideas, myself, and (in various senses) my kind. The reading practice founded on such basic demands and intuitions had necessarily to run against the grain of the most patent available formulae for young people's reading and life – against the grain, often, of the most accessible voices even in the texts themselves. At any rate, becoming a perverse reader was never a matter of my condescension to texts, rather of the surplus charge of my trust in them to remain powerful, refractory, and exemplary. And this doesn't seem an unusual way for ardent reading to function in relation to queer experience.

. . .

CHRISTMAS EFFECTS

What's 'queer'? Here's one train of thought about it. The depressing thing about the Christmas season – isn't it? – is that it's the time when all the institutions are speaking with one voice. The Church says what the Church says. But the State says the same thing: maybe not (in some ways it hardly matters) in the language of theology, but in the language the State talks: legal holidays, long school hiatus, special postage stamps, and all. And the language of commerce more than chimes in, as consumer purchasing is organized ever more narrowly around the final weeks of the calendar year, the Dow Jones aquiver over Americans' 'holiday mood'. The media, in turn, fall in triumphally behind the Christmas phalanx: ad-swollen magazines have oozing turkeys on the cover, while for the news industry every question turns into the Christmas question – Will hostages be free *for Christmas?* What did that flash flood or mass murder (umpty-ump people killed and maimed) do to those families' *Christmas?* And meanwhile, the pairing 'families/Christmas' becomes increasingly tautological, as families more and more constitute themselves according to the schedule, and in the endlessly iterated image, of the holiday itself constituted in the image of 'the' family.

The thing hasn't, finally, so much to do with propaganda for Christianity as with propaganda for Christmas itself. They all – religion, state, capital, ideology, domesticity, the discourses of power and legitimacy – line up with each other so neatly once a year, and the monolith so created is a thing one can come to view with unhappy eyes. What if instead there were a practice of valuing the ways in which meanings and institutions can be at loose ends with each other? What if the richest junctures weren't the ones where *everything means the same thing?* Think of that entity 'the family', an impacted social space in which all of the following are meant to line up perfectly with each other:

a surname
a sexual dyad
a legal unit based on state-regulated marriage
a circuit of blood relationships
a system of companionship and succor
a building
a proscenium between 'private' and 'public'
an economic unit of earning and taxation
the prime site of economic consumption
the prime site of cultural consumption
a mechanism to produce, care for, and acculturate children
a mechanism for accumulating material goods over several generations
a daily routine
a unit in a community of worship
a site of patriotic formation

and of course the list could go on. Looking at my own life, I see that – probably like most people – I have valued and pursued these various elements of family identity to quite differing degrees (e.g., no use at all for worship, much need of companionship). But what's been consistent in this particular life is an interest in *not* letting very many of these dimensions line up directly with each other at one time. I see it's been a ruling intuition for me that the most productive strategy (intellectually, emotionally) might be, whenever possible, to *dis*articulate them one from another, to *dis*engage them – the bonds of blood, of law, of habitation, of privacy, of companionship and succor – from the lockstep of their unanimity in the system called 'family'.

Or think of all the elements that are condensed in the notion of sexual identity, something that the common sense of our time presents as a unitary category. Yet, exerting any pressure at all on 'sexual identity', you see that its elements include

> your biological (e.g., chromosomal) sex, male or female;
>
> your self-perceived gender assignment, male or female (supposed to be the same as your biological sex);
>
> the preponderance of your traits of personality and appearance, mascu line or feminine (supposed to correspond to your sex and gender);
>
> the biological sex of your preferred partner;
>
> the gender assignment of your preferred partner (supposed to be the same as her/his biological sex);
>
> the masculinity or femininity of your preferred partner (supposed to be the opposite[1] of your own);
>
> your self-perception as gay or straight (supposed to correspond to whether your preferred partner is your sex or the opposite);
>
> your preferred partner's self-perception as gay or straight (supposed to be the same as yours);
>
> your procreative choice (supposed to be yes if straight, no if gay);
>
> your preferred sexual act(s) (supposed to be insertive if you are male or masculine, receptive if you are female or feminine);
>
> your most eroticized sexual organs (supposed to correspond to the procreative capabilities of your sex, and to your insertive/receptive assignment);
>
> your sexual fantasies (supposed to be highly congruent with your sexual practice, but stronger in intensity);
>
> your main locus of emotional bonds (supposed to reside in your preferred sexual partner);
>
> your enjoyment of power in sexual relations (supposed to be low if you are female or feminine, high if male or masculine);
>
> the people from whom you learn about your own gender and sex (supposed to correspond to yourself in both respects);
>
> your community of cultural and political identification (supposed to correspond to your own identity);

and – again – many more. Even this list is remarkable for the silent presumptions it has to make about a given person's sexuality, presumptions that are true only to varying degrees, and for many people not true at all: that everyone 'has a sexuality', for instance, and that it is implicated with each person's sense of overall identity in similar ways; that each person's most characteristic erotic expression will be oriented toward another person and not autoerotic; that if it is alloerotic, it will be oriented toward a single partner or kind of partner at a time; that its orientation will not change over time.[2] Normatively, as the parenthetical prescriptions in the list above suggest, it should be possible to deduce anybody's entire set of specs from the initial datum of biological sex alone – if one adds only the normative assumption that 'the biological sex of your preferred partner' will be the opposite of one's own. With or without that heterosexist assumption, though, what's striking is the number and *difference* of the dimensions that 'sexual identity' is supposed to organize into a seamless and univocal whole.

And if it doesn't?

That's one of the things that 'queer' can refer to: the open mesh of possibilities, gaps, overlaps, dissonances and resonances, lapses and excesses of meaning when the constituent elements of anyone's gender, of anyone's sexuality aren't made, (or *can't be* made) to signify monolithically. The experimental linguistic, epistemological, representational, political adventures attaching to the very many of us who may at times be moved to describe ourselves as (among many other possibilities) pushy femmes, radical faeries, fantasists, drags, clones, leatherfolk, ladies in tuxedoes, feminist women or feminist men, masturbators, bulldaggers, divas, Snap! queens, butch bottoms, storytellers, transsexuals, aunties, wannabes, lesbian-identified men or lesbians who sleep with men, or ... people able to relish, learn from, or identify with such.

Again, 'queer' can mean something different: a lot of the way I have used it so far in this dossier is to denote, almost simply, same-sex sexual object choice, lesbian or gay, whether or not it is organized around multiple criss-crossings of definitional lines. And given the historical and contemporary force of the prohibitions against *every* same-sex sexual expression, for anyone to disavow those meanings, or to displace them from the term's definitional center, would be to dematerialize any possibility of queerness itself.

At the same time, a lot of the most exciting recent work around 'queer' spins the term outward along dimensions that can't be subsumed under gender and sexuality at all: the ways that race, ethnicity, postcolonial nationality criss-cross with these *and other* identity-constituting, identity-fracturing discourses, for example. Intellectuals and artists of color whose sexual self-definition includes 'queer' – I think of an Isaac Julien, a Gloria Anzaldúa, a Richard Fung – are using the leverage of 'queer' to do a new kind of justice to the fractal intricacies of language, skin, migration, state. Thereby, the gravity (I mean the *gravitas*, the meaning, but also the *center* of gravity) of the term 'queer' itself deepens and shifts.

Another telling representational effect. A word so fraught as 'queer' is –

fraught with so many social and personal histories of exclusion, violence, defiance, excitement – never can only denote; nor even can it only connote; a part of its experimental force as a speech act is the way in which it dramatizes locutionary position itself. Anyone's use of 'queer' about themselves means differently from their use of it about someone else. This is true (as it might also be true of 'lesbian' or 'gay') because of the violently different connotative evaluations that seem to cluster around the category. But 'gay' and 'lesbian' still present themselves (however delusively) as objective, empirical categories governed by empirical rules of evidence (however contested). 'Queer' seems to hinge much more radically and explicitly on a person's undertaking particular, performative acts of experimental self-perception and filiation. A hypothesis worth making explicit: that there are important senses in which 'queer' can signify only *when attached to the first person*. One possible corollary: that what it takes – all it takes – to make the description 'queer' a true one is the impulsion *to* use it in the first person.

CURRENT: PROJECT 1

The Golden Bowl, J. L. Austin, Dr. Susan Love's *Breast Book*, and Mme de Sévigné are stacked up, open-faced, on the chair opposite me as I write. I've got three projects braiding and unbraiding in my mind ... I see them as an impetus into future work as well.

Project 1 ... is about desires and identifications that move across gender lines, including the desires of men for women and of women for men. In that sense, self-evidently, heterosexuality is one of the project's subjects. But the essays are queer ones. Their angle of approach is directed, not at reconfirming the self-evidence and 'naturalness' of heterosexual identity and desire, but rather at rendering those culturally central, apparently monolithic constructions newly accessible to analysis and interrogation.

The project is difficult partly because of the asymmetries between the speech relations surrounding heterosexuality and homosexuality. As Michel Foucault argues, during the eighteenth and nineteenth centuries in Europe:

> Of course, the array of practices and pleasures continued to be referred to [heterosexual monogamy] as their internal standard; but it was spoken of less and less, or in any case with a growing moderation. Efforts to find out its secrets were abandoned; nothing further was demanded of it than to define itself from day to day. The legitimate couple, with its regular sexuality, had a right to more discretion. It tended to function as a norm, one that was stricter, perhaps, but quieter ...
>
> Although not without delay and equivocation, the natural laws of matrimony and the immanent rules of sexuality began to be recorded on two separate registers. (1978, 38–40)

Thus, if we are receptive to Foucault's understanding of modern sexuality as the most intensive site of the demand for, and detection or discursive production of, the Truth of individual identity, it seems as though this silent, normative, uninterrogated 'regular' heterosexuality may not function as a sexuality at all. Think of how a culturally central concept like public/private is organized so as to preserve for heterosexuality the unproblematicalness, the apparent naturalness, of its *discretionary* choice between display and concealment: 'public' names the space where cross-sex couples *may*, whenever they feel like it, display affection freely, while same-sex couples *must* always conceal it; while 'privacy', to the degree that it is a right codified in U.S. law, has historically been centered on the protection-from-scrutiny of the married, cross-sex couple, a scrutiny to which (since the 1986 decision in *Bowers* v. *Hardwick*) same-sex relations on the other hand are unbendingly subject. Thus, heterosexuality is consolidated as the *opposite* of the 'sex' whose secret, Foucault says, 'the obligation to conceal ... was but another aspect of the duty to admit to' (1978, 61). To the degree that heterosexuality does not function as a sexuality, however, there are stubborn barriers to making it accountable, to making it so much as visible, in the framework of projects of historicizing and hence denaturalizing sexuality. The making historically visible of heterosexuality is difficult because, under its institutional pseudonyms such as Inheritance, Marriage, Dynasty, Family, Domesticity, and Population, heterosexuality has been permitted to masquerade so fully as History itself – when it has not presented itself as the totality of Romance.

PROJECT 2

Here I'm at a much earlier stage, busy with the negotiations involved in defining a new topic in a usable, heuristically productive way; it is still a series of hunches and overlaps; its working name is Queer Performativity. You can see the preoccupations that fuel the project already at work throughout *Epistemology of the Closet* as well as *Tendencies*, but I expect it to be the work of a next book to arrive at broadly usable formulations about them. Like a lot of theorists right now (Judith Butler and her important book *Gender Trouble* can, perhaps, stand in for a lot of the rest of us), I'm interested in the implications for gender and sexuality of a tradition of philosophical thought concerning certain utterances that do not merely describe, but actually perform the actions they name: '*J'accuse*'; 'Be it resolved ...'; 'I thee wed'; 'I apologize'; 'I dare you'. Discussions of linguistic performativity have become a place to reflect on ways in which language really can be said to produce effects: effects of identity, enforcement, seduction, challenge.[3] They also deal with how powerfully language *positions*: does it change the way we understand meaning, for instance, if the semantic force of a word like 'queer' is so different in a firstperson from what it is in a second- or third-person sentence?

My sense is that, in a span of thought that arches at least from Plato to Foucault, there are some distinctive linkages to be traced between linguistic performativity and histories of same-sex desire. I want to go further with an argument implicit in *Epistemology of the Closet*: that both the act of coming out, and closetedness itself, can be taken as dramatizing certain features of linguistic performativity in ways that have broadly applicable implications. Among the striking aspects of considering closetedness in this framework, for instance, is that the speech act in question is a series of silences! I'm the more eager to think about performativity, too, because it may offer some ways of describing what *critical* writing can effect (promising? smuggling?); anything that offers to make this genre more acute and experimental, less numb to itself, is a welcome prospect.

PROJECT 3

This project involves thinking and writing about something that's actually structured a lot of my daily life over the past year. Early in 1991 I was diagnosed, quite unexpectedly, with a breast cancer that had already spread to my lymph system, and the experiences of diagnosis, surgery, chemotherapy, and so forth, while draining and scary, have also proven just sheerly *interesting* with respect to exactly the issues of gender, sexuality, and identity formation that were already on my docket. (Forget the literal-mindedness of mastectomy, chemically induced menopause, etc.: I would warmly encourage anyone interested in the social construction of gender to find some way of spending half a year or so as a totally bald woman.) As a general principle, I don't like the idea of 'applying' theoretical models to particular situations or texts – it's always more interesting when the pressure of application goes in both directions – but all the same it's hard not to think of this continuing experience as, among other things, an adventure in applied deconstruction.[4] How could I have arrived at a more efficient demonstration of the instability of the supposed oppositions that structure an experience of the 'self'? – the part and the whole (when cancer so dramatically corrodes that distinction); safety and danger (when fewer than half of the women diagnosed with breast cancer display any of the statistically defined 'risk factors' for the disease); fear and hope (when I feel – I've got a quarterly physical coming up – so much less prepared to deal with the news that a lump or rash *isn't* a metastasis than that it is); past and future (when a person anticipating the possibility of death, and the people who care for her, occupy temporalities that more and more radically diverge); thought and act (the words in my head are aswirl with fatalism, but at the gym I'm striding treadmills and lifting weights); or the natural and the technological (what with the exoskeleton of the bone-scan machine, the uncanny appendage of the IV drip, the bionic implant of the Port-a-cath, all in the service of imaging and recovering my 'natural' healthy body in the face of its spontaneous and endogenous threat against itself). Problematics of undecidability present themselves in a new, unfacile way with a disease whose very *best* outcome – since breast cancer doesn't respect the five-year statute of limitations that constitutes cure for some other cancers – will be decades and decades of free-fall interpretive panic.

Part of what I want to see, though, is what's to be learned from turning this experience of dealing with cancer, in all its (and my) marked historical specificity, and with all the uncircumscribableness of the turbulence and threat involved, back toward a confrontation with the theoretical models that have helped me make sense of the world so far. The phenomenology of life-threatening illness; the performativity of a life threatened, relatively early on, by illness; the recent crystallization of a politics explicitly oriented around grave illness: exploring these connections *has* (at least for me it has) to mean hurling my energies outward to inhabit the very farthest of the loose ends where representation, identity, gender, sexuality, and the body can't be made to line up neatly together.

It's probably not surprising that gender is so strongly, so multiply valenced in the experience of breast cancer today. Received wisdom has it that being a breast cancer patient, even while it is supposed to pose unique challenges to one's sense of 'femininity', nonetheless plunges one into an experience of almost archetypal Femaleness. Judith Frank is the friend whom I like to think of as Betty Ford to my Happy Rockefeller – the friend, that is, whose decision to be public about her own breast cancer diagnosis impelled me to the doctor with my worrisome lump; she and her lover, Sasha Torres, are only two of many women who have made this experience survivable for me: compañeras, friends, advisors, visitors, students, lovers, correspondents, relatives, caregivers (these being anything but discrete categories). Some of these are indeed people I have come to love in feminist- and/or lesbian-defined contexts; beyond that, a lot of the knowledge and skills that keep making these women's support so beautifully apropos derive from distinctive feminist, lesbian, and women's histories. (I'd single out, in this connection, the contributions of the women's health movement of the 70s – its trenchant analyses, its grass-roots and antiracist politics, its publications,[5] the attitudes and institutions it built and some of the careers it seems to have inspired.)

At the same time, though, another kind of identification was plaited inextricably across this one – not just for me, but for others of the women I have been close to as well. Probably my own most formative influence from a quite early age has been a viscerally intense, highly speculative (not to say inventive) cross-identification with gay men and gay male cultures as I inferred, imagined, and later came to know them. It wouldn't have required quite so overdetermined a trajectory, though, for almost any forty year old facing a protracted, life-threatening illness in 1991 to realize that the people with whom she had perhaps most in common, and from whom she might well have most to learn, are people living with AIDS, AIDS activists, and others whose lives had been profoundly reorganized by AIDS in the course of the 1980s.

As, indeed, had been my own life and those of most of the people closest to me. 'Why me?' is the cri de coeur that is popularly supposed to represent Everywoman's deepest response to a breast cancer diagnosis – so much so that not only does a popular book on the subject have that title, but the national breast cancer information and support hotline is called Y-ME! Yet 'Why me?'

was not something it could have occurred to me to ask in a world where so many companions of my own age were already dealing with fear, debilitation, and death. I wonder, too, whether it characterizes the responses of the urban women of color forced by violence, by drugs, by state indifference or hostility, by AIDS and other illnesses, into familiarity with the rhythms of early death. At the time of my diagnosis the most immediate things that were going on in my life were, first, that I was coteaching (with Michael Moon) a graduate course in queer theory, including such AIDS-related material as Cindy Patton's stunning *Inventing AIDS*. Second, that we and many of the students in the class, students who indeed provided the preponderance of the group's leadership and energy at that time, were intensely wrapped up in the work (demonstrating, organizing, lobbying) of a very new local chapter of the AIDS activist organization ACT UP. And third, that at the distance of far too many miles I was struggling to communicate some comfort or vitality to a beloved friend, Michael Lynch, a pioneer in gay studies and AIDS activism, who seemed to be within days of death from an AIDS-related infection in Toronto.

... the framework in which I largely experienced my diagnosis ... was very much shaped by AIDS and the critical politics surrounding it, including the politics of homophobia and of queer assertiveness. The AIDS activist movement, in turn, owes much to the women's health movement of the 70s; and in another turn, an activist politics of breast cancer, spearheaded by lesbians, seems in the last year or two to have been emerging based on the model of AIDS activism.[6] The dialectical epistemology of the two diseases, too – the kinds of secret each has constituted; the kinds of *outness* each has required and inspired – has made an intimate motive for me ...

MY WAR AGAINST WESTERN CIVILIZATION

That there were such people [who neither loved one, nor liked one, nor wished one well] – that, indeed, the public discourse of my country was increasingly dominated by them – got harder and harder to ignore during the months of my diagnosis and initial treatment. For the first time, it was becoming routine to find my actual name, and not just the labels of my kind, on those journalistic lists of who was to be considered more dangerous than Saddam Hussein. In some ways, the timing of the diagnosis couldn't have been better: if I'd needed a reminder I had one that, sure enough, life *is* too short, at least mine is, for going head-to-head with people whose highest approbation, even, would offer no intellectual or moral support in which I could find value. Physically, I was feeling out of it enough that the decision to let this journalism wash over me was hardly a real choice – however I might find myself misspelled, misquoted, mis-paraphrased, or (in one hallucinatory account) married to Stanley Fish. It was the easier to deal psychically with having all these journalists scandalize my name because it was clear most of them wouldn't have been caught dead reading my work: the essay of mine that got the most free publicity, 'Jane Austen and the Masturbating Girl', did so without having been read by a single one of the people who invoked it: it reached its peak of currency in hack circles months before it was published, and Roger Kimball's *Tenured Radicals*, which first singled it out for ridicule, seems to have gone to press before the essay was so much as *written* (Kimball, 1990, 145–6).

Not that I imagine a few cozy hours reading *Epistemology of the Closet* would have won me rafts of fans amongst the punditterati. The attacks on me personally were based on such scummy evidential procedures that the most thin-skinned of scholars – so long as her livelihood was secure – could hardly have taken them to heart; the worst of their effects on me at the time was to give an improbable cosmic ratification (yes, actually, everything *is* about me!) to the self-absorption that forms, at best, an unavoidable feature of serious illness. If the journalistic hologram bearing my name seemed a relatively easy thing to disidentify from, though, I couldn't help registering with much greater intimacy a much more lethal damage. I don't know a gentler way to say it than that at a time when I've needed to make especially deep draughts on the reservoir of a desire to live and thrive, that resource has shown the cumulative effects of my culture's wasting depletion of it. It *is* different to experience from the vantage point of one's own bodily illness and need, all the brutality of a society's big and tiny decisions, explicit and encoded ones, about which lives have or have not value. Those decisions carry not only institutional and economic but psychic and, I don't doubt, somatic consequences. A thousand things make it impossible to mistake the verdict on queer lives and on women's lives, as on the lives of those who are poor or are not white. The hecatombs of queer youth; a decade squandered in a killing inaction on AIDS; the rapacious seizure from women of our defense against forced childbirth; tens of millions of adults and children excluded from the health care economy; treatment of homeless people as unsanitary refuse to be dealt with by periodic 'sweeps'; refusal of condoms in prisons, persecution of needle exchange programs; denial and trivialization of histories of racism; or merely the pivot of a disavowing pronoun in a newspaper editorial: such things as these are facts, but at the same time they are piercing or murmuring voices in the heads of those of us struggling to marshal 'our' resources against illness, dread, and devaluation. They speak to us. They have an amazing clarity.

A CRAZY LITTLE THING CALLED RESSENTIMENT

There was something especially devastating about the wave of anti-'PC' journalism in the absolutely open contempt it displayed, and propagated, for *every* tool that has been so painstakingly assembled in the resistance against these devaluations. Through raucously orchestrated, electronically amplified campaigns of mock-incredulous scorn, intellectual and artistic as well as political possibilities, skills, ambitions, and knowledges have been laid waste with a relishing wantonness. No great difficulty in recognizing those aspects of the anti-'PC' craze that are functioning as covers for a rightist ideological putsch; but it has surprised me that so few people seem to view the recent developments as, among other things, part of an overarching history of anti-intellectualism: anti-intellectualism left as well as right. No twentieth-century political movement, after all, can afford not to play the card of populism, whether or not the popular welfare is what it has mainly at heart (indeed, perhaps especially where it is least so). And anti-intellectual pogroms, like anti-Semitic or queer-bashing ones, are quick, efficient, distracting, and almost universally understood signifiers for a populist solidarity that may boil down to nothing by the time it reaches the soup pot. It takes care and intellectual scrupulosity to forge an egalitarian politics not founded on such telegraphic slanders. Rightists today like to invoke the threatening specter of a propaganda-ridden socialist realism, but both they and the anti-intellectuals of the left might meditate on why the Nazis' campaign against 'degenerate art' (Jewish, gay, modernist) was couched, as their own arguments are, in terms of assuring the instant, unmediated, and universal accessibility of all the sign systems of art (Goebbels even banning all art criticism in 1936, on the grounds that art is self-explanatory). It's hard to tell which assumption is more insultingly wrong: that the People (always considered, of course, as a mono-lithic unit) have no need and no faculty for engaging with work that is untransparent; or that the work most genuinely expressive of the People would be so univocal and so limpidly vacant as quite to obviate the labors and pleasures of interpretation. Anti-intellectuals today, at any rate, are happy to dispense with the interpretive process and depend instead on appeals to the supposedly self-evident: legislating against '*patently* offensive' art (no second looks allowed); citing titles as if they were texts; appealing to potted summaries and garbled trots as if they were variorum editions in the original Aramaic. The most self-evident things, as always, are taken – as if unanswerably – to be the shaming risibility of any form of oblique or obscure expression; and the flat inadmissability of openly queer articulation.

THOUGHT AS PRIVILEGE

These histories of anti-intellectualism cut across the 'political correctness' debate in complicated ways. The term 'politically correct' originated, after all, in the mockery by which experimentally and theoretically minded femin-ists, queers, and leftists (of every color, class, and sexuality) fought back against the stultifications of feminist and left anti-intellectualism. The hector-ing, would-be-populist derision that difficult, ambitious, or sexually charged writing today encounters from the right is not always very different from the reception it has already met with from the left. It seems as if many academic feminists and leftists must be grinding their teeth at the way the right has willy-nilly conjoined their discursive fate with that of theorists and 'deconstruc-tionists' – just as, to be fair, many theorists who have betrayed no previous interest in the politics of class, race, gender, or sexuality may be more than bemused at turning up under the headings of 'Marxism' or 'multiculturalism'. The right's success in grouping so many, so contestable, movements under the rubric 'politically correct' is a coup of cynical slovenliness unmatched since the artistic and academic purges of Germany and Russia in the thirties.

What the American intellectual right has added to this hackneyed populist semiotic of *ressentiment* is an iridescent oilslick of elitist self-regard. Trying to revoke every available cognitive and institutional affordance for reflection, speculation, experimentation, contradiction, embroidery, daring, textual aggression, textual delight, double entendre, close reading, free association, wit – the family of creative activities that might, for purposes of brevity, more simply be called *thought* – they yet stake their claim as the only inheritors, defenders, and dispensers of a luscious heritage of thought that most of them would allow to be read only in the dead light of its pieties and its exclusiveness. Through a deafeningly populist rhetoric, they advertise the mean pleasures of ranking and gatekeeping as available to all. But the gates that we are invited to invigorate ourselves by cudgeling barbarians at open onto nothing but a *Goodbye, Mr. Chips* theme park.

What is the scarcity that fuels all this *ressentiment?* The leveraged burnout of the eighties certainly took its toll, economically, on universities as well as on other professions and industries. In secretaries' offices, in hospitals and HMOs, in network news bureaus, in Silicon Valley laboratories and beyond, the bottom line has moved much closer to a lot of people's work lives – impinging not just on whether they *have* work, but on what they do when they're there. But academic faculty, in our decentralized institutions, with our relatively diffuse status economy and our somewhat archaic tangle of traditions and prerogatives, have had, it seems, more inertial resistance to offer against the wholesale reorientation of our work practices around the abstractions of profit and the market. For some faculty at some colleges and universities, it is still strikingly true that our labor is divided up by task orientation (we may work on the book till it's done, explain to the student till she understands) rather than by a draconian time discipline; that what we produce is described and judged in qualitative as much as quantitative terms; that there is a valued place for affective expressiveness, and an intellectually productive permeability in the boundaries between public and private; that there are opportunities for collaborative work; and most importantly, that we can expend some substantial part of our paid labor on projects we ourselves have conceived, relating to questions whose urgency and interest make a claim on our own minds, imaginations, and consciences.

Millions of people today struggle to carve out – barely, at great cost to themselves – the time, permission, and resources, 'after work' or instead of decently-paying work, for creativity and thought that will not be in the service of corporate profit, nor structured by its rhythms. Many, many more are scarred by the prohibitive difficulty of doing so. No two people, no two groups would make the same use of these resources, furthermore, so that no one can really pretend to be utilizing them 'for' another. I see that some must find enraging the spectacle of people for whom such possibilities are, to a degree, built into the structure of our regular paid labor. Another way to understand that spectacle, though, would be as one remaining form of insistence that it is not inevitable – it is not a simple fact of nature – for the facilities of creativity and thought to represent rare or exorbitant *privilege*. Their economy should not and need not be one of scarcity.

The flamboyance with which some critical writers – I'm one of them – like to laminate our most ambitious work derives something, I think, from this situation. Many people doing all kinds of work are able to take pleasure in aspects of their work; but something different happens when the pleasure is not only taken but openly displayed. I like to make that different thing happen. Some readers identify strongly with the possibility of a pleasure so displayed; others disidentify from it with violent repudiations; still others find themselves occupying less stable positions in the circuit of contagion, fun, voyeurism, envy, participation, and stimulation. When the pleasure is attached to medi-tative or artistic productions that deal, not always in an effortlessly accessible way, with difficult and painful realities among others, then readers' responses become even more complex and dramatic, more productive for the author and for themselves. Little wonder then that sexuality, the locus of so many showy pleasures and untidy identities and of so much bedrock confrontation, opacity, and loss, should bear so much representational weight in arguments about the structure of intellectual work and life. Sexuality in this sense, perhaps, can *only* mean queer sexuality: so many of us have the need for spaces of thought and work where everything doesn't mean the same thing!

So many people of varying sexual practices, too, enjoy incorrigibly absorb-ing imaginative, artistic, intellectual, and affective lives that have been richly nourished by queer energies – and that are savagely diminished when the queerness of those energies is trashed or disavowed. In the very first of the big 'political correctness' scare pieces in the mainstream press, *Newsweek* ponti-ficated that under the reign of multiculturalism in colleges, 'it would not be enough for a student to refrain from insulting homosexuals ... He or she would be expected to ... study their literature and culture alongside that of Plato, Shakespeare, and Locke' (Adler et al., 1990, 48).[7] *Alongside?* Read any Sonnets lately? You dip into the *Phaedrus* often?

To invoke the utopian bedroom scene of Chuck Berry's immortal *aubade:* Roll over, Beethoven, and tell Tchaikovsky the news.

NOTES

1. The binary calculus I'm describing here depends on the notion that the male and female sexes are each other's 'opposites', but I do want to register a specific demurral against that bit of easy common sense. Under no matter what cultural construction, women and men are more like each other than chalk is to cheese, than ratiocination is like raisins, than up is like down, or than 1 is like 0. The biological, psychological, and cognitive attributes of men overlap with those of women by vastly more than they differ from them.
2. A related list that amplifies some of the issues raised in this one appears in the introduction to *Epistemology of the Closet* (1990, 25–6).
3. One of the most provocative discussions of performativity in relation to literary

criticism is Shoshana Felman (1982); most of the current work being done on performativity in relation to sexuality and gender is much indebted to Judith Butler's *Gender Trouble: Feminism and the Subversion of Identity* (1989).

4. That deconstruction can offer crucial resources of thought for survival under duress will sound astonishing, I know, to anyone who knows it mostly from the journalism on the subject – journalism that always depicts 'deconstructionism', not as a group of usable intellectual tools, but as a set of beliefs involving a patently absurd dogma ('nothing really exists'), loopy as Christian Science but as exotically aggressive as (American journalism would also have us find) Islam. I came to my encounter with breast cancer not as a member of a credal sect of 'deconstructionists' but as someone who needed all the cognitive skills she could get. I found, as often before, that I had some good and relevant ones from my deconstructive training.

5. The work of this movement is mostly available today through books like the Boston Women's Health Book Collective's *The New Our Bodies, Ourselves: Updated and Expanded for the Nineties* (1992). An immensely important account of dealing with breast cancer in the context of feminist, antiracist, and lesbian activism is Audre Lorde, *The Cancer Journals*, 2nd edn (1988) and *A Burst of Light* (1988).

6. On this, see Alisa Solomon (1991, 22–7); Judy Brady, ed. (1991); Midge Stocker, ed. (1991); and Sandra Butler and Barbara Rosenblum (1991).

7. 'Queer and Now' was written in 1991 Ken Wissoker thought up the title, and Mark Seltzer cheered me on with it.

11.2

POST/MODERN: ON THE GAY SENSIBILITY, OR THE PERVERT'S REVENGE ON AUTHENTICITY – WILDE, GENET, ORTON, AND OTHERS

Jonathan Dollimore

To be really modern one should have no soul. (Wilde, 'Maxims')

Will he force me to think that homosexuals have more imagination than the ... others? No, but they are more frequently called upon to exercise it. (André Gide, *Journals*, 1931)

THE ELUSIVE HOMOSEXUAL SENSIBILITY

Separately and in different ways, Susan Sontag and George Steiner have suggested that a (or 'the') homosexual sensibility is a major influence in the formation of modern culture. In 1964 Sontag wrote that 'Jews and homosexuals are the outstanding creative minorities in contemporary urban culture. Creative, that is, in the truest sense: they are creators of sensibilities. The two pioneering forces of modern sensibility are Jewish moral seriousness and homosexual aestheticism and irony.' She seeks to substantiate this claim in the famous essay from which it is taken (1996, 290).

For Steiner homosexuality is if anything even more central to, and definitive of, the modern. 'Since about 1890', he believes, 'homosexuality has played a vital part in Western culture.' Whereas 'heterosexuality is the very essence of ... classic realism', a 'radical homosexuality' figures in modernity, particularly in its self-referentiality and narcissism; indeed 'homosexuality could be construed as a creative rejection of the philosophic and conventional realism, of the *mundanity* and extroversion of classic and nineteenth century feeling'. Further,

Extract from Jonathan Dollimore, *Sexual Dissidence: Augustine to Wilde, Freud to Foucault* (Oxford University Press, 1991), pp. 307–25.

homosexuality in part made possible 'that exercise in solipsism, that remorse-less mockery of philistine common sense and bourgeois realism which is modern art' (1978, 115, 117, 118). Steiner's association of homosexuality with narcissism, solipsism, and the refusal of referentiality obviously suggests reservations about both modernism (as he conceives it) and the efficacy of the homosexual influence upon it, and it comes as no surprise that in his most recent book he launches a strong attack on the former. Steiner now contends that two historical moments, the one epitomized in Mallarmé's 'disjunction of language from external reference', and the other in Rimbaud's 'deconstruction of the self' – *je est un autre* (I is (an)other) – splinter the foundations of the Western tradition and precipitate it into the crisis of modernity. Rimbaud would seem to be especially culpable since 'the deconstructions of semantic forms, the destabilizations of meaning, as we have known them during the past decades, derive from Rimbaud's dissolution of the self'. Compared to these two cultural moments, 'even the political revolutions and great wars in modern European history are, I would venture, of the surface' (1989, 101, 94–6).

Steiner and Sontag are in a sense correct about the centrality of homosexu-ality to modern culture. But [my] argument ... is that its centrality is quite otherwise than they suggest. Steiner's ludicrous generalizations stem in part from the very notion of defining cultures and history in terms of a sensibility. Even a cursory look at gay history and culture suggests that the sweep and conclusions of his argument are questionable at virtually every turn, as indeed is the very notion of a homosexual sensibility.

Sontag's article at least has the virtue of tentativeness; it is in the form of notes (dedicated to Oscar Wilde), and acknowledges the difficulty of defining a sensibility, especially one as 'fugitive' as this (1966, 277). But still questions abound: is this sensibility transcultural, or historically rooted in the (varying) histories of the representation of homosexuality? Is it a direct expression of homosexuality, or an indirect expression of its repression and/or sublimation? Is it defined in terms of the sexuality of (say) the individual or artist who expresses or possesses it – and does that mean that no non-homosexual can possess/express it? I shall suggest that there is a sense in which the very notion of a homosexual sensibility is a contradiction in terms. I am interested in an aspect of it which exists, if at all, in terms *of* that contradiction – of a parodic critique of the essence of sensibility as conventionally understood.

Michel Foucault argues that in the modern period sex has become definitive of the truth of our being ... As such, sexuality in its normative forms constitutes a 'truth' connecting inextricably with other truths and norms not explicitly sexual. This is a major reason why sexual deviance is found threatening: in deviating from normative truth and the 'nature' which underpins it, such deviance shifts and confuses the norms of truth and being throughout culture. Wilde's transgressive aesthetic simultaneously confirmed and exploited this inextricable connection between the sexual and the (apparently) non-sexual, between sexual perversion and social subversion, and does so through Wilde's own version of that connection: 'what paradox was to me in the sphere of thought, perversity became to me in the sphere of passion' (1962, 466).

If I had to give a single criterion of that dubious category, the homosexual sensibility, it would be this connection between perversity and paradox – if only because it suggests why that sensibility does not exist as such ... Wilde's transgressive aesthetic writes desire into a discourse of liberation inseparable from an inversion and displacement of dominant categories of subjective depth (the depth model). It is from just these categories that notions of sensibility traditionally take their meaning. Additionally for Wilde, perverse desire is not only an agency of displacement, it is partly constituted by that displacement and the transgressive aesthetic which informs it. Just as in reverse discourse the categories of subordination are turned back upon the regimes of truth which disqualify, so this 'other' sensibility is in part affirmed as an inversion and absence of sensibility's traditional criteria. Perverse desire is transvalued, socially, sexually, and aesthetically. *Dorian Gray* describes moments when 'the passion for sin, or for what the world calls sin' is utterly overwhelming

> and conscience is either killed, or, if it lives at all, lives but to give rebellion its fascination, and disobedience its charm. For all sins, as theologians weary not of reminding us, are sins of disobedience. When that high spirit, that morning-star of evil, fell from heaven, it was as a rebel that he fell. (1949, 210)

Law and conscience are subjected to the perverse dynamic, being made to enable and intensify the rebellion they were supposed to prevent; likewise with Wilde's transgressive aesthetic in the realm of desire and culture.

Wilde lived an anarchic and a political homosexuality simultaneously. Richard Ellmann describes him as 'conducting, in the most civilized way, an anatomy of his society, and a radical reconsideration of its ethics ... His greatness as a writer is partly the result of the enlargement of sympathy which he demanded for society's victims' (1987, xiv). I agree, and this can stand as a cogent if incomplete description of what is meant by a political homosexuality. But Wilde also fashioned his transgressive aesthetic into a celebration of anarchic deviance, and this is yet another factor which makes it difficult to identify the sensibility involved. There is a positive desire to transgress and disrupt, and a destructiveness, even a running to one's own destruction, paradoxically creative. Though in a different way, what we have seen to be true of Gide was also true of Wilde: 'running foul of the law in his sexual life was a stimulus to thought on every subject ... His new sexual direction liberated his art. It also liberated his critical faculty' (1987, 270).

Conformity angered and bored Wilde. It is not clear which, the anger or the boredom, was thought to be the more insulting, but both were expressed as that arrogance for which he was often hated. Yeats recalls receiving a letter from Lionel Johnson 'denouncing Wilde with great bitterness'; Johnson believed that Wilde got a '"sense of triumph and power, at every dinner-table he dominated, from the knowledge that he was guilty of that sin which, more than any other possible to man, would turn all those people against him if they but knew"' (1955, 285). Maybe Johnson was paranoid; that does not stop him being correct. Gide at the end of his life remarked that Wilde only began to live after dark as it were, away from most of those who knew him (1960, 27). But the point here is that Wilde also lived in terms of the discrepancy between his 'public' and 'private' selves, and took pleasure from it – from having a sexual identity elsewhere at the same time as being socially 'here'.

The anarchic and the political, the anger and the boredom, are all active in Wilde's transgressive aesthetic, and most especially when the survival strategies of subordination – subterfuge, lying, evasion – are aesthetically transvalued into weapons of attack, but ever working obliquely through irony, ambiguity, mimicry, and impersonation.

Which brings us to camp, considered by some to be the essence of the homosexual sensibility, by others, both within and without gay culture, as virtually the opposite: the quintessence of an alienated, inadequate sensibility ... The definition of camp is as elusive as the sensibility itself, one reason being simply that there are different kinds of camp. I am concerned here with that mode of camp which undermines the categories which exclude it, and does so through parody and mimicry. But not from the outside: this kind of camp undermines the depth model of identity from inside, being a kind of parody and mimicry which hollows out from within, making depth recede into its surfaces. Rather than a direct repudiation of depth, there is a performance of it to excess: depth is undermined by being taken to and beyond its own limits. The masquerade of camp becomes less a self-concealment than a kind of attack, and untruth a virtue: many a young man, says Wilde, 'starts with the natural gift of exaggeration which, if encouraged could flourish. Unfortunately he usually comes to nothing, either falling into the bad habit of accuracy, or frequents the society of the aged and well informed' (1968, 294). Compare John Mitzel: 'gay people are, I have learned, in the truest sense of the word, *fabulous* ... The controlling agents of the status quo may know the *power* of lies; dissident sub-cultures, however, are closer to knowing their value' (cit. Bronski, 1984, 41).

The hollowing-out of the deep self is pure pleasure, a release from the subjective correlatives of dominant morality (normality, authenticity, etc.) – one reason why camp also mocks the *Angst*-ridden spiritual emptiness which characterizes the existential lament. Camp thereby negotiates some of the lived contradictions of subordination, simultaneously refashioning as a weapon of attack an oppressive identity inherited *as* subordination, and hollowing out dominant formations responsible for that identity in the first instance. So it is misleading to say that camp *is* the gay sensibility; camp is an invasion and subversion of other sensibilities, and works via parody, pastiche, and exaggeration.

Jack Babuscio has suggested that the homosexual experience of passing for straight leads to a 'heightened awareness and appreciation for disguise, impersonation, the projection of personality, and the distinctions to be made between instinctive and theatrical behaviour' (1977, 45). Richard Dyer remarks, in relation to Babuscio, that the gay sensibility 'holds together qualities that are elsewhere felt as antithetical: theatricality and authenticity ... intensity and irony, a fierce assertion of extreme feeling with a deprecating sense of its absurdity' (1987, 154). I would add that camp is often also a turning of the second set of categories – theatricality, irony, and a sense of the absurdity of extreme feeling – onto the first, such that the latter – authenticity, intensity, the fierce assertion of extreme feeling – if they remain at all, do so in a transformed state. In this respect camp, as Andrew Ross observes, anticipated many of the recent debates of sexual politics: 'in fact, camp could be seen as a much earlier, highly coded way of addressing those questions about sexual difference which have engaged non-essentialist feminists in recent years' (1989, 161).

Camp integrates this aspect of gender with aesthetics; in a sense it renders gender a question of aesthetics. Common in aesthetic involvement is the recognition that what seemed like mimetic realism is actually an effect of convention, genre, form, or some other kind of artifice. For some this is a moment of disappointment in which the real, the true, and the authentic are surrendered to, or contaminated by, the factitious and the contrived. But camp comes to life around that recognition; it is situated at the point of emergence of the artificial from the real, culture from nature – or rather when and where the real collapses into artifice, nature into culture; camp restores vitality to artifice, and vice versa, deriving the artificial from, and feeding it back into or as, the real. The reality is the pleasure of unreality. And the primacy of fantasy: as the inheritor of a religious impulse, 'modern' sexual desire seeks to universalize and naturalize itself. Camp knows and takes pleasure in the fact that desire is culturally relative, and never more so than when, in cathecting contemporary style, it mistakes itself, and the style, for the natural.

Camp is not the same as gender inversion, but it often connects with it, and with good reason. Like ... cross-dressing ... gender inversion remains controversial because it allegedly only inverts, rather than displaces, the gender binary. But again, in (historical) practice to invert may also be to displace. Mario Mieli quotes an unnamed gay writer: 'we [gay men] demand our "femininity", the same thing that women reject, and *at the same time* we declare that these roles are devoid of sense' (1980, 46). An appropriate inversion becomes a deconstructive displacement.

So it is futile to try to define the homosexual sensibility according to the standards of conventional sensibility: first because the latter has sought to exclude the former; second because, in retaliation, the former has often worked to undermine the latter and, in the process, challenged the very nature of the aesthetic, fashioning in the process new and sometimes oppositional mutations of it. The search for the nature of the distinctively gay sensibility can be productively redirected as an exploration of the limitations of the aesthetic as conventionally understood, especially the way it is said to transcend the sociopolitical, and used in support of the proposition that discrimination is the essence of culture. Further, rather than seeking such a sensibility in an 'inner condition', we might more usefully identify it outwardly and in relation to other strategies of survival and subversion, especially the masquerade of femininity, and the mimicry of the colonial subject. What it might be found to share with the first is a simultaneous avoidance and acting out of the ambivalence which constitutes subordination, and a pushing of that ambivalence to the point of transgressive insight and possibly reinscribed escape.[1] As for the colonial context, Homi Bhabha argues that here mimicry is both a strategy of colonial subjection – an appropriation, regulation, and reform of the other – and, potentially, a way of menacing colonial discourse in and through an inappropriate imitation by the native, one which reveals the normative structure of colonial control. As such, mimicry becomes, in Bhabha's memorable phrase, 'at once resemblance and menace'.[2]

KNOWLEDGE AND PLEASURE IN JEAN GENET

In so many respects utterly different from Wilde, Genet nevertheless also subverts the depth model of identity via the perverse dynamic, and perhaps more so than any other writer since Wilde. Like the latter, Genet inverts and subverts the surface/depth binary, confirming and exploiting the connections between the paradoxical and the perverse, and turning them against the regimes, heterosexual and otherwise, which outlaw the deviant. Genet, also like Wilde, produces both anarchic pleasure and subversive knowledge inseparably.

Charles Marowitz once identified a crucial characteristic of Genet's work:

> In perhaps one of the most shocking hypotheses ever put forward in the drama, Genet suggests that the only thing that distinguishes the sexual pervert who masquerades as priest, king, or hero from his legitimate social counterpart, is a certain timidity. The sexual pervert lives his fantasies in private and is therefore harmless; whereas the social personages play out their roles in public. (1965, 173)

This facilitates and in part constitutes the challenge of the perverse:

> the highest ideal in *The Balcony* is for characters to attain that point of social definition at which others desire to impersonate them. Reality corresponds to the density of one's artifice. When a man achieves his highest reality he can serve as a fantasy for another man; and in a frightening Genetic turnabout, both then become equal. (173)

They become equal because fictions of selfhood are transvalued. Genet said of himself: 'Dehumanizing myself is my own most fundamental tendency' (1966, 82). The transgressive drive in his work is not a quest for the authentic self, but almost the reverse:

> The mechanism was somewhat as follows (I have used it since): to every charge brought against me, unjust though it be, from the bottom of my

heart I shall answer yes. Hardly had I uttered the word – or the phrase signifying it – than I felt within me the need to become what I had been accused of being ... I owned to being the coward, traitor, thief and fairy they saw in me. (1967, 145)

To be sure, the characteristics of the transcendent self remain in play: to become what others saw him as being required great self-discipline 'similar to spiritual exercises'; eventually he aspires to a classical stoic independence of spirit, a kind of sainthood (146). But then in *Our Lady of the Flowers* 'the gesture of solitude that makes you sufficient unto yourself' is not abstinence or retreat, but masturbation (124). Inversion and substitution are intensely narcissistic; despite that – or rather because of it, since Genet also transvalues narcissism – they extend far beyond the self. Of Divine, the anti-hero/ine drag queen of *Our Lady*, it is said:

> her carnal pleasures never made her fear the wrath of God, the scorn of Jesus, or the candied disgust of the Holy Virgin ... for as soon as she recognized the presence within her of seeds of these fears (divine wrath, scorn, disgust), Divine made of her loves a god above God, Jesus, and the Holy Virgin, to whom they were submissive like everyone else. (138)

Here, the figures who act as transcendent foils to a mundane inauthenticity, abjection, and subjection are themselves brought low, made to submit to what they once subjected. Notions of the freedom and autonomy of the self are at one and the same time inverted and used to pervert the ethical and metaphysical values which such a self is or was supposed to instantiate. Authentic selfhood is denied and then reconstituted in a perverse, parodic form – and then perhaps denied again, transformed from other to same and then back to a (different) other. Genet reinscribes himself within the violent hierarchies of his oppression, installing himself there relentlessly to invert and pervert them.

He writes in *Our Lady*: 'We are, after all, familiar enough with the tragedy of a certain feeling which is obliged to borrow its expression from the opposite feeling so as to escape from the myrmidons of the law. It disguises itself in the trappings of its rival' (113). Such incorporation facilitates a specific kind of transgressive reinscription. As in this passage, Genet not only disguises himself in terms of the law, but internalizes the disguise. What transpires is not the sacrilege which pays testimony to the sacred (i.e. containment), but a sacrilege inscribed within the sacred. Inside the church

> the [priest's] sprinkler is always moist with a tiny droplet, like Alberto's prick which is stiff in the morning and which has just pissed.
>
> The vaults and walls of the chapel of the Virgin are white-washed, and the Virgin has an apron as blue as a sailor's collar.
>
> Facing the faithful, the altar is neatly arranged; facing God, it is a jumble of wood in the dust and spider webs. (161)

In the description of the sprinkler and the apron, and especially the altar, the internalization of law (as disguise) results in this sacrilege within reverence, an intimacy with law which can blow apart its ideological effect (revealing the hidden side of the altar) – and with a strange knowing innocence strangely inseparable from that intimacy.

ORTON'S BLACK CAMP

Joe Orton, so different again from Wilde or Genet, nevertheless shares their transgressive commitment to inversion and the critique of authenticity. His *What the Butler Saw* (1969) becomes a kind of orgy of cross-dressing, gender confusion, and hierarchical inversion. It is also an angry repudiation of sexual repressiveness as enforced by the ideology of authentic, normal sexuality, now ratified by state law and the medical professions. But once again anger works through irony, parody, and pastiche, and is held together not by a unified dramatic voice but by a stylistic blankness, a kind of black camp. Here, as in his and Halliwell's notorious defacement of library books (for which they were imprisoned), and in Orton's theory of montage, there is an anticipation of that effect of pastiche which Fredric Jameson identifies as a defining criterion of the post-modern:

> Pastiche is, like parody, the imitation of a peculiar or unique style, the wearing of a stylistic mask, speech in a dead language: but it is a neutral practice of mimicry, without parody's ulterior motive, without the satirical impulse, without laughter, without that still latent feeling that there exists something *normal* compared to which what is being imitated is rather comic. Pastiche is black parody, parody that has lost its humor. (1983, 114)

The difference is that Orton's pastiche *is* comic but in a way which interrogates rather than presupposes the norm. As Jane Feuer points out, camp involves a kind of sensibility in which 'blank mimicry and a critical edge may coexist', and thereby resembles that form of postmodern parody which Linda Hutcheon defines as a 'repetition with critical distance that allows ironic signalling of difference at the very heart of similarity' (cit. Feuer, 1989, 455–6). Thereby camp may also, either implicitly or directly, interrogate the norm which, according to Jameson, traditional parody assumes. This is only one respect in which camp delights in the selfsame artifice which others distrust.

Orton's intention was to outrage. Had he been alive he would doubtless have been delighted at the response of the leading conservative theatre critic to *What the Butler Saw* (1969): 'Orton's terrible obsession with perversion, which is regarded as having brought his life to an end and choked his very high talent, poisons the atmosphere of the play. And what should have been a piece of gaily irresponsible nonsense becomes impregnated with evil.'[3] Perhaps Hobson spoke truer than he knew, for the play is a kind of gay non-sense:

[DR] RANCE. When Dr Prentice asked you to pose as a woman did he give a reason?

NICK. No.

RANCE. Didn't you consider his request strange?

NICK. No.

RANCE. Have you aided other men in their perverted follies?

NICK. During my last term at school I was the slave of a corporal in the Welsh Fusiliers.

RANCE. Were you never warned of the dangers inherent in such relationships?

NICK. When he was posted abroad he gave me a copy of 'The Way to Healthy Manhood'.

By insisting on the arbitrariness and narrowness of gender roles, and that they are socially ascribed rather than naturally given, Orton expresses a central motif in the sexual politics of that time. *What the Butler Saw* becomes an orgy of confused and *refused* gender identities:

GERALDINE [dressed as a boy]. I must be a boy. I like girls.

RANCE. I can't quite follow the reasoning there.

PRENTICE. Many men imagine their preference for women is, *ipso facto*, a proof of virility.

Cross-dressing leads to wholesale gender confusion, while Dr Rance's precisely inappropriate assumptions about madness, the natural, and 'the order of things' discredit the claims of psychiatry:

RANCE. Were you present when Dr Prentice used this youth unnaturally?

NICK. What is unnatural?

RANCE. How disturbing the questions of the mad can be. (*To* Nick [disguised as a girl]) Suppose I made an indecent suggestion to you? If you agreed something might occur which, by and large, would be regarded as natural. If, on the other hand, I approached this child – (*he* smiles at Geraldine [disguised as a boy]) – my action could result only in a gross violation of the order of things.

In the 1960s psychiatry was attacked for being a form of social policing which, with the aid of pseudo-scientific categories, mystified socially desirable behaviour as natural, and undesirable behaviour as the result of abnormal psychosexual development (a deviation from 'The Way to Healthy Manhood'). R. D. Laing wrote in *The Divided Self*:

Psychiatry can so easily be a technique of brainwashing, of inducing behaviour that is adjusted, by (preferably) non-injurious torture … I would wish to emphasize that our 'normal' 'adjusted' state is too often the abdication of ecstasy, the betrayal of *our true potentialities*, that many of us are only too successful in acquiring a false self to adapt the false realities. (12, my emphasis)

Orton goes further than Laing, for his plays transgress accepted norms at every point yet refuse to replace them with 'our true potentialities'; Laing is still preoccupied with the authentic self, the repressed human essence. Orton refuses that long-established kind of transgression which, in the very sincerity of its non-conformity, revalidates society's lapsed moral integrity. As John Milton put it centuries before: 'Men of most renowned vertu have sometimes by transgressing, most truly kept the law' (1953–82, iv. 75).

A significant contemporary manifestation of that belief, and a vivid instance of how 'modern' sexuality became a surrogate religion, somewhere for an essentially religious notion of integrity to survive in a mutated and displaced form, was at the prosecution for obscenity of D. H. Lawrence's *Lady Chatterley's Lover* (1960) (see Sinfield, 1990, 268–71). In that trial the author was defended on the grounds that he had to transgress moral respectability in order to be moral at a deeper, more authentic level dictated by personal conscience. Even the indignation of satire might assume the same moral perspective as that of the order being challenged, or at least an alternative to it. But, as his diaries indicate, Orton's indignation was too anarchic to be recuperated in such terms. In *What the Butler Saw*, sexuality, like language, becomes decentred and therefore radically contingent: it not only escapes from, but disorientates the medical and legal attempts to define and regulate it.

Not surprisingly, Orton's anarchic irresponsibility was thought by some to go too far, not just in what he actually *did*, but in the refusal in his work to confront established morality with an earnest moral alternative. What we find instead is a kind of delinquent black camp. In the article referred to at the outset, Susan Sontag remarks that camp 'is a solvent of morality. It neutralizes moral indignation, sponsors playfulness' (1966, 275, 280, 290). Orton's camp is indeed constituted by playfulness and it acts as a solvent of morality – but it does this to provoke rather than disarm moral indignation. 'No first night of the sixties was more volcanic than that of *What the Butler Saw*', says Orton's biographer, John Lahr; while Stanley Baxter, who played Dr Prentice, has recalled the 'militant hate' of the audience, some of whom 'wanted to jump on the stage and kill us' (Lahr, 1980, 333–4).

HOSTILE EROTICISM

As a style, and even more as a politics, the transgressive reinscriptions practised by such writers have proved controversial, especially when grounded in the celebration of a perverse inauthenticity disturbingly implicated in authenticity itself, as in Genet. On the positive side there are those like Kate Millett who find in Genet's deviants a subversive inversion of dominant heterosexuality, especially its masculine component (1977, 16–22, ch. 8). Thus inverted, these structures are shorn of their ideological legitimation; in effect the world of normality, beyond which Genet lives in exile, is ridiculed and contradicted in the very process of being imitated. Genet's femininity for instance 'is, as Sartre phrases it, a "hostile eroticism", delighted to ridicule and betray the very myth of virility it pretends to serve' (1977, 18, 349). All this means that, for Millett, Genet is 'the only living male writer of first class literary gifts to have transcended the sexual myths of our era' (22). Conversely, for Hans Mayer, Genet's commitment to inversion makes him deeply conservative: 'Genet's books are the exact opposite of literature of indignation and rebellion. The author has no intention of making accusations or unmasking society. He is a true believer in the bourgeois order, not a critic' (1982, 255).[4] More critical still are those like Walter Heist who conclude that Genet is pervaded with fascism (cited by Mayer (1982, 225), who dissents from the view).

Certainly there is a crucial sense in which Genet presupposes what he would challenge: 'I am steeped in an idea of property while I loot property. I recreate the absent proprietor', he says in *The Thief's Journal* (129); and in a 1975 interview: 'I would like the world, and pay attention to the way I'm saying it, I would like the world not to change so that I can be against the world' (1978, 79).

There is an ambivalence in Genet which his critics always misread and his defenders often overlook. Such ambivalence often figures within transgressive reinscription, and is one reason why it rarely approximates to a straightfor-wardly 'correct' political attitude. Consider two kinds of ambivalent transgres-sive reinscription within gay culture, camp and machismo. As styles they are very different, virtual alternatives in fact. But both have been regarded as politically reprehensible, camp because allegedly insulting to women, machis-mo because allegedly aping the masculinity oppressive of women (lesbian and straight) and gays. Defenders of camp and machismo point out that they are parodic critiques – in the first case of what is allegedly insulted (femininity), in the second of what is allegedly aped (masculinity). Certainly both gay camp and gay machismo can and do problematize femininity and masculinity as tradi-tionally understood. Thus Richard Dyer has argued of gay machismo that, by taking the traditional signs of masculinity and 'eroticising them in a blatantly homosexual context, much mischief is done to the security with which "men" are defined in society, and by which their power is secured' (1981, 61).

Throughout *Gender Trouble* Judith Butler offers – and for, rather than against, feminism – a similar defence of practices like drag, cross-dressing, and, in lesbian culture, butch/femme sexual stylization. She contests the view that these practices are 'either degrading to women, in the case of drag and cross-dressing, or an uncritical appropriation of sex-role stereotyping from within the practice of heterosexuality, especially in the case of butch/femme lesbian identities' (137). Thus she reads drag as playing with a threefold distinction: anatomical sex, gender identity, and gender performance:

> If the anatomy of the performer is already distinct from the gender of the performer, and both of those are distinct from the gender of the performance, then the performance suggests a dissonance not only between sex and performance, but sex and gender, and gender and

performance ... In imitating gender drag implicitly reveals the imitative structure of gender itself – as well as its contingency. (137)

Butler sees deviant sexualities more generally as involving this same process of denaturalizing, as parodic subversive repetitions which displace rather than consolidate heterosexual norms. The parody of deviant sex, far from presupposing and ratifying an original natural sexuality, exposes it as a fiction. Thus 'gay is to straight *not* as copy is to original, but, rather, as copy is to copy' (31). Additionally, the parody encourages a 'proliferation and subversive play of gendered meaning' (33). Most controversially of all, this argument has been extended to sado-masochistic sexuality which, far from ratifying the 'real' violence of society, theatricalizes and demystifies it.

In certain respects this argument replays for a post/modern politics Wilde's transgressive aesthetic and the gay (anti)sensibility which it helped inaugurate. It also resembles the strategy of the early modern female cross-dresser for whom sexual difference was not derived from natural and divine law, but produced by 'custom', that is, culture. Here then is a continuity between the early modern and the post/modern, one often overlooked when we concentrate on the differences in the way sexuality is conceptualized in the two periods. But crucial differences remain, and it was because the early modern transvestite was not conceptualized in terms of a pathological sexual subjectivity – the modern 'homosexual' – that her transgression was regarded, albeit with paranoia, as more social than sexual. The connections between gender and class were apparent enough in the early modern period, and if the transvestite was a pervert or invert it was precisely in the pre-sexological senses of these ideas; whether actually or only in the paranoid imagination of the dominant, she was regarded as upsetting the entire social domain, even when her sexual 'orientation' was not the issue.

So when it is argued today that the sexual deviant challenges sexual difference by denaturalizing it through parody, the realization of the early modern transvestite that both the deviant and the difference are effects of culture rather than nature is being revived and sophisticated. But a residual effect of the 'privatizing' of sexuality, and in particular of the construction of sexual deviance as an identity, a pathology of being, rather than a kind of behaviour in principle open to all, is that the challenge to this construction often itself remains imprisoned by the public/private dichotomy. So while the whole point of the argument, and rightly, is that when gender is understood as culture rather than nature we see that gender is implicated in all aspects of culture, in practice the argument rarely gets off the bed. As we shall see shortly, the way out of the bedroom is via the wider cultures, rather than the specific sexual acts, of transgressive reinscription – for example, the writings of Wilde, Genet, and others, the subculture from which they emerge and help to form and transform.

First there is another objection to be considered: do deviant identities and sexualities really denaturalize through theatrical parody as straight-forwardly as is sometimes suggested? Leo Bersani thinks not, at least where camp and gay machismo are concerned. He concedes a potentially subversive dimension to camp, but one inseparable from a more problematic and ambivalent relation to both femininity and women:

> the gay male parody of a certain femininity, which, as others have argued, may itself be an elaborate social construct, is both a way of giving vent to the hostility toward women that probably afflicts every male (and which male heterosexuals have of course expressed in infinitely nastier and more effective ways) *and* could paradoxically be thought of as helping to deconstruct that image for women themselves ... The gay male bitch desublimates and desexualizes a type of femininity glamorized by movie stars, whom he thus lovingly assassinates with his style.

Of the subversive claims for gay machismo, Bersani is even more sceptical, since he regards it as involving not a parodic repudiation of straight machismo, but a profound respect for it. But, crucially, and this reminds us of Genet, Bersani locates a challenge inseparable from a certain ambivalence: if gay males threaten male heterosexual identity, it is not because they offer a detached parody of that identity, but rather because 'from within their nearly mad identification with it, *they never cease to feel the appeal of its being violated*' (1987, 208–9, his emphasis). Bersani arrives at this position because he sees gay male sexuality as enacting insights into sexuality *per se* which heterosexual culture has to repress ruthlessly ...

The cultural dynamics of transgressive reinscription suggest how both positions are correct: identification with, and desire *for*, may coexist with parodic subversion *of*, since a culture is not reducible to the specific desires of the individuals comprising it – desires which anyway differ considerably – and even less to the 'truth' of desire itself. Gay culture is in part constituted by a self-reflexive, ironic representation of desire itself, gay and straight, and of the objects of desire, again both gay and straight. This is especially so of its involvement with masculinity. In one and the same gay milieu one is likely to encounter identification with, desire for, and parodies of masculinity. Among numerous other things, gay *subcultures* (as opposed to the illusory 'truth' of a unitary homosexual *desire*) include all three, and sometimes indistinguishably. And if those subcultures discredit any notion of an essential or unitary gay desire, they also constitute a crucial enabling condition of transgressive re-inscription. More than that, they help constitute it. This is why transgressive reinscription should not be understood in terms of discrete transgressive acts which 'succeed' or 'fail' in some immediate sense. Reinscription is an opposi-tional practice which is also a perspective and language (sensibility?) con-stantly interpreting and re-presenting all sections of a culture including its dominant and subordinate fractions, its conventional (e.g. heterosexual) as well as deviant (e.g. homosexual) identities. Butler remarks the importance of *repetition* in the process of resistance and transformation: 'The task is ... to repeat and, through a radical proliferation of gender, to *displace* the very gender norms that enable the repetition itself' (1990, 148). Certainly, but that displacement can only occur if it is also a struggle in and for representation – specifically, the representation of the repetition *as* re-presentation/inversion/ displacement of the norm. In short, the displacing repetition still has to be culturally construed as such. In the process the transgression and the norm are both re-presented. And this, far from being a containment (transgression presupposing and thereby ratifying the norm it contravenes), is one condition of the norm's undoing.

Transgressive reinscription will always remain controversial, if only because it raises such disturbing questions about desire itself, making it profoundly social and thereby asking equally disturbing questions about culture, representation, and social process. This is even more so when, as I have argued with homosexuality, so many dimensions of a culture have been displaced and/or condensed into the identity of the transgressor. But then there is no transgression from the position of the subordinate that is not controversial; it is a virtually inevitable consequence of the disempowered mounting a challenge at all.

THINKING TRANSGRESSIVE REINSCRIPTION

Consider two similarities, the first between two post-structuralists whose work is in most other respects incompatible, the second between post-structuralism and the post/modern. This is Foucault:

> Rules are empty in themselves, violent and unfinalized; they are impersonal and can be bent to any purpose. The successes of history belong to those who are capable of seizing these rules, to replace those who had used them, *to disguise themselves so as to pervert them, invert their meaning, and redirect them against those who had initially imposed them . . . so as to overcome the rulers through their own rules.* (1977, 151, my emphasis)

Elsewhere he writes:

> There are no relations of power without resistances; the latter are all the more real and effective because they are formed right at the point where relations of power are exercised; resistance to power does not have to come from elsewhere to be real, nor is it inexorably frustrated through being the compatriot of power. It exists all the more by being in the same place as power. (1980, 142)

Now compare Foucault with Derrida:

> Our discourse irreducibly belongs to the system of metaphysical oppositions. The break with this structure of belonging can be announced only through a *certain* organisation, a certain *strategic* arrangement which, within the field of metaphysical opposition, uses the strengths of the field

to turn its own stratagems against it, producing a force of dislocation that spreads itself throughout the entire system, fissuring it in every direction and thoroughly *delimiting* it. (1978, 20)

And then both Foucault and Derrida with Baudrillard:

a system is abolished only by pushing it into hyperlogic, by forcing it into an excessive practice which is equivalent to a brutal amortization ...

A parody and a paradox: it is by their very inertia in the ways of the social laid out for them that the masses go beyond its logic and its limits, and destroy its whole edifice. A destructive hypersimulation, a destructive hyperconformity ... that has all the appearance of a victorious challenge – no one can measure the strength of this challenge ...

There lies the genuine stake today, in this underhand, inescapable confrontation between the silent majority and the social imposed on them, in this hypersimulation reduplicating simulation and exterminating it according to its *own logic – not in any class struggle nor in the molecular hodge-podge of desire-breaching minorities*. This revolution ... proceeds by inertia, and not from a new and joyous negativity. (1983, 46–7, 47–8, 49)

Transgressive reinscription: a *turning back* upon something and a perverting of it typically if not exclusively through inversion and displacement. The idea seems strange: is not transgression a liberation from, a moving beyond; a breaking out, perhaps even a progression? As we saw in relation to Gide, even in a secularized philosophy of transgression, metaphors of transcendence abound. In comparison, the idea of turning back upon, or into, seems regressive – literally reactionary. But transgressive reinscription appropriates reaction for resistance, thereby substituting agency for autonomy.

The early modern transvestite and the post/modern gay (anti)sensibility suggest some of the ways in which transgressive reinscriptions have been around for much longer than post-modernism has been fashionable. There are of course others: such reinscription has worked via minimalist perversion – for instance, the complete defacement via minimum change as in the street graffito which blackens one tooth of the billboard toothpaste ad, or the MLA panel paper: 'A thing of beauty is a boy forever' – a difference of barely more (or less) than a single inverted letter. Then there have been the more elaborate perversions which parody the sophistication of high art – Joe Orton's and Kenneth Halliwell's defacing of library books, Duchamp's moustache on *Mona Lisa*.

A principal medium of transgressive reinscription is fantasy – but again, not the fantasy of transcendence so much as the inherently perverse, transgressive reordering of fantasy's conventional opposite, the mundane. Rosemary Jackson is surely right to remind us that 'fantasy is not ... transcendental. It has to do with inverting elements of this world, re-combining its constitutive features.' Fantastic literature 'does not introduce novelty, so much as uncover all that needs to remain hidden if the world is to be comfortably "known" ... As the term "paraxis" has already suggested, fantasy lies alongside the axis of the real ... This area, according to Freud, is one of concealed desire' (1981, 8, 65; see also 78). Jackson quotes Freud's view that something has to be added to what is novel and unfamiliar to make it uncanny; this something is 'nothing new or alien, but something which is familiar and old – established in the mind and become alienated from it through the process of repression' (66).

Fantasy may itself be a kind of transgressive reinscription, one presupposing a radical impurity in all identity, not excluding the transgressor's. It knows too the impurity of transgressive desire, and most of all perhaps the impurity of dominant forms of identity, be they white, heterosexual, whatever. The very impurity which the radical humanist seeks to transcend, only despairingly to rediscover at the very centre of his or her being – this impurity, for the fantasies of transgressive reinscription, is not the ground of its failure but the material upon which it works. This is partly the inevitable consequence of gender being socially constructed. As many have observed, the recognition that gender is so constructed implies that it can be altered. What is less often conceded or, if conceded, considered – Bersani being a significant exception – is that if gender is socially constituted *so too is desire*. Desire is informed by the same oppressive constructions of gender that we would willingly dispense with. Desire is of its 'nature' saturated by the social. It is just this which allows subversive potential to parodic repetition but which also means that the parody will typically be inflected with the ambivalence I have described and, partly because of that ambivalence, oscillate between the political and the anarchic.

To liberate desire from oppression is not – could never be – a matter of resuming or regaining a desire/subjectivity as it existed prior to discrimination. If oppression is imagined as a distortion of the self, then the lifting of oppression might be imagined to result in the self resuming its natural undistorted form. But, even assuming, first, that the oppression has indeed been lifted, second, that we can speak of, and know, a time when that desire was ever free, and third, that we can speak meaningfully of a 'natural' or a 'liberated' desire (and my argument questions all three assumptions), even assuming all this, *liberated desire would still always be different from its pre-oppression counterpart*. It will bear the history of that oppression, not necessarily as that which disables desire (though it may), but as desire itself. All desire bears its histories, the desires of the exploited and the repressed no less than the desires of those who exploit and repress. But differently in each case ... The proposition that the history of sexual oppression will always inhere in the sexual desire of the oppressed, most powerfully in the form of self-oppression, confesses to tragedy. There is truth in that, also in the proposition that in Western culture the 'tragic vision' has been one of the most powerful means of containing and sublimating desire. But never completely: in turning back upon his or her own desire the deviant knows how to read the history within it. Included there is a history of heterosexuality hardly known to itself.

NOTES

1. On masquerade and femininity, see Rivière (1986); Irigaray (1985; Irigaray also explores femininity in relation to mimicry); Heath (1986), Modleski (1986); Ross (1989, ch. 5, esp. 161); Butler (1989, esp. 46–54; includes a thoughtful discussion of the links between the masquerading woman and the homosexual man).
2. See also 'Sly Civility' (1994, 93–101). [The reader is referred to 'Of Mimicry and Man', reproduced in this volume in the section on postcolonial criticism, and the discussion of that essay by Gail Ching-Liang Low. JW]
3. Harold Hobson (19 March 1969) ... alluding to the fact that Orton was beaten to death by his lover.
4. For a more perceptive and helpful introduction to Genet, see Adams (1980, 182–205).

11.3

CRITICALLY QUEER

Judith Butler

Discourse is not life; its time is not yours.
—Michel Foucault, *Politics and the Study of Discourse*

... The temporality of the term ['queer'] is precisely what concerns me here: how is it that a term that signaled degradation has been turned – 'refunctioned' in the Brechtian sense – to signify a new and affirmative set of meanings? Is this a simple reversal of valuations such that 'queer' means either a past degradation or a present or future affirmation? Is this a reversal that retains and reiterates the abjected history of the term? When the term has been used as a paralyzing slur, as the mundane interpellation of pathologized sexuality, it has produced the user of the term as the emblem and vehicle of normalization; the occasion of its utterance, as the discursive regulation of the boundaries of sexual legitimacy. Much of the straight world has always needed the queers it has sought to repudiate through the performative force of the term. If the term is now subject to a reappropriation, what are the conditions and limits of that significant reversal? Does the reversal reiterate the logic of repudiation by which it was spawned? Can the term overcome its constitutive history of injury? Does it present the discursive occasion for a powerful and compelling fantasy of historical reparation? When and how does a term like 'queer' become subject to an affirmative resignification for some when a term like 'nigger', despite some recent efforts at reclamation, appears capable of only reinscribing its pain? How and where does discourse reiterate injury such that

Extract from Judith Butler, *Bodies that Matter: On the Discursive Limits of 'Sex'* (Routledge, 1993), pp. 223–42.

the various efforts to recontextualize and resignify a given term meet their limit in this other, more brutal, and relentless form of repetition?

In *On the Genealogy of Morals*, Nietzsche introduces the notion of the 'sign-chain' in which one might read a utopian investment in discourse, one that reemerges within Foucault's conception of discursive power. Nietzsche writes, 'the entire history of a "thing," an organ, a custom can be a continuous sign-chain of ever new interpretations and adaptations whose causes do not even have to be related to one another but, on the contrary, in some cases succeed and alternate with one another in a purely chance fashion' (1989, 77). The 'ever new' possibilities of resignification are derived from the postulated historical discontinuity of the term. But is this postulation itself suspect? Can resignifiability be derived from a pure historicity of 'signs'? Or must there be a way to think about the constraints on and in resignification that takes account of its propensity to return to the 'ever old' in relations of social power? And can Foucault help us here or does he, rather, reiterate Nietzchean hopefulness within the discourse of power? Investing power with a kind of vitalism, Foucault echoes Nietzsche as he refers to power as 'ceaseless struggles and confrontations ... produced from one moment to the next, at every point, or rather in every relation from one point to another' (1980, 92–3).

Neither power nor discourse are rendered anew at every moment; they are not as weightless as the utopics of radical resignification might imply. And yet how are we to understand their convergent force as an accumulated effect of usage that both constrains and enables their reworking? How is it that the apparently injurious effects of discourse become the painful resources by which a resignifying practice is wrought? Here it is not only a question of how discourse injures bodies, but how certain injuries establish certain bodies at the limits of available ontologies, available schemes of intelligibility. And further, how is it that the abjected come to make their claim through and against the discourses that have sought their repudiation?

PERFORMATIVE POWER

Eve Sedgwick's recent reflections on queer performativity ask us not only to consider how a certain theory of speech acts applies to queer practices, but how it is that 'queering' persists as a defining moment of performativity.[1] The centrality of the marriage ceremony in J. L. Austin's examples of performativity suggests that the heterosexualization of the social bond is the paradigmatic form for those speech acts which bring about what they name. 'I pronounce you ...' puts into effect the relation that it names. But from where and when does such a performative draw its force, and what happens to the performative when its purpose is precisely to undo the presumptive force of the heterosexual ceremonial?

Performative acts are forms of authoritative speech: most performatives, for instance, are statements that, in the uttering, also perform a certain action and exercise a binding power.[2] Implicated in a network of authorization and punishment, performatives tend to include legal sentences, baptisms, inaugurations, declarations of ownership, statements which not only perform an action, but confer a binding power on the action performed. If the power of discourse to produce that which it names is linked with the question of performativity, then the performative is one domain in which power acts *as* discourse.

Importantly, however, there is no power, construed as a subject, that acts, but only, to repeat an earlier phrase, a reiterated acting that *is* power in its persistence and instability. This is less an 'act', singular and deliberate, than a nexus of power and discourse that repeats or mimes the discursive gestures of power. Hence, the judge who authorizes and installs the situation he names invariably *cites* the law that he applies, and it is the power of this citation that gives the performative its binding or conferring power. And though it may appear that the binding power of his words is derived from the force of his will or from a prior authority, the opposite is more true: it is *through* the citation of the law that the figure of the judge's 'will' is produced and that the 'priority' of textual authority is established.[3] Indeed, it is through the invocation of convention that the speech act of the judge derives its binding power; that binding power is to be found neither in the subject of the judge nor in his will, but in the citational legacy by which a contemporary 'act' emerges in the context of a chain of binding conventions.

Where there is an 'I' who utters or speaks and thereby produces an effect in discourse, there is first a discourse which precedes and enables that 'I' and forms in language the constraining trajectory of its will. Thus there is no 'I' who stands *behind* discourse and executes its volition or will *through* discourse. On the contrary, the 'I' only comes into being through being called, named, interpellated, to use the Althusserian term, and this discursive constitution takes place prior to the 'I'; it is the transitive invocation of the 'I'. Indeed, I can only say 'I' to the extent that I have first been addressed, and that address has mobilized my place in speech; paradoxically, the discursive condition of social recognition *precedes and conditions* the formation of the subject: recognition is not conferred on a subject, but forms that subject. Further, the impossibility of a full recognition, that is, of ever fully inhabiting the name by which one's social identity is inaugurated and mobilized, implies the instability and incompleteness of subject-formation. The 'I' is thus a citation of the place of the 'I' in speech, where that place has a certain priority and anonymity with respect to the life it animates: it is the historically revisable possibility of a name that precedes and exceeds me, but without which I cannot speak.

QUEER TROUBLE

The term 'queer' emerges as an interpellation that raises the question of the status of force and opposition, of stability and variability, *within* performativity. The term 'queer' has operated as one linguistic practice whose purpose has been the shaming of the subject it names or, rather, the producing of a subject *through* that shaming interpellation. 'Queer' derives its force precisely through the repeated invocation by which it has become linked to accusation, pathologization, insult. This is an invocation by which a social bond among homophobic communities is formed through time. The interpellation echoes past interpellations, and binds the speakers, as if they spoke in unison across time. In this sense, it is always an imaginary chorus that taunts 'queer!' To what extent, then, has the performative 'queer' operated alongside, as a deformation of, the 'I pronounce you ...' of the marriage ceremony? If the performative operates as the sanction that performs the heterosexualization of the social bond, perhaps it also comes into play precisely as the shaming taboo which 'queers' those who resist or oppose that social form as well as those who occupy it without hegemonic social sanction.

On that note, let us remember that reiterations are never simply replicas of the same. And the 'act' by which a name authorizes or deauthorizes a set of social or sexual relations is, of necessity, *a repetition*. 'Could a performative succeed', asks Derrida, 'if its formulation did not repeat a "coded" or iterable utterance ... if it were not identifiable in some way as a "citation"?' (1992, 18). If a performative provisionally succeeds (and I will suggest that 'success' is always and only provisional), then it is not because an intention successfully governs the action of speech, but only because that action echoes prior actions, and *accumulates the force of authority through the repetition or citation of a prior, authoritative set of practices*. What this means, then, is that a performative 'works' to the extent that it *draws on and covers over* the constitutive conventions by which it is mobilized. In this sense, no term or statement can function performatively without the accumulating and dissimulating historicity of force.

This view of performativity implies that discourse has a history[4] that not only precedes but conditions its contemporary usages, and that this history effectively decenters the presentist view of the subject as the exclusive origin or owner of what is said.[5] What it also means is that the terms to which we do, nevertheless, lay claim, the terms through which we insist on politicizing identity and desire, often demand a turn *against* this constitutive historicity. Those of us who have questioned the presentist assumptions in contemporary identity categories are, therefore, sometimes charged with depoliticizing theory. And yet, if the genealogical critique of the subject is the interrogation of those constitutive and exclusionary relations of power through which contemporary discursive resources are formed, then it follows that the critique of the queer subject is crucial to the continuing *democratization* of queer politics. As much as identity terms must be used, as much as 'outness' is to be affirmed, these same notions must become subject to a critique of the exclusionary operations of their own production: For whom is outness a historically available and affordable option? Is there an unmarked class character to the demand for universal 'outness'? Who is represented by *which* use of the term, and who is excluded? For whom does the term present an impossible conflict between racial, ethnic, or religious affiliation and sexual politics? What kinds of policies are enabled by what kinds of usages, and which are backgrounded or erased from view? In this sense, the genealogical critique of the queer subject will be central to queer politics to the extent that it constitutes a self-critical dimension within activism, a persistent reminder to take the time to consider the exclusionary force of one of activism's most treasured contemporary premises.

As much as it is necessary to assert political demands through recourse to identity categories, and to lay claim to the power to name oneself and determine the conditions under which that name is used, it is also impossible to sustain that kind of mastery over the trajectory of those categories within discourse. This is not an argument *against* using identity categories, but it is a reminder of the risk that attends every such use. The expectation of self-determination that self-naming arouses is paradoxically contested by the historicity of the name itself: by the history of the usages that one never controlled, but that constrain the very usage that now emblematizes autonomy; by the future efforts to deploy the term against the grain of the current ones, and that will exceed the control of those who seek to set the course of the terms in the present.

If the term 'queer' is to be a site of collective contestation, the point of depar-ture for a set of historical reflections and futural imaginings, it will have to remain that which is, in the present, never fully owned, but always and only redeployed, twisted, queered from a prior usage and in the direction of urgent and expanding political purposes. This also means that it will doubtless have to be yielded in favor of terms that do that political work more effectively. Such a yielding may well become necessary in order to accommodate – without domesticating – democratizing contestations that have and will redraw the contours of the movement in ways that can never be fully anticipated in advance.

It may be that the conceit of autonomy implied by self-naming is the para-digmatically presentist conceit, that is, the belief that there is a one who arrives in the world, in discourse, without a history, that this one makes oneself in and through the magic of the name, that language expresses a 'will' or a 'choice' rather than a complex and constitutive history of discourse and power which compose the invariably ambivalent resources through which a queer and queering agency is forged and reworked. To recast queer agency in this chain of historicity is thus to avow a set of constraints on the past and the future that mark at once the *limits* of agency and its most *enabling conditions*. As expansive as the term 'queer' is meant to be, it is used in ways that enforce a set of overlapping divisions: in some contexts, the term appeals to a younger genera-tion who want to resist the more institutionalized and reformist politics some-times signified by 'lesbian and gay'; in some contexts, sometimes the same, it has marked a predominantly white movement that has not fully addressed the way in which 'queer' plays – or fails to play – within non-white communities; and whereas in some instances it has mobilized a lesbian activism, in others the term represents a false unity of women and men. Indeed, it may be that the critique of the term will initiate a resurgence of both feminist and anti-racist mobilization within lesbian and gay politics or open up new possibilities for coalitional alliances that do not presume that these constituencies are radically distinct from one another. The term will be revised, dispelled, rendered obsolete to the extent that it yields to the demands which resist the term precisely because of the exclusions by which it is mobilized.

We no more create from nothing the political terms that come to represent our 'freedom' than we are responsible for the terms that carry the pain of social injury. And yet, neither of those terms are as a result any less necessary to work and rework within political discourse.

In this sense, it remains politically necessary to lay claim to 'women', 'queer', 'gay', and 'lesbian', precisely because of the way these terms, as it were, lay their claim on us prior to our full knowing. Laying claim to such terms in reverse will be necessary to refute homophobic deployments of the terms in law, public policy, on the street, in 'private' life. But the necessity to mobilize the necessary error of identity (Spivak's term) will always be in tension with the democratic contestation of the term which works against its deployments in racist and misogynist discursive regimes. If 'queer' politics postures independently of these other modalities of power, it will lose its democratizing force. The political deconstruction of 'queer' ought not to paralyze the use of such terms, but, ideally, to extend its range, to make us consider at what expense and for what purposes the terms are used, and through what relations of power such categories have been wrought ... Such an inquiry does not suspend or ban the term, although it does insist that an inquiry into formation is linked to the contemporary question of what is at stake in the term. The point may be taken for queer studies as well, such that 'queering' might signal an inquiry into (a) the *formation* of homosexualities (a historical inquiry which cannot take the stability of the term for granted, despite the political pressure to do so) and (b) the *deformative* and *misappropriative* power that the term currently enjoys. At stake in such a history will be the differential formation of homosexuality across racial boundaries, including the question of how racial and reproductive relations become articulated through one another.

One might be tempted to say that identity categories are insufficient because every subject position is the site of converging relations of power that are not univocal. But such a formulation underestimates the radical challenge to the subject that such converging relations imply. For there is no self-identical subject who houses or bears these relations, no site at which such relations converge. This converging and interarticulation *is* the contemporary fate of the subject. In other words, the subject as a self-identical entity is no more.

It is in this sense that the temporary totalization performed by identity categories is a necessary error. And if identity is a necessary error, then the assertion of 'queer' will be necessary as a term of affiliation, but it will not fully describe those it purports to represent. As a result, it will be necessary to affirm the contingency of the term: to let it be vanquished by those who are excluded by the term but who justifiably expect representation by it, to let it take on meanings that cannot now be anticipated by a younger generation whose political vocabulary may well carry a very different set of investments. Indeed, the term 'queer' itself has been precisely the discursive rallying point for younger lesbians and gay men and, in yet other contexts, for lesbian interventions and, in yet other contexts, for bisexuals and straights for whom the term expresses an affiliation with anti-homophobic politics. That it can become such a discursive site whose uses are not fully constrained in advance ought to be safeguarded not only for the purposes of continuing to democratize queer politics, but also to expose, affirm, and rework the specific historicity of the term.

GENDER PERFORMATIVITY AND DRAG

How, if at all, is the notion of discursive resignification linked to the notion of gender parody or impersonation? First, what is meant by understanding gender as an impersonation? Does this mean that one puts on a mask or persona, that there is a 'one' who precedes that 'putting on', who is something other than its gender from the start? Or does this miming, this impersonating precede and form the 'one', operating as its formative precondition rather than its dispensable artifice?

The construal of gender-as-drag according to the first model appears to be the effect of a number of circumstances. One of them I brought on myself by citing drag as an example of performativity, a move that was taken then, by some, to be *exemplary* of performativity. If drag is performative, that does not mean that all performativity is to be understood as drag. The publication of *Gender Trouble* coincided with a number of publications that did assert that 'clothes make the woman', but I never did think that gender was like clothes, or that clothes make the woman ...

The practice by which gendering occurs, the embodying of norms, is a compulsory practice, a forcible production, but not for that reason fully determining. To the extent that gender is an assignment, it is an assignment which is never quite carried out according to expectation, whose addressee never quite inhabits the ideal s/he is compelled to approximate. Moreover, this embodying is a repeated process. And one might construe repetition as precisely that which *undermines* the conceit of voluntarist mastery designated by the subject in language.

As *Paris Is Burning* made clear, drag is not unproblematically subversive. It serves a subversive function to the extent that it reflects the mundane impersonations by which heterosexually ideal genders are performed and naturalized and undermines their power by virtue of effecting that exposure. But there is no guarantee that exposing the naturalized status of heterosexuality will lead to its subversion. Heterosexuality can augment its hegemony *through* its denaturalization, as when we see denaturalizing parodies that reidealize heterosexual norms *without* calling them into question.

On other occasions, though, the transferability of a gender ideal or gender norm calls into question the abjecting power that it sustains. For an occupation or reterritorialization of a term that has been used to abject a population can become the site of resistance, the possibility of an enabling social and political resignification. And this has happened to a certain extent with the notion of 'queer'. The contemporary redeployment enacts a prohibition and a degradation against itself, spawning a different order of values, a political affirmation from and through the very term which in a prior usage had as it final aim the eradication of precisely such an affirmation.

It may seem, however, that there is a difference between the embodying or performing of gender norms and the performative use of discourse. Are these two different senses of 'performativity', or do they converge as modes of citationality in which the compulsory character of certain social imperatives becomes subject to a more promising deregulation? Gender norms operate by requiring the embodiment of certain ideals of femininity and masculinity, ones that are almost always related to the idealization of the heterosexual bond. In this sense, the initiatory performative, 'It's a girl!' anticipates the eventual arrival of the sanction, 'I pronounce you man and wife.' Hence, also, the peculiar pleasure of the cartoon strip in which the infant is first interpellated into discourse with 'It's a lesbian!' Far from an essentialist joke, the queer appropriation of the performative mimes and exposes both the binding power of the heterosexualizing law *and its expropriability*.

To the extent that the naming of the 'girl' is transitive, that is, initiates the process by which a certain 'girling' is compelled, the term or, rather, its symbolic power, governs the formation of a corporeally enacted femininity that never fully approximates the norm. This is a 'girl', however, who is compelled to 'cite' the norm in order to qualify and remain a viable subject. Femininity is thus not the product of a choice, but the forcible citation of a norm, one whose complex historicity is indissociable from relations of discipline, regulation, punishment. Indeed, there is no 'one' who takes on a gender norm. On the contrary, this citation of the gender norm is necessary in order to qualify as a 'one', to become viable as a 'one', where subject-formation is dependent on the prior operation of legitimating gender norms.

It is in terms of a norm that compels a certain 'citation' in order for a viable subject to be produced that the notion of gender performativity calls to be rethought. And precisely in relation to such a compulsory citationality that the theatricality of gender is also to be explained. Theatricality need not be conflated with self-display or self-creation. Within queer politics, indeed, within the very signification that is 'queer', we read a resignifying practice in which the desanctioning power of the name 'queer' is reversed to sanction a contestation of the terms of sexual legitimacy. Paradoxically, but also with great promise, the subject who is 'queered' into public discourse through homophobic interpellations of various kinds *takes up* or *cites* that very term as the discursive basis for an opposition. This kind of citation will emerge as *theatrical* to the extent that it *mimes and renders hyperbolic* the discursive convention that it also *reverses*. The hyperbolic gesture is crucial to the exposure of the homophobic 'law' that can no longer control the terms of its own abjecting strategies.

To oppose the theatrical to the political within contemporary queer politics is, I would argue, an impossibility: the hyperbolic 'performance' of death in the practice of 'die-ins' and the theatrical 'outness' by which queer activism has disrupted the closeting distinction between public and private space have proliferated sites of politicization and AIDS awareness throughout the public realm. Indeed, an important set of histories might be told in which the increasing politicization *of* theatricality for queers is at stake (more productive, I think, than an insistence on the two as polar opposites within queerness). Such a history might include traditions of cross-dressing, drag balls, street walking, butch-femme spectacles, the sliding between the 'march' (New York City) and the parade (San Francisco); die-ins by ACT UP, kiss-ins by Queer Nation; drag performance benefits for AIDS . . . ; the convergence of theatrical work with theatrical activism; performing excessive lesbian sexuality and iconography that effectively counters the desexualization of the lesbian; tactical interruptions of public forums by lesbian and gay activists in favor of drawing public attention and outrage to the failure of government funding of AIDS research and outreach.

The increasing theatricalization of political rage in response to the killing inattention of public policy-makers on the issue of AIDS is allegorized in the recontextualization of 'queer' from its place within a homophobic strategy of abjection and annihilation to an insistent and public severing of that interpellation from the effect of shame. To the extent that shame is produced as the stigma not only of AIDS, but also of queerness, where the latter is understood through homophobic causalities as the 'cause' and 'manifestation' of the illness, theatrical rage is part of the public resistance to that interpellation of shame. Mobilized by the injuries of homophobia, theatrical rage reiterates those injuries precisely through an 'acting out', one that does not merely repeat or recite those injuries, but that also deploys a hyperbolic display of death and injury to overwhelm the epistemic resistance to AIDS and to the graphics of suffering, or a hyperbolic display of kissing to shatter the epistemic blindness to an increasingly graphic and public homosexuality.

MELANCHOLIA AND THE LIMITS OF PERFORMANCE

The critical potential of 'drag' centrally concerns a critique of a prevailing truth-regime of 'sex', one that I take to be pervasively heterosexist: the distinction between the 'inside' truth of femininity, considered as psychic disposition or ego-core, and the 'outside' truth, considered as appearance or presentation, produces a contradictory formation of gender in which no fixed 'truth' can be established. Gender is neither a purely psychic truth, conceived as 'internal' and 'hidden', nor is it reducible to a surface appearance; on the contrary, its undecidability is to be traced as the play *between* psyche and appearance (where the latter domain includes what appears *in words*). Further, this will be a 'play' regulated by heterosexist constraints though not, for that reason, fully reducible to them.

In no sense can it be concluded that the part of gender that is performed is therefore the 'truth' of gender; performance as bounded 'act' is distinguished from performativity insofar as the latter consists in a reiteration of norms which precede, constrain, and exceed the performer and in that sense cannot be taken as the fabrication of the performer's 'will' or 'choice'; further, what is 'performed' works to conceal, if not to disavow, what remains opaque, unconscious, unperformable. The reduction of performativity to performance would be a mistake.

The rejection of an expressive model of drag which holds that some interior truth is exteriorized in performance needs, however, to be referred to a psychoanalytic consideration on the relationship between how gender *appears* and what gender *signifies*. Psychoanalysis insists that the opacity of the unconscious sets limits to the exteriorization of the psyche. It also argues, rightly I think, that what is exteriorized or performed can only be understood through reference to what is barred from the signifier and from the domain of corporeal legibility.

How precisely do repudiated identifications, identifications that do not 'show', circumscribe and materialize the identifications that do? Here it seems useful to rethink the notion of gender-as-drag in terms of the analysis of gender melancholia (Butler, 1989, 57–65). Given the iconographic figure of the melancholic drag queen, one might consider whether and how these terms work together. Here, one might ask also after the disavowal that occasions performance and that performance might be said to enact, where performance engages 'acting out' in the psychoanalytic sense.[6] If melancholia in Freud's sense is the effect of an ungrieved loss (a sustaining of the lost object/Other as a psychic figure with the consequence of heightened identification with that Other, self-beratement, and the acting out of unresolved anger and love),[7] it may be that performance, understood as 'acting out', is significantly related to the problem of unacknowledged loss. Where there is an ungrieved loss in drag performance (and I am sure that such a generalization cannot be universalized), perhaps it is a loss that is refused and incorporated in the performed identification, one that reiterates a gendered idealization and its radical uninhabitability. This is neither a territorialization of the feminine by the masculine nor an 'envy' of the masculine by the feminine, nor a sign of the essential plasticity of gender. What it does suggest is that gender performance allegorizes a loss it cannot grieve, allegorizes the incorporative fantasy of melancholia whereby an object is phantasmatically taken in or on as a way of refusing to let it go.

The analysis above is a risky one because it suggests that for a 'man' performing femininity or for a 'woman' performing masculinity (the latter is always, in effect, to perform a little less, given that femininity is often cast as the spectacular gender) there is an attachment to and a loss and refusal of the figure of femininity by the man, or the figure of masculinity by the woman. Thus, it is important to underscore that drag is an effort to negotiate cross-gendered identification, but that cross-gendered identification is not the exemplary paradigm for thinking about homosexuality, although it may be one. In this sense, drag allegorizes some set of melancholic incorporative fantasies that stabilize *gender*. Not only are a vast number of drag performers straight, but it would be a mistake to think that homosexuality is best explained through the performativity that is drag. What does seem useful in this analysis, however, is that drag exposes or allegorizes the mundane psychic and performative practices by which heterosexualized genders form themselves through the renunciation of the *possibility* of homosexuality, a foreclosure that produces a field of heterosexual objects at the same time that it produces a domain of those whom it would be impossible to love. Drag thus allegorizes *heterosexual melancholy*, the melancholy by which a masculine gender is formed from the refusal to grieve the masculine as a possibility of love; a feminine gender is formed (taken on, assumed) through the incorporative fantasy by which the feminine is excluded as a possible object of love, an exclusion never grieved, but 'preserved' through the heightening of feminine identification itself. In this sense, the 'truest' lesbian melancholic is the strictly straight woman, and the 'truest' gay male melancholic is the strictly straight man.

What drag exposes, however, is the 'normal' constitution of gender presentation in which the gender performed is in many ways constituted by a set of disavowed attachments or identifications that constitute a different domain of the 'unperformable'. Indeed, it may well be that what constitutes the *sexually* unperformable is performed instead as *gender identification*. To the extent that homosexual attachments remain unacknowledged within normative heterosexuality, they are not merely constituted as desires that emerge and subsequently become prohibited. Rather, these are desires that are proscribed from the start. And when they do emerge on the far side of the censor, they may well carry that mark of impossibility with them, performing, as it were, as the impossible within the possible. As such, they will not be attachments that can be openly grieved. This is, then, less *the refusal* to grieve (a formulation that accents the choice involved) than a preemption of grief performed by the absence of cultural conventions for avowing the loss of homosexual love. And it is this absence that produces a culture of heterosexual melancholy, one that can be read in the hyperbolic identifications by which mundane heterosexual masculinity and femininity confirm themselves. The straight man *becomes* (mimes, cites, appropriates, assumes the status of) the man he 'never' loved and 'never' grieved; the straight woman *becomes* the woman she 'never' loved and 'never' grieved. It is in this sense, then, that what is most apparently performed as gender is the sign and symptom of a pervasive disavowal.

Moreover, it is precisely to counter this pervasive cultural risk of gay melancholia (what the newspapers generalize as 'depression') that there has been an insistent publicization and politicization of grief over those who have died from AIDS; the NAMES Project Quilt is exemplary, ritualizing and repeating the name itself as a way of publically avowing the limitless loss (see Crimp, 1989, 97–107).

Insofar as grief remains unspeakable, the rage over the loss can redouble by virtue of remaining unavowed. And if that very rage over loss is publically proscribed, the melancholic effects of such a proscription can achieve suicidal proportions. The emergence of collective institutions for grieving are thus crucial to survival, to the reassembling of community, the reworking of kinship, the reweaving of sustaining relations. And insofar as they involve the publicization and dramatization of death, they call to be read as life-affirming rejoinders to the dire psychic consequences of a grieving process culturally thwarted and proscribed.

GENDERED AND SEXUAL PERFORMATIVITY

How then does one link the trope by which discourse is described as 'performing' and that theatrical sense of performance in which the hyperbolic status of gender norms seems central? What is 'performed' in drag is, of course, *the sign* of gender, a sign that is not the same as the body that it figures, but that cannot be read without it. The sign, understood as a gender imperative – 'girl!' – reads less as an assignment than as a command and, as such, produces its own insubordinations. The hyperbolic conformity to the command can reveal the hyperbolic status of the norm itself, indeed, can become the cultural sign by which that cultural imperative might become legible. Insofar as heterosexual gender norms produce inapproximable ideals, heterosexuality can be said to operate through the regulated production of hyperbolic versions of 'man' and 'woman'. These are for the most part compulsory performances, ones which none of us choose, but which each of us is forced to negotiate. I write 'forced to negotiate' because the compulsory character of these norms does not always make them efficacious. Such norms are continually haunted by their own inefficacy; hence, the anxiously repeated effort to install and augment their jurisdiction.

The resignification of norms is thus a function of their *inefficacy*, and so the question of subversion, of *working the weakness in the norm*, becomes a matter of inhabiting the practices of its rearticulation. The critical promise of drag does not have to do with the proliferation of genders, as if a sheer increase in numbers would do the job, but rather with the exposure or the failure of heterosexual regimes ever fully to legislate or contain their own ideals. Hence, it is not that drag *opposes* heterosexuality, or that the proliferation of drag will bring down heterosexuality; on the contrary, drag tends to be the allegorization of heterosexuality and its constitutive melancholia. As an allegory that works through the hyperbolic, drag brings into relief what is, after all, determined only in relation to the hyperbolic: the understated, taken-for-granted quality of heterosexual performativity. At its best, then, drag can be read for the way in which hyperbolic norms are dissimulated as the heterosexual mundane. At the same time these same norms, taken not as commands to be obeyed, but as imperatives to be 'cited', twisted, queered, brought into relief as heterosexual imperatives, are not, for that reason, necessarily subverted in the process.

It is important to emphasize that although heterosexuality operates in part through the stabilization of gender norms, gender designates a dense site of significations that contain and exceed the heterosexual matrix. Although forms of sexuality do not unilaterally determine gender, a non-causal and non-reductive connection between sexuality and gender is nevertheless crucial to maintain. Precisely because homophobia often operates through the attribution of a damaged, failed, or otherwise abject gender to homosexuals, that is, calling gay men 'feminine' or calling lesbians 'masculine', and because the homophobic terror over performing homosexual acts, where it exists, is often also a terror over losing proper gender ('no longer being a real or proper man' or 'no longer being a real and proper woman'), it seems crucial to retain a theoretical apparatus that will account for how sexuality is regulated through the policing and the shaming of gender.

We might want to claim that certain kinds of sexual practices link people more strongly than gender affiliation, but such claims can only be negotiated, if they can, in relation to specific occasions for affiliation; there is nothing in either sexual practice or in gender to privilege one over the other. Sexual practices, however, will invariably be experienced differentially depending on the relations of gender in which they occur. And there may be forms of 'gender' within homosexuality which call for a theorization that moves beyond the categories of 'masculine' and 'feminine'. If we seek to privilege sexual practice as a way of transcending gender, we might ask at what cost the *analytic* separability of the two domains is taken to be a distinction in fact. Is there perhaps a specific gender pain that provokes such fantasies of a sexual practice that would transcend gender difference altogether, in which the marks of masculinity and femininity would no longer be legible? Would this not be a sexual practice paradigmatically fetishistic, trying not to know what it knows, but knowing it all the same? This question is not meant to demean the fetish (where would we be without it?), but it does mean to ask whether it is only according to a logic of the fetish that the radical separability of sexuality and gender can be thought.

In theories such as Catharine MacKinnon's, sexual relations of subordination are understood to establish differential gender categories, such that 'men' are those defined in a sexually dominating social position and 'women' are those defined in subordination. Her highly deterministic account leaves no room for relations of sexuality to be theorized apart from the rigid framework of gender difference or for kinds of sexual regulation that do not take gender as their primary objects (i.e., the prohibition of sodomy, public sex, consensual homosexuality). Hence, Gayle Rubin's influential distinction between the domains of sexuality and gender in 'Thinking Sex' and Sedgwick's reformulation of that position have constituted important theoretical opposition to MacKinnon's deterministic form of structuralism.[8]

My sense is that now this very opposition needs to be rethought in order to muddle the lines between queer theory and feminism.[9] For surely it is as unacceptable to insist that relations of sexual subordination determine gender position as it is to separate radically forms of sexuality from the workings of gender norms. The relation between sexual practice and gender is surely not a structurally determined one, but the destabilizing of the heterosexual presumption of that very structuralism still requires a way to think the two in a dynamic relation to one another.

In psychoanalytic terms, the relation between gender and sexuality is in part negotiated through the question of the relationship between identification and desire. And here it becomes clear why refusing to draw lines of causal implication between these two domains is as important as keeping open an investigation of their complex interimplication. For, if to identify as a woman is not necessarily to desire a man, and if to desire a woman does not necessarily signal the constituting presence of a masculine identification, whatever that is, then the heterosexual matrix proves to be an *imaginary* logic that insistently issues forth its own unmanageability. The heterosexual logic that requires that identification and desire be mutually exclusive is one of the most reductive of heterosexism's psychological instruments: if one identifies *as* a given gender, one must desire a different gender. On the one hand, there is no one femininity with which to identify, which is to say that femininity might itself offer an array of identificatory sites, as the proliferation of lesbian femme possibilities attests. On the other hand, it is hardly descriptive of the complex dynamic exchanges of lesbian and gay relationships to presume that homosexual identifications 'mirror' or replicate one another. The vocabulary for describing the difficult play, crossing, and destabilization of masculine and feminine identifications within homosexuality has only begun to emerge within theoretical language: the non-academic language historically embedded in gay communities is here much more instructive. The thought of sexual difference *within* homosexuality has yet to be theorized in its complexity.

For one deciding issue will be whether social strategies of regulation, abjection, and normalization will not continue to relink gender and sexuality such that the oppositional analysis will continue to be under pressure to theorize their interrelations. This will not be the same as reducing gender to prevailing forms of sexual relations such that one 'is' the effect of the sexual position one is said to occupy. Resisting such a reduction, it ought to be possible to assert a set of non-causal and non-reductive relations between gender and sexuality, not only to link feminism and queer theory, as one might link two separate enterprises, but to establish their constitutive interrelationship. Similarly, the inquiry into both homosexuality and gender will need to cede the priority of *both* terms in the service of a more complex mapping of power that interrogates the formation of each in specified racial regimes and geopolitical spatializations. And the task, of course, does not stop here, for no one term can serve as foundational, and the success of any given analysis that centers on any one term may well be the marking of its own limitations as an exclusive point of departure.

The goal of this analysis, then, cannot be pure subversion, as if an under-mining were enough to establish and direct political struggle. Rather than denaturalization or proliferation, it seems that the question for thinking discourse and power in terms of the future has several paths to follow: how to think power as resignification together with power as the convergence or interarticulation of relations of regulation, domination, constitution? How to know what might qualify as an affirmative resignification – with all the weight and difficulty of that labor – and how to run the risk of reinstalling the abject at the site of its opposition? But how, also, to rethink the terms that establish and sustain bodies that matter?

The film *Paris Is Burning* has been interesting to read less for the ways in which it deploys denaturalizing strategies to reidealize whiteness and hetero-sexual gender norms than for the less stabilizing rearticulations of kinship it occasioned. The drag balls themselves at times produce high femininity as a function of whiteness and deflect homosexuality through a transgendering that *reidealizes* certain bourgeois forms of heterosexual exchange. And yet, if those performances are not immediately or obviously subversive, it may be that it is rather in the *reformulation of kinship*, in particular, the redefining of the 'house' and its forms of collectivity, mothering, mopping, reading, and becoming legendary, that the appropriation and redeployment of the categories of dominant culture enable the formation of kinship relations that function quite supportively as oppositional discourse. In this sense, it would be interesting to read *Paris Is Burning* against, say, Nancy Chodorow's *The Reproduction of Mothering* and ask what happens to psychoanalysis and kinship as a result. In the former, the categories like 'house' and 'mother' are derived from that family scene, but also deployed to form alternative households and community. This *resignification* marks the workings of an agency that is (a) not the same as voluntarism, and that (b) though *implicated* in the very relations of power it seeks to rival, is not, as a consequence, reducible to those dominant forms.

Performativity describes this relation of being implicated in that which one opposes, this turning of power against itself to produce alternative modalities of power, to establish a kind of political contestation that is not a 'pure' opposition, a 'transcendence' of contemporary relations of power, but a difficult labor of forging a future from resources inevitably impure.

How will we know the difference between the power we promote and the power we oppose? Is it, one might rejoin, a matter of 'knowing'? For one is, as it were, in power even as one opposes it, formed by it as one reworks it, and it is this simultaneity that is at once the condition of our partiality, the measure of our political unknowingness, and also the condition of action itself. The incalculable effects of action are as much a part of their subversive promise as those that we plan in advance.

The effects of performatives, understood as discursive productions, do not conclude at the terminus of a given statement or utterance, the passing of legislation, the announcement of a birth. The reach of their signifiability cannot be controlled by the one who utters or writes, since such productions are not owned by the one who utters them. They continue to signify in spite of their authors, and sometimes against their authors' most precious intentions.

It is one of the ambivalent implications of the decentering of the subject to have one's writing be the site of a necessary and inevitable expropriation. But this yielding of ownership over what one writes has an important set of political corollaries, for the taking up, reforming, deforming of one's words does open up a difficult future terrain of community, one in which the hope of ever fully recognizing oneself in the terms by which one signifies is sure to be disappointed. This not owning of one's words is there from the start, however, since speaking is always in some ways the speaking of a stranger through and as oneself, the melancholic reiteration of a language that one never chose, that one does not find as an instrument to be used, but that one is, as it were, used by, expropriated in, as the unstable and continuing condition of the 'one' and the 'we', the ambivalent condition of the power that binds.

NOTES

1. See Eve Kosofsky Sedgwick's 'Queer Performativity' ... (1993). I am indebted to her provocative work and for prompting me to rethink the relationship between gender and performativity.
2. It is, of course, never quite right to say that language or discourse 'performs', since it is unclear that language is primarily constituted as a set of 'acts'. After all, this description of an 'act' cannot be sustained through the trope that established the act as a singular event, for the act will turn out to refer to prior acts and to a reiteration of 'acts' that is perhaps more suitably described as a citational chain. [...]
3. In what follows, that set of performatives that Austin terms illocutionary will be at issue, those in which the binding power of the act *appears* to be derived from the intention or will of the speaker. In 'Signature, Event, Context' [in *Margins of Philosophy* (1992), JW]. Derrida argues that the binding power that Austin attributes to the speaker's intention in such illocutionary acts is more properly attributable to a citational force of the speaking, the iterability that establishes the authority of the speech act, but which establishes the non-singular character of that act. In this sense, every 'act' is an echo or citational chain, and it is its citationality that constitutes its performative force.
4. The historicity of discourse implies the way in which history is constitutive of discourse itself. It is not simply that discourses are located *in* histories, but that they have their own constitutive historical character. Historicity is a term which directly implies the constitutive character of history in discursive practice, that is, a condition in which a 'practice' could not exist apart from the sedimentation of conventions by which it is produced and becomes legible.
5. My understanding of the charge of presentism is that an inquiry is presentist to the extent that it (a) universalizes a set of claims regardless of historical and cultural challenges to that universalization or (b) takes a historically specific set of terms and universalizes them falsely. It may be that both gestures in a given instance are the same. It would, however, be a mistake to claim that all conceptual language or philosophical language is 'presentist', a claim which would be tantamount to prescribing that all philosophy become history. My understanding of Foucault's notion of genealogy is that it is a specifically philosophical exercise in exposing and tracing the installation and operation of false universals. My thanks to Mary Poovey and Joan W. Scott for explaining this concept to me.

6. I thank Laura Mulvey for asking me to consider the relation between performativity and disavowal, and Wendy Brown for encouraging me to think about the relation between melancholia and drag and for asking whether the denaturalization of gender norms is the same as their subversion. I also thank Mandy Merck for numerous enlightening questions that led to these speculations, including the suggestion that if disavowal conditions performativity, then perhaps gender itself might be understood on the model of the fetish.

7. 'Freud and the Melancholia of Gender' in *Gender Trouble* (1989).

8. See Gayle Rubin (1984, 267–319); Eve Kosofsky Sedgwick (1990).

9. Toward the end of the short theoretical conclusion of 'Thinking Sex', Rubin returns to feminism in a gestural way, suggesting that 'in the long run, feminism's critique of gender hierarchy must be incorporated into a radical theory of sex, and the critique of sexual oppression should enrich feminism. But an autonomous theory and politics specific to sexuality must be developed' (1984, 309).

ANNOTATED BIBLIOGRAPHY

Bristow, Joseph, ed. *Sexual Sameness: Textual Differences in Lesbian and Gay Writing.* London, 1992.

An informative and useful collection of gay and lesbian readings examining the (textual) politics of representation of same-sex experience across a range of English and American literature by writers such as Shakespeare, Oscar Wilde, E. M. Forster, Virginia Woolf, Sylvia Townsend Warner, Joe Orton, H.D., Adrienne Rich, and Audre Lorde. Contributors include David Bergman, Diana Collecott, Terry Castle, Jonathan Dollimore, Sherron E. Knopp, Alan Sinfield and Liz Yorke.

Garber, Marjorie. *Vested Interests: Cross-Dressing and Cultural Anxiety.* London, 1992.

This incisively argued and beautifully illustrated book is a landmark study of the cultural significance of transvestism across a broad range of literature, art, film and television. Garber explores gay and lesbian theories and identities in relation to her much cited and debated central thesis that cross-dressing does not (as some theorists have argued) position the subject in one constructed gender identity or the other (masculine or feminine), but in fact constitutes a third category of identity – one which undoes or defies gender categorisation altogether. Garber's controversial work has met with mixed reception from gay, lesbian and queer theorists.

Sedgwick, Eve Kosofsky, ed. *Novel Gazing: Queer Readings in Fiction.* Durham, NC, and London, 1997.

A lively collection of essays making diverse and imaginative use of queer theory to explore a range of British, French and American novels by both canonical and esoteric authors, including Willa Cather, Benjamin Constant, William Gibson, Henry James, Toni Morrison, Marcel Proust, T. H. White and Virginia Woolf. The contributors are: Stephen Barber, Renu Bora, Anne Chandler, James Creech, Jonathan Goldberg, Joseph Litvak, Michael Lucey, Jeff Nunokawa, Cindy Patton, Jacob Press, Robert F. Reid-Pharr, Eve Kosofsky Sedgwick, Melissa Solomon, Tyler Stevens, Kathryn Bond Stockton, John Vincent, Maurice Wallace, Barry Weller.

Warner, Michael, ed. *Fear of a Queer Planet: Queer Politics and Social Theory.* Minneapolis, MN, 1993.

An important collection of interdisciplinary essays by some of the leading names in queer theory. Warner's helpful introductory essay has been much cited, and stands as a useful introduction to the field. The book sets out to 'queer' social theory by offering queer perspectives on traditions in various disciplines including anthropology, Marxism, psychoanalysis, psychology and law, and by inviting new engagements with the politics of identity, race, ethnicity, nationalism, gender and sexuality. The first part, 'Get Over It: Heterosexuality', includes Jonathan Goldberg on 'Sodomy in the New World', Diane Fuss on 'Freud's Fallen Women' and Eve Sedgwick on 'How to Bring Your Kids Up Gay'. The second part, 'Get Used to It: The New Queer Politics', includes Cathy Griggers on 'Lesbian Bodies in the Age of (Post)mechanical Reproduction', Henry Louis Gates on 'The Black Man's Burden' and Phillip Brian Harper on 'Black Nationalism and the Homophobic Impulse'. Other contributors are Laurent Berlant and Elizabeth Freeman, Douglas Crimp, Janet E. Halley, Andrew Parker, Cindy Patton, Steven Seidman and Robert Schwartzwarld.

Wittig, Monique. *The Straight Mind and Other Essays.* Hemel Hempstead, 1992.

The French writer, Monique Wittig, is a novelist and playwright as well as a theorist and critic whose work is considered a radical engagement with the French feminist tradition established by Simone de Beauvoir. She has been a significant influence on many Anglo-American feminist, lesbian and queer theorists, including Judith Butler. The title essay in this entertainingly provocative and readable selection includes Wittig's most famous declaration: 'Lesbians are not women'.

·

SUPPLEMENTARY BIBLIOGRAPHY

Abelove, Henry, Michèle Aina Barale and David M. Halperin, eds. *The Lesbian and Gay Studies Reader*. New York, 1993.

Beemyn, Brett and Mickey Eliason, eds. *Queer Studies: A Lesbian, Gay, Bisexual, and Transgender Anthology*. New York, 1996.

Bredbeck, Gregory W. 'The new queer narrative: intervention and critique', *Textual Practice*, 9: 3, 1995.

Bristow, Joseph, ed. *Sexual Sameness: Textual Differences in Lesbian and Gay Writing*. London, 1992.

———. *Sexuality*. London, 1997.

Butler, Judith. *Gender Trouble: Feminism and the Subversion of Identity*. London, 1990.

———. 'Imitation and gender insubordination', in *Inside/Out: Lesbian Theories*, ed. Diana Fuss. New York, 1991.

———. 'Against Proper Objects', *differences: A Journal of Feminist and Cultural Studies*, 6, 1994.

Castle, Terry. *The Apparitional Lesbian: Female Homosexuality and Modern Culture*. New York, 1993.

Creekmur, Corey K. and Alexander Doty, eds. *Out in Culture: Gay, Lesbian, and Queer Essays on Popular Culture*. London, 1995.

de Lauretis, Teresa. 'Queer Theory: Lesbian and Gay Sexualities', *differences: A Journal of Feminist and Cultural Studies*, 3: 2, 1991.

Dollimore, Jonathan. 'Bisexuality, heterosexuality, and wishful theory', *Textual Practice*, 10: 3, 1996.

Dorenkamp, Monica and Richard Henke, eds. *Negotiating Lesbian and Gay Subjects*. New York, 1995.

Fuss, Diana. *Essentially Speaking: Feminism, Nature and Difference*. New York, 1989.

———, ed. *Inside/Out: Lesbian Theories, Gay Theories*. New York, 1991.

Geltmaker, T. 'The Queer Nation Acts Up: Health Care, Politics, and Sexual Diversity in the County of Angels', *Society and Space*, 10, 1992.

Goldberg, Jonathan. *Sodometries: Renaissance Texts, Modern Sexualities*. Stanford, CA, 1992.

Hall, Donald E. and Maria Pramaggiore, eds. *RePresenting Bisexualities: Subjects and Cultures of Fluid Desire*. New York, 1996.

Harper, Phillip Brian, E. Francis White and Margaret Cerullo. 'Multi/Queer/Culture', *Radical America*, 24: 4, 1993.

Jeffreys, Sheila. 'The Queer Disappearance of Lesbians: Sexuality in the Academy', *Women's Studies International Forum*, 17, 1994.

Luckhurst, Roger. 'Queer Theory (and Oscar Wilde): Review Essay', *Journal of Gender Studies*, 4: 3, 1995.

Martin, Biddy. 'Sexualities without Gender and Other Queer Utopias', *Diacritics*, 24: 2/3, 1994.

Nordquist, Jean. *Queer Theory: A Bibliography*. Santa Cruz, CA, 1997.

O'Driscoll, Sally. 'Outlaw Readings: Beyond Queer Theory', *Signs: Journal of Women, Culture and Society*, 22: 1, 1996.

Phelan, S. *Playing With Fire: Queer Politics, Queer Theories*. London, 1997.

Rich, Adrienne. 'Compulsory Heterosexuality and Lesbian Existence', in *Blood, Bread and Poetry: Selected Prose 1979–1985*. London, 1987.

Savoy, Eric. 'You Can't Go Homo Again: Queer Theory and the Foreclosure of Gay Studies', *English Studies in Canada*, 20: 2, 1994.

Sedgwick, Eve Kosofsky. *Between Men: English Literature and Male Homosocial Desire*. New York, 1985.

––––––. *Epistemology of the Closet*. Berkeley, CA, 1990.

––––––, ed. *Studies in the Novel*, 28: 3, 1996.

––––––, ed. *Novel Gazing: Queer Readings in Fiction*. Durham, NC, 1997.

Segal, Lynne: *Cultural Politics – Queer Reading*. London, 1994.

––––––. *The Wilde Century: Effeminacy, Oscar Wilde and the Queer Moment*. London, 1994.

––––––. *Straight Sex: The Politics of Pleasure*. London, 1994.

––––––. 'Diaspora and Hybridity: Queer Identities and the Ethnicity Model', *Textual Practice*, 10: 2, 1996.

Smith-Rosenberg, Carroll. 'The Female World of Love and Ritual: Relations Between Women in Nineteenth Century America', in *Disorderly Conduct: Visions of Gender in Victorian America*. New York, 1985.

Walters, Suzanne Danuta. 'From Here to Queer: Radical Feminism, Postmodernism, and the Lesbian Menace (Or, Why Can't a Woman Be More Like a Fag?)', *Signs: Journal of Women, Culture and Society*, 21: 4, 1996.

Warner, Michael, ed. *Fear of a Queer Planet: Queer Politics and Social Theory*. Minneapolis, MN, 1993.

Weed, Elizabeth, and Naomi Schor, eds. *Feminism Meets Queer Theory*. Bloomington, IN, 1997.

Wittig, Monique. *The Straight Mind and Other Essays*. Hemel Hempstead, 1992.

PART 12
CULTURAL STUDIES

INTRODUCTION: THEORISING CULTURE, READING OURSELVES

Kenneth Womack

Cultural studies, by encouraging readers to look outwardly at the social, artistic, political, economic and linguistic *mélange*, simultaneously challenges us to reflect inwardly upon the ethical norms and biases that constitute our selves. As the 1990s come to a close, this wide-ranging field of study continues to dominate the contemporary direction of literary criticism and its examination of the politics of difference that define our senses of individual and cultural identity. Cultural studies manifests itself in a wide array of interpretative dimensions, including such intersecting fields of inquiry as gender studies, postcolonialism, race and ethnic studies, pedagogy, ecocriticism, the politics of nationalism, popular culture, postmodernism and historical criticism, among a variety of other topics. Concerned with the exploration of a given culture's artistic achievements, institutional structures, belief systems and linguistic practices, cultural studies highlights the interrelationships and tensions that exist between cultures and their effects upon not only the literary works that we consume, but also the authentic texts of our lives. A genuinely international and interdisciplinary phenomenon, the interpretative lens of cultural studies provides us with a means for exploring the cultural codes of a given work, as well as for investigating the institutional, linguistic, historical and sociological forces that inform that work's publication and critical reception. The reconstruction and analysis of the conditions of literary production afford us, then, with a venue in which to address the social and political contexts of literary works. This venue, fraught as it is with the ideology of difference inherent in an increasingly global society, comprises cultural studies.

The contemporary theoretical predominance of cultural studies finds its origins in the various processes that shaped the direction of our postwar global culture, including modernisation, industrialisation, urbanisation and the unparalleled rise of technology and mass communication during the latter half of the twentieth century. Fuelled by the necessity of massive historical change, cultural studies emerged initially as a means for responding to the rapid shifts in the ways we live our lives, to the sudden transformation of the humanistic and historical norms that once governed – and, indeed, provided constancy for – our social practices. Scholars often locate the rise of cultural studies to late-1950s Great Britain and the publication of seminal works by Richard Hoggart and Raymond Williams. Hoggart and Williams composed their early cultural studies manifestos in an era dominated by the monolithic critical ideology of F. R. Leavis and a renewed interest in 'cultural capital', or the dissemination of literary knowledge for the express purpose of enhancing the moral sensibilities of the nation's readers. In *The Great Tradition* (1948), Leavis argues for a restricted literary canon that shuns the experimental excesses of modernism in favour of the traditional humanism espoused by such writers as Jane Austen, Charles Dickens, Alexander Pope and George Eliot. Responding to the social didacticism of 'Leavisism', writers such as Hoggart and Williams recognised the inability of Leavis's aesthetic vision, with its express reliance upon an abbreviated cultural canon, to respond to the many facets of mass culture intrinsic to postwar life.

In *The Uses of Literacy* (1957), Hoggart explores postwar shifts in the lives of working-class Britons confronted with the changes inherent in modernisation, as well as with the disintegration of traditional familial roles and social practices. Williams's *Culture and Society: 1780–1950* (1958) offers a critique of the radical consequences of making distinctions between conventional notions of 'culture' and 'society', and between 'high culture' and 'low culture'. Williams also discusses the demise of the 'knowable communities' that characterise prewar life, arguing that an increasingly politicised culture and the emergence of new forms of global imperialism will ultimately replace prewar conceptions of politics and society. In *Marxism and Literature* (1977), Williams explores the ideology of 'cultural materialism', or the concept that economic forces and modes of production inevitably impinge upon cultural products such as literary works. Proponents of cultural materialism contend that as a cultural artifact literature functions as a means for subverting social and political norms. 'At the very centre of a major area of modern thought and practice, which it is habitually used to describe, is a concept, "culture," which in itself, through variation and complication embodies not only the issues but the contradictions through which it has developed,' Williams writes in *Marxism and Literature*. 'The concept at once fuses and confuses the radically different experiences and tendencies of its formation' (1977, 11).

During the 1960s and 1970s, cultural studies continued to evolve as a viable interpretative paradigm. In 1964, for example, Hoggart and Stuart Hall founded Birmingham University's Centre for Contemporary Cultural Studies, an institution that soon became synonymous with the cultural studies movement of that era. The 1960s also saw the publication of E. P. Thompson's influential *The Making of the English Working Class* (1964), a volume that examines the political and economic components of the working-class identity and argues that conceptions of individuality have become fragmented in the postwar world and no longer restrict themselves to notions of shared cultural interests and value systems. During the 1970s, literary critics often discussed cultural criticism in terms of 'hegemony', the Italian Marxist Antonio Gramsci's term denoting invisible relations of cultural or intellectual domination. The 1970s also witnessed the emergence of various structuralist modes of cultural criticism that intersected with the ideological theories of Louis Althusser and the psychoanalytic arguments of Jacques Lacan. While Althusser examines ideology as both a means of cultural identification and of social control, Lacan discusses the psychological anxieties of resolving individual and familial tensions in a modern world that lacks traditional and comforting social structures. The theoretical insights of writers such as Gramsci, Althusser and Lacan finally accorded cultural studies a terminology for exploring the emergence of literary art forms within a given culture and for addressing the social contexts within which a particular text is written, produced and ultimately read.

With the advent of poststructuralist interpretative modes and the arrival of the multicultural movement during the 1980s, cultural studies emerged as one of literary criticism's primary fields of critical inquiry. Cultural studies also owes its theoretical hegemony during the 1980s to the international rise of the 'new right', the political movement in the United States and the United Kingdom led by President Ronald Reagan and Prime Minister Margaret Thatcher respectively. As a political ideology, the new right advocated minimal governmental involvement in the lives of citizens in order to allow market forces to define the nature of social interrelations and economic exchange. At the same time, proponents of the new right promoted strong senses of nationalism in an effort to eschew any internal differences that might threaten national unity. Yet, as Simon During astutely recognises in his introduction to *The Cultural Studies Reader*, the policies of the new right contain an 'internal contradiction' between its economic rationalism and its strident sense of nationalism: 'The more the market is freed from state intervention and trade and finance cross national boundaries,' During writes, 'the more the nation will be exposed to foreign influences and the greater the gap between rich and poor' (1993, 14). This internal contradiction subsequently threatened our individual senses of cultural identity by sublimating them via the nationalist rubrics of 'Americanness' and 'Englishness'. Suddenly, cultural studies – with its accent upon personal identity and the study of our rich diversity of cultural artifacts – provided readers and critics alike with an appealing form of intellectual cachet; it offered both a decentred view of culture in sharp contrast with the monocultural themes of nationalism, as well as an arena for investigating the politics of difference highlighted by the increasing social and economic globalisation that resulted from the new right's conservative fiscal policies.

The new right's political pre-eminence during this era also served as the catalyst for the culture wars of the 1980s and early 1990s that tested the resiliency of cultural studies and multiculturalism while also challenging the intellectual dominion of the academy. Students of the culture wars typically attribute the inauguration of the intellectual crisis in higher education to Secretary of Education William J. Bennett's 1984 governmental report on the humanities, *To Reclaim a Legacy*, in which he fans the flames of nationalism and charges American academics with having lost their senses of moral and intellectual purpose when they enacted policies of canon expansion and multicultural study. While the power and publicity concomitant with Bennett's cabinet post provided him with the public voice necessary to strike a strident initial chord within the American public, Allan Bloom's *The Closing of the American Mind: How Higher Education Has Failed Democracy and Impoverished the Souls of Today's Students* imbued the culture wars with the intellectual cachet of a scholarly voice. Bloom, then a distinguished professor in the Committee on Social Thought and the College at the University of Chicago, derided the contemporary state of the humanities as an 'almost submerged old Atlantis' (1987, 371). In addition to arguing that higher education wallows in a state of chaos with little evidence of a scholarly or an ethical agenda, Bloom attacked the pluralistic motives of canon revisionists. As with the cultural warriors who follow the ideological lead of *The Closing of the American Mind*, Bloom championed the literary touchstones of western civilisation and the cultural capital that they would ostensibly impart to the minds of young readers. In *ProfScam: Professors and the Demise of Higher Education*, Charles J. Sykes similarly attacks what he perceives to be the professoriate's 'relentless drive for advancement [which] has turned American universities into vast factories of junkthink, the byproduct of academe's endless capacity to take even the richest elements of civilization and disfigure them into an image of itself' (1988, 7). In addition to calling for the broad abolition of tenure, Sykes refuses to address the policies of the multicultural project when he demands the unequivocal restoration of a Eurocentric canon and curriculum: 'Without apology', he writes, 'the undergraduate curriculum should be centred on the intellectual tradition of Western civilization. Quite simply,' he adds, 'there are certain books and certain authors that every college graduate should read if he is to be considered truly educated' (1988, 260).

As the culture wars advanced into the 1990s, proponents of the new right continued the culture warriors' onslaught against canon revision, while also increasingly objecting to the manner in which contemporary scholars resorted to the politicisation of literary and cultural studies. In *Tenured Radicals: How Politics Has Corrupted Higher Education*, Roger Kimball laments what he considers to be a concerted leftist effort to dismantle the traditional curriculum and institutionalize radical feminism, to ban politically unacceptable speech and propagate the tenets of deconstruction and similar exercises in cynical obscurantism' (1990, 167). In his divisive volume, *Illiberal Education: The*

Politics of Race and Sex on Campus, Dinesh D'Souza challenges the politicisation of literary studies by contemporary scholars: 'The problem is that many of the younger generation of faculty in the universities express lack of interest, if not contempt, for the Western classics,' he writes. 'Either they regard the books as flawed for their failure to endorse the full emancipation of approved minorities,' he continues, 'or they reject their metaphysical questions as outdated and irrelevant' (1991, 255). Finally, in *Telling the Truth: Why Our Culture and Our Country Have Stopped Making Sense – and What We can Do about It*, Lynne V. Cheney, the former director of the National Endowment for the Humanities, continues Bennett and Bloom's attacks on canon revision and the politicisation of academic scholarship. In the conclusion to her study, Cheney remarks: 'The virtues that we have increasingly come to believe we must nurture if we are to be successful as a culture simply make no sense if we turn away from reason and reality' (1995, 206).

In each instance, the culture warriors argued in favour of the new right's nationalistic aims and its affirmation of a singular cultural identity. Yet their remarkably narrow approach to culture – particularly in light of the intense era of globalisation that marked the 1980s and 1990s – only succeeded in underscoring the ideologies of difference that compose our divergent senses of identity. 'We face the outraged reactions of those custodians of Western culture who protest that the canon, that transparent decanter of Western values, may become – breathe the word – *politicized*,' Henry Louis Gates, Jr, observes (1992, 195). Gates's arguments underscore the manner in which ideology, despite the culture warriors' vehement claims to the contrary, invariably influences the selection and historical survival of cultural artifacts. Ironically, the culture wars not only resulted in a renewed interest in cultural studies, but also in the institutionalisation of the aims of the multicultural project. 'Whether the topic is language; the construction of readers, writers, and texts; canon formation; curriculum; institutions; or the social positions of women, African Americans, and other marginalized groups,' Isaiah Smithson writes in his introduction to *English Studies/Culture Studies: Institutionalizing Dissent*, 'teachers and students are exploring the cultural relations of texts rather than settling for what are ultimately naturalist and essentialist explanations' (1994, 9). By responding to the explicit threats posed by the culture wars waged by the new right – the dominant ideology and the purveyors of the new nationalism – cultural studies strengthened its interpretative claims and clarified its position as an ideologically based form of critique.

As cultural studies continues to develop as an interpretative mode during the 1990s, its proponents celebrate the remarkable heterogeneity that characterises its contemporary nature. In dramatic contrast with its earliest manifestations in the late 1950s, cultural studies currently intersects a variety of disciplines and political forms of literary criticism, from deconstruction and postmodernism to gender studies and environmental criticism. In the wake of the globalisation spurred on by the new right's economic policies and by unprecedented developments in technology and mass communications during the 1980s, cultural studies enjoys theoretical hegemony because of its capacity for addressing the issues that define the closing decades of the twentieth century. 'Whether we are discussing the multinational corporation, global agricultural development, the protection of endangered species, religious toleration, the well-being of women, or simply how to run a firm efficiently,' Martha C. Nussbaum remarks in *Cultivating Humanity: A Classical Defense of Reform in Liberal Education*, 'we increasingly find that we need comparative knowledge of many cultures to answer the questions we ask' (1997, 15). Cultural studies provides precisely such a mechanism, with its simultaneous interests in 'high' and 'low' culture, as well as in the nexus that it reveals between culture and society.

As the 1990s come to a close, cultural studies continues to evolve in a number of intriguing and significant directions. In addition to its ongoing academic institutionalisation, cultural studies confronts contemporary scholars with a variety of pedagogical implications while continuing to engage other, ostensibly separate fields of inquiry in interdisciplinary forms of critique. North American universities and colleges actively support the aims of cultural studies as they create American Studies programmes and provide students with curricula that offer multicultural studies options. As Elizabeth Fox-Genovese notes, 'Scholars have succeeded in imaginatively reclaiming the voices, representations, productions, and values of the oppressed and excluded, and they have demonstration the cultural strength and richness of those who have been ignored' (1990, 9). Cultural studies also provides the professoriate with an encouraging theoretical mode for exploring the politics of difference depicted by a variety of previously disenfranchised literary works. Simply put, cultural studies – rather than forcing instructors to engage literature in neutral, depoliticised terms – challenges teachers to investigate a given text's ideological properties in the classroom. Cultural studies, then, 'invokes the standard sense of the pedagogical contract,' Jeffrey Williams writes, 'that we can catalyze and generate social change via our relations with students. This possibility – to reach the minds of the young to effect social change – is perhaps the great hope of education and why it is cast as having significant stakes, from Socrates on' (1997, 301). By necessarily challenging literary critics to merge various interpretative modes, cultural criticism affords teachers and theorists alike with the opportunity to approach the act of reading in a multidisciplinary fashion. In this manner, cultural studies provides us with a valuable means for reinvigorating both our literary critiques and our classroom pedagogies.

While cultural criticism confronts the contemporary academy with a variety of interesting pedagogical implications, it nevertheless presents a number of ideological dilemmas regarding the ways in which we theorise literary study and the cultural discourses of the academy. The inevitable professionalisation of culture studies, for instance, has resulted in a blurring and convolution of the movement's principal aims. As Gisela Ecker observes, 'All too often references to "gender, race, and class" have degenerated into a mere litany which has to turn up in academic work as a sign of belonging to a supposedly progressive group' (1994, 41). In short, the elevation of cultural studies has engendered a form of political correctness that requires theorists to address particular cultural issues in their critiques; this necessity invariably manifests itself in the iteration of requisite subjects, including 'gender, race and class'. While cultural studies clearly seeks to elevate these important social issues within the critical and social main, their repetition as an academic mantra only serves to mitigate their considerable intellectual import. Popular culture's apotheosis within the academy presents yet another dilemma. Although cultural studies certainly provides a forum for investigating the significant social and political meanings inherent in various forms of 'low' culture, the elevation of popular culture under cultural studies' rubric calls into question many of the movement's most important scholarly goals. 'What "cultural studies," as an academic profession (in North America), clearly lacks,' Paul Bové cautions, 'is "high intellectual" effort' (1997, 53). Clearly, the study of popular culture offers much insight into our contemporary approaches to art, politics and society; yet, as Bové warns, its overemphasis may ultimately dilute the attention afforded to other past and present cultural forms and their impact upon our cultural selves.

In the essays that follow, J. Hillis Miller, Iain Chambers and Alan Sinfield demonstrate the interdisciplinary possibilities of cultural studies, as well as the theoretical elasticity of the paradigm as a means for interpreting our various senses of cultural identity. In 'Cultural Studies and Reading' (1997), Miller continues his analysis of the cultural and ethical properties inherent in the act of reading that he began in such works as *The Ethics of Reading: Kant, de Man, Eliot, Trollope, James, and Benjamin* (1987) and *Versions of Pygmalion* (1990). Having achieved academic renown during the 1980s for his 'deconstructive' critiques of literature and culture, Miller has devoted much of his recent work to positing an 'ethics of reading' that seeks to explain the reflexive process that occurs between the text and the reader, in addition to offering testimony to the ethical possibilities of poststructuralism, particularly deconstruction. For Miller, such an activity allows readers – the *de facto* authors of the texts that they appraise – to offer relevant conclusions about the moral properties of literary works and the ethical sensibilities of their theoretical premises. In 'Cultural Studies and Reading', Miller underscores the cultural import of the act of reading, the process via which we consume contemporary culture even as technology continues to transform the textures of our lives. While Miller recognises the many ways in which cultural studies has irrevocably altered the shape of the modern university and its curriculum, he argues that reading – indeed, the act of interpretation – still functions as the transaction that allows us to interact not only with 'literary or exclusively verbal texts but also works in visual or aural media like film, television, popular music, or advertising'.

Although he concedes that it provides a meaningful bridge between contemporary forms of 'high' and 'low' culture, Miller nevertheless sees cultural studies and its impact upon literary theory as potentially unsettling forces as we approach the new millennium. 'The universalizing idea of culture in cultural studies may be so all-inclusive as to be virtually empty,' Miller cautions. 'This process may occur even though all cultures and all persons may be seen as to some degree hybrid, not as univocal or essential'. In short, Miller argues, cultural studies possesses the capacity for undermining our notions of self and individuality because of its emphasis upon culture in its larger sense. Miller fears that 'individual works may be seen as unproblematically representative of the culture they reflect. A few carefully chosen examples can thus stand for a whole culture and offer a means of understanding it and taking it in,' he adds. Such an uncritical approach to our cultural artifacts would clearly undermine the political and institutional aims of cultural studies. Miller maintains that one solution for this 'disabling double gesture' may be the act of 'genuine' reading, a process in which readers consume a given text in its 'original language' and within the proper historical context. According to Miller, 'Only such a reading can hope to transmit or preserve some of the force that original work had or can still have as an event'. By insisting that cultural theorists address the artifacts of our civilisation in such a manner, cultural studies may yet succeed in achieving its democratic ends. As Miller argues in 'Is There an Ethics of Reading?', as the millennium approaches 'it would be beneficial to the health of our society to have an abundance of good readers' (1988, 100).

In 'Cities without Maps' (1994), Iain Chambers constructs an elaborate reading of the city as a cultural metaphor. In addition to providing a useful analogy for an era of increasing globalisation, the contemporary metropolis offers a virtual sea of interconnected histories, languages and cultures. While the city functions as a complex linguistic and social metaphor for the modern world, Chambers argues, maps of cities contradict the particularly human qualities of the urban landscapes that they reference, shape and outline. Although maps create contexts for our metropolitan adventures, they can never truly capture the reality inherent in a given city's historical memory and its convoluted array of cultures, stories, languages and experiences. Chambers writes:

> Beyond the edges of the map, we enter the localities of the vibrant, everyday world and the disturbance of complexity. Here we find ourselves in the gendered city, the city of ethnicities, the territories of different social groups, shifting centres and peripheries – the city that is a fixed object of design (architecture, commerce, urban planning, state administration) and yet simultaneously plastic and mutable: the site of transitory events, movements, memories.

A genuinely living and fluid entity, the city – by virtue of its collective size and concentration of humanity – forces us to make cultural connections and to risk living our lives without maps. As Chambers notes, cities challenge us, like the larger cultures within which we live and work, to surrender portions of our identity in order to experience yet other, previously unrealised transcultural regions of our selves.

Chambers also offers a valuable defence of mass culture as the natural product of a historical era marked by globalisation and cultural expansion. Rather than denigrating mass media and modern culture as an 'ideological façade' or as an 'infinity of commodity exchange', Chambers sees the contemporary metropolis as having its own aesthetics and its own complex, often ambiguous value systems and intercultural rhythms. Chambers illustrates the mutability of urban life through his description of Naples as a cultural metaphor. Nestled as it is below Mount Vesuvius, Naples must constantly confront its own potential destruction while simultaneously evolving as a human community. 'To live under the volcano, daily reminded of one's own mortality,' Chambers writes, 'is that the key to the city's schizophrenic energy, its languages of exultation and despair, its extremes of physical violence and mental resignation?'. Yet attempting to capture the essence of Naples – indeed, of any city – constitutes a cultural exercise in futility. As with any cultural phenomenon, cities consist of an infinitely complex series of signs and signifiers; these cities without maps, Chambers argues, 'can only be caught in fragments, in the economy of disorder, in the mythical half-light of an imagined decadence.' Always 'the sum of its collective histories, memories, and monuments', the city – in contrast with its various maps, which attempt to ascribe reality upon its cultural farrago – essentially functions as an 'imaginary place', in Chambers's words, that 'has a language that calls for a mode of interpretation'.

In 'Art as Cultural Production' (1994), Sinfield offers a useful demonstration of cultural studies' intersections with Marxist literary criticism and queer theory, while also elaborating upon the intellectual history of cultural criticism. Much of Sinfield's argument finds its origins in his postulation of an 'entrapment model', his theory about the interrelations of ideology and power. The entrapment model theorises that attempts to challenge any prevailing ideological system only serve to maintain that system's locus of power, perhaps entrenching its power structures even deeper than before. Sinfield argues that the entrapment model functions as a barrier to dissidence, as a means for the ideology in power to sustain its oppressive constructions of class, race, gender and sexuality. Cultural materialism, according to Sinfield, provides readers and critics alike with a mechanism for understanding the power dynamics inherent in the entrapment model and for establishing the forms of cultural dissidence necessary for effecting genuine social change. Although cultural materialism reveals that 'there is no simple way through' the dominant's ideology's locus of power, Sinfield writes, it reminds us that there is 'every reason to go on trying'. Sinfield also offers several thoughtful conclusions about the degrees of value ascribed to art and literature by different cultures. Simply put, not all societies possess – or even attribute value to – cultural artifacts. According to

Sinfield, the effective practice of cultural materialism recognises this concept and understands that forceful cultural critiques investigate both modes of cultural production and the roles (or lack thereof) of art and literature in a given culture's social order.

As with Miller, Sinfield locates the genesis of contemporary cultural criticism to around 1980, when other political forms of critique, particularly feminism and gender studies, challenged the conventional norms of literary criticism and theory. 'Feminism created space for other kinds of question,' Sinfield writes. 'We saw that we didn't, after all, have to spend our psychic energy on ever more ingenious explanations of why Shakespeare on Shylock, or Joseph Conrad on Blacks, or D. H. Lawrence on women, or Alexander Pope on Sporus and effeminacy, is really expressing a profound universal truth'. In addition to discussing class variations regarding such concepts as masculinity and effeminacy, Sinfield considers what he perceives to be the misapplication of ideological critique by dissident cultural theorists. Cultural criticism falters, Sinfield argues, when it dismisses the cultural past as a useless means for addressing the 'world of material affairs' of the present in favour of texts grounded in the contemporary moment. Sinfield astutely undermines this contention, arguing that cultural critique demands the investigation of a given work's political context. 'Cultural materialists say that canonical texts have political projects,' he writes, 'and should not be allowed to circulate in the world today on the assumption that their representations of class, race, ethnicity, gender, and sexuality are simply authoritative.' Nevertheless, Sinfield reminds us, 'politics should be up for discussion' and 'textual analysis should address it'. Sinfield's remarks illustrate the decidedly *political* nature of cultural criticism. While literary critics – in our zeal for engendering democratic values and truths – often neglect this significant aspect of the interpretative act, cultural criticism, with its express interest in the circumstances of textual production, challenges us to contemplate a wider range of sociological, historical and ideological contexts.

As the essays by Miller, Chamber and Sinfield usefully demonstrate, cultural studies – with its capacity for illuminating our senses of self and their inextricable relations with the worlds in which we live – provides precisely such a venue for considering the various contexts of an increasingly diverse and heterogeneous global community. Although cultural studies emerged from the culture wars of the last decade with a renewed sense of purpose and with fully realised political and institutional aims, it must nevertheless continue to assert its interdisciplinarity in order to further its evolution as a viable and relevant interpretative paradigm. By highlighting the interpretative interconnections between the various subgenres of the theoretical project – and among such ostensibly divergent fields of poststructuralist inquiry as feminism, psychoanalysis, deconstruction and postmodernism – cultural studies offers a powerful means for comprehending the cultural realities that inform our perceptions of the world, as well as of the self. As Manthia Diawara observes, 'Cultural studies, in its attempts to draw attention to the material implications of the worldviews we assume, often delineates a literal and candid picture of ways of life that embarrass and baffle our previous theoretical understanding of those forms of life' (1995, 202). In addition to affording us with a context for finally reading the texts of our own lives, cultural studies provides us with a forum for reflecting upon the narrative spaces inhabited by the cultural others with whom we live.

12.1

CULTURAL STUDIES AND READING

J. Hillis Miller

The rapid rise of cultural studies is a concomitant of the weakening of the nation-state, that is, the rapid transition to a postnational condition. It is also one effect of the new technological regime of telecommunications. Why did the massive shift to cultural studies from language-based theory begin when it did, around 1980? The reorientation was no doubt overdetermined and even contradictory. Many factors contributed to it, such as the Vietnam War, the student movement of the 1960s, and the Civil Rights movement. Those who created cultural studies had been decisively marked by these events. Moreover, literature in the old-fashioned sense of canonical masterworks appears to play a smaller and smaller role in the emerging multicultural global society. It is natural that young scholars should not wish to spend their time on something that seems increasingly marginal.

Cultural studies is intertwined in the immense network of economic, ideological, and political forces within which the university is embedded. Moreover, cultural studies itself is a large, heterogeneous set of practices. It cannot be justly summarized under a single set of conceptual presuppositions. Its relation to the language-oriented theory that preceded it is particularly complex and diverse. One major force, however, in the rise of a cultural studies that tends to marginalize literature has been the growing influence of new communication technologies. Technology has been changing society throughout the nineteenth and twentieth centuries. No one doubts that. But the rate of

Extract from ADE *Bulletin*, 117 (Fall 1997), pp. 15–18.

change has greatly accelerated in recent years. The younger United States scholars who have turned so spontaneously and so universally to cultural studies are members of the first generation of university teachers and critics brought up with television and with new forms of commercialized popular music. Many of them as children and teenagers spent as much time watching television or listening to popular music as they did reading books. I do not say these activities are necessarily bad. They are just different. Reading books can be bad for you too, as Flaubert's Emma Bovary and Conrad's Lord Jim show. The critics of this new generation have been to a considerable degree formed by a new visual and aural culture. *Culture* has a somewhat new meaning now. It names the media part of a global consumerist economy. The new media include of course some counterhegemonic elements. This new electronic culture is fast replacing the culture of the book. It is not surprising that young scholars should wish to study what has largely made them what they are, in spite of their participation in the culture of the book. Clear evidence of literature's weakening force in the United States is the way many young scholars trained in literary study now feel so great a call to study popular culture that they more or less abandon canonical literature.

For cultural studies, literature is no longer the privileged expression of culture, as it was, say, for Matthew Arnold or for the United States university until recently. Literature is now viewed as just one symptom or product of culture among others, to be studied alongside not only film, video, television, advertising, magazines, and so on but also the myriad habits of everyday life that ethnographers investigate. As Alan Liu observes, literature is 'a category that has increasingly lost its distinction on the unbounded plane of cultural "discourse", "textuality", "information", "phrase regimes", and "general literature."' Cultural studies, as Liu puts it, 'make[s] literature seem just one of many equipollent registers of culture and multiculture – no more or less splendid, say, than the everyday practices of dressing, walking, cooking, or quilting' (2).

Though scholars in cultural studies tend to be defensive about the relation of this new field to the social sciences, it seems evident that as cultural studies becomes more and more dominant in the humanities, the humanities will move closer and closer to a merger with the social sciences, especially with anthropology. Anthropologists have learned much from colleagues in the humanities, and similarly, graduate-level training in the protocols of anthropology and sociology would be helpful for future practitioners of cultural studies – for example, training in statistical analysis, in the relation between data and generalization, in the ethics of using human subjects, in learning by hook or by crook the languages necessary for the work undertaken, and so on. A traditional Eurocentric literary education is not much help for many of the projects of cultural studies.

Scholars working in cultural studies will be quick to point out that the social sciences in the United States are complicit in many ways with American imperialism, just as Rey Chow observes that the study of non-Western languages and cultures is already institutionalized in the university as part of that imperialist project.[1] Anthropology has been struggling to confront this problem at least since Claude Lévi-Strauss's *Tristes tropiques*. Cultural studies has much to learn from anthropology's procedures and strategies, including those devised to deal with the discipline's ingrained Eurocentrism. Moreover, that social scientists have done cultural studies in the wrong way does not make cultural studies any less a social science in many of its features. There is no reason to be scandalized by this categorization of cultural studies. The standard division of the disciplines in United States universities is just one arrangement among others. It could be different. In the People's Republic of China, literary studies is part of the mission of the Chinese Academy of Social Sciences. Disciplinary divisions and affiliations in the humanities and social sciences in United States universities are in any case now rapidly changing.

At the same time new communication technologies are transforming the way research and teaching are carried on in the humanities. These transformations have accompanied and to some degree effected the replacement of the Humboldtian university by the new technologized transnational university that serves the global economy. This new kind of university is an important feature of the weakening of the nation-state. Since we are in the midst of these changes, it is difficult to see them clearly. As the epochal cultural change from the book age to the hypertext age has accelerated, we have been ushered ever more rapidly into a threatening living space. As Jacques Derrida and many others have argued, this new electronic space – the space of television, cinema, telephone, videos, fax, e-mail, hypertext, and the Internet – has profoundly altered the economies of the self, the home, the workplace, the university, and the nation-state's politics. These entities were traditionally ordered around the firm boundaries of an inside–outside dichotomy: for example, the walls between the home's privacy and the world outside or the borders between the nation-state and its neighbors. The new technologies invade the home and confound all these inside–outside divisions. On the one hand, no one is so alone as when watching television, talking on the telephone, or sitting before a computer screen reading e-mail or searching an Internet database. On the other hand, the private space of the home has been invaded and permeated by a vast crowd of verbal, aural, and visual images existing in cyberspace's simulacrum of presence. Those images cross national and ethnic boundaries. They come from all over the world with a spurious immediacy that makes them all seem equally close and equally distant. The global village is not out there but in here, or a clear distinction between inside and outside no longer operates. The new technologies bring the *unheimlich* other into the privacy of the home. They are a frightening threat to traditional ideas of the self as unified and as properly living rooted in one dear particular culture-bound place, participating in a single national culture, firmly protected from any alien otherness. They are threatening also to our assumption that political action is based in a single topographical location, a given nation-state with firm boundaries and ethnic and cultural unity.

One response to this uprooting, dislocation, and blurring of borders, also discussed by Derrida, is the violent return to nationalism, to ethnic purification, and to the fanatical militarized religions that are spawning such horrible bloodshed around the world. Another response is the hysterical return to isolationism among some groups in the United States. Yet another very different response, perhaps, is the rapid switch in university humanities departments from literary study, organized primarily around the separate study of national literatures, to cultural studies. Though it would seem that nothing could be more different from ethnic cleansing in Rwanda or Bosnia than a program in cultural studies, the development of such programs may to some degree be another, very different response to the transformations in daily life new communications technologies bring about. Cultural studies can function as a way to contain and tame the threat of that invasive otherness new technologies bring into our homes and workplaces.

This containing and taming takes a contradictory double form. On the one hand, it tends to reestablish firm boundaries between one nation and another, one ethnic group and another, one gender or sexual orientation and another. It may assume that anyone can be defined through affiliation with a national, gender, or other kind of group, therefore can be understood through understanding the ethos of that group. The tradition of dividing university disciplines along national, linguistic, generic, or ethnic lines remains to a considerable degree intact after the introduction of cultural studies, despite much talk about interdisciplinarity and much recognition of the problems of defining identity through membership in a given group or community. Often the traditional divisions are now simply expanded to include separate programs in women's studies, gay and lesbian studies, Native American studies, African American studies, Chicano and Chicana studies, Asian American studies, film studies or visual culture studies, and so on. All these others are given a place in the university, but they are fenced off in a firm reestablishment of the inside–outside dichotomy that the new technologies threaten. The others are kept safely outside. Interdisciplinarity still presupposes the separate integrity of the disciplines that interact, just as hybridity presupposes the fixed nature of genetic strains that are hybridized. Joint appointments (say in English and African American studies) may cause scholars to lead a hybrid double life, subject to the presuppositions and protocols of two different disciplines. One should not, however, underestimate the long-term transformative effect on national literature departments the presence of such scholars will cause.

On the other hand, the return, wherever it happens, to a mimetic, representational, descriptive methodology tends to turn those threatening others into something that in theory (for this methodology is a theory too) can be easily understood, translated, and appropriated. The universalizing idea of culture in cultural studies may be so all-inclusive as to be virtually empty, may be a place of exchange where the other turns into the same. This process may occur even though all cultures and all persons may be seen as to some degree hybrid, not as univocal or essential. Individual works may be seen as unproblematically representative of the culture they reflect. A few carefully chosen examples can thus stand for a whole culture and offer a means of understanding it and taking it in. This procedure depends on a thematic way of interpretation that sees texts of other cultural artifacts as directly reflecting a historical or social context open to understanding by way of the work, though of course separate study of the context is also necessary. This form of study also sometimes depends on uncritical acceptance of the extremely dubious trope of synecdoche, part for whole, just as does letting deconstruction stand for all of theory. The historical context can then by way of the representative work be easily transposed into the terms of the university discipline assigned to assimilate it. That such translation can occur without essential loss is the key presupposition here. Such forms of archival appropriation have been in place since the origin of the Humboldtian research university. They are part of the foundational heritage of the university whereby everything has its reason and can be brought to light, known, understood, and appropriated. This contradictory double gesture says that the other is really other and can be kept safely outside the traditional literary disciplines and at the same time that the other is not really other and can be made a *heimlich* member of the family.

Such a disabling double gesture is by no means universal in cultural studies. Theory of the 1960s, 1970s, and 1980s is still recognized as a used approach to cultural studies, even by those who are overtly hostile to it. Examples include the deep explication of culture by Raymond Williams and others in Britain,[2] as well as the studies of ideology by Louis Althusser and other Continental Marxists. Rey Chow, an advocate of cultural studies and a practitioner of postcolonial studies, strongly affirms the continuity of poststructuralist theory and cultural studies (112). Wherever the rejection of theory occurs, however, whether explicitly under the aegis of the 'revolt against theory' or just as a spontaneous defensive response to a perceived threat, it may disable the project of cultural studies, just as it would disable any other attempts to alter the status quo. It may also prevent cultural studies from reaching the goal of political and institutional change toward the better democracy to come that most people desire.

The acceptance by the university of cultural studies has been relatively rapid and easy, though no doubt it has not seemed that way, for example, to those who have had to fight for years for the institutional acceptance of women's studies. The firm establishment of cultural studies in the university has nevertheless taken only fifteen years or so, a relatively short time for such a genuinely revolutionary change. It may be that university administrators unconsciously view the introduction of cultural studies as a nonthreatening change that leaves old institutional structures more or less intact. If so, I think they have misjudged cultural studies' power to transform the university. Nevertheless, the university may even perceive cultural studies as a way of policing minority groups. Once the new disciplines have been set up, at least the authorities will know where to find members of those groups.

The rise of cultural studies has accompanied the technologizing and globalizing turn in the university and, where that turn is an antitheoretical return to mimetism, is a concomitant of it. Why does this antitheoretical turn disable cultural studies? For one thing, it is a regression to just that conservative hegemonic ideology cultural studies would contest. The right and certain components of the left are similar in their basic presuppositions about cultural forms. Both sometimes accept, for example, the notion that cultural artifacts unproblematically reflect their cultural contexts. Attempts to use a particular ideology to displace the proponents of that ideology inevitably fail. Wherever cultural studies deploys precritical notions of the self and its agency, of referentiality, or of cultural artifacts' transparency or the idea that it is possible to narrativize history unproblematically or to describe cultural artifacts exhaustively by a repertoire of themes, its work will be politically ineffective.

Fortunately much work in cultural studies has great theoretical sophistication and is able through interventionist acts of reading to pass on the dislocating energy of the cultural artifacts it discusses. *Reading* here names a transaction that may involve not just literary or exclusively verbal texts but also works in visual or aural media like film, television, popular music, or advertising. The extension of the term *reading* in this way may be acceptable as long as it is remembered that reading a film is not the same thing as reading a novel. Reading, moreover, must be distinguished from theory. Though theory may facilitate reading and should ideally have arisen from acts of reading, the two are not the same thing, nor are they by any means always in harmony. Genuine acts of reading are always to some degree sui generis, inaugural. They always to some extent disable or disqualify the theory that may have been the motivating presupposition of the reader. It is easy enough to sprinkle a text in cultural studies with cogent, correct, and forceful appeals to theory – for example, references to Foucault, Anderson, Bhabha, Jameson, Fanon, Said, or Irigaray – while performing acts of reading that are precritical, pretheoretical, and exclusively thematic. Simple tests make possible a distinction between the two kinds of reading. A thematic reading summarizes plots, describes characters as if they were real people, and, where the work is in a language other than that of the reader, may cite a translation without referring to the original text. What I am calling a 'genuine' reading must always resort to the original language of the work, however awkward and time-consuming this process may be and however much it may go against the powerful ideology of journals and of university and commercial presses. A thematic reading assumes that everything can be translated without loss into English. But recourse to the original language is necessary, because the force of the original work, its occurrence as a cultural event that to some extent exceeded the social context from which it arose, lies in its unique use of its own vernacular or idiom.

I call this unique use the irreducible otherness of the work, an otherness even to the culture that apparently generated it. Use of a translation uproots the work, denatures it, transforms it into a *hortus siccus*, a dried flower ready to be stored in the bottomless archives of a transnational university system that is more and more dominated by English. This argument for return to the original language in acts of reading is, however, only the most visible expression of a need, even in studying works in one's own language, to reach behind thematic reading to what might be called the materiality of the work. The work's force as an event bringing cultural value or meaning into existence depends on a certain performative use of language or other signs. Such use always exceeds the referential or mimetic dimension of signs. A materialist reading must pay attention to what is internally heterogeneous, contradictory, odd, anomalous about the work instead of presupposing some monolithic unity that directly reflects a cultural context. Only such a reading can hope to transmit or preserve some of the force the original work had or can still have as an event. The reading itself, recorded in an essay or lecture, may become a new event and thus may help to bring about what Jacques Derrida calls the democracy to come, which is, or ought to be, the goal of cultural studies.

NOTES

1. 'Already, in myriad forms for an extended period of time, the very disciplinary structures that we seek to challenge have been firmly established in the pedagogical practices related to non-Western languages and literatures ... "Qualifications" and "expertise" in so-called other cultures have been used as the means to legitimate entirely conservative institutional practices in hiring, tenure, promotion, reviewing, and publishing, as well as in teaching' (110–11).
2. At least these critics understand culture as it is embodied in the United Kingdom, a society whose social structure is very different from that of the United States. In the United States, race, gender, and ethnic particularity are much more important than class in the European sense is in determining the hierarchy of power and privilege. That distinction does not mean the United States is not a class society, but class membership is much more difficult to define in the United States than in Europe. Forster's Leonard Bast, in *Howards End*, has little hope of rising out of his class, whereas Fitzgerald's Jay Gatsby, in *The Great Gatsby*, or Faulkner's Thomas Sutpen, in *Absalom, Absalom!*, are exemplars of the American myth of upward mobility.

12.2

CITIES WITHOUT MAPS

Iain Chambers

To arrive at the 'purity' of the gaze is not difficult, it is impossible.

Walter Benjamin (1986, 609)

The city, the contemporary metropolis, is for many the chosen metaphor for the experience of the modern world. In its everyday details, its mixed histories, languages and cultures, its elaborate evidence of global tendencies and local distinctions, the figure of the city, as both a real and an imaginary place, apparently provides a ready map for reading, interpretation and comprehension. Yet the very idea of a map, with its implicit dependence upon the survey of a stable terrain, fixed referents and measurement, seems to contradict the palpable flux and fluidity of metropolitan life and cosmopolitan movement. You often need a map to get around a city, its subway system, its streets. Maps are full of references and indications, but they are not peopled. They project the changing disposition of space through historical time in a mixed geometry of political, economic and cultural powers: centre, periphery, suburbia, industrial zone, residential area, public housing, commercial district, railway station, motorway exits, airport. With a map in our hands we can begin to grasp an outline, a shape, some sort of location. But that preliminary orientation hardly exhausts the reality in which we find ourselves. For the city's denuded streets, buildings, bridges, monuments, squares and roads are also the contested sites of historical memory and provide the contexts, cultures, stories, languages, experiences, desires and hopes that course through the urban body. The

Extract from Iain Chambers, *Migrancy, Culture, Identity* (Routledge, 1994), pp. 92–114.

fluctuating contexts of languages and desires pierce the logic of cartography and spill over the borders of its tabular, taxonomic, space.

Beyond the edges of the map we enter the localities of the vibrant, everyday world and the disturbance of complexity. Here we find ourselves in the gendered city, the city of ethnicities, the territories of different social groups, shifting centres and peripheries – the city that is a fixed object of design (architecture, commerce, urban planning, state administration) and yet simultaneously plastic and mutable: the site of transitory events, movements, memories. This is therefore also a significant space for analysis, critical thought and understanding. I want therefore to reflect for a moment on this space and the opportunity it provides us in reconsidering the scope and sense of cultural analysis today.

The idea of both lived and intellectual complexity, of Edgar Morin's 'la pensée complexe', finds us continually circulating around a changing social ecology of being and knowledge. Here both thought and everyday activities move in the realm of uncertainty. Linear argument and certainty break down as we find ourselves orbiting in a perpetual paradox around the wheel of being: we bestow sense, and yet we can never be certain in our proclamations (1977). The idea of cultural complexity, most sharply on display in the arabesque patterns of the modern metropolis – and that includes Lagos as well as London, Beijing and Buenos Aires – weakens earlier schemata and paradigms, destabilises and decentres previous theories and sociologies. Here the narrow arrow of progressive time is displaced by the open spiral of heterogeneous collaborations and contaminations, and what Edward Said has recently referred to as 'atonal ensembles' (1990, 16). It is a reality that is multiform, heterotopic, diasporic. The city suggests an implosive disorder, sometimes liberating, often bewildering, that results in an interpolation in which the imagination carries you in every direction, even towards the previously unthought (Leopardi, cit. Rella, 1989, 33). Here, in the dissonance and interrogation that lies between what Donna Haraway calls 'situated' and 'disembodied knowledges', the very location of theory is disturbed (cit. Mani, 1989).

'JE SUIS UN BEUR!'

> If initially the world market sterilises local sources, in a second moment it revitalises them.
>
> Edgar Morin (1987, 92)

Barbès is the traditional Arab immigrant quarter of Paris, the home of the sounds of Algerian raï, of Cheb Khaled. Here was born the statement 'Je suis un beur!', where *beur* is not the exact inversion, but rather a deliberate mixing up, of the word *arabe*. The *beurs* are French born of Arab parents. *Beur* signifies a difference, a particular history and context, a sign of creolisation and cultural ambiguity.

There is also rap. BAB (*Bombe à Baiser*) is a member of the Zulu nation. He raps in French over an electronic instrumentation produced by his white,

Italian collaborator. There is NTM from St Denis: 'We speak in our own name.' There is the ABC Nation. Their members, aged between 17 and 20, come from the French Antilles, Cameroon and Mali. They sport wide jeans, baseball caps, basketball pumps, rectangular hair cuts: the 'Zulu look'. On the northern periphery of Paris, in areas such as St Denis, Aubervilliers, La Courneuve, all last stops on the Métro, is 'Zululand'.[1] It is here, in the *banlieues populaires*, the 'popular suburbs', on the edges of the city, that sounds and stories from West Africa, from the Antilles, from the Maghreb, are mixed up and mixed down in reggae, raï and rap. The references are to Dr Martin Luther King, rebel chants against Babylon and the police, in praise of Malcolm X ('prophet of rage'). The raps are in French, with occasional phrases in English, and much in a subcultural slang. It is part of a *mélange* that stretches from the Bronx to Brixton, to Barbès, to Brazzaville. Composed of connective rhythms and local inflections, it proposes instances of mixing, remixing, translating and transforming a shared tonality into particular voices and situations. It helps to articulate the dissonance of the experiences of a particular time and place: to be Arab *and* French, to be black *and* Parisian.

Such examples, easily verified in parallel, but distinct, histories in London or Los Angeles, where Third Worlds rumble beneath the poverty lines in metropolitan ghettos, do not suggest any obvious integration with an existing cultural consensus or obliteration in the mainstream of modern life, but rather propose the shifting, mixing, contaminating, experimenting, revisiting and recomposing that the wider horizons and the inter- and trans-cultural networks of the city both permit and encourage. In rage, joy, pride and pain they offer continual evidence of that 'magic in which the connection of certain social facts with certain sounds creates irresistible symbols of the transformation of social reality' (Marcus, 1989, 2).

To Journey Without Maps

> Ethics comes from *ethos* and Heidegger translates this Greek word not so much in the sense of 'the character that belongs to man', but as 'lodging', 'the place where one lives', 'the open region in which man dwells'.
> Pier Aldo Rovatti (1990, 39)

> To be simultaneously 'rooted and rootless'.
> Trinh T. Minh-ha (1990, 335)

The labyrinthine and contaminated quality of metropolitan life not only leads to new cultural connections, it also undermines the presumed purity of thought. If critical thought can entertain this encounter, and abandon a distanced monologue for dialogue, then it curves downwards into the more extensive regimes of the everyday world and a different register. To travel in this zone, without maps and charts, is to experience the dis-location of the intellectual subject and his – the gender is deliberate – mastery of the word/world. The illusions of identity organised around the privileged voice and stable subjectivity of the 'external' observer are swept up and broken down in a movement that no longer permits the obvious institution of self-identity between thought and reality. In this disjunctive moment, the object of the intellectual gaze – the cultures and habits of the 'natives' of local, national and global 'territories' – can no longer be confined to an obvious chart or map, and there freeze-dried as a fixed or essential component of 'knowledge' (Clifford, 1992).

To inhabit this world, both intellectually and ethically, individually and collectively, is, as Trinh T. Minh-ha puts it, to struggle to continue in its continuation (1989, 42). Here we as individuals do not dominate the situation, but rather begin to lose our initial 'selves' in a passage destined to reveal further parts of the self. It opens up the possibility of 'dislodging the inertia of the "I"' (Rovatti, 1990, 30). It leads to the release of diverse voices, an encounter with an 'other' side, an unfolding of the self, that negates the possibility of reducing diversity to the identical, to the singular source and authority of the *cogito*. Knowledge takes a holiday from the traditional ideas of truth and knowledge as unitary and transcendental entities. It travels, takes a sabbatical. Against the virility of a self-assured, strong thought, we can propose a weaker, but more extensive, transvaluation of thinking that is contaminated, heterotopic, contingent.[2]

While the intellectual condemnation of mass culture and the mass media is today more subdued, no longer as self-assured as 'the rhetorical violence that is unleashed in *Dialectic of Enlightenment*', it is nevertheless still quietly widespread (Daniel, 1992, 33). The Italian critic Franco Rella has recently pointed out that it is a line of argument based on principles that have yet to be demonstrated:

> the disappearance of the individual and the subject in the mass; the evil of technology. In the end the impression is not that of coming closer to the truth, but rather closer to a neurosis (or the diagnosis of a neurosis). (1989, 25)

Still, there remain many willing to berate the evils of mass culture, and to see in it merely an ideological façade masking the cynical logic of capital. Despite the often tortuous prose employed in unveiling the fetishist character of mass culture the conclusions are disarmingly simple. Their appeal is to a rigid obviousness in both moral and logical terms. It is this clarity that permitted the rapid slide of Adorno's judgement from the just dismissal of a particular mass politics (National Socialism) to the blind condemnation of a mass art (jazz). The verdict was as totalitarian as the totalitarianism it purported to denounce. Art, the mass media and the modern, urban culture of the day, so the argument runs, are all caught up in the infinity of commodity exchange. What other values they may have known are now completely overdetermined by this fact, reduced to the point of fetishist simulation in which 'false' values parade as 'real' ones. Rigorously argued, nothing, with the exception for Adorno of the dwindling possibilities of the art of the avant-garde, escapes this logic. At this point culture can no longer offer an alternative, only an idle diversion; it has been reduced to a technological display of human betrayal, an endless symbolisation of the extraction of surplus value. Believing itself to represent *something*, the sphere of culture actually represents nothing but the incessant variations of its own absorption in the nullifying circuits of capital.

To this we can oppose some countervailing observations. Technology is the web in which we are embedded, argues Heidegger. It is where we meet with all the ambiguities of being enframed by its languages and techniques, and where the truth of our condition is revealed in the simultaneous presence of its danger and saving power (1977). The technical reproduction that is inherent in modern mass culture involves a shattering of tradition and the secularisation of the image. This, in turn, as Benjamin goes on to elaborate, leads to a distracted reception in which we all in different ways become 'experts'. We all learn to move around inside the languages of the mass media, whether sitting at our desks denouncing them on our word processors or, later in the evening, zapping through the TV channels. This at least introduces us to the possibility of a 'metropolitan æsthetics', to a latent democratisation of the use of contemporary sounds, signs and images, and to the space for an unsuspected politics of everyday life (1969).

Opposed to the abstractions of an ideological critique of mass culture – invariably presented as a homogeneous totality, without contradictions or room for subtle, subaltern or alternative voices – are the details and differences that are historically revealed in how people go about using and inhabiting this culture, invariably domesticating and directing it in ways unforeseen by the producers of the 'culture industry'.

The critical monologue that drones on castigating contemporary culture as if it were a unique, ideological bloc subject to the rule of an unmediated, wholly rational, economic mechanism (Fredric Jameson's 'logic of late capitalism', David Harvey's 'condition of postmodernity'), is concerned with the philosophical fate of mankind (*sic*) and the alienation of MAN in the abstract.[3] It has little to say about how real women and men get by and make sense of the conditions in which they find themselves. It cannot speak to the lives, fears, hopes, passions and expressions revealed in the immediate culture of the everyday world. But what if contradictions lie not between capital and an imagined alternative or utopia, but in the very conditions of capitalist society? This is what Marx seems to be saying when he insists that the new society will emerge out of the old, as internal contradictions lead to new developments, new possibilities and a widened intercourse between those caught up in the social relations of modern capitalism (1973, 541–2). To adopt this argument is to propose a stepping away from the historical sense of intellectual mission intent on maintaining a clear distinction between culture and industry, art and commerce. For it is a perspective that insists on the awareness that industry, commerce and urbanisation are not extraneous, but rather integral, to the production of contemporary cultures, identities, possibilities, lives.

This debate runs throughout the whole course of what we might call modernity ... It was inaugurated by Romanticism around 1800, with its opposition to the mechanical body of industry (Dr Frankenstein's monster), but Romanticism itself also drew upon the separation, elaborated by Kant in the 1780s, between the rational and the æsthetic realms. This distinction rationally legitimated, and philosophically endorsed, the treatment of the sphere of culture as an independent and autonomous reality: the source of eternal values, untouched by immediate history and the dirty hands of industry, commerce and the city.

From this influential history we inherit a fundamentally transcendental view of art and culture as an atemporal, metaphysical reality, set apart from the more pressing relations and concerns of the everyday world. Whereas the argument that spills out of this rationalist containment, and floods up from below as it were, suggests an opposed, secular, more open and complex outlook. It begins with the details and different histories of popular cultures, subaltern worlds, displaced realities, and the changes induced in culture as a whole by industrialisation, urbanisation, capitalism and globalisation. Here culture, its presumed values and æsthetics, cannot be conceived as a timeless entity. As sound, brush stroke, word, image, it is caught up in the times and the restless activities of the world. Here there are no eternal values, no pure states: everything is destined to emerge, develop and die within this movement.

What we are now called upon to confront is the emergence of differences under the sign of 'homelessness'; that is, of subjects, languages, histories, acts, texts, events ... values that are forced to find their home in a world without guarantees. There emerges from here a radical shift in our understanding and interpretation of the languages of art, politics, culture and identity. These can no longer be associated with a stable epistemological point of view depending upon the presumptions of a transcendental, unique and homogeneous truth that ensures critical 'distance'. In its place there is the evocation of the idea of ontological truth that is inscribed in our being, in the continual becoming and mutation of our being in the languages in which we are formed. In this manner, for instance, the critique of consumerism comes necessarily to be based on consumerism itself, on the rules of the game and its languages of identity. In the same manner, the critique of technology is expressed through the deployment of technology ... Denied perennial positions or eternal truths, we find ourselves in shifting constellations of meaning that orbit around potential openings, interruptions, intervals – both break-downs and break-throughs – in the world, languages, histories and identities we have inherited, as we come to explore the tense truth of ambiguity.

Such an enframing of our lives suggests analyses attentive to the nuanced differences of languages and narratives that combine in writing out, simultaneously explaining and excluding, our lives. Here the commonplace, and apparently homogeneous, material of popular tastes and cultures, for example, can reveal more complex stories and ways of making sense than often credited.

As a minimum it involves, as Michel de Certeau insisted, listening to frequently overlooked activities that are hidden away in the label of the mundane, the banal, the quotidian: in other words, in the colloquial differentiation of the popular. For here we meet with activities that, while drawing upon the vocabularies of established lexicons and languages – cinema, television, music, the supermarket, the newspaper – and always remaining subject to those languages, nevertheless establish trajectories of interests and desires that are neither necessarily determined nor captured by the system in which they develop. It is this remaking, this transmutation, where translation always involves a travesty of any 'original' intent, that makes the experience of such languages and texts – the city, cinema, music: contemporary culture and the modern world – habitable; as though they offered a historical space borrowed by a transient, an immigrant, a nomad.

> The 'making' in question is a production, a *poiesis* – but a hidden one, because it is scattered over areas defined and occupied by systems of 'production' (television, urban development, commerce, etc.), and because the steadily increasing expansion of these systems no longer leaves 'consumers' any *place* in which they can indicate what they *make* or *do* with the products of these systems. To a rationalized, expansionist and at the same time centralized, clamorous and spectacular production corresponds *another* production, called 'consumption'. The latter is devious, it is dispersed, but it insinuates itself everywhere, silently and almost invisibly, because it does not manifest itself through its own products, but rather through its *ways of using* the products imposed by a dominant economic order. (1988, xii–xiii)

> And since one does not 'leave' this language, since one cannot find another place from which to interpret it, since there are therefore no separate groups of false interpretations and true interpretations, but only illusory interpretations, since in short there is no *way out*, the fact remains that we are *foreigners* on the inside – *but there is no outside*. (1988, 13–14)

In such unobserved historical passages and details, and their transitive constructions of home, we can begin to glimpse how to cut the older ideological knot between capital and culture, and so critically get beyond both the condemnations of everyday culture as ideology and its apologetic and merely populist defence.

This is to suggest that there is no exterior 'truth' to be salvaged from the immediate world of commerce and everyday popular culture: as though somehow and somewhere beneath the surface, inside the sign, there lurks a deeper and more consistent message. The argument, central to both the Marxist and Baudrillardian critique of the sign (fetishism, simulacrum), is that surfaces and appearances are the deceptive, seductive and mystifying manifestations of an underlying reality: the alienation of the human condition. The reduction of the apparent to a concealed, hidden value – the value of 'authenticity' supposedly masked by false appearances – denies the ontological reality of signs, surfaces and everyday life. It denies that they, too, are sites of sense, of meaning. To appreciate this opening, this particular possibility, means again taking a holiday from the ideological critique that has traditionally disciplined our attention.

HOLIDAYS IN JAPAN

The idea of letting go, of taking a holiday from the languages that usually position us, of drifting free from domestic meanings, is how Roland Barthes prefaces his writings on Japan: *Empire of Signs*. He refers to that *'loss of meaning* that Zen calls a *satori'*, and muses on the 'retreat of signs'. He uses his encounter with the 'Other' not to presume to explain that alterity, but rather to go beyond himself, his own language and sign culture, and thereby disturb and question the presumed stability of the symbolic order of which he is a part. Here differences remain as differences, irreducible to the same; they exist as an addition, an excess that causes 'knowledge, or the subject, to vacillate' (1982, 4).

This idea of facing the other, of acknowledging differences, and with them the diverse inscriptions that inhabit and constitute our world, is not merely a geographical encounter typical of the metropolitan intellectual. It is also a rendezvous to be found within the internal territories of our own cultures – on the 'other' side of the city, culture and languages we inhabit.

'Japan' offers the possibility of undoing our own 'reality' and displaces the usual position, or topology, of the subject, together with her or his voice and authority. What has been taken for granted, considered 'natural', hence universal, is revealed to be local and historical (1982, 6). This Barthesian awareness, to return to the earlier point, does not emerge from excavating beneath the surfaces of appearances so much as from putting surface to surface, sign to sign, and there in the lateral or horizontal plane registering the difference. These are the differences that Barthes discovers in appearances – what he calls the 'shimmer of the signifier' – as found in the ornamental and fragmented arrangement of food, in the ceremonial bow, in the painted ideogram, in the Pachinko players, in the disregard for the Western illusion of totality in the *Bunraku* theatre, in the transitory instance of the haiku and its temporary suspension of finality (what we in the West call 'meaning'): signs, as Barthes puts it in describing Tokyo, that remind us 'that the rational is merely one system among others' (1982, 33).

So, for Barthes, the plenitude of haiku, of these minimal expressions of the event, does not pertain to meaning but to language. These gestures of writing provide a space of pure fragments in which it is language itself that is celebrated in an 'exemption from meaning'. Or rather, its presence dissipates the Western desire for fullness and semantic arrest, for what is 'abolished is not meaning but any trace of finality'. There remains just a trace, a designation of words, where meaning is 'only a flash, a slash of light'. Without a centre or direction to grasp, there is just 'a repetition without origin, an event without cause, a memory without person, a language without moorings' (1982, 79–83).

Signs and language can be set free from immediate referents. This is what Barthes's particular 'Japan' permitted him to contemplate. This does not mean that we are necessarily condemned to joining Baudrillard and the cultural pessimists in announcing the end of meaning. What Barthes's text opens up is the opposite of a resigned nihilism: it proposes an excess of sense.[4] We become aware that signs can be cast loose from their moorings in one system of thought, language, culture and history and acquire other, sometimes unrecognisable, perhaps incomprehensible, ones elsewhere. Such a semiotic movement, of setting sign to sign, and appearance to appearance, on the surfaces of language and culture, does not avoid the question of significance, but rather supplements, extends and complicates it.

. . .

The city I propose to walk in is Naples: arguably an atypical metropolis, but then what city is not specific, unique?

Under Vesuvius

The city lived under Vesuvius, and its existence was therefore constantly threatened. As a consequence it participated in the diffusion of the technical and economic development of Europe in piecemeal fashion, because it was impossible to know whether the year would not be interrupted by a catastrophe.

Alfred Sohn-Rethel (1991, 21)

Now it occurred to me that perhaps this was what happened when cities died. They didn't die with a bang; they didn't die only when they were abandoned. Perhaps they died like this: when everybody was suffering, when transport was so hard that working people gave up jobs they needed because they feared the suffering of the travel; when no one had clean water or air; and no one could go walking. Perhaps cities died when they lost the amenities that cities provided, the visual excitement, the heightened sense of human possibility, and became simply places where there were too many people, and people suffered.

V. S. Naipaul (1990, 347)

Naples is a piecemeal city attached to the edge of southern Europe. It has often provided a favourite site for examining the loose ends of European society, where civil society and the state apparently wither away. For it is here that the urban web tends to come undone and expose a living museum of archaic fragments, customs and practices. Yesterday, its ruined landscapes were the source of the Romantic sublime (Goethe), or later of a disenchanted capitalism (Benjamin). Today, it attracts the gaze of anthropologists as they retreat from previous peripheries to considering Europe's own internal frontiers and the peculiar rituals of its own native populations. Yet Naples is not merely the laboratory of the archaic, or a zoo of arrested urban development. Its crumbling historical core toasting in the sun has also been abruptly interrupted by the modern skyline punctuation of a Japanese-conceived commercial and administrative centre. With its violent mixture of antiquated street rites and global design capital, Naples confronts us as an enigma. Its sphinx-like qualities, reflecting back to us what we hope, and fear, to see, reveal an unstable hubris dissected by different cultures and historical rhythms. A precarious water supply, an erratic public transport system, seventeenth-century streets and sewers blocked with the traffic of twentieth-century pollution are coupled with a fanatical private cleanliness oblivious to public filth. Although managed by capital the city seems frequently to be out of control. Only an exasperated individualism, everyone free to invent his or her own highway code, manages to leave its mark. The rational organisation of urban space, of production, labour and profit, is constantly interrupted, decomposed and deviated by innumerable pockets of mercantilism, barter, corruption and crime: the corner deal concluded on the cellular phone, black market couriers on their Vespas, the buying and selling of favours, the institutionalised bribe. This is the tangled undergrowth of another city and of a cultural formation that loses its strands in the labyrinth of kinship, street culture, local identities, popular memory and urban folklore.

To be open to this dimension, to the collective narration of identities and exchange of memories that pass under the name of 'Napoli', is clearly to abandon the possibility of conducting all these strands into a single conduit, a unique narrative able to explain such details. Of course, we can employ terms like 'uneven development' and refer to the local, national and international concatenations of mixed temporalities, of structural inequalities and the peculiarities of historical and political formations, but the particular syntax of these conditions, their 'Neapolitan' mix, can only find inconclusive explanations in these categories.

Like many Mediterranean cities, Naples refers to itself and its local hinterland long before the nation state appears in its sense of identity (Matvejevic, 1987, 1991). Even the Nativity scene becomes a Neapolitan scene: *il presepe*. The papier mâché models and ceramic figures of biblical Bethlehem are invariably populated with local markets, piazzas and pizzas. Two myths are fused into a miniaturised language of representation in which the religious and the secular, the past and the present, the distant and the immediate, the dead and the living, share the same world (Esposito, 1992). Once a capital city, Naples is now without a kingdom. Seemingly robbed of its destiny, its trajectory has stopped short. As a defunct centre, as a corpse, it is perpetually ready to 'enter into the homeland of allegory' (Benjamin, 1990, 217). The visceral gestures of self-referentiality, and the *presepe* and its local literature are only the most documented exposure of this everyday practice, continue to propose all the pathos of that loss. This is to suggest that there is no overall project or unifying design able to encompass the Neapolitan experience. It is a story that can only be caught in fragments, in the economy of disorder, in the mythical half-light of an imagined decadence.

Seen under this aspect the city is not experienced merely as a physical reality, the sum of its collective histories, memories and monuments, but more in the instance of what the Situationists referred to as psychogeography: the practice of drifting that leads to rewriting the urban text in terms of a desire that snares the unexpected, the incalculable, the situation. The value of Naples, both socially and æsthetically (and are they really divisible?), may lie not in its pretended uniqueness but in its capacity for dispersal, for losing itself and thereby escaping the predictable. Here the city does not stand for a unique, rational, firm referent, but slips through predictable schemata to become a floating signifier, drifting through a hundred interpretations, a thousand stories. It exists beyond the rude physicality of its streets in the interior architecture that provides the scaffolding of the imaginary. Still, this imaginary place, like all dream material, has a language that calls for a mode of interpretation.

Alfred Sohn-Rethel's linking of the city of Naples to the idea of catastrophe, to imminent destruction and decay, draws us into the language of the ruin, the language of the baroque. This is how Walter Benjamin, who wrote much of his book on baroque theatre in 1925 while staying on Capri and frequently visiting Naples, comments on the centrality of the ruin in the figural economy of the baroque:

> In the ruin history has physically merged into the setting. And in this guise history does not assume the form of the process of an eternal life so much as that of irresistible decay. Allegory thereby declares itself to be beyond beauty. Allegories are, in the realm of thoughts, what ruins are in the realm of things. This explains the baroque cult of the ruin. (1990, 177–8)

It is in the allegorical style of the baroque, in its insistence on ruin and decay, in the shrivelling up of history and life, that the 'maximum energy emerges due to it being a corpse' (Buci-Glucksmann, 1923, 71).

To live under the volcano, daily reminded of one's mortality: is that the key to the city's schizophrenic energy, its languages of exultation and despair, its extremes of physical violence and mental resignation? In Naples you are constantly aware of not simply living an urban experience, but also of living urban life as a problem, as an interrogation, as a provocation. This strangely echoes the American architect Frank Lloyd Wright's description of the city as 'the form universal of anxiety'.[5] It is a fact that Naples continually talks to itself, offering us the scene of endless analysis. Constructing and reassuring itself in words, the city itself is continually displaced in laments for the past and fantasies for the future, while the present passes unattended, abandoned. Self-absorbed, as though blocked in what Lacan calls the mirror stage – the glance of Narcissus that avoids the void, the abyss (Vesuvius?), the other that might challenge and decentre its uniqueness, its identity – Naples, witnessed from elsewhere, also becomes the dream-site of an imaginary city. For this city, despite all its specific details and insular claims on experience, cannot avoid acquiring a part in other stories, other idioms, other possibilities. It is ineluctably transformed from being a self-referring monument to becoming an intersection, a moment of rendezvous, a site of transit, in a wider network. Set loose from its moorings, the city begins to drift, to enter other accounts. The parochial hold on reality is compromised by economic and cultural forces that are being narrated elsewhere: in a global economy that is simultaneously signalled in the world stock exchanges and the world drug market. Inhabiting the baroque motif of the ruin, posed on the edge of Europe, on the threshold of disaster and decay, Naples perhaps becomes emblematic of the city in crisis, of the city as crisis. The self-conscious pathos of its language, its style, betrays the multiple histories and memories that swell up – 'as the rupture and revenge of signification' – into a profoundly metropolitan interrogation of the enigma of what Heidegger called the nebulous quality of life (Taussig, 1993, 5).

FROM THE STREET TO THE GLOBE

The question is whether the real development of London or Manchester can be understood without reference to India, Africa, and Latin America any more than can the development of Kingston (Jamaica) or Bombay be understood without reference to the former.

Anthony D. King (1991, 78)

There is now a world culture, but we had better make sure that we understand what this means. It is marked by an organisation of diversity rather than by a replication of uniformity. No total homogenisation of systems of meaning and expression has occurred, nor does it appear likely that there will be one any time soon. But the world has become one network of social relationships, and between its different regions there is a flow of meanings as well as of people and goods.

Ulf Hannerz (1990, 237)

The details, these psychogeographic and allegorical particularities of Neapolitan life, also represent a local twist in a far vaster tale. The formation of a city like Naples is not inseparable from its historical place in a Mediterranean, a European and, ultimately, a global economy. The clearest symbol of such 'globalisation' today is the increasing immigrant labour force that lives in the city and hinterland. In Naples the vast majority of immigrant domestic female labour employed comes from Cabo Verde, Somalia and the Philippines, while immigrant male labour employed in agriculture and street vending largely comes from West Africa. To hear Arabic in the buses, observe the turbans, veils and the vivid patterns of the cotton dresses of the women from Somalia at the post office sending money home, is to recognise an urban future destined to transform local coordinates.

The earlier linkage of the emergence of the modern city to European expansionism and colonialism, both at the 'centre' and in the 'periphery', has today been redistributed along the spatio–temporal–information axes of a world economy (1991). A direct spatial exercise of powers – from the metropolitan centre towards the colonial periphery – is increasingly being realigned amongst a proliferation of centres, nodal points and communication networks that are coordinated by the interconnected imperatives of finance, production, markets, property, leisure and life styles. The national, unilateral colonial model has been interrupted by the emergence of a transversal world that occupies a 'third space' (Bateson, Bhabha), a 'third culture' (Featherstone), beyond the confines of the nation state.[6]

There have always been inseparable connections between the world's cities. The political, cultural and economic development of an urban, economic and architectural reality such as London, New York, Madrid or Naples, on the one hand, and Singapore, New Delhi, Lima or Adelaide, on the other, cannot be understood apart from each other, or in isolation from a tendentially global economy and its cultural networks and agendas. In the landscapes of contemporary urban geography it is increasingly difficult to ignore once hidden populations, often distanced by the international division of labour, whose forgotten labour sustains the wardrobes, diets and life styles of most modern metropolises (1982). Simultaneously, at the centre semi-clandestine labour markets, employing the hands, bodies and brains of the ex-colonised, provide services for baby-sitting, house-keeping, prostitution, street vending, sweat shops and seasonal rural labour.[7] Here, at least, the living evidence of repressed histories and dead empires is not so easily consigned to oblivion: the 'natives' have come home to haunt their 'origins'. Previously identified and subjected by metropolitan power they now bring elements of the 'Third World' – the absence of health care, welfare, housing, education and employment – back to the centre. Here they share the same time, increasingly the same streets, buses and shops, as those of other members of the metropolis. These are the 16 million 'non-European people' who currently live and work in Europe ('Editorial', 1992, 3).

Urban life is being transformed under the impact of a global formation. If we are to talk of globalism, it is a globalism which refers not only to the powers and movement of capital and the international division of labour, but also to social and cultural forces, institutions, relations and ideas. Individual cities and their inhabitants increasingly exist within an inter- and transnational system of differentiated but global reference. Many may choose to mentally refuse the consequences of these processes, and racism, xenophobia and virulent nationalism are always ready to provide the languages of comprehension, but our destiny is now clearly elsewhere.

We are constantly reminded that 'social control, inequality and the constraints of social interaction in general are not simply a function of the expropriation of surplus value or economic exploitation but, perhaps more importantly, of symbolically rooted cultural practices and their reproduction' (Ulin, 1991, 80). The cosmopolitan authority, language and logic of the West European and North American intellectual, technocrat and administrator is increasingly interrogated by voices from India, Japan, Latin America, Africa. Histories, cultures, processes, texts are being read from the other side of the once presumed centre–periphery divide: from Tokyo, from Bombay, from Buenos Aires, from Lagos, from Cairo – in particular, from those cities that are setting the pattern for global urban development much more than such older settlements as, say, Paris, London or New York.

Rethinking the economic, social and cultural production of space in a shared time – 'the world' – we are pushed into contemplating cultural, economic and political forms in new terms (King, 1991, x). The co-presence of globalisation and differentiation both supplements and interrogates the limits of the nation state. We are drawn beyond ideas of nation, nationalism and national cultures, into a post-colonial set of realities, and a mode of critical thinking that is forced to rewrite the very grammar and language of modern thought in directing attention beyond the patriarchal boundaries of Eurocentric concerns and its presumptuous 'universalism'. However, this task, precisely because it does not represent the latest bulletin in the unfolding of 'progress', occurs in a para-doxical manner. For deterritorialisation produces both diasporic identities and a new fundamentalism, and here nothing is clear-cut or proceeds smoothly. Older formations stubbornly, often brutally, re-emerge and impose themselves on our differentiated but increasingly connected lives, forcing us to acknowl-edge murderous tendencies that insist on localised ethnicities, virulent nation-alisms and religious fundamentalism, as they seek to establish rigid identities, parochial communities and traditional imperatives. It is a forcible reminder that the rational 'dialectic' has broken down. No one has a complete hold on the situation. The simple clarity of binary logic fractures into the complexities of unique intensities and blood-stained details. Returning to those deadly resolutions and crippling localisms, the questions of 'whose time?', 'whose history?' is managing, identifying and interpreting, both the local street and the global clock return to us with a dramatic urgency.

Here the dark spoils of a European, and Romantic, understanding of authenticity and national identity return in the nightmare continuities of phobia and fear to carry us spiralling down into a morass of vicious sub-jectivities and inhuman communities. This is the world represented by armed Serbian nationalists 'ethnically cleansing' Bosnia-Herzegovina and claiming a street in Mostar or Sarajevo as theirs, 'because it was so in 1388' (the year before Serbia was overthrown by the Turks). That such a form of belonging and home, violently brandishing its dead version of time, also expresses needs that cannot simply be expunged from current accounts is undeniable; but that they voice a particular cultural formation and mode of identity on which we feel called to express historical and ethical judgement is also equally irrefu-table.

No Equation

... modernity resides in its ambiguous status as a demand for external guarantees inside a culture that has erased the ontological preconditions for them.

William E. Connolly (1989, 11)

The discourse of radical democracy is no longer the discourse of the universal; the epistemological niche from which 'universal' classes and subjects spoke has been eradicated, and it has been replaced by a polyphony of voices, each of which constructs its own irreducible ... identity. This point is decisive: there is no radical and plural democracy without renouncing the discourse of the universal and its implicit assumption of a privileged point of access to 'the truth'.

Ernesto Laclau and Chantal Mouffe (1985, 191–2)

Naturally, all this is a prelude, part of a reflection gathered from looking at the scene of contemporary cultural analyses, urban life, and the histories, prospects and lives that frame such work and experiences. I have tried to unpack some of the analytical baggage that is still being carried around in this landscape, and which frequently passes for critical 'common sense'. To query that language is hopefully already to reveal in the undoing other, more open, ways of engaging with our prospects. To move through such ruins, and to learn to live within them, is already to step through the gaps in the city into another place.

Notes

1. For a descriptive journey into these territories, see Maspero (1992).
2. This is to introduce the post-Nietzschean theme of 'weak-thought', most widely associated with the work of Italian philosopher Gianni Vattimo. See Vattimo (1988). For a further exploration of this trope in the context of cultural analyses, see Chambers (1990).
3. The 'logic of late capitalism' is, of course, a reference to Fredric Jameson's attempts to synthesize the world in a cartography of powers susceptible to political 'mapping' from a peerless point of view (see Jameson, 1992). Also see Meaghan Morris's brilliant and incisive review (1992) of David Harvey's *The Condition of Postmodernity* (1989).
4. For a more extensive account of Barthes's encounter with the Orient and the aperture it opens up, see Trinh T. Minh-ha (1991).
5. The expression comes from his pastoral-inspired diatribe against 'rented aggregations of hard cells on upended pavements overlooking hard pavements' (Wright, 1956, 20–1).
6. See Gregory Bateson (1944), Homi K. Bhabha (1990) and Mike Featherstone (1990).
7. 'In the early 1980s, half of all the immigrants lived in the 10 largest American cities compared to only 11 per cent of the US population as a whole. In the last twenty years, 2 million Third-World migrants from South-East Asia, the Middle East, and Latin America have moved into the Los Angeles region resulting in a major change in the ethnic, economic, and social composition of the city (in 1953, Los Angeles County was 85 per cent Anglo-Saxon; in 1983, Hispanics, Blacks and Asians comprised 50 per cent of the population)' (King 1991, 28).

12.3

ART AS CULTURAL PRODUCTION

Alan Sinfield

IDEOLOGY

Students and professors in the United States often ask me to explain cultural materialism. This is mainly because it comes up in discussions of new historicism – either as a lamentable extreme toward which new historicism declines, or as the positive vision which it fails to attain. This is partly because the success of new historicism in North America derives from its vagueness; it covers most clever work that is not celebrating the unity of the-text-on-the-page. However, cultural materialism cannot adequately be understood as a variation on new historicism. It is a response, within British Marxism and Cultural Studies, to broader historical circumstances.

The European war of 1939–45 was unprecedented in the way it involved the whole population; it was called in Britain 'the people's war'. On the right as well as the left, it was agreed that there should be no return to the conditions of the 1930s. Then there had seemed to be three kinds of future: fascism, communism, and a rejigging of capitalism to protect people against exploitation and slumps – welfare-capitalism. These three fought it out between 1917 and 1948: fascism was defeated, and Europe was divided between communism and welfare-capitalism. Both promised all the people a stake in the society, an adequate share of its resources as of right – a job, a pension or social security, a roof over your head, health-care, education. In communism these were to be secured through state management of the economy; in welfare-capitalism, by state

Extract from Alan Sinfield, *Cultural Politics – Queer Reading* (Routledge and University of Pennsylvania Press, 1994), pp. 21–39.

intervention in the capitalist economy in the manner proposed by John Maynard Keynes. In the United States, welfare-capitalism has often been imagined as socialism, but that is an index of the extent to which the Cold War wiped out the US left; actually welfare-capitalism is an attempt to ameliorate and preserve capitalism, by protecting against and compensating for its disadvantages.

It is popularly imagined that the west-European left has been crucially dismayed by the recent failure of the Soviet system. Actually, it is a long time since very many of us looked hopefully in that direction. Since the late 1950s, the west-European left has been preoccupied, whether its formal allegiance is constitutional or revolutionary, with the failure of our own system: welfare-capitalism. It seemed unable to produce either the general material wealth or the spirit of co-operative advance that had been anticipated. The good life got to be defined as more household gadgets; and the idea that we had attained, or were about to attain, the best possible society was being used by politicians to make dissidence appear unnecessary and destructive. Despite the promises of 1945, we were suffering the inefficiency and inhumanity of capitalism, of imperialism, of patriarchy.

By 1960 or so, therefore, it seemed evident that some further intervention of a socialist kind was still necessary. The first task was to define it in a way that did not run into the disadvantages we observed in the Soviet Bloc; that produced a nervousness about grappling with what was perceived as Marxism. The tougher problem was how to get an alternative program on the road. There were ample signs of social distress – crime and juvenile delinquency, strikes and bloody-mindedness, the dissolution of family and neighborhood bonds, drug abuse, racism. 'Arise ye starv'lings from your slumbers,' we cried. But for the most part they didn't – we didn't. We pondered the reasons, and deduced that people must have been got at. The revolution wasn't occurring because the continuing oppression of ordinary people was being obscured. It seemed, therefore, a failure *at the level of culture*. Hence the preoccupation, in the west-European left, with theories of ideology: that is what needs explaining.

The Frankfurt School blamed monopoly capitalism and the mass media: both high culture and traditional local cultures were being smothered, and with them any sense of individual dignity. This was widely believed (I am aware that Frankfurt School work was not a postwar, west-European product; I am referring to the way it was taken up within that situation). More interestingly, Herbert Marcuse, in his essay 'Repressive Tolerance' (1965), sought to explain the ineffectiveness of those who should have been dissident: liberals, who respected the utilitarian-bourgeois tradition. Though those values were still frequently invoked, Marcuse said, the structures of business, the military and the political system were overriding them. He summed up: 'The tolerance which is the great achievement of the liberal era is still professed and (with strong qualifications) practiced, while the economic and political process is subjected to an ubiquitous and effective administration in accordance with the predominant interests. The result is an objective contradiction between the economic and political structure on the one side, and the theory and practice of toleration on the other.' Even the exercise of such freedoms as we appear to have – such as writing to your senator – strengthens repressive tendencies 'by testifying to the existence of democratic liberties which, in reality, have changed their content and lost their effectiveness' (1969, 129, 98). The very traditions and institutions that seemed to manifest the promise of freedom were inveigling people into complicity.

Marcuse's was a humanistic Marxism, founded in the belief that our humanity is there – it just needs liberating. Such a theory could flip over, quite easily, into revolutionary optimism. In the enthusiasm of the worldwide disturbances that we call '1968' – on US campuses, in US ghettoes, in Paris, Vietnam, Czechoslovakia, Cuba, and China; in the enthusiasm of all that, Marcuse was to make that optimistic move (in *An Essay on Liberation*, 1969). The appeal of Louis Althusser's essay 'Ideology and Ideological State Appara- tuses' (trans. 1971), coming in the wake of 1968, lay in its pessimism: Althusser at least could not raise extravagant hopes. 'In order to exist', he declares, 'every social formation must reproduce the conditions of its production' (1971, 124). This means both material resources and labour power. Immediately, this is done by wages, which enable workers to keep body and soul together so that they can check in at the workplace as required. But also, workers must accept their place in the system: there must be 'a reproduction of submission to the ruling ideology for the workers, and a reproduction of the ability to manipulate the ruling ideology correctly for the agents of exploitation and repression' (127–8). People get socialized, in other words, into attitudes that facilitate maintenance of the system. Althusser's analysis here is very powerful indeed. By definition, societies that continue must be reproducing themselves ideologically as well as materi- ally; they develop ideological apparatuses to arrange this – churches, schools, the family, the law, the political system, trades unions, the communications system, cultural arrangements. If they did not, they would die out or be transformed. Of course, there are directly repressive apparatuses as well – the police, courts, prisons, army. But in our societies – and to the west-European left this was the problem – people seem mostly to do what they are supposed to do. That compliance is what Althusser is addressing.

Further, this theory is not to be understood, in humanist manner, as the free individual being swayed by ideology. For Althusser, there is no essential core of irrepressible humanity in the individual. He regards ideology as ultimately con- stitutive. We are born into it, come to consciousness within it; it is confirmed, continually, in the practices of everyday life. Our subjectivities – the very idea that we *have* subjectivities – all this is constructed in ideology. Hence we recognize ourselves as the kinds of people ideology needs us to be. The social formation reproduces itself by constituting subjects who 'work by themselves', says Althusser. There are '"bad subjects" who on occasion provoke the inter- vention of one of the detachments of the (repressive) State apparatus. But the vast majority of (good) subjects work all right "all by themselves", that is, by ideo- logy' (169). So ideology does not deceive us, we discover our selves through it.

Now, this argument addresses powerfully the question of why there is not more dissidence, but at the cost of making it hard to see how there can be any dissidence at all. For if our subjectivities are constituted within a language and social system that is already imbued with oppressive constructs of class, race, gender, and sexuality, then how can we expect to see past that, to the idea of a fairer society, let alone struggle to achieve it? How, indeed, could Althusser see what he did?

At this point, new historicism converges on Althusser, with respect to its preoccupation with what I call the 'entrapment model' of ideology and power. This model claims that even attempts to challenge the system help to maintain it; in fact, those attempts are distinctively complicit, insofar as they help the dominant to assert and police the boundaries of the deviant and the permissible. In the entrapment model, any move seems to have been anticipated by the power system – you only dig yourself in deeper. As Don Wayne puts it, new historicism has often shown 'how different kinds of discourse intersect, contradict, destabilise, cancel, or modify each other ... seek[ing] to demonstrate how a dominant ideology will give a certain rein to alternative discourses, ultimately appropriating their vitality and containing their oppositional force' (1987, 795).[1] Dissidence plays into the hands of containment.

Attitudes toward the entrapment model constitute a principal effective difference between cultural materialism and new historicism. For west-European Marxism and cultural materialism, the importance of Althusser and the entrapment model was manifest, as a way of theorizing the power of dominant ideologies. Even more important, though, was theorizing a way out of that – theorizing the scope for dissidence. This, centrally, is what Raymond Williams was concerned with in his later work. In the 1950s Williams elaborated an influential socialist-humanist protest against the cultural degradation which he associated with capitalism. This protest was parallel with Frankfurt School work, but maintained also a belief in the validity of 'lived experience' and an optimism about the potential of welfare-capitalism. After 1968, and specifically the inadequacies of the Labour administrations of 1964–70, Williams turned to the non-Stalinist Marxist tradition, in the writings of V. N. Vološinov and Antonio Gramsci, seeking a more theoretical and materialist understanding of ideology. Cultural materialism is his term.

In his essay 'Base and Superstructure in Marxist Cultural Theory' (1973), Williams argued against the tendency in Marxist analysis to regard culture as a mere effect and reflection of the economic organization. He believed this tendency derived from an inadequate conception of the 'productive forces' in society, overlooking 'the primary production of society itself, and of men themselves, the material production and reproduction of real life.' Thus far, Williams is close to Althusser, who in the course of just such an argument about the reproduction of people, posits 'a "relative autonomy" of the superstructure with respect to the base' and 'a "reciprocal action" of the superstructure on the base' (Williams, 1980, Althusser, 1971, 130). However,

Williams turns then to Gramsci's work on hegemony as a way of analyzing not only the power of ideology as 'deeply saturating the consciousness of a society', but also the scope for dissidence. 'We have to emphasize that hegemony is not singular; indeed that its own internal structures are highly complex, and have continually to be renewed, recreated and defended; and by the same token, that they can be continuously challenged and in certain respects modified,' says Williams (37–8). So while there is a 'dominant culture' – 'the central, effective and dominant systems of meanings and values, which are not merely abstract but which are organized and lived' (38) – its dominance depends on continuous processes of adjustment, reinterpretation, incorporation, dilution. And, furthermore, these processes are conducted in relation to 'alternative' and 'oppositional', 'residual' and 'emergent' cultural formations (40–42). The dominant may tolerate, repress, or incorporate these other formations, but that will be a continuous, urgent, and often strenuous project.

The relevant elaboration of the theory of ideology in response to the challenge of Althusser and the entrapment model, then, is this: conflict and contradiction stem from the very strategies through which dominant ideologies strive to contain the expectations that they need to generate. Despite their power, dominant ideological formations are always, in practice, under pressure from diverse disturbances. These disturbances do not derive from our irrepressible humanity, but from pressures and strains which the social order inevitably produces within itself, even as it attempts to secure itself. The successes and failures of dissidence in our own situations, therefore, derive not from ineluctable laws, making compliance the condition of any human society, but from relative strengths and weaknesses in determinate historical circumstances.

In recent years the question of dissidence versus containment has often been approached through the work of Michel Foucault. He has been taken as the theorist of entrapment, and is often used to underwrite new historicist concerns. This is because he writes: 'Where there is power, there is resistance, and yet, or rather consequently, this resistance is never in a position of exteriority in relation to power.' However, Foucault was a committed and active leftist, and his project here has to be understood within the framework I have been identifying. When he says there is 'no single locus of great Refusal, no soul of revolt, source of all rebellions, or pure law of the revolutionary,' he is repudiating Marcuse's belief that the events of 1968 amounted to 'the Great Refusal' and were grounds for anticipating the end of capitalist repression. (Foucault, 1978, 95–6; Marcuse, 1972, 9). (Similarly, Foucault's insistence that sex is produced, rather than repressed, in our societies is formulated partly with reference to Marcuse's ideas of sexual liberation.) Like Althusser, Foucault rejects the idea of an essential core of irrepressible humanity; like the British left, he is trying to locate a credible theory of dissidence in the wake of such enthusiasms and disappointments. There is, he says, 'a plurality of resistance'. They are 'distributed in irregular fashion: the points, knots, or focuses of resistance are spread over time and space at varying densities, at times mobilizing groups or individuals in a definitive way' (96).

This argument does not, Foucault insists, imply an entrapment model: these resistances are not 'only a reaction or rebound, forming with respect to the basic domination an underside that is in the end always passive, doomed to perpetual defeat.' On the contrary, even a discourse of stigma may be thrown into a reverse signification. Homosexuality, says Foucault, was elaborated in nineteenth-century legal, medical, and sexological discourses, making possible new forms of control. But this very process gave a voice to sexual dissidence: 'Homosexuality began to speak in its own behalf, to demand that its legitimacy or "naturality" be acknowledged, often in the same vocabulary, using the same categories by which it was medically disqualified.' Deviancy returns from abjection by deploying just those terms which relegated it in the first place. There may be 'great radical ruptures', occasionally; but it is 'the strategic codification of these points of resistance that makes a revolution possible'(1978, 96, 101; see Laclau and Mouffe, 1985, 105–44). This is an apposite message for the west-European left: there is no simple way through, but every reason to go on trying.

ART AND CULTURAL PRODUCTION

Despite their differences, Marcuse and Althusser both accord a uniquely privileged role to art. The Frankfurt School believed that the full humanity withheld from people under capitalism will obtrude nonetheless, though in oblique forms, as an intuition of utopia; and especially in the fullness of artworks. Fredric Jameson finds 'the Utopian impulse' even in the representations of leisure-class people in Marcel Proust's *A la recherche du temps perdu*; he takes them to reflect 'in the most distorted way the possibilities of a world in which alienated labour will have ceased to exist.' Jameson grants that 'the Proustian leisure class is a caricature of that classless society: how could it be otherwise? Yet since it is (at least in Proust's society) the only leisure culture which exists, it alone can serve as a source of concrete images of what such a Utopia might be like' (1971, 153–4). To which one might reply: If that's what utopia is going to be like, it's just as well we have plenty of time to think it over.

Althusser also accorded a special role to art and literature. It is not true, as at least two recent studies have asserted, that he thought of them as ideological state apparatuses. '*I do not rank real art among the ideologies,*' Althusser declares. Art '*alludes* to reality'; it 'makes us *see* ... the *ideology* from which it is born, in which it bathes, from which it detaches itself as art.' It does this by effecting an '*internal distantiation*'. Through its formal properties, art draws attention to the ideology in which it is constructed; thus it occupies a distinctive position between ideology and Marxist knowledge (1971, 203–4). This theory is anticipated by the Russian formalists and by Bertolt Brecht (in the *Verfremdumseffekt*), but Althusser derives it from Pierre Macherey's *Theory of Literary Production* (1966). Macherey argues that literary language 'imitates the everyday language which is the language of ideology. We could offer a provisional definition of literature as being characterized by this power of parody. Mingling the real uses of language in an endless confrontation, it concludes by *revealing* their truth.' Thus literature *'reveals* the gaps in ideology' (1978, 59–60). These ideas were very influential in the early phases of 'theory' in Britain – for instance in Colin MacCabe's essay 'Realism and the Cinema: Notes on Some Brechtian Theses' (*Screen*, 1974), Terry Eagleton's *Criticism and Ideology* (1976), Terry Hawkes's *Structuralism and Semiotics* (1977), and Catherine Belsey's *Critical Practice* (1980).

The flaw in the ideas of Marcuse, Althusser, and Macherey, from a cultural materialist standpoint, is that they assume that we all know what art and literature are ('I mean authentic art, not works of an average or mediocre level,' Althusser avers, unhelpfully). They carry over, virtually, the bourgeois-liberal notion. Marx, indeed, had done this, and most British socialists; the task, as they saw it, was to redefine the roles of an apparently-known entity – art – within a socialist theory (Althusser, 1971, 204). There was a further, partly alternative, tradition concerned with folk art, working-class writing, and music hall, but it appeared fatally weakened by the mass media. Williams in *Culture and Society* (1958) refuses the idea of 'proletarian' art, on the ground that 'the traditional popular culture of England was, if not annihilated, at least fragmented and weakened by the dislocations of the Industrial Revolution,' so that what remains 'is small and narrow in range'. He asserts the relevance of the central culture to everyone: 'The body of intellectual and imaginative work which each generation receives as its traditional culture is always, and necessarily, something more than the product of a single class' (1961, 307–8). Everyone, therefore, is entitled to share privileges hitherto appropriated by the upper classes. This is the welfare-capitalist move.

'The crucial theoretical break,' Williams wrote in 1977 – and it was a break for him too, which made it additionally significant – 'is the recognition of "literature" as a specializing social and historical category.' Macherey also came to see this, in an essay written with Etienne Balibar, in 1978 (Williams, 1977, 53, 54–5; Macherey and Balibar, 1978, 4–12).[2] In *Marxism and Literature*, Williams presents a history of literature that is not a historical situating of texts already-agreed to be literary, but a history of the concept 'Literature', showing it to be the product of economic, social, and political changes running through from the eighteenth century. Insistence on the processes through which a text achieves its current estimation is the key move in cultural materialism, and a principal difference in emphasis from new historicism.

For not all societies have art and literature. Very many value specially some objects and texts, usually in relation to religious and social hierarchies, and most ornament and elaborate some objects and texts far beyond usefulness. But they do not regard them as 'art' and 'literature'. To be sure, we have assimilated to our concepts diverse objects and texts from those other cultures – religious paintings are put into galleries, churches become artworks. But that is our doing. Literature is not an objective category of value, but a discourse we have been constructing – in order to assert, and contest, certain ranges of value in our cultures. Marx, famously, wondered why ancient Greek art remains potent for us; is it not an instance of art transcending historical conditions? Marx (evidently at a loss) thought it might be because the Greeks lived in 'the historic childhood of humanity' and hence exercise 'an eternal charm' (Marx, 1973, 110–11).[3] Cultural materialists say: Greek art is valued while we find it useful as a way of handling our own dilemmas and maintain an ongoing discourse that appropriates it. Actually, of course, the classics haven't been lasting so well lately. If you raise the question of the Greeks with students today you probably get: So ... erm ... which Greeks were those, exactly? That is because most people have found more convenient bodies of work – other writings – around which to conduct current cultural contests.

A reappraisal of operations then follows. When we ask: What are the truly literary qualities? we should ask also: Who says these are literary qualities, and why? Not just: What is it about this text that makes it literary? but: What is it in the social organization that makes some people regard this text as literary? Literature becomes one set of practices within the range of cultural production; a 'discourse', we might say, meaning the working assumptions of those involved in those practices, together with the institutions that sustain them. Notions of literature transcending society, history, and politics then appear, in themselves, as ideological maneuvers. And study of literature, like study of other modes of cultural production, will attend to how it functions in the social order – considering the kinds of human possibilities that it promotes, and may be made to promote; how it acts to sustain the prevailing power relations, and affords opportunity for dissidence and new understanding.

For many younger Englit academics, this reappraisal offered an exciting prospect. The expansion of higher education in the 1960s, we may now see, allowed into humanities teaching too many bright, upwardly-mobile people, who passed tests in Englit (we knew who wanted his pound of flesh), but whose class background had not conferred on them an inbred sensitivity to art; and whose student culture was organized, typically, around cinema, beat poetry, rock music, and the peace movement. At first this disjunction didn't notice too much, because the old guard was still very much in charge, because academia was becoming more of a profession and less of a gentlemanly hobby anyway, and because we worked hard at ventriloquizing establishment culture. This mimicry was often uncomfortable, producing a self-division between the initial class culture of family and neighborhood, the student culture of electronic reproduction and political activism, and the old, establishment culture. But we accepted, by and large, a Marcusean cultural politics: modern societies inhibit creativity, literature is creative, and so social progress means (among other things) having more literature.

Political disappointments, focused by the events of 1968, made this increasingly inadequate. Then, suddenly, the Women's Movement showed that the alleged universality of quality culture was, in large part, male presumption. In 1979, within a decade of Germaine Greer's *Female Eunuch* and Kate Millett's *Sexual Politics*, Elaine Showalter distinguished two kinds of currently burgeoning work. One kind considers how 'the hypothesis of a female reader changes our apprehension of a given text, awakening us to the significance of its sexual codes'; the other investigates 'woman as the producer of textual meaning' (1986, 128). It is salutary to recall, now, how far such topics were from customary critical procedures. Feminism created space for other kinds of question. We saw that we didn't, after all, have to spend our psychic energy on ever more ingenious explanations of why Shakespeare on Shylock, or Joseph Conrad on Blacks, or D. H. Lawrence on women, or Alexander Pope on Sporus and effeminacy, is really expressing a profound universal truth.

Drawing attention to such instances provoked violent and irrational responses in the establishment, so we knew we were onto something. From here, one route was into Cultural Studies. Initially this meant working-class culture, past and present; it was pursued notably by upwardly mobile boys who had been doing their schoolwork while the other kids were hanging out on the block, and consequently had made it through the academic system. They turned back from the sissified high-cultural tradition, toward the rough boys who had harassed them on their way home from school; somewhat romantically, they wondered how far such behavior might amount to a form of resistance. From this vein, Stuart Hall and his associates at the Centre for Contemporary Cultural Studies at the University of Birmingham quarried principal themes and theories in cultural materialism. The other route was to hang on and hijack Englit, enjoying the aggro and believing that it is a significant site of struggle. In fact, the choice of text doesn't matter nearly as much as what you do with it; the history of literary criticism shows, conclusively, that it is all too common to be stupid and insensitive about *King Lear*, and quite possible to be generous and thoughtful about *Some Like It Hot*.

THE POLITICS OF LITERATURE

In the first enthusiasm of political criticism, literature and Shakespeare especially were deplored by some as the conduit of everything reactionary – capital, patriarchy, nation, and empire. After all, Margaret Thatcher's chancellor, Nigel Lawson, did co-opt Shakespeare as 'a Tory, without any doubt', on the basis of Ulysses's order speech in *Troilus and Cressida* and 'the Tory virtues, the Roman virtues' in *Coriolanus*.[4] Shakespeare is widely used in politics and the heritage business to signify Englishness; he's what the English have left to feel proud about.

However, the idea that literature is promoted in order to strengthen the forces of reaction is too close to Althusser, in the sense of assuming too much ideological coherence and purpose. As Williams observes, classes are not culturally monolithic. Within them, groups may be rising or falling, and there may be alternative affiliations, in religion or sexuality for instance, that are not characteristic of the class as a whole; they produce class fractions (Williams discusses William Godwin and his circle, the pre-Raphaelites and Bloomsbury) (1961, 73–81). In fact, although literary culture has often been broadly complicit with establishment values, we don't actually expect our rulers, in business, government, or the military, to have a sensitive apprehension of literary values; usually they despise them. Literature has often been a dissident formation, of a particular kind. Since the late eighteenth century, when the French Revolution, land enclosures, the factory system, and urbanization helped to stimulate the Romantic movement, the middle class has thrown up a dissident fraction partly hostile to the hegemony of that class. The line runs through the pre-Raphaelites, the decadent and aesthetic movements, Fabianism, Bloomsbury, modernism, public (i.e., private-) school communists, Leavisism, various new lefts, feminisms, peace movements, the green movement. In conjunction with such middle-class, dissident movements, art and literature have been constituted (along with the spirit, nature, personal religion, intimate and family relations) as 'the human', in a broad opposition to mechanical, urban, industrial and commercial organization in the modern world. Middle-class dissidence sets culture against the brutality of the system.

The weakness of this dissidence is that it starts from an acknowledgment of the priority of the utilitarian analysis as the first term in the argument. It accepts that art is no good at addressing the real world of material affairs (that's why it is provocative to say that Shakespeare is political); art, it says, is the special province of the human, the spiritual, the personal. Thus it accepts the binary opposition that includes its own subordination. And, by so much, it is discouraged from addressing the main determinants of events, which are not the human, the spiritual and the personal, but the institutional power of big business, the military, and government. Nevertheless, middle-class dissidence has been and is a valid political formation in its own right, and it is a mistake to imagine that political rectitude is the prerogative of more obviously oppressed groups.

The embarrassment of middle-class cultural dissidence is that it is gendered; there is something 'feminine' about it. 'Manliness' is celebrated as the inspiration of industry, business, the military, and empire; and art finds itself, in counterpart, in a feminine stance. When Hermann Goering reaches for his gun, we reach for our culture. Consider Matthew Arnold's phraseology: he sets humanist sweetness and light against the philistines and the barbarians. The latter two may be vulgar, but they do sound like real men. Tennessee Williams found writing a refuge when he was young – 'From being called a sissy by the neighborhood kids, and Miss Nancy by my father, because I would rather read books in my grand-father's large and classical library than play marbles and baseball and other normal kid games' (1972, 3–4). Literary dissidence accepts – in the main very gingerly – a touch of the feminine. Its invocation of a 'human' protest depends on a strategic deployment of effeminacy: of culture against brutality, the spirit against the system, style against purpose, personal emotion against compulsion. Hence the commonplace that the great writer is androgynous. There musn't be too much of the 'wrong' sex, though. The trick in artistic dissidence is to appropriate sufficient of the radical aura of androgyny, without more than is necessary of the disabling stigma. The great writer embraces something of the feminine, it is often said – but not too much.

None of this has been to the advantage of women. Effeminacy ... is a misogynist construct whereby the sexuality of men is policed through the accusation of sliding back from the purposeful reasonableness that is supposed to constitute manliness, into the laxity and weakness conventionally attributed to women. Englit and literary culture have depended on an effeminacy which they also need to disavow, and hence the derogation of the writing and reading of women. In the eighteenth and nineteenth centuries, women were regarded as the natural producers of culture; it seemed an extension of their domestic and nurturing responsibilities. They contributed hugely to imaginative writing and, as the larger body of readers, arbitrated upon literary taste. The fashionable mid-nineteenth century writer Nathaniel Willis observed: 'It is the women who read. It is the women who are the tribunal of any question aside from politics or business. It is the women who give or withhold a literary reputation' (cit. Douglas, 1978, 122). Again, more enthusiastically: 'literature', Jessie Boucherette remarked, 'is followed, as a profession, by women, to an extent far greater than our readers are at the moment aware of. Magazines of the day are filled by them; one of the oldest and best of our weekly periodicals owes two-thirds of its content to their pens.' As Mary Poovey comments, even if such opinions were not wholly accurate, it is important that they were 'widely held' (1984, 124). The access of women to literary culture 'was due of course to the extreme cheapness of its professional requirements,' Virginia Woolf noted. 'Books, pens and paper are so cheap, reading and writing have been, since the eighteenth century at least, so universally taught in our class, that it was impossible for any body of men to corner the necessary knowledge or to refuse admittance, except on their own terms, to those who wished to read books or to write them' (1977, 103).

Through the nineteenth century, there was a spate of awkward male repudiations and negotiations. Charles Kingsley – author of *The Water Babies* – in his 'Thoughts on Shelley and Byron' (1853) declared that 'the age' is 'an effeminate one', and that this may be seen from the popular preference for Shelley over Byron. Kingsley finds in Byron 'the sturdy peer proud of his bull neck and his boxing, who kept bears and bull-dogs, drilled Greek ruffians at Missolonghi, and "had no objection to a pot of beer"'; all this went, it seems, with a strong sense of moral law. Of course, we know now that Byron had sexual relations with both women and men; the point is not what he did or didn't do, but the need for literary culture to set boundaries between itself and the unacceptably effeminate. The bad opposite of Byron, in Kingsley's view, is Shelley: his nature 'is utterly womanish. Not merely his weak points, but his strong ones, are those of a woman. Tender and pitiful as a woman; and yet, when angry, shrieking, railing, hysterical as a woman. The physical distaste for meat and fermented liquors, coupled with the hankering after physical horrors, are especially feminine' (1980, 43–4, 47, 51).[5] It is in the nature of such disavowals that they must continually be repeated. Often it was asserted that only false literature is feminine; in 1870 Alfred Austin lamented that whereas great art is 'manly', those were 'feminine, timorous, narrow, domesticated' times, and hence inclined to produce feminine poetry (1987, 120, 124).

Part of the project of literary modernism, as Sandra M. Gilbert and Susan Gubar have shown, was to repudiate nineteenth-century forbears generally as effeminate. T. E. Hulme complained that 'imitative poetry springs up like weeds, and women whimper and whine of you and I alas, and roses, roses all the way. It becomes the expression of sentimentality rather than of virile thought' (cit. Gilbert and Gubar, 1988, 154). Henry James, Ann Douglas points out, felt he had to insist 'to the reading public, and himself, that fiction, the traditional province of women, be accorded all the seriousness of history, the customary province of men' (1978, 314). However, the boundary still could not be secured; the symbolist vein runs through – observe, for instance, the critical difficulty in deciding at what point W. B. Yeats's poetry becomes acceptably 'modern'.

The anxiety about effeminacy was exacerbated by the wish to establish English Literature as the kind of thing that might properly be studied in universities. If it was soppy, girls' stuff, you couldn't plausibly offer it as an academic discipline. This, I suggest, was the abiding factor in the maneuverings of literary criticism in the first half of this century. Irving Babbitt lamented in 1908 that 'men of business' regard poetry as 'a pretty enough thing for our wives and daughters' while men take science courses and women literary courses. The latter, 'indeed, are known in some of these institutions as "sissy" courses. The man who took literature too seriously would be suspected of effeminacy. The really virile thing to be is an electrical engineer. One already sees the time when the typical teacher of literature will be some young dilettante who will interpret Keats and Shelley to a class of girls' (1908, 118–19). Babbitt found that 'the more vigorous and pushing teachers of language feel that they must assert their manhood by philological research' – though this was unnecessary, he believed, because the true humanist makes 'a vigorous and virile application of ideas to life', his mind being 'assimilative in the active and masculine sense' (119, 133, 135). In England, the project of F. R. Leavis was to make literature fit for a man to study. Once again, Shelley comes off badly. He is accused of 'tender, caressing, voluptuous effects', and of 'the conventional bathos of album poeticizing, not excluding banalities about ... the sad lot of woman'. Leavis's not-Shelley is Wordsworth: he evinces 'emotional discipline, critical exploration of his experience, pondered valuation and maturing reflection' (1936, 222, 221, 212). Much more manly; but the distinction is still not very safe. 'I wandered lonely as a cloud / That floats on high o'er vales and hills': William Wordsworth. It's nice, but not all *that* manly.

Professional Englit systematically disqualified or ignored all but a few women authors. In the view of the men who dominated Englit, this was a small price for keeping imputations of effeminacy at bay. By the 1970s when feminists challenged orthodox assumptions, it seemed that women had contributed little of significance to writing. These days we have theory, which of course is really hunky. Harold Bloom, for instance, imagines literature passing from father to son in an Oedipal romance uncontaminated by female mediation.

The thought that literature is unmanly has been more worrying and more marked in the United States because of the frontier tradition; it is un-American not to be manly. Further, writers are reckoned to have contributed in a major way to the whole idea of being 'American'. 'The American has a duty beyond and above that of inventing an anti-classical form,' William Carlos Williams wrote, 'that of honoring his country and its language' – of making 'Americans' from diverse peoples (cit. Fielder, 1967, 263–4). Walt Whitman seemed to have got it right in the nineteenth century: he celebrated a 'manly love' that invoked both the frontier tradition and the prospect of a democratic future. In fact, Whitman virtually made poetry possible for 'Americans' (as Hemingway was to do with the novel). To Whitmanians, Leslie Fiedler explained in 1964, 'being American means despising the culture of Europe, indeed, all high culture, finally the very notion of culture itself' (1967, 223; see Pease, 1985).

Even so, the question about whether Whitman had 'feminine traits' had been raised, for instance by Havelock Ellis in his *Sexual Inversion* (1897). Ellis's principal witness was John Addington Symonds – who, not content with hijacking Shakespeare's *Venus and Adonis*, had tried for eighteen years to get Whitman to admit that there is sexual love between men in his Calamus poems. The evidence appears inconclusive. Consider this letter from an associate of Whitman, which Ellis prints: 'I knew Walt Whitman personally. To me Mr. Whitman was one of the most robust and virile of men, extraordinarily so. He was from my standpoint not feminine at all, but physically masculine and robust. The difficulty is that a virile and strong man who is poetic in temperament, ardent and tender, may have phases and moods of passion and emotion which are apt to be misinterpreted' (1936, 57; see 51–6). Observe the difficulty: insofar as Whitman is poetic, he IS effeminate, after all – but not, of course, in an unmanly way.

These anxieties became unavoidable with the popularization of psychoanalysis in the mid-twentieth century. Mark van Doren attacked Whitman in 1935 in an essay, 'Walt Whitman, Stranger' – the title already has the poet cast out from the community of decent 'Americans'. Whitman has appeared 'robust and masculine, a representative male', van Doren says. But actually he was 'fastidious, eccentric and feminine', too interested in clothes, and given to wearing 'shirts with lace-edged collars, opening on a fine neck which he regularly bathed with eau de cologne and which he set off with a large pearl. He was a good cook, and during the Civil War, of course, he was a nurse. So, as time has gone on, he has been recognized as the inverted individual that in one degree or another he was ... There would be no good reason for speaking of this,' van Doren adds, 'were it not that Whitman has been at such pains to put himself forward as a representative or normal American' (1968, 71–3). That was the rub: the very writers who seemed to have created America had in fact been un-American – subversives planting queer passions in the American identity.

President Kennedy told his countrymen and women: 'we have thought of the artist as an idler and a dilettante and of the lover of the arts as somehow sissy or effete. We have done both an injustice' (cit. Fielder, 1967, 273). Kennedy didn't mean that it is all right to be sissy and effete, but that art has been wrongly linked to all that. Hence the notoriety of Allen Ginsberg, who takes up the Whitman manner while refusing to accept that either homosexuality or communism is shameful. 'It's true I don't want to join the Army,' he writes, but 'America I'm putting my queer shoulder to the wheel' (1959, 34). That was not what America had expected or wanted. And it doesn't want people like Ginsberg in the army.

TEXTS AND SILENCES

Thus far I have considered mainly how the cultural materialist will address cultural institutions. He or she will be equally interested in reading texts. The traditional practice of Englit – in fact its virtual *raison d'être* – has been helping the text into an acceptable coherence by supplying feasible ways of smoothing over gaps and silences. If the words scripted for Hamlet or Iago seem not to explain their actions to the satisfaction of the modern reader, you can imagine aspects of their characters that will help them into sense. If push comes to shove, and the poet says something right over the top, such as '"Beauty is truth, truth beauty," – that is all / Ye know on earth, and all ye need to know,' you can declare that Keats didn't really mean it, he was using irony and paradox.

It is axiomatic in cultural materialism, as generally in poststructuralist theory, that no text, literary or otherwise, can contain within its project all the potential significance that it must release in pursuance of that project. Closure is always inadequate. The complexity of the social formation and the multiaccentuality of language combine to produce an inevitable excess of meaning. Macherey theorized this back in 1966. 'When we explain the work, instead of ascending to a hidden centre which is the source of life (the interpretive fallacy is organicist and vitalist), we perceive its actual de-centred-ness ... The literary work gives the measure of a difference, reveals a determinate absence, resorts to an eloquent silence' (1978, 79). It is a technical point, almost: every inside is defined by its outside. The text cannot be self-sufficient, an ideal whole. Without gaps, silences, and absences – that which the text is not – it would not exist; they frame it. They inform us of 'the precise conditions for the appearance of an utterance, and thus its limits, giving its real significance' (86). This argument is continuous with the one about how ideology cannot but allow dissidence: all stories comprise within themselves the ghosts of the alternative stories they are trying to suppress.

This theory licenses two cultural materialist procedures. First, it supersedes traditional forms of the text/context dichotomy. History, Macherey shows us, is not in an external relation to the work; 'it is present in the work, in so far as the emergence of the work required this history, which is its only principle of reality' (93).

> Thus, it is not a question of introducing a historical explanation which is stuck onto the work from outside. On the contrary, we must show a sort of splitting within the work: this division is *its* unconscious, in so far as it possesses one – the unconscious which is history, the play of history beyond its edges, encroaching on those edges: this is why it is possible to trace the path which leads from the haunted work to that which haunts it. (94)

The problem with this formulation is that Macherey is inclined still, at this date, to counterpose literature and history (or ideology); 'the reverse side of what is written will be history itself,' he adds. Cultural materialism generally goes one stage further, arguing (1) that any text may be read deconstructively, and (2) that everything is 'history itself'.

Second, Macherey legitimates readings that will not respect the ostensive project of the text. It is not a matter of catching out the author, he insists: 'the work is not at fault in relation to another work in which the absences would be made good, the insufficiencies remedied' (128). True; but in a context where one's colleagues are asserting that Shakespeare has a profound intuitive insight into what love between women and men is really about, it is provocative to observe that Olivia in *Twelfth Night* falls improbably silent at just the moment when anything she might plausibly say would disrupt the normalizing patriarchal closure at the end of that play. Or, when it is widely supposed that Macbeth's rule of Scotland represents an aberrant refusal of 'natural' sociopolitical relations, it is provocative to observe that the Scottish state is as violent under its 'good' and 'legitimate' monarchs as it is under the usurper (see Sinfield, 1992, 64, 74, 95–108). The silences of the text manifest moments at which its ideological project is under special strain. For as Nicos Poulantzas observes, 'ideology has the precise function of hiding the real contradictions and of *reconstituting* on an imaginary level a relatively coherent discourse (1973, 207). Traditionally, critics read for coherence; cultural materialists read for incoherence. Macherey anticipates this approach in his essay on Tolstoy. If the text may be said to be a mirror, he says, it is a selective one. 'The mirror selects, it does not reflect everything. The selection itself is not fortuitous, it is symptomatic; it can tell us about the nature of the mirror. We already know the reasons for this selectivity; Tolstoy's version of his age is incomplete because of his personal and ideological relation to it' (120).

Cultural materialists say that canonical texts have political projects, and should not be allowed to circulate in the world today on the assumption that their representations of class, race, ethnicity, gender and sexuality are simply authoritative. We don't mind texts having political projects, of course; we believe that every representation, with its appeal for recognition – It is like *this*, isn't it? – is political. But we think the politics should be up for discussion, and that textual analysis should address it . . .

A HANDY TEST FOR MANLINESS?

In the meantime, men of letters may be reassured to hear of a tidy test for manliness – according to Havelock Ellis and other early sexologists. 'The frequent inability of male inverts to whistle was first pointed out by Ulrichs,' Ellis says, 'and Hirschfield has found it in 23 percent. Many of my cases confess to this inability.' 'Inverted women', conversely, 'are very often good whistlers; Hirschfield even knows two who are public performers in whistling' (1936, 291, 256; see also 110, 182, 190–1). John Addington Symonds, the hijacker of *Venus and Adonis*, took up the idea: 'My muscular build was slight, I could not throw a ball or stone like other boys. And, oddly enough, I could not learn to whistle like them. And yet I was by no means effeminate.' In *Antony and Cleopatra*, our manly hero finds himself stood up by Cleopatra: 'Antony, / Enthron'd i' the market place, did sit alone, / Whistling to the air' (1984, 85; Shakespeare, 1962, I. ii. 214–16). He was a real man (there may be a research topic here).

Unfortunately the test is not altogether reliable. For instance, Ellis's case-history F.R. (I don't think this can be F. R. Leavis): 'His tastes are chiefly of a literary character, and he has never had any liking for sports'; he thinks he has 'a feminine mind in a male body'. Yet F.R. 'is able to whistle' (95). It just won't add up. Then there is T.D. At the age of ten he formed attachments to other boys, he says, such as 'Shelley speaks of as preceding love in ardent natures.' Now, Shelley of course is a suspicious character, so no wonder T.D. grew up to 'derive great pleasure from all literary and pictorial art and architecture', show 'facility in writing personal lyrical verse', and love other guys. Yet T.D. 'can whistle easily and well' (118–19). Even so, Ellis evidently thinks, it would be a pity to relinquish the idea. After all, Shelley, no less, 'was unable to whistle, though he never gave an indication of inversion; but he was a person of somewhat abnormal and feminine organisation . . .' (291).

NOTES

1. See also Howard and O'Connor, 'Introduction' (1987); Wayne (1987); Cohen (1987); Montrose (1989); and Liu (1989).
2. See also Williams (1976, 150–4); Bennett (1979); Eagleton (1983).
3. Cf. Eagleton (1976, 10–13); Macherey (1978, 70–1); Williams (1977, 52).
4. Quoted by Margot Heinemann (Dollimore and Sinfield, eds, 1985, 203). I argue in *Faultlines* (1992, ch. 10) that bardic authority has been hijacked in distinctive ways in the United States.
5. I am grateful to David Alderson for drawing my attention to this essay.

ANNOTATED BIBLIOGRAPHY

Bourke, Joanna. *Working-Class Cultures in Britain, 1890–1960: Gender, Class, and Ethnicity*. London, 1994.

Drawing upon a variety of historical approaches and methods, Bourke examines the construction of class within the intimate contexts of the body, the home, the marketplace and the nation in order to address the subjective identity of the working class in Britain through seven decades of intense social, cultural and economic change. In addition to arguing that class essentially functions as a social and cultural rather than an institutional or political phenomenon, Bourke explores the significant roles of gender and ethnicity and our conceptions of class. Bourke supplements her survey with discussion about the manner in which historians use evidence to understand change, as well as with several useful chronologies, statistics and tables of interest to cultural and literary critics alike.

Chambers, Iain. *Migrancy, Culture, Identity*. London, 1994.

Chambers explores the ways in which our senses of place and identity shift as we traverse myriad languages, worlds and histories. In addition to examining the uncharted impact of cultural diversity on contemporary society, Chambers discusses the 'realistic' eye of social commentary, the 'scientific' approach of the cultural anthropologist and the critical distance of the historian. Chambers analyses the disturbance and dislocation of history, culture and identity, while also investigating the manner in which migration, marginality and homelessness undermine our shared sense of cultural identity by disrupting our faith in linear progress and rational thinking.

During, Simon, ed. *The Cultural Studies Reader*. London, 1993.

The wide range of essays collected in During's volume provide a useful introduction to cultural studies. In addition to featuring selections by such influential voices as Roland Barthes, Theodor Adorno, Jean-François Lyotard, Cornel West, Eve Kosofsky Sedgwick, Michel Foucault, Raymond Williams and Meaghan Morris, among others, During's volume impinges upon a vast array of topics, from sports to postmodernism, from museums to supermarkets, and from gay and lesbian literature to popular music. During's introduction to cultural studies investigates the history and development of the discipline, as well as its intersections with such contemporary issues as postcolonialism, globalisation and multiculturalism.

Easthope, Antony. *Literary into Cultural Studies*. London, 1991.

Easthope examines the necessary opposition in modern literary studies between 'high' and 'low' forms of culture, between canonical literary texts and popular culture. In addition to discussing the theory and culture wars of the 1970s and the 1980s, and particularly the advent of structuralist and poststructuralist theory, Easthope investigates the ways which literary critics attempt to transform the oppositional nature of this relationship. Easthope argues that cultural studies must delineate an interpretative methodology for its analysis of canonical and popular texts. Drawing upon a host of competing theories – including cultural studies, new historicism and cultural materialism – Easthope offers a wide range of cultural materialist readings, from analyses of Conrad's *Heart of Darkness* to Edgar Rice Burroughs's *Tarzan of the Apes*, among other works.

Smithson, Isaiah and Nancy Ruff, eds. *English Studies/Culture Studies: Institutionalizing Dissent*. Urbana, IL, 1994.

The essays in Smithson and Ruff's collection investigate cultural studies' role as a mechanism for registering dissent and for effecting social change. In addition to addressing a wide range of topics from Native-American cultural studies and autobiography to curricular reform and the institutionalisation of English literature, the selections in Smithson and Ruff's volume provide valuable insights into the future of cultural studies and the political hurdles that confront the discipline as the millennium approaches. Smithson's introduction offers a useful overview of the contemporary state of cultural studies and affords attention to such issues as multicultural pedagogy and literary theory's approach to ethnicity and gender studies.

SUPPLEMENTARY BIBLIOGRAPHY

Bloom, Allan. *The Closing of the American Mind: How Higher Education Has Failed Democracy and Impoverished the Souls of Today's Students*. New York, 1987.

Bourke, Joanna. *Working-Class Cultures in Britain, 1890–1960: Gender, Class, and Ethnicity*. London, 1994.

Bové, Paul. 'Should Cultural Studies Take Literature Seriously?', *Critical Quarterly*, 39, 1997.

Boyd, Todd. *Am I Black Enough for You?: Popular Culture from the 'Hood and Beyond*. Bloomington, IN, 1997.

Chambers, Iain. *Migrancy, Culture, Identity*. London, 1994.

Cheney, Lynne V. *Telling the Truth: Why Our Culture and Our Country Have Stopped Making Sense – and What We Can Do about It*. New York, 1995.

Diawara, Manthia. 'Cultural Studies/Black Studies', in *Borders, Boundaries, and Frames: Essays in Cultural Criticism and Cultural Studies*, ed. Mae G. Henderson. New York, 1995.

D'Souza, Dinesh. *Illiberal Education: The Politics of Race and Sex on Campus*. New York, 1991.

During, Simon, ed. *The Cultural Studies Reader*. London, 1993.

Easthope, Antony. *Literary into Cultural Studies*. London, 1991.

Ecker, Gisela. 'Cultural Studies and Feminism', *Journal for the Study of British Culture*, 1, 1994.

Fox-Genovese, Elizabeth. 'Between Individualism and Fragmentation: American Culture and the New Literary Studies of Race and Gender', *American Quarterly*, 42, 1990.

Fuss, Diana, ed. *Human All Too Human*. New York, 1996.

Gates, Henry Louis, Jr. 'Whose Canon Is It, Anyway?', in *Debating P.C.: The Controversy over Political Correctness on College Campuses*, ed. Paul Berman. New York, 1992.

Gordon, Avery F. *Ghostly Matters: Haunting and the Sociological Imagination*. Minneapolis, MN, 1997.

Halberstam, Judith and Ira Livingston, eds. *Posthuman Bodies*. Bloomington, IN, 1995.

Hall, Stuart. *Stuart Hall: Critical Dialogues in Cultural Studies*, eds David Morley and Kuan-Hsing Chen. London, 1996.

Hirsch, Marianne. *Family Frames: Photography, Narrative, and Postmemory*. Cambridge, MA, 1997.

Hoggart, Richard. *The Uses of Literacy: Aspects of Working-Class Life, with Special Reference to Publications and Entertainments*. London, 1957.

Kellner, Douglas. *Media Culture: Cultural Studies, Identity, and Politics between the Modern and the Postmodern*. London, 1995.

Kimball, Roger. *Tenured Radicals: How Politics Has Corrupted Higher Education*. New York, 1990.

Kincaid, James R. *Erotic Innocence: The Culture of Child Molesting*. Durham, NC, 1998.

Miller, J. Hillis. 'Is There an Ethics of Reading?', in *Reading Narrative: Form, Ethics, Ideology*, ed. James Phelan. Columbus, 1988.

Modleski, Tania. *Feminism without Women: Culture and Criticism in a 'Postfeminist' Age*. London, 1991.

Nussbaum, Martha C. *Cultivating Humanity: A Classical Defense of Reform in Liberal Education*. Cambridge, 1997.

Regan, Stephen, ed. *The Politics of Pleasure: Aesthetics and Cultural Theory*. Bristol, PA, 1992.

Sinfield, Alan. *Literature, Culture, and Politics in Postwar Britain*. Berkeley, CA, 1989.

Smith, Anna Marie. *New Right Discourse on Race and Sexuality: Britain, 1968–1980*. Cambridge, 1994.

Smithson, Isaiah and Nancy Ruff, eds. *English Studies/Culture Studies: Institutionalizing Dissent*. Urbana, IL, 1994.

Sykes, Charles J. *ProfScam: Professors and the Demise of Higher Education*. Washington, DC, 1988.

Thompson, E. P. *The Making of the English Working Class*. New York, 1964.

Williams, Jeffrey. 'Renegotiating the Pedagogical Contract', in *Class Issues: Pedagogy, Cultural Studies, and the Public Sphere*, ed. Amitava Kumar. New York, 1997.

Williams, Raymond. *Marxism and Literature*. Oxford, 1977.

———. *Culture and Society: 1780–1950*. New York, 1983.

WORKS CITED

Each of the contributors has supplied an annotated bibliography with short selections of titles together with a list of supplementary reading which offers the reader some of the key texts in each field. These bibliographies appear at the end of each chapter. This bibliography is a list of works cited in the essays that are reprinted in each of the parts, along with any additional works cited by contributors to the current volume, organized alphabetically. Where certain works are repeated from the contributors' supplementary bibliographies to the list of works cited, I have let these stand, for the purpose of clarity of reference. Also, on occasion, different versions, translations, editions of the same essay, article or book are provided; these have been retained. Finally, page numbers for journal and book articles which refer to the entire essay in question have been omitted. While this is not usual practice, it has been necessary due to restrictions on space and because page references are given to particular works throughout the collection of essays.

Abel, Elizabeth. *Virginia Woolf and the Fictions of Psychoanalysis*. Chicago, 1989.
Adams, Stephen. *The Homosexual as Hero in Contemporary Fiction*. London, 1980.
Adamson, Joseph. 'Deconstruction', in *Encyclopedia of Literary Theory: Approaches, Scholars, Terms*, ed. Irena R. Makaryk. Toronto, 1993.
Adler, Jerry et al. 'Taking Offense: Is This the New Enlightenment on Campus or the New McCarthyism?', *Newsweek*, 24 December 1990.
Althusser, Louis. *Lenin and Philosophy and Other Essays*, trans. Ben Brewster. London, 1971.

Anderson, Benedict. *Imagined Communities*. London, 1983.

Anon. 'Editorial'. *Third Text*, 18, Spring 1992.

Anon. *The Problemes of Aristotle, with other Philosophers and Phisitions*. London, 1597.

Anson, Margaret. *The Merry Order of St Bridget: Personal Recollections of the Use of the Rod*. York, 1857.

Apter, T. E. *Virginia Woolf: A Study of Her Novels*. London, 1979.

Arnold, David, 'European Orphans and Vagrants in India in the Nineteenth Century', *Journal of Imperial and Commonwealth History*, 7: 2, 1979.

Austin, Alfred. 'The Poetry of the Period', in *The Victorian Poet*, ed. Joseph Bristow. London, 1987.

Austin, J. L. *How To Do Things With Words*. Cambridge, MA, 1967.

Babbitt, Irving. *Literature and the American College*. Boston, MA, 1908.

Babuscio, Jack. 'Camp and Gay Sensibility', in *Gays and Film*, ed. Richard Dyer. London, 1977.

Bacon, Francis. *Felicem Memoriam Elizabethae (ca.* 1608): *The Works of Francis Bacon*, ed. James Spedding et al., 15 vols. Boston, MA, 1860.

Balibar, Renée, and D. Laporte. *Le Français national*. Paris, 1974.

————, G. Merlin and G. Tret. *Les Français fictifs*. Paris, 1974.

Bär, Eugen. 'Understanding Lacan', in *Psychoanalysis and Contemporary Science*, vol. 3, eds Leo Goldberger and Victor H. Rosen. New York, 1974.

Barmé, Geremie. 'The Greying of Chinese Culture', in *China Review 1992*, eds Kuan Hsin-chi and Maurice Brosseau. Hong Kong, 1992, Section 13.

Barthes, Roland. *S/Z*. Paris, 1970.

————. 'L'analyse structurale du récit: à propos d'*Actes* 10–11', in *Exégèse et Herméneutique*. Paris, 1971.

————. *S/Z*, trans. Richard Miller, preface Richard Howard. New York, 1974.

————. *Image Music Text*, trans. Stephen Heath. London, 1977.

————. *Empire of Signs*, trans. Richard Howard. New York, 1982.

Bascom, Tim. 'Secret Imperialism: The Reader's Response to the Narrator in "The Man Who Would Be King"', in *English Literature in Transition*. London, 1987.

Bateson, Gregory. 'Pidgin English and Cross-Cultural Communication', *Transactions of the New York Academy of Sciences*, 6, 1944.

Baudelaire, Charles. *Oeuvres Complètes*. Paris, 1951.

————. *Madame Bovary*. Paris, 1966.

————. *Madame Bovary*, ed. Leo Bersani, trans. Lowell Blair. Toronto, 1981.

Baudrillard, Jean. *In the Shadow of the Silent Majorities . . . or the End of the Social and Other Essays*, trans. Paul Foss, Paul Patton and John Johnston. New York, 1983.

Bauer, George H. 'Duchamp, Delay, and Overlay', *Mid-America: An Historical Review*, 60, April 1978.

Beardsley, Monroe. 'The Concept of Literature', in *Literary Theory and Structure: Essays in Honor of William K. Wimsatt*, eds Frank Brady, John Palmer and Martin Price. New Haven, CT, 1973.

Beckett, Samuel. *The Unnamable. Molloy, Malone Dies*. London, 1966.

————. *Watt*. London, 1976.

————. 'Ohio Impromptu', in *The Complete Dramatic Works*. London, 1986.

Benbow, Mark, ed. *The Araygnment of Paris*, by George Peele. New Haven, CT, 1970.

Benjamin, Walter. *Illuminations*, trans. Harry Zohn, intro. Hannah Arendt. New York, 1969, 1973.

————. *One-Way Street*, trans. Edmund Jephcott and Kingsley Shorter. London, 1979.

————. *Parigi. Capitale del XIX secolo*. Turin, 1986.

————. *The Origin of German Tragic Drama*, trans. Harry Zohn. London, 1990.

Bennett, Tony. *Formalism and Marxism*. London, 1979.

Bennington, Geoff. 'Deconstruction is Not What You Think', *Art & Design*, 4: 3/4, 1988.

Bennington, Geoffrey and Jacques Derrida. *Jacques Derrida*, trans. Geoffrey Bennington. Chicago, 1993.

———. 'Derridabase', in Geoffrey Bennington and Jacques Derrida, *Jacques Derrida*, trans. Geoffrey Bennington. Chicago, 1993.

———. 'X', in *Applying: to Derrida*, eds John Brannigan, Ruth Robbins and Julian Wolfreys. Basingstoke, 1996.

Bersani, Leo. 'Is the Rectum a Grave?', *October*, 43, 1987.

———. *The Culture of Redemption*. Cambridge, MA, 1990.

——— and Ulysse Dutoit. 'Beckett's Sociability', *Raritan*, 12: 1, Summer 1992.

Bhabha, Homi K. 'The Third Space: Interview with Homi Bhabha', in *Identity, Community, Difference*, ed. John Rutherford. London, 1990.

Blackmur. R. P. [no title], *Southern Review*, Summer 1940.

Blanchot, Maurice. *The Space of Literature*, trans. Ann Smock. Lincoln, NE, 1982.

Boston Women's Health Book Collective. *The New Our Bodies, Ourselves: Updated and Expanded for the Nineties*. New York, 1992.

Brady, Judy, ed. *1 in 3: Women with Cancer Confront an Epidemic*. Pittsburgh and San Francisco, 1991.

Brodhead, Richard. *The School of Hawthorne*. New York, 1986.

Bronski, Michael. *Culture-Clash: The Making of Gay Sensibility*. Boston, MA, 1984.

Brooks, David. 'From Western Lit to Westerns as Lit', *The Wall Street Journal*, 2 February 1988, 24, cols 3–5.

Brooks, Peter. *Psychoanalysis and Storytelling*. Oxford, 1994.

Brown, Douglas. *Thomas Hardy*. London, 1954.

Buci-Glucksmann, Christine. *La Raison baroque*. Paris, 1983.

Buck-Morss, Susan. *The Dialectics of Seeing: Walter Benjamin and the Arcades Project*. Cambridge, MA, 1989.

Butler, Judith. *Gender Trouble: Feminism and the Subversion of Identity*. New York, 1989.

Butler, Sandra, and Rosenblum, Barbara. *Cancer in Two Voices*. San Francisco, 1991.

Caputo, John D. 'A Commentary: Deconstruction in a Nutshell', in Jacques Derrida and John D. Caputo, *Deconstruction in a Nutshell: A Conversation with Jacques Derrida*. New York, 1997.

Carrington, Charles. *Rudyard Kipling*. Harmondsworth, 1970.

Césaire, Aimé. *Discourse on Colonialism*. New York, 1972.

Chambers, Iain. *Border Dialogues: Journeys in Postmodernity*. London, 1990.

Charcot, J. M. *Leçons sur les maladies du système nerveux. Oeuvres Complètes*, vol. 1. Paris, 1886.

Chazaud, Jacques. *Les Perversions sexuelles*. Toulouse, 1973.

Chow, Rey. 'In the Name of Comparative Literature', in *Comparative Literature in the Age of Multiculturalism*, ed. Charles Bernheimer. Baltimore, MD, 1995.

Cixous, Hélène. 'Le Sexe ou la tête?' *Les Cahiers du GRIF*, 13, October 1976.

———. 'Entretien avec Françoise van Russum-Guyon', *Revue des sciences humaines*, 168, 1977.

Clifford, James. 'Travelling Cultures' in *Cultural Studies*, eds Lawrence Grossberg, Cary Nelson and Paula Treichler. London, 1992.

Cohen, Walter. 'Political Criticism of Shakespeare', in *Shakespeare Reproduced: The Text in History and Ideology*, eds Jean E. Howard and Marion F. O'Connor. New York, 1987.

Coleridge, Samuel Taylor. *The Friend* II, ed. Henry Nelson Coleridge. London, 1863.

———. *The Table Talk and Omniana*. Oxford, 1917.

———. *Biographia Literaria* I, ed. J. Shawcross. Oxford, 1958.

———. *Shakespearean Criticism* II, ed. T. M. Raysor. London, 1967.

Colette. *My Mother's House and Sido*, trans. Una Vicenzo Troubridge and Enid McLeod. New York, 1953.

———. *Earthly Paradise: An Autobiography Drawn from Her Lifetime Writings*, trans. Herma Briffault, Derek Coltman et al., ed. Robert Phelps. New York, 1966.

Connolly, William E. *Political Theory and Modernity*. Oxford, 1989.

Conrad, Joseph. *The Nigger of the 'Narcissus,' Typhoon and Other Stories*. Harmondsworth, 1963a.

―――. *Nostromo*. Harmondsworth, 1963b.

―――. *Lord Jim*, ed. T. Moser. New York, 1968.

―――. *Nostromo*. London, 1979.

Cornell, Louis. *Kipling in India*. London, 1966.

Corsa, Helen Storm. 'To the Lighthouse: Death, Mourning, and Transfiguration', *Literature and Psychology*, 21, 1971.

Currie, Mark. *Postmodern Narrative Theory*. Basingstoke, 1998.

Daniel, Jamie Owen. 'Temporary Shelter: Adorno's Exile and the Language from Home', *New Formations*, 17, Summer 1992.

Davis, Sara de Saussure. 'The Bostonians Reconsidered', *Tulane Studies in English*, 23, 1978.

de Certeau, Michel. *The Practice of Everyday Life*. Berkeley, CA, 1988.

de Man, Paul. *Allegories of Reading: Figural Language in Rousseau, Nietzsche, Rilke, and Proust*. New Haven, CT, 1979.

―――. 'Sign and Symbol in Hegel's *Aesthetics*', *Critical Inquiry*, 8, Summer 1982.

―――. *Blindness and Insight: Essays in the Rhetoric of Contemporary Criticism*. Minneapolis, MN, 1983.

―――. *The Resistance to Theory*, foreword Wlad Godzich. Minneapolis, MN, 1986.

Deleuze, Gilles and Félix Guattari. *A Thousand Plateaus: Capitalism and Schizophrenia*, trans. Brian Massumi. Minneapolis, MN, 1988.

Derrida, Jacques. 'The Ends of Man', trans. E. Morot-Sir, W. C. Piersol, H. L. Dreyfus and B. Reid, *Philosophical and Phenomenological Research*, 30, 1969; rpt. in *Margins of Philosophy*, trans. Alan Bass. Chicago, 1982.

―――. *Positions*. Paris, 1972.

―――. *Writing and Difference*, trans. Alan Bass. London, 1978.

―――. *Spurs: Nietzsche's Styles/Eperons: Les Styles de Nietzsche*, trans. Barbara Harlow. Chicago, 1979a.

―――. 'Border Lines', trans. James Hulbert. Harold Bloom et al., in *Deconstruction and Criticism*. New York, 1979b.

―――. 'Living On', trans. James Hulbert, Harold Bloom et al., in *Deconstruction and Criticism*. New York, 1979b.

―――. *La carte postale: de Socrate à Freud et au-déla*. Paris, 1980.

―――. *Positions*, trans. Alan Bass. Chicago, 1981a.

―――. 'Télépathie', *Furor*, February 1981b.

―――. *Margins of Philosophy*, trans. and additional notes Alan Bass. Chicago, 1982.

―――. 'Deconstruction and the Other: Interview', in Richard Kearney, *Dialogues with Contemporary Continental Thinkers: The Phenomenological Heritage*. Manchester, 1983.

―――. *Signéponge/Signsponge*, trans. Richard Rand. New York, 1984.

―――. 'Des Tours de Babel', trans. Joseph F. Graham, in *Difference in Translation*, ed. Joseph F. Graham. Ithaca, NY, 1985a.

―――. 'Deconstruction in America: An Interview with Jacques Derrida', trans. James Creech. *Critical Exchange*, 17, 1985b.

―――. *Mémoires: for Paul de Man*, trans. Cecile Lindsay, Jonathan Culler and Eduardo Cadava. New York, 1986.

―――. *The Post Card: From Socrates to Freud and Beyond*, trans. and intro. Alan Bass. Chicago, 1987a.

―――. *The Truth in Painting*, trans. Geoffrey Bennington and Iain McLeod. Chicago, 1987b.

―――. *The Ear of the Other: Otobiography Transference Translation*, trans. Peggy Kamuf. Lincoln, NE, 1988.

————. 'Introduction: Desistance', trans. Christopher Fynsk, in Philippe Lacoue-Labarthe, *Typography: Mimesis, Philosophy, Politics*, trans. Christopher Fynsk et al. Cambridge, MA, 1989a.

————. *Of Spirit: Heidegger and the Question*, trans. Geoffrey Bennington and Rachel Bowlby. Chicago, 1989b.

————. 'Rhétorique de la drogue', in *L'Esprit des drogues: La Dépendence hors de la loi?*, ed. Jean-Michel Herviev. Paris, 1989c.

————. 'Psyche: Inventions of the Other', trans. Catherine Porter, in *Reading de Man Reading*, eds Lindsay Waters and Wlad Godzich. Minneapolis, MN, 1989d.

————. 'Right of Inspection' (with Marie-Françoise Plissart), trans. David Wills, *Art & Text*, 32, Autumn 1989e.

————. 'On Colleges and Philosophy: Jacques Derrida and Geoff Bennington', *Postmodernism: ICA Documents*, ed. Lisa Appignanesi. London, 1989f.

————. 'How to Avoid Speaking: Denials', trans. Ken Frieden, in *Languages of the Unsayable: The Play of Negativity in Literature and Literary Theory*, eds Sandford Budick and Wolfgang Iser. New York, 1989g.

————. 'Force of Law: The "Mystical Foundation of Authority"', trans. Mary Quaintance. *Cardozo Law Review*, 11: 5/6, 1990.

————. 'Letter to a Japanese Friend', in *A Derrida Reader: Between the Blinds*, ed. Peggy Kamuf. New York, 1991a.

————. 'At this very moment in this work here I am', trans. Ruben Berezdivin, in *Re-Reading Levinas*, ed. Robert Bernasconi and Simon Critchley. Bloomington, IN, 1991b.

————. 'Afterw.rds: or, at least, less than a letter about a letter less', trans. Geoffrey Bennington, in *Afterwords*, ed. Nicholas Royle. Tampere, 1992a.

————. 'An "Interview" with Jacques Derrida', *The Cambridge Review*, 113: 2318, October 1992b.

————. 'Passions: "An Oblique Offering"', trans. David Wood, in *Derrida: A Critical Reader*, ed. David Wood. Oxford, 1992c.

————. 'The Law of Genre', trans. Avital Ronell, in *Acts of Literature*, ed. Derek Attridge. London, 1992d.

————. 'This Strange Institution Called Literature', trans. Geoffrey Bennington and Rachel Bowlby, in *Acts of Literature*, ed. Derek Attridge. London, 1992d.

————. 'Circumfession', in Geoffrey Bennington and Jacques Derrida, *Jacques Derrida*, trans. Geoffrey Bennington. Chicago, 1993.

————. 'The Time is Out of Joint', trans Peggy Kamuf, in *Deconstruction is/in America: A New Sense of the Political*, ed. Anselm Haverkamp. New York, 1995.

————. '"*As if* I were dead": An Interview with Jacques Derrida', in *Applying: to Derrida*, eds John Brannigan, Ruth Robbins and Julian Wolfreys. Basingstoke, 1996.

DeSalvo, Louise A. '1897: Virginia Woolf at Fifteen', in *Virginia Woolf: A Feminist Slant*, ed. Jane Marcus. Lincoln, NE, 1983

Di Battista, Maria. *Virginia Woolf's Major Novels: The Fables of Anon*, New Haven, CT, 1980.

Diamantis, Irène. 'Recherches sur la fémininité', *Ornicar? – Analytica*, vol. 5.

Dick, Susan, ed. *The Original Holograph Draft of 'To the Lighthouse'*. Toronto, 1983.

Dickens, Charles. *Bleak House*. Oxford, 1948.

Dickinson, Emily. *The Complete Poems of Emily Dickinson*, ed. Thomas H. Johnson. Boston, MA, 1960.

Donzelot, Jacques. *The Policing of Families*, trans. Robert Hurley. New York, 1979.

Douglas, Ann. *The Feminization of American Culture*. New York, 1978.

Dubois, Ellen. 'The Radicalism of the Woman Suffrage Movement: Notes towards the Reconstruction of Nineteenth-Century Feminism', *Feminist Studies*, 3, Fall, 1975.

Durand, Régis. '"The Captive King": The Absent Father in Melville's Text', in *The Fictional Father: Lacanian Readings of the Text*, ed. Robert Con Davis. Amherst, MA, 1981.

Dyer, Richard. 'Getting Over the Rainbow: Identity and Pleasure in Gay Cultural Politics', *Silver Linings: Some Strategies for the Eighties*, eds George Bridges and Rosalind Brunt. London, 1981.

Dyer, Richard. *Heavenly Bodies: Film Stars and Society*. London, 1987.

Eagleton, Terry. *Marxism and Literary Criticism*. London, 1976.

————. 'Text, Ideology, Realism', *Literature and Society*, ed. Edward Said. Baltimore, MD, 1980.

————. *Walter Benjamin or Towards a Revolutionary Criticism*. London, 1981.

————. *Literary Theory: An Introduction*. Oxford, 1983.

Ebert, Teresa L. 'Metaphor, Metonymy, and Ideology: Language and Perception in *Mrs. Dalloway*', *Language and Style*, 18: 2, Spring 1985.

Ellis, Havelock. *Studies in the Psychology of Sex*, vol. 2. New York, 1936.

Ellmann, Richard. *Oscar Wilde*. London, 1987.

Elsaesser, Thomas. *New German Cinema: A History*. New Brunswick, NJ, 1989.

Esposito, Vincenzo. 'Il mondo una piazza: note sul presepe', conference paper, 'La Piazza nella storia'. Salerno, 10 December 1992.

Fabian, Johannes. *Time and the Other: How Anthropology Makes Its Object*. New York, 1983.

Fanon, Frantz. *Toward the African Revolution*, trans. H. Chevalier. London, 1967.

————. *Black Skin, White Masks*. London, 1970.

Featherstone, Mike. 'Global Culture: An Introduction', in *Global Culture, Nationalism, Globalization and Modernity*, ed. Mike Featherstone. London, 1990.

Felman, Shoshana. 'Turning the Screw of Interpretation', *Yale French Studies*, 55–6, 1977.

————. *The Literary Speech Act: Don Juan with J. L. Austin, or Seduction in Two Languages*, trans. Catherine Porter. Ithaca, NY, 1983.

Fenves, Peter, ed. *Raising the Tone of Philosophy: Late Essays by Immanuel Kant, Transformative Critique by Jacques Derrida*. Baltimore, MD, 1993.

Feuer, Jane. 'Reading *Dynasty*: Television and Reception Theory', *South Atlantic Quarterly*, 88, 1989.

Fielder, Leslie. *Waiting for the End*. Harmondsworth, 1967.

Fleishman, Avrom. *Virginia Woolf: A Critical Reading*. Baltimore, MD, 1975.

Fliess, Robert. *Erogeneity and Libido*. New York, 1956.

Foucault, Michel. *The Order of Things*, trans. A. M. Sheridan Smith. New York, 1971.

————. *Discipline and Punish*, trans. Alan Sheridan. New York, 1977a.

————. *Language, Counter-Memory, Practice: Selected Essays and Interviews*, ed. and intro. Donald F. Bouchard, trans. Donald F. Bouchard and Sherry Simon. Oxford, 1977b.

————. *The History of Sexuality*, vol. 1, trans. Robert Hurley. New York, 1978.

————. *Power/Knowledge: Selected Interviews and Other Writings 1972–1977*, ed. Colin Gordon. Brighton, 1980.

Freud, Sigmund. *Standard Edition of the Complete Psychological Works*, trans. under general editorship of James Strachey collaboration with Anna Freud, assisted by Alix Strachey and Alan Tyson, 24 vols. London, 1953–74.

Fuller, Margaret. 'Woman in the Nineteenth Century', in *The Norton Anthology of Literature by Women: The Tradition in English*, eds Sandra Gilbert and Susan Gubar. New York, 1985.

Galand, R. *Baudelaire: Poétique et poésie*. Paris, 1969.

Gallop, Jane. 'Beyond the *Jouissance* Principle', *Representations*, 7, Summer 1984.

Gascoigne, George. *The Complete Works of George Gascoigne*, ed. J. W. Cunliffe, 2 vols. Cambridge, 1910.

Genet, Jean. *Our Lady of the Flowers*, trans. Bernard Frechtman, intro. Jean-Paul Sartre. London, 1966.

————. *The Thief's Journal*, trans. Bernard Frechtman. Harmondsworth, 1967.

————. 'Interview with Hubert Fichte', in *Gay Sunshine Interviews*, vol. 1, ed. W. Leyland. San Francisco, 1978.

Gernsheim, H., ed. *Lewis Carroll Photographer*, New York, 1969.

Gibson, Paul. 'Gay Male and Lesbian Youth Suicide', US Department of Health and Human Services, *Report of the Secretary's Task Force on Youth Suicide*. Washington, DC, 1989, vol. 3.

Gide, André. *So Be It, or; The Chips are Down*, trans. with intro. and notes, Justin O'Brien. London, 1960.

Gilbert, Sandra M. and Susan Gubar. *No Man's Land. Vol. I: The War of the Words*. New Haven, CT, 1988.

Ginsberg, Allen. *'Howl' and Other Poems*. San Francisco, 1959.

Gliserman, Martin. 'Virginia Woolf's *To the Lighthouse*: Syntax and the Female Center', *American Imago*, 40: 1, 1983.

Grant, C. 'Observations on the State of Society among the Asiatic Subjects of Great Britain'. *Sessional Papers of the East India Company*, 10: 282, 1812–13.

Green, Roger Lancelyn, ed. *Kipling: the Critical Heritage*. London, 1971.

Greimas, A. J. and François Rastier. 'The Interaction of Semiotic Constraints', *Yale French Studies*, 41, 1968.

Greimas, A. J. *Du Sens*. Paris, 1970.

———. *Sémantique structurale*. Paris, 1986.

Guideri, Remo. 'Les sociétés primitives aujourd'hui', *Philosopher: les interrogations contemporaines*, eds Ch. Delacampagne and R. Maggiori. Paris, 1980.

Habegger, Alfred. *Henry James and the 'Woman Business'*, Cambridge, 1990.

Hannerz, Ulf. 'Cosmopolitans and Locals in World Culture', in *Global Culture, Nationalism, Globalization and Modernity*, ed. Mike Featherstone. London, 1990.

Hardy, F. E. *The Life of Thomas Hardy: 1840–1928*. London, 1965.

Hardy, Thomas. *The Complete Poems*, ed. J. Gibson. London, 1976.

Harrington, Henry R. 'The Central Line down the Middle of *To the Lighthouse*', *Contemporary Literature*, 21: 3, 1980.

Harington, Sir John. *The Letters and Epigrams of Sir John Harrington*, ed. N. E. McClure. Philadelphia, 1930.

Harvey, David. *The Condition of Postmodernity*. Oxford, 1989.

Hastrup, Kirsten. 'Anthropological Visions: Some Notes on Visual and Textual Authority', in *Film as Ethnography*, eds Peter Ian Crawford and David Turton. Manchester, 1992.

Heath, Stephen. 'Joan Rivière and the Masquerade', in *Formations of Fantasy*, eds Victor Burgin, James Donald and Cora Kaplan. London, 1986.

Hegel, G. W. F. *Vorlesungen über die Aesthetik. Sämtliche Werke*, vol. 13. Stuttgart, 1927–8.

Heidegger, Martin. *The Question Concerning Technology and Other Essays*, trans. William Lovitt. New York, 1977.

Heinemann, Margot. 'How Brecht Read Shakespeare', in *Political Shakespeare: New Essays in Cultural Materialism*, eds Jonathon Dollimore and Alan Sinfield. Manchester, 1985.

Hertz, Neil. 'Medusa's Head: Male Hysteria under Political Pressure', *Representations*, 4, Fall 1983, rpt. in Neil Hertz, *The End of the Line: Essays on Psychoanalysis and the Sublime*. New York, 1985.

Hill, Leslie. *Beckett's Fiction: Different Words*. Cambridge, 1990.

Hjelmslev, Louis. *Prolegomena to a Theory of Language*, trans. E. J. Whitfield. Madison, NI, 1961.

Hobson, Harold. 'Review of *What the Butler Saw*', *Christian Science Monitor*, 19 March 1969.

Holloway, John. *The Charted Mirror*. London, 1960.

Howard, Jean E. and Marion F.O'Connor, eds. *Shaksepare Reproduced*. New York, 1987.

Husserl, Edmund. *Phantasie, Bildbewusstsein, Erinnerung*, ed. Eduard Marbach. The Hague, 1980.

Irigaray, Luce. *Ce Sexe qui n'en est pas un.* Paris 1977.

――――. 'Interview'. *Les femmes, la pornographie, l'éroticisme*, eds M.-F. Hans and G. Lapouge. Paris, 1978.

――――. *This Sex Which is Not One*, trans. Catherine Porter with Carolyn Burke. Ithaca, NY, 1985.

Jackson, Rosemary. *Fantasy: The Literature of Subversion.* London, 1981.

Jakobson, Roman. *On Translation*, ed. Reuben A. Brower. Cambridge, MA, 1959.

――――. 'Linguistics and Poetics', in *Style in Language*, ed. Thomas A. Sebeok. Cambridge, MA, 1960.

――――. *Poetics, Poetyka.* Warsaw, 1961,

―――― and Claude Lévi-Strauss, 'Les Chats de Charles Baudelaire', *L'Homme*, 2, 1962.

James, Henry. *The Notebooks of Henry James*, eds F. O. Matthiessen and Kenneth S. Murdock. New York, 1947.

――――. *The Bostonians*, ed. Alfred Habegger. Indianapolis, IN, 1976.

Jameson, Fredric. *Marxism and Form*, Princeton, NJ, 1971.

――――. 'Imaginary and Symbolic in Lacan: Marxism, Psychoanalytic Criticism, and the Problem of the Subject', *Yale French Studies*, 55–6, 1977.

――――. *The Political Unconscious: Narrative as Socially Symbolic Act.* Ithaca, NY, 1981.

――――. 'Postmodernism and Consumer Society', in *The Anti-Aesthetic: Essays on Postmodern Culture*, ed. Hal Foster. Washington, DC, 1983.

――――. *Postmodernism, or the Cultural Logic of Late Capitalism.* London, 1992.

Johnson, Barbara. *The Critical Difference: Essays in the Contemporary Rhetoric of Reading.* Baltimore, MD, 1981.

――――. Taking Fidelity Philosophically', in *Difference in Translation*, ed. Joseph F. Graham. Ithaca, NY, 1985.

Johnson, Paul. *Elizabeth I: A Study in Power and Intellect.* London, 1974.

Jolles, André. *Einfache Formen.* Halle, 1929.

Jullian, Philippe. *Oscar Wilde*, trans. Violet Wyndham. New York, 1969.

Kafka, Franz. *Briefe an Milena*, ed. E. Hass. New York, 1952.

――――. *Letters to Milena*, eds W. Hass, trans. T. and J. Stern. New York, 1954.

Kamuf, Peggy, ed. *A Derrida Reader: Between the Blinds.* New York, 1991.

――――. 'Preface', in *A Derrida Reader: Between the Blinds*, ed. Peggy Kamuf. New York, 1991.

――――. *The Division of Literature or the University in Deconstruction.* Chicago, 1997.

Kelley, Alice Van Buren. *The Novels of Virginia Woolf: Fact and Vision.* Chicago, 1973.

Kellogg, T. A. et al. 'Prevalence of HIV-I Among Homosexual and Bisexual Men in the San Francisco Bay Area: Evidence of Infection Among Young Gay Men', *Seventh International AIDS Conference Abstract Book*, vol. 2. Geneva, 1991. W.C. 3010.

Kelsall, Malcolm, Martin Coyle, Peter Garside and John Peck, eds. *Encyclopedia of Literature and Criticism.* London, 1990.

Kimball, Roger. *Tenured Radicals: How Politics Has Corrupted Our Higher Education.* New York, 1990.

King, Anthony D. *Global Cities: Post-Imperialism and the Internationalization of London.* London, 1991.

――――. *Urbanism, Colonialism, and the World-Economy.* London, 1991.

――――, ed. *Culture, Globalization and the World-System.* Albany, NY, 1991.

Kipling, Rudyard. *Life's Handicap.* London, 1897.

――――. *Plain Tales from the Hills.* London, 1898.

――――. *Literary and General Essays.* London, 1890.

――――. *Wee Willie Winkie and Other Stories.* London, 1914.

――――. *From Sea to Sea: Letters of Travel*, 2 vols. London, 1919.

――――. *The Book of Words.* London, 1928.

————. *The Definitive Edition of Rudyard Kipling's Verse*. London, 1969.

————. *The Kipling Papers*, University of Sussex Manuscripts, University of Sussex, Brighton, Great Britain.

Lacan, Jacques. 'Discussion: Société Psychanalytique de Paris', *Revue Française de psychanalyse*, April–June 1949.

————. *Écrits*. Paris, 1966.

————. 'Of Structure as an Inmixing of an Otherness Prerequisite to Any Subject Whatsoever', in *The Structuralist Controversy: The Languages of Criticism and the Sciences of Man*, eds Richard Macksey and Eugenio Donato. Baltimore, MD, 1972.

————. *Le Séminaire livre XI*. Paris, 1973a.

————. 'L'étourdit', *Scilicet*, 4, 1973b.

————. *Le Séminaire livre XX*. Paris, 1975a.

————. *Le Séminaire livre I*. Paris, 1975b.

————. *Ornicar?*, 6, 1975c.

————. *Ornicar?*, 12/13, 1976a.

————. 'Faire Mouche', *Le Nouvel Observateur*, 594, 29 March – 4 April 1976b.

————. 'Desire and the Interpretation of Desire in *Hamlet*', *Yale French Studies*, 55–6, 1977a.

————. *Écrits: A Selection*, trans. Alan Sheridan. New York, 1977b.

————. *The Four Fundamental Concepts of Psychoanalysis*, trans. Alan Sheridan. London, 1977; New York, 1978a.

————. *Le Séminaire livre II*. Paris, 1978b.

————. *Le Séminaire livre III*, 1981.

Laclau, Ernesto, and Chantal Mouffe. *Hegemony and Socialist Strategy*. London, 1985.

Lahr, John. *Prick Up Your Ears*. Harmondsworth, 1980.

Laing, R. D. *The Divided Self*. Harmondsworth, 1965.

Laplanche, Jean. 'The Wall and the Arcade', trans. Mary Stanton, in *Seduction, Translation, Drives*, comp. John Fletcher and Martin Stanton. London, 1992.

Leaska, Mitchell A. *The Novels of Virginia Woolf: From Beginning to End*. New York, 1977.

Leavis, F. R. *Revaluation*. London, 1936.

Lehman, David. 'Deconstructing de Man's Life: An Academic Idol Falls Into Disgrace', *Newsweek*, 15 February 1988, p. 62.

Lemaire, Anika. *Jacques Lacan*, trans. David Macey. London, 1977.

Lemoine-Luccioni, Eugénie. *Partages des femmes*. Paris, 1976.

Leopardi, Giacomo. 'Zibaldone', cit. Franco Rella, *Asterischi*. Milan, 1989.

Lidoff, Joan. 'Virginia Woolf's Feminine Sentence: The Mother-Daughter World of *To the Lighthouse*', *Literature and Psychology*, 32, 1986.

Lilienfeld, Jane. '"The Deceptiveness of Beauty": Mother Love and Mother Hate in *To the Lighthouse*', *Twentieth-Century Literature*, 23: 3, 1977.

Liu, Alan. 'The Power of Formalism: The New Historicism', ELH, 56, 1989.

————. 'The Future Literary: Literary History and Postmodern Culture', unpublished book. 1996.

Long, E. *A History of Jamaica*. 1774.

Lorde, Audre. *A Burst of Light*. New York, 1988.

————. *The Cancer Journals*. 2nd edn. San Francisco, 1988.

Lucas, Hyppolite. 'La Femme adultère', *Les Français peints par eux-mêmes*, 8 vols. Paris, 1840, vol. 3.

Lukács, Georg. *The Theory of the Novel*, trans. A. Bostock. Cambridge, MA, 1971.

Macaulay, T. B. 'Minute on Education', *Sources of Indian Tradition*, vol. II, ed. W. Theodore de Bary. New York, 1958.

MacCannell, Juliet Flower. *Figuring Lacan: Criticism and the Cultural Unconscious*. Lincoln, NE, 1986.

Macherey, Pierre, *A Theory of Literary Production*, trans. Geoffrey Wall. London, 1978.

———— and Etienne Balibar. 'Literature as an Ideological Form: Some Marxist Propositions', *Oxford Literary Review*, 3, 1978.

Mallarmé, Stéphane. *Oeuvres complètes*. Paris, 1945.

Mallet, Philip, ed. *Kipling Considered*. London, 1989.

Mani, Lata. 'Multiple Mediations: Feminist Scholarship in the Age of Multinational Reception', *Inscriptions*, 5, 1989.

Marcus, Greil. *Lipstick Traces: A Secret History of the Twentieth Century*. London, 1989.

Marcus, Jane. *Virginia Woolf and the Languages of Patriarchy*. Bloomington, IN, 1987.

Marowitz, Charles. 'The Revenge of Jean Genet', in *The Encore Reader: A Chronicle of the New Drama*, eds Charles Marowitz et al. London, 1965.

Marx, Karl. *Grundrisse*, trans. Martin Nicolaus. Harmondsworth, 1973.

Maspero, François. *Beyond the Gates of Paris*, trans. Paul Jones. London, 1992.

Matvejevic, Predrag. *Mediteranski Brevijar*. Zagreb, 1987; *Mediterraneo*. Milan, 1991.

Mayer, Hans. *Outsiders: A Study in Life and Letters*, trans. Denis M. Sweet. Cambridge, MA, 1982.

Mehlman, Jeffrey. *A Structural Study of Autobiography: Proust, Leiris, Sartre, Lévi-Strauss*. Ithaca, NY, 1974.

————. *Walter Benjamin for Children: An Essay on His Radio Years*. Chicago, 1993.

Mieli, Mario. *Homosexuality and Liberation: Elements of a Gay Critique*, trans. David Fernbach. London, 1980.

Miller, D. A. *The Novel and the Police*. Berkeley, CA, 1987.

Miller, J. Hillis. *Theory Now and Then*. Hemel Hempstead, 1991.

————. 'Deconstruction Now? The States of Deconstruction or Thinking without Synecdoche', in Nicholas Royle, ed. *Afterwords*. Tampere, 1992.

Miller, Nancy K. *The Heroine's Text: Readings in the French and English Novel 1722–1782*. New York, 1980.

Millett, Kate. *Sexual Politics*. London, 1977.

Milner, M. 'Poetique de la chute', in *Regards sur Baudelaire*, ed. W. Bush. Paris, 1974.

Milton, John. *Complete Prose Works*, general ed. Don M. Wolfe. New Haven, CT, 1953–82.

Minh-ha, Trinh T. *Woman, Native, Other*. Bloomington, IN, 1989.

————. 'Cotton and Iron', in *Out There: Marginalization and Contemporary Cultures*, eds Russell Ferguson, Martha Gever, Trinh T. Minh-ha and Cornel West. Cambridge, MA, 1990.

————. *When the Moon Waxes Red*. London, 1991.

Minow-Pinkney, Mikiko. *Virginia Woolf and the Problem of the Subject*. Brighton, 1987.

Modleski, Tania. 'Femininity as Mas[s]querade: A Feminist Approach to Mass Culture', in *High Theory/Low Culture: Analysing Popular Television and Film*, ed. Colin MacCabe. Manchester, 1986.

Montrelay, Michèle. *L'Ombre et le nom: sur la fémininité*. Paris, 1977.

————. 'Inquiry into Femininity', trans. Parveen Adams, *m/f*, 1, 1978.

Montrose, Louis Adrian. 'Gifts and Reasons: The Contexts of Peele's *Araygnement of Paris*', ELH, 47, 1980.

————. '"The Place of a Brother" in *As You Like It*: Social Process and Comic Form', *Shakespeare Quarterly*, 32, 1981.

————. 'Professing the Renaissance: The Poetics and Politics of Culture', in *The New Historicism*, ed. H. Aram Veeser. New York, 1989.

Morin, Edgar. *La Méthode. 1. La nature de la nature*. Paris, 1977.

————. *Sociologie*. Paris, 1984; Rome, 1987.

Morrell, Roy. *Thomas Hardy: The Will and the Way*. Oxford, 1965.

Morris, Meaghan. 'The Man in the Mirror: David Harvey's "Condition" of Postmodernity'. *Theory, Culture & Society*, 9: 1, 1992.

Muller, John P. and William J. Richardson. *Lacan and Language: A Reader's Guide to 'Ecrits'*. New York, 1982.

Mulvey, Laura. 'Visual Pleasure and Narrative Cinema', in *Movies and Methods*, vol. 2, ed. Bill Nichols. Berkeley, CA, 1985.

Naipaul, V. S. *The Mimic Men*. London, 1976.

———. *India: A Million Mutinies Now*. London, 1990.

Naremore, James. *The World without a Self: Virginia Woolf and the Novel*. New Haven, CT, 1973.

Neale, J. E. *Elizabeth I and Her Parliaments 1559–1581*. New York, 1958.

Nichols, John. *The Progresses and Public Processions of Queen Elizabeth* (1823), 3 vols. New York, 1966.

Nietzsche, Friedrich. *Werke*, vol. 3, ed. K. Schlecta. Munich, 1966.

———. *The Will to Power*, trans. W. Kaufmann and R. J. Hollingdale. New York, 1968a.

———. *Twilight of the Idols/The Anti-Christ*, trans. R. J. Hollingdale. Harmondsworth, 1968b.

———. *The Gay Science*, trans. Walter Kaufmann. New York, 1974.

———. *On the Genealogy of Morals/Ecce Homo*, trans. W. Kaufmann and R. J. Hollingdale. New York, 1989.

Niranjana, Tejaswini. *Siting Translation: History, Post-Structuralism, and the Post-Colonial Context*. Berkeley, CA, 1992.

Norris, Christopher. 'Deconstruction, Post-Modernism and the Visual Arts', in Christopher Norris and Andrew Benjamin, *What is Deconstruction?* London, 1988, pp. 7–33.

Novak, Jane. *The Razor Edge of Balance: A Study of Virginia Woolf*. Coral Gables, FL, 1975.

Ohman, Richard. 'Speech, Literature, and the Space Between', *New Literary History*, 4, Autumn 1972.

Olsen, Tillie. *Silences*. New York, 1979.

Orton, Joe. *The Complete Plays*, intro John Lahr. London, 1976.

Parry, Benita. 'The Contents and Discontents of Kipling's Imperialism', *New Formations*, 6, Winter 1988.

Pater, Walter. *Studies in the History of the Renaissance*, 5th edn. London, 1973.

Paz, Octavio. '*water writes always* plural', in Anne d'Harnoncourt and Kynaston McShine, eds, *Marcel Duchamp: A Retrospective Exhibition, by the Philadelphia Museum of Art and the Museum of Modern Art, New York*. Philadelphia, 1973.

Pease, Donald E. '*Moby Dick* and the Cold War', in *The American Renaissance Reconsidered*, eds. Walter Benn Michaels and Donald E. Pease. Baltimore, MD, 1985.

Pechter, Edward. 'The New Historicism and Its Discontents: Politicizing Renaissance Drama', PMLA, 102, 1987.

Peele, George. *The Araygnment of Paris* (1584), ed. R. Mark Benbow, in *The Dramatic Works of George Peele*, general ed. C. T. Prouty. New Haven, CT, 1970.

Pollock, Griselda. 'What's Wrong with Images of Women?', *Screen Education*, 24, Autumn 1977.

Poovey, Mary. *Uneven Developments*. London, 1989.

Porter, Carolyn. 'Are We Being Historical Yet?', in *The States of 'Theory': History, Art, and Critical Discourse*, ed. David Caroll. New York, 1990.

Poulantzas, Nicos. *Political Power and Social Classes*, trans. Timothy O'Hagan. London, 1973.

Pratt, Annis. 'Sexual Imagery in *To the Lighthouse*', *Modern Fiction Studies*, 18, 1972.

Propp, Vladimir. *Morphology of the Folktale*, Trans. Laurence Scott, intro. Svatava Prankova-Jakobson. Austin, TX, 1968.

Proust, Marcel. *Du côté de chez Swann*. Paris, 1954.

Ragland-Sullivan, Ellie. *Jacques Lacan and the Philosophy of Psychoanalysis*. Urbana, IL, 1986.

Ralegh, Sir Walter. *The Discovery of the Large, Rich, and Beautiful Empire of Guiana* (1596), ed. Sir Robert H. Schomburgk. Hakluyt Society, first series, 3. 1848; rpt. New York, n.d.

Readings, Bill. 'The Politics of Deconstruction', in *Reading de Man Reading*, eds Lindsay Walters and Wlad Godzich. Minneapolis, MN, 1989.

Reboul, Jean. 'Sarrasine ou la castration personnifiée', *Cahiers pour l'Analyse*, March–April 1967).

Rella, Franco. *Asterischi*. Milan, 1989.

Remafedi, G. 'Male Homosexuality: The Adolescent's Perspective', unpublished manuscript, Adolescent Health Program, University of Minnesota, 1985.

Richards, I. A. *Coleridge on Imagination*. Bloomington, IN, 1960.

Rignall, John. *Realist Fiction and the Strolling Spectator*. London, 1992.

Rivière, Joan. 'Womanliness as Masquerade', in Victor Burgin, James Donald and Cora Kaplan, eds, *Formations of Fantasy*. London, 1986.

Rose, Jacqueline. 'Paranoia and the Film System', *Screen*, 17: 4, Winter 1976/7.

Rosenthal, Michael. *Virginia Woolf*. New York, 1979.

Ross, Andrew. *No Respect: Intellectuals and Popular Culture*. London, 1989.

Rovatti, Pier Aldo and Alssandro Dal Lago. *Elogio de pudore*. Milan, 1990.

Royle, Nicholas. *Telepathy and Literature: Essays on the Reading Mind*. Oxford, 1991.

————. *After Derrida*. Manchester, 1995.

Rubin, Gayle. 'Thinking Sex: Notes for a Radical Theory of the Politics of Sexuality', in *Pleasure and Danger*, ed. Carole S. Vance. New York, 1984.

Said, Edward. *Orientalism*. New York, 1978.

————. 'The Text, the World, the Critic', in *Textual Strategies*, ed. Josué V. Harari. Ithaca, NY, 1979.

————. 'Figures, Configurations, Transfigurations', *Class*, 32: 1, 1990.

Sartre, Jean-Paul. *The Psychology of Imagination*. London, 1972.

Schafer, Roy. *Aspects of Internalization*. New York, 1968.

Schelling, F. W. J. *Grundlegung der positiven Philosophie*, ed. H. Fuhrmans. Turin, 1972.

Schleiner, Winifried. '*Divina virago*: Queen Elizabeth as an Amazon', *Studies in Philology*, 75, 1978.

Schultz, W. *Aspekte der Angst*, 2nd edn. Munich, 1977.

Sedgwick, Eve Kosofsky. *Between Men: English Literature and Male Homosocial Desire*. New York, 1985.

————. *Epistemology of the Closet*. Berkeley, CA, 1990.

————. 'Queer Performativity', GLQ, 1: 1, Spring 1993.

Segar, Sir William. *Honor Military, and Civill* (1602), in John Nichols (1966, 3).

Shakespeare, William. *Antony and Cleopatra*, ed. M. R. Ridley. London, 1962.

Shipley, Joseph T. *The Origins of English Words: A Discursive Dictionary of Indo-European Roots*. Baltimore, MD, 1984.

Showalter, Elaine. 'Toward a Feminist Poetics', in *The New Feminist Criticism*, ed. Elaine Showalter. London, 1986.

Sinfield, Alan. 'Who was Afraid of Joe Orton?', *Textual Practice*, 4: 2, 1990.

————. *Faultlines: Cultural Materialism and the Politics of Dissident Reading*. Berkeley, CA 1992.

Sohn-Rethel, Alfred. *Napoli, la filosofia del rotto*. Naples, 1991.

Solomon, Alisa. 'The Politics of Breast Cancer', *Village Voice*, 14 May 1991.

Sontag, Susan. *Against Interpretation*. New York, 1966.

Spivak, Gayatri Chakravorty, translator's preface to Jacques Derrida, *Of Grammatology*. Baltimore, MD, 1978.

Sprinker, Michael. *Imaginary Relations: Aesthetics and Ideology in the Theory of Historical Materialism*. New York, 1987.

Starobinski, Jean. *Les mots sous les mots: Les anagrammes de Ferdinand de Saussure*. Paris, 1971.

Steegmuller, Francis. *Flaubert and Madame Bovary: A Double Portrait*. Chicago, 1977.

Steiner, George. *On Difficulty and Other Essays*. Oxford, 1978.

——. *Real Presences: Is There Anything in What We Say?* London, 1989.

Stocker, Midge, ed. *Cancer as a Women's Issue: Scratching the Surface*. Chicago, 1991.

Stokes, E. *The English Utilitarians and India*. Oxford, 1959.

——. *The Political Ideas of English Imperialism*. Oxford, 1960.

Strouse, Jean. *Alice James: A Biography*. New York, 1980.

Strouse, Louise F. 'Virginia Woolf – Her Voyage Back', *American Imago*, 38: 2, 1981.

Suleri, Sara. *The Rhetoric of English India*. Chicago, 1992.

Symonds, John Addington. *The Memoirs of John Addington Symonds*, ed. Phyllis Grosskurth. London, 1984.

Taussig, Michael. *Shamanism, Colonialism, and the Wild Man: A Study in Terror and Healing*. Chicago, 1991.

The American Heritage Dictionary of the English Language, 3rd edn. New York, 1992.

Thomason, Communication to Church Missionary Society, 5 September 1819, in *The Missionary Register*, 1821.

Ulin, Robert C. 'Critical Anthropology Twenty Years Later', *Critique of Anthropology*, 11: 1, 1991.

van Doren, Mark. *The Private Reader*. New York, 1968.

Vattimo, Gianni. *The End of Modernity: Nihilism and Hermeneutics in Post-Modern Culture*, trans. and intro. Jon R. Snyder. Oxford, 1988.

——. *The Transparent Society*, trans. David Webb. Cambridge, 1992.

Vaughan, Dai. 'The Aesthetics of Ambiguity', *Film as Ethnography*, ed. Peter Ian Crawford and David Turton. Manchester, 1992.

Venuti, Laurence. *Rethinking Translation: Discourse, Subjectivity, Ideology*. New York, 1992.

Waller, Marguerite. 'Academic Tootsie: The Denial of Difference and the Difference It Makes', *Diacritics*, 17: 1, 1987.

Warner, Sylvia Townsend. *Summer Will Show*. London, 1987.

Wayne, Don E. 'Power, Politics, and the Shakespearean Text: Recent Criticism in England and the United States', in *Shakespeare Reproduced*, eds Jean E. Howard and Marion F. O'Connor. London, 1987.

——. 'New Historicism', in *Encyclopedia of Literature and Criticism*, eds Malcolm Kelsall, Martin Coyle, Peter Garside and John Peck. London, 1990.

Weber, Samuel. 'The Sideshow, or: Remarks on a Canny Moment', *Modern Language Notes*, 88: 6, 1973.

——. *Institution and Interpretation*. Minneapolis, MN, 1987.

West, David. *An Introduction to Continental Philosophy*. Cambridge, 1996.

White, Hayden V. *Metahistory: The Historical Imagination in Nineteenth-Century Europe*. Baltimore, MD, 1973.

——. *Tropics of Discourse: Essays in Cultural Criticism*. Baltimore, MD, 1978.

Wilde, Oscar. *The Picture of Dorian Gray*. Harmondsworth, 1949.

——. *The Letters of Oscar Wilde* ed. Rupert Hart-Davis. New York, 1962.

——. *The Artist as Critic: Critical Writings of Oscar Wilde*, ed. Richard Ellmann. London, 1970.

Wilden, Anthony. 'Lacan and the Discourse of the Other', in Jacques Lacan, *Speech and Language in Psychoanalysis*, trans. Anthony Wilden. Baltimore, MD, 1981.

Williams, Raymond. *Culture and Society 1780–1950*. Harmondsworth, 1961.

——. *The English Novel from Dickens to Lawrence*. London, 1970.

——. *The Country and the City*. Oxford, 1975.

——. *Keywords*. London, 1976.

——. *Marxism and Literature*. Oxford, 1977.

——. *Problems in Materialism and Culture*. London, 1980.

Williams, Tennessee. *The Theatre of Tennessee Williams*, vol. 4. New York, 1972.

Wolf, Eric R. *Europe and the People without History*. Berkeley, CA, 1982.

Wolff, Robert Paul, Barrington Moore, Jr and Herbert Marcuse. *A Critique of Pure Tolerance*. London, 1969.

Wolfreys, Julian. 'An "Economics" of Snow and the Blank Page, or, "Writing" at the "Margins": "Deconstructing" "Richard Jefferies"?' in *Literary Theories: A Case Study in Critical Performance*, eds Julian Wolfreys and William Baker. Basingstoke, 1996.

———. 'Justifying the Unjustifiable: A Supplementary Introduction, of Sorts', in *The Derrida Reader: Writing Performances*, ed. Julian Wolfreys. Edinburgh University Press, 1998.

———. *Deconstruction ● Derrida*. Basingstoke, 1998.

Wood, David. 'Reading Derrida: an Introduction', in *Derrida: A Critical Reader*, ed. David Wood. Oxford, 1992.

Woolf, Virginia. *To the Lighthouse*. New York, 1927.

———. *Three Guineas*. Harmondsworth, 1977.

Wright, Frank, Lloyd. *The Living City*. New York, 1956.

Wyndham, Horace. *Speranza: A Biography of Lady Wilde*. New York, 1951.

Yeats, W.B. *Autobiographies*. London, 1955.

Žižek, Slavoj. *The Sublime of Ideology*. London, 1989.

NOTES ON CONTRIBUTORS

Jill Barker is a Senior Lecturer in Literary Studies at the University of Luton, specialising in early modern drama, and in feminist and psychoanalytic approaches to literature. Her graduate work at the University of Warwick was on concepts of 'otherness' in sixteenth-century dramatic texts. She has published on the gendering of stage representations, as well as a short introduction to using psychoanalytic literary theory in 'Does Edie Count? A Psychoanalytic Perspective on "Snowed Up"', in *Literary Theories: A Case Study in Critical Performance*, eds Wolfreys and Baker (Macmillan, 1996).

John Brannigan is Lecturer in Literary Studies and Irish Studies at the University of Luton. He is the author of *New Historicism and Cultural Materialism* (Macmillan, 1998), and has co-edited collections of essays on Jacques Derrida and James Joyce. He has also published a number of essays on Irish writing, colonialism in Ireland and contemporary literary theories. He is currently working on a book on literature in England in the 1950s.

Mark Currie is Lecturer in English at the University of Dundee. He is the author of *Postmodern Narrative Theory* (Macmillan, 1998) and the editor of *Metafiction* (Longman, 1995).

Jane Goldman is Lecturer in English at the University of Dundee. She is author of *The Feminist Aesthetics of Virginia Woolf: Modernism, Post-Impressionism and the Politics of the Visual*, and co-editor of *Modernism: An Anthology of Sources and Documents* (Edinburgh University Press).

Moyra Haslett is a lecturer in English at St Patrick's College, Drumcondra.

She is the author of *Byron's* Don Juan *and the Don Juan Legend* (Clarendon Press, 1997) and of *Marxist Literary and Cultural Theories* (Macmillan, 1999) and has published essays on a range of Irish writing. She is currently working on a book on eighteenth-century literature.

Gail Ching-Liang Low has taught at the University of Southampton, the University of East Anglia, the Open University, Staffordshire University and the University of Dundee where she currently teaches Postcolonial, Contemporary British and American Literature and Film. She is the author *of White Skins/ Black Masks: Representation and Colonialism* (Routledge, 1996) and is currently working on pedagogy and canon formation in the institutional transformation of 'Commonwealth' to 'Postcolonial' in Britain.

Martin McQuillan is a Lecturer in Literature at Staffordshire University. He is co-editor of *Post-Theory: New Directions in Criticism* (Edinburgh University Press, 1999) and is currently preparing *Deconstruction: A Reader* for EUP and *The Narrative Reader* for Routledge.

K. M. Newton is Professor of English at the University of Dundee. Among his publications are *George Eliot: Romantic Humanist* (Macmillan, 1981), *In Defence of Literary Interpretation* (Macmillan, 1986), *Interpreting the Text* (Harvester, 1990) and *Twentieth-Century Literary Theory: A Reader* (Macmillan, 1997).

Ruth Robbins is Lecturer in Literary Studies at the University of Luton. She has published widely in late-nineteenth-century literature. With Julian Wolfreys, she edited *Victorian Identities: Social and Cultural Formations in Nineteenth-Century Literature* (Macmillan, 1994) and *Victorian Gothic* (forthcoming), and with Julian Wolfreys and John Brannigan, *Applying: to Derrida* (Macmillan, 1996) and *The French Connections of Jacques Derrida* (State University of New York Press, 1999). Her book *Literary Feminisms: Politics and Poetics* is forthcoming (Macmillan, 1999).

Leah Wain is a postdoctoral candidate at Birkbeck College, London, completing work on her dissertation, the subject of which is the biblical intertexts of Victorian Women's poetry.

Julian Wolfreys is the author of *Being English: Narratives, Idioms and Performances from Coleridge to Trollope* (State University of New York Press, 1994), *The Rhetoric of Affirmative Resistance: Dissonant Identities from Carroll to Derrida* (Macmillan, 1997), *Deconstruction ● Derrida* (Macmillan, 1998) and *Writing London: the Trace of the Urban Text from Blake to Dickens* (Macmillan, 1998). He has edited or co-edited several books, including most recently, *The Derrida Reader: Writing Performances* (Edinburgh UP/Nebraska UP, 1998) and *The French Connections of Jacques Derrida* (with John Brannigan and Ruth Robbins; State University of New York Press, 1998).

Kenneth Womack is Assistant Professor of English at Pennsylvania State University, Altoona. In addition to co-authoring *Recent Work in Critical Theory, 1989–1995: An Annotated Bibliography* and co-editing *Nineteenth-Century British Book-Collectors and Bibliographers*, he has published articles in the *Yearbook of Comparative and General Literature, Biography, The International Fiction Review, Style, Literature/Film Quarterly, Cahiers Victoriens et Edouardiens, Bulletin of Bibliography* and *The Library Chronicle*. He also works as a Correspondent for the *World Shakespeare Bibliography* and serves as Associate Editor of *George Eliot–George Henry Lewes Studies*.

ACKNOWLEDGEMENTS

The editor and publisher gratefully acknowledge the following for permission to reprint either in whole or in part:

1.2 Roland Barthes, 'From Science to Literature', reprinted from *The Rustle of Language* (pp. 3–10) by Roland Barthes, translated by Richard Howard, University of California Press (1989), by permission of the estate of Roland Barthes and the publishers, Farrar, Strauss, and Giroux, © 1986, 1989, the estate of Roland Barthes and Farrar, Strauss, and Giroux;

1.3 Roland Barthes, extract reprinted from S/Z, (pp. 3–16) by Roland Barthes, translated by Richard Miller, Preface by Richard Howard, by permission of the estate of Roland Barthes and the publishers, Farrar, Strauss, and Giroux, © 1974, the estate of Roland Barthes and Farrar, Strauss, and Giroux;

2.2 Claire Kahane, 'Medusa's Voice: Male Hysteria in *The Bostonians*', reprinted from *Passions of the Voice: Hysteria, Narrative, and the Figure of the Speaking Woman 1850–1915* (pp. 64–79) by Claire Kahane, by permission of the publishers, The Johns Hopkins University Press, © 1995, The Johns Hopkins University Press;

2.3 Terry Castle, 'Sylvia Townsend Warner and the Counterplot of Lesbian Fiction', reprinted from *The Apparitional Lesbian: Female Homosexuality and Modern Culture* (pp. 66–91, 248–54) by Terry Castle, by permission of the publishers, Columbia University Press, © 1993, Columbia University Press;

2.4 Mary Lydon, 'Myself and M/Others: Colette, Wilde, and Duchamp', reprinted from *Skirting the Issue: Essays in Literary Theory* (pp. 42–51) by Mary Lydon, by permission of the publishers, The University of Wisconsin Press, © 1995, The University of Wisconsin Press;

3.2 Terry Eagleton, extract reprinted from *Walter Benjamin or, Towards a Revolutionary Criticism* (pp. 122–30) by Terry Eagleton, by permission of the publishers, Verso, © 1985, Verso;

3.3 Raymond Williams, 'Marxism and Literature', reprinted from *Politics and Letters: Interviews by the New Left Review* (pp. 324–58), by Raymond Williams, by permission of the publishers, Verso, © 1981, Verso;

4.2 Michael Riffaterre, 'Describing Poetic Structures: Two Approaches to Baude-laire's "Les Chats"', reprinted from *Yale French Studies*, 36–7 (1966), by permission of the author and the publishers, *Yale French Studies*, © 1966, *Yale French Studies*;

4.3 Hans-Robert Jauss, 'The Poetic Text within the Change of Horizons of Reading: The Example of Baudelaire's "Spleen II"', reprinted from *Toward an Aesthetic of Reception* (pp. 139–218), by Hans-Robert Jauss, by permission of the publishers, University of Minnesota Press, © 1982, University of Minnesota Press;

4.4 Wolfgang Iser, 'The Imaginary', reprinted from *The Fictive and the Imaginary: Charting Literary Anthropology* (pp. 171–204) by Wolfgang Iser, by permission of the publishers, The Johns Hopkins University Press, © 1993, The Johns Hopkins University Press;

5.2 Stephen Heath, 'Difference', reprinted from *Screen*, 19: 3 (1978), pp. 51–112, by permission of Stephen Heath and *Screen*, © 1978, *Screen*;

5.3 James M. Mellard, 'Using Lacan: Reading *To the Lighthouse*', reprinted from *Using Lacan, Reading Fiction* (pp. 140–94) by James M. Mellard, by permission of the author and the publishers, University of Illinois Press, © 1991, the Board of Trustees of the University of Illinois;

6.2 Jacques Derrida, 'Letter to a Japanese Friend', reprinted from *A Derrida Reader: Between the Blinds* (pp. 270–6), ed. Peggy Kamuf, by permission of the publishers, Columbia University Press © 1991, Columbia University Press;

6.3 J. Hillis Miller, 'Thomas Hardy, Jacques Derrida, and the "Dislocation of Souls"', reprinted from *Tropes, Parables, Performatives* (pp. 171–80) by J. Hillis Miller, by permission of Duke University Press, © 1991, Duke University Press;

6.4 Nicholas Royle, 'On Not Reading: Derrida and Beckett', reprinted from *After Derrida* (pp. 159–74), by permission of Manchester University Press, © 1995, Manchester University Press, Manchester, UK;

7.2 Paul de Man, 'Semiology and Rhetoric', reprinted from *Diacritics*, 3: 3, (Fall 1973), pp. 27–33, by permission of *Diacritics* and the publishers, The Johns Hopkins University Press, © 1973, The Johns Hopkins University Press;

7.3 Avital Ronell, 'Scoring Literature', reprinted from *Crack Wars: Literature, Addiction, Mania* (pp. 93–135, 172–5) by permission of University of Nebraska Press, © 1992, University of Nebraska Press;

8.2 Jean-François Lyotard, 'Answer to the Question, What is the Postmodern?', reprinted from *The Postmodern Explained* (pp. 1–16) by Jean-François Lyotard, by permission of University of Minnesota Press, © 1982, University of Minnesota Press and *The Postmodern Explained to Children* by Jean-François Lyotard, by permission of the Power Institute © 1992, Power Institute;

8.3 Jean Baudrillard, 'Simulacra and Simulations', reprinted from *Simulacra and Simulations* (pp. 1–13, 23–49) by Jean Baudrillard, trans. Paul Foss, Paul Patton and Philip Beitchman, by permission of Autonomedia/Sémiotext(e), © 1983, Autonomedia/Sémiotext(e);

8.4 Fredric Jameson, 'Nostalgia for the Present', reprinted from *Postmodernism, Or, The Cultural Logic of Late Capitalism* (pp. 279–96) by Fredric Jameson, by permission of Duke University Press, © 1991, Duke University Press;

9.2 Catherine Gallagher, 'Marxism and the New Historicism', reprinted from *The New Historicism* (pp. 37–48), ed. H. Aram Veeser, by permission of Routledge, Inc., © 1989, Routledge, Inc.;

9.3 Louis Adrian Montrose, '"Shaping Fantasies": Figurations of Power and Gender in Elizabethan Culture', reprinted from *Representations*, 2 (Spring 1983), pp. 61–94, by permission of Louis Adrian Montrose and The Regents of the University of California, © 1983, The Regents of the University of California;

10.2 Homi K. Bhabha, 'Of Mimicry and Man: The Ambivalence of Colonial Discourse', reprinted from *The Location of Culture* (pp. 85–92) by Homi K. Bhabha, by permission of Routledge, Inc., © 1994, Routledge, Inc.;

10.3 Gail Ching-Liang Low, 'Loafers and Story-Tellers', reprinted from *White Skins, Black Masks* (pp. 238–76) by Gail Ching-Liang Low, by permission of Gail Ching-Liang Low and Routledge, Inc., © 1996, Routledge, Inc.;

10.4 Rey Chow, 'Film as Ethnography; or, Translations Between Cultures in the Postcolonial World', reprinted from *Primitive Passions: Visuality, Sexuality, Ethnography, and Chinese Cinema* (pp. 176–202, 238–43) by Rey Chow, by permission of Columbia University Press, © 1995, Columbia University Press;

11.2 Eve Kosofsky Sedgwick, 'Queer and Now', reprinted from *Tendencies* (pp. 1–20) by Eve Kosofsky Sedgwick, by permission of Duke University Press, © 1993, Duke University Press;

11.3 Jonathan Dollimore, 'Post/Modern: On the Gay Sensibility, or the Pervert's Revenge on Authenticity – Wilde, Genet, Orton, and Others', reprinted from *Sexual Dissidence: Augustine to Wilde, Freud to Foucault* (pp. 307–25), by Jonathan Dollimore, by permission of Oxford University Press, © 1991, Oxford University Press;

11.4 Judith Butler, 'Critically Queer', reprinted from *Bodies that Matter: On the Discursive Limits of 'Sex'* (pp. 223–42) by Judith Butler, by permission of Routledge, Inc., © 1993, Routledge, Inc.;

12.2 J. Hillis Miller, 'Cultural Studies and Reading', reprinted from ADE *Bulletin*, 117 (Fall 1997), pp. 15–18, by permission of the Modern Languages Association, © 1997, MLA;

12.3 Iain Chambers, 'Cities without Maps', reprinted from *Migrancy, Culture, Identity* (pp. 92–114), by Iain Chambers, by permission of Iain Chambers and Routledge, Inc., © 1994, Routledge, Inc.;

12.4 Alan Sinfield, 'Art as Cultural Production', reprinted from *Cultural Politics – Queer Reading* (pp. 21–39) by Alan Sinfield, by permission of Alan Sinfield, Routledge, Inc. and University of Pennsylvania Press, © 1994, Routledge, Inc. and University of Pennsylvania Press.

All reasonable efforts have been made to contact the parties concerned. If any permissions are outstanding, the editor and publisher would be grateful if the relevant parties could make contact with Edinburgh University Press.

INDEX OF PROPER NAMES